STRUCTURE AND GROWTH OF PHILOSOPHIC SYSTEMS
FROM PLATO TO SPINOZA
IV

THE PHILOSOPHY OF THE KALAM

THE PHILOSOPHY OF THE KALAM

BY

HARRY AUSTRYN WOLFSON

HARVARD UNIVERSITY PRESS
CAMBRIDGE, MASSACHUSETTS
AND LONDON, ENGLAND
1976

Publication of this book has been
aided by a grant from the
Lucius N. Littauer Foundation

Library of Congress Catalog Card Number 74-78718
ISBN 0-674-66580-5
Printed in the United States of America

FOREWORD

The Philosophy of the Kalam embodies all those traits which have over the years riveted scholarly attention on the writings of Professor Harry A. Wolfson: philological precision, philosophical perceptivity, and historical imagination. This volume, like his earlier works, combines massive erudition with great intuition. This time, however, Professor Wolfson was called upon to apply his method of conjecture and verification to fragmentary, philosophically laconic, and recalcitrant texts; the challenge of fitting these texts, frequently quotations or reports found in late doxographies, into his conceptual framework was great and that accounts for the delay in the completion of this work. In keeping with his method, he had to be speculative in his unfolding of latent processes of philosophic reasoning and in his attempt to articulate mute witnesses. The resultant volume is studded with new interpretations of unexplored sources and imaginative approaches to unsolved problems; it calls attention to unperceived relationships in the history of philosophy and will surely stimulate further research in these areas. In light of its wide scope, its treatment of such figures as Ghazali and Averroes, it may be anticipated that students of the entire range of Islamic philosophy, not only of Kalam, will find this work indispensable.

I hope that the supplementary monograph on "Repercussions of the Kalam in Jewish Philosophy" will be published in the near future — a fitting finale to an extraordinarily versatile scholarly career which began with *Crescas' Critique of Aristotle*.

It should be noted that not only is this volume being published posthumously, much to the sorrow of Professor Wolfson's many friends and admirers, but also that the infirmities of old age and debilities of illness prevented him from giving the book the final careful review which he lavished upon all his writings. Professor Wolfson would regularly re-read an entire work *in page proof*, checking for consistency in translation and transliteration as well as elegance of formulation and precision of conceptualization. The author was continually reviewing, revising, and reformulating.

The index was prepared by Mrs. Eleanor Kewer; the bibliography was prepared by Steven Harvey, a doctoral candidate at Harvard University, together with Mrs. Kewer. Publication was made possible by the generous support of Mr. Harry Starr, President of the Littauer Foundation in New York.

ISADORE TWERSKY
Littauer Professor of
Hebrew Literature
and Jewish Philosophy

PREFACE

In the series of studies which I drafted between 1934 and 1944 as the basis of my planned "Structure and Growth of Philosophic Systems from Plato to Spinoza," the study of the Church Fathers was followed by a study of the Muslim philosophers, who in part were on the left of Philo, and within this study were included sections on the Mutakallimūn, who in part were on the right of Philo. No special study on the Kalam was then contemplated, and this for the reason that most of the Kalam literature was still in manuscript. But in the course of my publication of the two volumes on Philo and the first volume on the Church Fathers it dawned on me that by following the method of research which I had used in these two works I would be able, on the basis of the Kalam literature already available in print, to prepare a volume on the Kalam in which certain problems peculiar to the Kalam would be dealt with in their relation to similar problems as dealt with by Philo and the Church Fathers in their common attempt to interpret Scripture in terms of philosophy and to revise philosophy in conformity with Scripture. And so, on the publication of the first volume on "The Philosophy of the Church Fathers" in 1956, for reasons which seemed both to me and to some friends quite valid, instead of proceeding at once to prepare the manuscript of the second volume on the Church Fathers for the press I began to prepare this study of the Kalam and kept on working at it until its completion in 1964.

The problems which I selected for discussion in this work are six: Attributes, Koran, Creation, Atomism, Causality, Predestination and Free Will. The reason for selecting these problems and how they are related to the problems dealt with by Philo and the Church Fathers and what the method of research is that is made use of in dealing with these problems are fully discussed later in this work under the heading "Origin, Structure, Diversity" (pp. 70–79). However, the discussion of the method of research will bear repetition.

This method, which in technical language I described as "the hypothetico-deductive method" of text interpretation (cf. *Crescas' Critique of Aristotle*, 1929, p. 25), means in simple language the method of conjecture and verification. I compared it to what in science is called "control-experiment" (cf. *The Philosophy of Spinoza*, 1934, I, 26). Just as the scientist starts out on some experiment, say with a certain number of rabbits, so in our investigation of any topic we start out with a certain number of representative texts bearing upon that topic. Then, just as the scientific experimenter inoculates only one or some of his rabbits and uses the others as controls, so we also perform all our conjectural interpretation on one or some of our texts and use the others as controls and verifications. The literature of the Kalam available to me in print during the preparation of this work has furnished, with regard to the six problems dealt with in it, all the passages that were necessary as bases of conjectural interpretations as well as all the passages that were necessary as bases of controls and verifications. I hope that the new Kalam literature that has been published since the preparation of this work and that will be published in the future will be found to corroborate, or to be susceptible of interpretation in accordance with, my findings.

Thirteen sections of the eight chapters of this volume have already appeared in various publications. The chronological order of their appearance in those publications and the pages in this work in which the titles of these publications are given are as follows: 1943 (p. 373), 1946 (p. 359), 1956 (p. 112), 1959 (p. 395), 1960 (p. 291), 1960 (p. 337), 1964 (p. 559), 1965 (p. 147), 1965 (p. 337), 1967 (p. 8), 1967 (p. 476), 1967 (p. 624), 1969 (p. 593).

The text of this work as completed in 1964 contained

chapters under the heading "Repercussions of the Kalam in Jewish Philosophy." These chapters will be published separately as a supplementary monograph to this volume.

For counsel and assistance in Arabic textual problems I am deeply indebted to Professor Moshe Perlmann of the University of California at Los Angeles, formerly at Harvard, and to Professor Muhsin Sayyid Mahdi and Dr. Wilson Basta Bishai, both of Harvard. Unbounded thanks are due to Eleanor Dobson Kewer, formerly Chief Editor of the Harvard University Press, who with watchful and searching care steered through the press the succession of corrected galley proofs. But for her unremitting help, the publication of this book, which for various reasons has been delayed, would have been further delayed.

H. A. W.
April 1974

CONTENTS

CHAPTER I

CHAPTER II

CHAPTER III

CHAPTER V

How the belief in creation out of nothing appeared in Philo

THE PHILOSOPHY OF THE KALAM

CHAPTER I

THE KALAM

I. The Term Kalam

The term *kalām*, which literally means "speech" or "word," is used in Arabic translations of the works of Greek philosophers as a rendering of the term *logos* in its various senses of "word," "reason," and "argument." [1] The term *kalām* is also used in those Arabic translations from the Greek in the sense of any special branch of learning, and the plural participle, *mutakallimūn* (singular: *mutakallim*), is used as a designation of the masters or exponents of any special branch of learning. Thus the Greek expression "discussions about nature" (περὶ φύσεως λόγοι)[2] is translated by "the physical *kalām*" (*al-kalām al-ṭabīʿī*).[3] The Greek terms for "physicists" (φυσικοί;[4] φυσιολόγοι [5]) are sometimes translated by "masters of the physical *kalām*" (*aṣḥāb al-kalām al-ṭabīʿī*) [6] or by "the *mutakallimūn* in physics" (*al-mutakallimūn fī al-ṭabīʿiyyāt*).[7] Similarly, the Greek term for "theologians" (θεολόγοι) [8] is translated by "masters of the divine *kalām*" (*aṣḥāb al-kalām al-ilāhī*) [9] or by "the *mutakallimūn* in divinity" (*al-mutakallimūn fī al-ilāhiyyāt*).[10] In this sense the terms *kalām* and *mutakallimūn* came to be used, probably under the influence of these Arabic translations from the Greek, also by original Arabic writers. Thus Yaḥyā Ibn ʿAdī speaks of the "Christian *mutakallimūn*"; [11]

[1] Averroes, *In Metaphysica*, Arabic: *Tafsir ma baʿd at-tabiʿat*, ed. M. Bouyges, Index D, a, p. (264).

[2] *Metaph.* I, 8, 990a, 7.

[3] Averroes, *In Metaphysica*, I, Text. 20, p. 104, l. 16.

[4] *Metaph.* XII, 10, 1075b, 27.

[5] *Ibid.* I, 8, 989b, 30–31.

[6] Averroes, *In Metaphysica*, XII, Text. 57, p. 1728, l. 11.

[7] *Ibid.* I, Text. 19, p. 101, l. 11.

[8] *Metaph.* XII, 10, 1075b, 26; 6, 1071b, 27.

[9] Averroes, *In Metaphysica*, XII, Text. 57, p. 1728, ll. 10–11.

[10] *Ibid.*, Text. 30, p. 1563, l. 9.

[11] Périer, *Petits Traités Apologétiques de Yaḥyā ben ʿAdī*, p. 39, l. 4.

Shahrastānī speaks of "the *kalām* of Empedocles," [12] "the *kalām* of Aristotle," [13] and the *kalām* of the Christians on the union of the Word with the body in the incarnation; [14] Judah Halevi [15] speaks of people belonging to "the same school of *mutakallimūn* . . . such as the school of Pythagoras, the school of Empedocles, the school of Aristotle, the school of Plato or of other individual philosophers, the Stoics,[16] and the Peripatetics, the latter belonging to the school of Aristotle";[17] Averroes speaks of "the *mutakallimūn* of the people of our religion and the people of the religion of the Christians" [18] or "the *mutakallimūn* of the people of the three religions which exist today";[19] Maimonides speaks of "the first Mutakallimūn from among the Christianized Greeks and from among the Muslims";[20] Ibn Ḫaldūn speaks of "the *kalām* of philosophers in physics and metaphysics." [21] In addition to all this, the term *kalām*, without any qualification, was applied to a particular system of thought which arose in Islam prior to the rise of philosophy, and its exponents, called simply *mutakallimūn*, were contrasted with those who, beginning with al-Kindī (d. *ca.* 873), were called simply philosophers.

How this system of thought described simply as Kalam came into being and what it was may be pieced together from passages dealing with its history to be found in three works written in Arabic, two by Muslims, Shahrastānī (1086–1153) and Ibn Ḫaldūn (1332–1406), and one by a Jew, Maimonides (1135–1204).

[12] *Milal*, p. 262, l. 1.
[13] *Ibid.*, p. 286, l. 7.
[14] *Ibid.*, p. 172, l. 4.
[15] *Cuzari* V, 14, p. 328, ll. 23–26; p. 329, ll. 13–16.
[16] *aṣḥāb al-mizallah*: *ba'le ha-ṣel.*
[17] Arabic reading in printed text *al-mīṭān*, probably a corruption of *al-mashshā'ūn*, Hebrew: *ha-holekim.* Cf. Goldziher in *ZDMG*, 41:705 (1887).
[18] Averroes, *In XII Metaph.*, Comm. 18, Arabic, p. 1489, ll. 4–5; Latin, p. 304 F.
[19] *Ibid.*, Arabic, p. 1503, ll. 11–12; Latin, p. 305 F.
[20] *Moreh* I, 71, p. 123, ll. 10–11.
[21] *Mukaddimah* III, p. 41, l. 8.

II. The Kalam According to Shahrastānī and Ibn Ḫaldūn

The development of Islam, during the period covered in this study, falls into two stages: first, the emergence of a unified system of belief out of the various teachings scattered in the Koran; second, the rise of heresies.

The first stage was dominated by those called *al-salaf*,[1] literally, "the predecessors," a term applied to the "companions of Muhammad" (*al-ṣaḥābah*) and to those who came after the companions, called "the followers" (*al-tābi'ūn*).[2] What these *salaf* agreed upon is taken to constitute that which may be called the good old-time religion of Islam. We shall refer to the *salaf* either as early Muslims or as the followers of early Islam or simply as orthodox Islam or the orthodox Muslims, all as is required by the context.

The religion formed out of the teachings of the Koran consists, according to Ibn Ḫaldūn, of two kinds of duties, "duties of the body" (*al-takālīf al-badaniyyah*) and "duties of the heart" (*al-takālīf al-ḳalbiyyah*).[3] The former kind consists of "the divine laws that govern the actions of all duty-bound Muslims," and this is Fiḳh [4] — a term which from its original meaning of "understanding, knowledge," at first came to be used in the limited sense of *ijtihād*, that is, the decision of legal points by one's own judgment in the absence of any precedent bearing on the case in question, but later acquired the comprehensive sense of Muslim jurisprudence based on four sources: (1) the Koran; (2) tradition (*sunnah*);

[1] *Muḳaddimah* III, p. 37, l. 2.

[2] *Ibid.*, p. 36, l. 19.

[3] *Ibid.* II, p. 386, l. 14. The same distinction is described as "actions" (*a'māl*) of "the hearts" (*al-ḳulūb*) and of "the limbs" (*al-jawāriḥ*) by Muḥāsibī in *Al-Ri'āyah li-Ḥuḳuḳ Allāh*, p. 43, l. 15, and by Ghazālī in *Kitāb Sharḥ 'Ajā'ib al-Ḳalb* of *Iḥyā'*, III, p. 40, l. 9, and as *farā'iḍ*, "duties," of "the heart" and of "the limbs" by Baḥya in *Al-Hidāyah 'ilā Farā'iḍ al-Ḳulūb*, Introduction, p. 5, ll. 14–15. See also references in Goldziher, *Streitschrift des Gazâlī gegen die Bāṭinijja-Sekte*, p. 109.

[4] *Ibid.*, l. 13.

(3) analogy (*ķiyās*); (4) consensus (*ijmā'*).[5] The latter kind of duties concerns "faith" (*īmān*), which is defined as "an affirmation by the heart in agreement with what is spoken by the tongue" [6] and is said to consist of six articles, which, according to tradition, were drawn up by Muhammad himself. These articles are as follows: "the belief in (1) God, (2) His angels, (3) His Scriptures, (4) His apostles, (5) the Last Day, and (6) the belief in predestination (*al-ķadar*), be it good or bad." [7] Thus Kalam means theology in contradistinction to Fiķh, which means jurisprudence. It is the discussion of these articles of faith (*al-'aķā'id al-īmāniyyah*) that, according to Ibn Ḫaldūn, constitutes "the science of the Kalam." [8]

When exactly the term Kalam came to be used in that technical sense is, as far as I know, nowhere explicitly stated. From statements by Shahrastānī we gather that there was a Kalam prior to the founding of Mu'tazilism by Wāṣil b. 'Aṭā' (d. 748) [9] and that "the splendor of the science of the Kalam began" during the reign of Harūn al-Rashīd (786–809).[10] The existence of a pre-Mu'tazilite Kalam may perhaps also be inferred from the use of the term *mutakallimūn* by Ibn Sa'd (d. 845) as a designation of those who discussed the problem of the status of sinners in Islam raised by the pre-Mu'tazilite sect of the Murji'ites [11] and from the use of the term *yatakallam* by Ibn Ķutaybah (828–889) in connection with the discussion of the problem of free will by the pre-Mu'tazilite Ghaylān.[12]

[5] Cf. Goldziher in *EI*, *s. v.* FIĶH (Vol. II, pp. 109 f.).

[6] *Muķaddimah* III, p. 33, ll. 15–16; cf. p. 35, ll. 6–9.

[7] *Ibid.*, p. 35, ll. 9–11.

[8] *Ibid.* II, p. 386, l. 17; cf. III, p. 35, ll. 11–12. The implication of these statements is that this particular discipline is called "Kalam" because it deals with "faith," which, by definition, is a matter of "speech." Cf. below at n. 155. This explanation of the meaning of the term Kalam is not mentioned by Taftāzānī (p. 10, l. 3–p. 11, l. 8) among his various explanations, eight in number, of the meaning of the term.

[9] Cf. below, pp. 19–20.

[10] *Milal*, p. 19, ll. 12–13.

[11] Cf. Goldziher, *Vorlesungen über den Islam* (1910), p. 100 (English, p. 105).

[12] Cf. *Kitāb al-ma'ārif* (ed. F. Wustenfeld, 1850), p. 244, l. 6, quoted in Haarbrücker's translation of Shahrastānī, II, p. 389.

Similarly, Ibn Ḫaldūn refers to Mutakallimūn who flourished prior to the rise of Muʿtazilism.[13]

From Ibn Ḫaldūn, moreover, we learn not only of the existence of pre-Muʿtazilite Mutakallimūn but also of how the Kalam of those Mutakallimūn originated and what it was. Thus in a passage dealing with religious conditions in Islam prior to the rise of Muʿtazilism, he says that the early Muslims, in trying to explain the articles of faith, at first quoted verses from the Koran and reports from the Sunnah. Later, when differences of opinion occurred concerning details (*tafāṣil*) of these articles of faith, "argumentation formed by the intellect (*al-ʿaḳl*) began to be used in addition to the evidence derived from tradition, and in this way the science of Kalam originated." [14] Now the differences of opinion concerning details of the articles of faith, which, according to Ibn Ḫaldūn, led to the science of Kalam, quite evidently refer to such pre-Muʿtazilite problems as the state of sinners and freedom of the will mentioned above and the problem of Koranic anthropomorphisms to be mentioned later in the course of our discussion. As to what he means by "argumentation formed by the intellect in addition to proof-texts derived from tradition" which led to the Kalam and hence was used in the Kalam, it may be gathered from a distinction he draws elsewhere between "philosophical sciences" and "traditional sciences," [15] under the latter of which he includes both Fiḳh and Kalam, describing Fiḳh as "the root of all the traditional sciences." [16] In the philosophical sciences, he says, "the subject-matter of each of these sciences, the problems which they deal with, and the methods of demonstration which they use in solving those problems" all originate in man by reason of his being "a thinking human being." [17] As for the traditional sci-

[13] Cf. below, pp. 25–28.
[14] *Muḳaddimah* III, p. 36, ll. 10–15.
[15] *Muḳaddimah* II, p. 385, ll. 1–4.
[16] *Ibid.*, p. 385, l. 16 – p. 386, l. 13, and p. 386, ll. 14–17.
[17] *Ibid.*, p. 385, ll. 5–9.

ences, he says, "there is no place for the intellect (*al-'aḳl*) in them, save that the intellect may be used in connection with them to relate the branches (*al-furū'*) of their problems with the roots (*al-uṣūl*)," [18] that is, "the general tradition" (*al-naḳl al-kullī*); [19] but the results of this limited use of the intellect are subsequently described by him as "intellectual proofs" (*al-adillah al-'aḳliyyah*) used in Kalam with regard to matters of faith.[20]

The full implication of this contrast between the two sciences, as may be gathered from his statements about the traditional sciences immediately following the statement just quoted and from his statements in his later discussion of one of the philosophical sciences, logic,[21] may be restated as follows. Both these sciences try to derive something unknown from something known, or, to use Kalam terms, something absent (*al-ghā'ib*) from something present (*al-shāhid*).[22] The unknown in the philosophical sciences is called *maṭlūb*,[23] "that which is sought," and the known is called *muḳaddimah*,[24] "premise"; in the traditional sciences, as we have seen, the unknown is called *far'*, "branch," and the known is called *aṣl*, "root" or "general tradition." [25] Now the "premise" in the philosophical sciences is said by Ibn Ḫaldūn to be a universal which the human mind forms by means of abstraction from perceptible objects; [26] the "root" or "general tradition" in the traditional sciences is said by him to be "teachings (*shar'iyyāt*) of the Koran and the Sunnah which have been enjoined on us by God and His Apostle." [27] As a description

[18] *Ibid.*, ll. 11–12.

[19] *Ibid.*, l. 13.

[20] *Ibid.*, p. 386, l. 17.

[21] *Ibid.* III, p. 108, l. 8–p. 112, l. 3.

[22] *Mi'yar al-'Ilm*, p. 94, l. 10.

[23] *Muḳaddimah* III, p. 110, l. 19.

[24] *Ibid.*, l. 11. Thus also is the expression "intellectual premises" (*muḳaddimāt 'aḳliyyah*) used by Ibn Ḫaldūn as a description of the theories of the atom and the vacuum which were used by Bāḳillānī as the basis of certain arguments (*Muḳaddimah* III, p. 40, ll. 7–9).

[25] Cf above at n. 19 and *Ishārāt*, p. 65, l. 2.

[26] *Muḳaddimah* III, p. 108, l. 9–p. 109, l. 18.

[27] *Ibid.* II, p. 385, ll. 15–17. The term *shar'iyyāt* here, I take it, is not used by Ibn Ḫaldūn in the narrow sense of "laws," for under the "traditional sciences," of which the *shar'iyyāt* are said by him to be the "root," he in-

of the method of reasoning by which the unknown is derived from the known in both the philosophical and traditional sciences, Ibn Ḫaldūn uses the same Arabic term, *ḳiyās*.[28] But from other sources we know that the term *ḳiyās* has a different origin and a different meaning in each of these two sciences. In the traditional sciences, the term *ḳiyās* as a method of reasoning from data furnished by the Koran and the Sunnah appeared first in connection with legal problems in the Fiḳh, where it means "analogy," and the term in that sense, it has been shown, is a translation of the Hebrew *heḳḳesh*, which is used in that sense in Talmudic law.[29] In the philosophical sciences, *ḳiyās* is used as a translation of the Greek term *syllogismos*,[30] and it is used in that sense by Ibn Ḫaldūn in his discussion of the "science of Logic," [31] which he describes as "the first" of the philosophical sciences.[32]

Accordingly, when Ibn Ḫaldūn says that with the rise of differences of opinion in matters of faith there appeared the use of "argumentation formed by the intellect," he means that the participants in the discussions of those differences of opinion in matters of faith borrowed from the Fiḳh the method of *ḳiyās*, "analogy," where it was used in connection with problems of law, and applied it to problems of faith. And when he further says that "in this way the science of Kalam originated," he means thereby that the name Kalam was given to the application of the method of analogy to problems of faith in order to distinguish it from its use in the Fiḳh in connection with problems of law; for Kalam means "speech," and faith by definition, as we have seen, is "an affirmation by the heart in agreement with what is spoken by the tongue," [33]

---

cludes not only Fiḳh but also Kalam. Cf. similar broad use of *shar'iyyah* in Taftāzānī, pp. 7–8.

[28] *Ibid.* II, p. 385, l. 14; III, p. 110, l. 7.

[29] Margoliouth, "Omar's Instructions to the Kadi," *JRAS* (1910), p. 320; Schacht, *The Origins of Muhammadan Jurisprudence*, p. 99.

[30] Cf. Arabic translation of συλλογισμὸς in *Anal. Pri.* I, 2, 24b, 18, and *passim.*

[31] *Muḳaddimah* III, p. 108, l. 8; p. 110, ll. 7 ff.

[32] *Ibid.*, p. 87, ll. 4–5.

[33] Cf. above, p. 4.

whereas Fiḳh by contrast, refers to "action," for it consists of "the divine laws that govern the action of all duty-bound Muslims." [34] But it will be noticed that Ibn Ḫaldūn does not say who among the participants in the discussion of those newly arisen problems of faith used this new method of argumentation. The inference to be drawn from his silence on this point is that the new method of argumentation was used not only by those whom he describes as having introduced innovations (*bidaʿ*), but also by those who followed the teachings of the early Muslims (*al-salaf*). What he means here by "innovations" will be discussed later.[34a]

The sects which arose in Islam are many,[35] and still more are the differences of opinion concerning the articles of faith. But for the purpose of our present study, we shall deal only with certain differences of opinion relating to two articles of faith, the first and the sixth, namely, the belief in God, which means a belief in the right conception of God, and the belief in predestination, which means the belief in the power of God over human acts. Concerning both these two articles of faith, there arose differences of opinion in Islam even before the rise of Muʿtazilism, which differences of opinion gave rise to discussions termed Kalam.

The pre-Muʿtazilite differences of opinion concerning the right conception of God were, according to Ibn Ḫaldūn, about anthropomorphism. These differences of opinion arose, according to him, out of conflicting descriptions of God found in the Koran. On the one hand, "in many verses of the Koran, God is described as being devoid of any likeness to human beings (*tanzīh*)." [36] But, on the other hand, "there are a few other verses in the Koran suggesting a likeness of God to human beings (*tashbīh*)." [37] These conflicting verses gave rise, according to Ibn Ḫaldūn, to three views.

First, there were "the early Muslims," who, he says, gave preference to those verses indicating God's freedom from any

[34] Cf. above, p. 3.
[34a] Cf. below, pp. 10–11.
[35] *Farḳ*, p. 12, ll. 2–4.
[36] *Muḳaddimah* III, p. 36, ll. 16–17.
[37] *Ibid.*, l. 20–p. 37, l. 1.

likeness to human beings."[38] The reason given by him for that preference is that the anti-anthropomorphic verses are "many" (*kathīrah*),[39] whereas the anthropomorphic verses are "few" (*ḳalīlah*),[40] and also that the anti-anthropomorphic verses are "clear in meaning, requiring no interpretation . . . being as they all are negative in their form of expression."[41] This explanation, it must be said, only partly conforms to what we actually find in the Koran. The Koran, indeed, contains anti-anthropomorphic verses which are couched in negative form, namely, the verses "Nought is there like Him" (42:9); "And there is none like unto Him" (112:4), and these verses, indeed, are more explicit in their denial of anthropomorphism than the verses which describe God by terms in which there is only an implication of anthropomorphism. But certainly these explicit anti-anthropomorphic verses are not more numerous than those which imply anthropomorphism. In justification of his explanation it may be suggested that by verses implying anthropomorphism, Ibn Ḫaldūn meant only those verses which imply, as he happens to mention later, such crude anthropomorphism as "hands and feet and a face,"[42] and by explicit anti-anthropomorphic verses couched in negative language, he meant not only the two verses quoted above but also the verses condemning idolatry and the worship of other gods, which by implication means the negation of anthropomorphism. By such a use of terms, Ibn Ḫaldūn could have gotten the impression that the explicit anti-anthropomorphic verses expressed negatively are more numerous than the verses which only imply anthropomorphism, though statistically perhaps his statement may not be correct even in that sense. As for the anthropomorphic verses, these early Muslims maintained that nothing is to be done about them, for, says Ibn Ḫaldūn, "though they were aware

[38] *Ibid.*, p. 37, ll. 1–2.
[39] *Ibid.*, p. 36, l. 17; cf. p. 37, l. 2.
[40] *Ibid.*, p. 36, l. 20.
[41] *Ibid.*, ll. 17–18; cf. p. 37, l. 2.
[42] *Ibid.*, p. 37, l. 9.

of the absurdity of likening God to human beings, they declared those anthropomorphic verses to be the word of God, and therefore they believed in them and did not try to investigate or interpret their meaning." [43]

Second and third, besides those who held the preceding view, reports Ibn Ḫaldūn, there were a few "innovators" (*mubtadi'ah*).[44] Of these there were two main groups. One group professed outright anthropomorphism.[45] Another group tried to harmonize the anthropomorphic verses with the anti-anthropomorphic verses by interpreting the former.[46] Some, dealing with verses which ascribe to God parts of the human body, such as "hands and feet and a face," [47] interpreted them to mean that God has "a body unlike bodies"; [48] others, dealing with verses which describe God by terms which only imply His possession of a human body, such as "direction, sitting, descending, voice, sound," [49] interpreted them to mean "a voice unlike voices," "a direction unlike directions," "descending unlike descending." [50] Ibn Ḫaldūn rejects this method of harmonization, arguing that any formula like "a body unlike bodies" is an infringement upon the Law of Contradiction, for any such formula is tantamount to saying that God is both like other things and not like other things.[51]

The term "innovators," by which Ibn Ḫaldūn describes both the extreme anthropomorphists and those who used the formula "a body unlike bodies," would at first sight seem to have been used here in the sense of "heretics," for the term *bid'ah*, "innovation," is used by him later in connection with the Mu'tazilites in the special sense of "heresy." [52] However, in view of the fact that interpretation by the formula "a body

[43] *Ibid.*, ll. 2–4.

[44] *Ibid.*, l. 7. The account here of the appearance of new views regarding the anthropomorphic verses in the Koran refers, I take it, to what happened among the Sunnites prior to the rise of Mu'tazilism. In Shahrastānī, there is nothing to correspond to this account.

[45] *Ibid.*, ll. 8–10.

[46] *Ibid.*, ll. 13–14.

[47] *Ibid.*, ll. 8–9.

[48] *Ibid.*, ll. 14–15.

[49] *Ibid.*, p. 38, ll. 1–2.

[50] *Ibid.*, ll. 3–4.

[51] *Ibid.*, ll. 15–16.

[52] *Ibid.*, p. 44, l. 3; p. 47, l. 17.

unlike bodies" was later adopted by Ḥanbalites[53] and that it is also quoted in the name of Ash'arī,[54] it is quite clear that Ibn Ḫaldūn uses here the term "innovators" simply in the sense that they introduced something new.[55] From this account of his, it is quite clear that, according to his knowledge, the formula "a body unlike bodies" had been used by certain Sunnites in their opposition to downright anthropomorphism prior to its use by the Shi'ite Hishām b. al-Ḥakam,[56] who was a downright anthropomorphist.[57]

This conception of God as a body unlike other bodies, which Ibn Ḫaldūn reports in the name of some pre-Mu'tazilite orthodox Muslims, is not new in the history of religion. In Christianity it was boldly asserted by Tertullian,[58] and it is based, as I have explained elsewhere, upon the fact that in the Scriptures, both in the Old and in the New Testament, God is never described by a term meaning "incorporeal"; He is only described there, and directly so only in the Old Testament, as being unlike any of His created beings, from which Philo, and after him other scriptural philosophers, derived their belief in the incorporeality of God.[59] So also in the Koran, it may be added, God is not described by a term meaning "incorporeal"; He is only described as being unlike any of His created beings, and this is the prime meaning of *tanzīh*, namely, the elevation of God above any likeness to

[53] Cf. below, p. 77 at n. 17.

[54] Cf. below at nn. 69, 98, 154.

[55] So also Shahrastānī (*Nihāyat*, p. 313, l. 15) describes Ash'arī as one who "innovated" (*abdā'*) a certain belief with regard to the Koran in departure from the common belief of the Early Muslims and the Ḥanbalites, without any suggestion that his innovation was heresy. Probably also in its application to the extreme anthropomorphizers the term "innovators" was not used here by Ibn Ḫaldūn in the sense of heretics, seeing that a group of extreme anthropomorphizers who appeared after the Miḥnah are included by Shahrastānī among those who "adhered to the plain meanings of the Book and the Sunnah" (*Milal*, p. 19, l. 20 – p. 20, l. 1). Cf. below at nn. 130 and 138–141.

[56] *Maḳālāt*, p. 33, ll. 10–11; p. 208, l. 1.

[57] *Ibid.*, p. 31, ll. 12 ff.

[58] *Adv. Prax.* 7 (PL 2, 162 C).

[59] Cf. *Philo*, II, pp. 94–100, 151–152; *Religious Philosophy*, pp. 84–85.

created beings. But a Tertullian origin for this view in Islam is hardly possible, for all the Christian influences upon the Kalam come from Greek Christianity, not from Latin Christianity; and Tertullian's view was not current in Greek Christianity.[60] This method of interpreting anthropomorphisms must have arisen, therefore, within Islam itself. How it could have arisen within Islam itself, I shall now try to explain.

The Arabic term for "anthropomorphization," *tashbīh*, literally means "likening," that is, likening God to human beings. So also the Arabic phrase *āyāt al-tashbīh*,[60a] which refers to anthropomorphic verses in the Koran, literally means, "the verses of likening," that is, the Koranic verses in which God is described in the likeness of human beings. It is such verses that, according to Ibn Ḫaldūn, certain pre-Muʿtazilite orthodox interpreted by the formula "a body unlike bodies." Now "likeness" between things in general, and not necessarily "likeness" between God and human beings, is the basis of the legal reasoning by "analogy" as used in the Fiḳh from earliest times. Thus in a letter of instruction to judges, which is quoted by Ibn Ḫaldūn, Caliph ʿUmar is reported to have said: "Study similitudes (*amthāl*) and likenesses (*ashbāh*) and judge things by analogy (*ḳis*) with things similar (*naẓāʾir*) to them." [61] Let us then study the manner in which the concept of "likeness" is used in the Fiḳh and see whether it will throw any light upon the origin of the formula "a body un-

[60] Origen's argument against "some" who said that God "is of a corporeal nature rarified and ethereal" (*In Joan.* XIII, 21, PG 14, 432 C) does not refer to a view like Tertullian's, according to which God is a body *sui generis* (*Adv. Prax.* 7 [PL 2, 162 C]), for the body *sui generis* which Tertullian ascribes to God is a body unlike even any known body which Origen describes as "rarified and ethereal." What Origen refers to is rather a view like that of Theophrastus, the successor of Aristotle, who identifies God with "the heaven" or with "the stars and the constellations of the heaven" (Cicero, *De Nat. Deor.* I, 13, 35), all of which are what Origen describes as "of a corporeal nature rarified and ethereal." So also Athenagoras refers to "Aristotle and his followers" as saying that God's body is "the ethereal space and the planetary stars and the sphere of the fixed stars" (*Supplicatio* 6).

[60a] *Tahāfut al-Falāsifah* XX, 20, p. 355, l. 21.

[61] *Muḳaddimah* I, p. 398, ll. 6–7.

like bodies" used in the interpretation of the "likeness" implied in the Koranic anthropomorphic verses.

Now when we study the actual cases of analogy as used in the Fiḳh, we find that the likenesses upon which the analogies are based are certain special likenesses with regard to certain special aspects to be observed in things which on the whole are unlike. A good example of such a use of analogy in the Fiḳh is to be found in Ibn Ḫaldūn's own citation of a case in which the method of analogy is used in the Fiḳh. In the Koran (2:216; 5:92, 93), there is a prohibition of the drinking of *ḫamr*, which means "grape wine." In the Fiḳh, however, this prohibition is extended to include *nabīdh*, that is, "date wine," and this is done by the argument that, though *ḫamr* and *nabīdh* are unlike each other, there is an analogy (*ḳiyās*) between them insofar as they are alike with reference to the fact that both cause intoxication.[62] Another good example is to be found in Shāfiʿī's attempt to draw an analogy between two such unlike things as a dog and carrion with regard to the nonliability of the payment of damages if, in the case of a dog, one killed him and, in the case of carrion, one burned it, and this analogy is drawn on the ground that there is a likeness between a dog and carrion insofar as the keeping of a dog is prohibited except for certain necessary purposes and similarly the eating of carrion is prohibited except under certain circumstances of necessity.[63] Analogy in the Fiḳh thus does not mean simply likeness; it means some special aspect or aspects of likeness between things which in all other aspects are unlike.

Let us now imagine that that group of early orthodox Muslims who, as we have seen, even before the rise of Muʿtazilism were opposed to *tashbīh*, that is, to taking the anthropomorphic verses in the Koran literally, were at the same time also opposed to those who maintained that one must not

[62] *Ibid.* III, p. 288, ll. 12–16; see Rosenthal's translation and note, III, pp. 331–332.

[63] Quoted in Margoliouth, *The Early Development of Mohammedanism*, p. 97; see also list of examples of *ḳiyās* in Schacht, *Origins*, pp. 106–111.

look for an explanation of those verses. To them these verses had to be explained somehow. They were thus trying to find an explanation for these verses. The explanation that naturally suggested itself to them was that the likeness which is implied in the anthropomorphic verses in the Koran is not to be taken to mean a complete likeness in every respect but that the likeness which is explicitly prohibited in the Koran is to be taken to mean a complete likeness in every respect. Trained, however, as they were in the method used by the early Muslims with regard to the explanation of the articles of faith, they were looking for traditional evidence in support of their explanation that the likeness implied in the anthropomorphic Koranic verses is not to be taken to mean a complete likeness in every respect. And as they were looking for such supporting evidence, they suddenly reminded themselves of the likeness in the method of analogy of the Fiḳh, which they knew was not a likeness in every respect but a likeness only in some respects. Aha, they exclaimed, why not apply this conception of likeness to the likeness in the anthropomorphic verses in the Koran? They tried and found that it worked. The likeness between God and human beings which is allowed in the anthropomorphic verses in the Koran, they reasoned, does not mean a likeness between them in every respect; it means a likeness between them in only some respects. Similarly, the likeness between God and human beings which is prohibited in the anti-anthropomorphic verses in the Koran refers only to a likeness between them in every respect; it does not refer to a likeness between them in only some respects. It is this kind of reasoning that is implied in Maimonides' statement that those Mutakallimūn who explain anthropomorphisms by the formula "a body unlike bodies" challenge their opponents to prove that the likeness between God and His creatures that is prohibited means any likeness whatsoever "in anything" [64] and argue in effect that a likeness between God and any of His created beings is not to be

[64] *Moreh* I, 76 (2), p. 160, ll. 15–16.

prohibited if the created being "is not like Him in all respects." [65] With this qualification of the Koranic prohibition of likening God to other beings, some pre-Muʿtazilite orthodox Muslims argued that the attribution to God in some Koranic verses of such terms as hands and feet and a face or as sitting and descending and a voice does not mean that these terms in their attribution to God are in all respects like the same terms when attributed to men; their attribution to God is meant to be taken only according to what in the Fiḳh is called analogy, that is to say, in their attribution to God these terms are only in some respect like the same terms when attributed to men; in all other respects there is no likeness between them. It is to be noted, however, that they do not try to explain in what respect they are unlike. They are quite satisfied with the simple assertion that the likeness implied is not a likeness in every respect.

Thus the pre-Muʿtazilite Kalam method of explaining anthropomorphisms by the formula "a body unlike bodies" is the method of analogy used in the Fiḳh, and one may reasonably assume that it was borrowed from the Fiḳh.

Corroborative evidence that this method of explaining anthropomorphisms is the method of analogy used in the Fiḳh may be found in a passage in Ibn Ḥazm's *Fiṣal.*

The passage comes as a sequel to Ibn Ḥazm's discussion of the use of analogy (*ḳiyās*) in the Fiḳh. As a Zahirite, Ibn Ḥazm is opposed to the use of the analogical method of reasoning in Muslim jurisprudence, and so, after having said all he had to say against the use of analogy in the Fiḳh, he proceeds to argue against its use in the Kalam.[66] Setting up certain

[65] *Ibid.*, l. 19. The logical basis for this kind of reasoning is supplied by Juwaynī who, in answer to the question whether "of two unlike things one of them may have something in common with the other," says that "it is not impossible for a thing to share in common with that which is unlike it in some general characteristics" (*Irshād*, p. 21, ll. 10–11 and 21–22[44]). Cf. the following statement of Aristotle: "Things are like if, not being absolutely the same, nor without difference in their concrete substance, they are the same in form" (*Metaph.* X, 3, 1054b, 3–5).

[66] Cf. Goldziher, *Die Zahiriten*, pp. 156 ff.

Ash'arites as the target of his attack, he first restates and characterizes their view and then criticizes it.

In his restatement he says that "the Ash'arites proclaim that they reject any likeness between God and created beings (*al-tashbīh*) but then they themselves sink deeply into this sin, for they say: Inasmuch as none among human beings can be performing actions unless he is living and knowing and powerful, it must necessarily follow that the Creator, who is the author of all things, is living and knowing and powerful." [67]

This restatement of the view of the Ash'arites reflects some such passages as the following: (1) a passage like that in which Ash'arī himself, after declaring that "the Creator is unlike creatures," tries to show that He cannot be like them even "in some one respect," [68] the implication thus being that He is unlike them in every respect; (2) a passage like that in which Ash'arī is reported as saying that "God has a knowledge which is not like other knowledges, and a power which is not like other powers, and a hearing which is not like other hearings, and a sight which is not like other sights." [69]

In his criticism of this view of the Ash'arites, Ibn Ḥazm says: "This is the wording (or tenor) of their analogy (*ḳiyās*) — both elevating God above all creatures and likening Him to them. But those who make use of reasoning by analogy allow its use only when it is drawn between things which are alike. As for drawing an analogy between things which are different in every respect and are not alike in anything, this would not, according to the opinion of anyone, be admissible." [70]

In this criticism, Ibn Ḥazm alludes to the two passages which we have quoted as being reflected in his restatement of the Ash'arite view. Alluding first to the second passage,

[67] *Fiṣal* II, p. 158, ll. 10–13.
[68] *Luma'* 7.
[69] *Tabyīn*, p. 149, ll. 11–12 (171, 1).
[70] *Fiṣal* II, p. 158, ll. 13–17. Cf. Ibn Ḫaldūn's criticism of this formula above, p. 10.

namely, that "God has a knowledge which is not like other knowledges, etc.," he describes it as "their analogy." By this, I take it, he means that this statement of the Ash'arites is based upon the analogy of the Fiḳh, where it is applied to things which, though unlike in some respects, are alike in others. Then, alluding to the first passage, namely, that God is not like His creatures even "in some one respect," he tries to show that in the Fiḳh, analogy is never applied to "things which are different in every respect and are not alike in anything."

From all this it may be gathered that the interpretation of the Koranic anthropomorphic verses by the formula "a body unlike bodies" is linked with the method of analogy as used in the Fiḳh. What, therefore, those orthodox "innovators" of Ibn Ḫaldūn did was to take the method of analogy, already in use by their contemporaries in connection with problems in the Fiḳh, and apply it to the problem of the anthropomorphic verses in the Koran.

So much for the pre-Mu'tazilite difference of opinion with regard to the right conception of God, especially the problem of anthropomorphism.

The other difference of opinion which, according to both Shahrastānī and Ibn Ḫaldūn, appeared before Mu'tazilism, concerned the belief in the power of God. This difference of opinion also arose, as we shall see, out of conflicting statements in the Koran on the power of God. On the one hand, there are verses which state that certain facts about man's life and certain actions of man are predetermined by God; but, on the other hand, there are verses which state that man enjoys a certain freedom of action.[71] The original view in Islam, according to Shahrastānī, was to follow those verses which state that the power determining human action belongs to God, for we are told by him that it was only "in the latter days of the Companions" that "there arose the heresy of Ma'bad al-Juhanī [d. *ca.* 699] and Ghaylān al-Dimashḳī and

[71] Cf. below, pp. 601–602.

Jūnas al-Aswārī with regard to the doctrine of the *ḳadar*,"[72] and because they transferred the *ḳadar* from God to man, maintaining that man himself, and not God, determines man's own action, they came to be known as the Ḳadarites (*al-ḳadariyyah*).[73] We shall henceforth refer to these two groups as Predestinarians and Libertarians. What made those early Muslims choose the predestinarian verses in preference to the libertarian verses and what caused the rise of the libertarian heresy and how both the Predestinarians and the Libertarians tried to explain the Koranic verses opposed to those chosen by them will be discussed later.[74]

Thus prior to the rise of Muʿtazilism there appeared in what was called Kalam differences of opinion with regard to two articles of faith, namely, the first, dealing with the right conception of God, and the sixth, dealing with the power of God.

Then, during the first part of the eighth century, there appeared the Muʿtazilite sect, the founder of which was Wāṣil b. ʿAṭā', who died in 748/9.

Muʿtazilism, as well as its founder, is charged with many heresies,[75] but, with the exception of two, none has reference to any of the original six articles of faith. Of the two exceptions, one was the heresy with regard to the belief in the power of God, which the Muʿtazilites inherited from the Libertarians. We have already briefly explained the nature of this heresy. The other was a heresy with regard to the belief in the right conception of God. The nature of this heresy may be briefly explained as follows: It happens that early in its history, for reasons to be explained later,[76] there appeared in Islam the belief that, corresponding to the terms "living" and "knowing" or "living" and "powerful" or "knowing" and "powerful," there existed in God life and knowledge or life and power or knowledge and power as real, eternal things

[72] *Milal*, p. 17, ll. 12–13. Cf. *Muḳaddimah* III, p. 48, ll. 17–18.

[73] Cf. below, pp. 619–620.

[74] Cf. below, pp. 608–611.

[75] *Farḳ*, p. 93, l. 12–p. 94, l. 14; p. 96, l. 17–p. 100, l. 3; *Milal*. p. 30, l. 6–p. 34, l. 8.

[76] Cf. below, pp. 112 ff.

described as *maʿānī*, "things," and *ṣifāt*,[77] "characteristics." In view of the fact that the term *ṣifāt*, which I have provisionally translated by "characteristics," came to be translated into European languages, through the influence of the Latin translation of Maimonides' *Guide of the Perplexed*, by the term "attributes,"[78] this belief in *ṣifāt* is now generally known as the orthodox Muslim belief in attributes, of which, as we shall see, the belief in the eternity of a pre-existent Koran was a part.[79] It is this orthodox belief in attributes that the Muʿtazilites denied. The denial of it, as reported in the name of its founder, Wāṣil b. ʿAṭāʾ, reads: "He who posits a thing (*maʿnā*) and attribute (*ṣifah*) as eternal posits two gods."[80] It is with these two heresies, namely, the assertion of free will and the denial of attributes, that the name Muʿtazilites became identified, even though the term *muʿtazilah*, "Separatists," which the name literally means, is derived from the fact that Wāṣil b. ʿAṭāʾ "separated himself" (*iʿtāzal*) from the accepted view of the Muslim community on the question of the status of sinners in Islam.[81] And since their assertion of free will was supported by them on the ground of their particular conception of divine justice and their denial of attributes was supported by them on the ground of their particular conception of divine unity, the Muʿtazilites came to be called "the partisans of justice and unity" (*aṣḥāb al-ʿadl waʾl-tauḥīd*).[82]

About a century after Wāṣil b. ʿAṭāʾ, Muʿtazilism, we are told, came under the influence of Greek philosophy and assumed a new character. As described by Shahrastānī, the change came about as follows: "Then, some masters of the Muʿtazilites devoted themselves to the study of the works

[77] For these translations of the terms *maʿānī* and *ṣifāt*, see below, pp. 114 ff.

[78] See *Religious Philosophy*, pp. 56–58.

[79] Cf. below, p. 241.

[80] *Milal*, p. 31, l. 19.

[81] *Farḳ*, p. 98, ll. 4–13; *Milal*, p. 33, ll. 2–11. For modern discussions of the origin of the name Muʿtazilites, see Nallino, "Sull' origine del nome dei Muʿtaziliti," *Rivista degli Studi Orientali*, 7:429–454 (1916–1918); Gardet et Anawati, *Introduction à la Théologie Musulmane* (1948), pp. 46–47.

[82] *Milal*, p. 29, l. 18.

of the philosophers, which were made available (*fussirat*, literally, 'disclosed,' 'interpreted') in the days of al-Mā'mūn [813–833]. Blending the methods (*manāhij*) of the philosophers with the methods of the Kalam, they formed of the blend a special branch of science. They named that science Kalam, and this either because the principal problem which they discussed and battled over was the problem of God's speech (*al-kalām*) and therefore the entire range of problems discussed by them was called by the name of that particular problem, or because the Muʿtazilites followed the example of the philosophers, who called one branch of their scientific disciplines the discipline of *manṭiḳ* [that is, logic], for *manṭiḳ* and *kalām* are synonymous Arabic terms [both of them, like the Greek *logos*, meaning 'speech']." [83]

In this passage, it will be noticed, Muʿtazilism is divided into a nonphilosophical period and a philosophical period, and the Muʿtazilites during the nonphilosophical period are said to have employed methods which are described as "the methods of the Kalam." What these "methods of the Kalam" were we are not told. But knowing as we do that prior to the rise of Muʿtazilism there already existed a Kalam method of reasoning consisting of the Fiḳh method of analogy, we may assume that by "the methods of the Kalam," Shahrastānī refers to the various applications of that Fiḳh method of analogy, including, we may further assume, its application to the anthropomorphic verses in the Koran, by interpreting them according to the formula "a body unlike bodies." [84]

As for "the methods of the philosophers" with which the Muʿtazilites blended "the methods of the Kalam," we may assume that Shahrastānī meant by it two things.

First, we may assume that he meant by it that under the influence of the Arabic translations of Greek philosophical works, the Muʿtazilites began to use the term *ḳiyās* in the sense of "syllogism," and for *ḳiyās* in the old sense of "analogy," as used in the Fiḳh, they substituted the term *tam-*

[83] *Ibid.*, p. 18, ll. 2–6. [84] Cf. above, pp. 7 and 10.

thīl. Our justification for this assumption is to be found in the fact that others in Islam who came under the influence of these translations changed the meaning of *ḳiyās* from "analogy" to "syllogism," and for *ḳiyās* in its old Fiḳh sense of "analogy," they substituted the term *tamthīl*. Thus, for instance, both Avicenna and Ghazālī use *ḳiyās* in the sense of "syllogism" [85] and *tamthīl* in the sense of "analogy," based, as in the Fiḳh, on a likeness between things; [86] and, after mentioning the term *tamthīl*, Avicenna remarks that "it is this which people of our time call *ḳiyās*," [87] and Ghazālī remarks that "it is this which the masters of the Fiḳh and the masters of the Kalam call *ḳiyās*." [88]

Second, we may assume that Shahrastānī meant by it also that the philosophical Muʿtazilites became acquainted with Aristotle's own conception of analogy, for which the Arabic was *musāwāh*, "equality," and blended it for the analogy of the Fiḳh, for which the new term in Arabic was *tamthīl*, "likening." Now the analogy of Aristotle is not based, as that of the Fiḳh, upon the mere likeness between things. As defined by him in his *Nicomachean Ethics*, "analogy (ἀναλογία) is the equality of ratios (ἰσότης λόγων)," which he im-

[85] *Ishārāt*, p. 65, l. 4; *Maḳāṣid*, p. 28, ll. 4 ff.

[86] *Ishārāt*, p. 64, l. 16 – p. 65, l. 1; *Maḳāṣid*, p. 43, ll. 13–16. It is to be noted that *tamthīl*, "analogy," used by Avicenna in the Fiḳh sense of "likeness," is contrasted by him here with both "syllogism" and "induction" (*istiḳrāʾ*). This use of *tamthīl*, "analogy," as has been shown by Madkour (*L'Organon d'Aristote dans le monde arabe*, pp. 220–221), is due to a combination of the Fiḳh "analogy" with the Aristotelian "example" (παράδειγμα) in *Anal. Pri.* II, 24, 38 ff. It may, however, be added that in the Arabic translation of the *Organon* the term παράδειγμα in the passage quoted is rendered by *mithāl* and not by *tamthīl*. The change of *mithāl* to *tamthīl* as the new term for "analogy" is probably due to the fact that *mithāl* is also used as a translation of παράδειγμα in the Platonic sense of idea (cf. pseudo-Plutarch's *De Placitis Philosophorum* I, 5, 3, p. 292a, l. 3 [ed. Diels] in its Arabic translation, p. 106, l. 10 [ed. Badawi]) and hence also as a translation of the term ἰδέα (cf. Averroes, *In VII Metaph.*, Text. 53, Arabic, p. 983, l. 13, on *Metaph.* VII, 1040a, 8.) On *mathal* and *shibh* used respectively in the sense of the Greek γνώμη, "maxim," and παράδειγμα, "example," see my paper "The Double Faith Theory in Clement, Saadia, Averroes, and St. Thomas, and Its Origin in Aristotle and the Stoics," *JQR*, n.s., 33:246 (1942).

[87] *Ishārāt*, p. 64, ll. 15–16.

[88] *Maḳāṣid*, p. 43, ll. 12–13.

mediately illustrates by the proportion "A : B :: C : D";[89] and elsewhere he explains by the statement that when the term "good" is predicated of "intellect" and of "sight," it is done so by way of "analogy," for "intellect is to the soul as sight is to the body."[90] What, therefore, Shahrastānī means to say is that the philosophical Mu'tazilites blended the analogy used by the Fiḳh in the mere sense of likeness with the analogy used by Aristotle in the sense of equality of ratios or relations. Though it is uncertain whether the *Nicomachean Ethics* was translated into Arabic,[91] the same definition of analogy is implied in the explanation given by Aristotle in the *Metaphysics* of the expression "one according to analogy (κατ' ἀναλογίαν)," which in the Arabic translation reads: "And those which are one according to equality (*musāwāh*) are those whose relation (*nisbah*) is the same as the relation of one thing to another thing."[92] Averroes in his comment upon this passage first explains "one according to equality" to mean "one according to relationship or proportionality (*tanāsub*)" and then adds: "just as the relation of the ruler to the state and that of the pilot to the ship are said to be the same relationship."[93] This shows that Arab students of philosophy were acquainted with Aristotle's own conception of analogy as defined and explained by him in the *Nicomachean Ethics*, and this Greek term *analogia* was rendered into Arabic not only by *musāwāh*,[94] "equality," or *tanāsub*,[95] "relationship," "proportionality," but also by *muḳayāsah*,[96] "analogy."

[89] *Eth. Nic.* V, 6, 1131a, 31, and 1131b, 5–6.

[90] *Ibid.* I, 4, 1096b, 28–29.

[91] Cf. Steinschneider, *Die arabischen Übersetzungen aus dem Griechischen* (1897), § 36 (60).

[92] *Metaph.* V, 6, 1016b, 34–35; Averroes, *In V Metaph.*, Text. 12, Arabic, p. 544, l. 15–p. 545, l. 1.

[93] Averroes, *In V Metaph.*, Comm. 12, Arabic, p. 549, ll. 11–12.

[94] Cf. above at n. 92.

[95] *Anal. Post.* I, 12, 78a, 1, 2, 3, 5 (Arabic, p 347, ll. 42, 43, 45); *Metaph.* XII, 4, 1070a, 32 (Averroes *In XII Metaph.*, Text. 19, Arabic, p. 1505, l. 8).

[96] *Top.* V, 8, 138b, 24 (Arabic, p. 621). In his Epitome of Porphyry's *Isagoge* (MS. Munich, *Cod. Arab.* 650a), this Aristotelian type of analogy is described by the term *mutashābihah*. Cf. my paper "Amphibolous Terms,"

In further proof that Aristotle's conception of analogy was known to Arabic students of his works, that it was used by some of them in place of the old Fiḳh conception of analogy as an interpretation of the anthropomorphic verses in the Koran, and that it could have been known to Shahrastānī, we may quote a passage from Juwaynī, who flourished about two centuries after the rise of philosophical Muʿtazilism but who died a year before Shahrastānī was born and who is quoted by Shahrastānī in his *Nihāyat*.[97]

In that passage, as reproduced by Ibn ʿAsākir, Juwaynī enumerates three views with regard to such terms as "hand" and "face" and "descent" and "being seated on the throne" which are ascribed to God in the Koran. One view is that of those who take all these terms in their literal sense. Another view is that of Ashʿarī, who takes all these terms to mean that God has a hand and a face and a descent and is seated on the throne unlike other hands and faces and descents and unlike others who are seated on thrones. A third view is that of the Muʿtazilites, who take "hand" to mean "power and bounty," "face" to mean "existence," "descent" to mean "the descent of some of God's signs and angels," and "being seated [on the throne]" to mean "dominion."[98] Now of the second and third views, that of Ashʿarī follows the old explanation by the formula "a body unlike bodies," which, as we have seen, is based on reasoning by "analogy" in the Fiḳh sense of mere likeness. But the view ascribed here to the Muʿtazilites strikes one as being based upon analogy in the Aristotelian sense of equality of relations, for all their explanations of these terms are reducible to the form of equations, as follows: Power and bounty are to God as hand is to man; existence is to God as face is to man; descent of some

HTR, 31:162, n. 52 (1938). Ghazālī, as we shall see (below at nn. 99–101), uses *mithl* or *mathal* for the Aristotelian type of analogy.

[97] *Nihāyat*, p. 12, l. 7.

[98] *Tabyīn*, p. 150, ll. 2–14; cf. p. 149, ll. 11–12 (172–173, 4–6; cf. 171, 1). See Spitta, *Zur Geschichte Abu'l-Ḥasan al-Aš'arī's*, pp. 106–107; Arabic text: Anhang no. 13, p. 141, l. 19 – p. 142, l. 7.

of His signs and His angels is to God as descent is to man; dominion is to God as being seated on a throne is to a king.

Moreover, an allusion to this new kind of interpretation of Koranic anthropomorphisms under the influence of the new philosophic conception of "analogy" may be discerned in a passage by Juwaynī's pupil, Ghazālī. In that passage, Ghazālī makes those in Islam whom he calls "philosophers" say that "the anthropomorphic verses" in the Koran are to be interpreted as "*amthāl*." [99] Now the reference here could not be to the interpretation by the formula "a body unlike bodies," for that interpretation is ascribed by his own teacher, Juwaynī, to Ashʿarī, and consequently he could not ascribe it to the "philosophers." Undoubtedly the reference is to the kind of interpretation which Juwaynī ascribed to the Muʿtazilites, which was like that used by the Muslim philosophers, and this, as we have suggested, is based upon the Aristotelian conception of analogy. The term *mithl* or *mathal*, of which the term *amthāl* used here is the plural, is thus used by Ghazālī in the sense of the Aristotelian conception of analogy. Corroborative evidence that the reference here is to an interpretation by analogy in its Aristotelian sense may be discerned in his remark that the interpretation of the Koranic anthropomorphisms as *amthāl* are "after the manner of the usage of metaphors in Arabic" [100] — a remark which evidently reflects Aristotle's statement that "analogy" is one of the four kinds of metaphor and the most popular of them.[101]

And so, while it cannot be determined when this new interpretation of the Koranic anthropomorphic verses was introduced by the philosophical Muʿtazilites during the two centuries of their history prior to Juwaynī, it is quite clear that Shahrastānī could have had knowledge of it, and we may therefore assume that it is included in his statement about the Muʿtazilites' blending of the methods of the philosophers with the methods of the Kalam.

[99] *Tahāfut al-Falāsifah* XX, 20, p. 355, ll. 6–8.
[100] *Ibid.*, XX, 21, p. 355, ll. 10–11.
[101] *Rhet.* III, 10, 1410b, 36 – 1411a, 1; cf. *Poet.* 21, 1457b, 6–9.

The last statement in Shahrastānī's passage explaining why the Mu'tazilites called their system Kalam means that, while they rejected the old methods of the Kalam, they still retained the term Kalam but gave it a new meaning. The term Kalam, "speech," he says, was no longer used by them as a description of the application of the method of analogy to faith, which is a matter of speech, in contradistinction to its application to Fiḳh, which deals with action; it has now acquired with them a twofold new meaning, and it is used as a description of their new method of reasoning as well as a description of the subject matter of their system. As a description of their new method of reasoning, the term *kalām* is used by them, like its synonym *manṭiḳ*, in the sense of logic; as a description of the subject matter of their system, the term *kalām* is used in the sense of the divine attribute of speech, that is, the pre-existent Koran, the denial of whose eternity is the chief contention of their system.

All this is what may be gathered from Shahrastānī's passage describing the rise of Mu'tazilism.

Corresponding to this passage in Shahrastānī, there are two passages in Ibn Ḫaldūn, in one of which he deals with the rise of Mu'tazilism and in the other of which he alludes to a distinction in the history of Mu'tazilism between a non-philosophical period and a philosophical period.

The passage in which he deals with the rise of Mu'tazilism comes immediately after the passage in which he describes the views of those who before the rise of Mu'tazilism either refused to discuss the anthropomorphic verses in the Koran or interpreted them by the formula "a body unlike bodies." [102] The passage reads as follows: "Then sciences and arts increased and people were eager to put down their views in writing and to carry on discussions on all sorts of subjects and the Mutakallimūn wrote on deanthropomorphization (*al-tanzīh*). At that juncture, the Mu'tazilite heresy took place. The Mu'tazilites broadened the meaning of the dean-

[102] *Muḳaddimah* III, p. 37, l. 1 – p. 38, l. 11; cf. above, pp. 9–10.

thropomorphization (*al-tanzīh*) which is implied in the negative verses [such as 'Nought is there like Him' (42:9) and 'There is none equal with Him' (112:4)] and took it to mean the denial of [the existence of] attributes conceived as things (*ṣifāt al-maʿānī*), such as knowledge and power and will and life, in addition to [taking it to mean the mere denial of the literalness of] these terms used as predications (*zāʾidah ʿalā iḥkamihā*) [that is, used in the form of participles such as knowing and powerful and willing and living]," [103] to which he later refers as *al-ṣifāt al-maʿnawiyyah*.[103a]

In this passage, Ibn Ḫaldūn describes by means of four brief statements the cultural climate in Islam on the eve of the rise of Muʿtazilism, all of which, as we shall see, correspond to certain statements by which Shahrastānī introduces the rise of Muʿtazilism.

The first statement, namely, "sciences and arts increased," is Ibn Ḫaldūn's substitution of a more general statement for a correspondingly more specific statement in Shahrastānī that Wāṣil b. ʿAṭāʾ, the founder of Muʿtazilism, "studied sciences and traditions" under his teacher al-Ḥasan al-Baṣrī,[104] and it reflects his own statement elsewhere that prior to the first attempt to translate Greek philosophic works into Arabic during the reign of Caliph Manṣūr (754–775), that is, long before the rise of Muʿtazilism, the Muslims had already become versed in many different "arts and sciences." [105] The term "arts" used by Ibn Ḫaldūn here in his first statement, as may be judged from the second statement immediately following it, refers especially to what he elsewhere calls the art of writing (*al-kitābah*) [106] and the other arts relating to it, such as the art of calligraphy (*al-ḫaṭṭ*),[107] the art of the copyist

[103] *Ibid.*, p. 38, ll. 11–15.

[103a] *Ibid.*, p. 39, ll. 10 and 12, and see *Faḍālī, Kifāyat*, p. 56, l. 39 – p. 57, l. 4 (cf. Macdonald's *Development of Muslim Theology*, p. 337), but see also below, p. 178, n. 65. On Ibn Ḫaldūn's conception of Ash'arī's theory of attributes, see *Religious Philosophy*, pp. 181–185.

[104] *Milal*, p. 31, ll. 12–13.

[105] *Mukaddimah* III, p. 91, ll. 4–5.

[106] *Ibid.* II, p. 277, l. 2.

[107] *Ibid.*, p. 338, l. 1.

(*al-nassāḫ*),[108] and the art of book production (*al-warāḳah*).[109]

The second statement, namely, that "people were eager to put down their views in writing," corresponds to Shahrastānī's statement that Wāṣil b. ʿAṭā''s teacher, al-Ḥasan al-Baṣrī, sent a treatise (*risālah*) to Caliph ʿAbd al-Malik b. Merwān, in which he discussed the problem of free will and predestination, and that the Caliph answered him also in writing.[110] Similarly, from another source we learn that a contemporary of al-Ḥasan al-Baṣrī, Ghaylān al-Dimashḳī, sent a book (*kitāb*) to Caliph ʿUmar b. ʿAbd al-ʿAzīs in which he discussed the same problem of free will and predestination.[111]

The third statement, namely, that the people were also eager "to carry on discussions on all sorts of problems," quite clearly refers to the account found in Shahrastānī concerning the controversies that prior to the rise of Muʿtazilism raged in Islam over such problems as predestination and free will, the status of sinners, and the status of those who participated in the Battle of the Camel. In every one of these controversies Wāṣil b. ʿAṭā' took a position which was considered heretical, and, according to tradition, it was the fact that he "separated himself" (*iʿtazal*) from the orthodox view on the problem of the status of sinners in Islam that he and his followers came to be called *muʿtazilah*, "Separatists."[112]

The fourth statement, namely, that "the Mutakallimūn wrote on deanthropomorphization (*al-tanzīh*)," quite evidently refers to that pre-Muʿtazilite group which Ibn Ḥaldūn himself has described as interpreting the anthropomorphic verses in the Koran by the formula "a body unlike bodies."[113] From another source we gather that such an interpretation was described as *tanzīh*.[114] His additional statement as to how the newly appearing Muʿtazilites broadened the meaning of

[108] *Ibid.*, p. 313, l. 3.
[109] *Ibid.*, p. 316, l. 7.
[110] *Milal*, p. 32, ll. 13–16.
[111] Cf. below, p. 616.
[112] *Milal*, p. 33, ll. 1–11; *Farḳ*, p. 98, ll. 4–13.
[113] Cf. above at nn. 44–46.
[114] Cf. *Tabyīn*, p. 149, ll. 11–12 (171) and p. 362, ll. 12–13 (188).

the deanthropomorphization which was used before them by Mutakallimūn means that, while they agreed with the Mutakallimūn that such terms as "knowing" and "powerful" and "willing" and "living" when predicated of God should be interpreted as meaning knowing and powerful and willing and living unlike other knowing and powerful and willing and living, they disagreed with those Mutakallimūn by denying the latter's contention that the terms "knowing" and "powerful" and "willing" and "living" when predicated of God mean the existence in God of knowledge and power and will and life as real attributes. Thus Ibn Ḫaldūn, like Shahrastānī, reports that the newly appearing Muʿtazilites, prior to their becoming philosophical, used the method of the Kalam in interpreting the anthropomorphic verses in the Koran by the formula "a body unlike bodies."

Ibn Ḫaldūn's allusion to the distinction between a non-philosophical period and a philosophical period in the history of Muʿtazilism occurs in a passage where at first, when he mentions the name of Wāṣil b. ʿAṭā', he describes him simply as being one "of them," that is, one of the Muʿtazilites,[115] but then, when he mentions the name of Abū al-Hudhayl, he describes him as one who "followed the opinions of the philosophers," [116] and similarly, when he mentions the name of Naẓẓām, he describes him as one who "devoted himself to the study of the works of the philosophers." [117] Following Shahrastānī, he gives the same two reasons why the philosophical Muʿtazilites named their system Kalam or, rather, why they adopted for their system the old name Kalam. "Their system was called the science of the Kalam," he says, "either because it contained argumentation and disputation, which is what might be called speech (*kalām*) [in the sense of 'logic' after the analogy of the term *manṭiḳ*], or because the main principle of

[115] *Muḳaddimah* III, p. 48, l. 19. Wāṣil is said here by Ibn Ḫaldūn to have lived during the reign of Caliph ʿAbd al-Malik b. Merwān (685–705), which quite evidently refers only to the date of the birth of Wāṣil (699); the date of his death is 748.

[116] *Ibid.*, p. 49, l. 3.

[117] *Ibid.*, l. 5.

their system is the denial of the attribute of speech [that is, the eternity of the Koran]." [118] With the rise of the Muʿtazilite sect, which, as we have seen, used the method of the Kalam and has retained for its system the name Kalam even when that system became philosophized, the term Kalam gradually came to be identified with Muʿtazilism. Thus, when one of the chief masters of the Fiḳh, Shāfiʿi (727/8–820), speaks of the *ahl al-kalām*, "the people of the Kalam," [119] he means by it the Muʿtazilites, and, therefore, when he criticizes and condemns the Kalam, it is the Kalam of the Muʿtazilites that he criticizes and condemns.[120]

The upshot of our discussion is that the history of the Kalam to the time of its becoming identified with Muʿtazilism falls into three periods.

The first period is that of the pre-Muʿtazilite Kalam. It began when, in such problems as anthropomorphisms, free will, the status of sinners, and the status of the followers of both sides in the Battle of the Camel, the participants in the discussion of these problems, instead of merely quoting texts from the Koran and the Sunnah in the defense of their respective views, began to use a certain method of reasoning whereby inferences were drawn from those texts of the Koran and the Sunnah. That method of reasoning was borrowed from the Fiḳh, where, known as *ḳiyās*, "analogy," it was used in connection with problems of law, which governed action. As the problems of faith to which this method of analogy came to be newly applied were problems related to the spoken word, this new application of the method of analogy came to be known as Kalam, the literal meaning of which is "speech." It was the application of this analogical method of reasoning by some early Muslims to the problem of the anthropomorphic verses in the Koran that gave rise to the interpretation of these

[118] *Ibid.*, ll. 7–9.
[119] Cf. Schacht, *Origins*, p. 128.
[120] Cf. Ibn ʿAsākir's explanation of Shāfiʿī's condemnation of the Kalam, in *Tabyīn*, p. 336, ll. 12 ff.; McCarthy, *The Theology of al-Ashʿarī*, pp. 184 ff.

verses by the formula "a body unlike bodies." The chief characteristics of this method of analogy, both in the Fiḳh and in the Kalam, are that it is based upon mere likeness and that it reasons from data furnished by tradition.

The second period is that of the nonphilosophical Muʿtazilite Kalam. It lasted for about a century, from the time of the appearance of Muʿtazilism in the first half of the eighth century to the translation into Arabic of Greek philosophic works in the first half of the ninth century. Throughout this period, the Muʿtazilites used the old Kalam method of analogy, but they manipulated it for their own purpose, in support of their various heretical views.

The third period is that of philosophical Muʿtazilite Kalam, which began with the translation of Greek philosophic works into Arabic during the early part of the ninth century. From these philosophic works, the Muʿtazilites learned not only certain philosophic views but also two new methods of reasoning, namely, the method of syllogism and a new use of the method of analogy. Both these philosophic methods of reasoning differed from the Kalam method of analogy in that they both reasoned from philosophic data, whereas the Kalam method of analogy reasoned from Muslim religious data, and, with regard to the philosophic use of analogy, it differed from the Kalam use of analogy also in that it was based upon an equality of relations, whereas the Kalam use of analogy was based upon a mere likeness between things. The Muʿtazilites used these two philosophic methods of reasoning in a twofold manner — either they substituted them for the Kalam method of analogy, thus reasoning philosophically from philosophic data, or they blended them with the Kalam method of analogy, thus reasoning philosophically from Muslim religious data. But though the philosophical Muʿtazilites rejected or modified the method of reasoning used in what was known as Kalam, they appropriated the term Kalam, gave it two new meanings, and used it as the name of their entire system.

This is the story of the Kalam to the time it became identified with Muʿtazilism.

Then both Shahrastānī and Ibn Ḫaldūn report how certain caliphs adopted Muʿtazilism and tried to suppress orthodoxy and how the reaction of the orthodox to the oppression ultimately led to the establishment of an orthodox Kalam to rival that of the Muʿtazilites.

In Shahrastānī the oppression of orthodoxy by Muʿtazilite caliphs is told in two brief passages. In one of these, after mentioning the name of "Abū Musā al-Muzdār [al-Murdār], the monk of the Muʿtazilites" as one of the masters of Muʿtazilism, he adds: "In his days there occurred most of the persecutions of the orthodox on account of their belief in the eternity of the Koran." [121] In the other passage, speaking of the Muʿtazilites, he says that "a number of Abbasside caliphs supported them in their denial of attributes and [the affirmation of] the createdness of the Koran." [122] Corresponding to these passages, there is in Ibn Ḫaldūn the following passage: "Certain leading Muʿtazilites indoctrinated certain caliphs with the belief that the Koran was created, and the people were forced to adopt it. The orthodox religious leaders opposed them. Because of their opposition, it was considered lawful to flog and kill many of them." [123] The references in these passages are to three historical facts: (1) the issuance of an edict by Caliph Ma'mūn in 827, whereby Muʿtazilism was declared to be the religion of the state and orthodoxy was condemned as heretical; (2) the issuance by him of another edict in 833, the year of his death, whereby a sort of inquisition, known as Miḥnah, was instituted; (3) the continuance of the Miḥnah during the reigns of Caliph Muʿtaṣim and Caliph Wāthiḳ to the second year of the reign of Caliph Mutawakkil (847).[124]

[121] *Milal*, p. 18, l. 20 – p. 19, l. 1. On the reading of "Muzdār" or "Murdār," see Haarbrücker's note in his translation of the *Milal*, vol. II, p. 399, note to pp. 71 f.

[122] *Milal*, p. 75, ll. 16–17.

[123] *Muḳaddimah* III, p. 39, ll. 5–7.

[124] Cf. W. W. Patton, *Aḥmad Ibn Ḥanbal and the Miḥna* (1897).

How the orthodox reacted to the Miḥnah is briefly described by Ibn Ḫaldūn: "This caused the people of the Sunnah to rise in the defense of the articles of faith by the use of intellectual (*ʿaḳliyyah*) proofs in order to repulse the innovations." [125] As we already know that the expression "argumentation formed by the intellect (*ʿaḳl*)" is used by Ibn Ḫaldūn in the sense of the Fiḳh analogical method of reasoning on the basis of traditional data which had come into use prior to the rise of Muʿtazilism and acquired the name Kalam,[126] it is quite clear that what he means by his statements here is that now, as a result of the Miḥnah, leaders of orthodoxy adopted that pre-Muʿtazilite Kalam method of reasoning. In fact, right after this statement, Ibn Ḫaldūn refers to these "people of the Sunnah" as "Mutakallimūn," [127] and from another statement of his, it may be gathered that among "these people of Sunnah" or "Mutakallimūn" he included Ibn Kullāb, al-Ḳalānisī, and al-Muḥāsibī [128] — names which in a corresponding passage in Shahrastānī, upon which the statement of Ibn Ḫaldūn is evidently based, are described as "powerful in Kalam," [129] by which is meant, as we shall see, the pre-Muʿtazilite nonphilosophical type of Kalam.

Now, according to that corresponding passage in Shahrastānī, this group of Mutakallimūn, described also by him as consisting of Ibn Kullāb and al-Ḳalānisī and al-Muḥāsibī, is only one of three orthodox groups which in the aftermath of the Miḥnah battled with the Muʿtazilites over the problem of attributes,[130] including, of course, the problem of the eternity of the Koran.

Of these three orthodox groups, the first two are described by Shahrastānī as arguing against the Muʿtazilites "not according to the canon of the Kalam, but rather by persuasive speech (*ʿalā ḳaul iḳnāʿī*)." [131] The expression "persuasive speech,"

[125] *Muḳaddimah* III, p. 39, ll. 7–8.
[126] Cf. above, p. 7.
[127] *Muḳaddimah* III, p. 49, l. 13.
[128] *Ibid.*, ll. 13–14.
[129] Cf. below, at n. 143.
[130] *Milal*, p. 19, ll. 17–18.
[131] *Ibid.*, ll. 18–19.

we take it, refers to what Aristotle would call "rhetoric," for rhetoric is defined by him "as the faculty of discovering the possible means of persuasion in reference to any subject whatever." [132] Now one of the means of persuasion, of the type which Aristotle calls "nontechnical," is described by him as "witnesses," by which he means quotations from such authoritative sources as Homer and Plato.[133] Accordingly, what Shahrastānī means by his statement here is that these two groups of post-Miḥnah orthodox Muslims went back to the most primitive method of the early Muslims. Thus, instead of using "the canon of the Kalam," that is, the method of analogy which before the rise of Muʿtazilism had been used even by some orthodox,[134] they resorted to the primitive method of the early Muslims by quoting texts from the Koran and the Sunnah — a method analogous to one of the means of persuasion which Aristotle includes under "rhetoric." In fact, Shahrastānī himself, right after saying that these two groups used "persuasive speech," says that "they adhered to literal meanings of the Book and Sunnah." [135]

These two post-Miḥnah orthodox groups, though presenting a common disregard for "the canon of the Kalam," are described by Shahrastānī as differing between themselves.

The first of these post-Miḥnah orthodox groups is described as that which "took attributes to be real things (*maʿānī*) subsisting in the essence of God." [136] From the wording of this statement, as contrasted with that of the statement by which, as we shall see, he describes the second group, we may take this statement to mean that this group only asserted the reality of attributes, without asserting their corporeality. No names are mentioned here by Shahrastānī in connection with this group, but in another place he tells us that its leader was Ibn Ḥanbal (d. 855), the champion of orthodoxy during the Miḥnah. He is described by Shahras-

[132] *Rhet.* I, 2, 1355b, 26–27.
[133] *Ibid.* I, 2, 1355b, 37; 15, 1375a, 22–25; 1375b, 25–1376a, 33.
[134] Cf. above, pp. 10–11.
[135] *Milal*, p. 19, l. 20 – p. 20, l. 1.
[136] *Ibid.*, p. 19, ll. 19–20.

tānī as following the view of Mālik b. Anas (d. 795), who said: "The sitting on the throne is known, but the howness (*al-kayfiyyah*) is unknown; the belief in it is obligatory, but the questioning about it is heresy (*bid'ah*)." [137]

The second of these post-Miḥnah orthodox groups is described as that which "likened the attributes of God with those of created beings." [138] Again, no names are mentioned here by Shahrastānī. But elsewhere in his work he differentiates from the old type of heretical Likeners, that is, anthropomorphists, whom he describes as "one group of the Shī'ites, namely, the Ghāliyyah," a new type of orthodox Likeners, whom he describes as "one group of the adherents of the Ḥadith, namely, the Ḥashwiyyah," [139] and as exponents of this new type of Likeners, described by him as belonging to "the people of the Sunnah," he mentions "Muḍar, Kahmash, and Aḥmad al Hajīmī [140] — all of whom flourished up to about 860,[141] that is, after the time of the Miḥnah.

The third orthodox group which flourished after the Miḥnah consisted, according to Shahrastānī, of "'Abdallah b. Sa'īd b. Kullāb [d. 854] and Abū al-'Abbās al-Ḳalānisī and al-Ḥārith al-Muḥāsibī [d. 857]." [142] The members of this group

[137] *Milal*, p. 65, ll. 7–9, and p. 64, ll. 12–17; cf. above at n. 43. At the time of Averroes, however, Ḥanbalites adopted the interpretation of Koranic anthropomorphisms by the formula "a body unlike bodies." *Cf. Kashf*, p. 60, ll. 14–15.

[138] *Ibid.*, p. 19, l. 20.

[139] *Ibid.*, p. 76, ll. 16 ff. On the relation of the Ḥashwiyyah to orthodox Islam, see A. S. Halkin, "The Hashwiyya," *JAOS*, 54:1–28 (1934).

[140] *Ibid.*, ll. 18–19, where the printed "people of the Shī'ah" is to be emended to read "people of the Sunnah" (cf. Haarbrücker's note *ad loc.* in his translation, vol. II, p. 403). Cf. p. 64, ll. 17–20; p. 65, ll. 5–6.

[141] Cf. Horten, *Systeme*, p. 50, n. 1.

[142] *Milal*, p. 20, l. 1. Here Ḳalānisī is placed between one who died in 845 and another who died in 857. Ibn 'Asārik, however, in his *Tabyīn*, p. 398, ll. 7–9, says that Ḳalānisī was a contemporary of Ash'arī (d. 935), denying, however, al-Ahwāzī's statement that he was one of the followers of Ash'arī. See McCarthy, *The Theology of al-Ash'arī*, p. 200, and n. 83. The Ash'arite Baghdādī, in his *Uṣūl* (p. 230, l. 16), introduces Ḳalānisī by the title "our *shayḫ*," which would seem to make him an Ash'arite; in his *Farḳ* (p. 115, ll. 13–14), however, where Ash'arī is introduced by the title "our *shayḫ*), Ḳalānisī is not introduced by that title. Muḥammad b. Muḥammad al-Murtaḍā, in his *Ithāf al-Sāda*, 2, 6 (quoted in Tritton, *Muslim Theology*, p. 211.

are described by him as being "most powerful in Kalam"[143] and "belonging to the number of those who followed the tenets of the early Muslims, except that they occupied themselves with the science of the Kalam and supported the articles of faith of early Islam by arguments used in the Kalam and by demonstrations used by the people who deal with the fundamentals of religion,"[144] all of which means that they used the pre-Muʿtazilite Kalam method of analogy.

Thus at about the middle of the ninth century, Muslim orthodoxy was divided on the question of anthropomorphism into three groups: (1) the Ḫanbalites, who, while denying anthropomorphism, refused to discuss the anthropomorphic verses in the Koran; (2) an orthodox branch of the Ḥashwiyyah, who, taking the anthropomorphic verses in the Koran literally, refused to discuss those verses which prohibited anthropomorphism; (3) the Kullabites, who interpreted the anthropomorphic verses in the Koran according to the method of the Kalam, that is, the method of analogy as used in the Fiḳh and expressed by the formula "a body unlike bodies."

It is out of this Kullabite group of orthodox that about half a century later, in 912, the Ashʿarite Kalam arose. As stated by Shahrastānī: "Some members of this group [of Kullabites] wrote books and others gave oral instruction up to the time that an argument took place between Abū al-Ḥasan al-Ashʿarī and his teacher [al-Jubbāʾī] over the problem of God's concern for human welfare and what is best for man. As a result of this, they quarreled and Ashʿarī joined this group [of Kullabites] and supported their views by Kalam methods (*bi-manāhij kalāmiyyah*), and this became the doctrine of the followers of the Sunnah and the Muslim community."[145] In another place he similarly says that Ashʿarī, after he re-

---

p. 182), makes Ḳalānisī a contemporary of Bāḳillānī (d. 1013) and Ibn Fūrak (d. 1015/6). Horten gives the date of Ḳalānisī in one place of his *Systeme* (p. 194) as d. 870 and in another place (p. 375) as *ca.* 920.

[143] *Milal*, p. 20, l. 3.

[144] *Ibid.*, p. 65, ll. 10–12.

[145] *Ibid.*, ll. 12–15; cf. *Muḳaddimah* III, p. 49, ll. 11–12.

nounced Mu'tazilism, "joined the party of the orthodox (*al-salaf*) and defended their system in the manner of the Kalam, so that it became a special system of its own." [146] Similarly Ibn Ḫaldūn, in passages which quite evidently are based upon Shahrastānī, says that Ash'arī, after his conversion to orthodoxy, "followed the views of Abdallah b. Sa'īd b. Kullāb, Abū al-'Abbās al-Ḳalānisī, and al-Ḥārith b. Asad al-Muḥāsibī." [147]

A characterization by Ibn Ḫaldūn of Ash'arī's Kalam is to be found in two passages.

In one passage, after stating that Ash'arī was the leader of "the Mutakallimūn" consisting of the aforementioned group of three, he describes him as having disavowed anthropomorphism and as having confirmed the existence of attributes without any implication of anthropomorphism,[148] adding then that he confirmed the existence of all attributes, "by the method of [argumentation based on] the intellect (*al-'aḳl*) and tradition (*al-naḳl*)." [149] By "the method of [argumentation based on] the intellect and tradition" Ibn Ḫaldūn quite evidently means the same as "argumentation formed by the intellect" superadded to evidence derived from tradition which, as we have seen, is used by him as a description of the Fiḳh method of analogy.

In another passage, Ibn Ḫaldūn tries to explain why Ash'arī called his system Kalam. It reads as follows: "The whole of Ash'arī's system was called the science of the Kalam either because it included the disputation of innovations, and this is mere speech (*kalām*) and implies no action, or because the system was invented and cultivated as a consequence of dissension concerning the existence of the speech of the soul (*al-kalām al-nafsānī*)." [150] The expression "speech of the soul," as we shall see, reflects the philosophic expression "internal speech," as contrasted with "uttered speech," and it refers to

[146] *Milal*, p. 20, ll. 5–6.
[147] *Muḳaddimah* III, p. 49, ll. 13–14.
[148] *Ibid.*, p. 39, ll. 9–12.
[149] *Ibid.*, ll. 12–13.
[150] *Ibid.*, p. 40, ll. 1–4.

the "Word of God" used in the sense of the pre-existent eternal Koran.[151] Now, of these two reasons the second is exactly like one of the two reasons given by Ibn Ḫaldūn himself, and before him by Shahrastānī, in the case of the philosophical Muʿtazilites.[152] But as for his first reason, it contains an expression not used by him, nor before him by Shahrastānī, in their corresponding other reason in the case of the philosophical Muʿtazilites. There, in the case of the Muʿtazilites, Ibn Ḫaldūn simply says that the reason why their system was called Kalam is that "it included argumentation and disputation which might be called speech (*kalām*)" and saw no need to explain why argumentation and disputation might be called speech. But here, after saying that the reason why Ashʿarī's system was called Kalam is that "it included the disputation of innovations, and this is speech (*kalām*)," Ibn Ḫaldūn adds "and implies no action," by which he would seem to try to explain why the disputation of innovations is mere speech. The question therefore arises: What need was there for him to add this unnecessary explanation? Certainly he did not mean by it to explain that Ashʿarī conducted his disputation of innovations in the form of an oral discussion and not in that of a fistic encounter.

The answer that suggests itself to my mind is that the expression "and implies no action" is not used here as a reinforcement of his statement that "the disputation of innovations" is "mere speech" but is rather a reminiscent expression of another reason why Ashʿarī's system was called Kalam. It would seem that, while Ibn Ḫaldūn was trying to explain that Ashʿarī's system was called Kalam because it included "the disputation of innovations" which is "mere speech," there were lingering in the back of his mind the following reminiscences of his own earlier views: (1) that the Kalam originated when the method of analogy used in the Fiḳh in connection with action was applied to the problem of anthropomorphism

[151] Cf. below, p. 286.

[152] Cf. above, p. 28 and p. 20.

which was a matter of faith and mere speech;[153] and (2) that this gave rise to the formula "a body unlike bodies," which ever since the beginning of the Kalam had been used by the orthodox Muslims, including Ash'arī, in their disputations with the anthropoformistic innovators.[153a] And so, when his pen jotted down the expression "and this is mere speech," out of the depths of those lingering reminiscences sprang up the expression "and implies no action," which was added to it. If he were to spell out the undesignedly added reminiscent expression, he would say: Furthermore, the whole of his system was called Kalam because it included his explanation of the anthropomorphic verses in the Koran by the formula "a body unlike bodies" which has its origin in the application of the method of analogy of the Fiḳh, which deals with action, to the problem of anthropomorphism, which is a matter of faith and speech, without implying any action.

From all this is to be gathered that in the earliest stage of his system Ash'arī interpreted the anthropomorphic verses in the Koran by the old formula "a body unlike bodies." It is his use of this formula that is reflected in the statement which, as quoted by Ibn 'Asākir in the name of Juwaynī, reports that Ash'arī held that God has knowledge and power and hearing and sight which are not like other knowledges and powers and hearings and sights and that God also has a hand and a face which are not like other hands and faces.[154] When, therefore, in his *Ibānah* he expresses himself in favor of *bi-lā kayfa*,[155] it is to be assumed that it belongs to a later stage in the history of his thought.

This is Shahrastānī's and Ibn Ḫaldūn's explanation of how the Kalam has its origin in the application of the Fiḳh method of analogy to the problem of anthropomorphism and how the term Kalam was retained both by the Mu'tazilites and by

[153] Cf. above, p. 7.
[153a] Cf. above, pp. 10–11.
[154] *Tabyīn*, p. 149, ll. 11–12, and p. 150, ll. 7–9 (171, 1, and 172, 5).
[155] *Ibānah*, p. 8, l. 14 (50).

Ash'arī as a description of the whole of each of their respective systems.

In Ibn Ḫaldūn there is also a sketch of the subsequent history of Ash'arī's Kalam.

He starts out with a general characterization of that Kalam in a passage in which, after stating that Ash'arī's system as perfected by his followers "became one of the best speculative disciplines and religious sciences," he goes on to say: "However, the forms of its demonstration are, at times, not exactly in accordance with the art [of logic], and this because the scholars of the time of Ash'arī were simple people and also because the art of logic, by which arguments are probed and syllogisms are tested, had not yet made its appearance in the religion [that is, it was not used in Islam in connection with matters religious]. Moreover, even if some of it had made its appearance [in matters religious among Muslim philosophers], the Mutakallimūn would not have used it, for it was too closely related to the philosophical sciences, which are altogether different from the beliefs of revealed religion, and would therefore have been avoided by them." [156]

It is to be noted that Ibn Ḫaldūn does not say that the Ash'arite system did not draw upon philosophy in the framing of its arguments nor does he say that its arguments are at times logically faulty. All he says is that "its arguments are, at times, not exactly in accordance with the art [of logic]," by which is meant that "at times," when the arguments could or should have been presented in logical, that is, in syllogistic, form, they were not so presented. Ibn Ḫaldūn may have had in mind here the Kalam argument for the creation of the world described later as "the argument from the createdness of the accidents of the component parts of the world." As framed by the various Mutakallimūn, all of them Ash'arites, this argument is in non-syllogistic form. But the Christian Ibn Ṣuwar, in reproducing it in the name of the Mutakallimūn,

[156] *Muḳaddimah* III, p. 40, ll. 13–20.

arranged it in syllogistic form and, after having done so, remarked as follows: "This is their syllogism when their reasoning is arranged according to the art [of logic]." [157]

Then Ibn Ḫaldūn mentions two changes that were introduced into the Ash'arite Kalam.

One change was introduced by Bāḳillānī (d. 1013). Starting with a proposition which is evidently aimed at Aristotle's view that it is sometimes possible to derive true conclusions from false premises,[158] Bāḳillānī maintains that "the demonstrations of the articles of faith are reversible in the sense that, if the demonstrations are wrong, the things proved by them are wrong." [159] He thus concluded that the demonstrations of the articles of faith, or the premises upon which the demonstrations are based, "hold the same position as the articles of faith themselves" [160] or "are next to the articles of faith in the necessity of believing in them," [161] so that "an attack against them is an attack against the articles of faith." [162] Accordingly, Ibn Ḫaldūn's statement that Bāḳillānī "affirmed the existence of the atom and of the vacuum" [163] is to be taken to mean that Bāḳillānī made the belief in the existence of atoms obligatory by reason of its being used in the demonstration of certain religious beliefs. The reference is to the fact that the theory of atoms is, according to Ash'arī, to be used as the basis of the demonstration of the creation of the world and hence also of the existence of God.[164] Thus atomism, which for a long time had been part of the philosophic doctrine of the Kalam and was used as a basis of arguments in support of certain religious beliefs, was made by Bāḳillānī an

[157] Cf. below, p. 393.

[158] *Anal. Prior.* II, 2, 53b, 8.

[159] *Muḳaddimah* III, p. 114, ll. 13–15.

[160] *Ibid.*, l. 15.

[161] *Ibid.*, p. 40, ll. 11–12.

[162] *Ibid.*, p. 114, l. 16.

[163] *Ibid.*, p. 40, ll. 9–10.

[164] Cf. below, p. 386, where Ash'arī is reported to have proved the creation of the world by "the argument from the aggregation and separation of atoms." But see Schreiner (*Aš'aritenthum*, pp. 108–109) and Gardet et Anawati (*Introduction*, pp. 62–63) who take Ibn Ḫaldūn's statement that Bāḳillānī "affirmed the existence of the atom and the vacuum" to mean that he was the first to introduce atomism into the orthodox Kalam.

essential part of those religious beliefs in the proof of which it had been used as an argument.

The second change may be described as the philosophization of the Ashʿarite type of Kalam, which was introduced by Ghazālī (d. 1111). Unlike Bāḳillānī, who is described by Ibn Ḫaldūn as a "pupil"[165] of Ashʿarī and as one by whom Ashʿarī's method was "perfected,"[166] Ghazālī is described by him as one who introduced "the method of the later ones" (*ṭarīḳat al-mutaʾaḫḫirīn*).[167] What these later ones did is summed up by him as follows: First, "they refuted most of the premises which were used in the Kalam as basis of its arguments, and this they did by demonstrations derived from philosophical discussions of physics and metaphysics."[168] Ghazālī, we know, once refrained from using atomism as an argument for a certain religious belief on the pretext that atomism involved difficulties which would take too long to solve.[169] We shall thus see how John Philoponus' argument against the eternity of the world from the impossibility of an infinite by succession, which is used by the Ashʿarites only in support of an argument based on atomism, is used by Ghazālī as an independent argument.[170] Second, those later ones rejected the view advanced by Bāḳillānī that "if the arguments were wrong, then the thing sought to be proved by the arguments was also wrong."[171] The rejection of this view means that the aforementioned Aristotle's view about the possibility of deriving true conclusions from false premises is applicable to proofs of articles of faith. Third, the

[165] *Muḳaddimah* III, p. 40, ll. 4–7.
[166] *Ibid.*, l. 13.
[167] *Ibid.*, p. 41, ll. 12 and 15. See discussion of this statement in Gardet et Anawati, *Introduction*, pp. 72–76, under the heading of *Via antiqua et via moderna*. See Maimonides' reference to "a skillful one from among the later (*al-mutaʾaḫḫirīn*) Mutakallimūn" in *Moreh* II, 14(4), p. 200, l. 18, by which, as we shall see, is meant Ghazālī. Cf. below, p. 595.
[168] *Ibid.*, ll. 5–8.
[169] *Tahāfut al-Falāsifah* XVIII, 14, p. 306, ll. 2–9, and 27, p. 312, ll. 3–4. Cf. Carra de Vaux, *Gazali*, p. 119.
[170] Cf. below, pp. 410; 422.
[171] *Muḳaddimah* III, p. 41, ll. 9–10; cf. above.

method of the later ones "often included refutation of the philosophers where the opinions of the latter differed from the articles of faith." [172] This, of course, refers to Ghazālī's own work *The Destruction of Philosophers* (*Tahāfut al-Falāsifah*).

The first and third characteristics of "the method of the later ones" introduced by Ghazālī reflect Ghazālī's own description of his attitude toward the Kalam in his autobiography. Starting out by saying that he began as a student of the Kalam, of which he obtained a thorough knowledge, he goes on to say that, while he commends the Mutakallimūn for their defense of orthodoxy against heresy, he finds fault with them on two grounds. First, "they based their arguments on propositions which they had accepted unquestioningly from their opponents and [claimed that] they were compelled to admit them either by their reliance on authority, or by the consensus of the community, or by a bare acceptance of the Koran and traditions." [173] Atomism was undoubtedly a case in point which he had in mind. Second, "I have not seen any of the sages of Islam who has turned his attention and his thought to philosophy. Whenever the Mutakallimūn in their writings on the Kalam bestir themselves to refute the philosophers they do nothing but utter some unintelligible and incoherent phrases." [174] He himself tried to remedy this defect in his *Tahāfut al-Falāsifah*.

From Ghazālī's own description of his attitude toward both the Kalam and philosophy we gather that, with regard to the Kalam, while he disapproved of its methods, he approved of its views, whereas, with regard to philosophy, quite the opposite — while he disapproved of its views, he approved of its methods. This, on the whole, may also be considered as a characterization of the philosophized Ashʿarite Kalam which, according to Ibn Ḥaldūn, was inaugurated by Ghazālī. Thus,

[172] *Muḳaddimah* III, p. 41, ll. 12–13.
[173] *Al-Munḳidh min al-Ḍalāl*, ed. Beirut, 1959, p. 16, ll. 13–14.
[174] *Ibid.*, p. 25, ll. 12–14.

while in his relation to the Kalam he is, as characterized by Ibn Ḫaldūn, one who started it on a new period in its history, in his relation to philosophy he is, as characterized by himself in the title of his work *The Destruction of Philosophers*, its critic. Since, however, in preparing himself for the task of criticizing philosophy, he tried, as he himself says, to gain a knowledge of the subject and an understanding of its most intricate problems — in which, as he intimates, he often surpassed those who accounted themselves philosophers [175] — and since both in his work in which he expounds the views of the philosophers and in his work in which he criticizes the philosophers he often shows himself as one who has original interpretation of commonly current philosophic opinions, Ghazālī, historically, may be considered as belonging both to the Kalam and to philosophy. In the present work, therefore, we have included his defense of certain doctrines of the Kalam; his particular interpretation of certain philosophic teachings, however, will be dealt with in a volume to be devoted to Arabic philosophy.

III. The Kalam According to Maimonides

Both Shahrastānī and Ibn Ḫaldūn were aware of the difference between "Kalam" and "philosophy" and also of the difference between their respective exponents, the "Mutakallimūn" and the "philosophers." Shahrastānī's work contains, as a counterpart to his account of the Kalam, an account of the philosophy of Avicenna,[1] preceded by what he knew of Greek philosophy;[2] and Ibn Ḫaldūn, after his treatment of the Kalam [3] and Sufism,[4] deals, under the title "The Various Kinds of Intellectual Sciences," [5] with philosophy proper, mentioning "Alfarabi and Avicenna in the East and Averroes and Avempace in Spain" and describing them as being "among

[175] *Ibid.*, ll. 7–11 and 17 ff.
[1] *Milal*, pp. 348–429.
[2] *Ibid.*, pp. 251–348.
[3] *Muḳaddimah* III, p. 27, ll. 1 ff.
[4] *Ibid.*, p. 59, ll. 16 ff.
[5] *Ibid.*, p. 86, ll. 18 ff.

the greatest Muslim philosophers." [6] But neither of them followed the religious rationalization of these Arabic philosophers. Shahrastānī describes the Ash'arite Kalam as having become "the doctrine of the followers of the Sunnah and the Muslim community," [7] which evidently he himself followed, though not without occasionally differing from it.[8] Similarly, Ibn Ḫaldūn says of the Ash'arite Kalam that it is "one of the best of speculative disciplines and religious sciences," [9] and he explicitly rejects the religious rationalization of Alfarabi and Avicenna, declaring that they were led astray by God.[10] Both Shahrastānī in his *Milal* and Ibn Ḫaldūn in his *Muḳaddimah* present the Kalam not as a unified system in contrast to the religious rationalization of the philosophers but rather as a system split into contrasting views held by opposing sects. Common also to both of them in their presentation of the Kalam is that, while they refer to some philosophic influences upon it, neither of them mentions any Christian influence upon the Kalam in general, though Shahrastānī mentions Christian influence upon two individual Mutakallims [11] and Ibn Ḫaldūn refers indirectly to some kind of Christian influence upon the Kalam in general when in his attempt to explain why Greek works on the sciences, including philosophy, were translated into Arabic, he says that one of the reasons was that Muslims "had heard some mention of them by bishops and priests among their Christian subjects." [12]

In contradistinction to both of them, Maimonides belonged to those who in Islam at that time were called "philosophers," though with a religious philosophy of his own in which he differed from them on some fundamental beliefs. To that religious philosophy of his own, in which he differed also from the Mutakallimūn even with regard to beliefs that were com-

[6] *Ibid.*, p. 91, l. 19 – p. 92, l. 2.
[7] *Milal*, p. 65, l. 15.
[8] Cf. Guillaume's introduction to his edition of Shahrastānī's *Nihāyat*, pp. ix, xii.
[9] *Muḳaddimah* III, p. 40, ll. 13–14.
[10] *Ibid.*, p. 213, ll. 2–10.
[11] *Milal*, p. 42, ll. 8–14.
[12] *Muḳaddimah* III, p. 91, l. 6.

mon, as he says, to Judaism and Islam,[13] his presentation of the Kalam was to serve as foil.[14] Accordingly, he was going to present the Kalam not in its historical development through its two stages of existence, the nonphilosophical and the philosophical, but rather as it existed in his own time, in the twelfth century, when both its sects, the Muʿtazilites and the Ashʿarites, had, each in its own way, already become philosophized, the former ever since the tenth century and the latter ever since the eleventh century.[15] Nor was he going to include in his planned presentation of the Kalam the various views quarreled over by the Muʿtazilites and Ashʿarites. As he himself defines the scope of his planned presentation of the Kalam, he was going to deal only with the philosophical views of the Kalam that are common to both the Muʿtazilites and the Ashʿarites and that are necessary for their arguments in establishing four religious beliefs [16] that are common to Islam and Judaism and Christianity,[17] namely, the beliefs of the creation of the world and the existence, unity, and incorporeality of God.[18] Accordingly, religious beliefs that were matters of controversy in Islam, but concerning which Maimonides felt that they ought to be dealt with by him in connection with his attempt to define the Jewish position on them, are relegated by him to other parts of his work. Thus the problem of attributes is relegated by him to chapters [19] within those chapters in which he tries to show how scriptural terms and phrases can be interpreted philosophically [20] and which serve him as a general methodological prolegomenon to his own philosophy. Thus also the special problem of the attribute of speech or word, which in Islam constituted the problem of the uncreatedness of the Koran, is relegated by him, again, to that methodological prolegomenon, and is dealt with by him in a chapter devoted to the explanation of the term "speech" or "word" (*kalām: dibbur*) which in Scripture is

[13] *Moreh* I, 71, p. 123, l. 4.
[14] *Ibid.*, p. 126, ll. 10–13.
[15] Cf. above, pp. 19 and 41.
[16] *Moreh* I, 73, p. 134, ll. 23–25.
[17] *Ibid.*, 71, p. 123, ll. 4–10.
[18] Cf. below at nn. 32–33.
[19] *Moreh* I, 50–60.
[20] *Ibid.*, 1–70.

attributed to God.[21] The problem of predestination, however, had for him a twofold aspect. While as a religious belief it was a matter of controversy between the Ashʿarites and the Muʿtazilites, as a philosophic view it was connected with the denial of causality, and the denial of causality was common to both the Ashʿarites and the Muʿtazilites.[22] Moreover, though on the whole Maimonides agreed with the Muʿtazilites in denying predestination, he did not altogether agree with their particular conception of free will. Consequently, the problem of predestination and free will is dealt with by him in two places. First, at the close of his explanation of the denial of causality as it was held in common by both the Ashʿarites and the Muʿtazilites, he adds that, with regard to "the actions of man," these two sects are in disagreement, and he then goes on to describe briefly their respective views.[23] Second, in connection with his discussion of his own view of divine Providence, he gives a more elaborate exposition of the Ashʿarite and Muʿtazilite views with regard to the problem of predestination and free will, dwelling especially on the religious aspects of these views.[24]

His presentation of selected views of the Kalam, which is contained in four chapters (73–76), is preceded by two chapters (71–72) in which he deals with the following three topics: (1) an explanation of the relevancy of his interposition of the views of the Kalam between his general methodological prolegomenon in Part I, chapters 1–70, and the exposition of his own views in Parts II and III of his work; (2) an outline of the historical background of the Kalam views as they existed in his own time; (3) an analysis of some of the fundamental differences between the views of the Kalam and his own views.

His explanation of the relevancy of his presentation of the views of the Kalam emerges from the following context. At

[21] *Ibid.*, 65.
[22] Cf. below, p. 613.
[23] *Moreh* I, 73, Prop. 6, p. 141, l. 11 – p. 142, l. 2.
[24] *Ibid.* III, 17.

the end of his general methodological prolegomenon, after interpreting philosophically the scriptural description of God as "He who rides the heaven" (Deut. 33:26) to mean that God by His power and will causes the circular motion of the outermost, all-encompassing celestial sphere, he says that this scriptural expression so interpreted points to the philosophical proof for the existence of God from motion, which "constitutes the greatest proof by which the existence of God can be known . . . as I shall demonstrate." [25] Here Maimonides was ready to proceed with his own proposed philosophical interpretation of the scriptural teachings, which begins in Part II with his first proof of the existence of God from motion. But evidently feeling that he had to justify himself for what he was about to do, he tries to show how the equivalent of Greek philosophy had at one time existed in Judaism as an oral tradition by the side of the oral tradition known as the Oral Law, how like that Oral Law it was used as a means of interpreting the teachings of the Written Law embodied in the Scripture, how this oral philosophic tradition happened to disappear, and how only traces of it are to be found in the Talmud and Midrashim.[26] Then, trying to show how philosophy was later reintroduced into Judaism under foreign influence, he contrasts the spokesmen of Judaism in the East, "the Geonim and the Karaites," with the spokesmen of Judaism in Spain. The former, he says, "in their discussion of the unity of God and whatever is dependent upon it," followed "the Muʿtazilites" from among "the Mutakallimūn of Islam," [27] that is to say, those Muʿtazilites who by the tenth century had already "blended the methods of the Kalam with the methods of the philosophers," [28] whereas the latter, including himself, followed "the philosophers." [29] This contrast quite naturally called for an exposition of the views of the Kalam as it existed

[25] *Ibid.* I, 70, p. 120, l. 25 – p. 121, l. 6.
[26] *Ibid.*, 71, p. 121, ll. 9–28.
[27] *Ibid.*, p. 121, l. 28 – p. 122, l. 4.
[28] Cf. above, p. 19.
[29] *Moreh* I, 71, p. 122, ll. 9–13.

in his own time, with which his own views, based upon philosophy, were to be contrasted, and such an exposition quite naturally, again, called for some account of the historical background of the views expounded.

His outline of the historical background of the views of the Kalam as they existed in his own time begins with the following statement: "Know that all that the Muslims, both the Muʿtazilites and the Ashʿarites, have said on these subjects are opinions based upon certain propositions, which propositions are taken from the books of Greeks and Syrians who sought to oppose the views of the philosophers and to refute their assertions." [30]

In this passage, while the expression "these subjects" grammatically refers to the previous statement "the subject of the unity of God and whatever is dependent upon this subject," psychologically it is a proleptic reference to what he later in the same chapter describes as the Mutakallimūn's arguments in proving the creation of the world and the existence, unity, and incorporeality of God.[31] What Maimonides, therefore, really wants to say in this passage is that insofar as both the Muʿtazilites and Ashʿarites argue in a philosophic manner in support of the belief in the creation of the world, which most of the philosophers deny, or in support of the belief in the existence, unity, and incorporeality of God, which most of the philosophers admit, they follow in the footsteps of the Christian philosophers, either by appropriating some of their arguments or by adopting their method of framing new arguments. Thus also, later in the same chapter, as he was about to criticize the Mutakallimūn's arguments for these four beliefs, he begins his criticism with the statement that "in general, all the first Mutakallimūn from among the Christianized Greeks and from among the Muslims" [32] shared a certain common element in framing their arguments for these four beliefs, and he continues to speak of "the ancient Mutakalli-

[30] *Ibid.*, ll. 13–16.

[31] *Ibid.*, p. 124, ll. 6–10.

[32] *Ibid.*, p. 123, ll. 10–11.

mūn" [33] and "these Mutakallimūn" [34] and "the method of the Mutakallimūn" [35] before he comes to say: "This is the method of every Mutakallim from among the Muslims in anything concerning this kind of investigation." [36] And Maimonides, it must be noted, is right in this assertion of his. For it can be shown that the Mutakallimūn's contention that the creation of the world can be established by demonstration is traceable to the Church Fathers.[37] Similarly traceable to the Church Fathers is their argument for the existence of God only on the basis of creation; for the Church Fathers, while making use of the argument of creation and some other arguments, never use Aristotle's argument from the eternity of motion.[38] So also traceable to the Church Fathers are some of their basic arguments for the unity and the incorporeality of God. Thus, for instance, of the five arguments for the unity of God reproduced by Maimonides in their name, the first, described by him as "the method of mutual hindering" (*al-tamānuʿ*: *ha-himmonaʿ*),[39] is traceable to John of Damascus,[40] and the fifth, described by him as an argument from "need" (*al-iftiḳār*: *ha-ṣorek*) and as being only a variation of the argument from mutual hindering,[41] is also traceable to John of

[33] *Ibid.*, l. 28.

[34] *Ibid.*, p. 123, l. 30 – p. 124, l. 1.

[35] *Ibid.*, p. 124, l. 2.

[36] *Ibid.*, l. 9.

[37] Cf. my paper "The Patristic Arguments against the Eternity of the World," *HTR*, 59:351–367 (1966), and below at n. 59.

[38] Discussed in the chapter on the proofs of the existence of God in the unpublished Volume II of *The Philosophy of the Church Fathers.*

[39] *Moreh* I, 75 (1), p. 156, ll. 14–22. This type of argument occurs in Juwaynī's *Irshād*, p. 31, ll. 11–18 (58), where the term *tamānuʿ* occurs later (p. 32, l. 14) as a description of another version of the same argument. It also occurs in Shahrastānī's *Nihāyat*, p. 91, l. 18 – p. 92, l. 13. Averroes in his *Kashf*, p. 48, l. 20 – p. 49, l. 10, quotes it in the name of the Ashʿarites and describes it by the term *mumāniʿah*, "hindrance."

[40] *De Fide Orthodoxa* I, 5 (PG 94, 801 B).

[41] *Moreh* I, 75 (5), p. 158, ll. 17–20. This argument is introduced by Maimonides with the words: "One of the later ones thought that he had found a demonstrative (*burhāniyyān*) method for the belief in unity" (l. 16). A brief statement of this argument occurs in Juwaynī's *Irshād*, p. 31, ll. 18–19 (59). In a more elaborate form it occurs in Shahrastānī's *Nihāyat*, p. 93, l. 8 – p. 94, l. 13. In the last part of this argument, Shahrastānī says that if one of the gods did not participate in the creation of the world,

Damascus.[42] Similarly, his third of the Mutakallimūn's arguments for the incorporeality of God[43] is modeled after an argument by Gregory of Nazianzus.[44] Both of these arguments prove the incorporeality of God by reducing its opposite to absurdity, while each of them uses its own particular method of reasoning in reducing that opposite to absurdity; the Mutakallimūn, in their version of it, making use of their own theory of admissibility.[44a]

Maimonides then goes on to describe the origin of Christian philosophy: "When the Christian Church brought into its fold the Greek and Syrian nations, the profession of belief of the Christians was what it is known to be, while among those nations the opinions of the philosophers were widely accepted, seeing that it is among them that philosophy had arisen. Consequently, when kings intent upon the defense of religion arose and the learned men of those times among the Greeks and Syrians saw that their profession of belief consisted of assertions which are greatly and clearly opposed by the philosophic opinions, there arose among them this science of the Kalam. They thus began to set up propositions which would be useful to them in the support of what they themselves believed and by which they could also refute those opinions of the philosophers which were ruinous to the foundations of their religion."[45]

"he would be in need (*muftaḳirān*) . . . of the other, but need (*al-faḳr*) is inconsistent with deity." He then concludes: "This method supports the demonstration (*bayan*) by the method of sufficiency (*al-istighnā'*), and this is the best of what has been reported concerning this problem." Exactly like this, Maimonides argues here that if the world could not be created except by two gods working together, then each of them, "by reason of his being in need (*li-iftiḳārihi*) of the other," would by himself be incapable of creating, and he would thus not be "self-sufficient" (*mustaghniyyān bi-dhātihi*). In Averroes' *Kashf*, p. 49, ll. 9–10, this argument forms part of the argument from *mumāni'ah*, "hindrance," which he ascribes to the Ash'arites (p. 48, ll. 20–21). Cf. above n. 39.

[42] *De Fide Orthodoxa* I, 5 (PG 94, 801 A).

[43] *Moreh* I, 76 (3), p. 161, ll. 13–14.

[44] Gregory of Nazianzus, *Oratio* XXVIII, 7 (PG 36, 33 B).

[44a] *Moreh* I, 73, prop. 10.

[45] *Ibid.* I, 71, p. 122, ll. 16–22.

The historical facts behind this statement are as follows: Christian apologetical and polemical literature began to appear long before Constantine's conversion to Christianity and hence long before the Nicene Council. This literature was written in Greek by men who may be described as of the Greek nation, such as Quadratus and Aristides, and by a man who may be described as of the Syrian nation, namely, Theophilus of Antioch. There was also that type of literature in Latin written by such men as Tertullian, Arnobius, and Lactantius. Christian works in Syriac by men who may be described as of the Syrian nation began to appear in the fourth century, that is, after Constantine's conversion to Christianity and after the Nicene Council, by such men as Aphrates and Ephrem Syrus. Of these three linguistic groups of Christian literature, the Muslims came in contact only with those written in Greek and in Syriac, and, with regard to the works written in Greek, they came in contact with them either through translations made directly from the Greek by Syrian Christians or through translations made from Syriac translations from the Greek. One more significant fact is to be mentioned. None of the ante-Nicene apologetical and polemical writings were translated into Arabic.[46]

In the light of all this, we have reason to assume that Maimonides' statement here was not meant to describe the historical origin of Christian apologetical and polemical writings; it was meant only to describe the types of Christian apologetical and polemical literature with which the Muslim Mutakallimūn came to be acquainted, and these were all produced during the post-Nicene period, when indeed there were "kings intent upon the defense of religion."

Maimonides then tries to show how the Christian philosophy became known to the Muslims. Historically the facts are as follows: Translations from general Greek philosophic works began in the eighth century during the reign of Caliph Man-

[46] Graf, *Geschichte der christlichen arabischen Literatur*, I (1944), pp. 302–310.

ṣūr (745–775) and reached their highest point, though not their end, during the reign of Caliph Ma'mūn (813–833). Then, with Kindī (d. *ca.* 873), works originally written in Arabic, based upon the philosophic Greek writings, began to appear and continued to appear to the time of Maimonides. At about the same time, early in the ninth century, Christians under Muslim rule began to transmit the teachings of the Greek Church Fathers in works written in Arabic and also to translate some of the works of the Greek Church Fathers. The first of such Christian authors in Arabic are the Melkite Abū Ḳurra, known as Abucara (flourished during the first part of the ninth century),[47] the Nestorian Catholicus Timothy I (d. 823),[48] and the Jacobite Abū Rā'iṭa (a contemporary of Abucara).[49] These were followed by others until long after the time of Maimonides.[50] One such author before the time of Maimonides was the Jacobite Yaḥyā Ibn 'Adī (893–974).[51] Direct translations from Greek Patristic literature, sometimes only in the form of compilations, abridgments, and paraphrases, began to appear in the ninth century,[52] and in the course of time translations were made of various works of many Church Fathers[53] and also of the works of other Greek Christian writers, among them John Philoponus.[54] Reflecting all this, Maimonides makes two statements.

In his first statement he says: "When the religion of Islam appeared and the writings of the philosophers were transmitted (*nuḳilat*: *ne'eteḳu*) to its believers, there were also transmitted (*nuḳilat*: *ne'eteḳu*) to them those refutations composed against the writings of the philosophers."[55] It is to be noted that Maimonides does not use the term *turjimat*,[56] which

[47] *Ibid.* II, pp. 7 ff.

[48] *Ibid.*, pp. 114 ff.

[49] *Ibid.*, pp. 222 ff.

[50] *Ibid.* I, pp. 79–82.

[51] *Ibid.* II, pp. 233 ff.

[52] *Ibid.* I, pp. 299, 300.

[53] *Ibid.*, pp. 302–378.

[54] *Ibid.*, p. 417.

[55] *Moreh* I, 71, p. 122, ll. 22–24.

[56] Ibn Ḫaldūn, in referring to the Arabic translations of the Greek philosophers, uses the term *tarjam.* Cf. *Muḳaddimah* III, p. 91, l. 14; p. 101, ll. 11 and 13; p. 213, l. 5. The term *tarjam* is often used by Maimonides. Cf. *Moreh* I, 27, p. 39, l. 1; I, 48, p. 71, l. 20; II, 33, p. 257, l. 25; II, 47, p.

means only "were translated"; instead he uses the term *nuḳilat*, which means both "were transmitted" and "were translated." The latter term, we take it, was advisedly used by him, for, as we have seen, both Greek philosophic works and Christian philosophic writings in Greek were made known to Muslims partly through direct translations and partly through works originally written in Arabic. It is also to be noted that just as the statement "when the religion of Islam appeared and the writings of the philosophers were transmitted to its believers" does not mean that immediately upon the rise of Islam in the seventh century Greek philosophy all at once, both through translations into Arabic and through works originally written in Arabic, became known to Muslims, so also the statement "there were also transmitted to them those refutations composed against the writings of the philosophers" does not mean that at the same time Christian writings in Greek all at once, both through translations into Arabic and through works originally written in Arabic, became known to Muslims. What Maimonides really means to say is that some time after the rise of Islam there began to appear Arabic translations of Greek philosophic works followed by works on philosophy written originally in Arabic, that in the course of time there began to appear also Arabic translations of Christian Greek works as well as Christian works written originally in Arabic, and that this kind of literary activity, once begun, continued for many years, even unto his own time.

In his second statement he says: "Thus, having discovered the Kalam of John the Grammarian and of Ibn ʿAdī and of others on these subjects, they clutched it, thinking that they had gotten hold of something mighty useful for their quest." [57] This statement does not mean that both John the Grammarian and Ibn ʿAdī were taken by Maimonides to be among the

---

291, l. 20. Shahrastānī, as we have seen, uses the term *fusirat* (cf. above, p. 20).

[57] *Moreh* I, 71, p. 122, ll. 24–26.

first Christian authors who became known to the Muslims and from whom the Muslims first learned the method of philosophic argumentation. His explicit statement that "the Kalam" of these Christian writers was "on these subjects"—that is to say, on the Muslim Mutakallimūn's arguments for the creation of the world with its corollary the existence of God, and also their arguments for the unity and incorporeality of God—shows quite clearly that these two names are mentioned by him only as examples of Christian writers who had influenced the Muslim Mutakallimūn in the framing of their arguments for these four beliefs and probably also as examples of the two types of such Christian writers, namely, those whose works were translated from the Greek and those whose works were written originally in Arabic.

And no better examples illustrative of these two facts, it must be remarked, could Maimonides have found. John the Grammarian or John Philoponus (flourished *ca.* 500), one of the most prolific commentators on Aristotle, was a convert to Christianity who wrote works in refutation of the belief in the eternity of the world directed against Aristotle and Proclus. Both these works were translated into Arabic,[58] and one of his arguments against the eternity of the world ascribed by Maimonides to the Mutakallimūn is traceable to John Philoponus.[59] Yaḥyā Ibn ʿAdī (893–974) is described by Graf as "a star of the first magnitude in the sky of scholars of the Christian orient." [60] Besides his being the translator and author of purely philosophic works and the author of purely Christian works,[61] he was also the author of works dealing with beliefs common to both Christians and Muslims, such as the belief in God's knowledge of particulars [62] and in the unity of God.[63] Undoubtedly Maimonides considered

[58] Steinschneider, *Die arabischen Uebersetzungen aus dem Griechischen*, § 55 (79).

[59] Cf. below, pp. 410, 425–427.

[60] Graf, *Geschichte*, II, p. 220.

[61] *Ibid.*, pp. 233 ff.

[62] *Ibid.*, p. 243, No. 12.1. Cf. below, ch. IX, sec. V, 2.

[63] *Ibid.*, p. 239, No. 1; p. 243, No. 13; cf. below.

him as one of the main sources of the Muslims' knowledge of what he calls the Christian Kalam.

Thus John Philoponus and Yaḥyā Ibn ʿAdī are mentioned by Maimonides not as examples of those who were responsible for the rise of the Kalam but rather as examples of those whose influence helped to shape some of the arguments for the four beliefs which he was going to deal with.[64]

So far Maimonides has tried to show how the Muslim Mutakallimūn followed those whom he calls Christian Mutakallimūn. Now he goes on to show how the Muslim Mutakallimūn differed from their Christian preceptors.

He begins by showing how the Muslims differed from the Christians in their conception of the physical constitution of the universe. He thus says: "They also selected from among the opinions of the earlier philosophers whatever he who selected considered useful for his purpose, even though the later philosophers had already demonstrated its falsehood, as, for instance, the theory of the atom and of the vacuum, for they believed that these were common notions and propositions which every follower of a revealed religion would be in need of." [65] That the Muslim Mutakallimūn's acceptance of atomism was not shared by the so-called Christian Mutakallimūn must have been generally known by the time of Maimonides from such works as Yaḥyā Ibn ʿAdī's treaties against atomism,[66] so that Maimonides did not feel the need of explicitly stating here that the acceptance of atomism by the Muslim Mutakallimūn was not due to Christian influence.

Then he goes on to show how the Muslim Mutakallimūn differed from the so-called Christian Mutakallimūn also in their methods of proving the creation of the world and the

[64] Students of this chapter of the *Moreh*, taking it to be an account of the historical origin of the Muʿtazilite Kalam, find Maimonides' reference to Yaḥyā Ibn ʿAdī here to be an anachronism. Cf. Munk's note *ad loc.* in his French translation of the *Moreh* (*Guide des Égarés*, I, p. 341, n. 2) and similar notes by Friedländer, Weiss, and Pines in their respective translations *ad loc.*

[65] *Moreh* I, 71, p. 122, ll. 26–29.

[66] Cf. Périer, *Yaḥyā ben ʿAdī*, p. 75, Nos. 27, 28, 32, 33; p. 76, No. 35.

existence, unity, and incorporeality of God. Using the term *ṭuruḳ*, which literally means "roads" but which, throughout his discussion, is used by him in the sense of "methods," [67] that is, methods of reasoning or arguments, he says: "Moreover (*thumma*), as the Kalam developed, its exponents descended to other strange roads (*ṭuruḳ*), which the Mutakallimūn from among the Greeks and others, because of their closeness to the philosophers, had never taken." [68] By this he means that, though they followed the Christian Mutakallimūn in their main contention about the demonstrability of the creation of the world and about some of their basic arguments for the existence, unity, and incorporeality of God, they deviated from them in that they framed proofs upon premises not approved of by philosophers — such, for instance, as their proofs for creation based upon atomism — and also in that they perverted some of the good philosophic proofs for the unity and incorporeality of God.[69]

This concludes Maimonides' account of the historical background of the two sets of views he was going to discuss in his presentation of the views of the Mutakallimūn, namely, (1) their conception of the physical constitution of the universe; (2) their arguments for the creation of the world and the existence, unity, and incorporeality of God. Then comes the following passage: "Moreover (*thumma*), also, there arose among Muslims certain doctrines which were peculiar to them and which they felt called upon to defend, and since there sprang up diversity of opinions concerning these peculiar doctrines, each sect set up propositions which it found useful in the defense of its own view.[70]

This passage, as well as the passage preceding it, is introduced by the term *thumma*, which literally means "then" and which in both Hebrew versions of the work is translated by "after this." [71] But this passage, as we shall see, does not deal

[67] See, e.g., *Moreh* I, 73, p. 134, l. 23; p. 150, l. 7.
[68] *Moreh* I, 71, p. 122, l. 29 – p. 123, l. 1.
[69] *Ibid.*, 75, Argument 2; I, 76, Argument 3. [70] *Ibid.*, 71, p. 123, ll. 1–3.
[71] Cf. Ibn Tibbon's and Ḥarizi's Hebrew translations *ad loc.*

with something that happened subsequently but rather with something that happened additionally. I have therefore translated it in both places by "moreover." What Maimonides means to say here is that not only have the Mutakallimūn followed the Christian method of argumentation in support of the beliefs in the creation of the world and the existence and unity and incorporeality of God, of which he subsequently says that Islam shares them in common with Judaism and Christianity,[72] but they have also applied the same method of argumentation to beliefs of which he subsequently says that they are peculiar to Islam and that he is not going to deal with them in this work.[73] While no mention is made here of these peculiarly Muslim beliefs, we know from his subsequent statement that one of them is the belief in the eternity of the Koran.[74] Others, we may assume, are attributes, predestination, and certain phases of eschatology, about all of which there were sectarian controversies in Islam.

So much for his outline of the historical background of the Mutakallimūn's views which he has chosen to discuss. Now for his general analysis of some of the fundamental differences between the Mutakallimūn's views and his own views. As the views which he was going to ascribe to the Mutakallimūn fall, as we have seen, into two parts, his analysis of how he differs from them falls also into two parts. First, he shows how he differs from them with regard to their proofs for the creation of the world and the existence, unity, and incorporeality of God.[75] Second, he shows how his own conception of the constitution of the physical universe differs from that of the Mutakallimūn.[76]

In my analysis of Chapter 71 of Part I of the *Guide*, I tried to show that Maimonides' purpose was not to explain the origin of the Kalam and the history of its development but rather to explain the background of the conception of

[72] *Moreh* I, 71, p. 123, ll. 4–5.
[73] *Ibid.*, ll. 5–10.
[74] *Ibid.*, l. 7.
[75] *Ibid.*, p. 123, l. 10 – p. 124, l. 7.
[76] *Ibid.*, I, 72.

the constitution of the physical universe characteristic of the Mutakallimūn as well as of their characteristic arguments for the creation of the world and for the existence, unity, and incorporeality of God. He tries to show that while on the whole the Mutakallimūn followed the Church Fathers in trying to support four of their religious beliefs on the basis of philosophy and even borrowed from them some arguments, they deviate from them, first, in adopting certain views from antiquated Greek philosophy not used by the Christians and, second, in framing new arguments on unapproved philosophic premises and perverting some good philosophic arguments. Preliminary to these explanations, he describes how the Christian philosophy of the Church Fathers, based upon pagan Greek philosophy but opposed to it, both in Greek and in Syriac came into existence, and how both the pagan Greek philosophy and the Christian philosophy came to be known to the Muslims through translations into Arabic as well as through works originally written in Arabic. As an example of a Christian Greek author whose work came to be known to Muslims through translation he mentions John Philoponus and as an example of a Christian author who wrote his work originally in Arabic he mentions Yaḥyā Ibn ʿAdī. These two authors were selected by him as illustrative not only because he thought they were each most outstanding in his field but also because they were sources of arguments which he had in mind later to present as characteristic of the Mutakallimūn. Finally, alluding to certain beliefs peculiar to Islam, he remarks that even in connection with these beliefs the Muslims employed the method of argumentation which they had learned from the Christians.

IV. Influences

1. Christianity

The question whether there was any Christian influence upon the Kalam, which must inevitably arise in one's mind by comparing the account of its history as sketched by Shahrastānī and Ibn Ḫaldūn with that sketched by Maimonides, was actually raised by one of the earliest modern students of Arabic philosophy. In a work published in 1842, Schmölders writes: "I find nothing precise on the origin of the Mutakallims. Moses Maimonides, who has of them a rather extended account, connects them with the first Christian philosophers, maintaining that it is from them that the Mutakallims borrowed their arguments against the philosophers. Shahrastānī, however, a more competent judge, says nothing about it, and the fact becomes still more improbable when one examines the very works of the Mutakallims. We think on the contrary that there is no relation between them and the Christian apologists."[1] Mabilleau, in 1895, after quoting Maimonides' statement as to the Christian influence on the Muslim Kalam, says: "The assertion is curious and it has nothing at the bottom but a resemblance," but he admits that the Kalam may have borrowed from Christianity some arguments against philosophy.[2] This, as we have seen, is exactly what Maimonides claims. In the same year, Schreiner, after calling attention to Maimonides' view on the influence of Christianity on the Kalam, remarks that the Christian influence is to be found only in the later Muʿtazilites and Ashʿarites but not in the early founders of Muʿtazilism, such as Wāṣil b. ʿAṭāʾ and ʿAmr ibn ʿUbayd.[3] This, again, as we have seen, is exactly what Maimonides has meant to say.

However, all other modern historians of Arabic philosophy, as well as of Islam in general, agree that there was a Christian influence upon the Kalam, but the influence which they speak of, unlike that spoken of by Maimonides, is not the Christian influence upon the Mutakallimūn's argumentations against the philosophers or upon their argumentations against each other but rather the Christian influence upon the forma-

[1] Schmölders, *Essai* (1842), pp. 135–136.
[2] Mabilleau, *Histoire de la Philosophie atomistique* (1895), p. 325.
[3] Schreiner, *Der Kalam in der jüdischen Literatur* (1895), pp. 2–3.

tion of certain Muslim beliefs which subsequently became matters of controversy among the Mutakallimūn. How these modern scholars have arrived at such a view was most clearly stated by de Boer in 1901. "The similarity between the oldest doctrinal teachings in Islam and the dogmas in Christianity is too great to permit any one to deny that they are directly connected. In particular, the first question about which there was much dispute, among Muslim scholars, was that of the freedom of the will. Now the freedom of the will was almost universally accepted by Oriental Christians" and was discussed "from every point of view . . . in the Christian circles in the East at the time of the Muslim conquest. Besides these considerations which are partly of an *a priori* character, there are also detached notices which indicate that some of the earliest Muslims, who taught freedom of the will, had Christian teachers." [4] Sixteen years later, in 1917, de Boer added to the problem of freedom of the will three other problems which were influenced by Christianity, of which only two are relevant here to our purpose, namely, the problem of the eternity of the Koran and the problem of divine attributes.[5]

This represents the state of knowledge about the Christian influence on the Kalam in the year 1917. All students of Muslim philosophy who, either before that year or after that year, speak of a Christian influence upon the Kalam find that influence in either all or some of the three problems mentioned by de Boer, and their view as to the existence of such an influence rests, as de Boer says, either upon a general similarity between the problems discussed by both Muslims and Christians or upon some kind of evidence. Let us then examine what students of Muslim philosophy have to say upon this Christian influence with regard to these three problems and the evidence used by them.

With regard to the problem of predestination and free will,

[4] de Boer, *Geschichte der Philosophie im Islam* (1901), p. 43 (Eng., p. 42).

[5] de Boer, "Philosophy (Muslim)," *ERE*, IX, 878a. The fourth problem mentioned by him is "the relation of God to man and the world."

most modern scholars are of the opinion that the belief in free will arose under the influence of Christianity in opposition to the native Muslim belief in predestination. In proof of this, Kremer in 1873 [6] refers to John of Damascus, who in his *Disputatio Christiani et Saraceni* makes a Christian and Muslim debate this question, the Christian arguing for free will and the Muslim maintaining predestination. The same view is repeated by Becker in 1912,[7] by Guillaume in 1924,[8] by Sweetman in 1945,[9] and by Gardet and Anawati in 1948.[10] Goldziher in 1910,[11] Tritton in 1947,[12] and Watt in 1948 [13] take free will to have arisen from certain verses in the Koran itself, but, whereas Goldziher and Tritton suggest that Christian influence hastened the development of this view in Islam, Watt denies any Christian influence. As for the orthodox belief in predestination, Schreiner in 1900 suggests that it was due to the influence of pre-Islamic fatalism, which statements contrary to it in the Koran could not wipe away,[14] and similarly Goldziher in 1910 suggests that, while primarily arising from the Koran itself, it was also favored by some "mythical tradition,[15] by which he means some pre-Islamic fatalism. This suggestion of the survival of some pre-Islamic fatalism is presented anew, more elaborately, by Watt in 1948.[16]

With regard to attributes, some modern scholars think that

[6] Kremer, *Culturgeschichtliche Streitfüge auf dem Gebiete des Islams* (1873), pp. 7 ff.

[7] Becker, "Christliche Polemik und Islamische Dogmenbildung," *Zeitschrift für Assyriologie*, 26:184 (1912).

[8] Guillaume, "Some Remarks on Free Will and Predestination in Islam," *Journal of the Royal Asiatic Society*, 1924, pp. 43–49.

[9] J. W. Sweetman, *Islam and Christian Theology*, I, 1 (1945), pp. 61–63; I, 2 (1947), pp. 174–180.

[10] Gardet et Anawati, *Introduction à la Théologie Musulmane* (1948), p. 37.

[11] Goldziher, *Vorlesungen über den Islam* (1910), pp. 95–96. Wensinck's restatement (*Muslim Creed* [1932], p. 52) of the view of Goldziher is only partly correct.

[12] Tritton, *Muslim Theology* (1947), p. 54.

[13] Watt, *Free Will and Predestination in Early Islam* (1948), pp. 38, 58, n. 27.

[14] Schreiner, *Studien über Jeschu'a b. Jehuda*, p. 11.

[15] Goldziher, *Vorlesungen*, p. 95.

[16] Watt, *Free Will*, pp. 19 ff.

only the Muʿtazilite denial of attributes had a Christian origin. Of these, Kremer in 1873 tried to prove it by taking the Arabic term *taʿṭīl*, which is used as a description of the Muʿtazilite view on attributes, to be a translation of the Christian term κένωσις,[17] for both these terms are usually translated by "emptying." It may be remarked that in meaning these two are not the same. The Arabic term *taʿṭīl* was applied to the Muʿtazilites by their opponents, and it means that the Muʿtazilites, by denying the reality of attributes, emptied or divested God of attributes.[18] The Greek term κένωσις is used in Christianity in the sense that the Son of God emptied himself of the form of God and assumed the form of man. Macdonald in 1903 merely says that the origin of the denial of attributes "is obscure, although suggestive of discussions with Greek theologians." [19] Becker in 1912 tries to show that the Muʿtazilite denial of attributes is based upon the Christian view that the anthropomorphic expressions in Scripture are not to be taken literally.[20] Wensinck in 1932, however, seems to think that both the denial and the affirmation of attributes have a Christian origin, finding a resemblance between the Muʿtazilite denial of attributes and the views of Dionysius the Areopagite and John of Damascus,[21] adding "that, on the whole, the position of orthodox Islam is in agreement with Christian dogmatics." [22] Sweetman in 1945 collected all kinds of things on attributes outside of Islam in order to show "that neither Christian nor Muslim has a monopoly of ideas on the subject either way. Different schools of thought are to be found in both religions." [23] Tritton in 1947 says that John of Damascus anticipated the Muʿtazilite doctrine that attri-

[17] Kremer, *Culturgeschichtliche*, p. 8.

[18] In his *Ibānah*, Ashʿarī uses the term *taʿṭīl* not only in the sense of the denial of attributes (p. 54, ll. 13–17 [94]) but also in the sense of the denial of the visibility of God (p. 19, ll. 2–4 [68]).

[19] Macdonald, *Development of Muslim Theology* (1903), pp. 131–132.

[20] Becker, "Christliche Polemik," pp. 188–190.

[21] Wensinck, *Muslim Creed*, pp. 70–71.

[22] *Ibid.*, p. 73.

[23] Sweetman, *Islam and Christian Theology*, I, pp. 78–79.

butes "are not other than God." [24] Gardet and Anawati in 1948, following Becker, say that the problem of attributes in Islam arose out of Christian arguments against anthropomorphism.[25]

With regard to the problem of the Koran, Macdonald in 1903, speaking of the createdness of the Koran, says: "We can have no difficulty in recognizing that it is plainly derived from the Christian Logos and that the Greek Church, perhaps through John of Damascus, has again played a formative part. So in correspondence with the heavenly and uncreated Logos in the bosom of the Father, there stands the uncreated and eternal Word of God; to the earthly manifestation of Jesus corresponds the Qur'an, the Word of God which we read and recite." [26] Becker in 1912 tries to show that the entire problem, whether the Koran was created or uncreated, originated in Christianity from the fact that in John of Damascus' fictitious debate between a Christian and a Muslim, the Christian argues from the analogy between the Muslim problem of the Koran and the Christian problem of the Logos.[27] Guillaume in 1924 denies that the doctrine of the uncreatedness of the Koran was derived from John of Damascus on the ground that, according to John of Damascus' own testimony, there had already existed in Islam the heresy of the denial of the uncreatedness of the Koran.[28] Wensinck in 1932 explains the orthodox belief in the eternity of the Koran as being derived from the old oriental conception of pre-existence, mentioning especially the pre-existence of the Torah in Judaism and the pre-existence and eternity of Logos in Christianity, and the Mu'tazilite denial of the eternity of the Koran is explained by him as being a corollary of their belief that God alone is eternal.[29] Sweetman in 1947 takes

[24] Tritton, *Muslim Theology*, p. 57.
[25] Gardet et Anawati, *Introduction*, p. 38.
[26] Macdonald, *Development of Muslim Theology*, p. 146.
[27] Becker, "Christliche Polemik," pp. 186–188.
[28] Guillaume, "Free Will and Predestination," p. 49.
[29] Wensinck, *Muslim Creed*, pp. 77–78.

the orthodox belief in the uncreatedness of the Koran to have been derived from the Christian belief in the uncreatedness of the Logos and the Muʿtazilite denial of it to have been due to a reaction against that Christian belief.[30] Gardet and Anawati in 1948, quoting Becker, say that the belief in an uncreated Koran arose under the influence of the Christian Logos.[31]

And so all the evidence that has so far been marshaled for the Christian influence upon these three problems is that Muslims were in contact with Christians and that an assertion of free will, like that of the antipredestinationists in Islam, was taught by Christians, that a denial of attributes, like that of the Muʿtazilites, can be shown to be the view of John of Damascus or the Fathers in general, and that the Muslim belief in the eternity of the Koran has a resemblance to the Christian belief in the eternity of the Logos.

2. GREEK PHILOSOPHY

While in their speculation as to Christian influence on the Kalam modern historians, if they were at all bent upon referring to the testimony of Arabic sources, could have quoted only Maimonides, in their discussion of philosophic influence they had before them all the Arabic sources which happen to speak of influence. All those Arabic sources, besides their general statements of the influence of philosophy upon the Kalam which began with translations from the Greek philosophers, mention also philosophic origins of certain Kalam views. Thus the Kalam's theory of atoms is ascribed by Ibn Ḥazm to "some of the ancients," [1] and its theories of both "atoms and the vacuum" are ascribed by Maimonides to "the ancient philosophers." [2] Naẓẓām's denial of atoms is ascribed by Baghdādī to "the heathen (*mulḥidah*) philosophers." [3] Ibn Ḥazm, after ascribing to Naẓẓām the denial of

[30] Sweetman, *Islam and Christian Theology*, I, 2, p. 116.

[31] Gardet et Anawati, *Introduction*, p. 38.

[1] *Fiṣal* V, p. 69, l. 1.

[2] *Moreh* I, 71, p. 122, l. 26.

[3] *Farḳ*, p. 113, ll. 16–17.

atoms, ascribes it also to "every one who is well versed in the teachings of the ancients." [4] Shahrastānī says that in the denial of atoms, Naẓẓām "agreed with the philosophers." [5] Similarly, the theory of latency, which is identified with the name of Naẓẓām, is said by Ash'arī to have been held also by "many of the heathen (*al-mulḥidīn*)",[6] and Shahrastānī ascribes it to various "philosophers," [7] mentioning Anaxagoras [8] and Thales.[9] Shahrastānī finds also philosophic influences upon Abū al-Hudhayl's treatment of attributes,[10] upon Naẓẓām's denial of free will in God [11] and his description of any kind of action or change by the term "motion," [12] and upon Mu'ammar's statements about the soul.[13]

In the light of all these, it is not to be wondered that scattered references to various philosophers are to be found in almost every modern work dealing with the Kalam. Especially outstanding among modern students of the Kalam in their attempt to establish philosophic influence upon the Kalam are Horovitz and Horten. Horovitz in a number of studies tried to show how certain Mutakallimūn adopted certain Greek philosophic views, such, for instance, as how Naẓẓām adopted certain Stoic views [14] and Mu'ammar and Abū Hāshim adopted certain Platonic views: [15] or how certain Kalam concepts, such as *tawallud*, reflect certain Greek philosophic concepts; [16] or how Greek scepticism penetrated into the Kalam.[17] Horten, in *Die philosophischen Systeme der spekulativen Theologen im Islam* (1912), in the course of his analysis of the various views of the masters of the Kalam, comments briefly on their origin in Greek philosophy. Thus

[4] *Fiṣal* V, p. 92, ll. 18–19.

[5] *Milal*, p. 38, l. 19.

[6] *Maḳālāt*, p. 329, l. 4; cf. below, pp. 505–506.

[7] *Milal*, p. 39, ll. 13–15.

[8] *Ibid.*, p. 257, ll. 7–12.

[9] *Ibid.*, p. 258, ll. 4–6.

[10] *Ibid.*, p. 34, ll. 14–16.

[11] *Ibid.*, p. 37, l. 17–p. 38, l. 3.

[12] *Ibid.*, p. 38, ll. 7–9.

[13] *Ibid.*, p. 47, ll. 8–14.

[14] S. Horovitz, *Ueber den Einfluss der griechischen Philosophie auf die Entwicklung des Kalam* (1909), pp. 6–44.

[15] *Ibid.*, pp. 44–78.

[16] *Ibid.*, pp. 78–91.

[17] S. Horovitz, *Der Einfluss der griechischen Skepsis auf die Entwicklung der Philosophie bei den Arabern* (1915), pp. 5–42.

the index of that work lists numerous references to such Greek philosophers and Greek philosophic terms as Anaxagoras, Aristotle, Atomists, Carneades, Democritus, Empedocles, Galen, Greek philosophers, Heraclitus, Homoeomeries, Idea, Logos, Neoplatonists, Plato, Plotinus, Socrates, Sophists, Stoics. Needless to say, the search for philosophic influences is continued by recent students of the Kalam.

3. IRANIAN AND INDIAN RELIGIONS

Baghdādī, who, as we have seen, said of Naẓẓām that he had come under the influence of "the heathen philosophers," also said of him that "during his youth he mingled with some people of the Dualists."[1] Three views held by Naẓẓām are definitely ascribed by Baghdādī to the influence of those Dualists[2] and, with regard to a fourth view, he is in doubt whether it is due to the influence of the Dualists or to the influence of the Naturalists.[3] Baghdādī reports also that Naẓẓām has written a book on Dualism and in that book he criticized a certain view of "the Manichaeans."[4] Among modern historians of the Kalam, Horovitz, in an examination of those views of Naẓẓām which Baghdādī ascribes to the influence of Persian Dualism, tries to show that they are really to be ascribed to Stoic influence.[5] Horten quotes Baghdādī's statements as to the influence of Dualism upon Naẓẓām[6] and brings together all kinds of statements from original sources with regard to contacts between Mutakallimūn and Dualists, to disputations between them, and to the influence of Dualism upon certain individual Mutakallimūn, adding some of his own conjectures as to such influences.[7]

The question of Indian influence upon the Kalam was introduced into modern scholarship by Schmölders in 1842.

[1] *Farḳ*, p. 113, ll. 13–14.
[2] *Ibid.*, l. 18 – p. 114, l. 1; p. 119, l. 17 – p. 120, l. 3; p. 124, ll. 7–14.
[3] *Ibid.*, p. 121, ll. 2–10; cf. p. 124, ll. 3–7.
[4] *Ibid.*, p. 117, ll. 5–12; p. 123, l. 18 – p. 124, l. 3.
[5] Horovitz, *Einfluss*, pp. 29 ff.
[6] Horten, *Systeme*, pp. 200 ff.
[7] *Ibid.*, p. 631, col. 2, *s. v.* "Dualisten."

Quoting from several Arabic manuscripts statements attributed to people called Summaniyyah,[8] he makes the following comment: "It is said that the sect of the Sumanites is derived from India and, though for the present it is not easy to prove the truth of this assertion, yet I do not think that one could call it in question." He then goes on to show how the Sumanite sect can be traced to the Chārvākas in India.[9] In another place, Schmölders hints at other Indian influences upon the Kalam, besides that of the Sumanite sect, saying: "The Indian doctrines were not so unknown to the Arabs as one ordinarily seems to think. Several authors, and notably some Muʿtazilite leaders, had pretty accurate notions of it. I hope to have occasion to return to this question some other time." [10]

Schmölders never had occasion to take up again the question of Indian influence upon the Kalam. But the question was taken up by Mabilleau in 1895. In his study of the history of atomism, he tries to show that the atomism of the Kalam did not come from Greek atomism but rather from Indian atomism.[11] This view, greatly modified to read that certain elements in Kalam atomism came from India, has been generally accepted; a full exposition of it is given by Pines.[12] The main argument is that the Kalam atomism contains many features which are not found in Greek atomism but are found in Indian atomism, especially the view held by many in the Kalam that atoms have no extension.[13]

The subject of the Sumanites, which was first broached by Schmölders, was taken up, many years later, in 1910, by Horten,[14] who tried to establish by proof what Schmölders had only conjectured, that the Sumanites were an Indian sect. His proof is based on a report by Ibn al-Murtaḍā that Jahm

[8] Schmölders, *Essai*, pp. 111–115.

[9] *Ibid.*, p. 114.

[10] *Ibid.*, p. 99, n. 2.

[11] Mabilleau, *Histoire de la Philosophie atomistique*, pp. 328 ff.

[12] Pines, *Atomenlehre*, pp. 102 ff.

[13] Cf. below, pp. 472–473.

[14] Horten, "Der Skeptizismus der Sumanija nach der Darstellung des Rāzi, 1209," *Archiv für Geschichte der Philosophie*, 24:142–143; 144, n. 6 (1910). Cf. *idem.*, *Systeme*, pp. 93–96.

and Muʿammar held a debate with Sumanites in India [15] and also that another debate was held in India between a Sumanite and a Muslim.[16] In *Die philosophischen Systeme der spekulativen Theologen im Islam*, he tried to paste Indian labels on all kinds of Kalam views. But, as Massignon in his review of that book has remarked, all these are based on mere "similarities and isolated coincidents." [17]

4. JUDAISM

Finally there is the question of Jewish influence upon the Kalam — as distinguished from Jewish influence upon the Koran and the Ḥadīth concerning which there is no question.[1] Various opinions have been expressed with regard to Jewish influence on the following three outstanding problems in the Kalam: (1) anthropomorphism and anti-anthropomorphism; (2) eternal or created Koran; (3) predestination or free will. The last two of these problems, as we have seen, have also been discussed by modern scholars in connection with Christian influences.

With regard to anthropomorphism, Isfarāʾinī, who divides the Jews into two sects, one of which he describes as anthropomorphists (*mushabbihah*), says that the anthropomorphism of such Muslim sects as the Rawāfiḍ and others came from the Jews.[2] Shahrastānī, in one place, speaking of Muslim anthropomorphists, says that "most of their anthropomorphisms were borrowed from the Jews, for anthropomorphism is characteristic of them." [3] In another place, however, speaking again of Muslim anthropomorphists, he says that "anthropomorphism, in its sheer and utter form, had already existed among the Jews, not among all of them, but among the Karaites of them," [4] without adding that Muslim anthropomor-

[15] *Al Muʿtazillah*, p. 21, ll. 5 ff. (p. 34, ll. 9 ff.).

[16] *Ibid.*, p. 31, ll. 12 ff. (p. 55, ll. 4 ff.).

[17] *Der Islam*, 3:408 (1912).

[1] On Jewish influence on early commentaries on the Koran, see Ibn Ḥaldūn, *Muḳaddimah* II, p. 393.

[2] *Tabṣīr*, p. 133, ll. 3–6 and 11–12.

[3] *Milal*, p. 77, ll. 19–20.

[4] *Ibid.*, p. 64, l. 20 – p. 65, l. 1.

phism was borrowed from the Jews. In still another place, after stating that the Jews are anthropomorphists,[5] he merely says that "the Rabbanites among them correspond to the Muʿtazilites among us and the Karaites to the anthropomorphists among us." [6] Among modern scholars, Schreiner argues quite the opposite, that it was the anti-anthropomorphists among the Muslims who had been influenced by Jews, and in proof of this he quotes al-Subkī as stating that the denial of anthropomorphism originated with the Jew Labīd b. al-Aʿṣam.[7] Neumark agrees with Schreiner.[8]

With regard to the problem of the eternity or the createdness of the Koran, Schreiner quotes a statement from Ibn al-Athīr, according to which, again, Labīd b. al-Aʿṣam was the first to introduce into Islam the doctrine of the createdness of the Koran.[9] Neumark, following his own view that among Jews there were those who believed in the eternity of the Torah,[10] takes the controversy in the Kalam over the Koran to have arisen under the influence of the controversy in Judaism over the Torah.[11] We have already quoted Wensinck,[12] who includes the Jewish lore about the pre-existent Law as one of the sources of the belief in the eternal Koran.

With regard to predestination and free will, Masʿūdī says of the Karaites among the Jews that they "profess the doctrines of the justice and unity of God," [13] that is, they profess the same doctrines that are professed by the Muʿtazilites among the Muslims. Just the opposite of this is Shahrastānī's statement that with regard to free will, "the Rabbanites of theirs are like the Muʿtazilites among us and the Karaites are like the Compulsionists." [14] Neither of them makes Islam

[5] *Ibid.*, p. 164, ll. 14–16. [6] *Ibid.*, ll. 17–18.
[7] Schreiner, *Kalam*, p. 4, n. 2, quoting al-Subkī, *Ṭabaḳāt al-Shāfiʿyyah.*
[8] Neumark, *Geschichte*, I, p. 119; *Toledot*, I, p. 112.
[9] Schreiner, *Kalam*, p. 3; cf. below
[10] Cf. Neumark, *Geschichte*, I, p. 84; *Toledot*, I, p. 68.
[11] *Id.*, *Geschichte*, I, p. 119; *Toledot*, I, p. 111.
[12] Cf. above, p. 63.
[13] Masʿūdi, *Tanbīh*, p. 112, l. 13–p. 113, l. 1 (159).
[14] *Milal*, p. 164, ll. 16–18.

influenced by Judaism in this respect. Isfarā'inī, however, after saying that the second of the two sects into which he has divided the Jews are "the Libertarians" (*al-ḳadariyyah*), adds: "And the Libertarians who appeared in the Muslim domain have acquired their belief from that Jewish sect." [15] Among modern scholars, Schreiner tries to show that Wāṣil b. 'Aṭā''s statement on freedom of the will is almost a verbatim translation of a rabbinic statement.[16] Neumark, who, like Goldziher, takes predestination in Islam to be a pre-Islamic heritage,[17] agrees with Schreiner that free will was introduced under the influence of Judaism.[18]

V. Origin, Structure, Diversity

The task which I had set for myself in this work was not to trace influences but to describe the origin and structure and diversity of the teachings of the Kalam. Whenever in the course of my study of the Kalam I happened to come upon a certain belief which could not be found in the Koran or which could not have arisen spontaneously as an interpretation of something found in the Koran, I asked myself two questions, for which I tried to find answers.

The first question was, what is its origin? The answer to this question was not to be found in the discovery of something similar to it in some other system of thought of which it could have been an imitation. Beliefs and ideas are indeed contagious, and the history of beliefs and ideas is often a history of imitation by contagion. But for the contagiousness of a belief or an idea to take effect, there must be a predisposition and susceptibility on the part of those who are to be affected by it. In the case before us, we must always ask ourselves, what was there in Islam that made it susceptible to that particular foreign influence? Then, also, beliefs and ideas

[15] *Tabṣīr*, p. 133, ll. 7-10.
[16] Schreiner, *Kalam*, p. 4; cf. below
[17] Neumark, *Geschichte*, I, i, p. 119; *Toledot*, I, p. 111.
[18] *Idem.*, *Geschichte*, I, p. 119; *Toledot*, I, p. 112.

ride on the back of terms, and whenever there is a transmission of a belief or an idea from one linguistic setting to another, there is always a transmission of the fundamental terminology of the belief or the idea transmitted, either by translation or by mistranslation. In the case before us, therefore, no foreign influence can be definitely established unless it is substantiated by a terminological linkage. Then there was another consideration. The important problems of influence or origin that came up in the study of the Kalam did not, as a rule, concern simple beliefs expressed by single terms or by single phrases; they concerned rather complicated beliefs, tangled webs of beliefs, woven together of many strands of thought and many threads of reasoning. Moreover, whatever foreign influence suggested itself in the search of origin in the study of any of the Kalam problems, it seldom came directly by way of authentic literature; most often it came by way of distorted doxographies or by way of hearsay. In view of all this, a mere reference to single foreign passage or a quotation of it would not be sufficient to answer the first question.

Next to the question of origin was the question whether the variety of statements in the Kalam teaching on any particular subject could be forged and hammered and beaten into a coherent, though ramified, system of thought. Here, too, the answer is not to be found in collecting all the statements bearing on a given problem and arranging them according to some kind of plan. The nature of the source material makes such a procedure inadequate. It happens that the original works of the earliest masters of the Kalam are not extant. Their teachings are preserved in later doxographic collections, the earliest of which, so far published, dates from the tenth century, and restatements of their teachings, and perhaps also genuine quotations of their teachings, are scattered through various other kinds of works, extending over many centuries. The teachings of the masters of the Kalam are reported in these various kinds of work either directly or through some intermediary or through a chain of intermediaries in the form of isolated sayings in the name of certain individuals or in the name of certain schools or in the name of certain groups of certain schools. The reports of these sayings in the various successive doxographies, and sometimes even in the same doxography, are not always consistent. Sometimes they differ in terminology, and one has the problem of deciding what the original terms were. Sometimes they are contradictory, or seem to be contradictory, and one has the problem of deciding what the genuine view of the author or authors quoted was. Most often the sayings quoted are fragmentary, and one has the task of piecing them together. In view of all this, a mere collection of sayings, in whatever manner classified, would not yield an answer to the second question.

What is really necessary in answering both these questions is first to trace all the suggestions of foreign influence in the problems dealt with by the Mutakallimūn to all the possible sources available either directly to themselves or to those who may have been their oral informants; then, by the use of what may be called the hypothetico-deductive method of text interpretation, or more simply the method of conjecture and verification, which I have described elsewhere, to try to establish the origin and structure and diversity of the problems dealt with in the Kalam. Briefly stated, this method of text interpretation is analogous to what in science is called control-experiment. Just as the scientist starts out on some experiment, say, with a certain number of rabbits, so in our investigation of any topic we start out with a certain number of representative texts bearing upon that topic. Then just as the scientific experimenter inoculates only one or some of his rabbits and uses the others as controls, so we also perform all our conjectural interpretations on one or some of our texts and use the others as controls.

This is what I have set out do to in this work.

The problems dealt with by the Kalam are varied and many. Some of them are purely religious; some are purely philosophical; some are problems of religion treated in terms of philosophy. Of these three types of problems, I have selected as the subject of discussion in this work only problems of the third type. The first type of problems does not come within the range of problems dealt with in my series of studies to which this work belongs, and the second type of problems will be dealt with in the volume devoted to Arabic philosophy as distinguished from the philosophy of the Kalam. Even of the third type of problems, I have selected only those which are either exclusively characteristic of the Kalam or exhaustively treated in it. Problems which, though touched upon in the Kalam, have been more fully and more exhaustively treated later by the philosophers have been left for the aforementioned volume on Arabic philosophy. The problems thus selected for treatment in this work are six: Attributes; the Koran; Creation; Atomism; Causality; Predestination and Free Will. Each of these six problems, it may be remarked in passing, is included by both Maimonides [1] and Ibn Ḫaldūn [2] among their lists of topics on which the Kalam, according to them, held views especially characteristic of them as a sect. Finally, the problems thus selected are dealt with only insofar as they are characteristic of the Kalam as a whole or of a school within the Kalam or of a group within a school. Individual Mutakallimūn are dealt with only insofar as they represent the Kalam as a whole or a school within the Kalam or a group within a school or, occasionally, as expressing an important or interesting dissenting opinion.

These six problems are not new with the Kalam. They are old problems, and my discussion of them in this work is a continuation of my discussion of the same problems in my studies of Philo and the Church Fathers, to which this present study of the Kalam is a sequel. The problem of attributes here is a further development mainly of the problem dealt with in the chapter on "God, the World of Ideas, and the Logos," in *Philo*, I, and the chapters under the heading "The Trinity,

[1] Cf. below, pp. 78–79.

[2] *Muḳaddimah* III, p. 114, ll. 1–12.

the Logos, and the Platonic Ideas" in *The Philosophy of the Church Fathers*, I, and partly also of the discussion of "The Unknowability of God and Divine Predicates" both in *Philo*, II, and in *The Philosophy of the Church Fathers*, II.[3] The problem of the eternity of the Koran here is a further development partly of the problems dealt with in the aforementioned chapters in *Philo*, I, and *The Philosophy of the Church Fathers*, I, and partly of the problems dealt with in the section on the "Immanent Logos" in *Philo*, I, and in the chapter "The Mystery of the Incarnation" in *The Philosophy of the Church Fathers*, I. The problem of creation and atomism here is a further development of the problem dealt with in the chapters on "Creation and Structure of the World" both in *Philo*, I, and in *The Philosophy of the Church Fathers*, II. The problem of causality here is a further development of the discussion of laws of nature and miracles both in *Philo*, I, and in *The Philosophy of the Church Fathers*, II. The problem of predestination and free will here is a further development of the discussion of free will both in *Philo*, I, and in *The Philosophy of the Church Fathers*, II.

As part of a series of studies on the *Structure and Growth of Philosophic Systems from Plato to Spinoza*, this work presents a system of religious philosophy based upon certain scriptural presuppositions laid down by Philo. In Philo, these scriptural presuppositions are the following eight: (1) existence of God; (2) unity of God; (3) creation of the world; (4) divine Providence; (5) unity of the world; (6) existence of ideas; (7) revelation of the Law; (8) eternity of the Law.[4] Let us, then, see how many of these eight presuppositions were accepted by the Kalam.

In Christianity, as we have seen,[5] the eternity of the Law was rejected outright; the unity of the world, though assumed, is not included among the religious principles; and the exis-

[3] Volume II of *The Philosophy of the Church Fathers* referred to here is as yet unpublished.

[4] Cf. *Philo*, I, pp. 164–169.

[5] Cf. *The Philosophy of the Church Fathers*, I, pp. 80–96.

tence of ideas has survived in a modified form in the doctrine of the Trinity. As for the remaining five scriptural presuppositions, they were all accepted, but concerning the unity of God there arose certain deviations from Philo.

In Philo, the unity of God meant four things: (1) the denial of polytheism; (2) the denial of the dependence of God upon something else, that is to say, the assertion of the self-sufficiency of God; (3) the assertion that God alone is eternal, whence the identification of eternity with deity; (4) the assertion, as a result of the combination of the scriptural principle of the unlikeness of God to anything else with the philosophic analysis of the meaning of the term "one," that the unity of God means absolute simplicity, excluding from God not only the internal plurality that is implicit in the conception of corporeality but also any other kind of internal plurality. In Christianity, the Philonic conception of the unity of God as a denial of polytheism and as an assertion of self-sufficiency and as an identification of eternity with deity was generally accepted. But with regard to the unity of God in the sense of His absolute simplicity, it became a matter of controversy in its sectarian differences over the doctrine of the Trinity, orthodox Christianity rejecting it; heretical Christianity accepting it. And a verbal difference of opinion appeared in orthodox Christianity also over the propriety of applying to God the term "corporeal." One of them, Tertullian, argued that God could be described as corporeal, with the understanding that His corporeality was unlike the corporeality of bodies.[6]

Similarly in Islam, the principle of the eternity of the Law was rejected; [7] the principle of the unity of the world, though assumed, is not included among the religious beliefs; and the existence of ideas survived in a modified form in the doctrine of attributes and the eternity of the Koran. As for the re-

[6] *Adv. Prax.* 7 (PL 2, 162 C).

[7] Cf. Steinschneider, *Polemische*, pp. 322–325; Schreiner, *Polemik*, pp. 619, 647–648.

maining five Philonic scriptural presuppositions, again, as in Christianity, they were all accepted.

The existence of God, as in Philo,[8] means to Islam a rejection not only of atheism but also of scepticism. Thus it is common in Islam to distinguish among philosophers between those who believed in a Creator and those who did not believe in a Creator [9] and to include among infidels before the rise of Islam various types of sceptics, who are placed under the general term "Sophists." [10] But with regard to the unity of God, of the four aforementioned Philonic conceptions of it, the first, that of the denial of polytheism, is most emphatically stressed in the Koran.[11] Similarly emphasized in the Koran is the self-sufficiency of God, so that the term *al-ghanī*, "the Rich," that is, the Free of Want or the Self-Sufficient, is included among the ninety-nine most beautiful names of God.[12] However, the unity of God in the sense that God alone was eternal became a matter of controversy in its sectarian differences over the problem of attributes, most Attributists rejecting it,[13] while some Attributists [14] and all Antiattributists [15] accepted it. So also the unity of God in the sense of His absolute simplicity became a matter of controversy, again, in the problem of attributes, all the Attributists rejecting it; the Antiattributists accepting it.[16]

Then, as in Christianity, there arose in orthodox Islam a difference of opinion, perhaps a difference of opinion which is only verbal, as to whether God can be described as being corporeal or even as having a body. There were those among the orthodox who assumed that on the mere basis of the Koranic injunction against likening God to created beings (42:9; 112:4), it is permissible to conceive of God as corporeal or even as having a body, provided His corporeality or his body is taken to be unlike that of anything else. Thus Aver-

[8] Cf. *Philo*, I, pp. 165–171.
[9] *Farḳ*, p. 346, ll. 10–13.
[10] *Ibid.*, l. 6; cf. *Milal*, p. 202, l. 13.
[11] Surah 4:51; 20:7, and *passim.*
[12] Based on Surah 2:265, 270; 3:11, 92; 27:40; 39:9; 64:6.
[13] Cf. below, p. 130.
[14] Cf. below, pp. 143 ff.
[15] Cf. below, pp. 132 ff.
[16] Cf. below, pp. 133; 138–139.

roes, speaking of "many Muslims," such as "the Ḥanbalites and their many followers," says that they believed that "God is a body which is unlike other bodies." [17] Ibn Ḫaldūn, referring to certain Muslims, whom he describes as "corporealists" (*mujassimah*), says that "they affirm the corporeality [of God], but not like [that of] bodies," [18] and Ibn Ḥazm, who himself believed in the incorporeality of God, argues that "if a Koranic text was shown to us in which God was called a body, it would be our duty to profess this belief, but then to qualify it by saying that He is a body not like other bodies." [19] Reference to this view in Islam is to be found also in the works of Jewish philosophers writing in Arabic. Joseph al-Baṣīr, referring to some Mutakallimūn, says: "Their statement that God is a body not like all other bodies is unsustainable," [20] and Maimonides refers to this view in quoting some other Mutakallimūn, who were opposed to it, as arguing: "If you say that God is a body not like other bodies, you are self-contradictory." [21]

The principle of the creation of the world is explicitly stated in the Koran,[22] and, as in Philo and the Church Fathers, it became an established principle of Muslim belief, but, as in Judaism, there arose differences of opinion as to its meaning.[23] Also explicitly stated in the Koran is the belief in divine Providence,[24] under which are included the problems of causality, on both of which there arose in Islam difference of opinion.[25] Finally, explicitly stated in the Koran is the belief in revelation,[26] but on this belief, too, there arose differences of opinion as to its meaning.[27]

The philosophy of the Kalam is thus, like the philosophy

[17] *Kashf*, p. 60, ll. 13–15. So also the Rafiḍite Hishām b. al-Ḥakam is reported to have said that God "is a body unlike other bodies" (*Maḳālāt*, p. 33, ll. 10–11; p. 208, l. 1).

[18] *Muḳaddimah* III, p. 52, l. 20; cf. p. 38, ll. 1–4.

[19] *Fiṣal* II, p. 118, l. 25–p. 119, l. 1.

[20] *Maḥkimat Peti* 18, p. 114b.

[21] *Moreh* I, 76, 2nd Argument, p. 160, l. 11.

[22] Surah 13:3, 4, and *passim*.

[23] Cf. below, ch. V.

[24] Surah 6:59; 15:20, and *passim*.

[25] Cf. below, ch. VII.

[26] Surah 2:3, and *passim*.

[27] Cf. below, ch. III.

of the Church Fathers, based upon five of the eight scriptural presuppositions laid down by Philo. And so Maimonides, in a chapter in which he deals with the Muslim Kalam and the Christian Church Fathers, draws a distinction between beliefs which are common to Judaism, Christianity, and Islam and beliefs which are peculiar to Christianity and Islam. As an example of beliefs which are common to the three religions, he mentions "the doctrine of the creation of the world, on the truth of which depends the belief in the truth of miracles and other beliefs." [28] By the "other beliefs" which together with the belief in miracles are said by Maimonides to depend upon the belief in the creation of the world, we may assume he meant the existence and the unity of God, divine Providence, and revelation, for, even though Maimonides believes that the existence of God and the unity of God, which to him include also incorporeality, can be established indirectly on the assumption of the eternity of the world, the direct and real proof for these two principles, according to him, rests on the principle of the creation of the world in which he himself believed,[29] and, as for divine Providence and revelation, they are both admitted by Maimonides to be miraculous acts [30] and hence, like all miracles, are to him dependent upon the belief in creation. Of the beliefs which are peculiar to Christianity and Islam, Maimonides mentions the doctrine of the Trinity in the case of the former and the doctrine of the eternity of the Koran, which is part of the doctrine of attributes, in the case of the latter.[31] These two doctrines, as we have seen, mark the deviations in orthodox Christianity and orthodox Islam from some of the Philonic conceptions of the meaning of the unity of God. Thus, according to Maimonides, the

[28] *Moreh* I, 71, p. 123, l. 5.

[29] *Ibid.* II, 2, p. 175, l. 12 – p. 176, l. 2.

[30] As for Providence, see Maimonides' characterization of divine knowledge and Providence in *Moreh* III, 20, p. 351, ll. 1–11; III, 23, p. 360, ll. 18–24. As for revelation, see Maimonides' characterization of it in his introduction to his Commentary on *M. Sanhedrin* X and his description of the revelation on Mount Sinai in *Moreh* II, 33.

[31] *Moreh* I, 71, p. 123, ll. 5–7.

philosophy of the Church Fathers, as well as that of the Kalam, is based upon five principles which they share in common with Judaism, which five principles, as we have seen, are five of the eight scriptural presuppositions laid down by Philo.

VI. Christian and Jewish Kalam

Christian as well as Muslim and Jewish writers refer to Christian Mutakallimūn. Thus Yaḥyā Ibn ʿAdī speaks of "Christian Mutakallimūn"; [1] Averroes speaks of the Mutakallimūn of the people of the religion of the Christians" [2] or "the Mutakallimūn of the peoples of the three religions which exist today"; [3] and Maimonides speaks of "the first Mutakallimūn of both the Christian Greeks and the Muslims." [4] Now in these three quotations, the statements of Yaḥyā Ibn ʿAdī and Maimonides about Christian Mutakallimūn refer, as may be judged from the context, to the Christian Church Fathers. But Averroes' statement about "the Mutakallimūn of the peoples of the three religions," in which he says that they all agree upon the principle of creation *ex nihilo*, quite evidently refers to Christian and Jewish theologians who wrote in Arabic and with whose works he was acquainted; for, while he may have become acquainted with the Christian insistence upon the principle of creation *ex nihilo* from Arabic translations of the works of the Church Fathers, he could not have known of the Jewish insistence upon this principle except from the works written by Jewish theologians in Arabic.[5] Since these Christian and Jewish theologians are referred to as Mutakallimūn, we should like to know whether the literatures produced by them shared any of the characteristics of the Muslim Kalam.

[1] Périer, *Petits*, p. 39.
[2] *In XII Metaph.*, Comm. 18, Arabic, p. 1489, ll. 4–5; Latin, p. 304 F.
[3] *Ibid.*, Arabic, p. 1503, ll. 11–12; Latin, p. 305 F.
[4] *Moreh* I, 71, p. 123, ll. 10–11.
[5] Cf. Steinschneider, *Heb. Uebers.*, pp. 368–461.

1. CHRISTIAN KALAM

Christians in Muslim countries, prior to their coming under Muslim rule in the seventh century, used three literary languages, Greek, Syriac, and Coptic. But during the eighth century they began to use also Arabic. While at first their use of Arabic was confined to translations of scriptural and liturgical works, by the tenth century they began to use it for translations of the works of the Greek and Syriac Church Fathers and also for the writing of original works on theological problems.[1] Most of this literature has not been published. But from the few works that have been published and from descriptions of the unpublished works, one gathers the impression that it was a continuation of the teachings of the Church Fathers, without its having been affected by either the philosophical or theological teachings characteristic of the Kalam. Thus from the fact that Yaḥyā Ibn ʿAdī wrote several treatises dealing with the infinite divisibility of bodies[2] or the denial that bodies are composed of atoms[3] and that his pupil Abū al-Ḫair al-Ḥasan ibn Suwār wrote a brief treatise in which he refuted a Kalam argument for the creation of the world based on the theory of atoms,[4] it may be gathered that the Christian Mutakallimūn did not accept the atomism of the Muslim Kalam. Then also from the fact that certain Ashʿarites, who identified their attributes with the second and third persons of the Trinity, found fault with Christianity for its limiting the persons, which they supposed to be the same as attributes, only to two,[5] shows that the Christians in Muslim countries during the period of the Kalam continued in the

[1] See Graf, *Geschichte der christlichen arabischen Literatur*, I (1944), II (1947).

[2] Cf. Périer, *Yaḥyā ben ʿAdī*, p. 75, Nos. 27, 28.

[3] *Ibid.*, Nos. 31, 32; cf. also p. 76, No. 35.

[4] Bernhard Lewin, "La notion de *muḥdath* dans le kalām et dans la philosophie," *Donum Natalicium H. S. Nyberg oblatum* (1954), pp. 88–93; *Maḳālah l'Abī al-Ḫayir al-Ḥasan Ibn Suwār al-Baghdādī* in Badawi's *Neoplatonici apud Arabes* (1955), pp. 343–347; cf. below, pp. 393–394.

[5] *Fiṣal* IV, p. 207, ll. 22–23; cf. below

Patristic view that none of the terms predicated of God, outside the terms designating the persons of the Trinity, indicates the existence of real beings. Finally, from the fact that Abucara in the eighth century expounds the Christian conception of absolute free will [6] and that Yaḥyā Ibn ʿAdī in the tenth century refutes even the newfangled Kalam theory of "acquisition," [7] which as used by the Predestinarians of his time was meant to be a sort of concession to those who believed in free will,[8] it may be gathered that the so-called Christian Mutakallimūn were not affected by the Muslim orthodox Kalam doctrine of predestination.

Still, as a minority group in an overwhelmingly Muslim world, Christians could not help but be affected by the environing powerful Islam. For, as time went on and Muslims acquired a knowledge of logic and metaphysics as well as a skill in using these disciplines, their continued assault upon the Christian doctrine of the Trinity, for which they had the warrant of the Koran, grew more and more searching, more and more telling. Against this, the repetition of the old line of arguments in defense of this doctrine lost its effectiveness, especially since the Muslims had already learned of the puncturing of these arguments by heretics within Christianity itself. A new line of argumentation had to be taken up — one more resilient, more recessive, more concessive. Christians under Muslim rule, thereupon, without consciously deviating from their orthodoxy, began to accommodate their doctrine of the Trinity to the Muslim doctrine of attributes. They began to argue that, after all, there is no fundamental difference between the Christian persons of the Trinity and the Muslim attributes of God in their respective effects upon the unity of God in which both Christians and Muslims believe. Dexterously they began to reduce differences between persons and attributes to mere verbiage. Thus we shall see how a group of Nestorians reformulated their orthodox doctrine of

[6] Graf, *Geschichte*, II, p. 13, No. 9.

[7] Cf. Périer, *Yaḥyā ben ʿAdī*, p. 73, No. 7

[8] Cf. below, pp. 684 ff.

the Trinity in terms of one of the formulations of the doctrine of attributes in Islam, without, however, deviating from their original orthodox conception of the Trinity.[9] We shall still further see how that same group of Nestorians, in order to accommodate their conception of Jesus to that held by the Muslims, changed the prevailing Nestorian formulation of Christology for a formulation current only among certain Nestorians.[10]

2. JEWISH KALAM*

In their own literature, written in Hebrew or Aramaic or in a mixture of both, the Jews who came under Muslim rule in the seventh century had no philosophic works corresponding to the philosophic writings of the Church Fathers possessed by the Christians who came under Muslim rule at the same time. Toward the end of the ninth century, however, philosophic works in Arabic of a Jewish content began to appear among them and continued to flow, both in the East and in Spain, until the end of the twelfth century, though isolated works occasionally appeared even after that time.[1]

A characterization of that Jewish philosophic literature in Arabic from its very beginning to his own time is given by Maimonides in his introductory remarks to his systematic presentation of the Kalam in his *Moreh Nebukim.*

"As for the little bit of Kalam regarding the subject of the unity of God and whatever is dependent upon this subject, which you will find among the Geonim and the Karaites, it all consists of matters which they borrowed from the Mutakallimūn of Islam." [2] He then goes on to say that, since among the Muslim Mutakallimūn the first sect to appear was that of the Muʿtazilites, "it was from them that our correligionists borrowed whatever they borrowed and it was their method

[9] Cf. below, pp. 342–347. [10] Cf. below, pp. 347–349.

* Reprinted with some revision from *The Seventy-Fifth Anniversary Volume of the Jewish Quarterly Review*, 1967, pp. 544–573.

[1] Steinschneider, *Die arabische Literatur der Juden*, §§ 23 ff.

[2] *Moreh* I, 71, p. 121, l. 28 – p. 122, l. 2.

that they followed," [3] but, as for the new views which appeared later with the coming of the Ash'arites, "you will not find any of them among our correligionists, not because they judiciously chose the former view in preference to the latter but rather because it just happened that they had taken up the former view [first] and adopted it and assumed it to be something incontestably demonstrated." [4] Then, in contrast to those Jewish speculative theologians in the East, he says: "As for the Andalusians from among the people of our nation, they all hold on to the words of the philosophers and are favorably disposed to their views insofar as they are not contradictory to any fundamental article of religion, and you will not find them in any way at all to have followed the methods of the Mutakallimūn, the result being that in many things they follow pretty near our own method in the present treatise, [as may be noticed] in the few works that we have of their recent authors." [5]

In this passage, Maimonides makes three significant statements. First, the influence of the Mutakallimūn upon the speculative Jewish theologians of the East, namely, "the Geonim," that is, the Rabbanites, and their opponents, "the Karaites," is to be found only in their treatment of "the unity of God and whatever is dependent upon it." Second, with regard to "the unity of God and whatever is dependent upon it," both the Rabbanites and the Karaites of the East followed the Mu'tazilites, whereas "the people of our religious denomination," that is, the Rabbanites, in Spain followed the philosophers. Third, the preference of the Geonim and the Karaites for the views of the Mu'tazilites was not the result of a deliberate choice but rather of the mere chance of their having become acquainted with the Mu'tazilite views first.

Each of these statements calls for comment.

[3] *Ibid.*, p. 122, ll. 4–5.

[4] *Ibid.*, ll. 6–9.

[5] *Ibid.*, ll. 9–13. Cf. *Moreh* I, Introduction, p. 10, 26–27, where, after stating that his work deals with certain recondite topics, Maimonides adds: "on which no book has been composed by any one in our religious community during this length of captivity, insofar as their writings on such topics are extant among us."

The first statement was meant to exclude such characteristic views held by the Mutakallimūn as atomism and the denial of causality. With regard to atomism, while it was followed by "the Karaites" of the East, such as Joseph al-Baṣīr and Jeshua ben Judah, who were known to Maimonides, it was not followed by "the Geonim" nor, it may be added, by later Karaites, such as his own contemporary Judah Hadassi [6] and probably also others,[7] who were unknown to Maimonides. With regard to the denial of causality, it was definitely not followed by "the Geonim," and it is doubtful whether it was followed by "the Karaites" of the East known to Maimonides.[8]

The second statement is subject to several qualifications. The expression "the unity of God and whatever is dependent upon it," judged by what we actually find in the writings of the Geonim and the Karaites which reflect a Kalam background, refers not only to discussions of the meaning of the unity of God but also to discussions of proofs for the existence and incorporeality of God, proofs for the denial of the reality of attributes, and proofs for the creation of the world and the freedom of the human will. Now it is true that in all these discussions both the Rabbanites of the East and the Karaites followed the methods of the Muʿtazilite Mutakallimūn, but still there were certain differences between them. Thus, while both Rabbanites and Karaites deny the reality of attributes, Joseph al-Baṣīr, the Karaite, followed Abū Hāshim's theory of modes,[9] whereas Saadia, the Rabbanite, expresses himself in a way which excludes the theory of modes,[10] and so also does al-Muḳammaṣ.[11] Similarly, with regard to the proofs of the creation of the world, which serve also as proofs for the existence of God, while both the Rabbanites of the East and the Karaites use arguments which are characterized by Maimonides himself as those of the Kalam,[12] the Karaites,

[6] *Eshkol ha-Kofer* 28, p. 19c–d.

[7] *Eṣ Ḥayyim* 4, p. 18, ll. 4–5.

[8] Discussed in the as yet unpublished study, "Kalam Repercussions in Jewish Philosophy."

[9] *Ibid.*

[10] *Ibid.*

[11] *Ibid.*

[12] Cf. below, p. 373.

who adopted the Kalam theory of atoms, use these arguments in their original Kalam form as based upon atomism, whereas Saadia, rejecting atomism, uses the same arguments in a modified form, from which the theory of atoms was eliminated.[13]

So also, with reference to Maimonides' statement on the difference between the spokesmen of Judaism in the East and those in Andalusia, while it is true that some of the Jewish philosophers in Spain abandoned the Kalam method of proving the creation of the world and the existence of God,[14] two of them, Baḥya Ibn Paḳuda and Joseph Ibn Ṣaddik, like Saadia of the East, used the modified form of the Kalam arguments for the creation of the world and hence also for the existence of God.[15] Undoubtedly his generalization was meant to refer only to those whom he includes in what he describes as "their recent authors" and evidently Baḥya Ibn Paḳuda and Joseph Ibn Ṣaddiḳ were not included among them. With regard to the problem of attributes, though it would seem to be included in the subject of "the unity of God" and hence it would also seem to be included in his generalization about the difference between the spokesmen of Judaism in the East and those of Andalusia, it can be shown that it is really not included in that generalization, and this for the following two reasons. First, on the fundamental issue in the problem of attributes there was no difference between the Muʿtazilites and those whom Maimonides calls "the philosophers." Second, the generalization refers only to those topics which are dealt with in the subsequent chapters on the Kalam; attributes are dealt with by him in earlier chapters.

The third statement, implying that were it not for the fact that the Geonim and Karaites had committed themselves to the views of the Muʿtazilites before the rise of the Ashʿarites they might have followed the latter, is somewhat puzzling.

[13] Cf. below, pp. 397–398; 404 and 405.
[14] As, for instance, Abraham Ibn Daud.
[15] Cf. Munk, *Guide*, I, 71, p. 339, n. 1; cf. below, pp. 389–390; 403–404.

There is no difference between the Muʿtazilites and the Ashʿarites in their methods of proving the creation of the world and the existence and unity and incorporeality of God. There is a difference between them only on such general religious questions as attributes and the freedom of the will, and also on such a purely Muslim question as the eternity of the Koran. When, therefore, Maimonides, by implication, says that but for the prior appearance of the Muʿtazilites the Geonim and Karaites might have followed the Ashʿarites, does he mean to say that they might have followed the Ashʿarites in accepting their view on the reality of attributes and predestination? But there is no ground for such an assumption. The belief in the reality of attributes and the belief in predestination did not originate with the Ashʿarites. They had been well established in Islam even before the Muʿtazilites came into being.[16] The controversy in Islam over both these doctrines was known to the Geonim and the Karaites, and still they aligned themselves with the Muʿtazilites in rejecting the orthodox Muslim position, later espoused by the Ashʿarites, on both these doctrines. Moreover, while it is true that Ashʿarī's views may not have been known to Saadia at the time he wrote his *Emunot ve-Deʿot* in Baghdad during the year 933, though Ashʿarī's orthodox preaching and writing took place during the years 912–935, the last of which years he spent in Baghdad where he died, Joseph al-Baṣīr, the Karaite, quotes the Ashʿarites and refutes them.[17] How, then, could Maimonides say that the agreement of the Geonim and the Karaites with the Muʿtazilites was due to the mere chance that the Ashʿarites were unknown to them?

Reference to Jewish followers of the Muslim Kalam, with the mention of only the Karaites, is to be found also in Judah Halevi's *Cuzari*. At one place in this work, written in the form of a dialogue between a rabbi and the king of the Khazars, just as Halevi was about to make the rabbi expound for the King the Neoplatonized Aristotelian system of philosophy,

[16] Cf. above, pp. 17–19.

[17] *Neʿimot*, pp. 44a, l. 18 ff.; Arabic, pp. 98b, l. 9 ff.

he has the rabbi say: "I will not make you travel the road of the Karaites who went up to theology without a flight of steps (*daraj: madregah*), but I will provide you with a clear outline, which will allow you to form a clear conception of matter and form, then of the elements, then of nature, then of the soul, then of the intellect, then of theology." [18] On the face of it, the passage would imply that what he objected to was the fact that the Karaites plunged right into theology without a preliminary study of physics.[19] But this, if we take the works of Joseph al-Baṣīr and Jeshua ben Judah as examples, is not an exact description of their method. They do not plunge right into a discussion of theology. They rather start with a discussion of the need of rational speculation in dealing with theological problems. They then go on with explanations of certain terms and concepts used in the physical sciences, in the course of which they discuss the proofs for the creation of the world. It is only then that they take up the discussion of purely theological problems, such as the existence, the unity, the incorporeality of God, and attributes.[20] This indeed is the method of the Kalam, but it is this method that is also used by such non-Karaite Jewish philosophers as Saadia and Baḥya.

In explanation of Halevi's statement, it may be suggested that the expression "without *daraj*," which for the time being I have translated literally by "without a flight of steps," does not mean that the Karaites plunge right into theology without prefacing it by a preliminary discussion of physical concepts; it rather means that the physical concepts which the Karaites discuss preliminary to their discussion of theology are not those of a graded order of beings in a process of successive emanation, such as he himself describes later in his exposition of the Neoplatonized Aristotelian system of emanation, where he speaks of "the knowledge . . . of the rank (*martabah:*

[18] *Cuzari* V, 2, p. 294, l. 18 – p. 296, l. 1; p. 295, l. 18 – p. 297, l. 2.

[19] Cf. commentaries *ad. loc.*

[20] *Ne'imot*, Hebrew, pp. 1b–9a; Arabic, pp. 1a–11a; *Maḥkimat Peti*, 1–9, pp. 103b–109b.

madregah) of Intelligence in its relation to the Creator, the rank of soul in its relation to intelligence, the rank of nature in its relation to soul, and the rank of spheres and stars and generated things in their relation to matter and form." [21] The term *daraj* is thus used here as the equivalent of the term *martabah* in the sense of "rank," "order," "hierarchy." Both these terms, it will be noticed, are in the Hebrew version of the *Cuzari* translated by *madregah*. What Halevi means to say here is that, unlike the Karaites, such as Joseph al-Baṣīr and Jeshua ben Judah who, as followers of the Kalam, preface their exposition of theology by a discussion of such concepts as thing, existent and nonexistent, eternal and created, atom and accident, motion and rest, I shall preface my exposition of theology with a discussion of concepts more fashionable in the current philosophy of emanation and shall begin with the lowest, matter, and go up step by step to form and element and nature and soul and intellect until I ultimately arrive at a discussion of theology.

According to both Halevi and Maimonides, then, there were among Jews those who followed the Kalam. Halevi, confining his discussion in that place to purely philosophic problems, mentions only the Karaites; Maimonides, dealing also with theological problems, mentions both Rabbanites and Karaites, describing their writings on these problems as "a little bit of Kalam," by which he means that they are few in number, and characterizing them as belonging to the Muʿtazilite type of the Muslim Kalam, by which he means that they all maintain certain traditional Jewish views on the unity and incorporeality of God and on the freedom of the human will which agree with views which in Islam were maintained by the Muʿtazilites in opposition to the Ashʿarites, and that they all, in their attempts to support these Jewish traditional views, use arguments which they borrowed from the Muʿtazilites.

But the few written works of the Geonim and the Karaites

[21] *Cuzari* V, 12, p. 316, ll. 15–24; p. 317, ll. 9–18.

anonymously referred to by Maimonides, as well as those which are known to us and are still extant, are not to be taken as the measure by which we are to estimate the extent to which discussions of speculative theology were carried on among Jews in Arabic countries during the period that the Kalam flourished in Islam. That was an age when not all who discussed or even taught philosophy or theology, and had something new to say on either of these subjects, committed their thoughts to writing. In works of Muslim authors of that time we find references to Jewish philosophers and theologians, of whom some are known only through some casual quotations by other authors and some are mere names. Thus Masʿūdī (d. *ca.* 956) refers to a certain Abū Kathir Yaḥyā al-Kātib of Tiberias, whom he describes as a teacher of Saadia and as one with whom he "had many discussions in the lands of Palestine and the Jordan concerning the abrogation of the Law, the difference between the Hebrew concepts of *Torah* and *ʿAbodah*, and other subjects." [22] Nothing is known about him from other sources, though some modern Jewish scholars try to identify him with a certain Karaite Hebrew grammarian.[23] Masʿūdī also mentions two people whom he did not know personally, Da'ūd, surnamed al-Muḳammaṣ, who lived in Jerusalem, and Ibrahīm al-Baghdādī.[24] Of these two, the first is known as the author of a work of the Kalam type; [25] the latter is a mere name. He then mentions that at Rakka in Iraḳ [26] he discussed philosophy and medicine with a certain Yahuda ibn Yusūf, surnamed Ibn Abū al-Thanā, who was a pupil of Thābit ibn Ḳurra al-Ṣābī, and in the same city he held also discussions with Saʿid ibn ʿAlī, surnamed Ibn Ashlamia.[27] Of these two the first is known only through a

[22] Masʿūdī, *Al-Tanbīh wa'l-Ashrāf* (ed. M. J. de Goeje), p. 113, ll. 4–6, 13–15 (160–161). Cf. Munk, *Guide* I, 71, p. 337 n.

[23] Cf. Malter, *Saadia*, p. 53, nn. 22, 23.

[24] *Tanbīh*, p. 113, ll. 12–13. The name al-Muḳammaṣ is corrupted in the text.

[25] Cf. Schreiner, *Kalam*, pp. 22 ff.

[26] In the text of Masʿūdī it is erroneously described as in Egypt (cf. Steinschneider, *Die arabische Literatur der Juden*, § 24, n. 1, p. 37).

[27] *Tanbīh*, p. 113, ll. 15–18.

quotation in Ḳirḳisānī;[28] the latter is a mere name. Finally, he reports that he had discussions with "those of their [i.e., Jewish] Mutakallimūn whom we have met in Baghdad, such as Ya'ḳūb ibn Mardawaih and Yusūf ibn Kayyūmā," concluding with the following statement: "The last one of them, whom we have seen from among those who came to visit us from Baghdad after the year 300 [=912], is Ibrahīm al-Yahūdī . . . He was the most subtle in speculation, and more skillful in argumentation than all their Mutakallimūn in modern times."[29] Nothing is known about any of these three names. 'Īsā ibn Zur'a (943–1009) mentions a certain Abū al-Ḫayr Dāūd ibn Mūsaf, of whom he says that "he was one of the principal Mutakallimūn of the Jews and the foremost thinker among them."[30] Referred to as Abū al-Ḫayr al-Yahūdī, he is also mentioned by Abū Hayyān al-Tauḥīdī (d. 1009) as a member of a group of philosophers in Baghdad formed around Abū Sulaymān Muḥammad ibn Ṭāhir al-Sijistānī.[31] But there is no mention of him in Jewish literature. Moreover, Saadia himself discusses two views in connection with the doctrine of creation, of one of which he says that it has been reported to him of "certain persons of our own people,"[32] and of the other that it is entertained "by one of our people whom I have known."[33] Neither of these views is traceable to any written work. Similarly, toward the end of a Bodleian manuscript of the Arabic text of the first part of Maimonides'

[28] Cf. Steinschneider, *Die arabische Literatur der Juden*, § 24, p. 36.

[29] *Tanbīh*, p. 113, l. 18 – p. 114, l. 4.

[30] Quoted from a manuscript by Munk, *Guide* I, 71, p. 337 n.

[31] Cf. Goldziher, "Mélanges Judeo-arabe," *REJ*, 47:4–46 (1903).

[32] *Emunot* I, 3, 2nd Theory, p. 43, l. 17. Perhaps one of those "certain persons" referred to here by Saadia was Ibn Abī Sa'īd who, in a letter received by his addressee, Yaḥyā b. 'Adī in 952, ten years after the death of Saadia, shows an interest in the problem of creation, for one of the topics dealt with in that letter is an objection to Aristotle's eternity of the world which corresponds exactly to Saadia's first argument against eternity in his first theory of creation. Ibn Abī Sa'īd is described as a protégé of a family whose name is mentioned in a letter written by Saadia and one of whose members had close connections with Saadia. Cf. S. Pines, "A Tenth Century Philosophical Correspondence," *PAAJR*, 24 (1955), pp. 103–136.

[33] *Emunot* I, 3, 6th Theory, p. 57, l. 2.

Guide of the Perplexed, there is a marginal note, purported to have been written by Maimonides himself, in which among well-known Jewish theologians and philosophers he mentions two unknown philosophers, one of whom has been identified as a contemporary of Saadia, who is mentioned in some other source, and the other is not mentioned anywhere else.[34]

From all this we may gather that, besides those speculative theologians who have written books and whose books have come down to us, there were others who did not write books or whose books have not come down to us. We also gather that all those Jewish speculative theologians of that period, both the known and the unknown, were referred to as Mutakallimūn. We have seen how Mas'ūdī applies this term to those Jewish theologians of Baghdad. We also find that Ibn Ḥazm applies the term "Mutakallimūn" to Saadia, Muḳammaṣ, Ibrahīm al-Baghdādī, and Abū Kathir of Tiberius.[35] And so also Moses ibn Ezra, writing in Arabic, speaks of "the most glorious Mutakallimūn, Rabbi Saadia and Rabbi Hai and others."[36]

Knowing then as we do that besides those glorious Jewish Mutakallimūn who speak to us from the pages of their writings, there was among the Jews during the period of the Muslim Kalam a host of mute Mutakallimūn unknown to glory, we should like to find out whether all those unknown Jewish Mutakallimūn, like those known to us through their writings, represented in Judaism a kind of Kalam which was like that of Mu'tazilism in Islam or whether among them there were also those who deviated from that standard type of the Jewish Kalam. Moreover, knowing as we also do that the later Jewish religious thinkers in Spain, who are described by Maimonides as philosophers, while differing from the earlier Jewish religious thinkers of the East in their method

[34] Cf. Munk, *Guide* I, p. 462, n. to p. 459.

[35] *Fiṣal* III, p. 171, ll. 23–24; cf. I. Friedländer, *JQR*, n.s., 1:602, n. 5 (1910–1911).

[36] Quoted from his *Kitāb al-Muḥāḍarah wa'l-Mudhākarah* by Schreiner in *Polemik*, p. 602, n. 5.

of demonstration, did not differ from them in their views on problems which in Islam were a matter of controversy between Muʿtazilites and orthodox, we should like to know more generally whether among Arabic-speaking Jews from the time of Saadia to that of Maimonides there were any groups of people or any individuals who deviated from the common pattern of views which we find in the works of Jewish religious thinkers of that period.

That in general, corresponding to the influence of Muʿtazilism upon religious rationalization among Jews in Muslim countries, there was also an influence of Muslim orthodoxy upon those Jews who opposed religious rationalization may be gathered from the literature of the time. Early in the tenth century, when religious rationalization had just made its appearance among Jews, Saadia tried to forestall opposition to it by introducing a fictitious "some one," a Jew, who, he says, might question the advisability of probing rationally into matters religious on the ground that "there are people (*al-nās: ha-ʿam*) who disapprove of such an occupation, being of the opinion that speculation leads to unbelief and is conducive to heresy." [37] The term "people" here, as may be judged from Saadia's answer, refers to Muslims. What Saadia, therefore, does here is to make a Jew raise doubt concerning religious rationalization by citing against it the opinion of orthodox Muslims. In his answer, Saadia says: "Such an opinion is held only by the common people among them" [38] — that is, among the Muslims. Saadia then adds that should that some one try to infer an objection to religious rationalization from a certain passage in the Talmud, he can be shown to be wrong.[39] In his entire discussion of the problem, it will be noticed, Saadia never refers to the existence of actual opposition to religious rationalization among the Jews of his time. All he does is to set up a fictitious Jewish character who, having heard that among Muslims there were those who

[37] *Emunot*, Introduction 6, p. 20, ll. 18, 20–21.
[38] *Ibid.*, p. 21, l. 1.
[39] *Ibid.*, ll. 5 ff.

objected to religious rationalization, tried to find support for such objection in some rabbinic passage.

A century later, however, perhaps as a result of the effect of religious rationalization upon certain Jews, we find among Arabic-speaking Jews outspoken opposition to it, re-echoing sentiments like those heard among orthodox Muslims. Thus Ibn Janaḥ, himself a physician, logician, and philologist, the author in Arabic of one of the most important Hebrew grammars and lexicons, commenting upon the verse, which he takes to mean "beware of the making of many books without end" (Eccl. 12:12), says: "By this warning the sage prohibits only the preoccupation with the study of those books which, according to the claim of those who have made a study of them, lead to a knowledge of the principles and the elements whereby one may investigate most thoroughly the nature of the upper world and the lower world, for that is a matter of which the real truth one cannot come to know and the end of which one cannot attain. Moreover, it injures religion and destroys faith and wearies the soul without any compensation and without any satisfaction, as the verse continues to say, 'and much study is a weariness to the flesh.' It is to this, too, that the sage makes allusion in his statement, 'all things are full of weariness: man cannot utter them' (Eccl. 1:8), that is to say, they are things which cause weariness because they are incomprehensible. According to the sage, therefore, the proper thing is to abandon oneself to God, to obey that which has been commanded in the Law, and resignedly to cleave to faith, as he says subsequently: 'the end of the matter, all having been heard: fear God, and keep His commandments; for this is the whole man' (Eccl. 12:13) — and leave alone that the truth whereof is past comprehension."[40]

But still we should like to know how far did that opposition

[40] *Kitāb al-Luma'*, ed. J. Derenbourg, chap. xxiv, p. 267, ll. 11–21; *Sefer ha-Riḳmah*, ed. M. Wilensky, chap. xxiv (xxv), p. 282, ll. 9–16; cf. S. Munk, "Notice sur Abou'l-Walid Merwan Ibn-Djana'h," *Journal Asiatique*, 16: 45–46 (1850).

go. Was it merely against the use of rational methods of demonstration of religious beliefs? or was it also against certain rationalized beliefs themselves? We would especially like to know whether among these Jews who opposed philosophic rationalization of religion there were any who, like the orthodox in Islam, openly advocated the reality of attributes and predestination or, like some orthodox in Islam, also advocated openly the corporeality of God.

Let us examine these three questions one by one.

With regard to the belief in the reality of attributes, there is nothing in the Jewish Scripture, as in fact there is nothing in the Muslim Koran, that could provoke the rise of such a belief spontaneously. Nor is there to be found among the Jews of that time the particular external circumstance, namely, the influence of Christianity, which could have given rise to the doctrine of attributes among them as it did in Islam.[41] Nor is there any reason to assume that any of the simple-minded pious Jews could have acquired such a belief by having merely heard orthodox Muslims utter it in the recitation of their creed.[42] Still less is there reason to assume, without positive evidence, that any of the learned among Jews could have become persuaded by the arguments of orthodox Muslim theologians — arguments mainly defensive — to adopt a belief which constantly stood in need of defense. When, therefore, the spokesmen of Judaism of that time, in their published writings, with one voice reject the reality of attributes, we have reason to believe that no such belief found any followers in Judaism.

The case of predestination is somewhat different. Though the Jewish Scripture is more explicit than the Koran in its assertion of free choice by man, still, like the Koran, it is just as emphatic in its assertion of the pervasiveness of the power

[41] Cf. below, pp. 112 ff.

[42] Cf., e.g., the creed called *Fikh Akbar* (II) in Wensinck's *Muslim Creed*, pp. 188–189 (Arabic, p. 6, l. 1–p. 9, l. 2), and the creed of Nasafī in Elder's translation of Taftāzānī's commentary on it, pp. 49, 58 (Arabic, p. 69, l. 2 – p. 77, l. 9).

of God.[43] Even among the rabbinic assertions of free will, there is one in which the expression "freedom of choice is given" is qualified by the statement that "everything is foreseen." [44] Moreover, in rabbinic literature, despite its many explicit assertions of free will, there are certain statements which would seem to imply predestination, such, for instance, as the one discussed by Maimonides himself, namely, that God predesignates "the daughter of so and so to so and so and the wealth of so and so to so and so." [45] In the case of this problem, then, it would be reasonable to assume that when Arabic-speaking Jews became acquainted with the Muslim discussions about free will and predestination and got wind of how in Islam those who believed in predestination tried to interpret the Koranic verses that seemed to affirm free will, there would be some among them who would come to believe in a similar view of predestination. It happens, however, that among all the Jewish philosophers prior to Maimonides who argue against predestination, or against those who believe in predestination, there is not a single one who suggests, however slightly, that those against whom he argues are Jews.

Direct information with regard to the problem of predestination and free will among Jews in Muslim countries may be gathered from statements in two works of Maimonides.

In his Hebrew-written Code of Jewish Law, the *Mishneh Torah*, in the course of his exposition, on the basis of scriptural and rabbinic passages, of the traditional Jewish view of free will, Maimonides urges the reader to pay no heed to "that which is said by the ignorant (*ṭippeshim*) among the gentiles and by most of the uninformed (*gelamim*) among the Jews, to wit, that the Holy One decrees concerning man at the beginning of his formation in his mother's womb whether he should be righteous or wicked." [46] The Hebrew term *ṭippe-*

[43] Cf. above, n. 8.

[44] *M. Abot* III, 15.

[45] *Pesiḳta de-Rab Kahana*, ed. Buber, pp. 11b–12a; *Genesis Rabbah* 68, 4. Cf. *Teshubot ha-Rambam* 159 (*Ḳobeṣ* I, p. 34c), 348 (ed. Freimann, p. 309). Cf. also *Shemonah Peraḳim* 8 (p. 28, ll. 24 ff.).

[46] *Mishneh Torah*, *Teshubah* V, 2.

shim, literally "stupid ones," is used by him here, I take it, in the sense of "ignorant ones" and as the equivalent of the Arabic terms *bulh* and *jāhilūn* or *juhhāl*, which mean "stupid ones" as well as "ignorant ones," but are used by him in the original Arabic of his *Moreh Nebukim* in the sense of "ignorant ones," that is to say, in the sense of those who follow only tradition and are either ignorant of philosophy or through ignorance are opposed to it.[47] In other words, the term *ṭippeshim* is used by him here in the sense of nonrationalists or in the sense of antirationalists. As for the term *gelamim* in the expression "most of the *gelamim* among the Jews," it is quite clearly used by him in the sense of his own explanation of the term *golem* in his Commentary on *Abot* as meaning an "uneducated" and "uninformed" person who, on account of his lack of knowledge, unwittingly gives utterance to erroneous views, the term having acquired that meaning, he goes on to explain, after the analogy of its use in the sense of an unfinished vessel lacking in form.[48] Thus also in his responsum to the proselyte Obadiah, Maimonides describes any Jew who takes some Agadic statements literally as one who is the opposite of a person "who is a wise man with a

[47] Cf. Maimonides' use of these Arabic terms in *Moreh* I, 32, p. 47, l. 13; I, 50, p. 75, l. 2; I, 59, p. 96, l. 11. Samuel Ibn Tibbon translates them in all these places by the Hebrew *peta'im*, a term which means "simple ones" as well as "foolish ones." In I, 35, p. 54, l. 30, he translates *bulh* by the Hebrew *sekalim*, which means "foolish ones" as well as "ignorant ones" and of which the singular is translated in the Targum on Ecclesiastes 1:19 by *ṭippesh*. So also in his letter on astrology does Maimonides use the term *ṭippeshim* in the sense of those who are ignorant of philosophy as the opposite of the term *ḥakamim* in the sense of those who are versed in philosophy (*Ḳobeṣ* II, p. 25a). Similarly, Judah Ibn Tibbon translates the Arabic *jāhil* in *Ḥobot ha-Lebabot* I, 10, p. 75, l. 3, by the Hebrew *kesil*, which, again, means "foolish one" as well as "ignorant one." With all these, compare the statement by the Mu'tazilite Ibn 'Aḳil quoted in George Makdisi's edition of "Ibn Qudāma's Censure of Speculative Theology," § 28 (p. 18, ll. 4–5, of the Arabic text): "The stupid person (*al-aḥmaḳ*) is he who is bedazzled by his forebears and has blind faith in the teaching of his elders." Cf. English translation of the same passage on p. 12 of the English part.

[48] Commentary on *Abot* V, 7, whence his use in his *Mishneh Torah* of the term *golem* in the technical sense of "matter" as contrasted with "form" (*Yesode ha-Torah* IV, 8).

discerning mind capable of perceiving the way of truth."[49] Accordingly by "the *ṭippeshim* among the gentiles" he refers to the dominant orthodox sect in Islam, "The People of Tradition" (*ahl al-sunnah*), to whom the denial of free will was a fundamental doctrine which they upheld against all those who defended the principle of free will. By "most of the *gelamim* among Jews," however, he could not have referred to any group of Jews who openly opposed free will, for we have Maimonides' own testimony in his *Moreh Nebukim* that free will "is a fundamental principle to which, thank God, no opposition has ever been heard in our religious community."[50] The reference in "most of the *gelamim*" cannot be but to individual uneducated Jews who, with an inconsistency characteristic of simple-minded believers, professed a blind belief in God's power as extending over human action, without openly denying free will and, so much the more, without openly opposing those who profess a belief in free will.

It is thus clear that not even in Arabic-speaking countries, where belief in predestination dominated among non-Jews, was there open opposition to free will among Jews, though most of the ignorant among the Arabic-speaking Jews in those Arabic-speaking Muslim countries, while not openly denying free will, spoke like their non-Jewish neighbors of the extension of the power of God over the actions of man.

So also is the case of the problem of the incorporeality of God. In the Jewish Scripture as in the Muslim Koran, while there are direct injunctions against likening God to any created beings, God is constantly described in anthropomorphic terms. Similarly in the post-Biblical traditional Jewish literature, the rabbis, evidently in pursuance of their own principle that the scriptural anthropomorphisms should not be taken literally, allowed themselves to describe God in anthropomorphic terms, evidently expecting not to be taken

[49] *Teshubot ha-Rambam* 159 (*Ḳobeṣ* I, p. 34c), 348 (ed. Freimann, p. 309).
[50] *Moreh* III, 17, 5th Theory, p. 338, l. 30.

literally. In this case, too, it would be reasonable to assume that when Arabic-speaking Jews become acquainted with Muslim discussions about the problem of the corporeality and incorporeality of God and got wind of how in Islam those who believed in the corporeality of God interpreted the Koranic verses prohibiting the likening of God with other beings, there would be some among them who came to believe in a similar view of the corporeality of God. But whether there actually were such believers and who they were is a subject which bears investigation.

Let us then study and analyze certain passages which may have a bearing on this question.

The most promising passage is to be found in Saadia's *Emunot ve-De'ot*, written in Baghdad during the year 933. In the introduction to this work, after intimating that his work was written for the benefit of both non-Jews, to whom he refers as "my species, the species of rational beings," and Jews, to whom he refers as "our people, the children of Israel," [51] he enumerates three types of people, evidently among both non-Jews and Jews, whom he envisaged as readers of his book: first, "many believers whose belief was not pure and whose creeds were not sound"; second, "many deniers of the faith who boast of their unbelief and look down upon men of truth, although they were themselves in error"; third, "men sunk, as it were, in seas of doubt and overwhelmed by waves of confusion." [52]

Of these three types of readers envisaged by Saadia, only the first type may be assumed to include those who believed in the corporeality of God, and in fact there is one long passage which deals with this type of reader. We shall, therefore, have to find out whether that passage contains any reference to such believers among Jews. Now, the passage in question begins with a twofold division of those who believe in the corporeality of God: (1) "those who believe that they

[51] *Emunot*, Introduction 2, p. 4, ll. 15–16; cf. Kaufmann, *Attributenlehre*, p. 150; Malter, *Saadia*, p. 200, n. 470.

[52] *Ibid.*, p. 4, ll. 15–20.

can picture God in their imagination as a body" and (2) "those who, without expressly attributing to Him corporeality, yet they arrogate for God quantity or quality or place or time or other such categories; however, when they make these arrogations, they really insist upon His being corporeal, for such characteristics appertain only to body." [53] He then illustrates these two kinds of believers in the corporeality of God by mentioning two kinds of Christian Trinitarians, namely, "the common people among them" and "their elite," and by alluding indirectly also to two similar kinds of corporealists among the Muslim Attributists.[54] But no reference or allusion is made by him to similar believers in the corporeality of God among Jews. Of course, there existed during the time of Saadia the arch anthropomorphic work *Shi'ur Ḳomah*, which both Karaite and Muslim writers held up as evidence of the Jewish belief in the corporeality of God.[55] But this work does not preach the corporeality of God; it only describes God in corporeal terms, the like of which, though in a lesser degree, is to be found in certain passages of both the Bible and the Talmud, and Saadia is reported to have written a work, no longer extant, in which he maintains that if that work is really of the authorship of Rabbi Ishmael, and not of that of some irresponsible person who need not be paid attention to, then its corporeal descriptions of God should be interpreted figuratively in the same way as similar corporeal descriptions of God in Scripture are, according to Jewish tradition, to be interpreted figuratively.[56] Thus, according to Saadia, in any work of a responsible author, the mere use of anthropomorphic descriptions of God is not to be taken as a belief in the corporeality of God and still less as the advocacy of such a belief.

Baḥya, however, in his work *Ḥobot ha-Lebabot*, written in Saragossa during the latter part of the eleventh century,

[53] *Ibid.* II, Exordium, p. 76, l. 19 – p. 77, l. 2.

[54] *Ibid.* II, 5, p. 86, ll. 5, 7.

[55] *Fiṣal* I, p. 221, l. 2, and cf. above, n. 8.

[56] *Perush Sefer Yeṣirah* by Judah b. Barzillai, pp. 20–21.

alludes to a type of pious man among Jews, who, because of his failure to comprehend the figurativeness of scriptural anthropomorphisms, unkowingly forms a corporeal conception of God. But the pious believer of this type is described by him as "ignorant and foolish" (*al-jāhil al-ghabī*: *ha-kesil ha-peti*), one who, he says, is to be forgiven only when his ignorance is due to a lack of capacity to learn; but he is to be held responsible for his erroneous belief if he has the capacity to learn and to know better and fails to do so.[57] Quite evidently what he means by this is that no learned Jew, not one learned in philosophy but one learned in Jewish lore, could believe in the corporeality of God.

Similarly Abraham ibn Daud in his *Emunah Ramah*, which appeared in Toledo in 1168, says that "the belief of the common people (*he-hamon* [=*al-ʿāmmah*]), who are wont to follow the popular notion of God, is [that God is a body], for they think that whatever has no body has no existence. It is only when they are admonished [by citations from Scripture] that they come to believe in accordance with what has been transmitted by the teachings of the forebears and the rabbis. But still, if they are not guided [by philosophy], there will always stir in their minds doubts and confusing thoughts, and it is concerning such as these that Scripture says: 'Forasmuch this people draw near, and with their mouth honor me, but have removed their heart from me' " (Isa. 29:13).[58] Here, again, the implication is that the ordinary Jew would not openly profess the corporeality of God, even though, not being a philosopher, he cannot conceive of God as incorporeal.

Twelve years later, Maimonides, in his *Mishneh Torah*, composed in 1180, tries to establish two points with regard to the incorporeality of God. First, applying the scriptural denying of any likeness between God and other beings (Isa. 40:25) to the scriptural doctrine of the unity of God (Deut.

[57] *Ḥobot* I, 10, p. 74, l. 17 – p. 75, l. 5.
[58] *Emunah Ramah* II, 1, p. 47.

6:4), he shows that the mandatory belief that there is only one God must also include the belief that the one God is not a body.[59] Second, having in mind the Talmudic statement that an idolater is a heretic,[60] and taking the term "idolater" to include also a polytheist, and following his own view that the belief in one God must include also the belief that the one God is not a body, he declares that "anyone who says that God is one but that He is a body and possesses a figure" is a heretic.[61]

But it will be noticed that, whereas in his discussion of free will he makes a reference to ignorant Jews who "say," that God predetermines everything, in his discussion of the incorporeality of God, no reference is made by him to ignorant Jews who say that God has a body. This is undoubtedly due to the fact that no Jew, however ignorant and however unable to conceive of the existence of anything incorporeal, ever dared openly to assert that God was corporeal.

From all this we may gather that by the time of the composition of the *Mishneh Torah*, there was none among Arabic-speaking Jews who openly advocated the corporeality of God and that even the common people, who may not have been able to conceive of the subtlety of an incorporeal existence and may not also have been able to explain, or even to understand, the figurative interpretations of the scriptural anthropomorphisms, did not dare openly to express a belief in the corporeality of God.

A few years later, in his *Moreh Nebukim*, composed sometime between 1185 and 1190,[62] Maimonides refers to "people" who, because they "thought" that the term "form" in the verse (Gen. 1:26) "Let us make man in our form (*ṣelem*), after our likeness (*demut*)" [63] is to be taken literally, "came

[59] *Mishneh Torah, Yesode ha-Torah* I, 8.

[60] *'Abodah Zarah* 26b; cf. *Yesode ha-Torah* I, 6.

[61] *Mishneh Torah, Teshubah* III, 7.

[62] See D. H. Baneth's comment in his edition of *Iggerot ha-Rambam* I, p. 2, on the date 1185 established by Z. Diesendruck.

[63] We may assume that in the Arabic translation of the Pentateuch used by the people referred to here by Maimonides, the Hebrew *ṣelem*, "image,"

to believe that God has the form (*ṣūrah*) of man, that is to say, man's figure and shape . . . maintaining that, if they did not conceive of God as a body possessed of a face and a hand similar to their own figure and shape, they would reduce Him to nonexistence. However, He is, in their opinion, the greatest and most splendid [of bodies] and also His matter is not flesh and blood." [64] After explaining how the term "form" (*ṣelem: ṣūrah*) is not to be taken anthropomorphically, Maimonides goes on to explain how also the term "likeness" (*demut: shibh*) is not to be taken anthropomorphically.

Who were these "people"?

Here are some texts which will help us to answer this question.

Ibn Ḥazm, in his attempt to show that the Hebrew Bible has an anthropomorphic conception of God, quotes Genesis 1:26, which, in the Arabic used by him, reads: "Let me make sons of Adam after our form (*ṣūrah* = *ṣelem*), after our likeness (*shibh* = *demut*)." Commenting upon it, he says that if only the phrase "after our form" were used, there would be justification for interpreting it figuratively. But the phrase "after our likeness," which immediately follows it, "shuts out interpretations, blocks up loopholes, cuts off roads, and of necessity and inevitably must the phrase be taken to attribute the likeness of Adam to God. The absurdity of this, however, is immediately perceived by the understanding, for *shibh* and *mithl* mean the same thing [namely, likeness], and far be it from God that He should have a *mithl* or *shibh* [that is, a likeness]." [65] The conclusion he wants us to draw here is that, inasmuch as the term "likeness" cannot be taken figuratively, the term "form" is also not to be taken figuratively. The reason why, in the midst of his trying to prove the anthropomorphism of the Bible, he goes out of his way to concede that the phrase "after our form" by itself could be

---

in Genesis 1:26 was translated *ṣūrah*, "form," for so it is also translated by Saadia.

[64] *Moreh* I, 1, p. 14, ll. 5–11.

[65] Ibn Ḥazm, *Fiṣal* I, p. 117, l. 21–p. 118, l. 4.

interpreted figuratively, is to be found in the fact that two Jewish authors of works in Arabic, Saadia and Ḳirḳisānī, the former in his comment on the term *ṣelem* in Genesis 1:27, which is only a repetition of Genesis 1:26, and the latter in his comment on the term *ṣelem* both in Genesis 1:26 and in Genesis 1:27, interpret that term figuratively.[66] Ibn Ḥazm's certainty that the term *shibh*, "likeness," in Genesis 1:26, on account of its being synonymous with the term *mithl*, cannot be taken figuratively but must be taken literally, is undoubtedly due to his belief that the Koranic verse (42:9), "Nought is there like Him (*ka-mithlihi*)," was aimed at Genesis 1:26.

Here then we have a Muslim who dismisses the attempt of two Jewish authors to interpret the term "form" (*ṣelem*: *ṣūrah*) in Genesis 1:26 and 1:27 and, in opposition to them, insists that, like the term "likeness" (*demut*: *shibh*) in Genesis 1:26, the term "form" in the same verse must be taken literally.

Then there are passages from which it can be shown that the term *ṣelem* in Genesis 1:27, which, as remarked before, is only a repetition of Genesis 1:26, was taken by certain Muslims in an anthropomorphic sense.

Shahrastānī in his *Nihāyat* reports that several subsects of the Shi'ites, among them the Hishāmiyyah, as well as "the anthropomorphists among the Attributists," by which is meant a certain group of Sunnites, believed that "God has a form like the form of men," adding that this belief of theirs was based upon a statement attributed to Muhammad, of which there were two readings: (1) "God created Adam in His

[66] Saadia, *Emunot* II, 9, p. 94, ll. 14–18: "by way of conferring honor (*'alā ṭarīḳ al-tashrīf*)," which he goes on to explain as meaning that although all forms are created by God, "He honored one of them by saying 'This is My form,' by way of conferring distinction (*'alā sabīl al-taḥṣīṣ*)." Ḳirḳisānī, *Anwār* II, 28, 12, p. 176, ll. 7–8 (ed. Leon Nemoy): "by way of conferring distinction and honor (*'alā sabīl al-taḥṣīṣ wa'l-tashrīf*)." Ibn Ḥazm, *Fiṣal* I, p. 117, l. 24–p. 118, l. 1: "as one might say about a monkey and about something ugly as well as about something beautiful, This is the form of God, that is to say, this is a formation by God and a peculiarity of existence which is due to the power of God alone, He being solely responsible for its creation."

form (*ṣūrah*)"; (2) "God created Adam in the form of the Merciful."[67] One of these unnamed "anthropomorphists among the Attributists" can be identified with Dā'ūd al-Jawārī, who is quoted by Shahrastānī in his *Milal* as saying that "God is a body and flesh and blood, who has limbs and organs," and that the statement "God created Adam in the form of the Merciful," which tradition attributes to Muhammad, is to be taken in a literal sense.[68] Now the statement attributed to Muhammad, in either of its readings, is not to be found in the Koran. It can be traced, however, in both its readings, to Genesis 1:27. In English, this verse in Genesis reads: "And God created man (*ha-adam*) in His image (*ṣelem*), in the image of God created He him." Among the early Muslims, we may imagine, this verse, minus the last three words, which in Arabic would have been one word, was circulated orally in an Arabic version which read: "And God created Adam in His form (*ṣūrah*), in the form of the Merciful." Thus also in Saadia's Arabic translation of the Pentateuch, the first part of the verse reads: "And God created Adam in His form." As for the substitution of "the Merciful" for "God" in the second part, it was quite natural for Muslims used to the language of the Koran. Then, we may further imagine, the verse, in its oral circulation, was broken up into two parts, (1) "God created Adam in His form"; (2) "God created Adam in the form of the Merciful," and both these parts were attributed to Muhammad.

Ghazālī, commenting upon one of the readings of the statement traditionally attributed to Muhammad, says: "If [by the term form in] the Prophet's saying that 'God created Adam in His form' you understand the external form which is perceived by eye-sight, you will be an absolute anthropomorphist, as the one addressed in the saying, 'Be an out-and-out Jew, or else play not with the Torah'; but, if you understand by it the inner form, which is perceived by insight (*baṣā'ir*) and not by eye-sight (*abṣār*), you will be a man

[67] *Nihāyat*, p. 103, l. 11–p. 104, l. 1.

[68] *Milal*, p. 77, ll. 5–18.

who keeps himself free from anthropomorphism in every respect and declares God to be holy — yea, a perfect man, walking the straight way, for you are in the holy valley of Tuwwa [Surah 20:12]." [69] The quotation of the saying with its warning not to play with the Torah means, I take it, that those who take the statement of Muhammad anthropomorphically are like the Jews who take the corresponding statement in Genesis 1:27 anthropomorphically, thus reflecting a contention like that of Ibn Ḥazm, or perhaps Ibn Ḥazm's very contention, that the "form of God" in the story of the creation of Adam as told in Genesis was meant to be taken by Jews in an anthropomorphic sense.

Finally, the Hishāmiyyah, of whom Shahrastānī has reported that they took the "form of God" in the creation of Adam anthropomorphically, reports of Hishām that he said that "God is a body possessing parts and is of a certain size, but He is unlike any created thing and no created thing is like Him," [70] which means, as the same view is phrased by Ashʿarī, that "God is a body unlike other bodies." [71] Similarly al-Jawārī, of whom Shahrastānī has also reported that he took the "form of God" in the creation of Adam anthropomorphically, reports of him that he also said that "God is a body unlike other bodies, flesh unlike other flesh, blood unlike other blood." [72]

From these passages we gather that Ibn Ḥazm directly and Ghazālī indirectly contended that the term *ṣelem* = *ṣūrah*, "form," in Genesis 1:26 and 1:27 was meant to be taken in an anthropomorphic sense, and so does Ibn Ḥazm also contend with regard to the term *demut* = *shibh*, "likeness," in Genesis 1:26. Moreover, when a statement based upon Genesis 1:27 was attributed to Muhammad, some Muslims took the term "form" in it, which is the Hebrew *ṣelem*, in an anthropomorphic sense. Finally, those Muslims who took the

[69] *Iḥyā'*, XXXV: *Kitāb al-Tauḥīd wa'l-Tawakkul*, IV, p. 245, ll. 26–29 (ed. Cairo, 1358/1939).

[70] *Milal*, p. 141, ll. 7–8.

[71] *Maḳālāt*, p. 33, ll. 10–11; p. 208, l. 1.

[72] *Milal*, p. 77, l. 9.

term "form" in Genesis 1:26 and 1:27 anthropomorphically qualified their anthropomorphic conceptions of God by saying, in the words of one of them, that "God is a body unlike other bodies, flesh unlike other flesh, blood unlike other blood."

In the light of all this, when Maimonides refers to "people" who "thought" that the term "form" in the story of the creation of Adam in Genesis 1:26 is to be taken anthropomorphically, the people referred to are Muslims; when he also says that these people conceded that God is "the greatest and most splendid [of bodies] and also His matter is not flesh and blood," the reference is to the concession made by those Muslims who took the term "form" in the story of the creation of Adam anthropomorphically; and when he continues to argue that even the term *demut* = *shibh*, "likeness," is not to be taken anthropomorphically, the argument is aimed at Ibn Ḥazm. No "people" who interpreted Genesis 1:26 anthropomorphically can be traced to Jewish sources. Nor are we to assume that such an interpretation of Genesis 1:26 was communicated to him orally by some Jews or was reported to him orally in the name of some Jews, for when Maimonides deals with something that has been communicated to him orally, he usually says so.[73]

Reference, however, to certain individuals among Jews who openly either doubted or denied the incorporeality of God is to be found in his *Ma'mar Teḥiyyat ha-Metim*, composed at about 1190, in answer to certain critics of his *Mishneh Torah*. The passage in question reads as follows: "We have met some one who was looked upon as a learned Jewish scholar and, by the eternal God! he was familiar with the way of the traditional law and from his youth had participated, as he claimed, in disputes about the Law, and still he was in doubt whether God is a body, possessing eye, hand, foot, and entrails, as mentioned in some scriptural verses, or whether He is not a body. Moreover, others from among the people

[73] See *Moreh* I, 2 beginning, and quotation at the next note below.

of some countries whom I have met definitely decided that God is a body and declared anyone who disagreed with this to be an unbeliever, applying to him the various Hebrew terms for heretic, and took the anthropomorphic passages of the rabbis in their literal sense. Similar things I have heard about men whom I have not met." [74]

In this passage, the hesitant opponent of the incorporeality of God, with whom are contrasted those "others from among the people of some countries," was undoubtedly a countryman of Maimonides visiting him in Fostat from some other city in Egypt. The fact that Maimonides shows himself surprised that such a view could be held by one reputed to be versed in Jewish traditional law indicates that he suspected him to have fallen victim to some outside influence. We may similarly assume that the other opponents of incorporeality in this passage were also Jews from Muslim countries, though there is nothing to support this assumption except the fact that up to that time all opposition to Maimonides came from Jews in Muslim countries. Certainly by these "others from among the people of some countries" he could not have meant those visitors of whom he speaks with praise in his letter to Samuel Ibn Tibbon.[75] That Jews in Muslim countries were not altogether impervious to the influence of Islam in religious matters may be inferred from a responsum by Maimonides himself addressed to Rabbi Phinehas b. Mesullam of Alexandria.[76]

But it will be noticed that, while opposition to Maimonides' omission of dealing with bodily resurrection in his *Mishneh Torah*, as well as opposition to his description of the eternal life in the world to come as being incorporeal, appeared openly in writing,[77] the opposition to his denial of the corporeality of God was bruited about only orally. Maimonides refers to it only by saying "some people thought" or "we

[74] *Ma'amar Teḥiyyat ha-Metim* (*Ḳobeṣ* II, p. 8a; ed. Finkel, §§ 3–4).
[75] *Iggerot ha-Rambam* (*Ḳobeṣ* II, p. 27a). This letter was written in 1199.
[76] *Teshubot ha-Rambam* 140 (*Ḳobeṣ* I, p. 25b).
[77] *Ma'amar Teḥiyyat ha-Metim* (*Ḳobeṣ* II, pp. 8b, 8d; ed. Finkel, §§ 10, 16, 17.

have already met some one who . . . was in doubt" or "others . . . whom I have met have definitely concluded." Evidently no one, and certainly no man of stature, dared openly in writing to oppose the belief in the incorporeality of God, and still less to advocate or even to condone the belief in God's corporeality.

The first man of stature who dared openly in writing to oppose the belief in the incorporeality of God and to condone, if not directly to advocate, the belief in His corporeality was Rabbi Abraham ben David of Posquières. In his splenetic attacks upon Maimonides' *Mishneh Torah*, the composition of which attacks is placed after 1193,[78] commenting upon Maimonides' inclusion in his list of heretics "anyone who says that God is one but is a body and possesses a figure," he ejaculates: "Why does he call such a person a heretic, when many people, greater and better than he, followed such a conception (*maḥashabah*) of God on the ground of its being in accordance with what they had seen in the verses of Scripture and even more by reason of what they had seen in the words of those Agadot which set minds awondering?" [79]

I imagine that if the rabbi of Posquières were challenged to name anyone who openly professed a belief in the corporeality of God, he would be hard put to it to make good his statement. And should we assume that the expression which I have translated "followed such a conception of God" was used by him advisedly in order to indicate that, while nobody in Judaism ever openly said that God is a body, still there were many who, not being philosophers like Maimonides, could not but conceive of God, in their minds, as a corporeal being, then what reason had he for assuming

[78] Cf. H. Gross, "R. Abraham b. David aus Posquières," *MGWJ*, 23:20 and n. 2 (1874).

[79] *Hassagot* on *Mishneh Torah*: *Madda'*, *Teshubah* III, 7. The term *ha-meshabbetot*, I take it, is used here by Rabad after the analogy of the use of the term *shibbushim* in Judah Ibn Tibbon's Hebrew translation of Saadia, that is, in the sense of confusing the mind and causing doubt and wonder. Cf. *Emunot ve-De'ot*, *Haḳdamah* 2 and 3; IV, 6. Hence my translation: "which set minds awondering."

that Maimonides would attach heresy to merely conceiving of God as a body without actually saying so? Did not Maimonides use the expression "anyone who says"? [80] In fact, as I have shown elsewhere, the mere conception of God as corporeal by one who is, as described by Maimonides, incapable of conceiving of the existence of anything incorporeal is not regarded by him as heresy.[81]

And should it occur to us that by "many people greater and better than he" the rabbi referred to some post-Talmudic authors and liturgists known to him who, following the example of Scripture and the Agadot of the Talmud, did not hesitate to use anthropomorphic descriptions of God, then what reason had he for assuming that such descriptions are an indication of a belief in the corporeality of God? Why did he not assume that those authors and liturgists, because they interpreted the anthropomorphisms of Scripture and the Agadot of the Talmud figuratively, did themselves also describe God anthropomorphically in a figurative sense? Did not Saadia say, as quoted in a work undoubtedly known to him, that the anthropomorphisms in the Talmud as well as those in the *Shi'ur Ḳomah* are to be taken figuratively, even as are those in Scripture? [82]

If, again, the rabbi of Posquières were challenged to tell whether he himself believed that God is a body, then perhaps, even without the prompting of the Christian Tertullian [83] or of Muslim Mutakallimūn,[84] he could by his own wit hit upon the subtlety that, on the mere showing of scriptural teaching the unlikeness of God only meant that God is a body unlike

[80] Cf. above at n. 61.

[81] Cf. my paper "Maimonides on the Unity and Incorporeality of God," *JQR*, n. s., 56:112–136 (1965).

[82] *Perush Sefer Yeṣirah* by Judah b. Barzillai, pp. 20–21 and 34. A similar explanation of the anthropomorphism of the *Shi'ur Ḳomah* is suggested by Judah Halevi (*Cuzari* IV, 3 end). Saadia, as quoted by Judah b. Barzillai (*Perush*, p. 21, ll. 16–22), doubted R. Ishmael's authorship of the *Shi'ur Ḳomah*, and Maimonides was certain that R. Ishmael was not its author, declaring it to be "undoubtedly the work of one of the Byzantine [Jewish] preachers" (*Teshubot ha-Rambam* 373, p. 343 [ed. Freimann]).

[83] *Adv. Prax.* 7 (PL 2, 162 C).

[84] Cf. above at nn. 70–72.

other bodies.[85] But here, again, what reason had he for assuming that Maimonides, who derived the incorporeality of God from the scriptural teaching of His unlikeness, would include among his five classes of heretics one who said that God is a body unlike other bodies? In fact, as I have shown elsewhere, no heresy is attached by him to the assertion that God is a body unlike other bodies; he only requires that the term "body" be used in an equivocal sense.[86] It is, therefore, more reasonable to assume that if the rabbi of Posquières were so challenged, he would honestly and frankly admit that he did not believe that God is a body. Later, during the controversy over the *Moreh Nebukim*, none of the authoritative spokesmen of Judaism advocated a belief in the corporeality of God — not even those who were opposed to Maimonides' philosophical interpretation of anthropomorphisms in scriptural verses and Talmudic lore. When rumors reached Naḥmanides of French rabbis who objected to a certain anthropomorphic statement of Maimonides, he gently reasoned with them, politely showing that they were wrong, and thereafter nothing was heard of their objection.[87] And there is no reason to assume that Moses Taku's vehement assertion of his belief in the literalness of Agadic anthropomorphism found followers among German rabbis, though in their innocence of philosophy they may have tacitly assented to his arraignment of the interpretation of anthropomorphisms by Maimonides and others,[88] since the interpretations used by Maimonides and the others mentioned by Moses Taku are all based upon philosophy. Solomon of Montpellier and his pupil David ben Saul, two philosophic innocents who in the first flush of their opposition to Maimonides proclaimed their wholesale belief in the literalness of all the Agadot of the Talmud, including

[85] Various attempts have been made to explain what Abraham b. David meant by his statement; a collection of them is to be found in I. Twersky, *Rabad of Posquières* (1962), pp. 282–286.

[86] See reference in n. 80 above.

[87] *Iggeret ha-Ramban* in *Iggerot Kena'ot* (*Ḳobeṣ* III, pp. 9d–10a).

[88] *Ketab Tamin* in *Oṣar Neḥmad* III, 1860, pp. 58 ff.

the literalness of the corporeal terms used in the Agadic description of God,[89] later recanted and openly protested that "far be it from them to conceive of God as having a likeness or form or a hand or a foot or any of the other limbs which happen to be mentioned in the text of Scripture; never had they uttered such a view nor had such a thought ever entered their minds." [90] And perhaps more loftily than they, but at the same time also more uprightly than they, would the rabbi of Posquières have declared: "Many people, even as great and good as I, had oftentimes spoken hastily and said things which they later withdrew."

[89] *Milḥamot ha-Shem* by Abraham Maimonides in *Iggerot Ḳena'ot* (*Ḳobeṣ* III, pp. 17a–18a).

[90] *Ibid.*, p. 19c.

CHAPTER II

ATTRIBUTES

I. The Muslim Attributes and the Christian Trinity *

As early as the first part of the eighth century, as one may judge from the reports of teachings to which Wāṣil (d. 748) was opposed,[1] there arose in Islam the belief that certain terms which are attributed to God in the Koran stand for real incorporeal beings which exist in God from eternity. There is nothing in the Koran to warrant such a belief. Nor is there any warrant that at that early stage in the history of Islam the belief originated spontaneously by that kind of reasoning by which later Muslim theologians tried to defend it against opposition. The appearance of that belief at that time can be explained only on the ground of some external influence. Such an external influence could be either Greek philosophy or Judaism or Christianity. Greek philosophy is to be eliminated, for we have the testimony of Shahrastānī that it was not until later, among the followers of Wāṣil, that the problem of attributes came under the influence of Greek philosophy.[2] And so also must Judaism be eliminated, for the kind of Judaism with which Islam was in direct contact at that time contained nothing in its teachings which could have inspired that new belief. By a process of elimination it is to be assumed that Christianity was that external influence.

A suggestion as to the Christian origin of the belief in the reality of divine attributes is to be found in the discussion of that problem in the literature of the time when the problem was still a vital issue. The belief in the reality of divine attributes was characterized by those who were opposed to it as

* Reprinted with many additions from *The Harvard Theological Review*, 49:1–18 (1956).

[1] *Milal*, p. 31, ll. 17 ff.

[2] *Ibid.*, ll. 19 ff. Cf. Horten, *Systeme*, p. 133.

being analogous to the Christian doctrine of the Trinity. Abulfaraj, also known as Bar Hebraeus, speaking of the Muʿtazilites, who denied the reality of divine attributes, says that thereby they steered clear of "the persons (*aḳānīm*) of the Christians," [3] the implication being that the belief in the reality of divine attributes indirectly steers one into the belief of the Christian Trinity. ʿAḍad al-Dīn al-Ījī similarly reports that the Muʿtazilites accused those who believed in the reality of divine attributes of having fallen into the error of the Christian belief in the Trinity.[4] And prior to both of them, among the Jews, David al-Muḳammaṣ,[5] Saadia,[6] Joseph al-Bāṣir,[7] and Maimonides,[8] evidently reflecting still earlier Muslim sources, whenever they happen to mention the Muslim doctrine of the reality of divine attributes, compare it to the Christian doctrine of the Trinity. It is thus in the Christian doctrine of the Trinity that we must look for the origin of the Muslim doctrine of divine attributes.

But the words of opponents cannot always be taken at their face value, for opponents, especially in matters of religion, are in the habit of accusing one another of things which are not necessarily so. If we are to assume, on the basis of what its opponents said about it, that the Muslim doctrine of attributes had its origin in the Christian doctrine of the Trinity, we shall have to find some external evidence in support of that assumption. We shall especially have to find some logical reason, or at least some psychological motive, to explain how the Muslims, who had started with an outspoken negation of the Christian Trinity on the ground of its incompatibility

[3] Cf. E. Pocock, *Specimen Historiae Arabum sive Gregorii Abul Farajii Malatiensis de Origine et Moribus Arabum* (1650), p. 19, l. 12, referred to by Munk, *Guide des Égarés*, I, p. 180, n. 1.

[4] *Ibid.*, quoted from al-Ījī's *al-Mawāḳif fī ʿIlm al-Kalām*; referred to in Munk, *Guide*, p. 181, n. 1.

[5] Quoted from his *ʿIshrūn Maḳālāt* in Judah b. Barzillai, *Perush Sefer Yeṣirah*, p. 79.

[6] *Emunot* II, 5, p. 86, ll. 2 ff.

[7] Cf. P. F. Frankl, *Ein Muʿtazilitischen Kalam aus dem 10ten Jahrhundert* (1872), pp. 15 and 28.

[8] *Moreh* I, 50.

with the unity of God, happened to substitute for it a doctrine which involved the very same difficulty contained in the doctrine of the Trinity. To say that they did it only as an imitation of the Christian doctrine would not be sufficient. Imitation could be used as an explanation in a case when some peculiarly Christian belief, the like of which existed also in Islam or which at least was not directly rejected by Islam, happened to find its way into Islam. It cannot be used as an explanation in the present case, when nothing resembling the doctrine of the Trinity existed in Islam and, moreover, when that doctrine itself was openly rejected. Then also, ideas always ride on the back of terms, and so, whenever there is a transmission of an idea from one language to another, we should expect the transmission also of some fundamental terms either by translation or by transliteration or, as sometimes happens, by mistranslation. Can we, therefore, find any term used in the Muslim doctrine of attributes which is traceable to some term in the Christian doctrine of the Trinity?

Starting therefore with the assumption that the Muslim doctrine of attributes might have originated in the Christian doctrine of the Trinity, we shall try to find first some external evidence for that assumption and then some logical explanation for the transition from the Christian doctrine of the Trinity to the Muslim doctrine of attributes.

We shall take up first the evidence of terminology.

From the very beginning of the history of the problem of divine attributes in Islam two Arabic terms are used for what we call attribute, namely, (1) *ma'nā* and (2) *ṣifah*. Thus in the report of the earliest occurrence of the problem, it is said that Wāṣil maintained, in opposition to those who believed in the reality of attributes, that "he who posits a *ma'nā* and *ṣifah* as eternal posits two gods."[9] Now if there is any truth in the a priori assumption that the doctrine of attributes originated in the doctrine of the Trinity, we should have a right to expect that these two fundamental terms used in the doc-

[9] *Milal*, p. 31, l. 19.

trine of attributes would reflect similar fundamental terms in the doctrine of the Trinity, terms which were perhaps used haphazardly by Arabic-speaking Christians in their discussions with Muslims and perhaps not the best chosen terms, but still terms which can be traced to corresponding Greek terms of good usage in the formulation of the doctrine of the Trinity.

The Arabic term *maʿnā*, among its various meanings,[10] has also the general meaning of "thing," and it is used as the equivalent of the term *shay*. Thus both *maʿnā* and *shay* are used as translations of the Greek term *pragma*, "thing," in Aristotle's works — *maʿnā* by Isḥāḳ ibn Ḥunayn [11] and *shay* by other translators, among them perhaps also the same Isḥāḳ ibn Ḥunayn.[12] Now it happens that in Christianity, the term "things" (*πράγματα*, *res*) is used, in addition to the terms "hypostases" (*ὑποστάσεις*) and "persons" (*πρόσωπα*, *personae*), as a description of the three persons of the Trinity, in order to emphasize their reality. Thus of the two Church Fathers who for the first time tried to formulate the doctrine of the Trinity in philosophic language, Origen, writing in Greek, describes the Father and Son as "two things (*πράγματα*) by hypostases," [13] and Tertullian, writing in Latin, argues that the Word is not "a voice and sound of the mouth" but rather a "thing (*res*) and a person," [14] whence he describes each of the three persons as a "substantive thing" (*res*

[10] Here are examples of translations of the term *maʿnā* in the passage of Wāṣil quoted above: Haarbrücker, I, p. 45: "Begriff"; Horten, *Systeme*, p. 132: "geistige Realität (mana, Idee)"; cf. also Horten, "Was bedeutet *Maʿnā* als philosophischer Terminus," *ZDMG*, 64: 391–396 (1910); Sweetman, *Islam and Christian Theology*, I, 2 (1947), p. 232: "meaning," "nature . . . in the sense of the reality of a thing or its entity."

[11] *De Interpr.*, 1, 16a, 7, and 7, 17a, 38 (cf. Arabic text in *Die Hermenutik des Aristoteles in der arabischen Uebersetzung des Isḥāk ibn Ḥonein*, ed. Isidor Pollak; *Organon Aristotelis in versione Arabica antiqua*, ed. Badawi).

[12] *Anal. Pri.* II, 27, 70a, 32; *Top.* I, 5, 102a, 19; *De Soph. Elen.*, 16, 175a, 8 (cf. Arabic text in Badawi, *Organon*); *Metaph.* V, 29, 1024b, 17 (cf. Arabic text in *Averroès*: *Tafsir ma baʿd at-tabiʿat*, ed. Bouyges(1938–48), Dal, T. 34, p. 684, l. 5. The Arabic translation of the text included in this commentary of Averroes may have been made by Isḥāḳ ibn Ḥunayn. Cf. Steinschneider, *Die arabischen Uebersetzungen aus dem Griechischen*, § 35 (59).

[13] *Cont. Cels.* VIII, 12 (PG 11, 1533 C).

[14] *Adv. Prax.* 7 (PL 2, 162 A B).

substantiva).[15] Though the term *pragma* did not succeed in establishing itself as a technical term for the members of the Trinity, its use did not altogether disappear. It occurs in the *Formula Prolixa* of the Council of Antioch in 343 as the equivalent of the term *prosopon*,[16] and it is similarly used by Athanasius as the equivalent of *prosopon*.[17] Basil uses it in place of *hypostasis*, [18] and Cyril of Alexandria uses it as the equivalent of *hypostasis*.[19] But what is especially important for our purpose here is that Theodore Abucara, in a work originally written in Arabic but extant only in Greek, describes each of the three persons of the Trinity as *pragma*,[20] which quite evidently reflects either *shay* or *ma'nā* as the underlying Arabic term. We have, therefore, reason to believe that during the early part of the ninth century, at about the time of the rise of Mu'tazilism, Christians under Muslim rule used the term *pragmata* instead of, or by the side of, the terms *hypostaseis* and *prosopa* as a description of the members of the Trinity and that the term *pragmata* was translated by them into Arabic by *ashyā' or ma'ānī*. Accordingly it is also reasonable to assume that when under the influence of the Christian Trinity orthodox Muslims advanced the doctrine of the reality of attributes and described each attribute by the term *ma'nā*, the term was used by them as the equivalent of *shay* in the sense of "thing."

Corroborative evidence that *ma'nā* in the Muslim doctrine

[15] *Ibid.* 26 (PL 2, 189 B).

[16] Cf. A. Hahn, *Bibliothek der Symbole und Glaubensregeln der alten Kirche*[3], § 159, IV: τρία ὁμολογοῦντες πράγματα καὶ τρία πρόσωπα.

[17] *De Synodis* 26, IV (PG 26, 729 B), 26, VII (732 C).

[18] *Homilia* XVI, 4 (PG 31, 480 C); XXIV (604 D); *Epist.* 210, 4 (PG 32, 773 B).

[19] *Apologeticus contra Theodoretum pro XII Capitibus*, I (PG 76, 396 C): ἀλλὰ πραγμάτων, ἤγουν ὑποστάσεων γέγονε σύνοδος.

[20] *Opuscula* (PG 97, 1480 B). There is no parallel to this quotation in the Arabic works of Abucara published by P. Constantin Bacha (*Les Oeuvres Arabes de Theodore Aboucara*, Beyrouth, 1904). Cf. the analysis of parallels between those Arabic works and the Greek *Opuscula* in G. Graf, "Die arabischen Schriften des Abū Qurra" in *Forschungen zur Christlichen Literatur- und Dogmengeschichte*, 10:67–78 (1910). The technical terms for persons used in these Arabic works are *akānīm* and *wujūh* (cf. *ibid.*, p. 32).

of attributes is used in the sense of *shay* and that its use in that sense goes back to the use of *pragma* in the Christian doctrine of the Trinity may be found in the following two sets of statements. First, with regard to attributes, Ashʿarī in his *Majālis*, as quoted by Ibn Ḥazm, refers to attributes as *ashyāʾ*,[21] whereas in his *Lumaʿ* he refers to an attribute as *maʿnā*.[22] Second, with regard to the Trinity, Yaḥyā Ibn ʿAdī first describes its three members by the commonly used technical Arabic term *aḳānīm*, "hypostases,"[23] but then refers to them as *ashyāʾ*[24] and *maʿānī*,[25] that is, "things." So also Saadia[26] and Ibn Ḥazm[27] refer to the Son and the Holy Spirit of the Trinity as "two things" (*shayʾāni*), and Ibn Ḥazm refers to all the three members of the Trinity as "three things" (*ashyāʾ*).[28] In fact, it would seem that *maʿnā* and *shay* and *ṣifah* all became interchangeable terms used as a description of anything existing in a subject. It is thus reported by Ashʿarī that " ʿAbdallah Ibn Kullāb used to call the *maʿānī* that exist in bodies accidents and he used to call them things (*ashyāʾ*) and he used to call them attributes (*ṣifāt*)."[29]

It can similarly be shown that the term *ṣifah*, which together with the term *maʿnā* is used by Wāṣil as a description of any of those real attributes which are rejected by him, goes back also to the Christian terminology of the Trinity. The term *ṣifah* comes from the verb *waṣaf*, "to describe," which as a verb occurs in the Koran thirteen times and of which the substantive form *waṣf*, "description," occurs once; the form *ṣifah* never occurs in the Koran. While in most cases in the Koran, the verb *waṣaf* is used with reference to what people say about God, in all these cases its usage is always

[21] *Fiṣal* IV, p. 207, l. 13.
[22] *Lumaʿ* 26, p. 14, ll. 13–14 and 17.
[23] Périer, *Petits Traités Apologétiques de Yaḥyā ben ʿAdī*, p. 65, l. 2.
[24] *Ibid.*, p. 66, l. 7.
[25] *Ibid.*, p. 67, l. 2.
[26] *Emunot* II, 5, p. 86, l. 10.
[27] *Fiṣal* IV, p. 207, l. 22.
[28] *Ibid.*, I, p. 49, l. 1.
[29] *Maḳālāt*, p. 370, ll. 11–12. Saadia in his *Emunot* I, 3, 2nd Theory, 2nd Objection, p. 42, ll. 16–17, similarly describes accidental qualities as the *maʿānī* and *ṣifāt* of bodies.

with reference to something unlaudable which impious people say about God;[30] it never occurs with reference to something laudable said about God. The laudable terms by which God is described in the Koran are never referred to in the Koran by any form of the verb *waṣaf*; they are referred to as "the most beautiful names" (*al-asmāʾ al-ḥusnā*, 7:179; 17:110; 20:7), and Muslim tradition, quoting Muhammad, speaks of ninety-nine such "most beautiful names." The term *ṣifah*, which, through the Latin translation of Maimonides' *Moreh Nebukim* in the thirteenth century, came to be translated by the term "attribute,"[31] was thus a technical term coined to take the place of the Koranic term *ism*, "name." When that term was coined and by whom is not known. The earliest mention of the term *ṣifah*, as well as of the term *maʿnā* as its equivalent, occurs in the report of the teaching of the founder of Muʿtazilism Wāṣil b. ʿAṭāʾ (d. 748), quoted above. Evidently the term *ṣifah* was immediately adopted by all Attributists. Thus Hishām b. al-Ḥakam (d. 814), an Attributist of the Rafiḍite subsect of Shiʿites, is quoted by Ashʿarī in the name of Abū al-Kāsim al-Balḫī as saying that "the knowledge of God is His attribute (*ṣifah*)."[32] The first Sunnite Attributist to use the term *ṣifah*, as far as I could find out, is Ibn Kullāb (d. 854), who is reported by Ashʿarī as using the expressions "the names (*asmāʾ*) of God are His attributes (*ṣifāt*)"[33] and "the names and attributes of God,"[34] which sound as an expression of approval of the use of the term *ṣifah* for the term *ism*. According to Ibn Ḥazm, "the term *ṣifah* was devised by the Muʿtazilites and by Hishām [b. al-Ḥakam] and other leaders of the Rafidites like him, and in their way they followed some people from among the masters of the Kalam, thus deviating from the right way of the early

[30] Surah 2:18, 112; 6:100, 140; 21:22; 23:93; 37:159, 180; 43:82. Similarly in all the other instances the term is used with reference to evil things. Cf. 12:18, 77; 16:64, 117; 23:98.

[31] Cf. *Religious Philosophy*, pp. 56–57.

[32] *Maḳālāt*, p. 494, l. 1; cf. p. 37, l. 10.

[33] *Ibid.*, p. 173, l. 1; cf. p. 546, ll. 8–9.

[34] *Ibid.*, p. 169, ll. 10, 12; p. 172, ll. 12, 14.

Muslims, for in them there is nothing to serve as a pattern and model for this newly devised term." [35] Still, despite this statement of Ibn Ḥazm, the manner in which Wāṣil b. 'Aṭā' introduces the term *ṣifah* gives the impression that the term had been used before, in which case it must have been coined by the Attributists. But, be that as it may, we shall try to show that, like the term *ma'nā*, the term *ṣifah* is also derived from the vocabulary of the Christian Trinity.

In Christianity with the assumption that the three "things" or "persons" or "hypostases," though immaterial, are still distinct from each other and each of them an individual being, the question came up as to what was the "principle of differentiation" (λόγος διαφορᾶς) [36] between them to take the place of matter which ordinarily serves as a principle of differentiation between material individual beings. Such a principle of differentiation was found by the Church Fathers in certain properties which characterize each of the persons and distinguish them from each other — distinguishing properties which do not imply matter and which, while distinguishing one person from another, are identical with the respective essences of the persons of which they serve as descriptions. Various Greek terms and phrases are used by the Fathers in designating these distinguishing properties. But in John of Damascus, who may always be taken as the connecting link between the Church Fathers and early Islam,[37] the following two expressions occur as a description of these distinguishing properties: (1) "hypostatic properties" (ὑποστατικαὶ ἰδιότητες); (2) "that which is characteristic of the proper hypostasis" (τὸ χαρακτηριστικὸν τῆς ἰδίας ὑποστάσεως).[38] Thus each of the three persons has a "property" or a "characteristic" which makes it a "thing" distinguished from the two other persons. Now it can be shown that the Greek verb χαρακτηρίζω and noun χαρακτήρ or τὸ χαρακτηριστικόν

[35] *Fiṣal* II, p. 121, ll. 4–6.
[36] Basil, *Epist.* 38, 3 (PG 32, 328 C).
[37] Cf. Gardet et Anawati, *Introduction à la Théologie Musulmane*, p. 201.
[38] *De Fide Orthodoxa*, I, 8 (PG 94, 824 B).

were used as translations respectively of the Arabic verb *waṣaf* and noun *ṣifah* or *waṣf*. Thus Theodore Abucara in those works which were written in Arabic and exist only in Greek speaks of Paul as being described (χαρακτηρίζεται) by "properties" (ἰδιότητες) [39] and of gold, which was minted into coins, as being "qua gold" a "thing" which has not "the description (χαρακτῆρα) of coin." [40] In both these places, the Greek verb quite evidently represents the Arabic *waṣaf*, and the Greek noun quite evidently represents the Arabic *ṣifah* or *waṣf*. We may therefore assume that the term *ṣifah*, which is made use of by Wāṣil as a description of the realistic conception of attributes rejected by him, represents the Greek τὸ χαρακτηριστικόν. Corroborative evidence for this is to be found in Yaḥyā Ibn ʿAdī (893–974) who, in his representation of the Christian Trinity, says that according to the opinions of the Christians the three persons (*aḳānīm*) are *ḫawāṣṣ* and *ṣifāt*.[41] Of these two terms, the first, *ḫawāṣṣ*, is the established Arabic translation of the Greek ἰδιότητες, "properties," one of the terms used by John of Damascus for the "principle of differentiation." The term *ṣifāt* here undoubtedly represents the plural of the Greek τὸ χαρακτηριστικόν which is the other term used by John of Damascus for the principle of differentiation.

But more than that. When we try to find what these properties and characteristics of the three persons of the Trinity were, we shall find that they correspond exactly to the attributes which at first in Islam were held to be real things existing in God. Ordinarily among the Greek Fathers the properties or characteristics are the ungeneratedness of the Father, the generatedness of the Son from the Father, and the proceedingness of the Holy Spirit either again from the Father or from

[39] *Opuscula* (PG 97, 1473 D).

[40] *Ibid.* (1480 C). There are no parallels to these two quotations in Abucara's original works (cf. above n. 20).

[41] Cf. Périer, "Un Traité de Yaḥyā ben ʿAdī, Défense du Dogme de la Trinité contre les Objections d'al-Kindī" in *Revue de l'Orient Chrétien*, 22:5, ll. 2–4 (1920–21).

the Father through the Son or from both the Father and the Son. In the doctrine of the Christian Trinity which became known to the Muslims, these characteristics are indeed reproduced. But in addition to these a set of three other characteristics appears in the literature from the earliest time. This set of three characteristics is said to be "existence" or "essence" or "generosity" for the Father, "life" or "wisdom" (or its equivalent "knowledge" or "reason") for the Son, and "wisdom" (or its equivalent "knowledge") or "life" or "power" for the Holy Spirit. Thus Yaḥyā Ibn ʿAdī says that the property or characteristic of the Father is "generosity" (*jūd*), that of the Son is "wisdom" (*ḥikmah*), and that of the Holy Spirit is "power" *ḳudrah*).[42] Saadia describes them as (1) essence (*dhāt*), (2) life (*ḥayāh*), and (3) knowledge (*ʿilm*),[43] al-Muḳammaṣ describes the Son or Logos as wisdom (*ḥokmah*) and the Spirit as life (*ḥayyim*),[44] and Ḳirḳisānī describes the three persons of the Trinity respectively as substance (*jahuar*) and living (*ḥayy*) and knowing (*ʿālim*).[45] Eliyyah of Nisibis describes the Father as essence (*dhāt*) or self-existent (*ḳāʾim bi-nafsihi*) and the Son as life (*ḥayāh*) and the Holy Spirit as wisdom (*ḥikmah*).[46] Shahrastānī in one place describes the three persons as (1) "existence" (*wujūd*), (2) life (*ḥayāh*) and (4) knowledge (*ʿilm*),[47] and in another place describes them as (1) existence, (2) knowledge, and (3) life.[48] Ibn Ḥazm speaks of some Christians who call the Holy Spirit life and the Son knowledge.[49] Juwaynī reports that by existence the Christians understand the Father,

[42] *Ibid.*, ll. 4–5.
[43] *Emunot* II, 5, p. 86, ll. 9–10.
[44] *Op. cit.* (above, n. 5), p. 79, ll. 19–20.
[45] *Anwār* I, 8, 3 (p. 43, l. 11).
[46] P. Louis Cheikho, *Vingt Traités Théologiques d'Auteurs Arabes Chrétiens*, 2nd ed. (1920), p. 126, ll. 2–3; cf. L. E. Browne, *Eclipse of Christianity in Asia*, p. 124, where Eliyya of Nisibis is also quoted, from Cheikho's *Trois Traités*, p. 33, as describing the Father as essence, the Son as the Logos, and the Holy Spirit as life. Cf. also Sweetman, *Islam and Christian Theology*, I, 2, p. 92.
[47] *Milal*, p. 172, l. 10.
[48] *Ibid.*, p. 175, l. 11; cf. p. 173, ll. 15–16.
[49] *Fiṣal* I, p. 50, ll. 18–19.

by knowledge the Word, called by them also Son, and by life the Holy Spirit.[50] Paul Rahib of Antioch describes the Father as essence and the Son as reason (*nuṭḳ* = Logos) and the Holy Spirit as life.[51]

The origin of these sets of characteristics has so far not been established, for while the term "life" is applied in the New Testament to the Son [52] and "power" is applied in the New Testament to both the Son [53] and the Holy Spirit [54] and the term "wisdom" is applied in the New Testament to the Son [55] and by some Church Fathers also to the Holy Spirit,[56] no Greek Father has so far been discovered who characterized the three persons by those properties by which they are characterized in the passages quoted from Arabic sources. About eighty years ago, David Kaufmann, commenting upon the passage quoted above from Saadia, made the assertion that Saadia's identification of the three persons with "essence," "life," and "knowledge" has no parallel in the history of Christian doctrine, and this assertion was corroborated by Professor Hermann Reuter of Breslau, though Professor Franz Delitzsch of Leipzig suggested two irrelevant passages, one from Augustine and the other from Gregory of Nyssa.[57] I myself, in the course of my reading, have come across only one Christian Church Father, and him writing in Latin, who uses terms like those quoted above from Arabic authors in connection with the three persons of the Trinity. That Latin Father is Marius Victorinus who in one place explains the unity of the three persons in God after the analogy of the soul in which existence (*esse*), life (*vita*), and intelligence (*intelligentia*), though distinct, are still united by their relation to each other,[58] and in another place says that the three persons are three powers, namely,

[50] *Irshād*, p. 28, ll. 10–12 (53).

[51] Cheikho, *Vingt Traités*, p. 20, ll. 9–10.

[52] John 1:4; Col. 3:4; cf. John 11:25; 14:6.

[53] I Cor. 1:24.

[54] Luke 1:35.

[55] I Cor. 1:24.

[56] Cf. Theophilus, *Ad Autol.* II. 15 and 18; Irenaeus, *Adv. Haer.* IV, 20, 3; cf. IV, 7, 4; IV, 20, 1.

[57] Cf. Kaufmann, *Attributenlehre*, p. 41, n. 77.

[58] *Adversus Arium* I, 63 (PL 8, 1087 D).

existence (*esse*), life (*vivere*), and intelligence (*intelligere*).[59] It is probably under the influence of this statement of Marius Victorinus that John Scotus Erigena says that "those who inquired into the truth have handed down that by essence (*essentiam*) is to be understood the Father, by wisdom (*sapientiam*) the Son, and by life (*vitam*) the Holy Spirit." [60] While Marius Victorinus cannot be considered as the source of the descriptions of the Trinity known to the Muslims — for the Muslim contact with Christianity was with its Greek and not with its Latin branch — still from Victorinus as well as Erigena we may get some clue as to how that description of the Trinity may have reached the Muslims. Marius Victorinus as well as John Scotus Erigena were under the influence of Neoplatonism. Moreover Erigena's words "those who inquired into the truth have handed down" (*inquisitores veritatis tradiderunt*) would seem to indicate that this description of the Trinity was not something that could be found in the standard works of the Fathers but rather something that only "those who inquired into the truth," namely, those who like himself searched for the truth in the writings of the Neoplatonists, "have handed down" as a sort of esoteric knowledge, which he was divulging. Now Neoplatonism is characterized by triads which were not unlike the Trinity of Christianity. Let us then study these Neoplatonic triads [61] to see whether they might not furnish us with some information.

The Neoplatonists whom we shall bring into play in this connection are Jamblichus, Theodore of Asine, and Proclus.

Jamblichus, as quoted by Damascius, describes his triad as (1) Father or subsistence (ὕπαρξις), (2) power (δύναμις), and (3) intellect (νοῦς) or intelligence (νόησις).[62] Theodore of Asine, as quoted by Proclus, describes his triad as (1)

[59] *Ibid.* IV, 21 (1128 D); cf. I, 13 (1048 B).
[60] *De Divisione Naturae* I, 13 (PL 122, 455 C).
[61] On the Neoplatonic triads, see Zeller, *Phil. d. Gr.* III, 2^4, pp. 748, 784, 857–858.
[62] Damascius, *Philosophi Platonici Quaestiones de Primis Principiis*, 54 (ed. Jos. Kopp, 1826), p. 144.

existence (τὸ εἶναι), (2) intelligence (τό νοεῖν), and (3) life (τὸ ζῆν).[63] Proclus himself has several descriptions of the triad. In three passages, which we shall combine and treat together, his triad is described as follows: (1) essence (οὐσία)[64] or the existent (τὸ ὄν)[65] or subsistence (ὕπαρξις)[66] or existence (τὸ εἶναι);[67] (2) life (ζωή)[68] or power (δύναμις);[69] (3) intellect (νοῦς)[70] or intelligence (τὸ νοεῖν).[71] In another passage, he describes his triad as goodness (ἀγαθότης), power (δύναμις), and knowledge (γνῶσις).[72] This last triad, it will be noticed, corresponds to Yaḥyā Ibn ʿAdī's Trinity of "generosity" (= goodness), "wisdom" (= knowledge), and "power," quoted above.

It is in these Neoplatonic triads that we may find the origin of the *ṣifāt* of the Christian Trinity as it became known to the Muslims as well as the origin of the descriptions of the Trinity which we have quoted from Victorinus and Erigena. The Arabic goodness (*jūd*) and essence (*dhāt*) and self-existent (*ḳāʾim bi-nafsihi*) and existence (*wujūd*) used as a description of the first person of the Trinity reflect the Greek ἀγαθότης, οὐσία, τὸ ὄν and τὸ εἶναι or ὕπαρξις used as a description of the first member of the Neoplatonic triad. The Arabic life (*ḥayāt*) and wisdom (*ḥikmah*) or reason (*nuṭḳ*) or knowledge (*ʿilm*) used as a description of either the second or the third person of the Trinity reflect the Greek τὸ ζῆν and νοῦς or νόησις, or γνῶσις used as a description of either the second or the third member of the Neoplatonic triad. Again, the Arabic power (*ḳudrah*) used as a description of the third person of the Trinity reflects the Greek δύναμις used as

[63] Proclus, *In Timaeum*, 225 B.

[64] *Plat. Theol.* III, 14, p. 146; IV, 1, p. 179.

[65] *Ibid.* IV, 1, p. 180; *Inst. Theol.* 103. From the context of this latter reference, it is evident that τὸ ὄν is to be taken here in the sense of "the existent" rather than in the sense of "existence."

[66] *Plat. Theol.* IV, 1, p. 180.

[67] *Inst. Theol.* 103.

[68] *Plat. Theol.* III, 14, p. 146; IV, 1, pp. 179, 180; *Inst. Theol.* 103.

[69] *Plat. Theol.* IV, 1, p. 180.

[70] *Plat. Theol.* III, 14, p. 146; IV, 1, pp. 179, 180; *Inst. Theol.* 103.

[71] *Inst. Theol.* 103.

[72] Proclus, *In Timaeum*, 118 E.

a description of the second member of the Neoplatonic triad.

But whether we are right or not in our explanation of the origin of the *ṣifāt* of the three persons of the Christian Trinity which occurs in Arabic literature, it is quite evident that in these Arabic restatements of the Christian doctrine of the Trinity the term "self-existent" or "existence" or "essence" or "goodness" was used as a description of the Father, and the term "life" or "wisdom" or "knowledge" was used as a description either of the Son or of the Holy Spirit, and the term "power" was used as a description of the Holy Spirit.

Now when we study the reports of the teachings of the earliest individual opponents of real attributes, we shall find that they contain, in various twofold or threefold combinations, only the terms "life," "wisdom" or "knowledge," and "power," those very same terms which we have met with as descriptions of the second and third persons of the Trinity.

In his report of Wāṣil, Shahrastānī at first simply states that he denied the existence of real attributes, without mentioning what these attributes were, but then he goes on to say that the followers of Wāṣil, under the influence of philosophy, not only denied the existence of real attributes but also undertook to explain how the terms "knowledge" and "power," which are predicated of God in the Koran, should be understood.[73] The inference to be drawn from this statement is that "knowledge" and "power" were the only terms which formed the subject of controversy between Wāṣil and the Attributists. Indeed, prior to his restatement of the individual view of Wāṣil and of the particular view of his immediate followers, Shahrastānī says of the Wāṣilites in general that they were for "the denial of the attributes of God, such as knowledge, power, will, and life." [74] But when he immediately adds that "this view was at first not fully developed," [75] he indicates that the four terms he mentioned belonged to a later period when, we know, a list of four terms existed. Ḍirār, as reported

[73] *Milal*, p. 31, l. 19–p. 32, l. 2.

[74] *Ibid.*, p. 31, ll. 16–17.

[75] *Ibid.*

by al-Ashʿarī, stated his antirealistic explanation of attributes only with regard to the terms "knowledge," "power," and "life," [76] or only with regard to the terms "knowledge" and "power." [77] It is quite evident that in the passage in which three attributes are mentioned, "power" and "life" are used as alternative terms. Similarly Abū-al-Hudhayl is reported to have stated his antirealistic conception of attributes either only with regard to the terms "knowledge," "power," and "life," [78] or only with regard to the terms "knowledge" and "power." [79] Al-Muḳammaṣ in the statement of his antirealistic conception of attributes, reflecting the Muʿtazilite influence, concentrates on the terms "living" and "wise," even though in the course of his discussion he introduces from the lists current in his own time such terms as "seeing" and "hearing." [80] Similarly Saadia in the statement of his antirealistic conception of attributes, again reflecting the influence of the Muʿtazilites, mentions only the terms "living," "powerful," and "knowing." [81] Here, too, "living" and "powerful" are to be taken as alternative terms. It is to be noted that Jahm b. Ṣafwān, who has arrived at his denial of attributes independently, on the ground of the Koranic prohibition of likening God to other beings, does not confine himself to the terms "life," "knowledge," and "power." [82] Still Shahrastānī, after quoting him as saying that "it is not permissible that the Creator should be described by terms by which His creatures are described, for this would constitute an act of likening [God to other beings]," concludes in his own words: "He therefore denies that He is living and knowing." [83] These concluding words of Shahrastānī would seem to be an echo of the early discussion of attributes among the Muʿtazilites, when the controversy turned only on the terms "life" and "knowledge."

[76] *Maḳālāt*, p. 166, ll. 14–15.
[77] *Ibid*., p. 487, l. 15–p. 488, l. 1; cf. *Milal*, p. 63, ll. 6–7.
[78] *Maḳālāt*, p. 165, ll. 5–6; *Milal*, p. 34, ll. 13–14.
[79] *Farḳ*, p. 108, ll. 7–9.
[80] *Op. cit.* (above, n. 5), pp. 78–79.
[81] *Emunot*, II, 4, p. 84, l. 15.
[82] Cf. passages quoted below p. 221 at nn. 77 and 79.
[83] *Milal*, p. 60, ll. 8–9.

That the original controversy about attributes turned only on the terms "knowledge," "power," and "life" may be also gathered from Shahrastānī's general statement about the Muʿtazilites. Wishing to explain how the Muʿtazilites, who "deny eternal attributes altogether," interpret the terms predicated of God in the Koran, he mentions only the terms "knowledge," "power," and "life." [84] The fact that at the time of Shahrastānī lists of more than three terms, a list of four terms and a list of seven terms, formed the subject of controversy between the Muʿtazilites and Attributists, and still in his restatement of the Muʿtazilite view he mentions only these three terms, shows that originally only these three terms formed the subject of controversy on the problem of attributes and that only these three terms were claimed by the Attributists to represent eternal real beings in God. Indeed, in another place Shahrastānī says that the Muʿtazilites deny the attributes of knowledge, power, will, life, hearing, and seeing,[85] but these six attributes are quite evidently taken from the list of seven attributes current in his own time and do not represent the original list of attributes which formed the subject of discussion in the early stage of the problem. Similarly, when Ghazālī says that the Muʿtazilites, in agreement with the philosophers, denied the attributes of knowledge (*ʿilm*), power (*ḳudrah*), and will (*irādah*),[86] we may assume that only the mention of "three" represents the original view of the Muʿtazilites, whereas the term "will" is taken from the later list of four or seven, current at the time of Ghazālī, and substituted for "life" of the original list.

Comparing the list of terms in the earliest statements of the problem of attributes and the list of terms in the statements of the doctrine of the Trinity as known to Muslims, we find that both of them contain the terms "life," "power," and "knowledge," or also "wisdom" and "reason" as the equivalents of "knowledge." Quite evidently there is some kind of

[84] *Ibid.*, p. 30, ll. 7–8.
[85] *Ibid.*, p. 61, l. 20–p. 62, l. 1.
[86] *Tahāfut al-Falāsifah* VI, 1, p. 163, ll. 2–3.

relation between the Muslim belief in attributes and the Christian belief in the Trinity. Moreover, when we scrutinize the list of these terms in the Christian Trinity, we find that it is the Son and the Holy Spirit that are described respectively either as "life" and "knowledge" or as "knowledge" and "life" or as "knowledge" and "power." Quite evidently it is these two persons of the Trinity, the Son and the Holy Spirit, that were transformed into Muslim attributes, for, as we have seen, in the earliest discussion of the problem of attributes the attributes mentioned are either "life" and "knowledge" or "knowledge" and "life" or "life," "knowledge," and "power." The question now is, how was the transformation effected? What was the reason that has led the Muslims to adopt a Christian doctrine, which is explicitly rejected in the Koran, and transform it into a Muslim doctrine?

Let us then reconstruct the logical situation which could have led to the substitution in Muslim theology of divine attributes for the Christian Trinity.

From the passages quoted, as well as from other passages, we may gather some of the main features of the Christian doctrine of the Trinity as it was presented to the Muslims. These main features were four. First, there was the orthodox Christian belief in the equality of the Father and the Son and the Holy Spirit, each of them being God.[87] Second, the Father and the Son and the Holy Spirit are each a hypostasis or person (*aḳnūm*) or a thing (*ma'nā*); that which is common to all three is called their common essence or substance.[88] Third,

[87] Cf. Yaḥyā Ibn 'Adī's quotation of the following statement by Muslims: "The hypostases are according to them equal in all respects" (Périer, *Petits*, p. 36). That the Christians called each person of the Trinity God is implied in the Koran; cf. below at nn. 91, 92.

[88] In the Arabic translations of the Greek formula μία οὐσία, τρεῖς ὑποστάσεις, the term *hypostases* is translated by *aḳānīm*, but, as for the term *ousia*, it is translated either by *jauhar*, "substance" used in the sense of "essence" (cf. Yaḥyā Ibn 'Adī in *Petits*, p. 36, l. 8; *Milal*, p. 172, l. 9, and p. 176, l. 8) or by *dhāt*, "essence" (cf. Paul Rahib of Antioch in *Vingt Traités*, p. 27, l. 11). Similarly in Latin versions of the formula, *ousia* is translated either *substantia* or *essentia* (cf. Augustine, *De Trinit.* V, 8, 10–V, 9, 10). Sometimes it is translated by *kiyān* (Eliyya of Nisibis in *Vingt Traités*, p.

the "principle of differentiation" between these three persons or things is that the Father is "goodness" or "essence" or "self-existence" or "existence"; the Son is "life" or "wisdom" or "knowledge" or "reason"; the Holy Spirit is "life" or "wisdom" or "knowledge" or "power." [89] Fourth, these three sets of terms by which the three persons or things are described are called "properties" (*ḫawāṣṣ*) or characteristics (*ṣifāt*).[90]

Now from the *Disputatio Christiani et Saraceni* by John of Damascus (d. *ca.* 754) we learn that in Syria, after its conquest by the Muslims in 635, there were debates between Christians and Muslims on the Christian doctrine of the Trinity. Let us then sketch some such typical debate between a Christian and a Muslim. In such a debate the Christian presumably begins by explaining that of the three hypostases in the Trinitarian formula, namely, Father, Son, and Holy Spirit, by Father is meant what is generally referred to by both Christians and Muslims as God and by Son and Holy Spirit are meant the properties life and knowledge or life and power or knowledge and power. Turning then to the Muslim, the Christian asks him if he has any objection to the Christian application of these properties to God. Immediately the Muslim answers that he has no objection, adding that the Koran explicitly describes God as "the living" (*al-ḥayy*),[91] as "the knowing" (*al-ʿalīm*),[92] and as "the powerful" (*al-ḳadīr*).[93]

126, l. 3), which, as a literal translation of *ousia*, may be taken to mean both "essence" and "substance."

[89] Cf. above at nn. 42–51. It is to be noted that, in these Arabic descriptions of the hypostases, some of them identify the Father with "essence," that is, the Greek *ousia* of the Trinitarian formula, whereas others identify the Father with "generosity" (Yaḥyā Ibn ʿAdī) or with "existence" (Juwaynī, Shahrastānī) or with both "essence" and "self-existence" (Eliyya of Nisibis). In Christianity there were two views with regard to the relation of the *ousia* of the formula "one *ousia*, three hypostases" to the hypostases. To most of the Church Fathers, the *ousia* is identified with the Father; to Augustine and the author of the Quicunque or the so-called Athanasian Creed, the *ousia* is the common substratum of all the three hypostases (cf. *The Philosophy of the Church Fathers*, I, pp. 352–354).

[90] Cf. above at nn. 36–41.

[91] Surah 2:256.

[92] Surah 2:30.

[93] Surah 30:53.

The Christian then goes on to report how among the Christians there is a difference of opinion with regard to the nature of the second and third hypostases, by which, as he has already explained, are meant various combinations of the properties life, knowledge, and power. Some Christians, branded as heretics,[94] maintain that these two hypostases are mere names of God. Most Christians, however, and they are the people of right belief, regard these two hypostases as real things which, while distinct from the essence of God, are inseparable from it. Turning again to the Muslim, the Christian asks him whether he has any objection to the view that life, knowledge, and power, as properties of God, are real things inseparable from the essence of God. After some deliberation the Muslim answers that there is nothing in the Koran which could be taken to mean opposition to such a view and consequently he is willing to agree with the people of right belief among the Christians that life, knowledge, and power as properties of God are real things.[95]

The Christian continues by reporting that among those Christians who regard the second and third hypostases as real things there are some, again branded as heretics,[96] who maintain that these two hypostases are created, whereas all the others, and they are again the people of right belief, maintain that the second and third hypostases are coeternal with the first hypostasis. Turning once more to the Muslim, the Christian asks him what his view is with regard to the origin of life, knowledge, and power as properties of God. Immediately the Muslim answers that, inasmuch as Muslims believe that God is eternally living and eternally knowing and eternally powerful,[97] these three properties, already admitted by him to be real things, are also admitted by him to be coeternal with God.

The Christian is then about to conclude his argument. First, he says, inasmuch as Christians believe that anything eternal

[94] That is, Sabellians.

[95] Cf. below, pp. 138–139.

[96] That is, Arians.

[97] The theory of created attributes appeared later. Cf. below, pp. 143–146.

is to be called God, the second and third hypostases are each to be called God,[98] thus the three hypostases are to be called three Gods. Second, he says, he is going to prove by arguments that these three Gods are really one God. But at this point the Muslim interrupts him by saying: Spare your arguments, for whatever they may be, the Prophet has warned us against them by his statement that "they surely are infidels who say, God is the third of three, for there is no God but one God." [99]

Thus gradually in the course of such debates Muslims came to admit that life, knowledge, and power as properties of God are real things but to deny that they are to be called Gods, which admission and denial constitute the Muslim belief in real attributes as distinguished from the Christian belief in the Trinity.

This is how the doctrine of real attributes was introduced into Islam.

Originally, as we have seen, only three terms, variously arranged in lists of two terms, were declared to be real attributes, and this because these three terms in various combinations were, to the knowledge of the Muslims, used by Christians, in their formulation of the doctrine of the Trinity, as designations of the second and the third persons, namely, the Son and the Holy Spirit. Two other terms, speech (or word) and will, were soon added, as we shall see,[100] to the original list of real attributes, and this, again, because these terms were used by Christians as designations of one of the persons of the Trinity, the Son, and were thus brought into play in the debates between Muslims and Christians. Gradually other new terms were added and various lists of attributes were drawn up, all of them based, as says Maimonides, upon "the text of some book," [101] that is to say, some text of the Koran or of the Sunnah as recorded in a *Ṣaḥīḥ*. From Baghdādī we may further gather that while the orthodox Attributists confined their lists of attributes to those terms by which

[98] Cf. below, p. 133, at n. 8; p. 137, at n. 25.
[99] Surah 5:77.
[100] Cf. below, pp. 236–238.
[101] *Moreh* I, 53, p. 82, l. 21.

God is described in the Koran and the Sunnah — and any term so used in them could be included in a list of attributes — the Baṣra Muʿtazilites allowed description of God by terms not found in the Koran and the Sunnah, and one of them, al-Fuwaṭi, on the other hand, forbade description of God even by some terms found in these two sources.[102]

Thus the orthodox Muslim belief in the reality of attributes is traceable to the Christian doctrine of the Trinity. Should we then say that, just as the orthodox Muslim belief in attributes is traceable to the orthodox Christian doctrine of the Trinity, the Muʿtazilite denial of the reality of attributes is similarly traceable to heretical Christian views which denied the reality of the second and third persons of the Trinity? This is a question which we shall discuss in the next section.

II. Denial of the Reality of Attributes

The orthodox Muslim view of the reality and eternity of attributes, as we have seen, had its origin in the conciliar Christian doctrine of the reality of the second and third persons of the Trinity, the Word and the Spirit, and hence it must have arisen during the early encounter of Islam with Christianity. The denial of attributes arose during the first half of the eighth century and it is generally ascribed to Wāṣil b. ʿAṭāʾ of Baṣra, the founder of Muʿtazilism.[1] The fact, however, that the denial of the eternity of the Koran (which, as we shall see, arose in consequence of the denial of attributes) [2] is ascribed to two non-Muʿtazilite and non-Baṣraite contemporaries of Wāṣil (to one of whom is also ascribed the denial of attributes) [3] would seem to show that the founder of Muʿtazilism was not the first to deny attributes. Still, the formal

[102] *Farḳ*, p. 145, ll. 7–15.

[1] Cf. above, pp. 18–19.

[2] Cf. below, p. 240.

[3] Cf. below, p. 241, on Jaʿd b. Dirham's and Jahm b. Ṣafwān's denial of the eternity of the Koran and below, p. 140, on Jahm's denial of attributes. So also the reference in John of Damascus to Muslim heretics who denied the eternity of the Koran does not seem to be to the Muʿtazilites (cf. below p. 242).

argument for the denial of attributes comes to us from the Muʿtazilites.

The Muʿtazilite argument against the existence of eternal real attributes in God falls into two parts. First, it assumes that anything eternal must be a God. Second, it assumes that the unity of God excludes any internal plurality in God, even if these plural parts are inseparably united from eternity. As briefly stated by Wāṣil, the argument reads as follows: "He who posits a thing and attribute as eternal posits two gods." [4] More fully is the argument restated as follows: "God is eternal (*ḳadīm*) and eternity is the most peculiar description of His essence and consequently the Muʿtazilites deny eternal attributes altogether . . . for if the attributes shared with God in eternity, which is the most peculiar of His descriptions, they would also have a share in divinity (*al-illāhiyyah*)." [5] And so, in order to safeguard that unity, the Muʿtazilites denied the reality of attributes, regarding them either as mere names or as modes. It is because of this rigid conception of the unity of God that they are called "the partisans of unity" (*aṣḥāb al-tauḥīd*).[6]

Both parts of the argument have their historical background in Philo through the intermediacy of the Church Fathers.

The background of the first part of the argument is the principle laid down by Philo that God "alone is eternal," [7] with the implication that if anything is described as eternal it must be God. It is this principle that John of Damascus, in his fictitious disputation between a Christian and a Muslim, after proving that the Word must be uncreated, uses to prove that it is God, for, he says, "everything that is not created, but uncreated, is God." [8] It is also this Philonic principle that is used by the Church Fathers, in various ways, as

[4] *Milal*, p. 31, l, 19.
[5] *Milal*, p. 30, ll. 6–9; cf. *Nihāyat*, p. 199, ll. 12–15.
[6] *Ibid.*, p. 29, l. 18.
[7] *De Virtutibus*, 39, 214; cf. *Philo*, I, p. 172.
[8] *Disputatio Christiani et Saraceni* I (PG 94, 1586 A). This sentence is missing in *Disputatio Saraceni et Christiani* (PG 96, 1341 D).

an argument against the eternity of matter. Typical examples of the use of this argument by the Greek Church Fathers are to be found in Justin Martyr's statement that "God alone is unbegotten and uncorruptible and therefore He is God, but all other things after Him are created and corruptible," [9] in Theophilus' statement with regard to those who believe in an eternal matter that, "nor, so far as their opinions hold, is the monarchy of God established," [10] and in Basil's statement that "if matter were uncreated, then it would be equal to God and would deserve the same veneration." [11] Among the Latin Fathers it is found in Tertullian's argument against the eternity of matter, which reads that "since this [that is, eternity] is a property of God, it will belong to God alone." [12]

The background of the second part of the Muʿtazilite argument is, again, a principle laid down by Philo to the effect that the unity of God is an absolute kind of unity, which excludes any kind of composition, even a composition of parts which are inseparably united from eternity.[13] Here, again, this principle must have reached the Muʿtazilites through the intermediacy of Christianity, but in this case it was through the intermediacy of those heretics in Christianity who were opposed to the orthodox belief in the reality of the second and third persons of the Trinity — the latter belief, as we have seen, was the origin of the orthodox Muslim belief in the reality of attributes.

The argument of those Christian heretics [14] who were opposed to what ultimately became the orthodox Christian belief, as reproduced by Origen, reads as follows: "Now there is that which disturbs many who sincerely profess to be lovers of God. They are afraid that they may be proclaiming two gods." [15] This fear, continues Origen, has driven those professedly sincere lovers of God "into doctrines

[9] *Dial.* 5.

[10] *Ad Autol.* II, 4.

[11] *Hexaemeron* II, 2.

[12] *Adv. Hermog.* 4.

[13] Cf. *Philo*, II, pp. 94 ff.

[14] Cf. *The Philosophy of the Church Fathers*, I, pp. 581 ff.

[15] *In Joan.* II, 2 (PG 14, 108 C–109 A).

which are false and wicked: either (*a*) they deny that the hypostasis of the Son is different from that of the Father, and make him whom they call the Son God in all but the name; or (*b*) they deny the divinity of the Son, giving his hypostasis and essence a sphere of existence which falls outside of the Father." [16] In other words, either (*a*) they denied any reality to the Son, identifying him completely with God and reducing the difference between them to a difference in names only; or (*b*) they denied that he was eternal like God and hence denied that he was God, making him only a creature of God. The first of these views, which Origen describes as false and wicked, has many exponents, chief among them Sabellius, who is reported to have maintained that "the Father is Son and the Son Father, in hypostasis one, in name two." [17] The second of these views is that which came to be known as Arianism, which taught that the second person of the Trinity, the Son or Word, was only a creature of God.[18]

Both these Christian heresies were known to the Muslims. The first was known to them either under the name of Sabellius, who is described as asserting that "the Eternal is a single substance, a single hypostasis, having three properties," [19] or under the name of Paul of Samosata, whose doctrine is described as "absolute and genuine unity." [20] The second heresy was known to them correctly as having been founded by Arius, who is described as maintaining that "God is one" and that the pre-existent Christ who is "the Word of God . . . was created before the creation of the world" [21] or that he "was a created servant and was the Word of God by whom He created the heavens and the earth." [22]

It is by the same insistence upon the absolute unity of God by which Sabellianism and Arianism denied the reality or the eternity of the second and third persons of the Trinity

[16] *Ibid.*
[17] Cf. Athanasius, *Orat. cont. Arian.* IV, 25 (PG 26, 505 C).
[18] Cf. *ibid.* I, 5 (21 AB).
[19] *Milal*, p. 178, l. 14.
[20] *Fiṣal* I, p. 48, l. 13.
[21] *Milal*, p. 178, ll. 15–17.
[22] *Fiṣal* I, p. 48, ll. 9–10.

that the Muʿtazilites denied the reality and eternity of attributes. In their positive conception of attributes, however, the Muʿtazilites, on the whole, arrived at a view which corresponds to that of Sabellianism rather than to that of Arianism. The attributes, on the whole, were taken by them to be not created real things distinct from God but rather mere names of God.[23] The exception made by most of the Muʿtazilites with

[23] Cf. below, pp. 217–218.

C. H. Becker in his paper on "Christliche Polemik und islamische Dogmenbildung" (*Zeitschrift fur Assyriologie*, 26: 188–190 [1912]) suggests that the Muʿtazilite denial of attributes has its origin in the Christian view that anthropomorphisms are not to be taken literally. In support of this he quotes from an Arabic work of Abucara (*Mimar* VII, 7–11, Arabic by Bacha, *Oeuvres Arabes*, pp. 94–97; German by G. Graf in *Forschungen zur Christlichen Literatur- und Dogmengeschichte* 10: 188–191 [1910]) in which Abucara argues with some unnamed interlocutor, who denied the generation of the pre-existent Christ from God on the ground of its incompatibility with the conception of God as an incorporeal being. Abucara's answer to this is that, just as those heretics do not hesitate to affirm that God is living and hearing and seeing and knowing and creating in the sense that His life and hearing and seeing and knowing and creating are unlike those of other beings, so should they also not hesitate to affirm that God can generate a son in a manner unlike the generation in the case of animal beings. The unnamed interlocutor against whom Abucara argues here is assumed to be some Christian heretic against whom Abucara argues from what is generally admitted by all Christians, including that Christian heretic, namely, that one is to deny the literalness and hence the corporeality and hence also the reality of terms predicated of God. The Muʿtazilites, it is assumed, adopted this general Christian denial of the reality of attributes and thus came out against those of their own religion who affirmed the reality of attributes.

Two things are wrong with this suggestion.

First, it confuses the problem of the incorporeality of God with the problem of the unity of God and hence confuses also the problem of anthropomorphism with the problem of the reality of attributes. But these two problems are independent of each other. There were those in Islam who believed in attributes and still interpreted the attributes in a nonliteral sense. A mere denial of the literalness of anthropomorphic expressions would therefore not lead to a denial of the reality of attributes.

Second, the unnamed interlocutor in this particular *Mimar* of Abucara's Arabic work is not a Christian heretic, but rather a Muslim, as may be judged from parallel passages in this *Mimar* and in Abucara's Greek work (*Opuscula* XXV, PG 97, 1560 C–1561 B), in the latter of which the interlocutor is explicitly described as a Muslim. Consequently, in the argument quoted, the Muslim interlocutor is already assumed to deny the literalness of anthropomorphisms, and consequently that argument cannot be taken to be the source of the denial of anthropomorphism as well as the reality of attributes among Muslims.

regard to the Word of God in the sense of the pre-existent Koran, on which their view corresponds to that of Arianism on the Word of God in the sense of the pre-existent Christ, will be discussed later in a section of the chapter on the Koran.

Since the arguments used by the Muʿtazilites for the denial of the reality of attributes were based upon their own particular conception of the meaning of "eternity" and of the meaning of the "unity of God," the Attributists, in their refutation of the Muʿtazilites, attack the Muʿtazilite conception of the meaning of these two terms.

First, they reject the Muʿtazilite claim that eternity means deity. To quote: "Your argument that if a real attribute is eternal it must be God is a bare assertion and is subject to dispute, and your assertion that eternity is a description most peculiar to God is an assertion for which there is no demonstration." [24] This exchange of opinion between the Muʿtazilites and the Attributists with regard to eternity is, in its historical context, a debate over the question whether to accept the established Christian view, inherited from Philo, that eternity spells deity. For the Church Fathers, as we have seen, without any recorded opposition, adopted this Philonic view, so that John of Damascus, in a debate supposed to be held between a Christian and a Muslim, makes the Christian force the Muslim to admit that the Word of God is uncreated, that is, eternal, and then, on the basis of this admission, forces him to admit that the Word of God is God, on the ground that "everything that is not created, but uncreated, is God." [25] The Muʿtazilites accept this Christian principle and hence argue that the attributes of the Attributists must be Gods, whereas the Attributists reject this Christian conception of eternity and hence refute the Muʿtazilite argument. It must, however, be remarked that while the orthodox, on the basis of their denial of the identity of eternity with deity, admit the existence of eternal attributes which are adjoined

[24] *Nihāyat*, p. 201, ll. 6–8.

[25] *Disputatio Christiani et Saraceni* (PG 94, 1586 A); cf. below, p. 310.

to the essence of God and inseparable therefrom, they do not thereby admit the existence of an antemundane eternal matter conceived as something apart from God.[26] Similarly, while the Muʿtazilites, on the basis of their identification of eternity with deity, do not admit the existence of eternal attributes which are inseparable from God,[27] they do admit the existence of an eternal antemundane matter which is separate from God and subject to His action upon it.[28]

Second, they reject the Muʿtazilite rigid conception of the unity of God. On this point, there was no unanimity of opinion in Christianity. The heretical Christian Sabellians and Arians, as we have seen, insisted upon this Philonic conception of the absolute unity of God. Orthodox Christianity, however, rejected this Philonic principle. Now the Muʿtazilites, as we have seen, followed the heretical Sabellians and Arians on this point. Orthodox Islam, however, followed orthodox Christianity. Accordingly, just as the Muʿtazilites rejected the reality of attributes by arguments by which Christian heretics rejected the reality of the second and third persons of the Trinity, so the orthodox Muslims defended the reality of attributes by arguments by which Christian orthodoxy defended the reality of the second and third persons. The orthodox Christian defense of the reality of the second and third persons of the Trinity consisted in rejecting the Philonic conception of the absolute unity of God and by maintaining that the unity of God is only a relative kind of unity, a conception of unity which does not exclude from God, who is one, the composition of three elements which from eternity existed together and were never separated.[29] So also the orthodox Muslim defense of the reality of attributes, as it was ultimately given expression by Ghazālī, reduces itself to an insistence upon a relative conception of the unity of God, which does not exclude its being internally composed of real attributes which existed together from eternity and

[26] Cf. below, pp. 359 ff. [27] Cf. below, pp. 133 ff. [28] Cf. below, pp. 359 ff.
[29] Cf. *The Philosophy of the Church Fathers*, I, pp. 311 ff.

were never separated. Thus, starting out with his own view that the description of God as "the necessary of existence" means only a denial of the dependence of God upon some cause of His existence, Ghazālī addresses himself to "the philosophers," who deny the existence of eternal attributes in God, as follows: "If the expression 'the necessary of existence' is, as it should be, taken by you to mean that which has no efficient cause, then what reason have you to derive therefrom that God has no attributes? Why should it be impossible to say that just as the essence of Him who is necessary of existence is eternal and has no efficient cause, so also His attribute exists with Him from eternity and has no efficient cause?" [30] and "just as the mind is capable of the conception of an eternal Being who has no cause for His existence, so it is also capable of the conception of an eternal Being endowed with attributes, who has no cause for the existence of both His essence and His attributes." [31]

And so, the views of the orthodox Muslims and the Muʿtazilites on the problem of attributes, as well as the arguments employed by them, correspond exactly to the views of orthodox Christians and the heretical Sabellians on the question of the persons of the Word and the Holy Spirit in the Trinity. The issue between the Attributists and the Antiattributists was thus clearly defined. It was an issue whether the unity of God was absolute or only relative. To the Attributists the unity of God was a relative unity, and hence they assumed in God the existence from eternity of real attributes. To the Antiattributists the unity of God was an absolute unity, and hence the terms attributed to God were mere names. There were, however, some modified views among the Attributists as well as some modified views among the Antiattributists. Among the Attributists, there were some who, while believing in the reality of attributes, denied that they were uncreated. This we shall discuss later.[32] Among the Antiattributists there

[30] *Tahāfut al-Falāsifah* V, 7, p. 166, ll. 6–8.
[31] *Ibid.* VI, 12.
[32] Cf. below, pp. 143–146.

were some who, while denying that attributes were real things, denied also that they were mere names and advanced a theory known as that of modes. This, too, we shall discuss later.[33] Others among the Antiattributists made an exception of certain terms predicated of God and treated them as things which are real and created. The terms treated by them in such an exceptional manner are (1) "knowledge," (2) "will," and (3) "word." This we shall discuss now.

The exceptional nature of the term "knowledge" is ascribed to Jahm. On the problem of attributes in general, Jahm is said to agree with the Muʿtazilites in denying their existence.[34] But, with regard to knowledge, he is reported in several sources to have said that "God's knowledge is originated (*muḥdath*)," [35] or that it is "distinct from God and originated (*muḥdath*) or created (*maḫlūḳ*)," [36] or that it is something "originated (*ḥādith*) not in an abode (*lā fī maḥall*)." [37] What he means by its being created not in an abode is that it is a created incorporeal being outside God. In contrast to this, as we shall see,[38] Jahm considers God's created word, that is to say, the Koran, as having been created by God in an abode, where by "abode" is meant the Preserved Tablet in heaven.

The first about whom the exceptional nature of the term "will" is reported is Abū al-Hudhayl. On the problem of attributes in general, Abū al-Hudhayl held a view, which, according to Shahrastānī, anticipated Abū Hāshim's theory of modes.[39] But with respect to "will," it is reported in one source that "he assumes wills (*irādāt*) without an abode, whereby God is a willing being." [40] From other sources,

[33] Cf. below, pp. 167 ff.

[34] *Milal*, p. 60, ll. 7–8.

[35] *Maḳālāt*, p. 280, l. 3; cf. *Farḳ*, p. 199, l. 10 (*ḥādith*).

[36] *Fiṣal* II, p. 126, l. 19. Ibn Ḥazm mentions also others who held the same view as Jahm about "knowledge."

[37] *Milal*, p. 60, l. 11. The Arabic term *maḥall*, as I have suggested, reflects Plato's χώρα and ἕδρα in *Timaeus* 52 A (cf. my paper, "Goichon's Three Books on Avicenna's Philosophy," *The Moslem World*, 31: 35–36 (1941).

[38] Cf. below, pp. 266–267 and 269.

[39] *Milal*, p. 34, ll. 19–20; cf. below, pp. 179–181.

[40] *Ibid.*, l. 20–p. 35, l. 1.

we gather that any one of these wills is an "origination" (*ḥudūth*) [41] and that it does not exist in God.[42] The will of God is thus neither a mere word predicated of God nor an eternal real attribute within God; it rather exists as an incorporeal real being created by God outside himself. We are told that "Abū al-Hudhayl was the first to express this view, in which others later followed him." [43] The same view is ascribed also to Jubbā'ī and his son Abū Hāshim.[44] Baghdādī ascribes it to the Muʿtazilites of Baṣra.[45] Later, this view is ascribed by Murtaḍā to the Muʿtazilites in general.[46]

With regard to the third exceptional attribute, "word," Abū al-Hudhayl, again, is the first to have dealt with it. It is reported of him that he divided the term "word" (*kalām*), attributed in the Koran to God, into two kinds. One kind is the word (*ḳaul*) "Be" which God says to a thing when he is about to create it. The other kind is the word in the sense of "command (*amr*), prohibition, narration, and inquiry," which God through the Prophet in the Koran addresses to man. The first kind of word is described as "the creative command" (*amr al-takwīn*); the second kind is described as "the obligative command" (*amr al-taklīf*). While both these kinds of word or command are created, according to Abū al-Hudhayl, the creative word or command is created not in an abode, that is to say, it is a created incorporeal being, whereas the obligative word or command, that is to say, the Koran, is created in an abode, where by "abode" is again meant the Preserved Tablet in heaven.[47]

How all those who denied the reality of attributes happen to make an exception of these three attributes of "knowledge," "will," and "word," endowing them with an incorporeal, though created, reality, would seem to need an ex-

[41] *Farḳ*, p. 109, l. 3.

[42] *Maḳālāt*, p. 190, ll. 2–4; p. 364, l. 2; but some of his followers take it to exist in God (*ibid*., p. 190, l. 2).

[43] *Milal*, p. 35, ll. 1–2.

[44] *Ibid*., p. 54, l. 9.

[45] *Farḳ*, p. 217, ll. 6–12.

[46] Cf. Horten, *Probleme*, p. 125.

[47] *Milal*, p. 35, ll. 2–4; *Farḳ*, p. 108, ll. 15–18.

planation. Certainly they could not have come by it on purely religious grounds, for on purely religious grounds there was no more reason to maintain a belief in a created real incorporeal "knowledge" or "will" or "word" than in that of the other attributes. They undoubtedly must have come by it on some other ground. What was that ground?

The ground, we should like to suggest, was a certain version of Neoplatonism which had drifted into Islam by that time, perhaps by mere hearsay, and was adopted by some of its thinkers and adjusted to their own particular religious beliefs.

It happens that among the early protagonists of Neoplatonism there were those who attempted to interpose between the One and the Intelligence of Plotinus some other hypostases or principles. Proclus interposes between them several hypostases,[48] each of which is said by him to possess a "divine knowledge"[49] (*γνῶσις θεία*) as something peculiarly belonging to it as a property.[50] Amelius, as quoted by Proclus,[51] distinguishes within the Intelligence itself three Intelligences,[52] thus interposing between the One or God and the Intelligence in the system of Plotinus two other Intelligences. Of these two interposing Intelligences, one is described by him as creating by will (*βουλήσει*) and the other as creating by command (*ἐπιτάξει*).[53] This interpretation of Plotinus by Proclus is reflected in the tradition reported later by Shahrastānī that according to both Plato and Aristotle, that is to say, according to Neoplatonism, will (*irādah*) and production (*fi'l*) are forms which have real existence (*ḳā'imtān*),[54] and that both of them come into existence from God without any intermediary.[55]

[48] *Plat. Theol.* III, 1.

[49] *Inst. Theol.* 113.

[50] *Ibid.*, 114.

[51] *Ibid.*, 124.

[52] Proclus, *In Timaeum* 93 D.

[53] *Ibid.* 110 A.

[54] *Milal*, p. 289, ll. 5–6.

[55] Based upon Shahrastānī's subsequent statement (*Milal*, p. 289, ll. 12–15) that Parmenides the Younger agrees with Plato and Aristotle with regard to "will," maintaining that it comes into existence (*takūn*) from God without any intermediary, though he disagrees with them with regard to "production," maintaining that it is through an intermediary.

Here, then, we have two philosophic views which maintain the existence of various real incorporeal beings described either as having "knowledge" or as creating "by will" or as creating "by command." We may assume that when these two philosophic views reached the Arabs, the real incorporeal beings came to be described simply as "knowledge" (γνῶσις; Arabic: *ʿilm*) and "will" (βούλησις, Arabic: *irādah*) and "command" (ἐπίταγμα, Arabic: *amr*), the last of which in Arabic, as we have seen, is interchangeable with "word" (*kalām*). With this philosophic sanction, it can be easily seen how the view that the terms "knowledge" and "will" and "word" stand for three incorporeal beings which have real existence had penetrated even among those Muslim thinkers who on the whole denied the reality of attributes. But, inasmuch as these Muslim thinkers could not accept the eternity of these three attributes, for this would be against their contention that real attributes which are eternal mean a plurality of gods, they made them created incorporeal beings.

III. Created Attributes

Besides the theories of eternal attributes and the denial of attributes, there was also a theory of created attributes. The exponents of this theory are the Rāfiḍah and the Karrāmiyyah.

Of the Rāfidah, there are various reports about the belief of some of its subsects in created attributes. (1) With regard to the subsect named Hishamiyyah, their founder Hishām b. al-Ḥakam, as reported by Ashʿarī[1] and Baghdādī[2] and Shahrastānī,[3] believed that only the attribute of knowledge is created. In these three reports, two things are to be noted. First, in all of them, the created knowledge as held by Hishām b. al-Ḥakam is described as an attribute in God, whence it differs from the created knowledge as held by Jahm b. Ṣafwān,

[1] *Maḳālāt*, p. 493, l. 15 – p. 494, l. 1; cf. p. 37, ll. 8–10; *Intiṣār* 74, p. 85, ll. 15–17.

[2] *Farḳ*, p. 49, ll. 9–12.

[3] *Milal*, p. 141, ll. 12–13.

which, as we have seen, is something incorporeal created by God outside Himself.[4] When, therefore, Ibn Ḥazm, on the basis of information orally communicated to him, speaks of both Jahm b. Ṣafwān and Hishām b. al-Ḥakam as believing that knowledge is created by God outside Himself,[5] he quite evidently either misunderstood his informant or was misled by him. Second, while all these three reports mention knowledge as the attribute which was held by Hishām to be created, two of these reports differ as to whether he held the same view with regard to some other attributes. According to Shahrastānī, "Hishām's view with regard to power and life is not like his view with regard to knowledge, for he did not assert the originatedness of these two attributes," [6] Ashʿarī says that "some people report of Hishām that he asserted that God is living and powerful from eternity, but others deny that he said that." [7] (2) With regard to the subsect named Zurāriyyah, Ashʿarī reports that they "maintain that from eternity God continued to be not hearing and not knowing and not seeing until He created these attributes for Himself." [8] In Baghdādī, two reports describe the Zurāriyyah as well as their founder Zurārah b. Aʿyun, as believing that "life and power and knowledge and will and hearing and seeing are all created attributes." [9] In Shahrastānī a report on Zurārah reads that he "agreed with Hishām b. al-Ḥakam with regard to the originatedness of the knowledge of God, but went beyond him in asserting the originatedness of God's power and life and His other attributes, so that before He created these attributes He was not knowing, not powerful, not living, not hearing, not seeing, not willing, and not speaking." [10] (3) In Ashʿarī there is a report which reads that "a fourth subsect of the Rāfiḍah maintain that from eternity God continued to be not living then He became living." [11]

[4] Cf. above, p. 140.
[5] *Fiṣal* II, p. 126, ll. 18–20.
[6] *Milal*, p. 141, ll. 14–15.
[7] *Maḳālāt*, p. 38, ll. 3–4.
[8] *Ibid.*, p. 36, ll. 3–5.
[9] *Farḳ*, p. 52, ll. 10–14; p. 323, l. 18 – p. 324, l. 1.
[10] *Milal*, p. 142, ll. 11–14.
[11] *Maḳālāt*, p. 37, ll. 1–2.

Of the Karrāmiyyah, Baghdādī says in one part of his *Farḳ* that "it was from the principle [of the Zurāriyyah plus the Baṣra Ḳadariyyah] that the Karrāmiyyah derived their view of the originatedness of the utterance (*ḳaul*) of God and His will and His perceptions [of things as they come to be]." [12] To these originated utterance and will of God and also to what Baghdādī describes as God's generated perceptions the Karrāmiyyah, according to a report by Shahrastānī, applied the term "attributes." [12a] Then from Baghdādī's elaborate description of the view of the Karrāmiyyah in a later part of his *Farḳ*, supplemented by a parallel description in Shahrastānī, an orderly account of their view of created attributes can be pieced together.

In God, according to them, there is an eternal power (*ḳudrah*) to create, as well as to do all the other things which He does in the world.[13] This eternal power to create is also called creativeness (*ḫalḳiyyah*),[14] and so is also His eternal power to do all the other things He does in the world similarly expressed by an appropriate abstract noun. It is because of this eternal power to create that God had been a Creator even before anything was created,[15] that is to say, God is called eternal Creator proleptically.[16]

In contrast to the mere power to create which existed from eternity, the act-of-creation (*al-ḫalḳ*), as well as any other act-of-doing, originates in God through that eternal power,[17] and it subsists in God. By the act-of-creation is meant God's utterance (*ḳaul*) of the word "Be" (*kun*),[18] which is His command to anything not merely to come into existence but to come into existence according to a certain manner precon-

[12] *Ibid.*, p. 52, ll. 15–16.

[12a] *Nihāyat*, p. 114, ll. 2–12.

[13] *Farḳ*, p. 206, ll. 13–14; *Nihāyat*, p. 114, ll. 9–10; *Milal*, p. 81, ll. 6, 8, 10, where the word "eternal" is omitted.

[14] *Farḳ*, p. 206, l. 12; *Nihāyat*, p. 114, l. 18.

[15] *Farḳ*, p. 206, ll. 11 ff.

[16] Cf. below, p. 295.

[17] *Farḳ*, p. 206, l. 14.

[18] *Ibid.*, p. 204, ll. 14–15.

ceived by God.[19] This utterance of the word "Be," a word which in Arabic consists of two consonants, *kāf* and *nūn*, constitutes two of five attributes [20] which are created in the essence of God by that eternal power of His whenever He creates a body or an accident in the world.[21] The five attributes are: (1) a will (*irādah*) to produce the object to be produced; (2) the letter *kāf* and (3) the letter *nūn*, which are the two consonants of the Arabic word for "Be"; (4) vision, with which God will see the produced object, for if that vision were not created in Him, He could not see that object; (5) hearing, with which He will hear the produced object, if it is audible.[22] To differentiate between that which is created and subsists in the essence of God and that which is created by God in the world, the former is described by the term *ḥādith* and the latter by the term *muḥdath*.[23]

In our earlier discussion of the other two theories of attributes, we have shown how the orthodox Muslim affirmation of attributes corresponds to the orthodox Christian conception of the reality of the second and third persons of the Trinity and how the Muʿtazilite denial of attributes corresponds to the Sabellian denial of the second and third persons of the Trinity.[24] We may now add that the belief in created attributes by the Rāfiḍah and the Karrāmiyyah corresponds to the Arian conception of the createdness of the second and third persons of the Trinity, except that the Arian created persons are extradeical, whereas the created attributes are intradeical.

[19] *Ibid.*, p. 205, ll. 1–2.

[20] The expression "five attributes (*ṣifāt*)" is used in *Nihāyat*, p. 114, l. 15, and p. 104, l. 11; cf. also reference to some of these five as "attributes" on p. 114, l. 4. In *Fark*, p. 204, l. 18, they are referred to as "many accidents," and so also on p. 205, ll. 1–3, the mention of the term *kun* is followed by the explanation "and this utterance by Himself consists of many letters, each one of which is an accident originating in Him."

[21] *Fark*, p. 204, l. 18.

[22] *Fark*, p. 205, ll. 1–5; *Nihāyat*, p. 114, ll. 15–16.

[23] *Nihāyat*, p. 104, l. 12 – 105, l. 1.

[24] Cf. above, p. 139.

IV. Modes

1. MUʿAMMAR'S MAʿNĀ *

The Muslim doctrine of attributes, being, as we have seen, a development of the Christian doctrine of the Trinity, is ultimately a development, through Philo's Logos, of the Platonic theory of ideas. The orthodox affirmation of the reality of attributes represents the orthodox Christian conception of the Trinity and hence the orthodox Christian modification of the Philonic interpretation of the Platonic ideas. The Muʿtazilite denial of the reality of attributes represents the Sabellian conception of the Trinity and hence the Albinian interpretation of the Platonic ideas. But while all these are Platonic ideas by heredity, they are not always so by function. In Plato, the function of ideas was twofold, that of exemplar and that of cause. The attributes and pre-existent Koran are not exactly exemplars nor are they exactly causes of creation, though they are perhaps not altogether devoid of these functions. Still they are traceable to Platonic ideas. They are descendants of those denizens of a world beyond ours which in Plato were called ideas and which among the interpreters of Plato — Aristotle, Philo, Albinus, and Plotinus — became an object of discussion as to whether they were within God or outside of God and, if the latter, whether they were coexistent with God or brought into existence by Him.[1]

In Islam, so far, these descendants of the Platonic ideas knew not their father nor those who quarreled among themselves about their patrimony. Whatever reflection of the Platonic ideas may be discerned in the discussions about attributes or about the Koran during the early part of the

* Reprinted with additions and revisions from *Arabic and Islamic Studies in Honor of Hamilton A. R. Gibb* (1965), pp. 673–688.

[1] Cf. *The Philosophy of the Church Fathers*, I, pp. 252–286, and "Extradeical and Intradeical Interpretations of Platonic Ideas" in *Religious Philosophy*, pp. 27–68.

eighth century comes not directly from Greek philosophy but from the Church Fathers. But in the latter part of the eighth century, Greek philosophic works began to be translated. Plato's *Timaeus* was translated before 806, the *Republic* before 873, and the *Sophist* before 911. Other early sources of Platonism accessible to the Muslims were Porphyry's *Isagoge*, which was translated before 763; an abridgment of Plotinus' *Enneads*, known as the *Theology of Aristotle*, which was translated in 840; Aristotle's *Metaphysics*, which was translated before 911, probably together with Alexander's Commentary on it; and pseudo-Plutarch's *De Placitis Philosophorum*, which was translated before 912.[2] Undoubtedly, philosophic knowledge was transmitted orally to Muslim theologians even before philosophic works were translated, and it continued to be transmitted orally even after the work of translation had begun, as all this may be seen from the appearance of philosophic terms and phrases and apothegms and excerpts in the reports of the Muslim teachers of the eighth century. This new philosophic knowledge in its earliest appearance in the eighth century, and even for some time afterwards, was not as yet differentiated according to the various opposing schools of Greek philosophy to which it belonged. Statements of philosophers, however diverse in origin, were all treated as segments of a uniform system of thought called philosophy, as distinguished from another system of thought based upon the Koran and tradition. It was an eclecticism due at first to a lack of knowledge, which in the course of time grew into a conscious attempt at harmonization, such as found in Alfarabi's work entitled *Kitāb al-Jamʿ bayn Raʾy al-Ḥakīmayn Aflaṭūn al-Ilāhī wa-Arisṭūṭālīs*, "Book of the Agreement between the Opinions of Two Philosophers, the Divine Plato and Aristotle."

The influence of this new philosophic knowledge is soon discerned in the problem of attributes. It is first discerned in

[2] Cf. Steinschneider, *Die arabischen Übersetzungen aus dem Griechischen* (1897), *s. v.*

the ninth century in the various formulae by which the Muʿtazilites, in their denial of the existence in God of real attributes, sought to express their interpretation of the terms which are predicated of God. This will be dealt with by us later, in the section on the semantic aspect of the problem of divine attributes. Then it is discerned in the theory of modes, which appeared in the tenth century. This will be dealt with by us, again, later, in the section on Abū Hāshim's *aḥwāl*. But Abū Hāshim's theory of modes, as we shall see, is only a revision of Muʿammar's theory of *maʿnā* in the ninth century, though in itself Muʿammar's theory may have no direct connection with the problem of attributes. We shall, therefore, prior to our discussion of the theory of modes, take up in this chapter Muʿammar's theory of *maʿnā* and try to unfold the processes of reasoning by which, under the influence of this new philosophic knowledge derived from a variety of sources, Muʿammar has arrived at his theory of *maʿnā*.

I shall first reproduce in chronological order the necessary reports on Muʿammar's theory of *maʿnā* and then I shall discuss them.

The oldest reports on Muʿammar's theory of *maʿnā* are in Ḫayyāṭ's *Intiṣār* and Ashʿarī's *Maḳālāt*.

Ḫayyāṭ first quotes Ibn al-Rāwandī as saying that Muʿammar "maintains that no single act is produced in the world but that there are produced simultaneously a thousand times thousand acts; yea, an infinity of other acts." [3] He then explains it: "Know — and may God teach you what is good — that this view, which the author of the book [Ibn al-Rāwandī] reports as being that of Muʿammar, is the theory with regard to the *maʿānī*. The meaning of this theory may be explained as follows. Having observed that of two contiguous bodies at rest one begins to move, while the other does not, Muʿammar inferred that a *maʿnā* must inevitably abide in the one and not in the other, and it is on account of

[3] *Intiṣār* 34, p. 46, ll. 11–12.

that *maʿnā* that the former is moved, for were it not so, then the one would not be more capable of motion than the other. He further said: If this reasoning is sound, there must inevitably also be another *maʿnā* on account of which the motion abides in one of the bodies rather than in the other. He again said: Were it not so, then the abiding of the motion in one of the bodies would not be more appropriate than the abiding of it in the other. So also, he went on to say, if I were asked concerning the [second] *maʿnā* why it was the cause of the abiding of the motion in one of the bodies and not in the other, my answer would be: It is on account of another *maʿnā*. He finally said: So also, if I were further asked [the same question] concerning this [third] *maʿnā*, my answer would be with regard to this *maʿnā* like my answer with regard to the preceding *maʿnā* [and so on to infinity]." [4]

Two observations are to be made about Ḫayyāṭ's explanation. (1) The motion spoken of in it is a motion caused by some inner cause in the body of that which is set in motion, such, for instance, as what Aristotle calls the motion of generation and corruption in the category of substance or the motion of growth and diminution in the category of quantity or the motion of the various alterations in the category of quality or the natural upward and downward motions of things in the category of place. (2) As described in the report, two questions are raised by Muʿammar, to which two answers are given by him, in each of which he makes use of the *maʿnā*. The first question is, why a body at rest begins to move. To this the answer given is that it is set in motion by a *maʿnā*. The second question is, why of two contiguous bodies at rest, each of them presumably possessing a *maʿnā*, one is moved by its *maʿnā* at a certain particular time, while the other remains at rest at that particular time, though presumably it will be moved by its *maʿnā* at some other time. To this the answer

[4] *Ibid.*, ll. 16–24. My bracketed addition here is required by the opening statement of this report as well as by the other reports to be quoted. The brief reference to Muʿammar's theory of *maʿnā* in *Intiṣār* 9, p. 22, ll. 18 ff. is discussed below.

given is that this is due to an infinite series of *maʿānī*, for though such an infinite series of *maʿānī* would presumably exist in both these contiguous bodies, it would differ in them in accordance with the difference in the time of the originations of these bodies. The combination of the two mentioned uses of the *maʿnā* leads to the conclusion that any motion that takes place in any particular body at any particular time is caused by an infinite series of *maʿānī*. It is this conclusion, as briefly formulated by Ibn al-Rāwandī in terms of acts, that is quoted by Ḫayyāṭ at the beginning of his report.

More fully is the same theory reported by Ashʿarī. "Some say that a body, when it is moved, is moved only on account of a *maʿnā*, which is the [cause of the] motion. Were it not for this, there would be no reason for this body, rather than for another body, to be moved, nor would there be any reason for this body to be moved at the time at which it is moved rather than to have been moved at some prior time. Since this is so, it may similarly be reasoned with regard to the motion that, if there was no *maʿnā* on account of which it was the motion of the body moved, there would be no reason for it to be the motion of that body rather than the motion of some other body. And so this *maʿnā* is a *maʿnā* of the motion of the body moved on account of still another *maʿnā*, but there is no totality and sum to the *maʿānī*; and they take place at a single time. The same holds true of black and white, that is, of the fact that it is the black of one body rather than of another and that it is the white of one body rather than that of another. The same holds true of the difference (*muḫālafah*) between blackness and whiteness and similarly, according to them, does it hold true of other genera and accidents,[5] that is

[5] In the expression here "of other genera (*al-ajnās*) and accidents," the other accidents quite evidently mean accidents in addition to "blackness and whiteness" mentioned before. As for the other genera, it refers to "same," which is mentioned later together with "different" but is not mentioned before when he mentioned "difference." The description here of "different" and "same" as "genera" reflects Plato's description of "same" and "other" as γένη, "genera," in *Sophist* 254 E. But, while the term "gen-

to say, when two accidents are different (*iḫtalafā*) or are the same (*ittifaḳā*), inevitably one must assume the existence of *maʿānī* to which there is no totality. It is also their claim that the *maʿānī* to which there is no totality are produced by an act of the place in which they abide. The same similarly holds true of the predicates 'living' and 'dead,' for when we predicate of a person that he is living or dead, we must inevitably assume an infinite number of *maʿānī* which abide in him, for life cannot be life to him rather than to another except on account of a *maʿnā*, and that *maʿnā* [cannot be the *maʿnā* of that life rather than of another life except] on account of a *maʿnā*, and so on to infinity. This is the view of Muʿammar." [6]

This report, which is introduced with the words "Some say" and closes with the words "This is the view of Muʿam-

---

era" as a description of "different" and "same" is undoubtedly borrowed here from the *Sophist*, the terms meant to be included here under "genera" are not taken from the *Sophist*. To begin with, one of the genera here is "difference" (*muḫālafah*), for which the Greek would be διαφορά, whereas the corresponding one of the genera in the *Sophist* is "other" (θάτερον). Then, the expression "other genera" here quite evidently alludes to some genera in addition to the single other genus "same" mentioned thereafter, but among the five genera enumerated in the *Sophist*, namely, being, motion, rest, same, and other, there is none which could be added here to "same." The allusion to several genera here in the expression "other genera" is to the terms "same," "other," "different," "like," "contrary" discussed by Aristotle in *Metaphysics* V, 9–10. The Arabic translation of these chapters in the *Metaphysics* is missing in Bouyges' edition of *Averroes: Tafsir Ma baʿd at-Tabiʿat* (1938–48), but in other parts of the *Metaphysics*, of which Bouyges' edition contains the Arabic translations, we get the Arabic for the following Greek terms:

(1) αἱ αὐταί, *muttafiḳah*, "the same" (III, 4, 1000a, 21, Text. 15);
(2) τὸ ὅμοιον, *al-mithl*, "the like" (V, 15, 1021a, 10, Text. 20);
(3) διαφορά, *al-iḫtilāf*, "difference" (X, 3, 1054b, 23, Text. 12);
(4) ἑτερότης, *al-ghayriyyah*, "otherness" (ibid.);
(5) ἡ ἐναντίωσις, *al-ḍiddiyyah*, "contrariety" (*ibid.*, 32, Text. 13).

The Arabic terms, it will be noticed, are the same as those used here by Ashʿarī and later by Shahrastānī and Rāzī (cf. below at nn. 8 and 24).

[6] *Maḳālāt*, p. 372, l. 2 – p. 373, l. 2. Again, an allusion to his theory of *maʿnā* is to be found in Muʿammar's statement, quoted by Ashʿarī, that "God creates a creation by a cause and there is a cause to that cause, but there is no limit and totality to the causes" (*Maḳālāt*, p. 253, ll. 3–4; cf. p. 364, ll. 12–13, and p. 511, ll. 8–9) and also in his statement, again quoted by Ashʿarī, that "to that which ceases to exist there is a destruction and to this destruction there is another destruction, and so on without limit" (*Maḳālāt*, p. 367, ll. 5–6).

mar," makes it quite clear that Muʿammar's theory of *maʿnā*, originally presented as an explanation of the difference in bodies with reference to motion, was taken by those "some" of his followers to have meant to serve also as an explanation of the difference or otherness or contrariety, as well as of the sameness and likeness, in bodies with reference to accidents in general, among which they included as accidents the predicates "living and dead," for, while "life" is said by Aristotle to be a "property" of "living being,"[6a] the duration of life in any living being, which quite evidently is meant here by the term "living" in the contrasting predicates "living and dead," is to be considered as an accident in individual living beings, whose various durations of life are determined, according to Aristotle, by various causes.[6b]

The same view is variously reported in the name of Muʿammar by later authors, such as Baghdādī, Ibn Ḥazm, and Shahrastānī. Baghdādī reproduces Muʿammar's view in two places in his *Farḳ*, and in one of the places his reproduction bears a resemblance to that which occurs later in Shahrastānī's *Milal*, which would make it seem that either Shahrastānī drew upon Baghdādī or Baghdādī and Shahrastānī drew upon a common source.

Both Baghdādī and Shahrastānī start with a general restatement of the main conclusion of Muʿammar's view, which in Baghdādī reads that "every species of accidents existing in bodies is infinite in number,"[7] and in Shahrastānī reads that "accidents are infinite in every species."[8] The statement here by both Baghdādī and Shahrastānī that accidents, according to Muʿammar, are infinite in number quite evidently refers to their statement subsequently that, according to Muʿammar, each accident is caused by an infinite chain of *maʿānī*. The inference, therefore, to be drawn from this is that the term "accidents" is used by them here in the sense of *maʿānī*. A

[6a] *Top.* V, 5, 134a, 32, and cf. *Soph. Elench.* 5, 167b, 33.
[6b] *De Long. et Brev. Vitae* I–VI; *De Respiratione* XVII–XVIII.
[7] *Farḳ*, p. 137, ll. 16–17.
[8] *Milal*, p. 46, l. 15.

justification for their description of *ma'ānī* as accidents would seem to be found in the fact that one of the formal definitions of accident is that "it is always subsisting in a subject," [9] plus the fact that the infinite *ma'ānī*, according to Mu'ammar, subsist in the same subject as the accidents which are produced by them, so that it was quite natural to conclude that the *ma'ānī* also could be described as accidents.

Then both Baghdādī and Shahrastānī restate the reasoning by which Mu'ammar was led to his conclusion. In Baghdādī, Mu'ammar is represented as trying to show how motion, color, taste, smell, and any other accident require the existence of an infinite chain of *ma'ānī* in the subject of the motion and color and taste and smell as well as of any other accident.[10] In Shahrastānī, he is represented simply as saying something to the effect that every accident requires the existence of a *ma'nā* and that this leads to an uninterrupted concatination (*al-tasalsul*). In Shahrastānī, however, there is the additional statement that "on account of this view, Mu'ammar and his followers were called the partisans of *ma'ānī* (*aṣḥāb al-ma'ānī*)." [11]

Finally, after these two passages quoted from Baghdādī and Shahrastānī, there are in both of them passages which reflect a common source. In Baghdādī the passage reads: "Al-Ka'bī, in his treatise, reports in the name of Mu'ammar that motion, according to him, differs from rest only in virtue of a *ma'nā* outside of it and in the same way rest differs from motion in virtue of a *ma'nā* outside of it, and that these two *ma'ānī* differ from two *ma'ānī* other than they. This reasoning, according to him, may go on to infinity." [12] The parallel passage in Shahrastānī reads: "And he [=Mu'ammar] adds thereto saying: motion differs from rest not in virtue of its essence but only in virtue of a *ma'nā* which necessitates the difference." [13] Shahrastānī then continues: "By the same token,

[9] Porphyry, *Isagoge*, p. 13, l. 5.
[10] *Fark*, p. 137, l. 17–p. 138, l. 4.
[11] *Milal*, p. 46, ll. 16–17.
[12] *Fark*, p. 183, ll. 4–8.
[13] *Milal*, p. 46, ll. 17–18.

the otherness (*mughāyarah*) between like things and the likeness (*mumāthalah*) between them and the contrariety (*taḍādd*) between two contrary things are all, according to his opinion, due to a *maʿnā*."[14] This additional statement, which may be based upon the same treatise of Kaʿbī, corresponds to the expression "other genera" used in the passage quoted above from Ashʿarī,[15] which we have explained to mean the extension by some followers of Muʿammar of their master's theory of *maʿnā* from its original use as an explanation of the difference in bodies with reference to motion to its use as an explanation of "otherness" or "contrariety" as well as "sameness" and "likeness" in bodies with reference to accidents in general.[16]

In another place in his *Farḳ*, Baghdādī represents Muʿammar as trying to show how the assumption of the existence of an infinite series of *maʿānī* is required in order to explain why one person rather than another possesses a certain special kind of knowledge.[17]

Ibn Ḥazm reproduces Muʿammar's theory of *maʿnā* in two places in his *Fiṣal*. In one of these places, he represents Muʿammar as arguing from motion and rest and from the differences between accidents for the existence of *maʿānī*, but, in the course of his exposition, he remarks that the *maʿānī* are "existent things" (*ashyāʾ maujūdah*), and hence he says that from this Muʿammar and his followers "conclude the existence in the world of an infinite number of things (*ashyāʾ*) at any given time."[18] In the other place in his *Fiṣal*, he merely reports of Muʿammar as saying that "in the world there are existent things (*ashyāʾ maujūdah*) to which there is no limit . . . and to which there is no measure and no number."[19] In both these places he thus uses *ashyāʾ* as the equivalent of *maʿānī*. Similarly, when he describes the persons of the Christian Trinity as *ashyāʾ*,[20] he uses *ashyāʾ* as the equivalent of *maʿānī*, as these

[14] *Ibid.*, l. 19.

[15] Cf. above n. 5.

[16] Cf. above, pp. 152–153.

[17] *Farḳ*, p. 181, ll. 12–17.

[18] *Fiṣal* V, p. 56, ll. 15–22.

[19] *Ibid.* IV, p. 194, ll. 2–4.

[20] *Fiṣal* I, p. 49, l. 1; cf. IV, p. 207, l. 22.

two terms are also used by Yaḥyā b. ʿAdī.[21] Similarly, also, when Ashʿarī is quoted by him as calling the attributes *ashyāʾ*,[22] the term *ashyāʾ* is used as the equivalent of *maʿānī*, for, in Shahrastānī, Ashʿarī is quoted as calling them *maʿānī*.[23]

Drawing upon all these sources, Rāzī (d. 1209) presents the theory of *maʿnā* as follows: "Some of them maintain that two things which are mutually other (*al-ghayrayni*) are mutually other by means of a *maʿnā* and the same holds true of two like things (*al-mathalāni*) or two contrary things (*al-ḍiddāni*) or two different things (*al-muḫtalifāni*). In proof of this they argue that the statement that black and white are black and white does not mean the same as the statement that they are mutually other and different and contrary, and in proof that the two statements are not the same they argue from the fact that otherness and difference and contrariety occur also in other things [besides blackness and whiteness]. It is thus evident that otherness is not something negative: it is rather something positive; and so it has been established that two things which are mutually other (*al-mutaghāyirayni*) are mutually other by means of a *maʿnā*. By the same token two things which are alike correspond to each other (*muḳābilāni*) by means of a *maʿnā*. They then argue that this *maʿnā* must inevitably be other than anything else, whence it follows that its otherness from anything else is [due to] to a [second] *maʿnā* existing by means of the [first] *maʿnā*. Now this [second] *maʿnā* must inevitably be either like another *maʿnā* or other than it and different from it. But [as shown before] its likeness as well as its otherness and difference is [due to] a [third] *maʿnā* existing by means of the [second] *maʿnā*. And the same reasoning is to be applied to this *maʿnā* as it was to the one before it, whence there results the assertion of an infinite number of *maʿānī*." [24] Ṭūsī (d. 1273) in his comment upon this passage of Rāzī identifies the view described therein as that of "Muʿammar and others" and restates Rāzī's con-

[21] Cf. above, p. 117.

[22] *Ibid*. IV, p. 207, l. 13.

[23] *Nihāyat*, p. 181, l. 4.

[24] *Muḥaṣṣal*, p. 104, ll. 2–8.

cluding statement as a view which maintains that "accidents exist by means of accidents up to infinity," in which the *maʿānī* are thus called "accidents." [25]

From all this we gather that Muʿammar was troubled by the question why things differ from each other. The differences between things mentioned by him, according to the two earliest reports of his view, are motion and rest, blackness and whiteness, and life and death. According to one of these earliest reports, he was troubled also by the question as to what accounts for the difference between accidents and the sameness of accidents, mentioning especially the accidents of blackness and whiteness. The answer given by him is that things differ and accidents both differ and are the same because of what he calls *maʿnā*. This *maʿnā* is described by him as abiding in bodies, from within which it acts as the cause of motion and rest and all the other accidents of the bodies in which it abides. Muʿammar is further reported to have said that at any given moment that an accident is produced in a body by a *maʿnā*, there is behind that *maʿnā* an infinite chain of *maʿānī*. In later reports, the *maʿānī* are also called *ashyāʾ*, "things," and, evidently because they exist in bodies as their subject, they are also called "accidents."

We thus find that Muʿammar has raised a question, the like of which was not raised by any other of his contemporary Mutakallimūn, and this question is answered by him by an elaborate theory, which is couched in language bristling with terms easily recognizable as reflecting Greek philosophic terminology.

The first thing, then, we should like to know is how it happened that of all of his contemporaries Muʿammar alone was troubled by the question of why things are different or the same. All his contemporaries, we imagine, would simply say that this is how they are made by God. Why then did not Muʿammar say the same thing?

In attempting to explain this peculiarity about the question

[25] Ṭūsī on *Muḥaṣṣal*, p. 104, n. 2, ll. 1–2. Cf. above at nn. 7, 8, 9.

raised by Muʿammar, let us assemble all the bits of information that we have of Muʿammar's philosophy and see whether we cannot find among them something which impelled him to raise his question.

We know that Muʿammar, like nearly all the Mutakallimūn, was an atomist. In fact, he is reported to have believed that the atom itself is not a body,[26] but that eight atoms make up a body.[27] How atoms came into existence we are told in his name: they were created by God.[28] We are similarly told in his name how bodies come into existence — they are also created.[29] Accidents, however, we are told in his name, are not created by God [30] but that "when the atoms are aggregated, accidents follow by necessity; the atoms produce them by the necessity of [their] nature, each atom by its own self producing whatever accident resides in it," [31] or that accidents are "the action of substances (i. e., atoms) by their nature," [32] or that "any accident of a body comes from the action of the body by its nature." [33] From the combination of these passages we may gather that in every atom there resides a nature, and it is this nature that produces accidents when atoms are aggregated and form a body. Elsewhere Muʿammar says in effect that bodies are perceptible only through their accidents.[34] Among the accidents mentioned as being produced by the atoms when they are formed into a body or as being produced by the body formed out of atoms are "life," "death," "color," "taste," and "smell." [35] It can similarly be shown that "motion" is also an act of the body in accordance with its nature, for it is reported of him that, in opposition to those who said that the motion in a moving

[26] *Maḳālāt,* p. 307, ll. 10–12.

[27] *Ibid.,* p. 303, l. 9.

[28] *Ibid.,* p. 548, ll. 9–10.

[29] *Milal,* p. 46, ll. 3–4.

[30] *Maḳālāt,* p. 548, l. 10; *Fiṣāl* IV, p. 194, ll. 9–13; *Farḳ,* p. 136, l. 18–p. 137, l. 1; *Milal,* p. 46, ll. 3–4.

[31] *Maḳālāt,* p. 303, ll. 10–11.

[32] *Ibid.,* p. 548, l. 12.

[33] *Farḳ,* p. 136, l. 15; cf. *Milal,* p. 46, l. 4; *Fiṣal* IV, p. 194, ll. 12–13.

[34] *Maḳālāt,* p. 362, ll. 7–8: "Only accidents of a body are perceived; as for body, it cannot be perceived."

[35] *Ibid.,* p. 548, ll. 11–12; *Fiṣal* IV, p. 194, ll. 9–12.

body is produced by God, he maintained that "the moving body produces it within itself," [36] by which he quite evidently means that it produces it within itself in accordance with its nature, though, in the case of living beings, he says that their "motion and rest and aggregation and segregation" are "of the creations of bodies," not "by nature" (*ṭabʿan*) but "by choice" (*iḫtiyāran*). It is to be noted, however, that, while in these passages, as well as in the passages quoted above, Muʿammar speaks of both the motion and the rest of bodies, there is another passage where, evidently in opposition to the view current in the Kalam that "the modes of being (*al-akwān*) are motion and rest and aggregation and segregation," [37] he says that "all modes of being (*al-akwān*) consist of rest and that some of them are called motions only in language and not in truth." [38] It may be remarked that this denial of motion and its description as being only in language and not in truth reflect the statement in pseudo-Plutarch's *Placita* that "Parmenides, Melissus, and Zeno deny that there are any such things as generation and corruption, for they suppose that the All is immovable," [39] plus the distinction said to have been made by Parmenides between one part of philosophy which deals with "truth" and another which deals with "opinion." [40]

We thus know that, according to his own philosophy, no accident, whether motion or rest or color or taste or smell or life or death, is produced in bodies by God; all accidents are

[36] *Milal*, p. 46, ll. 4–6. So also the statement that Muʿammar "was accustomed to say that man has no action other than will (*al-irādah*) and that all the other accidents are the actions of bodies by nature" (*Farḳ*, p. 138, ll. 16–17) is to be understood to mean that in man accidents are the work of the body by will, whereas in inanimate things accidents are the work of the body by nature.

[37] *Irshād*, p. 10, ll. 9–10; *Moreh*, I, 73, Prop. 1; cf. M. Schreiner, *Der Kalam in der jüdischen Literatur* (1895), p. 45, n. 3.

[38] *Maḳālāt*, p. 347, ll. 9–10; cf. p. 355, ll. 1–2; Ibn Ḥazm, *Fiṣal* IV, p. 204, ll. 4–5.

[39] Diels, *Doxographi Graeci* I, 24, 1, p. 320a, ll. 11–13; Arabic translation in *Aristotelis De Anima et Plutarci De Placitis Philosophorum*, ed. Badawi, 1954, p. 120, ll. 14–15.

[40] Diogenes Laertius, *De Vita et Moribus Philosophorum* IX, 22.

produced by the nature of the atoms which make up bodies or, as he loosely also says, by the nature of bodies. With this his view as to the origin of accidents, the question, as was to be expected, occurred to him, What is that "nature" which in bodies formed of atoms produces such a variety of accidents? As we shall see later,[41] a similar question was raised by Naẓẓām, who, like Muʿammar, believed that things have a nature; his answer, however, is different.

This is the reason why Muʿammar was troubled by the question as to the origin of likenesses and differences in things occasioned by the variety of accidents.

The answer to this question, we shall now try to show, he found in the new philosophic knowledge which he had acquired either by reading or by hearsay.

From Aristotle's definition of nature as that which is "a certain principle and cause of motion and rest to that in which it is primarily inherent essentially and not according to accident" [42] he has gathered that any event in the world which Aristotle calls motion has an inner cause which he calls nature. This view is adopted by him and is expressed in his above-quoted various statements to the effect that bodies are moved by their nature.

But, though in those quoted statements Muʿammar makes use of Aristotle's terms "motion" and "nature," he differs from Aristotle in the meaning of both these terms.[42a] To Aristotle, with his belief in a matter conceived of as potentiality, motion is a transition from potentiality to actuality [43] and the inner cause of that transition, which he calls nature, is identified by him with form,[44] which form itself, in the continuous course of motion, is changed from being something actual with reference to a matter preceding it into being something potential

[41] Cf. below, pp. 561 ff. [42] *Phys.* II, 1, 192b, 20–23.

[42a] The explanation given here for Muʿammar's substitution of the term *maʿnā* for "nature" differs from the explanation given by me in the article published in the volume in honor of Gibb, pp. 62–63.

[43] *Phys.* III, 1, 201a, 10–11.

[44] *Ibid.* II, 1, 193b, 3–5.

with reference to a form following it. To Muʿammar, however, with his adherence to the Kalam theory of atoms, there is no potential matter, and hence there is no form conceived of as the opposite of matter. To him, as to all the Mutakallimūn who believed in atoms, the Aristotelian contrast of matter and form is replaced by the contrast of atom and accident. Motion, therefore, to him is not a transition from potentiality to actuality; it is a succession from one state of actual existence to another state of actual existence.[44a] And so the term nature, which he retained in some of his statements, quite evidently using it in a sense of his own, had to be replaced by some term which had the meaning of actual existence. In the course of his search for such a term, he hit upon the term *maʿnā*. Now ever since the rise of the problem of attributes, as we have seen,[45] this term *maʿnā*, as a translation of the Greek term πρᾶγμα, "thing," and along with it the term *ṣifah*, as a translation of the Greek term τὸ χαρακτηριστικόν had been used by the Attributists in the sense of something which has real existence, in this case real existence in God. What Muʿammar did was to take the term *maʿnā*, which as a Muʿtazilite he denied to be something of real existence in God, and make it something of real existence in things. As a result of this, the two terms, *ṣifah* and *maʿnā*, which had started together on their technical career in Islam, parted company and each of them carved out for itself a different career as a technical term. The term *ṣifah* retained the meaning it acquired in its connection with the problem of attributes and thus formed part of the expression *aṣḥāb al-ṣifāt*,[46] "partisans of attributes," used as the equivalent of the term *al-ṣifātiyyah*,[47] "Attributists," whereas the term *maʿnā* formed part of the expression *aṣḥāb al-maʿānī*,[48] "Partisans of *maʿānī*," used as a description

[44a] "Motion," as defined by the Mutakallimūn, "is the transition of an atom belonging to those [atomic] particles [which constitute a body] from one atom [of the distance over which the body moves] to another atom next to it" (*Moreh* I, 73, Prop. 3, p. 137, ll. 1–2). Cf. below, p. 494 at n. 55.

[45] Cf. above, pp. 115 f.

[46] *Maḳālāt*, p. 171, l. 12.

[47] *Milal*, p. 64, l. 5.

[48] *Ibid.*, p. 46, l. 17.

of Muʿammar and those who agreed with him in this particular theory of his.

Then, by a continuation of that kind of reasoning by which he had arrived at the existence of a *maʿnā* as the cause of the motion in a body, Muʿammar arrived at the conclusion that each *maʿnā* must be preceded by a series of infinite *maʿānī*, the result thus being that in this world of ours, which to Muʿammar was created, there were various series of infinite *maʿānī*. It is this conception of infinite *maʿānī* that became the target of attack by the opponent of this theory of his.

The attack was on two main grounds. First, argues Baghdādī in his *Farḳ*, the conception of an infinite number of *maʿānī* in a world created by God is contrary to the Koranic statement about God that "He counted all things in number" (72:28),[49] and so also Ibn Ḥazm quotes against it the Koranic statement about God that "with Him everything is in measure" (13:9).[50] Second, having in mind his own description of Muʿammar's *maʿānī* as accidents,[51] again in his *Farḳ*, Baghdādī argues as follows: "If, now, Muʿammar says that the combination of infinite accidents in a body is possible, he cannot refute the claim of the followers of appearance (*ẓuhūr*) and hiding (*kumūn*) that it is possible for infinite accidents of the kind called appearance and hiding to be in one and the same abode. But this view carried to its legitimate conclusion leads to the assertion of the eternal pre-existence (*ḳidam*) of accidents — which is a heresy."[52] The "followers of appearance and hiding" referred to by Baghdādī in this passage of his *Farḳ* are that group of the Dahriyyah, described as "Eternalists" (*azaliyyah*), who in his *Uṣūl* are quoted by him as saying that "the accidents are eternally pre-existent (*ḳadīmah*), except that they hide in bodies and appear."[53] It is this same group of Dahriyyah, we may assume, that Ibn Ḥazm has reference to when, having in mind his own description of Muʿammar's *maʿānī* as things,[54] says that "the Dahriyyah agree with Muʿam-

[49] *Farḳ*, p. 138, l. 10.
[50] *Fiṣal* IV, p. 194, l. 6.
[51] Cf. above at nn. 7–9.
[52] *Farḳ*, p. 139, ll. 14–18.
[53] *Uṣūl*, p. 55, ll. 12–13.
[54] Cf. above at nn. 18–23.

mar in their assertion of an infinite number of things."[55] It is to be noted that neither Baghdādī nor Ibn Ḥazm accuses Muʿammar of actually assenting to the theory of "appearance and hiding" and hence of also believing in the eternity of accidents, which means the eternity of the world. All they both try to say is that the assertion of an infinity of *maʿānī* implies the assertion of their eternity, and hence Muʿammar, who believes in the creation of the world, contradicts himself.[55a] Later, in my discussion of the theory of appearance and hiding,[56] to which I refer as the theory of latency, I try to show three things: (1) that this theory started as an attempt to restate in popular language Aristotle's theory of the eternity of motion as an eternal process of transitions from potentiality to actuality and (2) that, when Naẓẓām adopted it, he adjusted it to his belief in the creation of the world; I also try to show (3) that, though Muʿammar, too, had a theory of appearance and hiding, his theory had nothing in it of the Aristotelian theory of potentiality and actuality.

All the foregoing reports on Muʿammar's theory of *maʿnā*, it will have been noticed, deal only with its application to created beings. In none of them is there any suggestion that the theory was applied by Muʿammar also to God. As a Muʿtazilite, he could hardly be expected to apply it to God, inasmuch as such an application would mean the assertion of the existence in God of *maʿānī* which would cause the existence in Him of attributes. Surprising, therefore, is it to find in Ashʿarī a statement which reads as follows: "It is reported of Muʿammar that he said that God is knowing in virtue of knowledge and that His knowledge is knowledge to Him in virtue of a *maʿnā* and that there is a *maʿnā* to a *maʿnā* to

[55] *Fiṣal* IV, p. 194, l. 7.

[55a] Ibn al-Rāwandī, as quoted by Ḫayyāṭ (*Intiṣār* 7, p. 21, ll. 11–12), testifies that Muʿammar, together with some other Muʿtazilites, held that "it is conceivable that the body [of the world] is in motion from eternity and that its motion is created," a sort of conception of eternal creation analogous to the Plotinian and the Christian conception of eternal generation. Ḫayyāṭ, however, denies the truth of Ibn al-Rāwandī's testimony (*ibid.*, ll. 13 ff.).

[56] Cf. below, pp. 498 ff.

infinity. And so was also his view with regard to the other attributes." But evidently being in doubt as to the authenticity of the report, Ashʿarī adds: "Concerning this I was told by Abū ʿAmr al-Furātī in the name of Muḥammad b. ʿĪsā al-Ṣairāfī that this is what Muʿammar said." [57]

According to Baghdādī, however, Muʿammar "denied the eternal attributes of God, just as the rest of the Muʿtazilites denied them," [58] and similarly, according to Shahrastānī, he was "the greatest" among those who argued for "the remotion of attributes." [59]

This is what seems to me to be the origin and meaning of Muʿammar's theory of *maʿnā*. Essentially Muʿammar's theory of *maʿnā* is Aristotle's theory of nature, which he adopted as a substitution for his rejected Kalam theory that every event in the world is directly created by God, but in which the term *maʿnā* was substituted by him for the term nature because of his rejection of Aristotle's theory of matter and form which was involved in the term "nature."

Let us now consider two other interpretations, that of Horovitz [60] and that of Horten.[61]

Horovitz finds that Muʿammar's theory of *maʿnā* is based solely upon Plato's theory of ideas as represented in *Sophist* 254 B – 256 E. We shall reproduce here his arguments in support of his interpretation and comment upon each of these arguments.

First, basing his interpretation on the reports in Shahrastānī, Baghdādī, and Ibn Ḥazm, for Ḥayyāṭ's *Intiṣār* and Ashʿarī's *Maḳālāt* had not as yet been published, Horovitz takes the terms "motion," "rest," "otherness," "likeness," and "contrariety" used in Shahrastānī's restatement of Muʿammar's argument for *maʿnā* to reflect the last four of the terms

[57] *Maḳālāt*, p. 168, ll. 9–12.

[58] *Farḳ*, p. 137, ll. 5–6.

[59] *Milal*, p. 46, ll. 1–2.

[60] S. Horovitz, *Kalam* (1909), pp. 44–54.

[61] M. Horten, "Die sogenannte Ideenlehre des Muammar," *Archiv für systematische Philosophie*, 15: 469–483 [1909]; *Die philosophischen Systeme der spekulativen Theologen im Islam* (1912), pp. 277–278.

"being," "motion," "rest," "same," and "other" used in the *Sophist* in the argument for ideas.

That Muʿammar knew the *Sophist* we have shown by his use, in Ashʿarī's reproduction of his theory, of the term "genera" as a description of "same" and "difference."[62] But at the same time we have also shown how his use of the term "difference" rather than the term "other" and how also his use of the plural "genera" in the expression "and other genera," when it is followed by only one genus, indicate that what he really had in mind was a list of terms enumerated by Aristotle in his *Metaphysics* and that only the designation of these terms as "genera" was borrowed from the *Sophist*. To this list of terms in the *Metaphysics*, we have further shown, belong also the terms "otherness," "likeness," and "contrariety" used by Shahrastānī. We have similarly shown an Aristotelian origin for the terms "motion" and "rest" used by Muʿammar, according to all the restatements of his theory. Finally, the use of the term "accidents" in Ashʿarī's restatement of Muʿammar's theory, as well as in later restatements, is definitely of an Aristotelian, and not of a Platonic, origin.

Second, quoting from Shahrastānī the statement that "accidents are infinite in every species," Horovitz takes it to reflect the statement in *Sophist* 256 E that "in each of the species being is many and not-being is infinite in multitude" and interprets the term "accidents" in Shahrastānī's statement to mean the same as the term "not-being" in Plato's statement, and this on the ground of a statement by Maimonides to the effect that, according to the Kalam, the negation of an accident is an accident,[63] whence, presumably, Plato's "not-being" was changed by Muʿammar to "accidents."

Perhaps one would have had to resort to this explanation if the statement, as phrased by Shahrastānī, had actually been used by Muʿammar and if, moreover, it had been used by him in addition to, and as something different from, his statement that the *maʿānī* are infinite in number. But, as we have seen,

[62] Cf. above n. 5.

[63] *Moreh* I, 73, Prop. 4, p. 138, ll. 8–17.

the statement about the infinity of accidents occurs in neither of the two oldest reports of Muʿammar's theory, namely, those by Ḫayyāṭ and Ashʿarī. As I have suggested above, the statement about the infinity of accidents both in Shahrastānī and Baghdādī, just as the similar statement in Ṭūsī, represents a later substitution for Muʿammar's original statement about the infinite number of *maʿānī*. As for Muʿammar's own statement, it is based, as we have shown, upon his own reasoning.

Third, Horovitz takes the expression *aṣḥāb al-maʿānī*, which, according to Shahrastānī, was applied to Muʿammar and his followers, to reflect the expression *οἱ εἰδῶν φίλοι*, "the friends of ideas," in *Sophist* 248 A.

There is nothing peculiar about *aṣḥāb al-maʿānī* to have to be explained by *οἱ εἰδῶν φίλοι*, of which, by the way, it is not a literal translation. The use of *aṣḥāb* in combination with some other term as a description of partisans or followers of some theory is common in Arabic, and in Ashʿarī's *Maḳālāt* there occur seventeen such combinations.[64]

Finally, the problem here is not solely the origin of certain terms or expressions used by Muʿammar in the exposition of his theory of *maʿnā*; the problem is the origin and meaning of the theory itself. With regard to this, quite definitely, his theory of *maʿnā* is not the same as the theory of ideas in the *Sophist*. *Maʿnā* is represented by Muʿammar as existing only in bodies; the ideas have an existence apart from bodies — a criticism already raised by Horten against Horovitz' interpretation of the *maʿnā* theory.

Now for Horten's own interpretation of Muʿammar's theory of *maʿnā*. He takes it to have been formed under the influence of what he describes as the Vaiśeṣika category of inherence in Indian philosophy.

Horten, it may be remarked, while claiming an Indian origin for Muʿammar's theory, does not claim that any of the terms used by Muʿammar in the exposition of his theory reflect some term in any of the languages through which the

[64] Cf. Index to *Maḳālāt*, pp. 55–56.

Vaiśeṣika theory could have been transmitted to him. In contradistinction to this, as we have seen, every term used in connection with Muʿammar's theory can be shown to have come from the Greek. Consequently, unless it is absolutely impossible to explain the theory of *maʿnā* on the basis of a Greek origin, there is no need of resorting to the assumption of an Indian origin.

Since the time of Horovitz and Horten, as far as I know, two other scholars, Tritton and Nader, have dealt with Muʿammar's theory of *maʿnā*. Tritton refers to both Horovitz and Horten. The interpretation of Horovitz is dismissed by him as follows: "This is ingenious and meets the case; there is no evidence for it and it must stand on its own merits." [65] The interpretation of Horten is approved of by him as follows: "Indian influence in other branches of knowledge is certain so it is not surprising to find it in philosophy, even if undigested." [66] Nader interprets Muʿammar's theory of *maʿnā* as a sort of Leibnizian principle of sufficient reason.[67]

2. ABŪ HĀSHIM'S *Aḥwāl*

About a century after Muʿammar, speculation on the question raised by Muʿammar and his followers led Abū Hāshim to a criticism of Muʿammar's theory of *maʿnā* and to a new theory, to be referred to as the theory of modes (*aḥwāl*).[1]

[65] A. S. Tritton, *Muslim Theology* (1947), p. 101, n. 2.

[66] *Ibid.*, p. 100.

[67] Albert N. Nader, *Le Système Philosophique des Muʿtazila* (1956), pp. 208–210, under the chapter heading: "Le Principe de Raison Suffisante."

[1] In Arabic dictionaries, *ḥāl*, singular of *aḥwāl*, is translated as "state," "condition," "circumstance," "position," "present time." In connection with the problem of attributes, modern scholars from the earliest time adopted the term "state" as its translation: Schmölders, *Essai* (1842), p. 150: "*état*"; Haarbrücker, *Scharastani's Religionspartheien*, I (1850), p. 83: "*Zustand*"; Munk, *Guide*, I, 51 (1856), p. 185: "*conditions*," but *Melanges* (1859), p. 328: "*condition, état ou circonstance*"; Macdonald, *Development of Muslim Theology* (1903), p. 160: "states"; Horovitz, *Der Einfluss der griechischen Philosophie auf die Entwicklung des Kalam* (1909), p 57: "*Zustand*." This translation is followed by many later scholars. But the term "mode" is used by the following: de Boer, *Geschichte der Philosophie im Islam* (1901), p. 54, "*Zustande oder Modi*"; Horten, "Die Modus-Theorie des abū Hāschim" in *ZDMG*, 63: 303 ff. (1909); Nader, *Muʿtazila*, p. 211: "*le mode*." I have

Once he had developed this theory of modes as a general theory of predication, he applied it to the problem of divine attributes, arriving at a view opposed at once to that of the Attributists and to that of the Antiattributists.

We shall deal first with his general theory of modes and then with its application to the problem of attributes.

Baghdādī, who was himself an Ash'arite and refers to Ash'arī as "our master" (*shayḫunā*),[2] introduces Abū Hāshim's theory of modes with the statement that this view "was considered heretical by his fellow Mu'tazilites as well as by other sects." [3] He then quotes two reports as to the origin of the theory of modes.

Both reports open with an announcement to the effect that they are going to explain "what forced" Abū Hāshim into his theory of *aḥwāl*. Their common explanation is that he was forced into it by a criticism of Mu'ammar's theory of *ma'nā*. Mu'ammar's theory of *ma'nā* is then presented in both these reports as an attempt to answer a question which in the first report is quoted as a question put "by our fellow orthodox (*aṣḥabunā*) to the old Mu'tazilites" [4] and in the second report is quoted as a question raised by Mu'ammar himself.[5] The question as phrased in the first report reads, "whether he who is knowing among us differs from him who is ignorant, with regard to his knowledge, in virtue of himself or in virtue of some [external] cause," [6] and as phrased in the second report reads, "whether the knowledge of Zayd belongs to him rather than to 'Amr in virtue of himself or in virtue of a *ma'nā* or neither in virtue of himself nor in virtue of a *ma'nā*." [7] The answer as clearly stated in the first report and as implied in the second report is that it is neither in virtue of himself nor in virtue of some external cause but in virtue of a *ma'nā*. Two

---

chosen to use the term "mode," though, as will be shown later in Appendix III, the term was originally used by Abū Hāshim in the sense of "disposition" and then he extended its meaning and used it in the sense of "state."

[2] *Farḳ*, p. 200, ll. 6–7.

[3] *Ibid*., p. 180, ll. 17–18.

[4] *Ibid*., p. 181, l. 1.

[5] *Ibid*., ll. 11–12.

[6] *Ibid*., ll. 1–2.

[7] *Ibid*., ll. 12–13.

criticisms of this conclusion are briefly and only allusively reported. One of these criticisms reads that "if it is in virtue of a *ma'nā*, then Mu'ammar would be right in his assertion that one *ma'nā* is connected with another *ma'nā* up to infinity." [8] Abū Hāshim's objection to an infinity of *ma'ānī* is quite evidently based upon the Koranic teaching about God that "He counteth all things in number (72:28).[9] As a result of his criticisms of Mu'ammar's theory of *ma'nā*, Abū Hāshim was led to his new theory which as phrased in the first report reads that "he who is knowing differs from him who is ignorant only in virtue of a *ḥāl* in which he is [that is to say, by his being disposed to knowledge]" [10] and as phrased in the second report reads that "knowledge belongs to Zayd [who is the knower] in virtue of a *ḥāl* [that is to say, by a disposition]." [11]

What follows this account of how the theory of *aḥwāl* arose differs in the two reports. In the first report what follows is a passage which is introduced as a sort of conclusion from what has preceded. To quote: "And so he established the *ḥāl* with reference to three situations. The first situation is that in which a subject is described by a certain predicate in virtue of the subject itself, and the subject deserves the predicate in virtue of a *ḥāl* in which it is [that is to say, by being disposed to it]. The second situation is that in which a subject described by a certain thing as its predicate in virtue of a *ma'nā* has come to possess that *ma'nā* in virtue of a *ḥāl*. The third situation is that in which the subject deserves a certain pred-

[8] *Ibid.*, ll. 14–15. In the printed edition of the *Farḳ*, this criticism appears only, and as the only criticism, in the second report. But the opening words in the printed edition of the only criticism in the first report, which reads "and it necessarily follows also," shows that it was preceded by a missing other criticism. This missing criticism is included in Horten's German translation of Baghdādī's first report from a Berlin manuscript (cf. his "Neues zur Modustheorie des abu Háschim," p. 49).

[9] Cf. below, p. 470, n. 25.

[10] For the technical meaning of the underlying Arabic expression *li-ḥāl kāna 'alayhā* upon which this bracketed interpretation is based, see below, Appendix III.

[11] *Ibid.*, l. 17.

icate neither in virtue of itself nor in virtue of a *maʿnā*, but possesses that predicate rather than some other predicate, according to Abū Hāshim, in virtue of a *ḥāl*." [12] On the basis of a twofold division of Abū Hāshim's modes reported by Juwaynī [13] and by Shahrastānī,[14] it can be shown, I believe, that the threefold division reported here by Baghdādī refers respectively (1) to modes in the sense of predicates which are properties, (2) to modes in the sense of predicates which are certain accidents in living beings, and (3) to modes in the sense of predicates which are genera or species. Thus Abū Hāshim's theory of modes as a general theory of predication applies to four of the five predicables enumerated by Porphyry.

It is probably because modes are terms predicated of a subject and all terms predicated of a subject, except proper names, are universal terms that the term modes (*aḥwāl*) came to be used by Abū Hāshim and his followers in the sense of universals. Such a use of the term *aḥwāl* is directly mentioned by Ghazālī in his statement that "the intellectual faculty apprehends the general intellectual universals, which the Muʿtakallimūn call modes." [15] It is so also directly mentioned by Maimonides in his use of the expression "modes, that is, universal concepts (*al-maʿānī al-kulliyyah*)." [16] It is implied in a statement by Ibn Ḥazm which reads that "one of the absurdities of the Ashʿarites is their assertion that it is possible for men to believe in modes and [universal] concepts (*al-maʿānī* [*al-kulliyyah*]) which are neither existent nor nonexistent." [17] It is similarly implied in a statement by Averroes which reads that "those who deny modes (*al-aḥwāl*) deny the belief in existence in general and color in general, whereas those who affirm modes say that existence in general and color in general are neither existent nor nonexistent." [18] This nega-

[12] *Ibid.*, ll. 7–11.
[13] Cf. below, pp. 183 ff.
[14] *Ibid.*
[15] *Tahāfut al-Falāsifah* XVIII, 62, p. 328, ll. 13–14.
[16] *Moreh* I, 51, p. 76, ll. 26–27.
[17] *Fiṣal*, IV, p. 208, ll. 5–6.
[18] *Tahāfut al-Tahāfut* III, 233, p. 258, ll. 10–11.

tive description of universals has, as we shall see later,[19] an affirmative meaning, namely, that of ascribing to universals intramental existence, in opposition both to those who ascribe to them extramental existence and to those who maintain that they are mere words.

In the second report, the account of the origin of the theory of *aḥwāl* is followed by a number of challenging questions put to Abū Hāshim by "our fellow orthodox." [20] Each of the questions is answered by Abū Hāshim and each answer contains some additional information about the theory of modes. Thus in answer to one question, Abū Hāshim makes the statement that "neither does he say that the modes are existent nor does he say that they are nonexistent." [21] Then, in the course of this questioning by "our fellow orthodox," Abū Hāshim seems to have begun to apply his theory of modes to the problem of divine attributes and to speak of "the *aḥwāl* of the Creator" [22] and, in answer to a direct question with regard to the modes in their application to the Creator, he said that "they are neither He nor other than He." [23] This, as we shall see later,[24] is an old formula, which had been used by the Attributists as a denial of the Christian belief that the second and third persons of the Trinity are each God but to which Abū Hāshim gave a new meaning as a denial of both the reality of attributes as conceived of by the Attributists and the verbality of attributes as conceived of by the Muʿtazilites. Undoubtedly in the course of his answers to the various challenging questions he also had occasion to say that the modes in their application to divine attributes, like the modes as a general theory of predication, are "neither existent nor nonexistent," for elsewhere it is directly reported that "Abū Hāshim posited modes as attributes which are neither existent [nor nonexistent]." [25]

Thus Abū Hāshim by his theory of modes has placed

[19] Cf. below, p. 197.
[20] *Farḳ*, p. 181, l. 17.
[21] *Ibid.*, p. 182, l. 5.
[22] *Ibid.*, l. 9.
[23] *Ibid.*, l. 14.
[24] Cf. below, p. 211.
[25] *Milal*, p. 56, l. 3.

himself in opposition to the conception of attributes of both the Attributists and the Muʿtazilites. But here a question arises in our minds. Inasmuch as Abū Hāshim's theory of modes is a denial of the verbality of attributes as conceived of by the Muʿtazilites, it must follow that the differences between the various modes predicated of God are not mere nominal or verbal differences, and hence also the plurality of modes in God is not a mere nominal or verbal plurality. How then would Abū Hāshim have met the Muʿtazilite argument that, inasmuch as the unity of God includes internal unity in the sense of absolute simplicity, a plurality in God of modes like those conceived of by Abū Hāshim would be incompatible with the internal unity and simplicity of God? Now, as we have seen,[26] when the Attributists were confronted by the Muʿtazilites with this argument, they downrightly denied that the unity of God includes internal unity in the sense of absolute simplicity, maintaining that the unity of God, according to their own conception of it, does not exclude from Him a plurality of parts which from eternity have been united with each other and with the essence of God. The question, therefore, is how Abū Hāshim would have dealt with this argument. Would he have found himself compelled to resort, like the Attributists, to a denial of the absolute simplicity of God, or would he have discovered some other way of fending off that argument of the Muʿtazilites?

An answer to this question is to be found in a statement quoted repeatedly in the name of Abū Hāshim by Shahrastānī both in his *Milal* and in his *Nihāyat*. In his *Milal*, after stating that Abū Hāshim "posited modes as attributes which are neither existent [nor nonexistent] and neither cognizable nor incognizable," [27] he adds: "Then Abū Hāshim posits of God another mode (*ḥālah*) which necessarily causes (*aujabat*) these modes." [28] Almost in the same words he says in his *Nihāyat* that "Abū Hāshim posits another mode (*ḥālah*)

[26] Cf. above, pp. 138–139.

[27] *Milal*, p. 56, ll. 3–4.

[28] *Ibid.*, l. 12.

which necessarily causes these modes." [29] In another place in his *Nihāyat*, he quotes Abū Hāshim as saying: "Knowingness is a mode and powerfulness is a mode, and benefiting both of them is a mode (*ḥāl*) which necessarily causes all the modes." [30] In still another place in the same work, he makes an opponent of modes say: "Did not Abū Hāshim posit of God a mode (*ḥāl*) which necessarily causes His being knowing and willing?" [31] An allusion to the difference between the plurality of modes as applied to God and the plurality of modes as applied to other beings is also to be found, I believe, in a passage in which, after stating that the terms "existing," "living," and "knowing" predicated of God by a certain Nestorius are used by him in the sense of Abū Hāshim's modes, Shahrastānī adds the following: "His statement ultimately amounts to the assertion that God's being existing and living and [knowing used in the sense of] rational is as the philosophers say in the definition of man [that he is living and rational], except that in respect to man the things predicated of him differ, seeing that man is composite, whereas [in respect to God they do not differ], seeing that God is a simple substance, incomposite." [32] The difference spoken of by him in that passage is undoubtedly due to what he says in his statements here that all the various modes predicated of God stem from one single mode.

Statements parallel to those of Shahrastānī are to be found in Rāzī. In one place, he attributes to Abū Hāshim the view that "knowingness, powerfulness, livingness, and existingness are caused by a fifth mode (*ḥālah*), and this notwithstanding the fact that all the modes are eternal," [33] the implication being that the four modes mentioned are eternally caused by the fifth mode. In another place, he says: "Abū Hāshim maintains that God's essence is like other essences in essentiality and that it differs from them only by a mode (*ḥālah*) which necessarily causes four modes, namely, livingness, knowing-

[29] *Nihāyat*, p. 180, ll. 12–13.
[30] *Ibid.*, p. 198, ll. 2–3.
[31] *Ibid.*, p. 140, ll. 3–4.
[32] *Milal*, p. 175, ll. 18–20.
[33] *Muḥaṣṣal*, p. 55, l. 17.

ness, existingness, and powerfulness." [34] In none of these passages, it will be noticed, are we told what that underlying causative mode in God is. This information, however, is furnished by Ṭūsī in his comment on the second passage quoted from Rāzī. Using the term "attribute" for the term "mode" in Rāzī's passage, he remarks: "The attribute which Abū Hāshim alone, and no other, ascribes to God is the attribute of Godhood (*al-ilāhiyyah*)." [35] Described as "Godhood," this single mode thus belongs to God alone and as such it is what Aristotle would call a "property" (*ἴδιον* = *ḫāṣṣiyyah*), which, as defined by him, means a term predicated of a thing and belonging "to that thing alone." [36] In fact, as we shall see, Juwaynī describes that single mode of Abū Hāshim as being God's "most proper" (*aḫaṣṣ*) description.[37]

According to these statements, then, the theory of modes introduced two innovations.

First, it gave a new meaning to the old formula "neither God nor other than God" and it also framed the new formula "neither existent nor nonexistent," using both of these formulae as a description of modes in their contrast to attributes as conceived by both the Attributists and the Muʿtazilites.

Second, it introduced the view that modes, the new name for attributes, are related to God as effects to their cause. That was something new, for to the Attributists there was no causal relationship between God and His attributes. From the earliest times the attributes are spoken of as being coeternal with God or as subsisting in His essence or as being superadded to His essence, without any suggestion that they were proceeding from Him as from a cause. Only with reference to the attribute of word or speech, in the sense of the eternal Koran, is God conceived of as the cause of that attribute. The absence of any conception of causal relationship between the essence of God and His attributes among the orthodox Attributists is clearly implied in Ibn Kullāb's description of

[34] *Ibid.*, p. 111, ll. 13–14.
[35] *Ibid.*, p. 111, n. 2, l. 2.
[36] *Topics* I, 5, 102a, 18–19; cf. *Philo*, II, p. 131.
[37] *Irshād*, p. 47, l. 4 (80).

the divine attributes as being "ceaselessly uncreated," [38] that is to say, eternally uncaused. It is more clearly brought out in Ghazālī who openly discusses the problem of the relation between the attributes of God and His essence. The view which he maintains in effect is that the essence is not in need of the attributes for its existence, whereas the attributes are in need of the essence for their existence, for as attributes they are in need of a subject (*mauṣūf*) in which to exist.[39] But the existence of attributes in a subject, he goes on to explain, does not establish between them a causal relationship in the true sense of the term, that is, in the sense of the relationship between an effect and its "efficient cause" (*'illah fā'iliyyah*), even though, he adds, philosophers in their artificial terminology call the subject of which an attribute is predicated a "receptive cause" (*'illah ḳabliyyah*) and the attribute predicated of the subject a "caused thing" (*ma'lūl*).[40]

It is to be noted that, in the opposition aroused by the theory of *aḥwāl* among the Attributists, only the question of formula became a matter of discussion; the question of a causal relationship between God and His attributes is never discussed. This would seem to indicate that this difference, though it existed, was not considered as a matter of religious significance. In fact, about three centuries later, the Hanbalite Ibn Ḳudāma (d. 1223), without any trace of influence by Abū Hāshim's modalism, out of his own orthodox faith says that "His attributes are from Him (*minhu*)," [41] that is to say, they proceed from God as their cause.

The theory of modes which arose among the Mu'tazilites as a moderate form of their denial of attributes was, according to the testimony of Ibn Ḥazm,[42] adopted by some Ash'arites as a moderate form of their affirmation of attributes. Two of such Ash'arites, Bāḳillānī and Juwaynī, are mentioned by Shahrastānī in his *Nihāyat*. Of Bāḳillānī he says that after some hesitation he accepted the theory of modes [43] and of

[38] *Fiṣal*, IV, p. 208, ll. 4–5.
[39] *Tahāfut al-Falāsifah* VI, 5, p. 166, ll. 2–4.
[40] *Ibid.*, 8–9, p. 166, l. 12 – p. 167, l. 6.
[41] *Taḥrīm* 19, p. 12, l. 12.
[42] Cf. below, pp. 215–216.
[43] *Nihāyat*, p. 131, ll. 5–6.

Juwaynī he says that at first he affirmed modes and later he denied them.[44] Rāzī similarly describes both Bāḳillānī and Juwaynī as those who adopted the theory of modes.[45]

But, as we shall see, though both of them in adopting the theory of modes tried to harmonize it with their own belief in attributes, the manner of their harmonization was not the same.

The manner in which Bāḳillānī harmonized it with his belief in attributes may be gathered from a tripartite passage in Shahrastānī's *Milal*. First, it reproduces from a work of Bāḳillānī Ash'arī's argument against the modalistic formula that the modes are neither existent nor nonexistent on the ground that it is in violation of the Law of Excluded Middle. Second, it refers to the fact that Bāḳillānī refuted that argument and established his own view of modes without actually giving up his belief in attributes as being real things (*ma'ānī*) in God. Third, it quotes Bāḳillānī as saying: "The mode posited by Abū Hāshim, when he posited a mode which necessarily causes those [modes which we call] attributes, is that which we call attribute in particular." [46]

Thus whatever else his own formulated theory of modes may have contained, it was primarily based upon Abū Hāshim's conception of a single mode as the cause of all the other modes.

Juwaynī's harmonization of modes with attributes, unlike that of Bāḳillānī, is not based upon an acceptance of Abū Hāshim's view of a single mode as the cause of all other modes. That view is rejected by him as heretical. Thus in his *Irshād*, after stating that "the Mu'tazilites and the heretics who follow them agree upon the denial of attributes," [47] he enumerates three such heretical groups, one of which, the second, is described by him as follows: "Others express themselves by saying that these predicative terms are affirmed of the essence of God on account of His having a mode (*ḥālah*) which is

[44] *Ibid.*, ll. 8–9.

[45] *Muḥaṣṣal*, p. 38, ll. 19–20.

[46] *Milal*, p. 67, ll. 2–8.

[47] *Irshād*, p. 46, l. 20 – p. 47, l. 1 (80).

the most proper (*aḫaṣṣ*) of His descriptions and this mode necessarily causes Him to be described as living, knowing, and powerful." [48] The view thus described is quite evidently that of Abū Hāshim.

The manner in which Juwaynī does harmonize modes with attributes may be gathered from a study of two chapters in his *Irshād*, of which one deals with divine attributes under the heading "Attributes Necessary of God" [49] and the other deals with modes as a general theory of predication under the heading "The Establishment of the Knowledge of Attributes." [50] Now the very phrasing of the headings of these two chapters would seem to indicate that terms predicated of God, which are referred to by Juwaynī as attributes, are regarded by him as modes in their use in the general theory of predication. But his treatment of attributes as modes emerges more clearly from a close comparison of his description and illustration of what he finds to be the two kinds of divine attributes with his description and illustration of what he finds to be the two kinds of modes. From such a comparison we learn that what with regard to divine attributes he calls *ṣifāt nafsiyyah* [51] — "attributes of the subject itself," such as "eternally preexistent," [52] "one," [53] and "eternally post-existent" [54] — corresponds to what with regard to the general theory of modes constitutes the first form of "uncaused modes," namely, properties.[55] Thus attributes of this kind are regarded by him as modes which are described by him as neither existent nor nonexistent.[56] Similarly what with regard to divine attributes he calls *ṣifāt ma'nawiyyah* [57] — such as "knowing," "powerful," "living," [58] "willing," [59] "hearing," [60] "seeing," [61] and "speaking" [62] — is with regard to the general theory of modes

[48] *Ibid.*, p. 47, ll. 3–5.
[49] *Ibid.*, p. 17, l. 16 (38).
[50] *Ibid.*, p. 46, l. 18
[51] *Ibid.*, p. 17, l. 17
[52] *Ibid.*, p. 18, l. 19
[53] *Ibid.*, p. 30, l. 15 (57).
[54] *Ibid.*, p. 46, l. 9 (78).
[55] *Ibid.*, p. 47, ll. 13 and 16–18 (81); cf. below, p. 187.
[56] *Ibid.*, l. 12.
[57] *Ibid.*, p. 17, l. 17
[58] *Ibid.*, p. 37, ll. 7–8 (66).
[59] *Ibid.*, l. 12.
[60] *Ibid.*, p. 43, l. 1 (74).
[61] *Ibid.*, p. 45, l. 17 (78).
[62] *Ibid.*, p. 58, l. 4 (98).

called by him "caused modes," [63] the cause of which he calls *maʿnā*,[64] from which we have reason to infer that by *ṣifāt maʿnawiyyah* he means *maʿnā*-caused attributes.[65] Accordingly, such attributes as knowing, powerful, living, willing, hearing, seeing, and speaking are modes which are neither existent nor nonexistent, but each of these modes is caused by a corresponding *maʿnā*, such as "knowledge, power, life, will, audition, sight, and speech," and each of these *maʿānī* is a real attribute existing in God. This is how Juwaynī harmonized modes with attributes. Of course, it is to be understood that in the case of modes as a theory of divine attributes the causal relation between the *maʿnā* and its corresponding mode is an eternal relation, analogous to the eternal causal relationship implied in the concept of eternal generation as used in Christianity and in Plotinus.[66] It is Juwaynī's type of harmonization of modes with attributes that Rāzī quite evidently had in mind when, after referring "to those who support modes among the orthodox," he says, evidently with reference only to what Juwaynī calls *ṣifāt maʿnawiyyah*, that "they maintain that knowingness is an attribute caused by a *maʿnā* subsisting in God and this *maʿnā* is knowledge." [66a]

A precise exposition of what quite obviously is Juwaynī's harmonization of modes with attributes is to be found in Faḍālī's discussion of the attributes powerful, willing, know-

[63] *Ibid*., p. 47, l. 12

[64] *Ibid*., ll. 12 and 13–14.

[65] Here the term *maʿnāwiyyah* quite evidently means "*maʿnā*-caused," referring as it does to such predicative modes as "knowing," "powerful," and the like, which have "knowledge," "power," and the like, each of which is a *maʿnā*, as their respective causes. It is in this sense of such predicative modes as "knowing" and "powerful" that the expression *ṣifāt maʿnāwiyyah* is used in Faḍālī's *Kifāyat*, p. 57, l. 4, in contrast to the expression *ṣifāt al-maʿānī*, which is used on p. 56, l. 39, in the sense of such substantive terms as "knowledge" and "power." However, in a passage to be quoted later from *Kashf*, p. 56, l. 4 (cf. below, p. 215 at n. 39), where Averroes uses the term *maʿnāwiyyah* as a description of Ashʿarī's belief in the reality of attributes, it is quite evidently used in the sense of "real," that is to say, as an adjective of *maʿnā*, where *maʿnā* is used in the sense of *shay*, "thing," of which it is used as an equivalent (cf. above, p. 115).

[66] Cf. below, p. 299.

[66a] *Muḥaṣṣal*, p. 131, ll. 7–9.

ing, living, hearing, seeing, and speaking. His discussion may be restated as follows.

Whenever in the essence of a subject there is power (*ḳudrah*), the subject is said to be powerful (*ḳadir*). There is, however, a difference between the substantive term power and the predicative term powerful. Power is something actually existent [and is thus a real attribute (*maʿnā*)];[66b] powerful is neither existent nor nonexistent and is thus a mode (*ḥāl*). There is also a difference between the interrelationship of these two terms in their application to created beings and their interrelationship in their application to God. In the case of their application to created beings, both the power in them and their being powerful are created, and the relation of power to powerful is that of cause (*ʿillah*); in the case of their application to God, wherein both the power in Him and His being powerful are eternal, "power is not said to be a cause in His being powerful; it is only said that between power and His being powerful there is a necessary interrelation (*talāzum*)."[66c] What has thus been said about the predicative term powerful holds true also of the other six predicative terms mentioned above, all of which are modes.[66d] Then, also, all these modes are to be described as *ṣifāt maʿnawiyyah*, attributes derived from their respectively corresponding substantive terms, which are *ṣifāt al-maʿānī*, attributes in the sense of real things, and of which the relation to their respective modes is in the case of created beings that of cause and in the case of God that of a mere necessary interrelationship.[66e]

The theory of modes is associated with the name of Abū Hāshim, and Shahrastānī in one of his works says explicitly that prior to Abū Hāshim ibn al-Jubbāʾī there is no mention of the theory of modes.[67] Still Shahrastānī himself in another work tries to show that Abū al-Hudhayl, who lived about a

[66b] Cf. below at n. 66[e].

[66c] *Kifayat*, p. 55, ll. 7–26 and 26–30.

[66d] *Ibid.*, p. 55, l. 37 – p. 56, l. 39.

[66e] *Ibid.*, p. 56, l. 39 – p. 57, l. 8; cf. above, n. 65.

[67] *Nihāyat*, p. 131, ll. 3–5.

century before Abū Hāshim, held a view which is like the theory of modes of Abū Hāshim,[68] or, in other words, that Abū al-Hudhayl anticipated Abū Hāshim's theory of modes.

The original view of Abū al-Hudhayl is reported by Ash'arī as follows: "God is knowing by a knowledge which is He and He is powerful by a power which is He and He is living by a life which is He." [69] In Baghdādī only the second part of the formula is reproduced. It reads: "The knowledge of God is God and His power is He." [70] In Ibn Ḥazm the formula is paraphrased to read: "The knowledge of God is eternal and it is God." [71] In Shahrastānī it reads: "The Creator is knowing by a knowledge which is himself (*nafsuhu*)" [72] or "the Creator is knowing by knowledge and His knowledge is His essence (*dhātuhu*), powerful by power and His power is His essence, living by life and His life is His essence." [73]

Upon this last formulation of Abū al-Hudhayl's theory of attributes, Shahrastānī makes the following comment: "The difference between the statement of him who says that God is knowing in virtue of His essence and not in virtue of knowledge and the statement of him who says [that is, Abū al-Hudhayl] that He is knowing in virtue of a knowledge which is His essence is that the former statement is a denial of attributes, whereas the latter statement is an affirmation either of essence as being itself attribute or of attribute as being itself essence. But if Abū al-Hudhayl takes these attributes to be aspects (*wujūh*) of the essence, then they are the same as the hypostases (*aḳānīm*) of the Christians or the modes (*aḥwāl*) of Abū Hāshim." [74]

What he means to say is this. When the expression "knowing in virtue of His essence" is qualified by the expression "and not in virtue of knowledge," which is the formula used by Naẓẓām [75] but is ascribed by Shahrastānī himself to the

[68] *Milal*, p. 34, ll. 19–20.

[69] *Maḳālāt*, p. 165, ll. 5–6; cf. p. 188, ll. 11–13.

[70] *Farḳ*, p. 108, ll. 7–8.

[71] *Fiṣal* II, p. 126, ll. 24–25.

[72] *Nihāyat*, p. 180, l. 6.

[73] *Milal*, p. 34, ll. 13–14.

[74] *Ibid.*, ll. 17–20.

[75] *Maḳālāt*, p. 486, ll. 11–12.

Mu'tazilites in general,[76] it means that attributes are nonexistent, that they are mere verbal utterances (*al-alfāẓ*) or what would be described in Latin as a mere emission of voice (*flatus vocis*), so that when they are predicated of God, each predicate of God is only a name of God. Not so, however, is the view of Abū al-Hudhayl. When he begins by saying that "God is knowing in virtue of knowledge" and then proceeds to qualify that statement by saying that "that knowledge is His essence" or that it is "himself," then what he says lends itself to two interpretations.

First, it may mean that knowledge is God himself — an interpretation which, as we shall see, is given to it by Ibn al-Rāwandī. But this interpretation, as we shall also see, is refuted by Ḫayyāṭ as well as by Shahrastānī himself.[77]

Second, it may mean that "knowledge," or any other attribute, on the one hand, is other than the essence of God and, on the other, is the same as the essence of God; in other words, that, on the one hand, it is existent and, on the other, it is nonexistent, or that it is neither existent nor nonexistent, and hence neither other than God nor the same as God. But such an interpretation, Shahrastānī goes on to say, implies that knowledge and all the other terms predicated of God are considered by Abū al-Hudhayl as "aspects of the essence" and thus they are what Abū Hāshim later came to call "modes," for modes are described by the Modalists as "aspects." [78] His mention here of "the hypostases of the Christians" refers to those Christians whose formulation of the Trinity, as we shall see,[79] is compared by Shahrastānī to Abū Hāshim's formulation of modes and hence he infers that the hypostases would similarly be described by them as "aspects."

This is what one may get out of Baghdādī and Juwaynī and Shahrastānī as to the history and meaning of Abū Hāshim's theory of *Aḥwāl* in its bearing upon the problem of attributes. Essential points in its history are three. (1) It was started by

[76] *Milal*, p. 30, ll. 7–8.
[77] Cf. below, pp. 230–231.
[78] Cf. below, pp. 231–232.
[79] Cf. below, pp. 338–339.

Abū Hāshim, in his criticism of Muʿammar's theory of *Maʿnā*, as a general theory of predication. (2) It was then applied by him to divine attributes as a sort of moderation of his fellow Muʿtazilites' thorough denial of attributes. (3) Subsequently it was adopted in some form or other by certain Attributists as a sort of moderation of their fellow Attributists' belief in the extreme reality of attributes.

Brief summaries of other explanations of Abū Hāshim's theory of modes are by the following: (1) A. Schmölders, who simply says: "Le mot *état* est la plus compliqué par l'étendue de sa signification. C'est pour me servir du langage d'Aristotle, le δυνάμει ὄν, ou plutôt le terme générique de cette manière d'être" (cf. his *Essai* [1842], p. 197); (2) S. Horovitz, who takes it to be all based upon Plato's theory of ideas (cf. his *Kalam* [1909], pp. 54–69); (3) M. Horten, who, after several long studies on the subject ("Die Modus-Theorie des abū Hāschim," *ZDMG*, 63:303–324 [1909]; *Systeme* [1912], pp. 411–418; "Neues zur Modustheorie des abū Hāschim," *Festgabe zur 60. Geburtstag Clemens Baeumker* [1913], pp. 45–53), has arrived at the following conclusion: "Aus Gedanken, die der Inhärenzlehre der Vaišeṣika nahestehen, sind die Theorien Muʿammar und abū Hāšim entstanden" (*Die Philosophie des Islam* [1924], p. 185; cf. also, *Systeme*, p. 416, n. 2); (4) Simon van den Bergh, who takes the term *ḥāl* to be a translation of the Stoic πὼς ἔχον and theory based upon that term *ḥāl* to reflect the Stoic discussion of the λεκτά (Averroes' *Tahāfut al-Tahāfut* [1954], vol. II, p. 4);[80] (5) A. N. Nader, who, of the two types of modes in Shahrastānī's *Nihāyat* (cf. below, pp. 183ff.), says that they bring to mind "les jugements synthétiques dont parle Kant" and "les jugements analytiques dont parle Kant," and, with regard to the divine modes, says: "Pour mieux comprendre 'les modes' on peut les rapprocher des jugements analytiques chez Kant" (*Le Système Philosophique des Muʿtazila* [1956], pp. 211–212, and p. 212, n. 1).

[80] Cf. below, p. 202, n. 18a.

APPENDIX A. *The Threefold and the Twofold Classification of Modes*

From Baghdādī's two reports on Abū Hāshim quoted above we gather that the term *ḥāl*, conventionally translated by "mode," is used by Abū Hāshim as a designation of something existing in a person in virtue of which he differs from another person, which difference is expressed by a certain term predicated of him, so that that term predicated of him is called *ḥāl*. With this use of the term mode in mind, Abū Hāshim, as reported by Baghdādī, divides modes into three classes, of which each class is distinguished by the special manner in which the predicative term is predicated of its subject. In the first class, it is predicated of its subject "in virtue of the subject itself"; in the second class, it is predicated of its subject "in virtue of a *ma'nā*"; in the third class, it is predicated of its subject "neither in virtue of the subject itself nor in virtue of a *ma'nā*." What these three vague phrases mean is not explained in this threefold classification of modes as reported by Baghdādī, but an explanation of them is furnished in the twofold explanation of the same modes as reported by Juwaynī and Shahrastānī.

Both Juwaynī and Shahrastānī begin with a classification of modes into those which are "caused" and those which are "not caused." [1] Then Juwaynī goes on to say briefly that, "as for the mode which is caused, it includes every predicate (*ḥukm*) affirmed of the essence [of a subject] in virtue of a *ma'nā* subsisting in it, as, for instance, the affirmation that a living being is living and that a powerful being is powerful." [2] Of these two predicates mentioned by him, it is to be noted, "living," used, as we have explained above,[3] in the sense of the duration of life, is an accident in living beings as is "powerful." In Shahrastānī, the corresponding explanation of caused modes reads as follows: "As for the first class of

[1] *Irshād*, p. 47, ll. 12–13 (81); *Nihāyat*, p. 132, ll. 2–3.
[2] *Irshād*, p. 47, ll. 13–14.
[3] Cf. above, p. 153.

modes, it includes every predicate (*ḥukm*) [affirmed of a subject] in virtue of a cause subsisting in the essence [of a subject] which, according to Abū Hāshim, has life as a condition for its existence, as, for instance, the affirmation that a living being is living, knowing, powerful, willing, hearing, and seeing . . . so that life subsists in a subject and necessitates the subject to be living, and the same holds true of knowledge and power and will and of everything else of whose existence life is a condition. These predicates (*al-aḥkām*) are called modes (*aḥwāl*), that is, attributes (*ṣifāt*) superadded to the *ma'ānī* which necessitate them." [4] According to the report in Shahrastānī, then, by the *ma'nā* is meant the substantive terms life, knowledge, power, will, audition, and sight from which the corresponding adjectival predicative modes living, knowing, willing, hearing, and seeing are derived.

Then both Juwaynī and Shahrastānī go on to say, the former that "according to our opinion" and the latter that "according to the opinion of the Ḳāḍī [Bāḳillānī]," the conception of caused modes should not be restricted to living beings or, as they express themselves, it should not be restricted to beings in the case of which the *ma'nā* in them has "life as a condition" for its existence. It should be extended to non-living beings, so that the terms "moving" and "black" predicated of an inanimate body are to be called modes, the causes of which are the *ma'ānī*,[5] by which is meant "motion" and "blackness."

From all this we gather that the caused modes of Abū Hāshim as reported by Juwaynī and Shahrastānī consist of predicates, including among them the predicate "knowing," all of which are accidents in living beings and each of which is caused by a *ma'nā*. This quite evidently corresponds to Abū Hāshim's second class of modes as reported by Baghdādī in the second part of his first report, where they are said to

[4] *Nihāyat*, p. 132, ll. 5–10.
[5] *Irshād*, p. 47, ll. 14–16; *Nihāyat*, p. 132, ll. 10–13.

refer to a situation in which "a certain thing" is predicated of a subject "in virtue of a *maʿnā*," where the "certain thing" is, as in the first part of this same first report, the term "knowing" and the *maʿnā* is, as in Shahrastānī's classification of modes, the term "knowledge."

So much for Abū Hāshim's caused modes.

As for his uncaused modes, they are illustrated both in Juwaynī and in Shahrastānī by two kinds of predicates.

In Juwaynī, the first kind of predicate is illustrated by "the space-occupancy (*taḥayyuz*) of substance," [6] that is, by the predicate in the proposition "the atom is space-occupying." Now the space-occupancy of substance, that is, of the atom, is used by him earlier in the same work with reference to divine attributes as an illustration of what he calls "the attributes of the self (*ṣifāt nafsiyyah*)," that is to say, attributes of the subject itself, which is described by him as "every attribute affirmed of the subject itself, which belongs to the subject itself as long as the subject lasts and which is uncaused." [6a] Since the term "self" in the expression "attribute of the self" here refers to God, the term "attribute" in it cannot be taken as genus or species; it must be taken as property, that is, as belonging to God alone. The expression "attribute of the self," therefore, quite evidently reflects Aristotle's description of property as "whatever belongs to each thing in virtue of itself (καθ' αὑτό) but is not in its essence (οὐσίᾳ)," [7] in contrast to his use of the same phrase "in virtue of itself" in the sense of "whatever is present in what anything is (ἐν τῷ τί ἐστιν)," that is to say, whatever is part of a definition, such, for instance, as the term "animal" predicated of an individual human being, "for animal is present in the for-

[6] *Irshād*, p. 47, l. 17.

[6a] *Irshād*, p. 17, ll. 17–18 (38–39).

[7] *Metaph.* V, 30, 1025a, 31–32. In the Arabic version of the *Metaphysics*, καθ' αὑτό is translated by *bi-dhātihi*, "in virtue of its essence," and οὐσίᾳ is translated by *fī al-jauhar*, "in the substance" (cf. *Averroes' Long Commentary on Metaphysics* V, Text. 35, p. 693, ll. 4–5). But *bi-dhātihi* and *bi-nafsihi* are used interchangeably (cf. below, pp. 225–226, and n. 9 below).

mula that defines him."[8] The use of the space-occupancy of the atom as an example of the Aristotelian conception of property as a predicative term is in accordance with a view current in the Kalam.[9]

The second form of predicates of uncaused modes in Juwaynī is illustrated by the proposition that "an existent thing (*al-maujūd*) is accident, color, blackness, a state of being (*kaun*), knowledge, et cetera."[10] Reflected in this proposition is his own statement earlier in the same work, that the world consists of substances (that is, atoms) and accidents and that "accident" includes "colors, tastes, odors, life, death, knowledges, wills, powers," and also "states of being (*al-akwan*)," that is to say, "motion, rest, aggregation, and segregation."[11] As Juwaynī undoubtedly was already acquainted with the terms genus, species, specific difference, and subaltern genera and species used in philosophy in connection with its classification of things, we may assume that by the term "accident" in his classification of accidents he meant genus, that by the plural "colors" he meant "blackness" and "whiteness" and the other colors, which he regarded as subaltern species under the species "color," that by the plural "states of being" he meant that each of the four states of being mentioned by him is a subaltern species under the species "state of being," and so also with the other plural terms mentioned by him in his classification of accidents. Accordingly, in the proposition quoted above, in which the predicative terms "accident" and "color" and "blackness" and "state of being" and "knowledge" are used by him as illustrations of the second form of his uncaused modes, by "accident" he means genus, by "color" and "state of being" and "knowledge" he means species, and

[8] *Ibid.* V, 18, 1022a, 27–29.

[9] The expression commonly used as a description of the space-occupancy of the atom is *ṣifah dhātiyyah*, but this expression is used in the sense of Aristotle's καθ' αὑτό as a description of property and as the equivalent of *li-nafsihi* (cf. Biram's n. 3 on pp. 18–19 of the German part of his edition of Abū Rashīd's *Masā'il*).

[10] *Irshād*, p. 47, ll. 19–20 (81).

[11] *Ibid.*, p. 10, ll. 7–10 (28).

by "blackness" he means subaltern species under the species "color." [12]

Thus by the first form of his uncaused modes Juwaynī means properties and by the second form he means genera and species.

So also in Shahrastānī, the first form of uncaused modes is illustrated by the example of "the space-occupancy of the atom" [13] and is explained by the statement that "any existent thing which has a property (*ḥāṣṣiyyah*) by which it is distinguished from another thing is distinguished from that other thing by a property which is only a mode." [14] Similarly the second form of uncaused modes is illustrated by the proposition that "an existent thing [*al-maujūd*] is accident and color and blackness" [15] and is explained by the statement that "so also that by which like things are alike and different things are different is a mode, and such modes are what we call attributes pertaining to genera and species." [16]

The two forms of Juwaynī's and Shahrastānī's uncaused modes, we shall now try to show, correspond respectively to Baghdādī's first and third classes of modes.[17]

As for the first form, namely, properties, it corresponds to Baghdādī's description of his first class of modes as referring to predicates affirmed of a subject "in virtue of itself (*li-nafsihi*)." The phrase "in virtue of itself," as we have seen, reflects a phrase used by Aristotle as a description of property.

As for the second form of uncaused modes, namely, genera and species, it corresponds to Baghdādī's third class of modes, which, in contrast to the first class (namely, properties) and the second class (namely, accidents), is said by him to be that in which a subject described by a certain predicate

[12] Cf. Porphyry, *Isagoge*, p. 1, l. 17 – p. 13, l. 8.

[13] *Nihāyat*, p. 132, l. 19.

[14] *Ibid.*, p. 133, ll. 1–2.

[15] *Ibid.*, p. 132, l. 19 – p. 133, l. 1. The bracketed term *al-maujūd* is an emendation of the term *al-'araḍ*, "accident," of the printed text and the underlying manuscripts. I have made this emendation on the basis of the corresponding passage in Juwaynī quoted above at n. 10.

[16] *Ibid.*, ll. 2–3.

[17] See quotation of Baghdādī's text above, pp. 169–170.

"possesses that predicate rather than some other predicate in virtue of a *ḥāl*." This is a fitting description of predicative terms which are genera and species in contrast to those which are properties and accidents, for, while a subject can be said to have many different properties and many different accidents, no subject can be said to belong to more than one genus and to more than one species, for subaltern species are, according to Aristotle, one and the same species,[18] and this is true also of subaltern genera. It is to be noted how in his description of the function of *ḥāl* in the first two classes of modes, Baghdādī carefully says that, in the case of the first class, it is simply to explain why the subject deserves its predicate and similarly, in the case of the second class, it is simply to explain why the subject came to possess the *maʿnā* in virtue of which it is described by a certain predicate. In neither of these cases does he say, as he does in the case of the third class, that it is that predicate rather than some other predicate that the subject deserves or is described by.

And so the threefold classification of modes in Baghdādī are reducible to the twofold classification of modes in Juwaynī and Shahrastānī. Baghdādī's first and third classes mean the same as what they call uncaused modes, and these include predicates which are either properties (Baghdādī's first type) or predicates which are genera or species (Baghdādī's third type). Baghdādī's second class of mode means the same as what in the twofold classifications is described as caused modes, and these include predicates which are accidents. All these types of modes thus correspond to four of Porphyry's five predicables.

APPENDIX B. *Relation of Abū Hāshim's Theory of* Aḥwāl *to Muʿammar's Theory of* Maʿnā

In the first of Baghdādī's two reports, which we have analyzed above, one could not have failed to notice a discon-

[18] *Metaph.* V, 10, 1018a, 1 and 7–8.

gruity between its two parts, and this despite the fact that the second part is introduced as a consequence following from the first. In the first part, Abū Hāshim is reported to have rejected Muʿammar's *maʿnā*, substituting for it the *ḥāl*; in the second part, he is reported to have retained Muʿammar's *maʿnā* in the second of his three classes of modes, using the *ḥāl* only as supplementary to it. The non sequitur of the second part from the first is quite evident. The explanation that suggests itself to me is that in the source of Baghdādī's first report, its first part, like the first part in his second report, was followed by a series of questions and answers, and it was from Abū Hāshim's answers to questions that the second part followed as a consequence. The discongruity that now appears between the two parts of Baghdādī's first report is thus due to the omission of the intervening questions and answers that must have existed in the source of that report.

I shall not attempt to task the reader with having to wade through the boresome questions and answers which I have reconstructed in order to satisfy myself that the threefold classification of modes in the second part of the first report could have logically followed from them. What alone is really necessary for the purpose at hand is to show how the threefold classification of modes as reported in the second part, granted to have immediately arisen from an assumed missing series of questions and answers, has ultimately grown out of Abū Hāshim's criticism of Muʿammar's theory of *maʿnā* as reported in the first part. This is what we shall now try to show.

In his theory of *maʿnā*, as we have seen, Muʿammar deals only with accidents, for which he uses the example of motion. With regard to accidents, he raises two questions, in answer to each of which questions he makes use of the *maʿnā*, but the use he makes of the *maʿnā* differs in each of these answers. The first question raised is why accidents come into existence in a subject after their not having existed in it, to which his answer is that they come into existence by a *maʿnā*. The *maʿnā* thus serves as the cause of the coming into existence of accidents in a subject of which they are used as predicates. The second question raised is why of two subjects, each of them possessing a *maʿnā*, only one of them is moved by its *maʿnā* at a certain particular time, whereas the other is moved by its *maʿnā* at some other time, to which his answer is that this is due to an infinite series of *maʿānī*. The infinite series of *maʿānī* thus serves as the cause of the difference between two subjects with reference to predicates which are accidents. Now Abū Hāshim admits with Muʿammar that the coming into existence of accidents as predicates of a subject, for which he uses as an example the predicate "knowing," is due to a *maʿnā*. He rejects, however, Muʿammar's explanation of the difference between subjects with reference to predicates which are accidents as being due to an infinite series of *maʿānī*. To him it is due to *ḥāl*. This adoption of Muʿammar's single *maʿnā* and rejection of his infinite series of *maʿānī* by substituting for it *ḥāl* has resulted in Abū Hāshim's second and third classes of modes, which in some respect may be regarded as being only modified forms of Muʿammar's theory of *maʿnā*.

Now predicates which are properties or genera and species, unlike predicates which are accidents, are coexistent with their subjects, and hence are not in need of a *maʿnā* to bring about their existence in their subjects. But still, in the case of property, there is need of an explanation why subjects differ with respect to properties. The answer given by Abū Hāshim is the same as the answer given by him to the question why subjects differ with respect to accidents, namely, that it is due to a *ḥāl*. This constitutes his first class of modes. In the case of genus and species, however, the question is, as we have seen, why a subject is described by one genus or species as its predicate rather than by another genus or species. The answer given by him, again, is that it is due to a *ḥāl*. This constitutes his third class of attributes.

This is how Abū Hāshim's threefold classification of modes has grown out of his criticism of Muʿammar's theory of *maʿnā*.

But here a question rises in our mind. Muʿammar's theory of *maʿnā*, as we have tried to show, originated as a result of his view that bodies have a nature which produces their accidents. This conception of a nature means, as we shall see later,[1] a belief in causality, in opposition to those in the Kalam who denied causality. Now Abū Hāshim, for all we know, like almost all the Muʿtazilites, except Muʿammar and Naẓẓām, did deny causality. What need, therefore, was there for him to assume a *maʿnā* plus a *ḥāl* to explain why subjects have accidents as predicates and to assume a *ḥāl* to explain why subjects have genera and species and specific differences and properties as predicates? Why did not he simply say that they are directly created by God in their subjects?

In answer to this question, the following three things are to be noted with regard to the denial of causality in the Kalam: (1) that the denial of causality does not mean an unawareness of the commonly observed fact that events in the world directly created by God follow a certain order of succession; (2) that this commonly observed order of succession is explained by a theory of "custom" which is attributed either to the Ashʿarites in general or to Ashʿarī himself; (3) that, while Ghazālī, in accordance with his denial of causality, insists that, in that commonly observed order of succession of events, every preceding event is not the "cause" of the event following it but only a "condition" thereof, he himself is sometimes found to be using the term "cause" as descriptive of the relation between two successive events, which quite evidently means that in those instances he uses the term "cause" rather loosely.[2] It is in the light of this conception of the denial of causality that we are to understand Abū Hāshim's use of his *maʿnā* and *ḥāl*. In the order of succession in which, according to him, it is the custom of God to create events in the world, he maintains that a *maʿnā* plus a *ḥāl* or only a *ḥāl* is created by God prior to His creation of certain predicates in subjects; and, while he is using ex-

[1] Cf. below, pp. 559 ff. [2] Cf. below, pp. 544–551.

pressions which imply that the *maʿnā* and *ḥāl* are causes, such as the expression "caused modes" and the expressions "in virtue of a *maʿnā*" and "in virtue of a *ḥāl*," the "cause" implied in the use of such expressions should be taken as a cause used in a loose sense. That the coinage of the term "custom" is ascribed to Ashʿarites does not mean that Ashʿarī's stepbrother and fellow-student, Abū Hāshim, and even others before him, did not have the idea of custom in their minds, even if there is no record of their having used the term custom. Similarly there is nothing against the assumption that the term "cause" was used by Abū Hāshim, and even by others before him, in a loose sense, even as it was so used later by Ghazālī. In fact, in Greek philosophy, the Epicureans, despite their denial of causality, sometimes use the term cause in a loose sense.[3]

So interpreted, the term *maʿnā*, as used by Abū Hāshim in his "caused modes" as reported by Juwaynī and Shahrastānī, and in his second class of modes as reported by Baghdādī, though borrowed from Muʿammar, is not used by him in the same way that it is used by Muʿammar. As used by Muʿammar, each *maʿnā* is implanted by God in each body at the time of the creation of that body and the *maʿnā* acts by its own power as the cause of some appropriate accident in that body.[4] As used by Abū Hāshim, each *maʿnā* is created by God in each body in connection with His creation of some accident in that body. But it is to be assumed that, once the accident and the *maʿnā* and also the *ḥāl* connected with it are created, all of them, the accident and the *maʿnā* and the *ḥāl*, have duration and need not be continuously created, for, as we shall see, the masters of the School of Baṣra, among whom Abū Hāshim is to be included, as well as Abū Hāshim's father, Jubbāʾī, held that creation involves duration.[5] Similarly in the case of the application of *ḥāl* to properties and to genera and species, all

[3] Such as the expressions *causa salutis* (Lucretius, *De Rer. Nat.* III, 348) and *morbi causa* (*ibid.*, 502).

[4] Cf. below, pp. 565 and 572 ff.

[5] Cf. below, pp. 533 and 537.

of which are created simultaneously with the creation of their subjects, it is to be assumed that, once a subject and the *ḥāl* connected with it are created, both the subject and the *ḥāl* have duration.

APPENDIX C. *The Term* Ḥāl

The question of the origin of the term *ḥāl* was raised by Ibn Ḥazm who, in his criticism of the theory of modes, says: "Before everything and after everything, one may ask them: Where did you get the term *aḥwāl*?"[1] In attempting to answer this question, let us see what are some of the special features which characterize Abū Hāshim's use of the term *ḥāl*.

From the reports of Baghdādī we gather that the term *ḥāl* was introduced by Abū Hāshim in connection with a proposition in which the predicate is the term "knowing," for which the examples used by him are "he who is knowing"; "Zayd is knowing."[2] From Baghdādī's first report we further gather that the term "knowing" is predicated of him who is knowing "in virtue of a *ḥāl* in which he is (*li-ḥāl kāna ʿalay-hā*),"[3] which phrase calls for an explanation. Then, from a comparison of Abū Hāshim's second class of mode in the second part of Baghdādī's first report with the caused modes in Juwaynī's and Shahrastānī's reports, we gather that in a proposition like "Zayd is knowing" the term *ḥāl* would be applied by Abū Hāshim to the predicate "knowing" in virtue of a *maʿnā*, by which he meant "knowledge," and the subject Zayd would, according to him, come to possess that *maʿnā* of knowledge "in virtue of a *ḥāl* [in which he is]."[4] The question before us, therefore, is whether we can find in Greek philosophy a term the application of which to the term "knowing" predicated of a subject will explain the meaning of Abū Hāshim's phrase "in virtue of a *ḥāl* in which he is."

[1] *Fiṣal* V, p. 51, ll. 23–24.
[2] Cf. above, p. 168 at nn. 6 and 7.
[3] *Ibid.*, n. 10.
[4] Cf. above, Appendix A.

The most obvious candidate for such a term would be the Greek term διάθεσις, "disposition," which by the time of Abū Hāshim had already been translated, in the Arabic versions of Aristotle, by the term *ḥāl*, in contrast to the term *malakah*, which was used as a translation of the Greek ἕξις, "habit" or "state." Let us then see how the term *diathesis*, "disposition," is used by Aristotle.

In his *Categories*, Aristotle says that habit and disposition apply to a certain kind of quality,[5] which means that they apply to a certain kind of accident. Since quality is defined by him as "that in virtue of which people are said to be such and such,"[6] habit and disposition apply not only to a substantive term which designates a quality possessed by a subject but also to an adjectival term which is derived from that substantive term and is predicated of the subject which possesses the quality. Among the examples of a quality described as a habit he mentions "knowledge"[7] and among the examples of a quality described as a disposition he mentions "heat,"[8] so that not only "knowledge" but also "knowing" would be a habit and not only "heat" but also "hot" would be a disposition.[9] "Habit differs from disposition," he says, "in that it is more lasting and stable."[10] Still, he subsequently adds, "habits are also dispositions," for "those who have habits are disposed (διάκεινται) in some manner or other in virtue of them,"[11] which statement, in the Arabic translation of the *Categories*, reads that "he who has a habit is in virtue of that also in a certain *ḥāl* (*man kanat la-hu malakah fa-huwa bi-hā bi-ḥāl mā ayḍan min al-aḥwal*)."[12] Accordingly, knowledge, which in the statement quoted above, is used by Aristotle as

[5] *Categ.*, 8, 8b, 26–27.

[6] *Ibid.*, 25.

[7] *Ibid.*, 29.

[8] *Ibid.*, 36.

[9] See also *ibid.*, 8b, 39, where the term "disposition" is applied to the term θερμός, "hot."

[10] *Ibid.*, 8b, 27–28.

[11] *Ibid.*, 9a, 10 and 11–12.

[12] It may be added that *ibid.*, 9a, 7–8, for the Greek "they are disposed (διάκεινται) in some manner" the Arabic has "to him there is a certain *ḥāl*" and *ibid.*, 8b, 37–38, for the Greek "a man is disposed (διάκειται)" the Arabic has "a man receives a *ḥāl*."

an example of habit, is in other places described by him either both as a habit and as a disposition or only as a disposition. To quote: (1) "Knowledge is called knowledge of the object of knowledge, but it is called a habit and a disposition not of the object of knowledge but of the soul"; [13] (2) "Every disposition . . . is formed naturally in that of which it is a disposition . . . as knowledge is formed in the soul, being a disposition of the soul"; [14] "Disposition is the genus of knowledge"; [15] "Both knowledge itself and its genera, as disposition and habit, are predicated of a certain thing." [16]

Thus, according to Aristotle, the term disposition is applied to the predicate knowing because he who is knowing is disposed to knowledge. Adopting this Aristotelian application of the term disposition — for which the Arabic term is *ḥāl* — to the predicate knowing, Abū Hāshim makes use of it for his own purpose in two ways.

First, directly in opposition to Muʿammar's view that the reason why the term knowing is predicated of A rather than of B is that in A there is an infinite series of *maʿānī*, he maintains that the term knowing is predicated of A rather than of B "only in virtue of a *ḥāl* in which he is," [17] which, as we have seen, is the Arabic way of saying that it is only in virtue of his being disposed to knowledge, for, according to Aristotle, he who has the habit of knowledge, that is, he who is knowing, is thereby disposed to knowledge. This, as we have seen, is what he describes as the second class of modes, namely, accidents.

Second, extending the use of the term *ḥāl*, he applies it to two other types of predicates, namely, (1) properties and (2) genera and species, both of which types are, like the habit knowledge, stable and lasting, but, unlike knowledge, require no *maʿānī* for their coming into existence. These, as we have

[13] *Top.* IV, 4, 124b, 33–34.
[14] *Ibid.* VI, 6, 145a, 34–37.
[15] *Ibid.* II, 4, 111a, 23.
[17] Cf. above, p. 169.

seen, are what he describes respectively as the first and third classes of modes.

The term *ḥāl* is thus used by Abū Hāshim neither simply in the sense of disposition nor simply in the sense of habit or state. It is, therefore, to be translated by the term mode, whose literal meaning "a manner" of existence would be taken to mean a state of existence containing a disposition for that state of existence.

Since the term *ḥāl* was originally applied by Abū Hāshim to predicates which are accidents and since also the term *ḥāl* was originally used by him in the technical sense of disposition, which Aristotle describes as a kind of quality and hence as an accident,[18] it was quite natural for Abū Hāshim to describe *aḥwāl* as not being "things" (*ashyā'*) [19] and as being "neither existent nor nonexistent," [20] so as to contrast them with Mu'ammar's *ma'ānī* which are described as "existent things" (*ashyā' maujūdah*).[21] That Abū Hāshim should, on account of their being accidents, describe *aḥwāl* as not being "things" and as being "neither existent nor nonexistent" may be explained on the ground of such Aristotelian statements about accident as that it "is only as it were a mere name," [22] that it is "closely akin to the nonexistent," [23] and that it "may not exist." [24] Without being conscious of any difficulty, Abū Hāshim retained the same negative description of *ḥāl* when he applied that term to predicates which are properties, for, whatever differences there may be between accident and property, he knew that, as far as their existence was concerned, both property and inseparable accident have in common, as stated by Porphyry, "not to subsist without those things in which they are beheld." [25] But when he came to describe *ḥāl* in its application to genera and species, that is,

[18] Cf. above, Appendix B and Appendix C.

[19] *Farḳ*, p. 182, ll. 2–3; *Nihāyat*, p. 133, l. 4.

[20] *Farḳ*, p. 182, l. 5; *Nihāyat*, p. 133, l. 4; p. 198, ll. 4–5.

[21] Cf. above, p. 155.

[22] *Metaph.* VI, 2, 1026b, 13–14.

[23] *Ibid.*, 22.

[24] *Phys.* VIII, 5, 256b, 10.

[25] *Isagoge*, p. 21, ll. 9–10.

universals, as being neither existent nor nonexistent, he was confronted with Porphyry's enumeration of the various views about their existence, of which one view maintained that they have substantive existence apart from objects of sense and another view maintained that they reside merely in naked mental conceptions,[26] which was taken by some opponent of Abū Hāshim to mean that they are mere words. As against both these views Abū Hāshim argued that his negative description of genera and species really has a positive meaning, for it means that they have a special kind of existence, an intramental existence, which is unlike both the nonexistence of mere words and the extramental existence of objects of sense.[27]

3. OPPOSITION TO ABŪ HĀSHIM

Abū Hāshim, who formally advanced a theory of modes, was a Muʿtazilite. The theory itself, however, was a veering away from the extreme nominalist position on attributes of the Muʿtazilites toward orthodoxy, but never reaching the extreme realist position of orthodoxy. The fate of any intermediate position has consequently overtaken it. It was disowned by both the Muʿtazilites and the orthodox. According to Baghdādī, it "was considered heretic by Abū Hāshim's fellow Muʿtazilites as well as by the other sects." [1] It has thus become the target of attack from both sides. But, as we have seen, there is a theory of modes as a mere theory of universals and there is a theory of modes as a theory of divine predicates, and of the latter, as we have also seen,[2] there are two versions: (1) the commonly accepted version, which was in opposition to both the orthodox Attributists and the Muʿtazilite Antiattributists; (2) the version by which Bāḳillānī and Juwaynī tried to harmonize modes with the orthodox belief in attributes, but which was rejected by Rāzī. The recorded criticisms of the theory of modes which we shall

[26] *Ibid.*, p. 1, ll. 9–11.
[27] Cf. below, pp. 201–202.

[1] *Farḳ*, p. 180, ll. 17–18.
[2] Cf. above, pp. 171 and 175.

deal with here are aimed at it either as a theory of universals in general or as a theory of divine predicates according to its commonly accepted version.

The spokesman for the Muʿtazilites who opposed Abū Hāshim's theory of modes is Abū Hāshim's own father, Jubbā'ī. Three main arguments against modes are reported in the name of Jubbā'ī and others.

First, the theory of modes involves the same difficulty of an infinite regress as the theory of Muʿammar. For, with regard to any subject but God, Abū Hāshim assumes that the modes are many in number. Since they are many in number, they must have something which they share in common and something by which they differ. But that difference between the modes will have to be explained by another mode; that other mode will introduce new differences, and these new differences will have to be explained by still another mode, and so it will go on to infinity.[3]

Second, the modes cannot be, as claimed by Abū Hāshim, neither existent nor nonexistent; they cannot but be nonexistent. This argument[4] may be restated as follows. Since Abū Hāshim has rejected the orthodox view that predicates of God are *maʿānī* or *ṣifāt*, that is, real things or attributes, and substituted for them modes, his modes must inevitably be either of the following two: either (a) they are mere words (*al-alfāẓ*), which, as common terms, are each predicable of many things because of their being rooted in one primary meaning of a word (*aṣl*), which is shared in common by all the different subjects of which the mode is predicated;[5] or (b) they are intellectual aspects (*wujūh*) and considerations (*iʿtibārāt*), that is to say, they are the concepts formed in our mind (*al-mafhūmah*) when we judge things as being alike by participation (*al-ishtirāk*) or as being unlike by separation (*al-iftirāḳ*).[6] "But these aspects," he adds, "are like relation-

[3] *Milal*, p. 56, ll. 14–16; cf. *Nihāyat*, p. 133, ll. 17–19.
[4] *Milal*, p. 56, l. 16–p. 57, l. 1.
[5] *Ibid.*, ll. 16–17.
[6] *Ibid.*, ll. 18–19.

ship (*al-nasab*), correlationships (*al-iḍāfāt*), proximity (*al-ḳurb*), remoteness (*al-buʿd*), and the like, which, according to the consensus of opinion, are not to be counted among real attributes" [7] — a statement which would seem to show that the early Muʿtazilite Antiattributists, like the later Alfarabi and Avicenna, agreed that there is no implication of a belief in attributes by interpreting terms predicated of God as relations.[8] Elsewhere, this second alternative is put as a separate argument addressed to the Modalists by their opponents, and it reads as follows: "What do you mean by saying that separation (*al-iftirāḳ*) and participation (*al-ishtirāk*) are an intellectual judgment? If you mean by it that a thing may be known from one aspect and unknown from another aspect, then [they are intellectual aspects, and] intellectual aspects (*al-wujūh al-ʿaḳliyyah*) are mental and estimative considerations (*iʿtibārāt dhihniyyah wa-taḳdīriyyah*), but these do not require to be taken as attributes firmly and they are like relationships and correlationships, such as proximity and remoteness between substances." [9] The argument, in other words, is this: Since modes are not "real things called attributes," they must be either mere "words" or "intellectual aspects and considerations," but, even if they are "intellectual aspects and considerations," they are nonexistent, in the same way that "relations" are nonexistent.

Third, the theory of modes is contrary to the Law of Excluded Middle. To quote: "According to the opinion of those who maintain the theory of modes, it is a mode which cannot be described either by existence or by nonexistence, but this, as you see, is a contradiction (*tanāḳuḍ*) and an absurdity." [10] The contradiction and absurdity we are expected

[7] *Ibid.*, l. 19 – p. 57, l. 1.

[8] Cf. Alfarabi, *Siyāsat*, p. 19, l. 15 – p. 20, l. 8; Avicenna, *Najāt*, p. 410, ll. 3–6 and 12–17 (see pp. 552–554 of my paper "Avicenna, Algazali, and Averroes on Divine Attributes," *Homenaje Millás Vallicrosa*, II [1956], 545–571).

[9] *Nihāyat*, p. 135, ll. 2–5.

[10] *Milal*, p. 57, ll. 5–6; cf. *Farḳ*, p. 182, ll. 1–7.

to see here is that according to the Law of Excluded Middle, already enunciated by Aristotle, "there cannot be an intermediate between contradictories, but of one subject we must either affirm or deny any one predicate." [11] In his *Nihāyat*, Shahrastānī restates this argument more fully as follows: "We know intuitively (*bi'l-badihah*) that there is no intermediate between negation and affirmation and between nonexistence and existence, yet you believe that the mode is neither existent nor nonexistent, which is contrary (*mutanāḳiḍ*) to what is known by intuition." [12]

In consequence of this criticism of modes, Jubbā'ī and others reaffirmed the old Mu'tazilite conception of attributes, restating it as a theory of universals and predicables. As reported by Shahrastānī in the *Milal*, "they take participation (*al-ishtirāk*) and separation (*al-iftirāḳ*) to refer to words (*al-alfāẓ*) and names of genera (*asmā' al-ajnās*)." [13] What they mean to say is that universal terms by which things are described as being similar or different are mere "words and generic names." The "intellectual aspects and considerations" which Abū Hāshim regards as a special kind of existence, a conceptual existence, an existence which is only in the mind, is an empty phrase. Things either have extramental existence or have no extramental existence. Mental or conceptual existence means a mere verbal existence, a mere emission of sound (*flatus vocis*), as the Scholastics would describe it. Thus the attributes, when called modes, would have to be described as nonexistent.

A similar rejection, by the opponents of modes, of conceptual existence and its reduction to a mere nominal existence is to be found also in the following statement in Shahrastānī's *Nihāyat*: "Those [among the Mu'tazilites] who deny modes are of the opinion that things are different or similar by their individual essences. As for names of genera and species, the generality of the former refers only to words by which similar

[11] *Metaph.* IV, 7, 1011b, 23–24.
[12] *Nihāyat*, p. 134, ll. 12–14.
[13] *Milal*, p. 56, ll. 13–14.

things are designated, and so also is the peculiarity of the latter. Sometimes indeed a thing is known from one aspect and unknown from another aspect, but these aspects are considerations which do not refer to attributes surnamed modes peculiarly belonging to essences." [14] What all this amounts to is a rejection of the modalistic conception of universals.

The three arguments against modes which we have quoted above did not remain unanswered by the Modalists.

The first argument, namely, that the theory of modes would have to lead to an infinite regress,[15] is answered as follows: "Generality and peculiarity in mode is like genericity and specificity in genera and species. Genericity in genera is not a genus, so that every genus would demand a genus, which would lead to an infinite regress, and similarly specificity in species is not a species, so that every species would demand a species. By the same token, we conclude, the modality of modes does not demand a mode, so that it would lead to an infinite regress." [16]

The answer may be spelled out as follows: Modes are universals, such as genera and species, and should be treated like genera and species. Now, if you take the Tree of Porphyry and turn it upside down, beginning with individuals and tracing backward the succession of species and genera, then no matter how long a series of intermediate subaltern species and genera you may get, it will not be infinite, for you are ultimately bound to reach a *summum genus*.

The second argument, namely, that "intellectual judgments" are only "intellectual aspects," which in turn are only "mental and estimative considerations" like relations, such as "proximity and remoteness between substances," [17] is answered as follows: "These aspects are not abstract words subsisting in him who speaks but rather cognizable and intelligible relations, which, while they do not exist independently nor are known separately, are attributes by which essences are

[14] *Nihāyat*, p. 133, ll. 6–10.

[15] Cf. above, p. 198.

[16] *Nihāyat*, p. 141, l. 16–p. 142, l. 1.

[17] Cf. above, pp. 198–199.

described. Accordingly, what you call aspects, we call modes, for these cognizable realities are distinct from each other, even though the essence is the same, and the distinction between them points to the numerical difference of the two aspects or modes, being as they are, two real cognizables to which two distinct cognitions attach, one necessary, the other derived. Modes are thus unlike relations and correlations, for the latter refer to abstract words, in which there is no real knowledge attaching to a real cognizable." [18]

The Modalists are thus willing to describe the modes as "intellectual aspects and considerations" but, unlike the Nominalists, who use this expression as a designation of mere "words," the Modalists use it as a designation of a special kind of existence, an intramental existence, which is distinct from both mere "words" and extramental reality.[18a]

But while the Modalists were not opposed to the use of the term "aspects," provided it is properly understood, the term in its general use was taken to have a nominalistic meaning. Thus Shahrastānī, who in one of his works, as we have just seen, uses the *wujūh*, "aspects," as a description of Abū al-Hudhayl's theory of modes,[19] in another of his works uses it as a description of the nominalistic theory of attributes as opposed to the modes of Abū Hāshim. He thus says: "The Muʿtazilites held different opinions as to whether terms predicated of the [divine] essence are (1) modes (*aḥwāl*) of the essence or (2) aspects (*wujūh*) and considerations (*iʿtibārāt*). Most of them said that they are [aspects and considerations, that is,] names and judgments formed regarding the essence

[18] *Nihāyat*, p. 137, l. 14–p. 138, l. 3.

[18a] The discussion about the existence of *ḥāl* is similar, as has been suggested by van den Bergh (see above, p. 182), to the Stoic discussion about the existence of λεκτόν, "verbal expression." But the two are not the same. The Stoic discussion about the "verbal expression" gave rise to the formula that "the verbal expression is midway between a thought and a thing" (Arnim, *Fragmenta* II, p. 48, ll. 34–35), whereas the discussion here about the *ḥāl* has led to the conclusion that it is neither a word nor a thing but a thought.

[19] Cf. above, p. 180, at n. 74.

. . . Abū Hāshim said: They are modes firmly and permanently attached to the essence."[20]

The third argument, namely, that the description of modes as neither existent nor nonexistent and as neither knowable nor unknowable violates the Law of Excluded Middle,[21] is answered as follows: "Arguments by logical division compelled us to establish the existence of modes, but necessity bid us not say that they are existent by themselves and knowable by themselves. For a thing is sometimes knowable along with something else and is not knowable by itself, as is the junction between substances and the contact and proximity and remoteness between them, for no junction and no contact can be known in a substance as long as no other substance gets joined to it. And if this obtains in the case of the kind of attributes which are essences and conceivable accidents, how much more so must it obtain in the case of attributes which are not essences but predications concerning essences?"[22]

What this passage means may be restated as follows: Inasmuch as the Modalists assume that modes have a conceptual existence and inasmuch as they also assume that a conceptual existence is distinct both from the existence of real extramental things and from the nonexistence of mere uttered words, what they mean then by their formula that "modes are neither existent nor nonexistent" is that they are neither existent like real things nor nonexistent like mere words. So understood, their formula does not violate the Law of Excluded Middle, for the Law, as phrased by Aristotle, reads as follows: "There cannot be an intermediate between contradictories (ἀντιφάσεως), but of one subject we must either affirm or deny any one predicate."[23] The meaning of this is that only in the case of "contradictories" — that is, in the case of the affirmation and negation of the same predicate of the same subject,[24] — between which, by definition, there is no inter-

[20] *Nihāyat*, p. 180, ll. 8–12.
[21] Cf. above, p. 199.
[22] *Nihāyat*, p. 137, ll. 6–12.
[23] *Metaph.* IV, 7, 1011b, 23–24.
[24] *De Interpr.*, 6, 17a, 31–37.

mediate, does the Law of Excluded Middle apply, so that one cannot say: "A neither is black nor is not black." But in the case of "contraries" (ἐναντία), between which, by definition, there are intermediates, the Law of Excluded Middle does not apply, so that one can say: "A neither is black nor is white" or "A neither is just nor is unjust." [25] Now, inasmuch as modes have a conceptual existence which is intermediate between the existence of real beings and the nonexistence of verbal beings, the proposition that "modes are neither existent nor nonexistent" does not violate the Law of Excluded Middle.

So much for the Muʿtazilite opposition to modes. Now for the orthodox opposition.

The chief exponent of the opposition to modes from among the orthodox attributists was Ashʿarī. As restated by Shahrastānī in his *Milal*, Ashʿarī begins with a statement that all those in Islam who participated in the discussion of the problem of attributes begin with the common premise that there is a Creator who is to be described as powerful and knowing and willing.[26] He then proceeds to argue that these three terms predicated of God must differ from each other in meaning,[27] whence, he wants us to conclude, they must differ also from the essence of God of which they are predicated. The question, therefore, is only as to what the nature of that difference is. Three alternative answers are enumerated by him. The predicates may be each either (1) a mere word (*lafẓ*), which is the view of Jubbāʾī, or (2) a mode (*ḥāl*), which is the view of Abū Hāshim, or (3) a real attribute (*ṣifah*),[28] the view which he himself is going to defend, after he has refuted both Jubbāʾī and Abū Hāshim.

In his criticism of Jubbāʾī, Ashʿarī contends that distinctions conceived by the mind reflect certain realities which are quite independent of the words by which these distinctions are

[25] *Categ.* 10, 12a, 9–25.

[26] *Milal*, p. 66, ll. 3–8; cf. similar argument in Ashʿarī's *Lumaʿ* 3, 13, 14, 18, and 23.

[27] *Milal*, p. 66, ll. 15–19.

[28] *Ibid.*, ll. 19–20.

expressed, and so distinctions cannot be mere words. To quote: "The intellect determines what difference of meaning there is between two concepts, and were it supposed that there was no word at all, the intellect would still be in no doubt [as to the meaning of the differences] in its conceptions." [29] This is exactly like the Modalists' argument against the view that universals are mere words as quoted by Rāzī.[30]

In his criticism of Abū Hāshim, Ash'arī repeats the argument already raised by the Mu'tazilites against the theory of modes,[31] namely, that it is contrary to the Law of Excluded Middle. His argument, as reported by Shahrastānī, reads as follows: "The assumption of an attribute which can be described neither by existence nor by nonexistence is the assumption of something which is in the middle between existence and nonexistence, between affirmation and negation, but this is something absurd." [32]

With the elimination of these two alternative possibilities, Ash'arī is left with the third possibility, namely, the old orthodox conception of attributes as being real things subsisting in God from eternity.

V. The Semantic Aspect of the Problem of Attributes *

The problem of divine attributes in the Kalam has a twofold aspect, an ontological and a semantic aspect. A third aspect, a logical one, was introduced later by those who are called "Philosophers," as distinguished from those known as "Mutakallimūn." [1]

[29] *Ibid.*, l. 20–p. 67, l. 2.

[30] *Muḥaṣṣal*, p. 39, ll. 9–12.

[31] Cf. above at nn. 10–12.

[32] *Milal*, p. 67, ll. 2–3.

* The part on the Antiattributists in this section (pp. 217 ff.) is reprinted here, with revisions, from *JAOS*, 79: 73–80 (1959), where it appeared under the title "Philosophical Implications of the Problems of Divine Attributes in the Kalam."

[1] Cf. my papers "Avicenna, Algazali, and Averroes on Divine Attributes,"

The ontological aspect of the problem deals with the question whether terms predicated of God in the Koran, such as "living" and "knowing" and "powerful," imply the existence in God of life and knowledge and power as real incorporeal beings, which, though inseparable from the essence of God, are distinct from it. No basis for this problem is to be found in the Koran. It originated under the influence of the Christian doctrine of the Trinity,[2] and in the early part of the eighth century there were already Attributists and Antiattributists.

The semantic aspect of the problem appears, in the Kalam, in two forms.

The first form of the problem is how one is to take the Koranic terms which describe God in the likeness of created beings. The basis of this form of the problem is the Koranic teaching, re-echoing a teaching in the Hebrew Scripture, that there is no likeness between God and other beings, which is expressed in such verses in the Koran as "Nought is there like Him" (42:9), and "There is none equal with Him" (112:4).

Among the Attributists there were various opinions on this form of the problem. There were some who, disregarding the verses condemning the likening of God to other beings, took the terms predicated of God in their extreme literalness. These were repudiated by other Attributists and were referred to by them derogatorily as "the Likeners" (*al-mushabbihah*).[3] But these repudiators of the Likeners were themselves divided into two groups. One group was satisfied with the mere assertion that all the terms predicated of God, while not establishing a likeness between God and other beings, should be taken literally to mean exactly what they say, adding with a shrug of the shoulders, *bi-lā kayfa*, "without questioning how."[4] Another group was willing to say explicitly that any term

---

Homenaje a Millás-Vallicrosa, II, 1956, pp. 545–571; "Crescas on the Problem of Divine Attributes," *Jewish Quarterly Review*, n.s., 7: 1–44, 175–221 (1916).

[2] Cf. above, Section I.

[3] Cf. *Farḳ*, p. 304, l. 10.

[4] Cf., e.g., *Ibānah*, p. 8, ll. 14 and 15 (50).

predicated of God is unlike the same term predicated of any other being, without, however, giving it a new unlike meaning, their common formula being "a body unlike other bodies." [5]

Among the Antiattributists there was no division of opinion on this form of the problem. They all agreed that common terms predicated of God are not only not to be taken literally but are also to be given new non-literal meanings.[6]

The second form of the semantic aspect of the problem, for both the Attributists and the Antiattributists, was the search for a formula which would express their respective conceptions of attributes.

The first dated formula for attributes is that used by Sulaymān b. Jarīr al-Zaydī, who flourished at about 785. In one place in his *Maḳālāt*, Ashʿarī reports him as saying that "God's knowledge is not God himself," [7] but this is evidently an incomplete statement, for in other places he reports him as saying that "God's knowledge is neither God nor other than God" [8] and also that "God is eternally willing in virtue of a will of which it cannot be said that it is God nor can it be said that it is other than God." [9] Similarly, his followers are reported by Ashʿarī as saying that "the Creator is knowing in virtue of a knowledge which is neither He himself nor other than He" to which Ashʿarī adds: "and like that they say with regard to all the other attributes." [10]

The same formula is used by Hishām b. al-Ḥakam (d. 814). In Ashʿarī there are two reports on his use of this formula. First, with regard to the attribute knowledge, he says: "God knows things only after His not having known them and He knows them in virtue of knowledge and the knowledge is one of His attributes, which is neither He nor other than He nor a part of Him, and His knowledge can [not] be described either as eternal or as created, for it is an attribute and an attribute, according to him, is not subject to predica-

[5] Cf. above, pp. 10–11.
[6] *Milal*, p. 30, ll. 14–16.
[7] *Maḳālāt*, p. 171, l. 6.
[8] *Ibid.*, p. 547, l. 14.
[9] *Ibid.*, p. 514, ll. 15–16.
[10] *Ibid.*, p. 70, ll. 8–10.

tion." [11] This last statement, it may be remarked in the passing, reflects his own view that "the so-called accidents are only attributes of the body which are neither the body nor other than the body" [12] plus Aristotle's statement that "an accident cannot be an accident of an accident," [13] from the combination of which it follows that an attribute is not subject to predication. Second, with regard to such attributes as power and life and hearing and seeing and willing, which, unlike knowledge, are, according to him, coeternal with God also *a parte ante*, he says that "they are attributes of God which are neither God nor other than God." [14]

The next one to use this formula is Ibn Kullāb (d. 854), a Sunnite. In one place, coupling him with the Shi'ite Sulaymān b. Jarīr, Ash'arī reports him as saying that "God is eternally willing in virtue of a will of which it cannot be said that it is God nor can it be said that it is other than God." [15] In another place, Ash'arī reports him as saying: "The meaning of 'God is knowing' is that He possesses knowledge and the meaning of 'He is powerful' is that He possesses power and the meaning of 'He is living' is that He possesses life, and so it is to be said with regard to all His other names." Ash'arī then goes on to report: "And Ibn Kullāb used to say that the names and attributes of God are in virtue of His essence (*li-dhātihi*); they are neither God nor other than God; they subsist in God, and it is impossible for attributes to subsist in attributes." [16] The same formula, without the phrase "in virtue of His essence," is also reported by Ash'arī in the name of a group of Ibn Kullāb's followers. According to one of these groups, "the names of the Creator are neither He nor other than He"; [17] according to another group, "one is not to say that the names of the Creator are He nor is one to say that they are not He," to which Ash'arī adds: "and they refrained

[11] *Ibid.*, p. 37, ll. 9–12; cf. p. 493, l. 15–p. 494, l. 3.
[12] *Ibid.*, p. 344, ll. 9–11.
[13] *Metaph.* IV, 4, 1007b, 2–3.
[14] *Maḳālāt*, p. 38, ll. 1–2.
[15] *Ibid.*, p. 514, ll. 15–16.
[16] *Ibid.*, p. 169, ll. 10–13; cf. p. 546, ll. 9, 11; p. 548, ll. 1–2.
[17] *Ibid.*, p. 172, ll. 7–8; cf. p. 546, l. 13.

from saying: 'They are not He and they are not other than He.'"[18]

Henceforth the formula that attributes are neither God nor other than God will be referred to as the Kullabite formula.

Of these three, Ibn Kullāb is known from another source to have been an Attributist on the ontological aspect of the problem,[19] and his use here of the expression that the attributes "subsist in God" corroborates it.

As for Sulaymān b. Jarīr al-Zaydī, one would at first sight take him to be an Antiattributist, for the founder of the Zaydiyyah was a pupil of Wāṣil b. 'Aṭā', and there was a close relationship between the Zaydiyyah and the Muʿtazilites.[20] But from the fact that Ashʿarī associates him here with Ibn Kullāb in asserting that "God is eternally willing in virtue of a will' and that he also reports him as saying that "God's knowledge is a thing and His power is a thing and His life is a thing,"[21] it is to be inferred that on the ontological aspect of the problem he was an Attributist.

Hishām b. al-Ḥakam is reported by Ibn Ḥazm as having joined the Muʿtazilites on the problem of attributes.[22] But in the same passage he includes also "the Ashʿarites" among those who have joined the Muʿtazilites on the problem of attributes, by which he means, as I shall show later, only those Ashʿarites who adopted the theory of modes, which theory was to him an exclusively Muʿtazilite theory.[23] So also what he says about Hishām b. al-Ḥakam as having joined the Muʿtazilites on the problem of attributes may merely mean that he took Hishām to be a follower of the theory of modes, and this on the mere

[18] *Ibid.*, p. 172, ll. 8–10. [19] Cf. below, p. 248.

[20] Cf. I. Friedlaender, "The Heterodoxies of the Shiites in the Presentation of Ibn Hazm," *JAOS*, 29: 11 (1908).

[21] *Maḳālāt*, p. 171, ll. 11–12.

[22] *Fiṣal* II, p. 112, ll. 19–20; cf. below. The reference in Baghdādī's *Farḳ*, p. 49, l. 10, to Hishām b. al-Ḥakam's having erred about "attributes" means, as may be judged from the context, not that he denied the reality of attributes but rather that he erred about some phase of the doctrine of real attributes in which he believed.

[23] Cf. below, p. 216.

ground that the formula "neither God nor other than God," as we shall see, came to be known later, after the time of Abū Hāshim, as an exclusively modalistic formula. From his own description of the attribute knowledge, which to him has a temporary beginning, it is quite evident that he regarded that attribute as a real attribute and so also quite evidently must he have regarded all the attributes which he admitted to be beginningless.

Since this formula is ascribed to three persons, two Shiʿites and one Sunnite, who quite evidently used it independently of each other as a description of their belief in the reality of attributes, it is to be assumed that none of them was its original author. They must have come upon it as an old formula, probably as old as, if not older than, the formula that "the Koran is neither a creator nor created" which is quoted on the authority of a man who died in 712.[24] Now this latter formula about the Koran, as we shall show, is aimed at the Christian belief that the second person of the Trinity, the Word, is a creator.[24a] We may, therefore, assume that this present formula about attributes, too, is aimed at some Christian belief in connection with the Trinity, and hence we may further assume that this formula was framed by those early Muslims who, as we have tried to show,[24b] arrived at the belief in the reality of attributes as a result of their debates with Christians on the Koranic rejection of the Christian Trinity. Accordingly, the first part of the formula, which reads "neither God," is to be taken to mean that, unlike the second and third persons of the Trinity, the attributes are not each God. The second part of the formula, which reads "nor other than God," is to be taken to mean that, though the attributes, unlike the second and third persons of the Trinity, are not each God, still, like those two persons, they are not separable from the essence of God and are not created beings. It is to be assumed, however, that with these three users of this old

[24] *Ibānah*, p. 38, ll. 5–7 (79).

[24a] Cf. below, p. 244.

[24b] Cf. above, pp. 129–132.

formula, all of whom flourished after the rise of Muʿtazilism, the first part of the formula, namely, the expression "neither God," has taken on an additional meaning, namely, that of an answer to the Muʿtazilite charge that a belief in attributes means a belief in more than one God. It may also be added that in the case of Hishām b. al-Ḥakam's formula for the created attribute of knowledge, the expression "nor other than He nor a part of Him" is to be taken to mean that, though knowledge is created and not eternal, it is not "other than He," that is, not outside of God, nor is it "a part of Him," that is, not a separate part of the eternal essence of God; it is an attribute created by God in Himself.

About a century later, the Kullabite formula was adopted by Abū Hāshim (d. 933). With him, however, this formula no longer meant to describe a belief in the reality of attributes; it rather meant to describe a belief in a new theory, his own theory of modes, which, on the one hand, was a denial of the extreme reality of attributes as conceived by the Attributists and, on the other hand, was a denial of the extreme verbality of attributes as conceived by the Antiattributists. Utilizing the old Kullabite formula, but changing the term "attribute" to "mode," Abū Hāshim says of modes that they are "neither God nor other than God." [25] This formula, however, is no longer aimed at the Christian doctrine of the Trinity; it is now aimed at the two opposite conceptions of the Muslim doctrine of attributes. Thus the first part of the formula, which reads "neither God," is a denial of the Muʿtazilites' view that terms predicated of God are mere names designating the essence of God; the second part of the formula, which reads "nor other than God," is a denial of the Attributists' view that terms predicated of God indicate the existence of real attributes in God which are distinct from His essence.[26]

At about the time that Abū Hāshim adopted the Kullabite formula and used it for his new theory of modes, Ashʿarī

[25] *Farḳ*, p. 182, l. 14.

[26] Cf. above, p. 139.

used that Kullabite formula and also another formula. As quoted by Ibn Ḥazm from one of his works, of which no title is given, Ash'arī says, with regard to the knowledge of God, that "one is not to say that it is God nor is one to say that it is other than God," [27] which is only another way of phrasing the formula that "it is neither God nor other than God" quoted just before it by Ibn Ḥazm in the name of some "groups from among the Sunnites." [28] However, from another work of his, of which, again, no title is given, Ibn Ḥazm quotes Ash'arī as saying that "the knowledge of God is other (*ghayr*) than God and different (*ḫilāf*) from God, but despite this it is uncreated and eternal." [29] The same view, as quoted, again, by Ibn Ḥazm from a work of Ash'arī's entitled *Al-Majālis*, reads: "Coexistent with God are things (*ashyā'* = attributes) other than Himself (*siwahu*), which are eternal as He is eternal." [30] Similarly, speaking for himself in his *Al-Luma'*, Ash'arī first affirms that "God is knowing in virtue of a knowledge which cannot be Himself" and then denies that "God is knowing neither in virtue of Himself nor in virtue of a thing (*ma'nā* = attribute) which cannot be Himself," [31] by which he means that for the attribute of knowledge or for any other attribute one is to use the formula "it is other than God" and not the formula "it is neither God nor other than God." A modified form of Ash'arī's formula in his *Luma'*, one according to which the otherness of attributes in their relation to God is to be implicitly asserted but not explicitly expressed, is to be found in Shahrastānī. Thus, quoting Ash'arī first as saying that the formulation of one's conception of every attribute is to be modeled after the formula "God is knowing in virtue of knowledge," by which is meant that attributes are real and hence other than God, he then quotes Ash'arī as saying with regard to attributes that "it is not to

[27] *Fiṣal* II, p. 126, ll. 21–22.
[28] *Ibid.*, ll. 20–21.
[29] *Ibid.*, ll. 22–24.
[30] *Ibid.* IV, p. 207, ll. 13–14.
[31] *Luma'* 25–26, p. 14, ll. 11–4.

be said that they are He or other than He or not He or not other than He." [32]

Now Abū Hāshim and Ash'arī were stepbrothers and fellow students under their father and stepfather, Jubbā'ī, who was a Mu'tazilite and Antiattributist. Both of them, we may assume, while students under Jubbā'ī, were Mu'tazilites and Antiattributists. Both of them, we know, later abandoned the Antiattributism of their master. Abū Hāshim, at some unknown time, became the founder of the theory of modes, to which he applied the Kullabite formula in its new meaning; Ash'arī, in 912, became completely converted to orthodoxy, accepting all its teachings, including the reality of attributes. When, therefore, Ash'arī uses two formulae, one a new formula in two forms asserting or implying that attributes are "other than God," the other the Kullabite formula asserting that attributes are "neither God nor other than God," we are certain that his new formula comes from the period after his conversion, when he came to believe in the reality of attributes and with the zeal of a new convert dropped the ambiguous Kullabite formula and proclaimed that attributes are to be described as "other than God" and as "different from God." But, with regard to his use of the Kullabite formula, the following question may be raised. Is it used by him in its original Kullabite sense, as an affirmation of attributes, and hence comes from the period following his conversion to orthodoxy? This would seem to be corroborated by the fact that the orthodox Ash'arī is described by Ibn Ḫaldūn as following Ibn Kullāb.[33] Or is it used by him in its Hashimite sense, as a description of modes? This would mean that for a while, prior to his conversion to orthodoxy, Ash'arī joined his stepbrother and fellow student in advocating the theory of modes. Changes of mind on the problem of modes are reported to have occurred later among some of his followers.[34] Or, on the assumption, again, that it was used by

[32] *Milal*, p. 67, ll. 8–10.

[33] Cf. above, p. 36.

[34] Cf. below at n. 49.

him in its Hashimite sense as modes, does it mean that after his conversion to orthodoxy, Ashʿarī modified his view on attributes and adopted modes? A similar modification of his original orthodox views has been noted in connection with other problems.[35]

The uncertainty as to what Ashʿarī meant by his use of the Kullabite formula created among his followers three different views on the problem of attributes.

Some of his followers were Attributists and used Ashʿarī's new formula as an expression of their view. Thus Bāḳillānī (d. 1013), after being introduced by Ibn Ḥazm (d. 1064) as "the greatest" of the Ashʿarites, is reported by him as saying: "God has fifteen attributes, all of them coeternal with God *a parte ante* and *a parte post*, and all of them other (*ghayr*) than God and different (*ḫilāf*) from God, and every one of them other than the others and different from the rest, and God is other than they and different from them." [36] Similarly, in another place, after quoting from one of Ashʿarī's works his non-Kullabite formula that "the knowledge of God is other than God and besides God, but despite this it is uncreated and ceaseless," Ibn Ḥazm adds that "Bāḳillānī and the majority of his followers are in agreement with him on this." [37] The same non-Kullabite formula, but with the substitution of the phrase "superadded to" for the phrase "other than" is ascribed to the Ashʿarites by both Shahrastānī (d. 1153) and Averroes (d. 1198). Thus Shahrastānī in his *Nihāyat* reports in the name of the Ashʿarites as follows: "The Creator is knowing in virtue of knowledge, powerful in virtue of power, living in virtue of life, hearing in virtue of hearing, seeing in virtue of sight, willing in virtue of will, speaking in virtue of speech, and these [seven] attributes are superadded (*zāʾidah*) to God's essence and they are attributes (*ṣifāt*) eternally existent and things (*maʿānī*) subsisting in His essence." [38] And as restated by Averroes in the name of the

[35] Cf. Wensinck, *The Muslim Creed*, pp. 91–94.
[36] *Fiṣal* IV, p. 207, ll. 7–10.
[37] *Ibid.* II, p. 126, ll. 22–23.
[38] *Nihāyat*, p. 181, ll. 1–4.

Ash'arites, the attributes are "real" (*ma'nawiyyah*),[39] "superadded (*zā'idah*) to the essence," [40] each of them "subsisting" (*ḳā'im*) in the essence.[41]

Other followers of Ash'arī, also Attributists, used the Kullabite formula, which, as we have seen, was at one time used by Ash'arī. This we gather from Taftāzānī's commentary on Nasafī's *Creed*. It happens that Nasafī (d. 1142), who was not an Ash'arite, uses the Kullabite formula that attributes "are neither God nor other than God" [42] as an expression of his belief that God "has attributes subsisting in His essence from all eternity." [43] Commenting on this formula, Taftāzānī (d. 1388) says that it is the same as that of the Ash'arites, whom he quotes, with regard to attributes, as denying "both their otherness [from God] and their sameness [with God]." [44] Somewhat later, Ibn Ḫaldūn (d. 1406), in answer to the Mu'tazilite argument that the belief in real attributes is tantamount to a belief in many gods, says: "The argument is refuted by the view that the attributes are neither identical with the essence [of God] nor other than it." [45] From the context it is evident that he reproduces the view of the Ash'arites.

With regard to these two formulae used by these two groups of followers of Ash'arī, Mula Aḥmad al-Jundī, in his supercommentary on Taftāzānī, remarks that the formula that attributes "are neither God nor other than God" represents the view of "the earlier Ash'arites," whereas "the later ones maintain that the attributes are other than the essence [of God]." [46]

Besides these two groups of Ash'arites who were Attributists, there were also Ash'arites who were Modalists. Ibn Ḥazm refers to them as follows: "One of the stupidities of

[39] *Kashf*, p. 56, l. 4. Cf. above, p. 178, n. 65.

[40] *Ibid.*, ll. 3 and 7.

[41] *Ibid.*, l. 6.

[42] Taftāzānī, p. 70, l. 3.

[43] *Ibid.*, p. 69, l. 2; p. 70, ll. 6, 7.

[44] *Ibid.*, p. 72, l. 10.

[45] *Muḳaddimah* III, p. 38, ll. 16–17.

[46] Jundī, p. 109, quoted by Elder, p. 53, n. 9.

the Ashʿarites is their assertion that [it is possible] for men [to believe in] modes (*al-aḥwāl*) and [universal] concepts (*al-maʿānī*) which are neither existent nor nonexistent, neither known nor unknown, neither created nor uncreated, neither beginningless nor originated, and neither real nor unreal." [47] Another reference in Ibn Ḥazm to Ashʿarites as upholders of the theory of modes is in the following statement: "As for the modes (*al-aḥwāl*) which the Ashʿarites adopted as their own (*iddaʿathā*), they said that there are modes which are neither real nor unreal, neither created nor uncreated, neither existent nor nonexistent, neither known or unknown, neither things nor not-things." [48] A reference to two known Ashʿarites who were Modalists is to be found in Shahrastānī's statement that although Ashʿarī himself and the generality of his followers opposed Abū Hāshim's theory of modes, Bāḳillānī supported it after some hesitation, and Juwaynī first supported it and then opposed it.[49] Both Bāḳillānī and Juwaynī are known as Ashʿarites. Bāḳillānī and Juwaynī are mentioned also by Rāzī as "two foremost from among us [orthodox]" who supported the theory of modes.[50] As we have seen,[51] both Bāḳillānī and Juwaynī, each in his own way, tried to harmonize modes with their own belief in attributes.

In one place, Ibn Ḥazm includes "the Ashʿarites" among those who followed the Muʿtazilites on the problem of divine attributes.[52] The reference undoubtedly is here again to those Ashʿarites who adopted the theory of modes, which was regarded by him as a Muʿtazilite theory.

On the whole, one gets the impression that while the theory

[47] *Fiṣal* IV, p. 208, ll. 5–7. By "modes and [universal] concepts," I take it, Ibn Ḥazm means here modes as applied to divine predicates and modes in the sense of universals. On the relation between these two senses of modes, see above pp. 170–171. Maimonides, in a passage where he refers only to modes in the sense of universals, uses the expression "the modes (*al-aḥwāl*), that is, the universal concepts (*al-maʿānī al-kulliyyah*)." Cf. *Moreh* I, 51, p. 76, ll. 26–27.

[48] *Fiṣal* V, p. 49, ll. 2–4.

[49] *Nihāyat*, p. 131, ll. 5–9.

[50] *Muḥaṣṣal*, p. 38, ll. 19–20.

[51] Cf. above, pp. 175 ff.

[52] *Fiṣal* II, p. 112, ll. 19–20. Cf. above

of modes in its application to divine predicates started as a moderate Muʿtazilite view, it came to be regarded as a sort of moderate orthodox view. Ibn Ḫaldūn, it is to be noted, includes both the belief in the reality of attributes [53] and the belief in modes [54] among what he considers common characteristics of the Kalam; and perhaps, when in the passage quoted above he ascribes to Ashʿarites the formula that "the attributes are neither identical with the essence [of God] nor other than it," it is the theory of modes that he means by it.[54a]

So much for the treatment of the semantic aspect of the problem of attributes by the Attributists. Let us now take up its treatment by the Antiattributists.

Since the arguments of the Muslim Antiattributists against the reality of attributes were framed, as we have seen, under the influence of the arguments of heretical Christians against the reality of the persons of the Trinity, the formulae used by them to express their denial of the reality of attributes were modeled after the formulae used by those heretical Christians to express their denial of the reality of the persons of the Trinity. Now in the various formulae used by those heretical Christians, they tried either to emphasize the sameness of the persons of the Trinity or to reduce the differences between them to mere names.[55] They thus say that "the Father and the Son so-called are one and the same, not another from another," [56] or that "the Father is Son and again the Son Father, in hypostasis one, in name two," [57] or that the second person, the Word, is "but a voice and sound of the mouth." [58] Similarly, the Antiattributists are reported as saying that "the knowledge of the Creator is the Creator," [59] or that the attributes are "the very essence of God," [60] or that the terms predicated of God are "names and judgments formed of the

[53] *Muḳaddimah* III, p. 114, l. 6.
[54] *Ibid.*, l. 11.
[54a] Cf. *Religious Philosophy*, pp. 182–184.
[55] Cf. *The Philosophy of the Church Fathers*, I, pp. 580–585.
[56] Noetus in Hippolytus, *Refutatio Omnium Haeresium* IX, 10, 11.
[57] Sabellius in Athanasius, *Orat. cont. Arian.* IV, 25 (PG 26, 505 C).
[58] Praxeas in Tertullian, *Adv. Prax.* 7.
[59] *Maḳālāt*, p. 173, l. 15.
[60] *Ibid.*, p. 174, ll. 9–10.

essence," [61] or that "the names and attributes are only words (*al-aḳwāl*), and this is what is meant when we say: God is knowing, God is powerful, and the like." [62]

But a name must have meaning, and different names must have different meanings. What then are the different meanings of the different names which are predicated of God and which are all said to be the very essence of God?

The question had already been raised in the mind of those Christian heretics who considered the persons of the Trinity as being only different names. The answer suggested by at least one of them, Sabellius, is to be found in a statement reported in his name, which says in effect that the terms "Father" and "Son" and "Holy Spirit" are only names, but names which designate different actions (ἐνέργειαι), those different actions into which the one single action of God manifests itself in the world.[63]

The same question was raised also in the mind of the orthodox Fathers with regard to all those predications of God which were not terms designating the persons of the Trinity. For while with respect to the terms designating the persons of the Trinity, the Fathers of the Church believed that they stand for real beings, with respect to all other terms predicated of God, such as great and merciful and the like, they considered them as mere words or names, so that with regard to this kind of terms the Fathers of the Church were what in Islam would be described as deniers of attributes. The distinction between these two kinds of terms is clearly brought out by John of Damascus who, after dealing with the "Word" and the "Holy Spirit" and the whole "Trinity," takes up "What is Affirmed of God" [64] to which he subsequently refers as the "names" of God.[65] But, inasmuch as these predicates are common terms which are equally predicated of other beings, the Fathers of the Church were faced with the problem of how

[61] *Nihāyat*, p. 180, l. 9.
[62] *Makālāt*, p. 172, ll. 14–15.
[63] Epiphanius, *Adv. Haer. Pan.* LXII, 1 (PG 41, 1052 B).
[64] *De Fide Orthodoxa* I, 6–8.
[65] *Ibid.* I, 9 (PG, 94, 833 B – 836 A, l. 12).

to eliminate from their use as predications of God the implication of any likeness between God and other beings.

The solution offered by the Fathers of the Church is that terms predicated of God should be expressed either in the form of (1) actions or in the form of (2) negations and, if they are not expressed in either of these two forms, they should be interpreted as being actions or negations in meaning. Thus, again, John of Damascus, in his classification of terms which can be predicated of God, mentions (1) terms signifying "action" (ἐνέργεια)[66] and (2) terms signifying "what God is not."[67] It may be remarked here in passing that the active interpretation of divine predicates is ultimately traceable to Philo, and the reason given by him why action may be predicated of God without fear of likening Him to other beings is that to act is a property which belongs to God alone, for man's power to act freely is a gift to man by God,[68] whence to describe God as acting does not imply a likeness between Him and created beings. As for the negative interpretation of terms predicated of God in the Scriptures affirmatively, it is generally ascribed to pseudo-Dionysius, who is reputed to be the father of the so-called negative theology. But, in truth, he is not its real father; he is only its stepfather. Before him was Plotinus. But even Plotinus is not its real father; he is only its foster father. Before Plotinus was Albinus, and it is Albinus who is its real father.[69]

These two solutions are openly and directly discussed later in Arabic philosophy. But we shall try to show how they came to be introduced into Islam during the Kalam period.

It is interesting to note that Wāṣil ibn ʿAṭāʾ (d. 748), who, according to extant reports, was the first to discuss the problem of attributes in its ontological aspect, does not touch upon its semantic aspect. All that is reported of him is his

[66] *Ibid.* (837 A, l. 12). [67] *Ibid.* (l. 15).

[68] Cf. *Philo*, II, pp. 133–134.

[69] Cf. my papers "Albinus and Plotinus on Divine Attributes," *Harvard Theological Review*, 45: 115–130 (1952), and "Negative Attributes in the Church Fathers and the Gnostic Basilides," *ibid.*, 50: 145–156 (1957).

rejection of the existence of real attributes on the ground of its implication of polytheism.[70]

A contemporary of Wāṣil, however, Jahm ibn Ṣafwān, is reported to have expressed himself in a way which implies that he was conscious of the semantic aspect of the problem and attempted to solve it. Jahm is not included among the Muʿtazilites,[71] and, though on some problems he is at one with them, on others he differs with them. He is at one with them, for instance, on the problem of the createdness of the Koran, but he differs with them on the problem of free will. As for the problem of attributes, Ibn Ḥazm[72] and Shahrastānī[73] testify that he agreed with the Muʿtazilites in the denial of the reality of attributes.[74] Jahm himself, however, is never quoted directly as saying that attributes are to be denied on the ground, as usually stated by the Muʿtazilites, that they violate the true conception of the unity of God. From the statements quoted in his name, it may be gathered that his denial of attributes was based on the ground that the assumption of their existence and their predication of God would be contradictory to the Koranic injunction against likening God to other beings.

Statements ascribed to him, or made concerning him, which indicate that he was conscious of the semantic aspect of the problem of attributes and tried to solve it are as follows: (1) "I will not say that God is a thing, for this is likening Him to things";[75] (2) "Since the Jahmiyyah say that God has neither knowledge nor power, they believed that He is neither

[70] *Milal*, p. 31, ll. 17 ff.

[71] He is explicitly excluded from the Muʿtazilites by Ḫayyāṭ (*Intiṣār* 83, p. 92, ll. 22–24). Baghdādī (*Farḳ*, p. 93, ll. 4–12) does not include him among the founders of the twenty Muʿtazilite sects. Nor does Shahrastānī (*Milal*, p. 29, ll. 18 ff. and p. 60, ll. 6 ff.) include him among the Muʿtazilites.

[72] *Fiṣal* II, p. 112, ll. 19–21.

[73] See below at n. 79.

[74] With regard to knowledge, it is to be noted, he is quoted as saying that it is created and other than God (*Maḳālāt*, p. 222, l. 9; p. 204, l. 10; *Intiṣār* 83, p. 92, ll. 21–22); the meaning of this statement is discussed above on p. 140 and p. 144. Cf. Pines, *Atomenlehre*, p. 125, n. 1.

[75] *Maḳālāt*, p. 280, ll. 2–3; p. 181, ll. 2–3; p. 518, ll. 5–6.

knowing nor powerful," even though "the fear of the sword restrains them" from expressing publicly the true implication of their statement; [76] (3) "He refrained from applying to God the description that He is a thing, or that He is living or knowing or willing, saying 'I shall not describe Him by a description which may be applied to others, such as existent thing, living, knowing, willing, and others like them.' But he described Him as being powerful and causing existence and acting and creating and causing life and causing death"; [77] "Jahm ibn Ṣafwān arrived at the opinion that a thing is that which has come into existence and that the Creator is He who makes the thing a thing"; [78] (5) "He agreed with the Muʿtazilites in the denial of eternal real attributes, but went further than they in some matters. One of these is his statement that it is not permissible that the Creator should be described by terms by which His creatures are described, for this would lead to an act of likening (*tashbīh*). He therefore denies that He is living and knowing. He affirms, however, that He is powerful, doing, and creating, for none of His creatures is describable by the terms 'power,' 'doing,' and 'creating.' " [79] Followers of Jahm are quoted by Ibn Ḥanbal as expressing their denial of attributes by using such formulae as "God is the whole of Him (*kulluhū*) face, the whole of Him light, the whole of Him power," [80] in which the expression "the whole of Him" is quite evidently used as the equivalent of the expression "in virtue of himself" (*li-nafsihi*) which was introduced, as we shall see, by Najjār and Ḍirār.[81]

Combining these various reports, we may restate Jahm's view as follows: He agreed with the Muʿtazilites, that is, Wāṣil and his followers, on the ontological aspect of the problem of divine attributes, but he added to this aspect of the problem also the discussion of its semantic aspect. With

[76] *Ibānah*, p. 54, ll. 11–12 (94).

[77] *Farḳ*, p. 199, ll. 10–13.

[78] *Nihāyat*, p. 151, ll. 9–10.

[79] *Milal*, p. 60, ll. 6–11.

[80] Quoted by Pines, *Atomenlehre*, pp. 124–125, from Ibn Ḥanbal's *Al-Radd ʿalā al-Zanādiḳah wa'l-Jahmiyyah*, p. 315, ll. 10–11. Cf. below at n. 109.

[81] Cf. below at nn. 86 and 88.

reference to this semantic aspect of the problem, we are told that he prohibited the predication of God of any of such terms as "thing," "existent," "living," and "knowing," but he allowed to affirm of God that He is "causing existence" and "causing life," and, by the same token, we may assume, also "causing knowledge," "causing will," and their like. The terms "powerful," "doing," and "creating," however, are treated by him as exceptions. Their predication of God is allowed by him, and this evidently on the ground that they describe God not as what He is but rather as what He does. Undoubtedly even in the case of the terms "existent," "knowing," and "living," Jahm would not insist upon the actual use of the expressions "causing existence," "causing knowledge," and "causing life"; he would allow their use as divine predicates if they were only understood to mean "causing existence," "causing knowledge," and "causing life."

The reason given by Jahm for assuming that terms describing God as what He does do not imply His likeness to other beings is in accordance with his own particular view that apart from God, no other being, including man, has any power of his own to act, so that every act of man is directly created by God.[82] This is only a modified form of the reason given by Philo in justifying the predication of action of God, for, according to him, while man has the power to act freely, that power is a special gift with which the human species has been endowed by God.[83]

Jahm was thus the first to introduce into Arabic philosophy the semantic aspect of the problem of attributes and to offer the active interpretation, already established by Philo, Albinus, Plotinus, and the Church Fathers, as a solution of the problem. We may therefore assume that all the philosophic reasoning used by his predecessors in justifying the active interpretation of divine predicates is behind Jahm's statements.

Jahm died, or rather he was executed, in 746. Shortly after

[82] Cf. below, p. 606.

[83] Cf. *Philo*, I, pp. 424–462; II, pp. 133–134; above n. 68.

that the negative interpretation of affirmative predicates was introduced by two contemporaries, Najjār and Ḍirār, who flourished between 750 and 840.

Of Najjār or of his followers we have the following reports: (1) "Of the views which they share with the Ḳadarites is the remotion of God's attribute of knowledge and His attribute of power and His attribute of life and His other eternal attributes";[84] (2) "God is continuously generous in the sense that avarice is remote from Him and He is continuously speaking in the sense that He is never powerless for speech";[85] (3) "The Creator is willing in virtue of himself (*li-nafsihi*) just as He is knowing in virtue of himself"[86] and "the meaning of His being willing is that He is not feeling an aversion nor is He being compelled."[87]

Combining these reports, we may restate Najjār's view as follows. He denied the existence of real attributes in God. Consequently he used two types of formula: (1) the simple affirmation of a predicate; (2) the affirmation of a predicate followed by the qualifying phrase "in virtue of himself," but, in either of these formulae, the affirmative proposition in which a positive term is predicated of God is to be taken as being negative in meaning.

Of Ḍirār it is reported that "he maintained that the meaning of the statement that God is knowing or powerful is that He is not ignorant and not powerless and so did he say with regard to the other predicates of the Creator which are in virtue of himself (*li-nafsihi*)."[88]

Najjār and Ḍirār were thus the first to introduce the negative interpretation of affirmative predicates into Arabic philosophy.

Where they got this negative interpretation of attributes we are not told in these reports. In a doxography of Greek philosophers reproduced by Shahrastānī there is the statement

[84] *Farḳ*, p. 196, ll. 1–2.
[85] *Maḳālāt*, p. 284, ll. 15–16.
[86] *Milal*, p. 62, l. 2.
[87] *Ibid.*, ll. 3–4.
[88] *Maḳālāt*, p. 281, ll. 13–14; cf. *Farḳ*, p. 202, ll. 6–8; *Milal*, p. 63, l. 7.

that Plato in his *Laws* says that "God can be known only by negation, that is to say, He has no likeness and no resemblance." [89] If the Arabic version of the *Laws* did actually contain such a statement, it might perhaps have been known to both Najjār and Ḍirār, for the *Laws* was translated by Ḥunayn ibn Isḥāḳ (809–873),[90] probably during the lifetime of Najjār and Ḍirār. However, no such statement is actually to be found in Plato. Undoubtedly, like the very problem of attributes in Islam, this conception of the negative interpretation held by Najjār and Ḍirār had its immediate origin in the Church Fathers. Corroborative evidence for this may be in the fact that another report of the teaching of Ḍirār ascribes to him the statement that "God has a quiddity (*māhiyyah*) which no other but He knows." [91] Rephrased into more familiar terms, this statement means that God's essence is unknowable, and undoubtedly this statement is meant to be the reason for his other statement, that God must be described negatively. Now this is the underlying reason for the use of the negative interpretation by John of Damascus,[92] as well as by others. Incidentally, it may be remarked that the principle of the unknowability of God's essence does not occur in Greek philosophy before Philo.[93] It was introduced by Philo as a philosophic inference from the scriptural teaching of the unlikeness of God.[94] We may therefore assume, again, that all the philosophic reasoning used by their predecessors in justifying the negative interpretation of divine predicates is behind the statements of Najjār and Ḍirār.

The negative interpretation of affirmative predicates, which was introduced by Najjār and Ḍirār, became the subject of

[89] *Milal*, p. 288, ll. 16–17.

[90] Cf. M. Steinschneider, *Die arabischen Uebersetzungen aus dem Griechischen*, p. 18.

[91] *Farḳ*, p. 201, l. 18–p. 202, l. 1; cf. *Milal*, p. 63, ll. 7–8; *Maḳālāt*, p. 216, ll. 3–4, and p. 154, l. 2.

[92] *De Fide Orthodoxa* I, 2 (PG 94, 792 C, 793 B) and I, 12 (845 BD).

[93] Cf. my paper "The Knowability and Describability of God in Plato and Aristotle," *Harvard Studies in Classical Philology*, 56–57: 233–249 (1947).

[94] Cf. *Philo*, II, pp. 94–164.

tacit controversy between two of their younger contemporaries, al-Naẓẓām (d. 845) and Abū al-Hudhayl (d. 849).

Of Naẓẓām it is reported as follows: "He denies knowledge, power, life, hearing, seeing, and the [other] essential attributes [of God] and says that God is continuously knowing, living, powerful, hearing, and eternal in virtue of himself (*bi-nafsihi*), but not in virtue of knowledge, power, life, hearing, seeing, and eternity, and so is his view with regard to the [other] essential attributes." [95]

Of Abū al-Hudhayl we have the following reports: (1) Ashʿarī: (a) "He affirms glory, majesty, splendor, greatness, and so does he also with regard to the other attributes by which God is described in virtue of himself (*li-nafsihi*)"; [96] (b) "God is knowing in virtue of a knowledge, which is himself (*hu*), and He is powerful in virtue of a power, which is himself, and He is living in virtue of a life, which is himself, and so does Abū al-Hudhayl say also with regard to God's hearing and His seeing and His eternity and His glory and His majesty and His splendor and His greatness and His other attributes which are in virtue of His essence (*li-dhātihi*)"; [97] (c) "God has knowledge [in virtue of a knowledge] which is himself"; [98] "The Creator's knowledge [which is in virtue of knowledge] is He himself." [99] (2) Shahrastānī: (a) "The Creator is knowing in virtue of a knowledge which is himself (*nafsuhu*)"; [100] (b) "The Creator is knowing in virtue of knowledge, and His knowledge is His essence (*dhātuhu*)." [101]

Though in the reports of their teachings neither of them makes reference to the other, it is quite clear that their formulae are in opposition to each other. Naẓẓām explicitly uses, in one part of his formula, the statement that God is knowing "not in virtue of knowledge," whereas Abū al-Hudhayl explicitly uses, in one part of his formula, the statement that God is knowing "in virtue of knowledge." Un-

[95] *Maḳālāt*, p. 486, ll. 10–13.
[96] *Ibid.*, p. 177, ll. 13–14.
[97] *Ibid.*, p. 165, ll. 5–7; cf. *Fiṣal* II, p. 126, ll. 24–25; p. 108, ll. 7–8.
[98] *Maḳālāt*, p. 188, l. 11.
[99] *Ibid.*, p. 484, l. 5.
[100] *Nihāyat*, p. 180, l. 6.
[101] *Milal*, p. 34, l. 13.

doubtedly, then, their formulae are in opposition to each other. Still both Naẓẓām and Abū al-Hudhayl, though using formulae which are in opposition to each other, describe the relation of the terms predicated of God to God by the same expression, namely, the expression "in virtue of himself," for which Abū al-Hudhayl in the passages quoted uses also as its equivalent, the expression "in virtue of His essence." [102] The expression "in virtue of himself," it will be recalled, is also used by Najjār and Ḍirār. Since then both Naẓẓām and Abū al-Hudhayl use the same expression, "in virtue of himself," as a description of the relation of such a predicate, for instance, as "knowing" to God, and still Naẓẓām infers therefrom that the term "knowing" is predicated of God "not in virtue of knowledge," whereas Abū al-Hudhayl infers therefrom that it is predicated of God "in virtue of knowledge," it is reasonable to assume that each of them has a different understanding of the meaning of the expression "in virtue of himself."

Let us then try to find out all we can about the expression "in virtue of himself" and see whether there is something in the background of that expression which would lead to the use of these two different formulae.

The Arabic term *li-nafsihi* or *bi-nafsihi*, which we have translated "in virtue of himself," is a direct translation of the Greek καθ' αὑτόν, which means "according to himself," "by himself," or "in virtue of himself." Now in his *Metaphysics*, Aristotle says that "life belongs (ὑπάρχει) to God, for the actuality of thought is life, and God is that actuality; and God's actuality in virtue of itself (καθ' αὑτὴν) is life most good and eternal," concluding that "we say therefore that God is a living being, eternal, most good" and that "this is God." [103] This statement of Aristotle is reflected in an Arabic doxography of Greek philosophers which attributes to Aristotle the statement that "God is living in virtue of His essence (*bi-dhātihi*) and is eternal in virtue of His essence." [104]

[102] Cf. above at n. 97 and below n. 112.

[103] *Metaph.* XII, 7, 1072b, 26–30.

[104] *Milal*, p. 315, ll. 13–14.

It happens, however, that in Aristotle the phrase καθ' αὑτό is used to signify either (1) that which is the definition of the subject, thus signifying its essence, or (2) that which is its genus and differentiae, or (3) that which is its property.[105] Now from the fact that in the passage quoted Aristotle says that life "belongs" (ὑπάρχει) to God "in virtue of itself," it may be inferred that he means by this statement that life is a property of God, for property is defined by Aristotle as "a predicate which does not signify the essence of a thing, but yet belongs (ὑπάρχει) to that thing alone"[106] or "that which belongs (ὑπάρχει) to each thing in virtue of itself, but is not in its essence."[107] Accordingly, when both Naẓẓām and Abū al-Hudhayl describe divine attributes as terms predicated of God "in virtue of himself," they mean thereby that each of these terms signifies a property of God. But what does it mean logically to say that any predicate of God, say the predicate "knowing," signifies a property of God? It is on this question that Naẓẓām and Abū al-Hudhayl differ. To Abū al-Hudhayl, Aristotle's definition of property as not signifying the essence of the subject of which it is predicated, but yet as belonging to that subject alone, means that in one respect property is other than the subject of which it is predicated but in another respect it is the same as the subject. In his formula, therefore, he first says that "the Creator is knowing in virtue of knowledge," indicating thereby that in this one respect knowledge is other than God, but then adds that "His knowledge is himself," thereby indicating that in this other respect knowledge is the same as God. Naẓẓām, however, seems to argue that whenever the subject of a property is God, who is a unique being and unlike any other being, the property predicated of Him, belonging as it does to Him alone, is to be taken to be the same as He in every respect. In the case of God, therefore, any term predicated of Him as a property is to be taken as signifying His very essence, for no term predicated of God as property is subject

[105] *Metaph.* V, 18, 1022a, 24–36.

[106] *Top.* I, 5, 102a, 18–19.

[107] *Metaph.* V, 30, 1025a, 31–32.

to the distinction made by Aristotle between a predicate which is a definition and a predicate which is a property. But inasmuch as God's essence is unknowable, the property predicated of Him cannot have a positive meaning. It must be interpreted negatively. He therefore maintains that when such a predicate as "knowing," for instance, is affirmed of God "in virtue of himself," it must be taken to mean that it is "not in virtue of knowledge." And this presumably is also the meaning given to the expression "in virtue of himself" by Najjār, who uses the active interpretation of attributes, and by Ḍirār, who uses the negative interpretation.

I am aware of the fact that the *Metaphysics* was not yet translated, or was only in the process of being translated, during the time of Naẓẓām and Abū al-Hudhayl. But it can be shown, I believe, on entirely independent grounds, that transmission of Greek philosophy to Arabic-speaking peoples preceded the actual translation of Greek philosophic works into Arabic.

Corroborative evidence that a difference in the interpretation of the Arabic word meaning "in virtue of himself" is involved in the difference of formula used by Naẓẓām and Abū al-Hudhayl may be found, I believe, in Ashʿarī and Shahrastānī.

Ashʿarī, after reproducing, incompletely, Abū al-Hudhayl's formula as quoted above,[108] adds the following: "This view of his is taken by Abū al-Hudhayl from Aristotle. For in one of his books, Aristotle says that the Creator is the whole of Him (*kulluhū*) knowledge, the whole of Him power, the whole of Him hearing, the whole of Him seeing. Abū al-Hudhayl thought he could improve upon this form of statement by saying that [God is knowing in virtue of knowledge, but] His knowledge is himself, [God is powerful in virtue of power, but] His power is himself." [109] Now the statement quoted by Ashʿarī from what he refers to as one of the books of Aristotle

[108] Cf. above at n. 99.

[109] *Maḳālāt*, p. 485, ll. 7–10. Cf. quotation from the followers of Jahm above at n. 80.

does not occur in any of Aristotle's works. Undoubtedly it is a paraphrase of the statement we have quoted above from the *Metaphysics* about life belonging to God in virtue of itself.[110] We thus have here an indication that Abū al-Hudhayl's formula is based upon Aristotle's statement that life belongs to God "in virtue of itself."

The corroborative evidence from Shahrastānī is still stronger. In his report on Abū al-Hudhayl's teaching, he suggests that the difference between Abū al-Hudhayl's formula and a formula he quotes anonymously, which can be identified as that of Naẓẓām, is that the former is an affirmation of what later Abū Hāshim called modes, whereas the latter is a denial of modes.[111] In other words, Shahrastānī makes Naẓẓām and Abū al-Hudhayl forerunners of Jubbā'ī and Abū Hāshim with regard to the problem of modes. Now, in his report on the teachings of Jubbā'ī and Abū Hāshim, Shahrastānī says that though both of them describe the relation of attributes to God by the expression "in virtue of His essence (*li-dhātihi*), which is used here as the equivalent of "in virtue of himself" (*li-nafsihi*),[112] they each interpret it differently. Jubbā'ī takes it to mean a denial of attributes even in the sense of modes, whereas Abū Hāshim takes it to mean only a denial of attributes in the sense of real attributes but not in the sense of modes.[113] And so, inasmuch as Naẓẓām and Abū al-Hudhayl are represented by Shahrastānī as forerunners of Jubbā'ī and Abū Hāshim, we may infer from him that the difference between Naẓẓām and Abū al-Hudhayl also turned on a difference in their interpretation of the expression "in virtue of himself" or its equivalent, "in virtue of His essence."

Three observations may be added here with regard to early discussions of certain aspects of the different formulae used by Naẓẓām and Abū al-Hudhayl.

[110] Cf. above at nn. 103 and 104.

[111] *Milal*, p. 34, ll. 17–20.

[112] Cf. quotations from Shahrastānī above nn. 100 and 101; cf. also quotations from Ash'arī above nn. 96 and 97. The term *li-nafsihi*, and not *li-dhātihi*, is used by Ash'arī in connection with Jubbā'ī (*Maḳālāt*, p. 179, l. 2) and by Baghdādī in connection with Abū Hāshim (*Farḳ*, p. 181, ll. 2 and 3).

[113] *Milal*, p. 55, l. 20–p. 56, l. 2.

First, while these two were tacitly battling over the phrase "in virtue of himself" or "in virtue of His essence" as to whether it has a negative meaning or an affirmative meaning, their contemporaries Abbād b. Sulaymān and Ibn Kullāb used it as having an affirmative meaning. From ʿAbbād b. Sulaymān's statement that "when I say God is knowing . . . He is powerful . . . He is living, it means a bestowal of a name upon God," [114] it is quite evident that he denied the reality of attributes and regarded them only as names of God. Accordingly, the formula used by him is: "God is knowing not in virtue of knowledge and powerful not in virtue of power and living not in virtue of life." [115] Still, it is reported of him that "he rejected the formula that God is knowing, powerful, and living in virtue of himself (*li-nafsihi*) or in virtue of His essence (*li-dhātihi*)." [116] This quite evidently shows that he takes these phrases to have an affirmative meaning. Ibn Kullāb, as we have seen above, is an Attributist, and so in one place he says that "God is eternally willing in virtue of will." [117] In another place, however, he says that "the names and attributes of God are in virtue of His essence." [118] This, again, shows that the phrases in question are taken by him as having an affirmative meaning.

Second, there was a difference of opinion as to the meaning of Abū al-Hudhayl's formula. Ibn al-Rāwandī, as quoted by Ḫayyāṭ, took Abū al-Hudhayl's statements about knowledge and power to mean that "the knowledge of God is God [himself] and His power is [also] himself," and hence he proceeded to argue that this would make knowledge and power to be the same, a view concerning which he says "I know of no man on earth before him who dared to suggest it." [119] Ḫayyāṭ, in his refutation of Ibn al-Rāwandī, offered his own interpretation of Abū al-Hudhayl's formulae. "Abū al-Hudhayl," he says, "having become convinced of the truth

[114] *Maḳālāt*, p. 166, ll. 6–8.
[115] *Ibid.*, ll. 1–2.
[116] *Ibid.*, l. 4.
[117] Cf. above at n. 15.
[118] Cf. above at n. 16.
[119] *Intiṣār* 48, p. 59, ll. 16–18.

that God is really knowing, but at the same time having also become convinced of the falsehood of both the assertion that God is knowing in virtue of an eternal knowledge, as maintained by the Nābitah, and the assertion that God is knowing in virtue of a created knowledge, as maintained by the Rafiḍites, arrived at the conclusion that it is true to assert that God is knowing in virtue of himself (*bi-nafsihi*)." [120] In other words, when Abū al-Hudhayl first says that "God is knowing in virtue of knowledge" and that "He is powerful in virtue of power," he merely means that God is truly knowing and that He is truly powerful; and, when he then says that "His knowledge is himself" and that "His power is himself," he merely means that He is knowing and powerful in virtue of himself and not in virtue of something added to himself as a real eternal or created attribute. Thus, according to Ḫayyāṭ, there is no difference between Naẓẓām's formula and Abū al-Hudhayl's formula; the difference between them is only verbal.

Ibn al-Rāwandī's interpretation of the meaning of Abū al-Hudhayl's formula is taken by Baghdādī to be a true interpretation of the meaning of that formula. He restates it as follows: "The fourth of Abū al-Hudhayl's heresies is that the knowledge of God is God [himself] and His power is [also] himself." [121] He then proceeds to repeat Ibn al-Rāwandī's argument against it, without taking any notice of Ḫayyāṭ's correction, though on two previous occasions, dealing with other topics, when he happened to repeat Ibn al-Rāwandī's arguments against Abū al-Hudhayl, he quoted Ḫayyāṭ's answers and refuted them.[122]

Later, Shahrastānī, evidently having in mind the misrepresentation of Abū al-Hudhayl's view by Ibn al-Rāwandī and Baghdādī, alludes to it both in his *Nihāyat* and in his *Milal*.

[120] *Ibid.*, ll. 18–20. On the Nābitah, see Halkin, "*The Ḥashwiyya*," *JAOS*, 54: 1–25 (1934). On created knowledge, see above, pp. 143–146.

[121] *Fark*, p. 108, ll. 7–8.

[122] Cf. *ibid.*, p. 103, ll. 10 ff., and *Intiṣār* 4; *Fark*, p. 105, ll. 15 ff., and *Intiṣār* 5.

In his *Nihāyat*, after saying that "Abū al-Hudhayl al-ʿAllāf walked in the highroads of the philosophers and said that the Creator is knowing in virtue of a knowledge which is He himself," he adds immediately "but His self is not to be called knowledge after the manner of the philosophers who say that He is the act of intellection (*ʿākil* = νόησις), the intellect (*ʿaḳl* = νοῦς), and the object of intellection (*maʿḳūl* = νοητόν, νοούμενον)." [123] In his *Milal*, similarly after restating the correct view of Abū al-Hudhayl, as expressed in the formula that "God is knowing in virtue of knowledge and His knowledge is His essence," he remarks that Abū al-Hudhayl "borrowed this view only from the philosophers, who believed that His essence is one, without there being in it any plurality in any respect, and that the attributes are not things (*maʿānī*) besides the essence, subsisting in the essence; they are rather His essence, reducing themselves to negations and consequents (*al-lawāzim*)," [124] that is to say, properties.[125] The implication of this passage is that neither is knowledge a real attribute in God nor is it identical with God himself after the manner of the philosophers' view quoted in the preceding passage. But it is to be noted that in neither of these twc passages is there any suggestion, made by Shahrastānī elsewhere,[126] that Abū al-Hudhayl's formula implies a theory like that of Abū Hāshim's modes.

Prior to Shahrastānī, a Jewish contemporary of Ḫayyāṭ, al-Muḳammaṣ, an Antiattributist, quotes with approval two anonymous formulae which can be identified as those of Abū al-Hudhayl and Naẓẓām. He then justifies his use of these two formulae by remarking that "while they differ in language, they do not differ in meaning." [127] The fact that he felt

[123] *Nihāyat*, p. 180, ll. 5–7. Cf. *Metaph.* XII, 7, 1078b, 19–24; XII, 9, 1075a, 3–5.

[124] *Milal*, p. 34, ll. 15–16.

[125] *Al-lāzim* = τὸ παρακολουθοῦν, which is contrasted by Aristotle with "genus" as "property" (ἴδιον) is contrasted by him with "genus" (*Top.* I, 5, 102a, 18–19 and 22–23). Cf. my paper "Avicenna, Algazali, and Averroes on Divine Attributes," *Homenaje a Millás-Vallicrosa*, II, p. 558.

[126] Cf. above at n. 111.

[127] Cf. Judah ben Barzillai's *Perush Sefer Yeṣirah*, p. 79, ll. 21–22.

called upon to justify his use of both these formulae shows that he knew that someone did not consider them to have the same meaning. The someone whom he quite evidently had in mind is Ibn al-Rāwandī.

In the light of the foregoing discussion of the various formulae used by the orthodox Attributists and the Muʿtazilite Antiattributists, it is rather puzzling to find in Ashʿarī the following statements: (1) "Some say: The names of God are He himself. This formula is followed by the majority of the adherents of the *Ḥadīth*." [128] (2) "Some say: The names of the Creator are other than He, and so are His attributes. This is the formula of the Muʿtazilites, the Ḫarijites, the majority of the Murjiites, and the majority of the Zaydiites." [129] (3) "The people of the *Ḥadīth* and the *Sunnah*" confess that "one must not say that the names of God are other than God, as do the Muʿtazilites and the Ḫarijites." [130] As we have seen, it is Ashʿarī himself who sometimes describes attributes as being "other" than God [131] and it is the Muʿtazilites who in various ways describe attributes as being the same as God.[132]

An explanation of these puzzling statements that suggests itself to me is that the term "other" is not used by Ashʿarī here in the same sense as the term "other" is used by him in the formula for attributes. There it is used as a description of his own belief in the real existence of attributes as something distinct from the essence of God; here it is used by him as a description of the Muʿtazilites' use of the allegorical interpretation of the names and attributes of God, that is to say, of their interpreting the names or attributes of God as meaning something "other" than what they obviously mean. Though the term *ta'wīl*, which is the Arabic for allegorical interpretation, does not contain anything corresponding to *allos*, "other," in the Greek term *allegoria*, so that literally *ta'wīl* means simply "explanation" or "interpretation," still it car-

[128] *Maḳālāt*, p. 172, ll. 6–7.

[129] *Ibid.*, ll. 10–11.

[130] *Ibid.*, p. 290, ll. 2, 13; cf. *Ibānah*, p. 8, l. 16, and *Uṣūl*, p. 114, l. 16 – p. 115, l. 13.

[131] Cf. above at nn. 29–31.

[132] Cf. above at nn. 59–62.

ried with it the sense of giving to one term the meaning of another term. Thus Ibn Ḳudāmah, in his criticism of the "allegorical interpretation" (*al-ta'wīl*) of attributes, argues that "the allegorical interpreter combines the ascription to God of an attribute which He did not ascribe or adjoin to Himself, with the negation of an attribute which God did adjoin to Himself." [133] In other words, the allegorical interpretation describes God in terms "other" than those by which God describes Himself. This, we may take it, is what Ash'arī means, in the statements quoted, by his contrast between the orthodox and the Mu'tazilites plus some other non-orthodox sects.

[133] *Taḥrīm* 58, p. 33, ll. 12–14 (23).

CHAPTER III

THE KORAN

I. The Uncreated Koran

1. ORIGIN OF THE DOCTRINE OF THE UNCREATED KORAN

In the preceding chapter, on the basis of statements expressing opposition to a prevailing manner of predicating certain terms of God, we have shown that early in the eighth century, and presumably before that, there existed in Islam a belief that two terms by which God is described in the Koran, namely, the terms "living" and "knowing" or the terms "living" and "powerful" or the terms "knowing" and "powerful," indicated that in God there existed either life and knowledge or life and power or knowledge and power as real eternal things distinct from His essence. We have also shown how these real eternal things were designated by the Arabic terms *maʿānī*, "things," and *ṣifāt*, "characteristics," the latter of which came to be translated, through a thirteenth-century Latin translation of a Hebrew translation of an Arabic work by Maimonides, by the term "attributes." We have also shown how this belief arose out of disputations between Muslims and Christians over the Christian doctrine of the Trinity, and how the connecting link between the Muslim doctrine of attributes and the Christian doctrine of the Trinity is to be found in two facts: (1) in the fact that the two Arabic terms *maʿānī* and *ṣifāt* are direct translations respectively of the Greek πράγματα, which is used as a designation of the persons of the Trinity, and the Greek χαρακτηριστικά, which is used as a designation of the distinctive properties of the persons; (2) in the fact that the two alternative sets of terms which occur in the earliest discussions of the problem of attributes, namely, life and knowledge or life and power or knowledge and power, correspond exactly to two alternative sets of terms by which the second and the third persons of the Trinity, namely, the Son and the Holy Spirit, were described in the earliest representations of the Trinity in Arabic. The term "knowledge," it may be remarked, is used synonymously with the term "wisdom."

But the second person of the Trinity is also described by two other terms, and these two terms are also predicated of God in the Koran. Thus the second person of the Trinity is called Word (λόγος) in the New Testament,[1] and the term "Word" (*kalimah*), which occurs in several verses in the Koran in connection with the birth of Jesus,[2] reflects that New Testament term. Among the Church Fathers, the second person is also called "will," for, as says Athanasius, "we have heard from the prophet that He is become the 'Angel of Great Counsel'[3] and is called the Will (θέλημα) of the Father."[4] Now, in the Koran, the terms "word" and "will" as predicates of God are also implied in the expressions "God spoke" (*kallama*)[5] and "God willed" (*arāda*).[6] Accordingly, if we were right in assuming that the three terms, "life," "knowledge-wisdom," and "power," upon which was centered the early controversy over attributes, were derived from the terms by which the second and third persons of the Trinity were described, we should expect that the terms "word" and "will" should also become a subject of controversy in the early history of the problem of attributes. That this is what happened may be gathered from reports about the terms used by Najjār (between 750 and 840) to illustrate how they are to be interpreted as negations by those who deny that they are real attributes.[6a] Thus in one report his followers are said to have agreed with those who denied of God "knowledge, power, life, and His other eternal

[1] John 1:1.

[2] Surah 4:169; 3:34; 3:40.

[3] Isa. 9:5(6).

[4] Athanasius, *Orat. cont. Ariano.* III, 6 (PG 26, 457 A). Cf. Marius Victorinum (*Adv. Arium* I, 32, PL 8, 1064 C): "The Father is God and the Son is His Will." Cf. *The Philosophy of the Church Fathers*, I, p. 193, n. 12, and p. 231.

[5] Surah 2:254 *et al.*

[6] Surah 36:82 *et al.*

[6a] Cf. above, p. 223.

attributes."[7] The three terms mentioned in this report are the original three terms which in various twofold combinations formed, as we have seen, the subject of controversy in the earliest stage of the problem. But in another report he is said to have believed that "God is continuously speaking in the sense that He is never incapable of issuing a word (*al-kalām*)."[8] In still another report he is said to have believed that "God is continuously willing (*murīd*) that what He knows would come to pass should come to pass and what He knows would not come to pass should not come to pass, and this willingness is in virtue of himself; it is not in virtue of a will; but it is in the sense that He is not reluctant or forced."[9] The fact, therefore, that, in addition to his denial that "knowledge" and "power" and "life" are real eternal attributes, Najjār went on to deny that also "word" and "will" are not real eternal attributes shows that also "word" and "will" had already come to be regarded as real eternal attributes, and quite evidently they had come to be so regarded as a result of the debates between Christians and Muslims on the Christian doctrine of the Trinity. Such debates, as may be inferred from the *Disputatio Christiani et Saraceni* by John of Damascus, began to appear in Syria after its conquest by the Muslims in 635, when the Muslims came in contact with learned spokesmen of Christianity. There is thus reason to assume that the belief in real eternal attributes, including the real eternal attribute "word," did not arise in Islam before that date, and presumably it was not long after that date that it did arise.

From all this it may be gathered that with the rise of the problem of attributes during the first half of the eighth century, those who are reported as the opponents of the orthodox belief in the reality of eternal attributes illustrated their denial of attributes by mentioning such attributes as knowledge-wisdom, life, power, will, and word-speech, all of

[7] *Farḳ*, p. 196, ll. 1–2.
[8] *Maḳālāt*, p. 284, ll. 15–16.
[9] *Ibid*., p. 514, ll. 12–13; cf. *Milal*, p. 62, l. 2.

which are derived from terms predicated of God in the Koran and all of which are also used in Christianity as descriptions of two of the three persons of the Trinity, some of them of the second person and some of the third person.

Independently of this belief in the reality of eternal attributes, and undoubtedly prior to it, there had already been current in Islam a belief in the existence of a Koran before its revelation and even before the creation of the world. However, unlike the belief in the reality of eternal attributes, which, as we have seen, arose under Christian influence, the belief in the pre-existence of the Koran had its basis in three statements in the Koran itself. First, the Koran describes itself as "an honorable Koran, in a Hidden (*maknūn*) Book" (56:76, 77). Second, it describes itself as "a glorious Koran, on a Preserved (*maḥfūẓ*) Tablet" (85:22). Third, it describes itself as "an Arabic Koran . . . in the Mother (*umm*) of the Book" (43:3).[10] All this quite naturally was taken to mean that the Koran, prior to its revelation, had existed in a sort of heavenly Koran invariably described as "a Hidden Book" or "a Preserved Tablet" or "the Mother of the Book." This conception of a pre-existent Koran is nothing but a reflection of the traditional Jewish belief in a pre-existent Torah,[11] for the Koran constantly describes its revelatory nature as being the same as that of the Torah.[12] A connecting link between the pre-existence of the Koran and the pre-existence of the Torah may be discerned in the use of the expressions "Hidden Book" and "Preserved Tablet" as descriptions of the pre-existent Koran and the use of the expressions "Preserved (*genuzah*) Treasure" [13] and "Hidden (*muṣnāʿ*) with God" [14] as descriptions of the pre-existent Torah. Now in Judaism, the Torah, though pre-existent, was still created; it was created prior to

[10] Cf. also 13:39. In 3:5 the expression "the Mother of the Koran" refers to clearly understood verses in the Koran as distinguished from ambiguous verses.

[11] Cf. below, n. 15.

[12] Surah 2:38; 5:72; 6:90–93; 10:94; 46:9–11.

[13] *Shabbat* 88b, 89a.

[14] *Genesis Rabbah* 1, 1.

the creation of the world.[15] We may, therefore, assume that the original teaching of the Koran about its own pre-existence, and also the original Muslim belief based upon that teaching, was that the pre-existent Koran was created prior to the creation of the world. There is nothing directly contradictory to such a view. The earliest reference to a belief in the uncreatedness of the Koran is contained in a tradition which ascribes it to Ibn Abbas who died in 687,[16] over fifty years after the conquest of Syria in 635, by which time the belief in the reality of eternal attributes, including the eternal real attribute of "Word" in the sense of an eternal pre-existent Koran, may have already been firmly established. Nor, as I shall try to show,[17] is there any evidence that the teaching of the createdness of the Koran by a son-in-law of a contemporary of Muhammad, which Ibn Athīr later branded as heretical, was really regarded as heretical at the time of the teaching. A survival of this original belief in a created pre-existent Koran is to be discerned in a tradition handed down in the name of the Prophet that the Preserved Tablet was created by God prior to His creation of the world.[18] Incidentally, this tradition is said to be shared "by the people of the Book, whether Jews, Christians, or Samaritans." [19]

It happens, however, that, following the Hebrew Scripture which refers to every one of its revelations as "the word of God," [20] the Koran also refers to the revelations contained therein either in the singular as "the word (*kalām*) of God," [21] or in the plural, as "the words (*kalimāt*) of God," [22] and, by

[15] *Pesaḥim* 54a *et al.*

[16] *Ibānah*, p. 38, ll. 2–3 (79).

[17] Cf. below, p. 265.

[18] *Farḳ*, p. 127, ll. 7–9.

[19] *Ibid.*

[20] Gen. 15:1 and *passim.*

[21] Surah 2:70; 9:6; 48:15.

[22] Surah 6:115; 7:158; 10:65; 18:26; 18:109; 31:26.

Generally, for "Word" or "Speech" in the sense of the pre-existent Koran the Arabic term used is *kalām*, and for "Word" in the sense of the pre-existent Christ the Arabic term used is *kalimah*, the latter being based upon Surah 3:34; 3:40; 4:169 (cf. below, p. 242). Arabic-speaking Christians, who as Christians believed that only "Word" in the sense of the pre-existent Christ is uncreated but that "Word" in the sense of the revealed Scripture is not uncreated (cf. John of Damascus, *Disputatio* [PG 96, 1344 A; 94,

implication, it uses also the same expression as a description of the Law [23] and the Psalms [24] and the Gospels.[25] So also, following his own reference to the Law of Moses as "the Book and Wisdom," [26] which is evidently based upon the verse in the Book of Proverbs where the Law of Moses is referred to as "wisdom," [27] Muhammad refers to the Koran as "the Book and Wisdom." [28] Moreover, in several places, directly or by implication, the Koran is described as being "knowledge" from God.[29] The Koran thus describes itself by the terms "word" and "wisdom" and "knowledge." With the rise, therefore, under the influence of the Christian Trinity, of the belief in eternal real attributes, the terms "word" and "wisdom" and "knowledge," which are predicated of God and are used to mean the Koran, came to mean eternal, uncreated attributes in God and hence also an eternal, uncreated pre-existent Koran. Thus the original belief in a pre-existent Koran which was created became a belief in an uncreated pre-existent Koran. Accordingly, just as the Anti-attributists argued that the belief in attributes does not differ from the Christian belief in the Trinity,[30] so also Caliph Ma'mūn (786–833), during his campaign against the belief in the uncreatedness of the Koran, in his third letter to the governor of Baghdad, argues that those who believe in the uncreatedness of the Koran are "like Christians when they

---

1588 B]), were careful about the use of these two Arabic terms. It is thus that Juwaynī says: "By *kalimah* the Christians do not mean *kalām*, for to them *kalām* is created" (*Irshād*, p. 28, ll. 12–13 [p. 53]). As for Muslims, though as a rule the term used by them for "Word" in the sense of the pre-existent Koran is *kalām*, they would have no objection to the use of the term *kalimah*, for, as we have seen, the plural form of this term is used in the Koran itself for divine revelations.

[23] Surah 32:23.

[24] Surah 17:56.

[25] Surah 5:50.

[26] Surah 4:57; cf. 33:23.

[27] Prov. 8:22.

[28] Surah 2:123; cf. 2:146; 2:231; 3:75; 3:158; 4:113; 17:41; 33:34; 54:5; 62:2.

[29] Surah 2:114; 13:37; 55:1–3, all quoted in the name of Ibn Ḥanbal in Patton, *Aḥmad Ibn Ḥanbal and the Miḥna* (1897), pp. 101 and 162. Cf. *Ibānah*, p. 34, l. 4, and p. 41, ll. 8–9, quoting Surah 29:48.

[30] Cf. above, p. 113.

claim that Jesus the son of Mary was not created (*maḫlūḳ*) because he was the Word of God." [31]

The upshot of our discussion is that the belief in a pre-existent uncreated Koran was a revision of an original belief in a pre-existent created Koran and that, while the original belief in a pre-existent created Koran was based directly upon the teaching of the Koran itself, the revised belief in a pre-existent uncreated Koran was an offshoot of the belief in eternal uncreated attributes, which belief, as we have seen, arose under the influence of the Christian doctrine of the Trinity. When exactly the belief in eternal, uncreated attributes and its corollary, the belief in an uncreated Koran, arose we do not know. I have already mentioned the tradition which refers to one who died in 687 as a believer in the uncreatedness of the Koran and I have also mentioned Ibn Athīr's unsupported view that the createdness of the Koran taught by a son-in-law of a contemporary of Muhammad was heretical at the time it was taught.[32] Historically, opposition to the belief in an uncreated Koran does not appear until the early part of the eighth century, with Jaʿd b. Dirham (d. 743) and Jahm b. Ṣafwān (d. 746).[33] Reference to the existence of a sectarian controversy in Islam over the problem of the uncreatedness of the Koran during the early part of the eighth century is also to be found in a fictional disputation between a Muslim and a Christian, in which its author, John of Damascus (d. *ca.* 754), instructs Christians how to carry on a religious debate with Muslims.[34]

[31] Ṭabarī, *Annales*, p. 118, ll. 10–11; cf. Patton, *Aḥmed Ibn Ḥanbal and the Miḥna*, p. 67. I take this statement of Ma'mūn to mean: "Jesus the son of Mary was not created because he was the [incarnation of the uncreated] Word of God." It thus reflects a knowledge of the Christian doctrine of the uncreatedness of the pre-existent Christ and its incarnation in Jesus, which was not derived from the Koran (cf. below, p. 305), and of the application of that doctrine to the Koranic statements about the Christian belief that Jesus was "begotten" of God, that he is God, and that he is the second person of the Trinity (cf. below, pp. 310–311).

[32] Cf. above at nn. 16 and 17.

[33] Cf. below, p. 265.

[34] *Disputatio Saraceni et Christiani* (PG 96, 1341; cf. PG 94, 1586 A–1587 A).

In that fictional disputation, John of Damascus advises the Christian to wrest from the Muslim the admission that Jesus is called in the Koran (4:169) the Word (*kalimah*) of God in the sense of a pre-existent Christ, just as the Koran is called in it the Word of God in the sense of a pre-existent Koran, and hence to try to force him to admit that the Word of God in the sense of a pre-existent Christ is uncreated, remarking that the Muslim interlocutor, as a good orthodox Muslim, is bound to reject the view that the Word of God in whatever sense used is created, "for," says John of Damascus, "those among the Saracens who maintain this are heretics and most abominable and despicable."[35] What John of Damascus means to say here is that the Muslim, to be consistent, would have to admit that the Word of God used in the Koran in the sense of the pre-existent Christ was uncreated, since the Word of God used in the Koran in the sense of the pre-existent Koran is regarded by orthodox Islam as uncreated and since also the denial of the uncreatedness of the Koran is regarded by it as heresy. A similar allusion by John of Damascus to the Muslim belief in an uncreated pre-existent Koran, after the analogy of the Christian belief in an uncreated pre-existent Christ, is to be found in his statement concerning the Koran that Muhammad declared that "a Scripture had been brought down to him from heaven."[36] The description of the Koran as having been brought down "from heaven," which John of Damascus attributes to Muhammad, undoubtedly means that it was eternal and uncreated, for the phrase "from heaven" is borrowed from the New Testament description of the pre-existent Christ as "he that came down from heaven,"[37] "he that cometh from heaven,"[38] and "the Lord from heaven,"[39] and this New Testament description of the pre-existent Christ is known to

[35] *Ibid.* Cf. C. H. Becker, "Christliche Polemik und islamische Dogmenbildung," *Zeitschrift für Assyriologie*, 26: 188 (1912).

[36] *De Haeresibus* 101 (PG 94, 765 A).

[37] John 3:13.

[38] John 3:31.

[39] I Cor. 15:47.

have meant to John of Damascus that the pre-existent Christ was eternal and uncreated.

Having thus made the Christian force the Muslim to admit that the Word of God used in the Koran in the sense of the pre-existent Christ is uncreated, John of Damascus then tries to make the Christian force the Muslim to admit that the uncreated pre-existent Christ is God, for "everything that is not created, but uncreated, is God." [40] What he means to say is that everything not created but eternally generated is coeternal with God and hence God, for eternity spells God. What the Muslim's answer would be to this reasoning of the Christian is not given here by John of Damascus, but from his statement elsewhere that the Muslims "call us Associaters (ἑταιριασταί = *al-mushrikūn*), because, they say, we bring in an associate to God when we claim that Christ is the Son of God and God," [41] we may gather that the Muslim's answer here, as in the case of attributes,[42] would be that even if one were to admit for the sake of argument that the pre-existent Christ was eternally generated and hence eternal, he would still not be God, for eternity does not mean deity. Then, also, the Muslim might have argued that, while the Word of God as applied in the Koran to itself can be shown to mean a pre-existent Koran,[43] the Word of God as applied in it to Christ only means the creative word "Be" by which all things in the world are created by God.[44]

From all this we may gather that already in the early part of the eighth century there existed in Islam two views with regard to the question as to whether the Word of God, by which is meant the pre-existent Koran, was uncreated or created, and that the denial of its uncreatedness was referred to by John of Damascus as a heretical Muslim view. We may further gather that, from such debates between Muslims and

[40] PG 94, 1586 A. Text in PG 96, 1341 D is here defective. Cf. also *De Haeresibus* 101 (PG 94, 768 C).

[41] *De Haeresibus* 101 (PG 94, 768 B).

[42] Cf. above, p. 137.

[43] *Ibānah*, p. 40, l. 17 ff. (80–81).

[44] Cf. below, p. 309.

Christians as that referred to by John of Damascus, Muslims came to know that Christians compared their belief in an uncreated Word of God in the sense of a pre-existent Christ to the Muslim belief in an uncreated Word of God in the sense of a pre-existent Koran. It is therefore quite reasonable to assume that from such debates as well as from the New Testament statement that "all things were made through Him" (John 1:3) the Muslims also learned that the pre-existent Christ was conceived of by Christians as being a creator. When we therefore find a statement, quoted by Ashʿarī in the name of men who died in 712, which reads that "the Koran is not a creator nor is it created," [45] it is, again, quite reasonable to assume that this statement was meant to contrast the Muslim conception of the pre-existent Koran with the Christian conception of the pre-existent Christ, analogous to the Koranic contrast between the Muslim conception of God and the Christian conception of God implied in the verse "He begetteth not, and He is not begotten" (111:3).

2. THE UNRAISED PROBLEM OF INLIBRATION

In the preceding section we have tried to explain how the history of the doctrine of the uncreatedness of the Koran falls into two stages. It started as mere belief in a pre-existent Koran conceived of as created. The belief in its uncreatedness arose later with the rise of the belief in real attributes co-eternal with God, when the Word of God, by which was meant the pre-existent Koran, was taken to be one of those real attributes co-eternal with God.

But here two questions arise in our mind.

The first question concerns the relation of the uncreated Word of God in the sense of the uncreated pre-existent Koran to the Preserved Tablet, and its equivalents, the Hidden Book and the Mother of the Book. In the Koran, quite clearly, the Preserved Tablet means that on which the Koran was written

[45] *Ibānah*, p. 38, ll. 5–7 (79). On Ibn Ḥazm's description of the Word of God in the sense of the pre-existent Koran as "creator," see below, p. 258.

and preserved, the term "Tablet" thus being used in the same sense as that of the "Tablets" of the Ten Commandments, on which, according to the Koran (7:142), were written an admonition and explanation of everything,[1] so that when tradition takes the Preserved Tablet to mean that on which the divine decrees were written, it may be assumed to reflect the influence of the Book of Jubilees (5:13–14).[2] But, according to a tradition handed down in the name of the Prophet, the Preserved Tablet, together with the "pen" and the "throne" and the "chair," was created by God before the creation of the world;[3] and, according to a statement by Baghdādī, this belief in the antemundane creation of "the tablet and the pen" was held by "the forebears of the Muslim community, as well as by the people of the Book, whether Jews, Christians, or Samaritans."[4] In the light of this, we should like to know how those who believed in an uncreated pre-existent Koran reconciled their belief with the Koranic statement that the pre-existent Koran, before its revelation, had its abode in the created Preserved Tablet.

The second question concerns the relation of the uncreated Word of God in the sense of a pre-existent Koran to the revealed Koran. In Christianty, the question of the relation of the uncreated Word of God in the sense of the pre-existent Christ to the born Christ gave rise to two main views. According to one view, the pre-existent Christ was incarnate in the born Christ, with the result that in the born Christ there were two natures, that of the pre-existent Christ, described as divine, and that of the born Christ, described as human. According to the other view, there was no incarnation or enfleshment of the kind that would result in two natures; the born Christ had only a human nature, though a nature

[1] There is similarly a rabbinic saying to the effect that the Ten Commandments contain all the laws of the Torah (*Canticles Rabbah* to Cant. 5:14)

[2] Cf. Wensinck, "*Lawh*," in *Encyclopedia of Islam*, III, 19.

[3] Quoted in Wensinck, *Muslim Creed*, p. 162.

[4] *Fark*, p. 127, ll. 7–9.

superior to that of any other human being. The first view was held only by those who believed in the eternity of the pre-existent Christ; the second view included among its followers not only those who believed in the createdness of the pre-existent Christ but also some of those who believed in his eternity.[5] Now it happens that in that fictitious disputation by John of Damascus the Muslim is made to ask, "How did God come down into the womb of a woman?"[6] whereupon the Christian explains to him the orthodox doctrine of the incarnation, concluding with the words: "For know that Christ is said to be twofold in matters pertaining to natures, but one in hypostasis."[7] From this we gather that by the time the problem of the eternity of the Koran became a matter of sectarian controversy, those who participated in that controversy had already gained a knowledge of the orthodox Christian doctrines of the incarnation and the two natures and undoubtedly they must have by that time also heard that among the Christians there were those who denied both the uncreatedness of the pre-existent Christ and the two natures in the born Christ. Consequently, in view of the fact that the controversy in Islam over the problem of whether the pre-existent Koran was uncreated or created is analogous to the Christian controversy over the problem of whether the pre-existent Christ was uncreated or created, the question arises in our mind whether similarly, in analogy to the Christian controversy over the problem of the incarnation and the problem of two natures, there was not also in Islam a controversy over the problem of the inlibration, that is, the embookment, of the pre-existent Koran in the revealed Koran and also over the problem of whether the revealed Koran had two natures, a divine and a man-made, or only one nature, a man-made nature.

Of these two questions, the first would seem to have been raised by those who believed in the uncreatedness of the

[5] Cf. *The Philosophy of the Church Fathers*, I, pp. 170–176, 364–372, 602–606.

[6] John of Damascus, *Disputatio* (PG 96, 1344 C; 94, 1587 C).

[7] *Ibid.* (PG 96, 1345 A; 94, 1589 A).

Koran, probably moved to do so by the fact that the Muʿtazilites made use of the Koranic reference to "a glorious Koran on the Preserved Tablet" (85:21, 22) in their view of the createdness of the Koran. The answer to this question, as given by Ashʿarī, reads as follows: "If anybody says, 'Tell us, do you believe that the Word of God is on the Preserved Tablet?' the answer is: That is what we believe, because God has said, 'Yet it is a glorious Koran on the Preserved Tablet' and therefore the Koran is on the Preserved Tablet." [8] What this answer means is that the uncreated Word of God in the sense of the pre-existent Koran had prior to its revelation a twofold stage of existence: first, from eternity as an attribute in God; second, with the creation of the Preserved Tablet prior to the creation of the world, as a book on that Preserved Tablet. How the transition from the one stage to the other was effected we are not told. In Christianity, it is to be noted, a similar conception of a twofold stage of existence in the uncreated Word of God in the sense of the pre-existent Christ prior to the incarnation was held by the Apologists and Arius, where the transition from the first stage of existence to the second was effected, according to the Apologists, by an act of generation but, according to Arius, by an act of creation.[9] Here, however, in the case of the uncreated Word of God in the sense of the pre-existent Koran, the transition could not be explained as having been effected either by an act of generation or by an act of creation.[10] Its effectuation would have to be explained, I imagine, by some kind of act whereby the Word would not cease to be an uncreated attribute in God.

As for the second question, the question about inlibration, it was not to my knowledge raised directly. But many passages dealing with the Koran, both by those who believe in its un-

[8] *Ibānah*, p. 41, ll. 5–6 (81).

[9] Cf. *The Philosophy of the Church Fathers*, I, pp. 192–198, 287–304, 585–587.

[10] The statement by the Kullabite Faḍālī that "the Glorious Expressions are written and created on the Preserved Tablet" (cf. below, p. 290, at n. 14) refers only to the "Expressions" and not to the uncreated simple "Word" which continues to be an attribute in God.

createdness and by those who deny its uncreatedness, contain statements which seem like answers in anticipation of such a question. We shall examine some such passages, beginning with those of two contemporaries who flourished during the first part of the ninth century, Ibn Kullāb and Ibn Ḥanbal.

In order to keep up the analogy between the problem of "inlibration" here and the Christian problem of "incarnation," I shall continue to translate the expression "the *kalām* of God" by "the Word of God" rather than by the more commonly used phrase "the Speech of God."

a. Ibn Kullāb and the Denial of Inlibration

Ibn Kullāb's view as reported by Ashʿarī falls into two parts, the first part dealing with the uncreated Word of God and the second with the post-revealed Koran.

In the first part, after stating that "the Word of God is an attribute which subsists in Him and that God and the Word are coeternal," he goes on to describe the Word as follows: "The Word of God is not made up of letters (*ḥurūf*), nor is it a voice. It is indivisible, it is impartible, it is indissectible, it is unalterable. It is one single thing (*maʿnā*) in God." [1]

In the second part, he deals with the post-revealed Koran in the following passages:

(1) "The impression (*rasm*) consists of various letters [and expressions] and it is the recital (*ḳirāʾah*) of the Koran . . . The expressions (*ʿibārāt*) used as substitutes for the Word of God contain variety and diversity, whereas the Word of God contains no variety and diversity, just as the liturgical glorification of God (*dhikr*) is expressed in various and diverse terms, whereas God the glorified is subject to no variation and diversification." [2] (2) "The recital [which is the impression of the Word of God] is different from the thing recited which subsists in God [namely, the Word of God], even as the liturgical glorification of God is different from God. For just as He who is glorified is beginningless and ceaselessly existent,

[1] *Maḳālāt*, p. 584, ll. 9–13.

[2] *Ibid.*, ll. 13–17.

whereas the glorification is originated, so also, with regard to the thing recited [which subsists in God, namely, the Word of God] God is eternally speaking it, whereas the recital is originated and created and it is an acquisition (*kasb*) on the part of man."[3] (3) "The Word of God is called Arabic only because the impression, which is the expression thereof and is the recital thereof, is in Arabic, and so it is called Arabic for a reason. Thus also is it called Hebrew for a reason, and that is because the impression, which is the expression thereof, is in Hebrew. Thus also is the Word of God called command for a reason, and it is called prohibition for a reason, and it is called narration for a reason. God was eternally speaking even before His Word came to be called command, and even before the existence of a reason for which His Word is called command, and the same holds true with regard to calling His Word prohibition and narration. I deny that God is eternally narrating or eternally prohibiting."[4] (4) "Abdallah b. Kullāb was of the opinion that what we hear recited by reciters is an expression used as a substitute for the Word of God, though Moses did indeed hear God uttering His Word; and, as for the Prophet's saying '[If any one of those who join gods with God ask an asylum of thee,] grant him an asylum, that he may hear the Word of God' (9:6), it means 'that he may understand (*yafham*) the Word of God,' or it may mean, according to his opinion, 'that he may hear the reciters recite it.'"[5]

These passages touch upon two topics: (1) the origin of the letters and expressions in the Koran; (2) the problem of inlibration.

With regard to the origin of the letters and expressions in the Koran, we gather from the third passage quoted that the impression — which consists of letters and expressions — of the uncreated simple Word of God was created at the time at which the Word of God was Arabicized, but, since the Arabicization of the Word of God was quite evidently due

[3] *Ibid.*, p. 601, l. 13 – p. 602, l. 3.
[4] *Ibid.*, p. 584, l. 17 – p. 585, l. 6.
[5] *Ibid.*, p. 585, ll. 8–11.

to Muhammad's recital of it, just as the Hebraicization of it is said by Ibn Kullāb to have been due to Moses' recital of it, it is to be inferred that it was Muhammad's recital of the Word of God — which Word of God, according to the fourth passage quoted, must have been heard by him as the Word of God was heard by Moses — that created the impression of the Word of God. It is, therefore, also to be inferred that, just as it is the Arabicized Word of God as it was created by Muhammad that any subsequent reciter of the Koran recites, so it is also the impression of the Word of God as it was created by Muhammad that any subsequent reciter of the Koran recites. Accordingly, when in the second passage quoted the uncreated Word of God is described as "the thing recited" (*al-maḳrū'*), in contrast to "the recital" (*al-ḳirā'ah*), this description is to be taken to mean that it is the ultimate and remote object of the recital, its immediate and proximate object being the impression of the Word of God. As for his statement in the same passage quoted that "the recital is originated and created, and it is an acquisition (*kasb*) on the part of man," it reflects a current theory, according to which all human acts are created by God but acquired by man.[6]

With regard to the problem of inlibration, Ibn Kullāb's denial of it is quite evident from his denial, in the fourth passage quoted, of the literalness of the Koranic statement "that he may hear the Word of God." A denial of inlibration may perhaps be discerned also in the contrast between his description of attributes in general, in which he says only that they are neither God nor other than God,[7] and his description here of the attribute of Word in the sense of the Koran, in which he says that "it is an error to say that it is God or a part of Him (*ba'ḍuhu*) or other than He." [8] This addition certainly calls for an explanation, and a plausible explanation could be found, I think, in taking the statement here that the Word of God is not a "part" of God to mean that it is not a "part"

[6] Cf. below, p. 673.
[7] Cf. above, p. 208.
[8] *Maḳālāt*, p. 584, ll. 14–15. So also in *Mughnī*, vol. 7, p. 4, ll. 3–4.

which is "separated" from God and is "transferred" from Him to something else — expressions which, as we shall see, were used by Ashʿarite followers of Ibn Kullāb in stating their denial of inlibration.[9]

b. Ibn Ḥanbal and the Affirmation of Inlibration

In contrast to the view of Ibn Kullāb is the view of Ibn Ḥanbal. We shall quote here three reports of his view.

First, Ibn Ḥazm reports him as saying that "the Word of God is His eternal knowledge and hence it is uncreated." [1]

Second, in Shahrastānī there is the following statement: "The early Muslims (*al-salaf*) and the Ḥanbalites said: Agreement has established that what is between the covers is the Word (*kalām*) of God, and what we read and hear and write is the very Word of God. It therefore follows that the [individual] words (*kalimāt*) and letters (*ḥurūf*) are the very Word of God. But inasmuch as agreement has established that the Word of God is uncreated, it follows that the [individual] words [and letters] are eternal and uncreated." [2]

Third, another statement in Shahrastānī, following shortly after the one just quoted and ascribed to the same "Early Muslims," reads as follows: "One is not to suppose that we assert the eternity of the letters and sounds which subsist in our tongues." [3] Though in this passage Shahrastānī does not repeat the words "and the Ḥanbalites" used by him in the preceding passage, we may assume that the view expressed in it is shared also by the Ḥanbalites.

From these three passages, three characteristic features of Ibn Ḥanbal's doctrine of the uncreated Koran may be gathered.

First, when in the first report quoted he says that "the Word of God is . . . eternal . . . and uncreated" and in the third report quoted he says by contrast that "one is not to suppose that we assert the eternity of the letters and sounds which subsist in our tongues," he quite clearly means to dis-

[9] Cf. below, p. 255.
[1] *Fiṣal* III, p. 5, ll. 5–6.
[2] *Nihāyat*, p. 313, ll. 4–8.
[3] *Ibid.*, p. 314, ll. 3–4.

tinguish, as does Ibn Kullāb, between an uncreated pre-existent Koran, which is the Word of God, and a created Koran which comes into existence whenever one recites it or hears it or memorizes it or writes it.

Second, in the light of this denial of the eternity of the Koran which comes into existence whenever one recites it or hears it or memorizes it or writes it, when in the second report quoted he says that "what is between the covers is the Word of God and what we hear and read and write is the very Word of God," he means to say that in every created Koran produced by reciting or hearing or memorizing or writing is embooked the uncreated Word of God, so that every created Koran consists of two natures, a created nature and an uncreated nature. This is a direct affirmation of inlibration, in opposition to Ibn Kullāb's denial of it.

Third, when therefore from his assertion of inlibration in the first part of the second report he infers in the second part of the same report that "the [individual] words and letters are the very Word of God" and are "eternal and uncreated," he merely means to assert that the differentiation of words and letters is already to be found in the uncreated Word of God, so that there is an inlibration of an uncreated individual Word and Letter in every created individual word and letter. This is in direct opposition to Ibn Kullāb who, as we have seen, maintains that the "uncreated Word" is "single" and "indivisible" and that all differentiations take place only in the recited Koran. It is for this reason that, in the first report quoted, Ibn Ḥanbal dwells only on the eternity and uncreatedness of the Word of God but makes no mention of its simplicity.

This conception of the doctrine of the uncreatedness of the Koran, which may be gathered from Ibn Ḥazm's and Shahrastānī's reports of the teaching of the Ḥanbalites, is confirmed by statements made by Ibn Ḥanbal himself, first, at his trial before Caliph al-Muʿtasim; [4] second, in a conversation

[4] Patton, *Aḥmad Ibn Ḥanbal and the Miḥna*, pp. 93 ff.

with Isḥaḳ ibn Ibrāhīm;[5] third, in his letter to ʿObaidallah ibn Yaḥya.[6]

To begin with, like Ibn Kullāb, he distinguishes between the uncreated Koran and a man-made Koran, for, in contrast to his insistence that "the Koran is uncreated" on the ground that "the Word (*kalām*) or Command (*amr*) of God" is uncreated,[7] he admits that "the utterance of the Koran" (*lafẓ al-Ḳu'rān*) is created.[8] The "utterance of the Koran" is the equivalent of Ibn Kullāb's "impression" or "expression." It is the Koran produced by reciting or hearing or memorizing or writing it.

But then, unlike Ibn Kullāb, who maintains that the uncreated Word of God is not embooked in the recited Koran, he maintains that the uncreated Word of God is embooked in the "utterance of the Koran." Thus in the verse "If any one of those who join gods with God ask an asylum of thee, grant him an asylum, that he may hear the Word of God" (9:6), he takes the expression "that he may hear the Word of God" literally,[9] in direct opposition to Ibn Kullāb, who interprets it figuratively.[10]

Thus, according to Ibn Ḥanbal, every recited Koran, and hence also every heard or memorized or written Koran, is of a twofold nature, a created one and an uncreated one. But, though one of the natures of these forms of the Koran was created, Ibn Ḥanbal refrained from applying to any such Koran the term "created." As reported of him by Ibn Ḫaldūn, "his scrupulousness prevented the imam Aḥmad [b. Ḥanbal] from applying the term 'created' to the Koran [in any of its forms], for [as far as authoritative doctrine was concerned] he had not heard from the ancient Muslims before his time [anything to the effect] that he [was to] say that the written copies of the Koran are eternally pre-existent, or that the

[5] *Ibid.*, pp. 139 ff.

[6] *Ibid.*, pp. 155 ff.

[7] *Ibid.*, pp. 139, 160, 161, 162, 163.

[8] *Ibid.*, pp. 32–35.

[9] *Ibid.*, p. 162. Cf. similar statement in Shahrastānī, *Milal*, p. 79, ll. 4 ff.

[10] Cf. above, p. 249.

recitation [of the Koran] which is done by [human] tongues was something eternally pre-existent." [11]

We have thus shown how by the middle of the ninth century there were two distinct conceptions of the orthodox Muslim belief in the uncreatedness of the Koran, that of Ibn Kullāb and that of Ibn Ḥanbal, one denying inlibration, the other affirming inlibration. We shall now try to show how subsequent orthodox believers in the uncreatedness of the Koran followed either Ibn Kullāb or Ibn Ḥanbal on the question of inlibration.

c. The Ḥanbalite Ashʿarī

The outstanding representative of the Ḥanbalite conception of the uncreatedness of the Koran is Ashʿarī in his work *Ibānah*. This is attested to by Ashʿarī himself, who, in one of the early parts of this work, declares that in his exposition of the beliefs of Islam he is following Ibn Ḥanbal.[1]

To begin with, like Ibn Ḥanbal, he does not consider the uncreated Word of God as simple. This may be gathered from the fact that he uses the verse "Should the sea become ink, to write the words of my Lord, the sea would surely fail ere the words of My Lord would fail" (18:109) as proof of the uncreatedness of the "Word" of God,[2] thus indicating that the uncreated Word, to him, was composed of words.

Then, while rejecting the use of Ibn Ḥanbal's expression "the utterance (*lafẓ*) of the Koran," [3] like Ibn Ḥanbal, he believes that the written or memorized or recited or heard Koran is created and that in it the uncreated Word of God is inlibrated. He thus says: "The Koran [used by him in the sense of the uncreated Word of God] is really written in our books, really preserved in our hearts, really read by our tongues, and really heard by us."[4] He thus also follows Ibn Ḥanbal's interpretation of the verse about giving asylum to a

[11] *Mukaddimah* III, p. 50, ll. 7–10. Cf. note *ad loc.* in Rosenthal's translation (III, p. 64). Cf. also, below, pp. 260–261.

[1] *Ibānah*, p. 8, ll. 3–4.

[2] *Ibid.*, p. 25, l. 13; p. 41, l. 1.

[3] *Ibid.*, p. 41, ll. 11–17.

[4] *Ibid.*, ll. 9–11.

polytheist (9:6) by taking the clause "that he may hear the Word of God" to mean literally that the very Word of God is heard when one hears the reading of the Koran.[5] Again, like Ibn Ḥanbal, he does not allow the application of the term "created" to any recited or heard or memorized or written Koran, even though any such Koran is of a twofold nature, a created one and an uncreated one. He thus asserts that "it may not be said, 'A part of the Koran is created,' because the Koran in its completeness is uncreated." [6]

d. The Kullabite Ashʿarī and Ashʿarites

While, speaking for himself in his *Ibānah*, Ashʿarī proved himself to be a Ḥanbalite on the problem of inlibration, there are reports both of him and of the Ashʿarites which show them to be Kullabites on that problem. Here are some of such reports.

As reported by Ibn Ḥazm, the Ashʿarites held that "the Word of God is an attribute of essence, eternal, uncreated . . . and God has only a single Word." [1]

They are then also reported by him as saying: "Gabriel did not bring down the Word of God into the heart of Muhammad; he brought down to him only something else, and that is an expression (*ʿibārah*) used as a substitute for the Word of God. Of that which we read in copies of the Koran and is written therein nothing is the Word of God. The Word of God . . . does not separate itself (*yuzāyil*) from the Creator, nor does it subsist in something else, nor does it abide in different places, nor is it transferred (*yuntaḳal*), nor does it consist of combined words." [2]

From these passages we gather that the Ashʿarites agreed with Ibn Kullāb both on the simplicity of the uncreated Word of God and on the denial of the inlibration of that uncreated simple Word of God in the recited or written revealed Koran, but that they disagreed with him on the origin of the "expressions." According to Ibn Kullāb, as the report on him

[5] *Ibid.*, l. 11.

[6] *Ibid.*, l. 18. Cf., below, pp. 260–261.

[1] *Fiṣal* III, p. 5, ll. 5–6.

[2] *Ibid.*, p. 6, ll. 10–16.

quoted above from the *Maḳālāt* [3] would seem to indicate, the expressions are created by the recital of the revealed Koran; according to the Ashʿarites here, they came into existence in the heavenly Koran prior to its revelation. Whether this difference was their conscious departure from Ibn Kullāb's view or whether it is based on some other version of the Kullabite view is a matter calling for investigation.

A similar Kullabite view is ascribed by Shahrastānī to both Ashʿarī himself and the Ashʿarites.

In his *Nihāyat*, in contrast to "the Early Muslims and the Ḥanbalites," whose views we have quoted above, he says of Ashʿarī that he "put forward something new (*abdaʿ*)" by asserting "the origination of the letters" and that "what we read is not the Word of God in reality but only metaphorically." [4] This view is quite evidently Kullabite, even though Shahrastānī declares it to be an innovation by Ashʿarī.

In his *Milal*, under the general heading "The Word of God," he quotes Ashʿarī as saying: "The Word of God is one and [despite its unity] it is command and prohibition, narration and inquiry, promise and threats; but [all these are aspects, and] these aspects refer only to various points of view from which His word may be considered and not to [a multiplicity of] number in the Word itself. The expressions (*al-ʿibārāt*) and utterances (*al-alfāẓ*) which are sent down to the prophets by means of the tongue of the angel are indications (*dalalāt*) of the eternal Word (*al-kalām*). The indication is created and originated; that which is indicated is beginningless and eternal. The distinction between the reading and that which is read and between the reciting and that which is recited is like the distinction between the liturgical glorification of God (*al-dhikr*) and God who is glorified (*al-madhkūr*), where the glorification is originated, and He who is glorified is eternal." [5] Later he adds that, according to the Ashʿarites, "what is in our hands is not really the Word of God." [6]

[3] See, above, pp. 249–250.
[4] *Nihāyat*, p. 313, ll. 15–17.
[5] *Milal*, p. 67, l. 20 – p. 68, l. 5.
[6] *Ibid.*, p. 78, ll. 12–13.

Thus Ashʿarī and the Ashʿarites of Shahrastānī, like the Ashʿarites of Ibn Ḥazm, agree with Ibn Kullāb on the simplicity of the uncreated Word of God and on the denial of inlibration but differ with him on the origin of the letters and expressions.

e. The Ḥanbalite Ibn Ḥazm

Another follower of the view of Ibn Ḥanbal is to be found in Ibn Ḥazm. Though his brief formal restatement of Ibn Ḥanbal's view on the Koran simply reads that "the Word of God is His eternal knowledge and hence it is uncreated," [1] his presentation of his own view touches upon the various other points in Ibn Ḥanbal's view, as we have reconstructed it on the basis of other sources, among them Ashʿarī's *Ibānah*.

His own view on the Koran is presented by Ibn Ḥazm in opposition to those called by him "the Ashʿarites," that is, the Kullabite Ashʿarites, whose view we have discussed in the preceding section.

First, he comes out in opposition to their Kullabite view of the simplicity of the uncreated Word of God. Quoting the Ashʿarites as saying that "God has only a single Word" [2] or that the Word of God does not consist of "combined letters," [3] he brands it as "sheer unbelief, for which there is no possible defense." [4] Maintaining, therefore, as does Ibn Ḥanbal, that the Word of God contains within itself innumerable words,[5] he supports himself by quoting the verse "Should the sea become ink, to write the words of my Lord, the sea would surely fail ere the words of my Lord would fail," [6] and the verse "If all the trees that are upon the earth were to become pens, and if God should after that swell the sea into seven seas [of ink], His words would not be exhausted," [7] in both of which verses the plural "words" is used. These are the same verses quoted by Ashʿarī in his *Ibānah* to prove directly that the

[1] Cf. p. 251, above.
[2] *Fiṣal* III, p. 5, l. 8.
[3] *Ibid.*, p. 6, ll. 15–16.
[4] *Ibid.*, l. 19.
[5] *Ibid.*, p. 5, l. 24 – p. 6, l. 9.
[6] Surah 18:109.
[7] Surah 31:26.

Word of God is uncreated and, indirectly, as we have seen,[8] also that the Word of God contains many words. Finally, like Ibn Ḥanbal, whom he himself has quoted as saying that "the Word of God is His eternal knowledge and hence uncreated," [9] he says of the Word of God that it is "His knowledge." [10] But inasmuch as Ibn Ḥazm, unlike Ibn Ḥanbal and all other Attributists, denies the reality of attributes,[11] it is to be assumed that, though like Ibn Ḥanbal he makes use of the same assertion that the Word of God is His knowledge, he does not mean by it the same thing. To Ibn Ḥanbal "word" and "knowledge" are real attributes in God; to Ibn Ḥazm, since they are not real attributes, they are identical with the essence of God, and as such they are to be interpreted as actions. This will explain why unlike those who, on account of their belief that the Word of God in the sense of the Koran is an attribute in God, deny that it is a creator,[11a] Ibn Ḥazm declares that it is a creator.[11b]

Second, he comes out in opposition to the Kullabite view of the Ashʿarites on the question of inlibration. Quoting "a certain group of Ashʿarites" as saying that "Gabriel did not bring down the Word of God" but only "the expression of the Word of God," he first dismisses this view with the comment that "this is sheer unbelief, for which there is no possible defense." [12] Then he proceeds to argue that "the Koran is the Word of God," and that it is this Koran which is the Word of God that is "recited in the mosques and written in books and preserved as a memory in hearts," [13] for it is this Koran which is the Word of God that was brought down by Gabriel.[14]

Thus Ibn Ḥazm, like Ibn Ḥanbal, distinguished between a pre-existent uncreated Koran identified with the Word of

[8] Cf. above at n. 1.

[9] *Fiṣal* III, p. 5, ll. 5–6.

[10] *Ibid.*, p. 8, l. 16.

[11] *Fiṣal* II, p. 120, l. 20 – p. 121, l. 19; p. 128, l. 4 – p. 129, l. 2; p. 140, ll. 1–16. Cf. Goldziher, *Zāhiriten*, pp. 143–145; Horten, *Systeme*, p. 577; Tritton, *Theology*, p. 197.

[11a] Cf. above, p. 244, at n. 45.

[11b] Cf. below at n. 31.

[12] *Fiṣal* III, p. 6, ll. 10–19.

[13] *Ibid.*, p. 6, l. 19 – p. 7, l. 2.

[14] *Ibid.*, p. 7, l. 11.

God and a man-made Koran produced by reciting and writing and memorizing the Koran, and undoubtedly also by hearing it, but makes no mention of the Preserved Tablet. Like Ibn Ḥanbal, too, he believes in the inlibration of the Word of God in the man-made Koran.

Ibn Ḥazm then goes on to explain more fully the distinction between the uncreated Koran and the man-made or, as he calls it, the created Koran, and to reassert the principle of inlibration.

Both the expression "the Word of God" and the term "Koran," he says, apply to the following five things: (1) the physical sound which is uttered and heard when one recites the Koran,[15] that is, the so-called "utterance (*lafẓ*) of the Koran"; (2) the expounding of the practical duties prescribed in the Koran, such, for instance, as almsgiving (*al-zakāt*), prayer (*al-ṣalāt*), and pilgrimage (*al-ḥajj*); [16] (3) the written copy of the Koran; [17] (4) the memorized Koran of one who knows it by heart; [18] (5) the Word of God which is His knowledge.[19] Of these five meanings of the term "Koran" as well as of the expression "the Word of God," only the fifth meaning refers to something uncreated; the first four meanings refer to things "created," that is, man-made, which are thus created or man-made Korans. Still, even these created or man-made Korans, he maintains, are to be described as the Word of God and not as mere "expressions" of the Word of God, as in the belief of those Ashʿarites who were quoted by himself as saying that "Gabriel did not bring down the Word of God" but only "the expression of the Word of God." Evidently having in mind another statement by the same Ashʿarites, one quoted by Shahrastānī but not by himself, namely, that "what we recite is the Word of God metaphorically not in truth," [20] Ibn Ḥazm says, in opposition to it, that what we recite or hear or memorize or write is "the Word of God in

[15] *Ibid.*, ll. 14–21.
[16] *Ibid.*, ll. 21–23.
[17] *Ibid.*, l. 23 – p. 8, l. 8.
[18] *Ibid.*, p. 8, ll. 8–16.
[19] *Ibid.*, l. 16.
[20] *Nihāyat*, p. 313, ll. 15–17.

truth,"[21] inasmuch as it is inlibrated or embooked in every form of the man-made Koran. Evidently, again, having in mind still another statement of the same Ash'arites, which was quoted by himself, namely, that "of that which we read in the copies of the Koran and is written therein nothing is the Word of God,"[22] he says, again, in opposition to it, that "the utterance that is heard is the Koran itself and the Word of God itself."[23] In support of this assertion he quotes the verse on giving asylum to the worshipper of many gods (9:6), in which, like Ibn Ḥanbal and unlike Ibn Kullāb,[24] he takes the expression "that he may hear the Word of God" to mean literally that he may really hear the Word of God.[25]

Then a question would seem to have arisen in the mind of Ibn Ḥazm. In view of the fact that the term "Koran" applies to five things, of which only one is uncreated but four are created, one would like to know, he would seem to have asked himself, whether, depending on the sense in which one uses the term "Koran," one could not say of the Koran either that it is uncreated or that it is created or that it is both uncreated and created. Already Ibn Ḥanbal, as we are told by Ibn Ḫaldūn, anticipated such a question, for, having in mind his own admission that "the utterance of the Koran" is created,[26] he "scrupulously refrained from applying the term created to the Koran,"[27] even when one meant by the term "Koran" the created utterance of it. In fact, there were some, as reported by Ash'arī in his *Maḳālāt*, who, because of their belief in the uncreatedness of the pre-existent Koran and the createdness of the utterance of it, expressed themselves by saying that "part of the Koran is created and part of it uncreated,"[28] and it is with evident reference to them that Ash'arī in his *Ibānah* concludes his discussion with the appendage: "And it

[21] *Fiṣal* III, p. 7, ll. 15, 21.

[22] *Ibid*., p. 6, ll. 12–13.

[23] *Ibid*., p. 11, l. 5.

[24] Cf. above, p. 253.

[25] *Fiṣal* III, p. 11, l. 6.

[26] Cf. above, p. 253.

[27] *Muḳaddimah* III, p. 50, ll. 7–8. Cf. discussion of the meaning of this passage in Rosenthal's note to his translation of the *Muḳaddimah*, *ad loc*. (Vol. III, p. 64, n. 405a).

[28] *Maḳālāt*, p. 585, l. 15 – p. 586, l. 1.

may not be said that part of the Koran is created, for the Koran in its entirety is uncreated,"[29] thus following Ibn Ḥanbal's view that one is not to predicate the term "created" of the Koran in any way whatsoever. Similarly Ibn Ḥazm follows the view of Ibn Ḥanbal, but, instead of explaining that view on the mere ground of religious scrupulousness, as in fact it is done later by Ibn Ḫaldūn,[30] he tries to explain it on the ground of some logical principle by which a proposition may be judged true or false.

The passage in which Ibn Ḥazm tries to explain the view of Ibn Ḥanbal by some logical principle reads as follows: "Inasmuch as the term Koran applies with equal appropriateness to five things, of which four are created and one is not created, it is definitely not allowed for any one to say that the Koran is created nor, by the same token, to say that the Word of God is created, for he who says this is a liar, since he applies the description of creation to something signified by the term Koran and by the expression Word of God, to which the term creation does not apply. And it is logically necessary that it should be said that the Koran is neither creator nor created and that the Word of God is neither creator nor created, for, inasmuch as four of the things which are named by these terms are not creators [even though the fifth thing, the Word of God, is creator], it is not allowed to apply unqualifiedly the term creator to the terms Koran and Word of God, and, inasmuch as the fifth thing [named by these terms] is not created, [it is not allowed to apply unqualifiedly the term created to the terms Koran and the Word of God]. And [in general] it is not [logically] admissible to apply to the subject as a whole any predicate that is true only of part of the subject and not of the whole of it; rather is it necessary that a predicate which is true only of part of a subject should be negated of the subject as a whole."[31] He then proceeds to

[29] *Ibānah*, p. 41, l. 18.
[30] *Muḳaddimah* III, p. 50, ll. 10–13. Cf. above, pp. 253–254.
[31] *Fiṣal* III, p. 9, l. 25 – p. 10, l. 8.

illustrate the truth of this general principle by a number of concrete propositions.

The reasoning underlying Ibn Ḥazm's general principle with its illustrative propositions is based, I think, upon Aristotle's discussion of the various meanings of the term "whole" (ὅλον, *al-kull*). "Whole," says Aristotle, may also be taken to mean "that which so contains the things it contains that they form a unity; and this in two ways." [32] In one way, the whole is any universal term, such as the term "man," which includes many individual human beings, all of whom form one single species referred to as man.[33] In another way, the whole may consist of "many things" which actually exist as many things, but have become a "whole" or "one" by having been made "artificially" into a bundle "by a band." [34]

Starting with this twofold meaning of the term "whole," Ibn Ḥazm argues that, in the case of a proposition in which the subject is a whole in either of these two ways and in which the predicate is not applicable to all the things that are contained in the subject, the proposition cannot be true if the predicate is affirmed of the subject; it can be true only if the predicate is negated of the subject. He illustrates his principles by propositions in which the subjects are "wholes" of the two kinds mentioned by Aristotle. First, taking the "whole" in the sense in which many actually existing things are artificially made into a unity by a band, he says that, if of five garments, that is to say, of five garments which have been artificially made into one whole, four are red and one is not red, then the proposition "these garments [conceived of as one whole] are red" is quite evidently false, but the proposition "these garments [again, conceived of as one whole] are not red" is quite evidently true.[35] Second, taking the "whole" in the sense of a universal which contains many individuals conceived of as one whole, such as genus or species, he says that the proposi-

[32] *Metaph.* V, 26, 1023b, 27–28.
[33] *Ibid.*, 29–32.
[34] *Ibid.*, 32–34; V, 6, 1015b, 36 – 1016a, 1.
[35] *Fiṣal* III, p. 10, ll. 12–14.

tion that "man [that is, the human species as a whole] is a physician" is quite evidently false, but the proposition that "man [that is, again, the human species as a whole] is not a physician" is quite evidently true.[36]

On the basis of the principle laid down by him, namely, that, in the case of a subject which answers to Aristotle's description of a "whole," a predicate which is true of only part of the subject may be negated of the subject but not affirmed of it, he concludes that, inasmuch as the term "Koran" or the expression "the Word of God" is a "whole" which includes four things which are created and one thing which is not created, one may say logically that "the Koran or the Word of God is not created" but one may not say "the Koran or the Word of God is created." [37]

II. The Created Koran

1. THE DENIAL OF THE UNCREATED KORAN AND THE DENIAL OF ETERNAL ATTRIBUTES

In the problem of attributes in general, those who denied their reality interpreted all terms attributed to God as mere names. In this, as we have seen, they developed a view which corresponds to that of the heretical Christian Sabellianism on the problem of the Trinity. In the problem of the particular attribute of Word, in the sense of the pre-existent Koran, those who denied its uncreatedness did not deny its reality. They admitted that there was a real pre-existent Koran, but it was created. They thus developed a view which corresponds to the heretical Christian Arianism on the problem of the Trinity and which, historically, is a return to what was probably the original conception of the Koran as taught in the Koran itself — a pre-existent created Koran modeled after the Jewish lore of a pre-existent created Law.[1]

[36] *Ibid.*, ll. 14–16.

[37] *Fiṣal* III, p. 10, ll. 20–22.

[1] Cf. Schreiner, *Kalam*, p. 3, n. 7, quoting Ibn al-Athīr (referred to below

In their opposition to an eternal, uncreated Koran, as in their opposition to the reality of eternal attributes, the Muʿtazilites argued that such a belief was contradictory to the conception of the unity of God. Thus Caliph al-Maʾmūn, in his third letter to the governor of Baghdad, says that "he has no belief in God's unity who does not confess that the Koran is created." [2] This, as we have seen, is the argument which in Christianity had led either to Sabellianism or to Arianism.[3]

And so, while with reference to all the other attributes, with the few exceptions mentioned above,[4] the Muʿtazilites denied their existence altogether, with reference to the attribute of Word in the sense of the pre-existent Koran, they did not deny its existence altogether; they only denied its eternity, maintaining that it was created.

2. THE CREATED KORAN AS A PRE-EXISTENT CREATED HEAVENLY KORAN

In the passage quoted above in which Abū al-Hudhayl distinguishes between the creative word "Be" and the Word in the sense of Koran, he also says that, while the creative word "Be" is created by God not in an abode (*maḥall*), the Word in the sense of Koran is created by God in an abode.[1] This description of the Koran as the Word of God which was created in an abode becomes the established characterization of the Muʿtazilite conception of the Koran. Thus Shahrastānī, in contrast to Ashʿarī whom he describes as maintaining that God is a speaker (*mutakallim*) by means of an uncreated Word which subsists in Him as an attribute,[2] describes the Muʿtazilites as maintaining that "God is a speaker by means of a Word which He created in an abode (*maḥall*)." [3] But as

p. 265, n. 4); cf. Patton, *Aḥmad Ibn Ḥanbal and the Miḥna*, p. 47; Watt, "Early Discussions," p. 29.

[2] Ṭabarī, *Annales*, p. 1120, ll. 10–11; Patton, *Aḥmad Ibn Ḥanbal and the Miḥna*, p. 69. Cf. *Milal*, p. 48, ll. 16–17, quoting al-Muzdār.

[3] Cf. above, pp. 134–135.

[4] Cf. above, pp. 140 ff.

[1] *Farḳ*, p. 108, ll. 15–18; *Milal*, p. 35, ll. 2–4; cf. above, p. 141.

[2] *Milal*, p. 68, ll. 6–8.

[3] *Nihāyat*, p. 269, l. 18.

to what that object was in which God created His Word we are not told.

In a passage in which Ibn al-Athīr traces the history of the doctrine of the createdness of the Koran prior to the rise of the Muʿtazilites, he says that "Jahm b. Safwān (d. 746) acquired it from Jaʿd b. Adham (probably a corruption of Jaʿd b. Dirham [d. 743]), Jaʿd acquired it from Abān b. Samʿān, Abān acquired it from Ṭalūb, the nephew and son-in-law of Labīd al-Aʿṣam, Ṭalūb acquired it from Labīd b. al-Aʿṣam, the Jew, who bewitched the Prophet. Labīd had taught the createdness of the Torah, but the first who composed a book on this (that is, on the createdness of the Koran) was Ṭalūb, and he was a *zindīḳ* (that is, an insincere convert to Islam and heretic) and consequently he spread the heresy [of the createdness of the Koran]." [4] Here then we have a historian's testimony to certain historical facts, namely, that under the influence of the Jewish tradition as to the createdness of the pre-existent Torah, a Jewish convert to Islam, a nephew and son-in-law of a Jewish contemporary of Muhammad, wrote a book on the createdness of the pre-existent Koran, through which the belief in the createdness of the pre-existent Koran was disseminated among Muslims. But it will be noticed that no mention is made by Ibn al-Athīr of any opposition to Ṭalūb's teaching of the createdness of the Koran on the part of his contemporary Muslims or of its having been decried by them as heretical; its description as heresy by Ibn al-Athīr quite evidently expresses a later judgment on it. His silence on these points would seem to show circumstantially, as do the above-mentioned evidences, all of them circumstantial, that the original belief about the pre-existent Koran was that it was created and that its uncreatedness was introduced later in consequence of the rise of the belief in uncreated attributes.

The earliest persons in Ibn al-Athīr's list concerning whose

[4] Ibn al-Athīr, *Al-Kāmil fī al-Tārīḫ*, ed. C. J. Tornberg, VII, p. 49, ll. 6–11; cf. Schreiner, *Kalam*, pp. 3–4.

belief in the createdness of the Koran there is some additional information are Jaʿd and Jahm.

Concerning Jaʿd — and this time his full name is given as Jaʿd b. Dirham — Ibn al-Athīr tells us elsewhere that he believed in "the createdness of the Koran" [5] and that he said that "God did not speak to Moses directly." [6] Quite evidently there was in his mind some relation between these two statements. What that relation was we are not told. But inasmuch as two similar statements are also ascribed to his contemporary Jahm, we may reasonably assume that he meant by them what, as we shall see, Jahm meant by them.

Concerning Jahm, Ashʿarī reports in his *Maḳālāt* that he believed in "the createdness of the Koran." [7] In his *Ibānah*, speaking not of Jahm himself but of his followers, the Jahmiyyah, Ashʿarī furnishes us with some further information about the doctrine of the createdness of the Koran. Referring to the Koranic account of God's speaking to Moses out of the bush,[8] he says: "The Jahmiyyah think the same way as the Christians, for the Christians think that the womb of Mary enclosed the [uncreated] Word of God, and the Jahmiyyah, going further than they, think that a created word of God took up its abode in the bush and the bush enclosed it." [9] Then after referring to that created Word of God speaking to Moses out of the bush as the Word of God created in a created bush,[10] he presents the Jahmiyyah's belief of the createdness of the Koran as a belief that the Word of God was created in a created thing.[11] From this we may gather that by the createdness of the Koran the followers of Jahm meant that it was revealed to Muhammad by means of a Word created in some created thing corresponding to the bush in which the Word of God to Moses was created. This would seem to be the general view of the Muʿtazilites with regard to the Koran, for, speaking of the Muʿtazilites in general, Ibn

[5] *Al-Kāmil*, V, p. 196, l. 25; p. 329, l. 2.
[6] *Ibid.*, p. 197, l. 5.
[7] *Maḳālāt*, p. 280, l. 4.
[8] Surah 28:30; Exod. 3:4.
[9] *Ibānah*, p. 26, ll. 2–4.
[10] *Ibid.*, ll. 6 and 9.
[11] *Ibid.*, ll. 12–14.

Ḥazm reports that "they said that the Word of God is an attribute of a created action and they said that God spoke to Moses with a word which He created in a bush," [12] by which is quite evidently meant that the Word of God in the sense of the Koran was created in some created thing just as the word of God spoken to Moses was created in a bush. But what that created thing was in which the Koran was created we are not told.

Information as to what that created thing was may be found in several passages of Ashʿarī's *Maḳālāt*, in which are reported the views of Jaʿfar ibn Ḥarb (d. 850), Jaʿfar ibn Mubashshir (d. 851), and Abū al-Hudhayl (d. 849).

In one of these passages, Ashʿarī reports in the name of Jaʿfar ibn Ḥarb and most of the Baghdadian Muʿtazilites that "the Word of God is an accident and that it is created." [13] In another passage, he reports in the name of both Jaʿfar ibn Ḥarb and Jaʿfar ibn Mubashshir and their followers that "the Koran was created by God on the Preserved Tablet," [14] with the additional statement elsewhere that according to Jaʿfar ibn Mubashshir the created Koran is a body.[15] Combining these passages, we may infer that the created abode in which, according to the Muʿtazilites, the Word of God was created was, according to the two Jaʿfars and their followers, the Preserved Tablet. On the basis of all these statements, we may assume that the Word of God or Koran was created on the Preserved Tablet and, inasmuch as the Preserved Tablet is among the things which were created before the creation of the world, the Koran was created before the creation of the world. The difference between the two Jaʿfars on the question whether this pre-existent created Koran is to be called accident or body, it may be assumed, does not affect their view as to the nature of the pre-existent created Koran, for the difference between them on this point rests only on the

[12] *Fiṣal* III, p. 5, ll. 3–5.
[13] *Maḳālāt*, p. 192, ll. 8 and 10–11.
[14] *Ibid.*, p. 599, l. 16 – p. 600, l. 1; cf. *Milal*, p. 49, ll. 4–5.
[15] *Maḳālāt*, p. 588, ll. 4 and 7.

question whether God can be said to be the creator of accidents, Jaʿfar b. Mubashshir being one of those who happen to believe that God creates only bodies.[16] It is this pre-existent Word of God or Koran, abiding on the Preserved Tablet, whether called accident or body, that, according to the two Jaʿfars, was subsequently revealed to Muhammad. It is also to be assumed that, according to the two Jaʿfars, the pre-existent created Word of God or Koran on the Preserved Tablet was an orderly, arranged text consisting of words and letters, for, according to the view ascribed to the generality of the Muʿtazilites, "just as the word (*kalām*) of man consists of letters (*ḥurūf*) so does also the Word of God." [17]

Then a number of passages in Ashʿarī and others deal with the Muʿtazilite conception of the relation of that created, pre-revealed heavenly Koran on the Preserved Tablet to the earthly Koran produced by man in reciting it or hearing it or memorizing it or writing it; in other words, with the problem of inlibration — the inlibration of the created heavenly Koran in the man-made earthly Koran.

In a passage in which he reports in the name of Jaʿfar ibn Ḥarb and most of the Baghdadian Muʿtazilites, Ashʿarī says: "And they consider it impossible that the Word of God should exist in two places at the same time and they assert also the impossibility of its transference and removal from the place in which it was created to take up existence in another place." [18] Of the two Jaʿfars and their followers, his report continues to say: "It is not possible for the [heavenly] Koran to be transferred (*yunḳal*) and it is not possible for it to exist in more than one place at the same time, for the existence of one thing at the same time in more than one place by way of indwelling (*ḥulūl*) and inhabitation (*tamakkun*) is impossible. In spite of this, however, they say that the Koran which is written in books and preserved in the hearts of believers and in what is heard from the reciter is the [pre-existent] Koran, and this is in accordance with what is agreed upon by most

[16] *Ibid.*, ll. 4–8. [17] *Ibid.*, p. 604, ll. 8–9. [18] *Ibid.*, p. 192, ll. 8–10.

of the Muslim community, except that the Jaʿfars mean by this saying of theirs that what is heard and memorized and written is an imitation (*ḥikāyah*) of the [pre-existent] Koran, from which nothing was torn away, and this imitation is the act of the writer and reciter and memorizer, whereas the pattern of the imitation (*al-maḥkīy*) is wherein God created it. They said: Sometimes, when a man has heard a word which corresponds to this word [of the Koran heard or memorized or written down], he says that it is that very word, in which case he is correct and faultless. So likewise, whenever we say that what is heard or written or memorized is the very same Koran that exists on the [Preserved] Tablet, it is so, because it is a likeness (*mithl*) and imitation (*ḥikāyah*) thereof." [19]

In Shahrastānī the same passage is restated briefly as follows: "It is not possible that it should be transferred, for it is impossible that one thing should be in two places at the same time (*ḥall*), and whatever we recite is an imitation (*ḥikāyah*) of that which was first written on the Preserved Tablet, and, as for this imitation, it is we who made and created it." [20]

In Ibn Ḥazm, the same view, quoted in the name of Jaʿfar ibn Mubashshir al-Ḳaṣabī, reads as follows: "The Koran is not in the pages of the book: what is in the pages of the book is something else, and that is the imitation of the Koran." [21]

From the combination of all these passages, we may gather that the Koran exists only in one place, in the place in which it was created, that is, on the Preserved Tablet, and that it is neither transferred from that place to the earthly Koran made by man through his writing it down or memorizing it or reciting it nor does it exist simultaneously in two places, that is, both on the Preserved Tablet in heaven and in the man-made Koran on earth. In fact, it does not exist in the man-made earthly Koran as in place, for there is no inlibration, and the man-made earthly Koran is only an imitation of the pre-existent heavenly Koran on the Preserved Tablet.

[19] *Ibid.*, p. 600, ll. 1–11.
[20] *Milal*, p. 49, ll. 5–7.
[21] *Fiṣal* IV, p. 197, ll. 9–10.

This is the view of a group of Muʿtazilites headed by the Jaʿfars — a group described by Ashʿarī as consisting of "most of the Baghdadians." A partly different view, we shall see, was held by a group of Muʿtazilites headed by Abū al-Hudhayl — a group undoubtedly consisting of members of the school of Baṣra.

We have already quoted passages from Shahrastānī and Baghdādī in which Abū al-Hudhayl is quoted as saying that the obligative word or command of God, that is, the word or command of God in the sense of the pre-existent Koran, was created in an abode.[22] In passages in Ashʿarī's *Maḳālāt*, he and his followers are quoted as saying that "the Koran was created by God on the Preserved Tablet and that it is an accident" and that "they refused to admit that it is a body." [23] Combining these two passages, we may gather from them the view that the Word of God or the pre-existent Koran was created by God, prior to its revelation, as an accident on the Preserved Tablet.

Thus, with regard to the general conception of a created pre-existent Koran, his view is the same as that of the two Jaʿfars and, with regard to the special question whether the pre-existent created Koran on the Preserved Tablet was an accident or a body, his view is the same as that of Jaʿfar b. Ḥarb. But, with regard to the question of inlibration, we shall try to show by passages from Ashʿarī's *Maḳālāt* that he differed from the Jaʿfars. These passages are rather obscure. In quoting them, we shall therefore add within brackets certain explanatory phrases, with a view to bringing out what we consider to be the meaning of these passages.

In one passage, Abū al-Hudhayl is reported to have said: "The Koran exists in three places: in the place wherein it is preserved as a memory, in the place wherein it is written, and in the place wherein it is recited and heard. The word of God thus exists in many places in the manner in which we have

[22] *Milal*, p. 35, ll. 2–4; *Farḳ*, p. 108, ll. 16–18; cf. above, p. 141.
[23] *Maḳālāt*, p. 598, ll. 11–12 and p. 192, ll. 1–2.

just explained, without implying that thereby the Koran is transferred or removed [from the Preserved Tablet] or that thereby it disappears [from it] in the true sense of these terms. Only as something written or recited or memorized does it exist in a place, so that if the Koran was blotted out from something on which it was written, it would no longer exist there as in a place, without, however, ceasing to exist [on the Preserved Tablet as in a place] and, by the same token, if the Koran was written down on something, it would thereby come to exist on it as in a place, without, however, having been transferred to it [from the Preserved Tablet]. The same observation applies also to remembering and reciting. Finally, if God destroyed all the places in which the Koran existed as something memorized or read or heard, the Koran would vanish [from those places] and no longer exist [in them, without, however, ceasing to exist on the Preserved Tablet as in a place]." [24]

In another passage, Abū al-Hudhayl and his followers are reported as follows: "And they thought that the Koran [which was created on the Preserved Tablet] exists in many places at the same time, namely, when a reciter recites it, it exists simultaneously with his reciting of it, and so also, when a writer writes it, it exists simultaneously with his writing of it, and so also, again, when a memorizer memorizes it, it exists simultaneously with his memorizing of it, for, through reciting and memorizing and writing, the Koran exists in places. However, transference [from the Preserved Tablet] and disappearance [from it] are inconceivable with regard to the Koran." [25]

In these passages, it will be noticed, Abū al-Hudhayl, like the two Jaʿfars, says that the pre-existent heavenly Koran cannot be "transferred" or "removed" from the Preserved Tablet in heaven on which it was created. But, unlike the Jaʿfars, who say that the earthly Koran made by man through writing or memorizing or reciting is not another place in

[24] *Ibid.*, p. 598, l. 12 – p. 599, l. 5.

[25] *Ibid.*, p. 192, ll. 2–6.

which the pre-existent created heavenly Koran takes up its abode and that hence the pre-existent Koran does not exist in two places, Abū al-Hudhayl says that these various forms of the earthly man-made Koran are places in which the pre-existent heavenly Koran takes up its abode and that hence the pre-existent Koran exists in many places at the same time. Then also, unlike the two Jaʿfars, he does not describe the earthly man-made Koran by the term "likeness" or "imitation." All this shows that while Abū al-Hudhayl and his followers believed in the createdness of the Koran, they also believed in its inlibration.

In the foregoing passages in which Ashʿarī reports on the teachings of the three contemporaries, the two Jaʿfars and Abū al-Hudhayl, we get the same explanation as to what is meant by the createdness of the Koran. It does not mean a denial of a pre-existent pre-revealed Koran. It only means that prior to its revelation the Word of God was created on the Preserved Tablet, probably simultaneously with the creation of the Preserved Tablet itself, which took place prior to the creation of the world, and it is from its abode on the Preserved Tablet that the Koran was subsequently revealed to Muhammad. From the same reports, we also gather that among those who believed in the createdness of the Koran, just as among those who believed in its eternity, there was a difference of opinion on the question of inlibration.

The problem of inlibration among those who believed in the createdness of the Koran is touched upon by Shahrastānī in two passages.

In one passage, Shahrastānī attributes to the Muʿtazilites the following views: "The word of God [that is, the pre-existent Koran] is originated and created in an abode [that is, on the Preserved Tablet] and it is letter (*ḥarf*) and sound (*ṣaut*), the likenesses (*amthāl*) of which are written down in books which are imitations (*ḥikāyāt*) thereof." [26] In this passage, Shahrastānī touches upon two topics: (1) the createdness of the

[26] *Milal*, p. 30, ll. 10–11.

pre-existent heavenly Koran; (2) its relation to the earthly man-written Koran. In his statement on the first topic, the singular terms "letter" (*ḥarf*) and "sound" (*ṣaut*), I take it, are either corruptions of the plural terms "letters" (*ḥurūf*) and "sounds" (*aṣwāt*) or are used by Shahrastānī in a generic sense; for from other sources we gather that the Koran, which, according to the Muʿtazilites, was created on the Preserved Tablet, consisted, according to them, of "letters" and "sounds." [27] In his statement on the second topic, the term "likenesses" as a description of the letters and sounds in the written books of the Koran and the term "imitations" as a description of the written books of the Koran themselves indicate that the Muʿtazilites spoken of by him here did not believe in inlibration. Thus the Muʿtazilites in this passage refer to the Baghdadians as represented by the Jaʿfars.

In another passage, contrasting the Muʿtazilites with the Ashʿarites, he says: "The Muʿtazilites agree with us in our belief that what is in our hands is the word of God and disagree with us as to the eternity of the Koran; they are, however, refuted by the consensus of the Muslim community. The Ashʿarites agree with us as to the eternity of the Koran and disagree with us in that they believe that what is in our hands is not really the word of God; they, too, are refuted by the consensus of the Muslim community." [28] According to this passage, then, the Muʿtazilites believed in inlibration, whereas the Ashʿarites did not believe in it, and Shahrastānī placed himself on the side of those who believed in it. In this passage, therefore, the Muʿtazilites spoken of are the Baṣraites as represented by Abū al-Hudhayl; the Ashʿarites spoken of are those we described as the Kullabite Ashʿarites, whose view, as we have seen, Shahrastānī himself characterized as an innovation; [29] those on whose side Shahrastānī places himself

[27] *Irshād*, p. 59, ll. 6–9; p. 60, ll. 8–9 (pp. 100, 102); Taftāzānī, p. 82, ll. 11–13; cf. above, p. 268.

[28] *Milal*, p. 78, ll. 10–13. On the denial of inlibration by the Ashʿarites, see above, pp. 255 ff.

[29] Cf., above, p. 256.

here are those whom he described as "the Early Muslims and the Ḥanbalites." [30]

3. THE DENIAL OF A PRE-EXISTENT HEAVENLY KORAN

Quite different from the conception of the createdness of the Koran held by the two Jaʿfars and Abū al-Hudhayl are two conceptions reported in the names of Naẓẓām and Muʿammar.

As quoted by Ashʿarī, Naẓẓām and his followers held that "the Word of the Creator is a body, and this body is a sound which is articulate, composite, audible, and it is the work of God and His creation. Man does only the reading, and the reading is a motion, and it is other than the Koran." [1] To this Ashʿarī adds that "al-Naẓẓām considers it impossible that the Word of God should at one and the same time be in many places or even in two places, maintaining that it is in the place wherein God created it." [2] In another passage, after quoting anonymously a view which in the first of the two foregoing passages he has ascribed to Naẓẓām and his followers, Ashʿarī says: "Ibn al-Rāwandī reports that he has heard that some one of the upholders of the aforesaid view thinks that it [that is, the Word of the Creator] is a word in the air and that the reader removes its obstacle by his reading and thereby it becomes audible." To this Ashʿarī adds: "And this is the view of Ibrahīm al-Naẓẓām most likely." [3] Naẓẓām is also reported to have denied the miraculous nature of the literary form of the Koran and to have maintained that a work of greater beauty and elegance could be produced by others. Not the external literary form of the Koran, he says, is proof of the reliability of Muhammad's claim to prophecy but only its contents which makes unknown things manifest.[4]

From these passages, we gather that to Naẓẓām the created-

[30] Cf. p. 256, above.

[1] *Maḳālāt*, p. 191, ll. 11–13; cf. p. 604, ll. 9–10.

[2] *Ibid.*, p. 191, ll. 13–15.

[3] *Ibid.*, p. 588, ll. 9–14.

[4] *Intiṣār* 15, p. 28, ll. 10–11; *Farḳ*, p. 128, ll. 5–14; p. 218, ll. 3–7; *Milal*, p. 39, ll. 15–18.

ness of the Koran did not mean that the Word of God was created on the Preserved Tablet. It was created in the air, and it was created there as a body, in the form of a combination of articulate sounds. When this Word was created in the air is not stated, but probably it was created at the time of the revelation of the Koran to Muhammad, when that Word was heard by him and he communicated it to the people in the form of a written book, the Koran. But though it is this created Word of God which was communicated to the people through the Koran, it is not inlibrated in the Koran, for the Word of God remains in the place wherein it was created. Only its contents are communicated to the people through the Koran, and they are communicated in the language of Muhammad's own choosing. From Ibn al-Rāwandī's report of a teaching, which Ashʿarī identified with that of Naẓẓām, we get the further information that the language in which the Koran is written is only an external shell of the created Word of God and an obstacle to its audibility. That shell, however, is broken, as it were, when one reads the Koran; the obstacle is then removed, and the created Word of God becomes audible to the reader, as it was to Muhammad, and the reader then clothes it in words of his own choosing, as did Muhammad. The upshot of all this is that, like the Jaʿfars and the Baghdadians, Naẓẓām denies the inlibration of the Word of God in the Koran, but, going further than they, he even denies that the Koran is an imitation of the Word of God, which to him was created not on the Preserved Tablet prior to the creation of the world but in the air at the time of its revelation.

Historically this explanation of the revelation of the Koran reflects three sources. First, it reflects the Philonic description of the revelation on Mount Sinai. For Philo in his *De Decalogo*, commenting upon the scriptural statement that at the revelation on Mount Sinai "Moses spoke and God answered him by a voice" (Exod. 19:19), explains it to mean that "at that time God wrought a miracle of a truly holy kind by bidding an invisible sound to be created in the air," which sound was "an articulate voice" which was "audible." [5] This Philonic explanation could have reached Naẓẓām by hearsay, even if the condensed Arabic translation of the *De Decalogo*, which we know to have existed,[6] was not made until later. Second, it reflects the Stoic denial of immateriality, which was followed by Naẓẓām, as implied in his views on accidents.[7] Accordingly, the articulate voice created in the air which by Philo is said to be "invisible," that is to say, "incorporeal," [8] is changed by Naẓẓām into a "body." Third, it reflects the teaching of the Church Fathers, which corresponds to a certain opinion of the rabbis, that the language by which the prophets expressed the divine communications was chosen by themselves.[9]

While to Naẓẓām the Word of God is a Word created by God in the air, to Muʿammar it is only a capacity created by God in man enabling him to produce a word which expresses the will and design of God.

We shall quote his view as reported by Ibn al-Rāwandī through Ḫayyāṭ and by Ashʿarī, Baghdādī, and Shahrastānī.

As reported by Ibn al-Rāwandī and Ḫayyāṭ: "Muʿammar maintains that the Koran is not the work of God, nor is it, as according to the view of the generality of the people, an attribute in the essence of God; it is rather the work of nature." [10] What this statement means is that Muʿammar is not only against the orthodox belief in the eternity of the Koran as an attribute in God but he is also against the Muʿtazilite belief that it is a Word created by God.

As reported by Ashʿarī: "The followers of Muʿammar claim that the Koran is an accident . . . But it is impossible that God should have made it in the true sense of the term, for

[5] *De Decalogo* 9, 33.

[6] Cf. H. Hirschfeld, "The Arabic Portion of the Cairo Genizah of Cambridge," *JQR*, 17: 65–66 (1905).

[7] Cf. Horovitz, *Einfluss*, pp. 10 ff.

[8] Cf. *Philo*, II, p. 37, n. 85.

[9] *The Philosophy of the Church Fathers*, I, pp. 92–94.

[10] *Intiṣār* 36, p. 48, ll. 2–3.

they consider it impossible that accidents should be an act of God. They think, therefore, that the Koran is an act of the place from which it is heard. If it is heard from the bush, then it is the act of the bush, and wherever it is heard it is the act of the abode in which it happens to be located." [11]

Also, as reported by Ashʿarī through Zurḳān: "Muʿammar said that God created substance but, as for accidents which are in it, they are the act of the substance, and verily they are the act of nature, so that the Koran is an act produced by the nature of the substance in which it is, and it is not a creator nor something created, but it is produced by the nature of the thing in which it abides." [12]

As reported by Baghdādī: "Inasmuch as Muʿammar thought that God created no accidents whatsoever and at the same time denied eternal attributes of God . . . it was inevitable that he should fall into this heresy, namely, that God has no Word, since he could not say that God's Word was an eternal attribute . . . seeing that he did not ascribe to God any eternal attribute, nor could he say that His Word was His act . . . since God, according to him, does not create any accidents whatsoever. The Koran, according to him, is the act of the body in which the Word happens to be located, but is not an act of God, nor an attribute," from which Baghdādī infers that, according to Muʿammar, God "has no Word" and "no power to command, to forbid, nor to impose any obligation." [13]

As reported by Shahrastānī: "God created nothing but bodies. As for accidents, they are the products of bodies, produced either by nature, as, for instance, fire produces burning and the sun heat and the moon the coloration of things, or by choice, as, for instance, animal beings produce motion and rest, aggregation and segregation." Then, like Baghdādī, Shahrastānī goes on to say: "Since he does not

[11] *Maḳālāt*, p. 192, l. 12 – p. 193, l. 2.
[12] *Ibid.*, p. 584, ll. 1–4.
[13] *Farḳ*, p. 137, ll. 4–13.

believe in the existence of eternal attributes nor in the creation of accidents, it follows that, according to him, God has no Word by which He speaks" and hence "there is no command or prohibition." [14]

Combining these various reports and taking them to be mutually complementary, we may restate the view of Muʿammar as follows: The Word of God is neither an uncreated attribute in God, as held by the orthodox, nor a created accident in the Preserved Tablet, as held by the Muʿtazilites, nor even, as Naẓẓām says, a body created by God in the air. In fact, there is no Word of God. What is called the Word of God is only a word produced by certain bodies which were especially created by God to be capable of producing out of themselves a word which would communicate to men certain messages from God. Such especially endowed bodies created by God for the purpose of communicating His Word to men were, for instance, the bush, through which God spoke to Moses, and the various prophets, including Muhammad, through whom He spoke to mankind. It was, however, only the body of the bush and the bodies of the prophets that were directly created by God and endowed by Him with a special power to produce out of themselves a Word which is figuratively called the Word of God. The act of producing the Word, however, is either by nature, as in the case of the bush, or by choice, as in the case of the prophets. The Koran therefore is a man-made work; it is divine in the sense that the Prophet who produced it was especially endowed by God with the power to produce it and also in the sense that it expresses the will and design of God. Since there is no Word of God in the true sense of the term, there is no room for the question concerning the relation of the Word of God to the man-made Koran, and so not only has Muʿammar no theory of inlibration but also no theory of imitation. Like Naẓẓām, he would maintain that the Koran in its literary form is a man-made work.

[14] *Milal*, p. 46, ll. 3–6, 12–14.

III. The Formal Creeds on Inlibration

In our analysis of the various statements on the problem whether the Koran is uncreated or created, we have seen how neither the assertions of its uncreatedness nor the assertions of its createdness represented one single and uniform view.

On the whole, those who professed a belief in an uncreated Koran conceived of it as a belief in an uncreated Word of God subsisting in Him as an attribute and all of them also believed that the post-revealed Koran when recited or heard or memorized or written down constituted a created Koran. But there was a difference of opinion among them on the following two points. Some of them believed that the uncreated Word of God was a simple word and that that simple Word was not inlibrated in the created Koran, whereas others believed that the uncreated Word of God consisted of letters and words and verses and that that composite Word was inlibrated in the created Koran. But among those who believed that the uncreated Word of God was simple there was a difference of opinion as to when it became composite, whether prior to its revelation or after its revelation. All of them, however, believed that the uncreated Word of God, which from eternity subsisted in God as an attribute, was prior to the creation of the world placed on the created Preserved Tablet upon which it remained until its revelation without thereby ceasing to continue to be an attribute in God.

Under the doctrine of the createdness of the Koran there were two main views. First, there was a view which admitted the existence of a pre-revealed Word of God, but conceived of that Word of God as having been created on the Preserved Tablet. As among those who believed in the uncreatedness of the Koran so also among those who held this view, there was a difference of opinion on the question of inlibration, some of them believing in inlibration, others not believing in it. Second, there was a view which denied the existence of a pre-revealed Word of God, even a created one. The Word of God, according to this view, was created at the time of the revelation of the Koran. But those who held this view differed among themselves as to the meaning of the Word of God and as to where it was created. According to one view, the Word of God was created as a real word in the air; according to another view, the Word of God only means the capacity with which God has endowed the Prophet to give utterance of His will by spoken word. To both these two classes of followers of the second view, the Koran in its literary form is a man-made book which is not inimitable.

In the light of this analysis of representative views of those who maintained the uncreatedness of the Koran as well as of those who maintained the createdness of the Koran, we shall examine certain formal creeds of Islam. We shall deal with the Waṣiyyah, al-Nasafī and his commentator al-Taftāzānī, and al-Faḍālī.

I. THE WAṢIYYAH [1]

The Creed known as the Waṣiyyah of Abū Ḥanīfah "seems," according to Wensinck, "to have originated in the period between Abū Ḥanīfah (d. 767) and Ahmad ibn Ḥanbal (d. 855), and probably belongs to the latter part of that period." [2] This does not seem to exclude the possibility of its having originated somewhat later, when the contrasting views of Ibn Kullāb and Ibn Ḥanbal on inlibration had already made their appearance.

The article on the Koran in the Waṣiyyah opens with the statement "The Koran, the Word of God, uncreated, . . . His real attribute," [3] wherein the understood copula "is" may be placed either after "The Koran" or after "the word of God," but in either case the statement quite clearly means that "the Koran," like "the Word of God," is uncreated. The question, therefore, arises in our mind whether the term "Ko-

[1] *Kitāb al-Waṣiyyah*, with a commentary by Molla Ḥusain ibn Iskandar al-Ḥanafī, Haidarabad (1321). English translation in Wensinck, *Muslim Creed*, pp. 125–131.

[2] Wensinck, *Muslim Creed*, p. 187.

[3] *Waṣiyyah*, p. 12, ll. 6–7.

ran" is used here in the sense of the post-revealed Koran, as a book composed of letters and words, and hence the "Word of God" is similarly used in the sense of its being composed of letters and words, or whether the "Word of God" is used in the sense of a simple word and hence the "Koran" is used here in the sense of the pre-revealed Koran conceived of as not being composed of letters and words. In other words, the question is whether this Creed is Ḫanbalite or Kullabite.

An answer to this question is to be found in the next few statements in the Waṣiyyah.

First, of the Koran which is, like the Word of God, uncreated it says: "Written in the copies, recited by the tongues, preserved in the heart, yet not residing in them. The ink, the paper, and the writing are created, for they are the work of men." [4] Here it is made clear that by "the Koran" which, like "the Word of God," is uncreated is meant the pre-revealed uncreated Koran, in contrast to that created Koran by which is meant the post-revealed Koran on its being written or recited or memorized; and, furthermore, that that pre-revealed Koran is not "residing," that is, it is not inlibrated, in that created Koran. This is the Kullabite view.

Second, it then goes on to add that, in contrast to "the ink, the paper, and the writing" which are created, "the Word of God is uncreated, for the writing and the letters and the words and the verses are a token (*dalālah*) of the Koran for the sake of human needs" and so also, with regard to the Word of God, "its meaning is understood (*mafhūm*) by means of these things." [5] Here, again, it is made clear that "the letters and the words and the verses," like "the writing," are created and are the work of men, so that the uncreated pre-revealed Koran and the Word of God are simple and without letters and words and verses. This, again, is the Kullabite view. Then, in addition to this, the previous direct denial of inlibration is repeated here indirectly by the following two descriptions

[4] *Ibid.*, p. 12, ll. 12–13, and p. 13, ll. 1–2.
[5] *Ibid.*, p. 13, ll. 2–3, and ll. 4–5.

of the relation between the created "letters and words and verses" and the uncreated pre-revealed Koran and the Word of God. (1) They are "a token (*dalālah*) of the Koran," which is but slightly different from the expression "indications (*dalālāt ʿalā*) of the eternal Word," [6] which is one of the ways by which the Kullabite Ashʿarites describe their denial of inlibration. (2) The "meaning" of the Word of God "is understood (*mafhūm*) by means of these things," which is but slightly different from the statement "that he may understand (*yafham*) the word of God" used by Ibn Kullāb as an interpretation of the Koranic statement "that he may hear the word of God" (9:6) in his harmonizing it with his denial of inlibration.[7]

The Waṣiyyah is thus Kullabite in its view on the simplicity of the uncreated Word of God, on the post-revealed origin of the letters and the other component parts of the text of the Koran, and on the denial of inlibration.

2. NASAFĪ AND TAFTĀZĀNĪ

Kullabite, too, in its view on the simplicity of the uncreated Word of God, on the post-revealed origin of the letters and the other component parts of the text of the Koran, and on the denial of inlibration is the Creed of Nasafī (d. 1142), which Kullabite character of it is emphasized by Taftāzānī (d. 1388) in his commentary.[1]

Nasafī begins with a general statement with regard to the attribute of "Word" (*kalām*),[2] saying that "God speaks with a Word which is an eternal attribute of His." [3] This is a reproduction of the common orthodox view and is directly a denial of the general Muʿtazilite view that the Word of God in the sense of the Koran is something created in an abode.[4]

[6] Cf. above, p. 256. [7] Cf. above, p. 249.

[1] Arabic Text of Taftāzānī's Commentary and the Text of Nasafī, Cairo, A. H. 1335. English translation, Earl Edgar Elder, *Sa'd al-Dīn al-Taftāzānī on the Creed of Najm al-Dīn al-Nasafī* (1950).

[2] Taftāzānī, p. 77, l. 9.

[3] *Ibid.*, p. 79, ll. 4, 6. [4] Cf. above, p. 264.

It does not commit itself either to the Kullabite view that the Word is simple or to the Ḥanbalite view that it is composite.[5] Taftāzānī, however, gives it a Kullabite meaning. Commenting on the term "Word," he says: "This is an eternal attribute of which expression is given (*'ubbir*) in an arrangement of words (*al-naẓm*) composed of letters, called Koran."[6] Here, then, we have a distinction, like that made by the Kullabites, between the Word of God, which is presumably simple, and the Koran, which is described as a literary composition and, as in the Kullabites, the literarily composed Koran is described as the expression of the Word of God.

Nasafī then adds that this Word of God is "not of the genus of letters and sounds" and that "it is the negation of silence and deficiency."[7] Taken by itself, this statement of Nasafī may only mean that the Word of God is not to be included under the same genus to which also belongs the word of man which consists of letters and sounds. In brief, it may only mean that the Word with which God speaks is not a physical kind of Word, like the human word, and it is to be understood only as a negation of any physical communication between God and man. It may thus only reflect the words of Ghazālī, who, in his discussion of the attribute of Word describes it as "subsisting in His essence" and then goes on to say: "It does not resemble the word of created beings, nor is it a sound arising from the commotion of the air or the collision of bodies, nor is it a letter articulated by the joining together of lips or by the motion of the tongue."[8] Taftāzānī, however, gives it another interpretation. He takes it to be "a refutation

[5] Cf. above, pp. 248, 251.

[6] *Taftāzānī*, p. 77, l. 9. But see Elder's translation.

[7] *Ibid*., p. 79, ll. 7, 10, 11.

[8] *Iḥyā'* II: *Kitāb Ḳawā'id al-'Aḳā'id*, Section 1, Vol. I, p. 90, ll. 25–26 (quoted in Macdonald's *Development of Muslim Theology* (1903), p. 303, and Sell's *The Faith of Islam*, 3rd ed. [1907], pp. 210–211). Cf. also Ghazālī's *Iḳtiṣād*, p. 57, l. 4. Cf. Philo's comment on "and God answered him by a voice" (Exod. 19:19): "Did He then do so, uttering himself some kind of voice? Away! let not such a thought ever enter our mind, for God is not like a man, in need of a mouth and of a tongue and of a windpipe" (*Decal.* 9, 32).

of the Ḥanbalites and the Karramites," who believed that the uncreated Word of God was composite or, as he puts it, they believed that "His Word is an accident of the genus sounds and letters, and yet in spite of that it is eternal." [9] Here, again, Nasafī's statement is given by Taftāzānī a Kullabite meaning.

Then Nasafī adds another statement: "God speaks with this attribute, commanding, prohibiting, and narrating." [10] This statement, at first sight, would seem to be in opposition to the Kullabite view that God's commanding and prohibiting and narrating were not from eternity.[11] Still, it will be noticed, Nasafī does not say explicitly that God's commanding and prohibiting and narrating were from eternity, and Taftāzānī, in his comment on it, explains it to mean that the division of the Word of God into commands, prohibitions, and narrations is not in the Word itself but in its relationship to men, whom God from eternity planned to create and to whom from eternity planned to reveal His Word.[12] This explanation is only a variation of the view of Ibn Kullāb and his followers, the Kullabite Ashʿarites, quoted above.[13]

The next statement of Nasafī, namely "the Koran, the Word of God, uncreated," [14] is an exact quotation of the opening statement in the Waṣiyyah. Now in the Waṣiyyah, as we have seen, its subsequent statements make it clear that the term "Koran" in the opening statement refers to the pre-revealed Koran. Similarly here, Taftāzānī tries to show that the term "Koran" in this statement of Nasafī refers to the pre-revealed Koran. Thus prefatory to his comment upon Nasafī's statement he remarks that "the term Koran is sometimes applied to the eternal speech of the soul [that is, to the uncreated Word of God] as it is applied to the originated text which is recited." [14a] Then, taking Nasafī's statement to mean that "The Koran [in the sense of] the Word of God [is] uncreated," he concludes that Nasafī is in agreement with

[9] Taftāzānī, p. 79, ll. 8–10.

[10] *Ibid.*, p. 80, l. 4.

[11] Cf. above, p. 249.

[12] Taftāzānī, p. 80, l. 4–p. 81, l. 10.

[13] Cf. above, p. 256.

[14] Taftāzānī, p. 81, ll. 11–12.

[14a] *Ibid.*, ll. 10–11; cf. below at nn. 29–33.

those whom he calls *al-mashāyiḫ*, the Early Theologians, literally, the Masters, to whom he ascribes the view that "one is to say that the Koran is the uncreated Word of God and one is not to say that the Koran is uncreated." [15] The reason given by him for their objection to the use of the expression "the Koran is uncreated" is their fear "lest the mind jumps to the conclusion that the thing composed of sounds and letters [that is, the text which is recited] is eternal," [16] to which, of course, the Early Theologians were opposed. The objection of the Early Theologians to any one saying that the Koran is uncreated is contrasted by Taftāzānī with "the position that the Ḥanbalites took out of ignorance and obstinacy," [17] which position is described by him later as the assertion that "the text which is composed and arranged in parts is eternal." [18]

This contrast between the Ḥanbalites and the Early Theologians as to whether "the thing composed of sound and letters" is eternal or created quite evidently reflects the controversy over the questions whether the uncreated Word of God is composed of sounds and letters or is simple and whether that uncreated Word of God is inlibrated or not. Now, as we have seen, the opponent of the Ḥanbalites on these questions, as reported by Shahrastānī, was Ashʿarī,[19] who evidently in some work of his followed Ibn Kullāb, even though in his *Ibānah* he followed the Ḥanbalites. Accordingly we may assume that the term *al-mashāyih*, literally, the Masters, used here by the Ashʿarite Taftāzānī includes both Ibn Kullāb and Ashʿarī, for the term *shayḫunā*, our Master, is applied by Ashʿarites to Ibn Kullāb [20] just as it is applied by them to Ashʿarī.[21] Then also, as we shall see later, a certain statement ascribed by Taftāzānī to the *mashāyiḫ* is a quotation from Ibn Kullāb [22] and a certain term ascribed by him to "one (*baʿḍ*) of the *mashāyiḫ*" is quoted by Shahrastānī in the name of Ashʿarī.[23]

[15] *Ibid.*, ll. 12–13.
[16] *Ibid.*, p. 82, l. 1.
[17] *Ibid.*
[18] *Ibid.*, p. 85, ll. 4–5.
[19] Cf. above, p. 256.
[20] *Nihāyat*, p. 303, l. 16.
[21] *Fark*, p. 200, ll. 6–7.
[22] Cf. below at nn. 40–41.
[23] Cf. below at nn. 52–53.

Finally, as in the Waṣiyyah, Nasafī says of the Koran, as well as of the Word of God, that "it is written in our volumes, preserved in our hearts, recited by our tongues, heard by our ears, yet not residing (*ḥāll*) in them." [24] This statement, as we have shown in our comment on the Waṣiyyah,[25] is quite definitely Kullabite and a denial of inlibration. Taftāzānī in his comment on this statement thus correctly gives it a Kullabite meaning. The Koran in the sense of the uncreated Word of God, he says, is "an eternal thing (*maʿnā*) subsisting in the essence of God, which is expressed and heard by means of the organized text which indicates it." [26] Taftāzānī explains the distinction between the uncreated Word of God and the recited or heard text of the Koran as follows: Suppose we write down the formula "fire is a burning substance" and we recite it and memorize it. This, he says, would not lead us to conclude that the real essence of fire is a sound and a letter.[27] This explanation, it is to be noted, is taken from Ghazālī.[28] He also explains the distinction between them by the analogy of the distinction between what he says is called "speech of the soul" (*kalām nafsī*) and "uttered speech" (*kalām lafẓī*),[29] in connection with which he quotes a line from the Arabic Christian poet al-Aḫṭal, in which "speech of the soul" is referred to as "speech" which is "in the heart." [30] Directly, both the analogy and the quotation are, again, taken from Ghazālī.[31] Ultimately, however, the analogy reflects the Stoic distinction between λόγος ἐνδιάθετος and λόγος προφορικός,[32] as it is used by those Church Fathers who believed in the twofold stage theory of the pre-existent Logos as an illustration of the distinction between these two stages in its pre-existence — the first stage, when it was in the mind of God,

[24] Taftāzānī, p. 83, ll. 3, 4, 5, 6.
[25] Cf. above, p. 281.
[26] Taftāzānī, p. 83, l. 6.
[27] *Ibid.*, ll. 8–9.
[28] *Iḳtiṣād*, p. 58, ll. 14–20.
[29] Taftāzānī, p. 78, l. 3, and p. 80, l. 2.
[30] *Ibid.*, p. 78, l. 5.
[31] *Iḳtiṣād*, p. 54, l. 21–p. 55, l. 2.
[32] Arnim, II, 135 and 223.

and the second stage, when it was generated as a real hypostatic being.[33]

The difference of opinion with regard to inlibration has led, as we have seen, to a difference of opinion as to whether the clause "that he may hear the Word of God" in the verse about giving asylum to a worshipper of many gods (9:6) should be taken literally or not.[34] In Taftāzānī there is a reference to this difference of opinion. "In regard to the eternal Word which is an attribute of God," he says, "al-Ash'arī took the position that it is possible for it to be heard." [35] This exactly represents the view of Ash'arī in his *Ibānah*.[36] He then goes on to say that "al-Ustādh abū Isḥāḳ al-Isfarā'inī denied it, and Abū Manṣūr [al-Māturīdī] also chose this [latter] position." [37] His statement with regard to Māturīdī may have to be qualified. According to another report, Māturīdī agrees with Ash'arī that the Word of God can be heard; he only adds that the Word heard is without sound.[38]

The Word of God is thus simple and uncreated, whereas the Koran is composed of sounds and letters and suras and verses and is created. Still, says Taftāzānī, even though "in reality" the expression "the Word of God" applies to the uncreated Word, "metaphorically" (*majāzan*) it applies also to the verbal utterance of the Koran [39] — a view which subsequently he ascribes to "one (*ba'ḍ*) of the Early Theologians." [40] This is exactly the view of the Kullabite Ash'arī, which we have quoted above.[41] But then, in order to obviate the objection that by "the Consensus" (*al-ijmā'*) of the Muslim people as well as by the implication of certain verses in the Koran (2:21; 17:90) the recited text of the Koran is to be regarded as the Word of God,[42] he says that, though in comparison with the uncreated Word of God the recited text

[33] Cf. *The Philosophy of the Church Fathers*, I, pp. 298 ff.
[34] Cf. above, p. 253.
[35] Taftāzānī, p. 84, ll. 3–4.
[36] Cf. above, pp. 254–255.
[37] Taftāzānī, p. 84, ll. 4–5.
[38] *Al-Rauḍah al-Bahiyyah*, p. 44, ll.3–6.
[39] Taftāzānī, p. 84, ll. 7–8.
[40] *Ibid.*, l. 14.
[41] Cf. above, p. 256, at n. 4.
[42] Taftāzānī, p. 84, ll. 7–11.

of the Koran is the word of God only in a metaphorical sense, still it is to be regarded as a real word of God in the sense of its being "something created by God and not one of the compositions of His creatures." [43] This last statement reflects Ibn Kullāb's statement that "the recital is originated and created [by God] and it is an acquisition (*kasb*) on the part of man." [44]

Like Ibn Kullāb and others, nowhere in their discussion of the Koran do Nasafī and Taftāzānī mention the Preserved Tablet, upon which, according to the Koran's own statement,[45] the Koran abided prior to its revelation. The Preserved Tablet is mentioned by Taftāzānī only in connection with the Muʿtazilites. "Since the Muʿtazilites," he says, "could not deny that God is a speaker, they held that God is a speaker in the sense of the creation of sounds and letters in their abodes or of the creation of the shapes of the characters on the Preserved Table," [46] that is to say, by the createdness of the Koran the Muʿtazilites mean either (1) the creation of the Word of God in some abode outside the Preserved Tablet, which is the view of Naẓẓām and Muʿammar,[47] or (2) its creation on the Preserved Tablet, which is the view of the Jaʿfars and Abū al-Hudhayl.[48]

The conception of the uncreatedness of the Koran as presented by Taftāzānī is thus like that of Ibn Kullāb and in opposition to that of Ibn Ḥanbal. Ibn Ḥanbal, as we have seen, is quoted by him as believing in the compositeness of the uncreated Word of God. He also quotes Ashʿarī as believing that the uncreated Word of God can be heard.[49] This, as we have seen, is the view of Ashʿarī in his *Ibānah*.[50] The name of Ibn Kullāb is not mentioned by Taftāzānī. But toward the end of his discussion, he refers to "some later theologians" (*al-muḥaḳḳiḳūn*) as reporting that "our early theologians" (*mashāyiḫunā*) distinguished between the Word of God, which

[43] *Ibid.*, ll. 12–13.
[44] Cf. above, p. 249, at n. 3.
[45] Surah 85:22.
[46] Taftāzānī, p. 82, ll. 11–13.
[47] Cf. above, pp. 274 ff.
[48] Cf. above, pp. 267 ff.
[49] Taftāzānī, p. 84, l. 4.
[50] Cf. above, pp. 254–255.

is simple and uncreated, and the arrangement of that Word of God into sounds and letters and suras and verses, which takes place only when one recites the Koran or meditates upon it.[51] He then concludes: "This is the meaning of their statement that that which is recited (*al-maḳrū'*) is eternal, but the recital (*al-ḳirā'ah*) is originated." [52] This is an accurate paraphrase of the statement of Ibn Kullāb quoted above,[53] and thus, indirectly, Taftāzānī identifies his interpretation of Nasafī with the view of Ibn Kullāb.

3. FAḌĀLĪ

Like the Waṣiyyah and the Creed of Nasafī in its view on the simplicity of the uncreated Word of God and on the denial of inlibration but unlike them in its view on the pre-revealed origin of the letters and words and verses and chapters of the Koran is the Creed of Faḍālī (d. 821).[1]

In his discussion of the attribute of Speech or Word (*kalām*), Faḍālī describes it as "eternally pre-existent," as "subsisting in God's essence," and as being "not a letter (*ḥarf*) or sound and far removed from priority and posteriority and from inflection and structure," [2] and as having "no verses and chapters." [3]

In contrast to that uncreated simple Word of God, there is what he calls "the Glorious Expressions (*al-alfāẓ*) revealed to the Prophet" which are "originated" and "embrace priority and posteriority and inflections and chapters and verses." [4] As to when these component parts of the Glorious Expressions originated, he says that "there is a conflict of opinion." [5] Some say that what Gabriel brought down to the Prophet was "only

[51] Taftāzānī, p. 85, ll. 2–5.

[52] *Ibid.*, l. 8.

[53] Cf. above, p. 249 at n. 3.

[1] *Kifāyat al-'awāmm min 'ilm al-kalām*, with the commentary of al-Bayjūrī, Cairo, A. H. 1315. English translation in D. B. Macdonald's *Development of Muslim Theology*, pp. 315–351. The section dealing with the Koran is on pp. 335–336.

[2] *Kifāyat*, p. 52, ll. 35–36.

[3] *Ibid.*, p. 53, ll. 4–5.

[4] *Ibid.*, p. 52, l. 37–p. 53, l. 6.

[5] *Ibid.*, p. 54, ll. 13–14.

the meaning (*al-maʿnā*)" [6] and that "the Prophet clothed the meaning with expressions of his own." [7] This, as will be recalled, is what we have found to be the view of Ibn Kullāb,[8] as well as of the Waṣiyyah [9] and Nasafī and Taftāzānī.[10] Others say that "he who clothed the meaning is Gabriel." [11] This, as we have seen, is the view of the Kullabite Ashʿarites.[12] Faḍālī adopts the latter view,[13] restating it as follows: "The Glorious Expressions are created and written on the Preserved Tablet; Gabriel brought them down to the Prophet." [14] Still, "both the Glorious Expressions and the eternal attribute are called Koran and the Word of God." [15] This reflects a view which Taftāzānī, as we have seen, ascribes to the Consensus (*al-ijmāʿ*) of the Muslim people.[16]

The problem of inlibration is dealt with by him in three passages, each of which, as we shall see, reflects a certain statement by some other author. Thus evidently having in mind some statement like that of Ibn Kullāb's, according to which the Koranic verse about granting an asylum to a polytheist "that he may hear the word of God" (9:6) is interpreted to mean that he may understand (*yafham*) the word of God,[17] he expresses his disagreement with it by saying: "And these Glorious Expressions do not indicate (*tadullu ʿalā*) the eternal attribute in the sense that the eternal attribute can be understood (*mafhūm*) from them." [18] But, then, evidently having in mind some statement like that in the Waṣiyyah where it says of the Word of God that "its meaning (*maʿnā-hu*) is understood (*mafhūm*) by means of these things," [19] that is, by means of the letters and words and verses, he expresses his agreement with it by saying, with regard to the Word of God, that "these expressions indicate its meaning

[6] *Ibid.*, ll. 12–13.
[7] *Ibid.*, ll. 14–17.
[8] Cf. above, pp. 249–250.
[9] Cf. above, p. 281.
[10] Cf. above, p. 286.
[11] *Kifāyat*, p. 54, ll. 17–19.
[12] Cf. above, pp. 255–256.
[13] *Kifāyat*, p. 54, ll. 19–20.
[14] *Ibid.*, p. 53, ll. 29–33.
[15] *Ibid.*, ll. 26–28.
[16] Cf. above, p. 287 at n. 42.
[17] Cf. above, p. 249 at n. 5.
[18] *Kifāyat*, p. 53, ll. 11–15.
[19] Cf. above, p. 281 at n. 5.

(*ma'nā*)."[20] Finally, evidently having in mind such a statement as that of the Kullabite Ash'arites that "what we read" is the Word of God "only metaphorically,"[21] he says that "what is understood from these expressions equals (*musāwī*) what would be understood from the eternal attribute if the veil were removed from us and we could hear it."[22] Here, then, a formal equation is drawn by Faḍālī between the relation of "the expressions" to "what is understood" and the relation of "the eternal attribute" to "what would be understood if . . . we could hear it [that is, the eternal attribute]." Now such an equation is what Aristotle calls "analogy," which he illustrates by the equation "the intellect is to the soul as sight is to the body."[23] But analogy, according to Aristotle, is one of the four kinds of metaphor,[24] and the most popular one.[25] Consequently, what Faḍālī means by his statement here is that "the expressions" are the Word of God "only metaphorically," which, as we have seen, is the view of the Kullabite Ash'arī.[26]

IV. The Terms Muḥdath, Ḥadath, and Ḥādith as Applied to the Koran *

In the preceding sections we have dealt with the various views of those who speak of the Koran as created or as uncreated. We have shown how, with a few exceptions, the controversy was mostly over the question whether the Koran, which prior to its revelation existed in heaven on the Preserved Tablet, was uncreated or created. In Arabic, the terms used for "uncreated" and "created" in their application to the Koran are *ghayr maḫlūḳ* and *maḫlūḳ*,[1] and for "uncreated" Ibn Kullāb is reported to have used *ghayr maḫlūḳ wa-lā muḥdath*.[1a] But there are reports, as we shall see, of certain people who,

[20] *Kifāyat*, p. 53, ll. 20–21.
[21] Cf. above, p. 256 at n. 4.
[22] *Kifāyat*, p. 53, ll. 15–19.
[23] *Eth. Nic.* I, 4, 1096b, 28–29.
[24] *Poet.*, 21, 1457b, 6–9.
[25] *Rhet.* III, 10, 1410b, 6–9.
[26] Cf. above, at n. 21.

* Revised reprint from *The Joshua Bloch Memorial Volume*, 1960, pp. 92–100.

[1] *Luma'* 27, ll. 4–5.
[1a] *Mughnī*, vol. VII, p. 4, l. 1.

while they were opposed to the use of both *maḫlūḳ* and *ghayr maḫlūḳ*, allowed themselves the use of *muḥdath* or *ḥadath* or *ḥādith*. Now the terms *al-ḫalḳ*, "creation," and *al-iḥdāth*, "origination," are both said to mean "the bringing of the nonexistent from nonexistence into existence." [2] We should, therefore, expect that those who used the term *muḥdath* or *ḥadath* or *ḥādith* as a description of the Koran would agree with those who used the term *maḫlūḳ* in the denial of the uncreatedness of the Koran. We can thus readily see why they should reject *ghayr maḫlūḳ*, "uncreated." But why they should reject *maḫlūḳ*, "created," and also why, having rejected *maḫlūḳ*, they should approve of *muḥdath*, "originated," or of *ḥadath* or of *ḥādith* is a question for which we shall try to find an answer.

Let us then examine the passages in which Ashʿarī reports on this change of terminology. We shall start with passages which report on the term *muḥdath*. We shall quote two such passages.

In one of these passages Ashʿarī reports: "Muḥammad b. Shajjaʿ al-Thaljī, and those from among the suspensors of judgment (*al-wāfiḳah*) who agreed with him, said that the Koran is the Word of God and that it is originated (*muḥdath*), namely, it was after it was not, and that it is God through whom it came to be and it is He who originated it, and they refrained from applying the term *maḫlūḳ* or the phrase *ghayr maḫlūḳ*. And Zahīr al-Athirī said that the Koran is the Word of God and that it is originated (*muḥdath*) but not created (*maḫlūḳ*)." [3]

In this passage, the fact that the use made of the term *muḥdath* by Thaljī is explained as meaning that the Word of God came into being after it had not been quite definitely places him among those who believed in the createdness of the Koran, most of whom expressed their belief by using the term *maḫlūḳ*, for believers in the createdness of the Koran who used the term *maḫlūḳ* are reported to have ex-

[2] Taftāzānī, p. 86, ll. 1–2.

[3] *Maḳālāt*, p. 583, ll. 3–6.

pressed themselves by saying that the Koran, which is the Word of God, "was not, then it was," [4] the very same expression used here by Thaljī. His apparent objection to the use of the term *maḫlūḳ*, while using the term *muḥdath* in the very same sense as the term *maḫlūḳ*, may be explained if we assume that Thaljī, like those suspensors of judgment who agreed with him, was himself a suspensor of judgment. In his *Ibānah*, dealing with the suspensors of judgment, Ash'arī says that the reason they refrain from using both *maḫlūḳ* and *ghayr maḫlūḳ* is that the Koran never describes itself explicitly either by the term *maḫlūḳ* or by the term *ghayr maḫlūḳ*.[5] In the light of this statement, then, Thaljī's refusal to use *maḫlūḳ*, despite his belief in the createdness of the Koran, is to be explained as being simply due to the fact that the term is not used in the Koran in connection with itself. This, however, raises the question why, having rejected the term *maḫlūḳ* on the ground that it is not used in the Koran in connection with itself, he should not have also rejected the term *muḥdath*, for this term, too, is not used in the Koran in connection with itself.

An explanation why the objection raised against *maḫlūḳ* on the score of its having no Koranic sanction was not applied by Thaljī to *muḥdath* may be found in a report of a controversy between Ibn Ḥanbal and those who believed in the createdness of the Koran as to the meaning of the term *dhikr*, "admonition," as qualified by the term *muḥdath*, "innovated," "new," "originated," which occurs twice in the Koran (21:2; 26:4). It would seem that there were some who took the term *dhikr*, "admonition," in these two places to mean the Koran and hence from the fact that in these two places *dhikr* is described as *muḥdath*, "innovated," "new," "originated," they inferred that the Koran was created. As against them, Ibn Ḥanbal argued that while indeed the definite *al-dhikr*, "the admonition," means the Koran, the indefinite *dhikr*, "admonition," which is used in the two verses in the Koran, does not

[4] *Ibid.*, p. 582, ll. 8–9.

[5] *Ibānah*, p. 40, ll. 5 ff.

mean the Koran.[6] Evidently Thaljī and those suspensors of judgment who agreed with him sided with the opponents of Ibn Ḥanbal in taking the term *dhikr* in the expression *dhikr muḥdath*, which occurs twice in the Koran, to refer to the Koran itself, and consequently they came to describe the Koran by the term *muḥdath*.

The other passage which reports on the use of the term *muḥdath* reads as follows: "And it came to my attention concerning one of the masters of the Fiḳh that he said that God is eternally a speaker in the sense that eternally He possesses the power to speak, and that he also said that the Word of God is *muḥdath* and not *maḫlūḳ*. This is the opinion of Da'ūd al-Iṣbahānī [=Da'ūd b. ʿAlī b. Ḫalaf al-Iṣbahānī al-Ẓāhirī]." [7]

This passage occurs amidst a group of passages, each of which begins with the statement "the Koran is the Word of God" and all of which are placed under the general heading "Discourse concerning the Koran." Moreover, according to a report quoted by al-Samʿānī, the statement attributed here to al-Ẓāhirī reads that "the Koran is *muḥdath*." [8] Consequently, the statement here that "the Word of God is *muḥdath*" means that "the Koran is the Word of God and it is *muḥdath* and not *maḫlūḳ*," thus expressing the same view as that of the preceding statement of Thaljī, namely, that the Koran was created. Undoubtedly the reason for the substitution here of *muḥdath* for *maḫlūḳ* is the same as in Thaljī, namely, that the term *maḫlūḳ* is not used in the Koran as a description of itself.

The additional statement, with which the passage opens, namely, that "God is eternally a speaker in the sense that eternally He possesses the power to speak" is of special significance. It is meant to be an answer to an objection that has been raised against the belief in the createdness of the Koran. The objection, as phrased by Ashʿarī in his *Ibānah*, reads as follows: "Know that, by the belief of the Jahmiyyah that the

[6] Cf. Patton, *Aḥmad Ibn Ḥanbal and the Miḥna*, p. 103.
[7] *Maḳālāt*, p. 583, ll. 8–10.
[8] Quoted in Goldziher, *Die Zahiriten*, p. 226, p. 9.

Word of God is created, they are compelled to admit that God would have been from all eternity like the idols, which have neither speech nor language . . . But how can one with reference to whom speech is impossible from eternity be a God?"[9] To this objection Ẓāhirī's answer here is that even though the Koran was created, God could still be described as being eternally a speaker if that description is taken to mean that eternally He possesses the power to speak, so that even before He was actually a speaker He could be called a speaker proleptically, in anticipation of the actual speaker that He was to become. The reasoning employed here by Ẓāhirī in his answer is analogous to the reasoning employed by Hippolytus and Novatian among the Church Fathers. Thus Hippolytus argues that even though before the incarnation the Logos was not yet a "perfect son," God still addressed him as son "because he was to be begotten in the future";[10] and Novatian, who believed in the twofold stage of existence in the pre-existent Logos, similarly argues that even though the Logos generated or proceeded from the Father only prior to the creation of the world, God could always be called Father in anticipation of the future generation of the Logos as son.[11] Whether Ẓāhirī's answer implies a twofold stage theory of the existence of the pre-revealed Koran analogous to the twofold stage theory of the existence of the preincarnational Christ[12] cannot be ascertained.[13]

[9] *Ibānah*, p. 27, ll. 3–10 (69). A similar argument is used by Athanasius against the Arian contention that the Word in the sense of the pre-existent Christ was created: "Has not a man himself lost his mind who even entertains the thought that God was without word (ἄλογον) and without wisdom (ἄσοφον)." Cf. *Orat. cont. Arian.* II, 32 (PG 26, 216 B). The same argument against both Arians and Muslims occurs also in John of Damascus, *Disputatio Saraceni et Christiani* (PG 96, 1341 D; cf. 94, 1587 A): "Before God created the Word and Spirit had He no Word and no Spirit?"

[10] *Cont. Haer. Noëti* 15 (PG 10, 824 B).

[11] *De Trinit.* 31. Cf. *The Philosophy of the Church Fathers*, I, pp. 196 and 205–206. Cf., above, p. 145 at n. 16.

[12] Cf. *The Philosophy of the Church Fathers*, I, pp. 192–198.

[13] In the earlier version of this paper, as published in the Bloch Memorial Volume, I assumed that Ẓāhirī's view implied a twofold-stage theory of the existence of the prerevelational Koran.

So much for the substitution of the term *muḥdath* for the term *maḫlūḳ*. Let us now take up the substitution of the term *ḥadath* for *maḫlūḳ*.

The passages which report on this substitution read as follows:

"Abū Muʿādh al-Tūmanī said: The Koran is the Word of God and it is an origination (*ḥadath*) and not that which was originated (*muḥdath*) and an action (*fiʿl*) and not that which was produced by an action (*mafʿūl*), and he refrained from saying that it is a creation (*ḫalḳ*). He says that it is neither a creation (*ḫalḳ*) nor that which was created (*maḫlūḳ*), that it subsists in God, and that it is impossible that God should speak with a word that subsists in something other than in Him, just as it is impossible that He should move with a movement which subsists in something other than in Him. And thus he also says with regard to will (*irādah*) and love (*maḥabbah*) and wrath (*bughḍ*) that they all subsist in God."[14] In another passage, al-Tūmanī is reported to have said that "the Word of God is neither an accident nor a body and it subsists in God; and it is impossible that the Word of God should subsist in something other than in Him, just as this is impossible in the case of His will (*irādah*) and His love (*maḥabbah*) and His wrath (*bughḍ*)."[15]

In the first of these passages, the fact that Tūmanī rejects both *maḫlūḳ* and *muḥdath* shows that he is against the createdness of the Koran as it is generally expressed in the statement quoted above: "It was not, then it was." The fact that he accepts the term *ḥadath* shows that the term which means "origination," unlike the term which means "originated," is not taken by him to mean the createdness of the Koran in its usual sense that it was not and then it was. That Tūmanī used the term *ḥadath* to express his opposition to the createdness of the Koran in its usual sense can be further shown from the fact that in both passages quoted he compares the Word, with reference to its subsistence in God, to the attributes of will

[14] *Maḳālāt*, p. 583, ll. 11–15.

[15] *Ibid.*, p. 593, ll. 10–13.

(*irādah*) and love (*maḥabbah*) and wrath (*bughḍ*), for a similar comparison is used by those who believed in the uncreatedness of the Koran as an argument against those who believed in its createdness. Thus, in opposition to the Jahmiyyah, who believed that the Word of God was created,[16] Ashʿarī argues that "since God's anger (*ghaḍab*) is uncreated, and likewise His favor (*riḍan*) and His displeasure (*suḫt*), why do you not believe that His Word is uncreated?" [17] The question that may be raised, why Tūmanī, who distinguishes between *muḥdath* "originated," and *ḥadath*, "origination," and, while rejecting the former, accepts the latter, should not also distinguish between *maḫlūḳ*, "created," and *ḫalḳ*, "creation," and thus also accept the latter, may be answered that the term *ḫalḳ*, unlike the term *ḥadath*, does not occur in the Koran in connection with itself. As for the question, why then did he accept the term *fiʿl*, "action," which like the term *ḫalḳ* is not used in the Koran in connection with itself, it may be answered that, though the verb *faʿal* is not used in the Koran in connection with itself, its equivalent, the verb *jaʿal*, is used in connection with the Koran in the verse "We have made it (*jaʿalnāhu*) an Arabic Koran that ye may understand." [18] In fact, Ibn Ḥanbal, in his defense of the uncreatedness of the Koran, argued that the word *jaʿal* does not mean the same as *ḫalaḳ*.[19]

In the second passage, the statement that "the Word of God is neither an accident nor a body and it subsists in God; and it is impossible that the Word of God should subsist in something other than God" is obviously aimed at the Jaʿfars and Abū al-Hudhayl who held that the Word of God was created either as an accident or as a body on the Preserved Tablet.[20]

But here a new question arises. If by *ḥadath*, "origination," Tūmanī meant the denial of the createdness of the Koran, why did he not use the already established phrase *ghayr*

[16] *Ibānah*, p. 26, ll. 1 ff. (68). [17] *Ibid.*, p. 31, ll. 11–12 (73).

[18] Surah 43:2.

[19] Cf. Patton, *Aḥmad Ibn Ḥanbal and the Miḥna*, p. 91.

[20] Cf. above, pp. 267 ff.

maḫlūḳ, "uncreated"? What need was there for him to introduce into the discussion of the problem this new and unheard of term *ḥadath*? And if he objected to the phrase *ghayr maḫlūḳ* because it is based upon a verb which is not used in the Koran in connection with itself, why then did he not use the phrase *ghayr muḥdath*, "unoriginated," which is more explicit and more meaningful than the term *ḥadath*, "origination," as a rejection of the createdness of the Koran? Since Tūmanī has chosen the term *ḥadath* in preference to the phrase *ghayr maḫlūḳ* or *ghayr muḥdath* to express his opposition to the createdness of the Koran, it is to be assumed that the opposition to the createdness of the Koran implied by the use of *ḥadath* is different from the opposition implied in *ghayr maḫlūḳ* or *ghayr muḥdath*. What then is the difference?

In order to discover some kind of difference between the denial of the createdness of the Koran implied in *ḥadath* and the denial of it implied in *ghayr maḫlūḳ* or *ghayr muḥdath*, we shall first try to find out if *ghayr maḫlūḳ* or *ghayr muḥdath* could have some other implication besides the mere denial of the createdness of the Koran in the sense that it had a beginning of existence, and if we find that it could have some other implication, we shall be justified in assuming that it is that other implication that the use of the term *ḥadath* proposes to eliminate.

Logically, the negative phrase *ghayr maḫlūḳ*, "not created," or *ghayr muḥdath*, "not originated," in itself could have a twofold meaning. It could mean not only a denial of a beginning of existence but also a denial of a cause of existence; for just as "created" or "originated" implies not only a beginning of existence but also a cause of existence, so also "uncreated" or "unoriginated" could imply not only a denial of a beginning of existence but also a denial of a cause of existence. Though those who believed in the uncreatedness of the Koran and expressed themselves by the use of *ghayr maḫlūḳ* quite certainly used that phrase in the exclusive sense of a denial of a beginning of existence, without meaning to deny thereby that the Koran had a cause for its existence, still the phrase *ghayr maḫlūḳ* used by them, as well as the phrase *ghayr muḥdath* that could be used by them, in itself is ambiguous and it might be taken to mean both "eternal" and "causeless." Tūmanī wanted to eliminate that ambiguity and so he was in search of some term that would describe the Koran as having no beginning of existence, while at the same time it would describe it also as having a cause of existence.

Now a problem similar to this faced here by Tūmanī had been faced long before him in Christianity by Origen and in Greek philosophy by Plotinus. Origen believed that the Logos was eternal, and Plotinus similarly believed that the Nous was eternal, but both of them believed that the Logos or the Nous was dependent upon God as its cause, for they both believed that the Logos or the Nous was generated from God. So what did they do? They coined a new Greek expression, *γέννησις ἀΐδιος*, "eternal generation," by which they described the generation of the Logos or of the Nous by or from God.[21] Now an Arabic translation of this expression would be *taulīd azalī* or *wilādah azaliyyah*, but no term meaning or implying "begetting" could Tūmanī, as a faithful Muslim, use in connection with God, for the Koran, in conformity with its oft-repeated disapprobation of the Christian conception of God as begetter,[21a] admonishingly proclaims: "God begets not (*lam yalid*)."[22] According to the Koran, God "made (*ja'ala*),"[23] God "created (*ḫalaḳa*),"[24] God "only says to a thing 'Be,' and it is,"[25] but God does not beget. And so the best Tūmanī could do was to use the term *ḥadath*, "origination," relying upon the reader to infer from the context that it is to be taken in the sense of "eternal origination." Whether, like the eternally generated Logos in Christianity,[26] the eter-

[21] Cf. *The Philosophy of the Church Fathers*, I, pp. 201–204, and passages quoted on pp. 219–223 which show that the term *γέννησις*, "generation," is used in the sense of both "begetting" and "being begotten."

[21a] Cf. below, pp. 305–306.

[22] Surah 112:3.

[23] Surah 2:20.

[24] Surah 2:27.

[25] Surah 2:111.

[26] Cf. *The Philosophy of the Church Fathers*, I, pp. 219–223.

nally originated Koran of Tūmanī also existed as a completely originated Word or whether it was in an eternal process of origination, there is no way of telling.[26a]

Now for those who use the term *ḥādith* as a description of the Koran.

Juwaynī in his *Irshād*, after reporting that among those who denied the eternity of "the Word of God" there were some who refrained from applying to it the term *maḫlūḳ* but applied to it the term *muḥdath*,[27] reports the view of the Karrāmiyyah, which, in the light of our discussion above of their view on attributes,[28] may be restated as follows.

As in their view on attributes they say that God is called eternal Creator because He has an eternal power to create, so also here they say that "the Word (*kalām*) of God is eternal" because He has an eternal "power to speak." [29] Again, as in their view on attributes they say that God's utterance (*ḳaul*) of the command "Be" is created and subsists in the essence of God, so also here they say that "the Koran, which is the utterance (*ḳaul*) of God and not the Word (*kalām*) of God . . . is created and subsists in the essence of God." [30] Then, following the distinction they made in their view on attributes between the term *ḥādith* and the term *muḥdath*, applying the former to that which is originated in the essence of God and the latter to that which is originated outside the essence of God, they say here that it is the term *ḥadith* that is to be applied to the utterance of God, which is the Koran; [31] for, as they explain, "everything which has a beginning of existence and which subsists in the essence of God is to be described as *ḥādith*, and not as *muḥdath*, by the [eternal] power [of God]." [32] Finally, just as in their view on attributes they say that the utterance (*ḳaul*) of the command "Be" is created by God in His essence when He creates any body or any accident in the world, so also here, we may assume, they

[26a] But see above, p. 174, bottom.

[27] *Irshād*, p. 85, ll. 13–16 (99).

[28] Cf. above, pp. 145–146.

[29] *Irshād*, p. 58, ll. 17–18 (99).

[30] *Ibid*., ll. 18–19.

[31] *Ibid*., l. 17.

[32] *Ibid*., ll. 20–21.

would say that the utterance (*ḳaul*) of the Koran was created in the essence of God when the Koran was put on the Preserved Tablet, assuming that the Karrāmiyyah followed the orthodox view on this point.[33] And so, though the statement of the Karrāmiyyah that "the Word of God" is His eternal "power to speak" is the same as the statement quoted above from Ẓāhirī,[34] the views meant to be expressed by this common statement are not the same. Ẓāhirī, with his use of the term *muḥdath*, rejected the orthodox belief in the uncreatedness of the Koran but agreed, as we have seen, with the Muʿtazilite belief that the Koran was created, that is, it was created on the Preserved Tablet; the Karrāmiyyah, with their use of the term *ḥādith*, disagree with both the orthodox and the Muʿtazilites, maintaining that the Koran was created in the essence of God.

References to the Karrāmiyyah's view on the Koran are to be found also in Baghdādī's and Shahrastānī's discussions of the Karrāmiyyah's view on attributes.

Baghdādī in his *Farḳ*, after stating, in the name of the Karrāmiyyah, that "God is eternally a Speaker because of a Word (*kalām*), which is His power-to-utter" but that "His utterance (*ḳaul*) consists of letters originating (*ḥādithah*) in Him," concludes that "the utterance of God, according to them, is therefore originating (*ḥādith*) in Him, but His Word is eternal."[35]

While Baghdādī, like Juwaynī, in reproducing the view of the Karrāmiyyah, distinguishes between "the Word of God" and "the utterance of God," Shahrastānī makes of that distinction two meanings of the expression "the Word of God." Thus in one place in his *Nihāyat* he distinguishes between "the Word (*kalām*) of God" in the sense of "the power-to-utter" and "the Word of God" in the sense of "utterance" (*ḳaul*), the latter of which is described as that which "orig-

[33] Cf. above, p. 247.
[34] Cf. above, at n. 7.
[35] *Farḳ*, p. 206, l. 18 – p. 207, l. 3; cf. p. 218, ll. 7–11.

inates in His essence,"[36] with the implication that the former is eternal. In another place in his *Nihāyat*, evidently using the expression "the Word of God" in the sense of God's "utterance," he says that "His Word consists of attributes which originate in Him — and these are expressions made up of consonants and vowels, according to some, or of consonants only, according to others — so that it is *ḥādith*, neither eternal nor *muḥdath*."[37]

Let us now recapitulate our discussion.

In addition to the two well-known views as to whether the Koran is *maḫlūḳ* or *ghayr maḫlūḳ*, there are reports of three other views, of which one says that the Koran is *muḥdath*, another that it is *ḥadath*, and a third that it is *ḥādith*. The first two views, as we have seen, are revisions respectively of the older two views as to whether the Koran was *maḫlūḳ*, "created," or *ghayr maḫlūḳ*, "uncreated," substituting, in the former case, the term *muḥdath* for *maḫlūḳ* and, in the latter case, the term *ḥadath* for the term *ghayr maḫlūḳ*. The reason for the substitution of *muḥdath* for *maḫlūḳ* as a description of the createdness or noneternity of the Koran is that in the Koran the term *maḫlūḳ* is never used as a description of the origin of the Koran, whereas the term *muḥdath* is used as such a description. The reason for the substitution of *ḥadath* for *ghayr maḫlūḳ* as a description of the uncreatedness or eternity of the Koran is that *ghayr maḫlūḳ* might mean eternal not only in the sense of beginningless but also in the sense of causeless, whereas *ḥadath*, taken in the sense of continuous origination, while it means eternal in the sense of beginningless, can never be taken to mean causeless.[38] The third view rejects both the orthodox view

[36] *Nihāyat*, p. 288, ll. 4–7.

[37] *Ibid.*, p. 104, l. 17 – p. 105, l. 1.

[38] In an article by W. Montgomery Watt, entitled "Early Discussions about the Qur'ān," *Muslim World*, 40 (1950), commenting upon the use of *muḥdath* by Zahīr al-Athirī (quoted above at n. 3) and upon the use of *ḥadath* by Abū Mu'ādh al-Tūmanī (quoted above at nn. 14, 15), the author says (pp. 38–39): "In general their position was similar to that of Aḥmad [b. Ḥanbal], but they were ready to make some concessions. Zahīr would

that the Koran was *ghayr maḫlūḳ*, "uncreated," and the Muʿtazilite view that it was *maḫlūḳ* (or its equivalent *muḥdath*), "created," that is, created on the Preserved Tablet, substituting for both of them the view that the Koran was *ḥādith*, meaning thereby that it was created in the essence of God.

not admit that the Qur'ān was 'created,' but in view of the fact that it had appeared in time he applied to it the word 'originated' (*muḥdath*). Abū Muʿādh did not quite go so far; the Qur'ān was not 'originated' but an 'origination' (or perhaps rather 'event'-*ḥadath*), not what is done in an act (*mafʿūl*) but the act itself (*fiʿl*); it was truly the Word of God, and was subsisting in God (*qāʾim bi-'llāh*), not in anything other than God. These views cannot be adequately criticized without fuller knowledge than we possess of the general position of the theologians in question; but it is fairly clear that while they are nobly trying to hold on to both the belief that the Qur'ān is the Word of God and the fact that it appeared at a definite point in time, they had not quite grasped the fundamental point Aḥmad was insisting upon — that the Qur'ān expresses something of the essential character of God."

According to our interpretation, Zahīr al-Athirī, with his use of *muḥdath*, and Abū Muʿādh al-Tūmanī, with his use of *ḥadath*, are diametrically opposed to each other. Zahīr al-Athirī belongs to those who maintained that the Koran was "created," but for a certain reason he objected to the use of the term *maḫlūḳ*. Abū Muʿādh al-Tūmanī belongs to those who maintained that the Koran was "uncreated," but again for a certain reason he objected to the use of the phrase *ghayr maḫlūḳ*.

CHAPTER IV

ISLAM AND CHRISTIANITY

I. Trinity and Incarnation in the Koran

The Christian doctrines of the Trinity and the Incarnation as represented in the Koran do not agree with these doctrines as formulated by the Church councils. With regard to the Christian Trinity as represented in the Koran, it consisted of God, Jesus, and Mary.[1] According to the conciliar formulation of the doctrine, the Trinity consisted of God, the Word, that is, the pre-existent Christ, and the Holy Spirit. No adequate explanation of the Koranic representation of the Christian Trinity has been advanced. The fact that a certain Christian sect, already extinct at the time of Muhammad, held such a view of the Trinity [2] could hardly explain it. All that one can say on this subject is that the two Koranic deviations from the conciliar conception of the Trinity are not without precedent. The substitution of Jesus, that is, the born Christ, for the pre-existent Christ as the second member of the Trinity has its precedent in the Trinitarian conception as it is found in the New Testament and in the Apostolic Fathers.[3] As for the substitution of Mary for the Holy Spirit as the third member of the Trinity, it may have its precedent in some such conception of the Trinity as may be reflected in Origen's quotation from the gospel of the Hebrews, where Christ is quoted as saying "My Mother, the Holy Spirit." [4] With regard to the doctrine of the Incarnation, which in Christianity meant the incarnation of a begotten pre-existent Christ in the born

[1] Surah 5:116.

[2] Cf. notes by G. Sale and E. M. Wherry in their translations of the Koran on Surah 4:169; L. Horst, *Des Metropoliten Elias von Nisibis Buch vom Beweis der Wahrheit des Glaubens* (1886), p. 6, n. 1.

[3] Cf. *The Philosophy of the Church Fathers*, I, pp. 155–191.

[4] Origen, *In Joan.* II, 6 (PG 14, 132 C); ed. Brooke, II, 12 (I, 73); ed. Preuschen.

Christ, resulting, according to the conciliar formulation of the doctrine, in two natures in Jesus, a divine and a human, as presented in the Koran, the Christians believed that Jesus himself was begotten of God and is the begotten son of God and that, as the begotten son of God, he is God like his Father,[5] that is, wholly God, thus being of one nature which is divine. This conception of one divine nature in Jesus ascribed in the Koran to the Christians in general reflects the view held by the Monophysites.

Besides restating these two doctrines, the Koran also undertakes to refute them, maintaining that these two Christian doctrines are later corruptions of the genuine teachings of Jesus about himself.

The verses in which opposition to these Christian doctrines of the Trinity and Incarnation is expressed are the following: (1) "Believe therefore in God and his apostles, and say not, Three" (4:169); (2) "They are infidels who say, God is the third of three, for there is no God but one God" (5:77); (3) "And when God shall say, O Jesus, son of Mary, hast thou said unto mankind, Take me and my mother for two gods beside God? he shall say, Glory unto Thee! it is not for me to say that which I knew to be not the truth" (5:116); (4) "They are infidels who say, God is the Messiah, son of Mary" (5:19); (5) "The Messiah, son of Mary, is only an apostle" (5:79); (6) "This is Jesus, the son of Mary . . . It beseemeth not God to beget a son" (19:35, 36); (7) "And they say, God hath a son. No!" (2:110); (8) "How, when He hath no consort, should He have a son" (6:101); (9) "The Jews say, Ezra is the son of God;[6] and the Christians say, The Messiah

[5] Surah 2:110; 6:101; 5:19; 5:116.

[6] The statement that the Jews believed that Ezra was the son of God has no basis in Jewish literature. For explanations of how Muhammad happened to make this statement, see notes by G. Sale, E. M. Wherry, and Maulvi Muhammad Ali in their translations of the Koran on Surah 9:30; A. Geiger, *Was hat Mohammed aus dem Judenthume aufgenommen*, pp. 16, 194 (1st ed.), pp. 15, 191 (2nd ed.); Steinschneider, *Polemische*, p. 176, n. 17; L. Ginsberg, *Legends of the Jews*, VI, 432, 446. According to Ibn Ḥazm (*Fiṣal* I, p. 91, ll. 5–6), the Sadducees, whom he places in the vicinity of Yemen, were the only ones among the Jews who said that Ezra was

is a son of God. Such is the sayings of their mouth! They resemble the saying of the infidels of old!" (9:30); (10) "He begetteth not, and He is not begotten" (112:3). This last statement may be taken as being aimed at the Christian admission that, while God is a begetter, He is not begotten,[7] thus arguing against them that God is not a begetter just as He is admittedly not begotten.

In addition to its restatement and refutation of these two Christian doctrines, the Koran advances its own account of the birth of Jesus. That account occurs in two versions. In one of these versions, the term "spirit" plays the main role in his birth and is thus traceable to Matthew and Luke, but more directly to Luke. In the other version, the term "Word" appears prominently and is thus traceable to John.

The verses in which the story of the birth of Jesus centers on the term "spirit" are the following: (1) "And we sent our spirit to her; and he took before her the form of a perfect man . . . Said he, I am only a messenger of thy Lord, that I may bestow on thee a holy son. Said she, How shall I have a son, when man hath never touched me, and when I am no harlot? He said, so shall it be. Thy Lord hath said: Easy is this with me; and we will make him a sign for mankind and a mercy from us. For it is a thing decreed. And she conceived him" (19:17–22). (2) "And [remember] her who kept her maidenhood, and into whom we breathed of our spirit and made her and her son a sign for all creatures" (21:91); (3)

---

the son of God (cf. S. Poznanski, "Ibn Ḥazm über jüdische Secten," *JQR*, 16: 769 (1903–04).

With reference to this Koranic verse, Maimonides, in a letter to a correspondent, after stating that the Muslims are not what is legally called "idolaters" that is, polytheists, adds: "And, because they falsify and lie and say that we say that God has a son, we shall not similarly lie about them and say that they are idolaters. It is with reference to such false accusers as they that Scripture testifies as to the existence of those 'whose mouth speaketh falsehood' [Ps. 144:8, 11], and it is with reference to our refraining from falsely accusing them that it testifies that 'the remnant of Israel shall not do iniquity, nor speak lies, neither shall a deceitful tongue be found in their mouth' [Zeph. 3: 13]." *Teshubot ha-Rambam,* no. 160, p. 34d (*Ḳobeṣ* I); no. 369, p. 335 (ed. Freimann).

[7] Cf. *The Philosophy of the Church Fathers*, I, pp. 292 and 339.

"And Mary, the daughter of Imram, who kept her maidenhood, and into whose womb we breathed of our spirit" (66:12).

In these three passages, the term "spirit" is used in two different senses. In the first passage, the spirit describes himself as a messenger (*rasūl*) of God sent down to announce to Mary the birth of Jesus, and in the performance of that mission, the spirit is said to have taken on the semblance of a man. This quite evidently makes the spirit in this passage identical with the angel Gabriel, who, according to Luke,[8] told Mary, "Behold, thou shalt conceive in thy womb, and bring forth a son, and shalt call his name Jesus." [9] The "messenger (*rasūl*) of God" here is thus, as elsewhere in the Koran, an angel of God,[10] who, like angels in the Hebrew Bible as well as in the Koran,[11] took on the form of a human being. Moreover, from the identification of the spirit with an angel, we may also gather that the spirit was a real but created being, for angels, according to the Koran, were real beings created by God like Adam.[12]

How Mary had conceived is not stated in this passage. The spirit's statement, "I am only a messenger of thy Lord, that I may bestow upon thee a holy son," only means that he came to announce that God would bestow upon her a son. In the other two passages, however, the spirit is said to have been breathed by God into Mary or into her womb and as a result of this Jesus was born. The expressions "into whom we breathed of our spirit" and "into whose womb we breathed of our spirit" used in these passages would seem to suggest the expression "and I breathed of my spirit into him" [13] used elsewhere in the Koran in connection with the creation of Adam, and there, in connection with the creation of Adam, the term "spirit," as may be judged from its parallel expression

[8] Luke 1:26–28.

[9] Luke 1:31. Thus also Luke 16:24 is reflected in Surah 7:48 and Luke 16:25 in Surah 46:19 (cf. Noldeke, *Sketches from Eastern History*, p. 31).

[10] Cf. Surah 11:72, 79, 83.

[11] Cf. Surah 6:9; 11:73.

[12] Surah 7:11.

[13] Surah 15:29; 38:72; cf. 32:8.

"and He breathed into his nostrils the breath of life" [14] in the Book of Genesis, undoubtedly merely means a life-giving soul. This would seem to indicate that, while following the Gospel according to Luke in its account that an angel had foretold to Mary the birth of Jesus, the Koran does not follow it in its account that the angel also told her, "The Holy Spirit shall come upon thee . . . therefore also the holy thing which shall be born of thee shall be called the Son of God." [15] According to the Koran, the birth of Jesus, like the creation of Adam, was effected by God's breathing into the womb of Mary a life-giving soul, and thereby creating Jesus as a human being. In another place the Koran says: "Verily, the likeness of Jesus with God is as the likeness of Adam. He created him of dust. He then said to him 'Be,' and he was" (3:52). This is the Koran's substitute for Luke's "The Holy Spirit shall come upon Thee."

The verses in which the story of the birth of Jesus centers on the term "Word" are the following: (1) the verse in which the angels are said to have called out to Zacharias that God promised him a son named John "who shall be a verifier of the Word (*kalimah*) from God" (3:34); (2) the verse in which an angel is reported to have said to Mary, "O Mary! verily, God gives thee the glad tidings of a Word from Him" (3:40); and (3) a verse in which it is reported: "She said, Lord! how can I have a son, when man has not touched me? He said, Thus God creates what He pleases. When He decrees a matter he only says Be (*kun*) and it is" (3:42).

These statements about the Word reflect a combination of Luke and John. From Luke the Koran borrowed the story of the announcement by the angel to Zacharias of the birth of his son John [16] and also of the announcement by the angel Gabriel to Mary that she should conceive and bring forth a son.[17] From John it borrowed the statement that John the Baptist "came for a witness, to bear witness of the light" [18]

[14] Gen. 2:7.
[15] Luke 1:35.
[16] Luke 1:11–13.
[17] Luke 1:26–31.
[18] John 1:7.

which was in the Word; [19] and, accordingly, of John the Son of Zacharias it says that he "shall be a verifier of the Word of God," and of the announcement to Mary of the conception and birth of a son it says "God gives thee the glad tidings of a Word from Him." But it does not follow the Gospel according to John in its description of the Word as a pre-existent Christ, a real being, who was incarnated in the born Jesus. The "Word" is taken in the Koran to mean the word "Be" (*kun*) by which God caused Jesus to be conceived and born without a human father. It is the same word, "Be" (*kun*), by which, according to the Koran, God created the heavens and the earth,[20] thus reflecting the Hebrew *yehi*, "let there be," repeatedly used in the creation story in the first chapter of the Book of Genesis. Similar suggestions that the miraculous birth of Jesus from a virgin was, like the miraculous creation of the world, by God's merely uttering the word "Be," occur also in other verses.[21]

From all these we may construct a connected story of the birth of Jesus as narrated in the Koran. God sent an angel, referred to as "our spirit" (19:17), to announce to Mary the birth of a son. That son to be born is referred to as "a mercy from Us" (19:21), as "the word from God" (3:34), and as "a word from Him" (3:40). The son was born miraculously from a virgin by God's breathing into his mother a soul, referred to as "of our spirit" (21:91; 66:12), and by His saying the word "Be" (3:42; 19:36; 110:111). This combined version of the birth of Jesus occurs in the following verse: "The Messiah, Jesus, son of Mary, is only an Apostle of God, and His word which He sent down to Mary, and a spirit from Him" (4:169). In the light of the other verses, this verse means that Jesus, who has been referred to as "the word from God," was sent down to Mary by God in a miraculous way by His saying "Be" and by his breathing into her a soul called "our spirit."

[19] John 1:4.

[20] Surah 36:81, 82.

[21] Surah 19:36; 110:111.

Thus in the Koran there is a denial of the divinity of Jesus, while yet affirming his miraculous birth from a virgin. Such a view is not unprecedented. Certain Ebionites, we are told, who did not accept the orthodox Christian view of the divinity of Jesus, still believed that "Jesus was born of a virgin." [22] Such also was the view of Theodotus of Byzantium, for he held that though Jesus was "born of a virgin according to the will of the Father," he was "a man" [23] or "a mere man." [24]

II. Trinity and Incarnation in the Kalam

Not long after the rise of Islam, with the conquest of Syria, Muslims came in contact with authoritative exponents of Christianity. From them the Muslims learned of the conciliar formulation of the Trinity, a Trinity of which the two other members besides God were a pre-existent Christ called the Word and a pre-existent Holy Spirit. How the Muslims happened to learn of the true meaning of the Christian doctrines of the Trinity and the Incarnation may be gathered from two sources, both of them dating from the eighth century: first, a fictional debate between a Muslim and a Christian composed by John of Damascus before 754; second, a real debate between Mar Timothy, the Catholicos of the East Syrian Church, with Caliph Mahdī, held in the year 781.

In the fictional debate between a Muslim and a Christian by John of Damascus, quoted above,[1] we have seen how the Christian imparted to the Muslim the information that, according to the Christian belief, the term "Word" as applied to Christ refers to a pre-existent Christ and how also he assumed, without being contradicted by the Muslim, that the term "Word" applied to Jesus in the Koran also refers to a pre-existent Christ. In the actual debate between Mar Timothy and Caliph Mahdī, we may similarly see how Timothy painstakingly explains to the Caliph that the Word by which the

[22] Origen, *Cont. Cels.* V, 61.
[23] Hippolytus, *Refut. Omn. Haer.* VII, 35, 2.
[24] *Idem*, *Adv. Haer. Noeti* 3.

[1] Cf. above, p. 242.

Son of God is described refers to a pre-existent Christ, who is to be distinguished from the born Christ.[2]

Again, in the fictional debate by John of Damascus, in answer to the Muslim's question "What do you call Christ?" the Christian says that Christ is "the Word of God." But, when in answer to the Christian's question "What is Christ called in your Scripture?" the Muslim is assumed by the Christian to be compelled to answer: "By my Scripture he is called the spirit and the word of God,"[3] the Christian lets it pass without any comment. In the actual debate, however, between Timothy and the Caliph, we notice how the Caliph is informed by Timothy that the term "Word" when applied to the Son refers to the pre-existent Christ; how immediately after that the Caliph, in mentioning the Trinity, speaks of it, in agreement with the conciliar formulation, as consisting of "Father, Son, and Holy Spirit"[4] rather than, in agreement with the Koranic formulations, as consisting of God, Jesus, and Mary; and how, with this conciliar formulation of the Trinity in mind, the Caliph proceeds to ask Timothy: "What is the difference between the Son and the Spirit, and how is it that the Son is not the Spirit nor the Spirit the Son?"[5]

These two sources give us some idea as to the manner in which early Muslims in their contact with authoritative spokesmen of Christianity had gradually learned of the true meaning of the Christian doctrine of the Trinity. How these early Muslims reconciled this newly acquired knowledge of the meaning of the Christian Trinity with the Trinity as presented in the Koran is unknown to me at the present writing.[6]

[2] Cf. A. Mingana, *Timothy's Apology for Christianity*, pp. 17–19.

[3] John of Damascus, *Disputatio* (PG 96, 1341 C; PG 94, 1586 A); cf. Abucara, *Opuscula* XXV (PG 97, 1592 B).

[4] Mingana, *Timothy's Apology*, p. 22.

[5] *Ibid*., p. 25.

[6] A modern Muslim, Maulvi Muhammad Ali, in his annotated translation of the Koran (p. 284, n. 751; p. 244, n. 654; p. 273, n. 723), argues that the verse "O Jesus, son of Mary, hast thou said unto mankind, Take me and my mother as two gods, beside God" (5:116) does not refer to the Christian doctrine of the Trinity, but rather to the Christian practice

From these authoritative spokesmen of Christianity, Muslims must have also learned that the Christian doctrine of the Incarnation did not mean, as stated in the Koran, that Jesus was wholly God but rather that a divine nature was embodied in his human body, so that Jesus had two natures, a divine nature and a human nature, and hence that he was both God and man. Thus from the same fictional debate by John of Damascus, we also learn how Christians imparted this kind of information to Muslims. The Muslim is supposed to ask: "If Christ was God, how did he eat and drink and sleep, and how was he crucified and how did he die, and the like?" In answer, the Christian was to explain the Christian doctrine of the Incarnation, whereby Jesus was "a perfect man, both animal and rational," though at the same time he was also "the Word of God," concluding: "For know Christ is said to be twofold in matters pertaining to natures, but one in hypostasis." [7] Similarly, in the actual debate between Timothy and the Caliph, the former explains the Christian doctrine of the Incarnation as meaning that in Jesus there are "two natures, one which belongs to the Word and the other one which is from Mary." [8] Still later, we know, the Muslims became acquainted with the differences within Christianity itself on the question of the Incarnation, the differences between the Dyophysites, the Monophysites, and the Nestorians.[9]

But this new information which the Muslims acquired about the true meaning of the Christian doctrines of the Trinity and the Incarnation did not change their attitude toward these doctrines. The Koranic condemnation of the Trinity of God, Jesus, and Mary was extended to apply also to the conciliar Trinity of God, the Word, and the Holy Spirit. Thus, when the Christian conception of a pre-existent Trinity gave rise in

---

of worshiping Jesus and Mary as gods. From Ḳirḳisānī (cf. *Anwār*, VIII, 3) it may be gathered that some Muslims still followed the Koran in considering Jesus as the second person of the Trinity.

[7] John of Damascus, *Disputatio* (PG 96, 1345 A; PG 94, 1589–1590).

[8] Mingana, *Timothy's Apology*, p. 19.

[9] Cf. *Fiṣal* I, p. 48, l. 23–p. 49, l. 13; *Milal*, p. 173, l. 14–p. 178, l. 7.

Islam to the theory of attributes, those who opposed that theory condemned it on the ground that it was like the Christian belief in the Trinity of God, the Word, and the Holy Spirit.[10] Similarly the Koranic arguments that God could not beget a "child," [11] that Jesus is only a "servant of God," [12] and that "there is no God but one God" [13] are repeated by Caliph Mahdī [14] even after he has learned from Timothy the Christian conception of the Incarnation and of the two natures in Jesus.

Still, despite the Koranic opposition to what it believed to be the Christian conception of the Trinity, the subsequently acquired new conception of this Christian doctrine was responsible, as we have seen, for the rise of what became two fundamental doctrines in Islam, that of the reality of attributes and that of the uncreatedness of the Koran. It was also the opposition in Christianity, on the part of certain heretics, to the reality or to the eternity of the second and third persons of the Trinity that similarly gave rise in Islam to an opposition to the reality of attributes and the uncreatedness of the Koran. Moreover, it was the same kind of arguments that were used in Christianity both for and against the reality or eternity of the second and third persons of the Trinity that were used also in Islam both for and against the reality of attributes and the uncreatedness of the Koran. Then also, it is quite possible that it was the newly acquired conception of the Christian doctrine of Incarnation and the opposition to it that has produced in Islam differences of opinion with regard to what we have chosen to call the problem of the "inlibration" of the pre-existent Koran in the revealed Koran.

In the problem of attributes, as we have noted, while Islam had taken over from Christianity the conception of the existence of real persons or hypostases in God, which it transformed into attributes, it constantly insisted, in opposition to

[10] Cf. above, pp. 112–113.

[11] Surah 4:170; 19:91, 93; 43:59.

[12] Surah 19:31.

[13] Surah 5:77.

[14] Cf. Mingana, *Timothy's Apology*, pp. 78, 80, 81.

Christianity, that they are not God. This was the fundamental distinction between the Christian Trinity and the Muslim attributes. In the course of time, however, among certain Muslims, who were regarded as orthodox, this difference between the Christian Trinity and the Muslim attributes was somewhat blurred. We gather this from the following statement in Ibn Ḥazm: "To one of the Ashʿarites I said: Since you say that coexistent with God are fifteen attributes, all of them other than He and all of them eternal, why do you find fault with the Christians when they say that God is 'the third of three'? [15] He said to me: We find fault with the Christians only because they assume that there coexist with God only two things and do not assume that there coexist with Him a greater number of things. Indeed, one of the Ashʿarites has already told me that the name 'God,' that is, our use of the term 'God,' is a word which applies to the essence of the Creator and the totality of His attributes, and not to His essence without His attributes." [16]

From these answers of the followers of the Ashʿarite teachings, we may gather that somehow within this orthodox group there were some who forgot that the original opposition to the Christian doctrine of the Trinity was on the ground of the application of the term "God" to the second and third persons. Quite oblivious of this fundamental opposition, they were willing to apply the term "God" as a common appellation of God and His attributes, which is only an adoption of the Christian view that the term "God" is to be used as a common appellation of the Father and the two other persons, though, I imagine, these Ashʿarites would still balk at calling each individual attribute "God." The emphasis that the term "God" is not to be applied to the essence alone without the attributes and the statement that the difference between their belief and that of the Christians consists only in the fact that the Muslim attributes are more numerous than the Christian

[15] This is a quotation from Surah 5:77.
[16] *Fiṣal* IV, p. 207, ll. 20–24.

persons indicate that in all other respects their attributes assume the character of the Christian persons.

It may be remarked that this Muslim objection to the Christian restriction of the persons surnamed attributes to three is answered by Elias of Nisibis, by drawing a distinction between the three terms by which the persons of the Trinity are described and all the other terms predicated of God. The terms by which the persons of the Trinity are described, he says, are "properties (*ḫawāṣṣ*) belonging to the essence of the Creator, in which none besides Him participates," whereas all the other terms, such as "Creator," "Merciful," "Powerful," are descriptive of some action.[17]

Besides these Christian influences in the various sects which are generally regarded as belonging to the community of Islam, there were wider Christian influences among sects whose inclusion within the community of Islam was a matter of doubt.[18] Among these sects, similar to the Christian belief in a pre-existent Christ through whom the world was created and who was incarnate in Jesus of whom there will be a second coming, there arose the belief that "God created Muhammad,"[19] evidently a pre-existent Muhammad, that "it is he, and not God, who created the world,"[20] by which is evidently meant who directly created the world, that God was incarnate in Muhammad as well as in ʿAlī, Fāṭimah, al-Ḥasan, and al-Ḥusayn,[21] and that ʿAlī, whose assassination was compared to the crucifixion of Jesus, would reappear.[22]

Another kind of infiltration of Christian influence, one not affecting any of the Islamic religious beliefs but affecting the Muslim conception of the birth of Jesus, is to be found in the

[17] Cf. Horst, *Des Metropoliten Elias von Nisibis Buch vom Beweis der Warheit des Glaubens*, p. 4. The Arabic terms *ḫawāṣṣ and ashḫāṣ* quoted in n. 1 are translated in German by Horst as "Attributen" and "Personen." More accurately, they should be translated, in English, as "properties" and "individuals." For the distinction drawn here by Elias, see below, p. 350.

[18] *Farḳ*, pp. 220 ff. [19] *Ibid.*, p. 238, l. 12. [20] *Ibid.*, l. 13.

[21] *Ibid.*, p. 239, ll. 8–9; cf. *Milal*, p. 135, ll. 8–9.

[22] *Farḳ*, p. 223, l. 14–p. 224, l. 6. For a history of this view, see J. Friedländer, "The Heterodoxies of the Shiites in the Presentation of Ibn Ḥazm," *JAOS*, 29: 23–28 (1908).

reports on the teachings of two disciples of Naẓẓām, Ibn Ḥā'iṭ and al-Ḥadathī,[23] both of whom died in the latter part of the ninth century. In the Koran, as we have seen, the verses stating that the Christian Messiah is the word of God (3:34, 3:40, 4:169) meant that Jesus was miraculously born by the word "Be" uttered by God,[24] and, while we know that the Muslims subsequently became acquainted with the Christian use of the term "word" in the sense of the pre-existent Christ and accepted that use, we do not know how many Christian teachings about the Word and the pre-existent Christ they accepted. But, as reported of these two, they accepted several Christian teachings about "the Word."

First, concerning both Ibn Ḥā'iṭ and Ḥadathī, it is reported that they believed that the world has two creators, one of them "God" and the other "the Word of God, the Messiah, Jesus, son of Mary, by whom the world was created." [25] This quite evidently means that they took John's statement about the Word that "all things were made by him" [26] and applied it to "the Messiah, Jesus, son of Mary," concerning whom the Koran (3:34; 3:40; 4:169) says that he is the "word" of God, thus interpreting the term "word" in this Koranic verse in its Christian sense of a pre-existent Messiah, by whom God effected the creation of the world. There were thus two creators. Of these two creators, God is described as "eternal" (*ḳadīm*) and the Word as "originated" (*ḥādith*,[27] *muḥdath* [28]) or as that which is created (*maḫlūḳ*).[29] This I take to reflect the Christian doctrine that, while both God and the Word

[23] In *Fiṣal* IV, p. 197, ll. 20–21 (cf. p. 192, l. 4), and *Milal*, p. 42, ll. 6–7, these two are treated under the general heading of Mu'tazilites. In *Fiṣal* II, p. 112, ll. 10–13, however, the followers of Ibn Ḥā'iṭ are included among those who are generally regarded as not belonging to Islam. In *Farḳ*, p. 260, ll. 3 ff., they are similarly treated among the sects that were excluded from the Muslim community.

[24] Cf. above, p. 308.

[25] *Fiṣal* IV, p. 197, ll. 21–22. In *Farḳ*, p. 260, l. 9, and in *Milal*, p. 42, l. 4, the expression "the Word of God" is omitted; the former merely has "Jesus the son of Mary" and the latter merely has "the Christ."

[26] John 1:3.

[27] *Fiṣal* IV, p. 197, l. 22.

[28] *Milal*, p. 42, l. 3.

[29] *Farḳ*, p. 260, l. 9.

are coeternal, there is a difference between them, God being ungenerated (ἀγέννητος) and the Word being generated (γεννητός) or rather eternally generated.[30] The description of the Word in the passages quoted as "originated" or "created" is not to be taken literally as reflecting the Arian conception of the second person of the Trinity; it is to be taken, I believe, in the sense of eternally generated or eternally created and hence as reflecting the orthodox Christian view of "eternal generation." In fact, Shahrastānī, who in one place, referred to above,[31] describes it as "originated," in another place describes it as "eternal" (*ḳadīmah*),[32] which may be taken as an indication that the term "originated" means eternally originated.

Second, not only have they given to the term "word," as used in the Koran with reference to Jesus, the Christian meaning of a pre-existent Christ who is a creator, but they have also accepted the Christian doctrine of the incarnation as accounting for the birth of Jesus. Of Ibn Ḥā'iṭ, with whom undoubtedly Ḥadathī agreed, it is reported that "he believed that the [pre-existent] Christ clad himself with bodily flesh and he is the eternal Word who was made flesh, as the Christians say." [33] What this statement means is that, departing from the Koran's account of the birth of Jesus by the word "Be," [34] Ibn Ḥā'iṭ and Ḥadathī adopted the Christian doctrine of the Incarnation as expressed in the verse "And the Word was made flesh" (John 1:14). The expression "clad himself" is used by the Church Fathers as a figure of speech for their various conceptions of the Incarnation, whether it be Dyophysite or Monophysite or Nestorian.[35] Baghdādī, commenting on the Christology of Ibn Ḥā'iṭ and Ḥadathī, says that "they believed the Messiah is the son of God by adoption

[30] Cf. *The Philosophy of the Church Fathers*, I, p. 339.
[31] Cf. above at nn. 27, 28.
[32] *Milal*, p. 42, l. 14.
[33] *Ibid.*, ll. 13–14.
[34] Cf. above
[35] Cf. *The Philosophy of the Church Fathers*, I, pp. 168–169.

(*al-tabannā*), and not by birth."[36] If this is a true interpretation of their view, then it means that as a concession to the Koran, which denies the Christian belief that Jesus was the son of God by birth,[37] they maintained that the true Christian belief about Jesus was not that of the Malkites (that is, the Dyophysites) nor that of the Jacobites (that is, the Monophysites) but rather that of the Nestorians, which, as expressed by their forerunner Theodore of Mopsuestia, maintains that the man Jesus, on account of his union with the Word of God or the pre-existent Christ, who is the true son of God, has acquired the right to be called son of God by adoption.[38] Baghdādī also reports that both Ibn Ḥā'iṭ and Ḥadathī "asserted that the [pre-existent] Messiah (i.e., the Word) clad himself with flesh, but before his clothing himself with flesh he was an Intellect (*'aḳl*)."[39]

III. The Philosopher Kindī and Yaḥyā Ibn 'Adī on the Trinity

The earliest disputations between Muslims and Christians at their first meetings consisted merely in bandying Biblical and Koranic verses and in calling each other names. The Muslims, using the Koranic term "associators" (*mushrikūn*) for polytheists (2:99) and bearing in mind the Koran's warning, "O my son! associate none with God, for, verily, association is a grievous iniquity" (31:12) and also the Koranic statement that the Christians "associate" with God another god by their belief that "the Messiah is a son of God" (9:30,

[36] *Farḳ*, p. 260, ll. 9–10; cf. Halkin's note in his translation *ad loc.* (p. 99, n. 5).

[37] Cf. above, pp. 305–306.

[38] Cf. *Theodorus Mopsuestenus in Ep. ad Galatas* 4:5 and *in Ep. ad Colossenes* 1:13 (ed. H. B. Swete, I, p. 63, l. 2–p. 64, l. 6; p. 260, ll. 4–6, and p. lxxxi).

[39] *Farḳ*, p. 261, ll. 1–2. The term *'aḳl* quite evidently stands here for the term *logos* by which the pre-existent Christ is known in Greek. This unusual translation of the Greek *logos* by the Arabic *'aḳl* occurs in another connection in *De Placitis Philosophorum* I, 3, 18, p. 285a, ll. 3 and 8 (Arabic, p. 102, ll. 11 and 13).

31) taunted the Christians by calling them "Associators" (ἑταιριασταί).[1] The Christians retorted by calling the Muslims "mutilators (κόπται) of God," arguing that, inasmuch as Christ is described in the Koran as the Word of God, he was inseparable from God and was God, and consequently the Muslims, by denying that he was God, mutilated God.[2]

This is how in the early part of the eighth century, as reported by John of Damascus, Muslims and Christians debated Christian doctrines.

But when Islam learned from Christians the art of argumentation and, in the course of arguing, partly yielded to the Christians by admitting the existence in God of eternal attributes, which were like the second and third persons of the Trinity in all but in their not being called God, the debate between Muslims and Christians took on a different character. The Muslims, instead of merely hurling at Christians the Koranic epithet "associators," began to justify the use of that epithet by trying to show how a belief in a trinity of persons, each of whom is conceived as God, is incompatible with the strict conception of the unity of God, in which Christians, no less than Muslims, professed a belief. The Christians, for their part, began to explain, by the use of certain analogies borrowed from the Church Fathers, how the three persons of the Trinity, each of them called God, could still be spoken of as one God. An early example of this new turn in the manner of debate between Muslims and Christians is to be found in the debate between the Catholicos Timothy and Caliph Mahdī in the latter part of the eighth century. Verses from Scripture and the Koran are indeed still quoted, and they are

[1] John of Damascus, *De Haeresibus* 101 (PG 94, 768 B).

For the Koranic use of the term "associator" (*mushrik*) in the sense of "polytheist," compare the rabbinic description of polytheism in the following statements: "He who associates (*ha-meshattef*) the name of God with something else will be uprooted from the world" (*Sanhedrin* 63a); "the verse in Exodus 32:8 does not say 'this is thy god,' but 'these are thy gods,' because they associated the golden calf with Him and said: 'God and the calf redeemed us'" (*Exodus Rabbah* 42, 3).

[2] *De Haeresibus* (768 B-D).

still the determining factors in the respective attitudes of the debaters. But there are in the debate attempts at logical reasoning. The Caliph is really curious to know how Christians would reconcile the Trinity with the unity of God.[3] The Catholicos tries to explain the reconcilability of these two beliefs by such analogies as that of a king, who, because his word and spirit are inseparable from him, is "one king with his own word and spirit, and not three kings" and as that of the sun, which, again, because its light and heat are inseparable from it, "is with its light and heat not called three suns but one sun."[4] All these analogies reflect the patristic method of explaining the contention that, while the distinction between the persons of the Trinity is real, and not nominal, God is still one, and this on the ground that the unity of God is a relative kind of unity, a unity which allows within itself a distinction of eternally inseparable parts.[5]

But when among the Muslims, during the reign of Ma'mūn (813–833), philosophy became a special discipline, independent of theology, the debate between Muslims and Christians on the problem of the Trinity took on a still newer aspect. Muslims, having by that time raised their own problem of attributes to a logical problem of universals and predication,[6] began to apply the same method of logical reasoning in their arguments against the Trinity, bolstering up their contentions by quotations from the logical writings of Aristotle. Christians found themselves compelled to employ the same method in their defense of the doctrine under attack. Thus a new type of debate between Muslims and Christians made its appearance in the ninth century. The chief exponent of this new type of debate on behalf of Islam was the philosopher al-Kindī (d. 873); the chief exponent on behalf of Christianity was Yaḥyā Ibn 'Adī (d. 974). Kindī's arguments against the Trinity are

[3] Mingana, *Timothy's Apology*, p. 22.

[4] *Ibid.* Cf. similar analogies in *The Philosophy of the Church Fathers*, I, pp. 359–361, and Abucara, *Mimar* III, 22.

[5] Cf. *The Philosophy of the Church Fathers*, I, pp. 311 ff.

[6] Cf. above, pp. 170–171.

known only from a work in which Yaḥyā Ibn ʿAdī undertook to refute them. We shall therefore begin here with an analysis of Kindī's arguments as restated by Ibn ʿAdī, and then proceed to analyze the refutation of these arguments by Ibn ʿAdī, in which we shall include an analysis of the refutation of some of the other Muslim arguments, which are to be found in Ibn ʿAdī's other works.[7]

Drawing upon the Arabic translation of the Cappadocian formula for the Trinity, Kindī opens his discussion with the statement that "all the Christian sects confess that three eternal hypostases (*aḳānīm*, ὑποστάσεις) are one substance (*jauhar*, οὐσία).[8] The expression "all the Christian sects," it may be remarked, refers to the Malkites, Nestorians, and Jacobites, all of whom were known to the Muslims as being orthodox in the doctrine of the Trinity; it does not include the Macedonians, the Sabellians, and the Arians, who were known to them as being unorthodox in the doctrine of the Trinity.[9]

Against this Christian doctrine of the Trinity thus formulated, Kindī raises the objection that the doctrine of the Trinity implies composition and whatever is composed cannot be eternal. Under this objection he has three arguments:

First, evidently having in mind a statement like that of John of Damascus, namely, that each hypostasis (ὑπόστασις) is an individual (ἄτομον) [10] and that the hypostases differ from each other by properties (ἰδιότητες) or characteristics (χαρακ-

[7] For a complete account of Yaḥyā Ibn ʿAdī's works, see G. Graf, *Geschichte der christlichen arabischen Literatur*, II (1947), pp. 233–249.

Works of Yaḥyā Ibn ʿAdī referred to in this section are as follows:

(1) *Defense*=*Defense of the Doctrine of the Trinity against the Objections of al-Kindī*. Arabic text with French translation by A. Périer in *Revue de l'Orient Chrétien*, 22: 3–21 (1920–21); revised French translation in *Petits* (item 4 below), pp. 118–128.

(2) *Unity*. Cf. A. Périer, *Yaḥyā ben ʿAdī: Un Philosophe arabe chrétien du X*^e^ *siècle* (1920), pp. 122–150.

(3) *Trinity*. Cf. *ibid*., pp. 150–191.

(4) *Petits* = *Petits Traités Apologétiques de Yaḥyā ben ʿAdī*, by A. Périer (1920), Arabic and French.

[8] *Defense*, p. 4, l. 10; "Substance" is used here in the sense of "essence" (cf. above, p. 128, n. 88).

[9] Cf. above, p. 337.

[10] *Dialect*. 43 (PG 94, 613 B).

τηριστικά),[11] Kindī says that "by hypostases they mean individuals (*ashḫāṣ*) and by one substance they mean that [in which] each one of the hypostases exists with its property (*ḫāṣṣah*)." [12] He then goes on to say: "Accordingly, the notion of substance exists in each one of the hypostases and it has the same meaning in each of them; and each of the hypostases has a property, which is eternal in it and which differentiates one hypostasis from the other. Whence it follows that each of the hypostases is composed of a substance, which is common to all of them, and a property, which is peculiar to each of them. But everything composed is the effect of a cause, and no effect of a cause can be eternal, whence it follows that neither is the Father eternal nor is the Son eternal nor is the Holy Spirit eternal. Thus things which have been assumed to be eternal are not eternal. But this is a most absurd impossibility." [13]

In his refutation, Yaḥyā admits that the hypostases consist of parts; thus, like all those orthodox Christians who believed in the reality of all the three hypostases, he takes the unity of God to be only a relative unity.[14] Still, he maintains, the three hypostases can be eternal; for, he argues, only that which is composed of parts which have previously existed separately cannot be eternal, but there is no reason why a thing could not be eternally composed of parts which had never existed separately. To quote: "If you mean by the term composed that which is produced by an act of composition, then this, by my religion, is something caused and created and not eternal, and your reasoning will be applicable to this as well as to any other case like this. Christians, however, do not agree with you that the Father and the Son and the Holy Spirit were produced as a result of the composition of the substance and the properties, for they only say that the substance is described by every one of these three attributes

[11] *De Fide Orthodoxa* I, 8 (PG 94, 824 B). Cf. above, pp. 119–120.
[12] *Defense*, p. 4, ll. 11–12.
[13] *Ibid.*, ll. 12–17.
[14] Cf. *The Philosophy of the Church Fathers*, I, pp. 311 ff.

(*al-ṣifāt*) and that these attributes are eternal, without their having been produced in it after they had not been." [15] It is this kind of argument, it may be remarked in passing, that is used later by Ghazālī in answer to a similar objection against the existence of eternal real attributes in God. Thus Ghazālī argues: "Why is it impossible that, just as the essence of Him Who is Necessary of Existence is eternal and has no efficient cause, so also any attribute of His coexists with Him from eternity and has no efficient cause." [16]

Second, referring to Porphyry's enumeration in his *Isagoge* [17] of the five predicables in logical propositions, Kindī reduces the Trinitarian formula to a logical proposition, in which the expression "the one substance" is the subject and the expression "three eternal hypostases" is the predicate, and the subject and predicate are combined by the copula "is." He then asks himself, "What are the three eternal hypostases which are predicated of the subject *ousia*?" Are they genera (*ajnās*)? [18] Are they species (*anwāʿ*)? [19] Are they differentiae (*fuṣūl*)? [20] Are they accidents in the general sense of the term (*aʿrāḍ ʿāmmiyyah*)? [21] Are they accidents in the peculiar sense of the term (*aʿrāḍ ḫāṣṣiyyah*), that is to say, properties (*ḫawāṣṣ*)? [22] To these he adds also the question whether of the hypostases some are genera and some either differences or species,[23] or whether they are all individuals of a species.[24] He shows that the hypostases cannot be taken as any of these, and this on the ground that if taken as any of these, each of the hypostases, assumed to be eternal, would have to be composed of parts, that is, of a subject and a predicate, and, as

[15] *Defense*, p. 6, ll. 9–14.
[16] *Tahāfut al-Falāsifah* VI, 7, p. 166, ll. 7–8.
[17] *Defense*, p. 6, ll. 18–20; p. 10, ll. 15–17.
[18] *Ibid.*, p. 6, l. 20–p. 7, l. 3.
[19] *Ibid.*, p. 7, ll. 7–11.
[20] *Ibid.*, p. 8, l. 18–p. 9, l. 3.
[21] *Ibid.*, p. 9, ll. 8–11.
[22] *Ibid.*, ll. 14–17. For the reference here to the use of the term "accident" in the sense of either "accident" or "property," see Aristotle, *Metaph.* V, 30, 1025a, 30–32.
[23] *Defense*, p. 9, l. 21 – p. 10, l. 2.
[24] *Ibid.*, p. 10, ll. 5–8.

before, he concludes, nothing composed of parts can be eternal.

In his refutation of this argument, Yaḥyā repeats his previous contention that an eternal uncaused composition is possible.[25] In addition to this general refutation, he denies unqualifiedly that the hypostases are considered by Christians as genera [26] or as species [27] or as what Kindī calls accidents in the general sense of the term.[28] With regard, however, to what Kindī calls "accidents in the particular sense of the term, that is to say, properties," Yaḥyā says: "The Christians do not also say that the hypostases are accidents in the particular sense of the term, for, while they apply to them the term property, they do not mean thereby that they are accidents; they rather consider each of the hypostases a substance," [29] by which is meant what Aristotle would call a "first substance," that is, an individual.[29a] In this passage, his statement that the Christians apply to the three hypostases the term "property" refers to the common use of the term "property" (*al-ḥāṣṣ*, ἰδιότης) as a designation of that which is peculiar to each of the three hypostases and by which they are distinguished from each other.[30] Similarly, with regard to description of the hypostases as individuals, Yaḥyā cautiously says: "The Christians do not also say that the hypostases are individuals in the sense given by al-Kindī to that term." [31] Behind this cautious statement of Yaḥyā is the view running throughout the history of the discussion of the Trinity that the orthodox conception of the reality of the hypostases means that they are conceived as individuals, but individuals in the sense of individual species.[32]

Third, evidently having in mind Aristotle's statement in the *Metaphysics* that to the term "one" (ἕν, Arabic: *wāḥid*)

[25] *Ibid.*, p. 7, l. 13–p. 8, l. 17; p. 9, ll. 4–7; p. 10, ll. 3–4, 12.
[26] *Ibid.*, p. 7, ll. 4–6.
[27] *Ibid.*, ll. 12–13.
[28] *Ibid.*, p. 9, ll. 12–13.
[29] *Ibid.*, ll. 18–20.
[29a] *Categ.* 5, 2a, 11–14.
[30] Cf. above at n. 11.
[31] *Defense*, p. 10, ll. 9–10.
[32] Cf. *The Philosophy of the Church Fathers*, I, pp. 305–365.

belongs the term "same" (*ταὐτό*; Arabic: *huwa huwa*) [33] and drawing directly upon Aristotle's statement in the *Topics* that "the same" (*ταὐτόν*) is used either "in species" (*εἴδει*) or "in genus" (*γένει*) or "in number" (*ἀριθμῷ*),[34] Kindī argues against the Christian belief that "three are one and one is three" as follows: "That which we call one and the same (*huwa huwa wāḥid*) we call one only in three senses, as it is said in the Book of *Topics* (*ṭaubīḳa*), which is the fifth [Book of Aristotle's *Organon*], namely, it is called one and the same in number (*bi'l-ʿadad*), as the unit is called one; or it is called one and the same in species (*bi'l-nauʿ*), as Ḫalid and Zayd are one, because they are included under a common species, which is man; or it is called one and the same in genus (*bi'l-jins*), as man and ass are one, because they are included under a common genus, which is animal." [35] Kindī then tries to show how the oneness of the three hypostases cannot be understood in any of these three senses of one enumerated by Aristotle. Against the last two senses of one, the one in species and the one in genus, he repeats his previous argument that one in either of these two senses would imply composition and hence could not be eternal.[36] But against the first of the three Aristotelian senses of one, the one in number, he has a new argument, in which, starting with the statement that three is a multiple of one and one is a part of three, he says something to the effect that the affirmation of both three and one of a subject is "an affirmation of repugnant absurdity and evident impossibility." [37]

More fully and clearly is this argument reproduced by Yaḥyā in the name of those whom he terms "the adversaries of the Christians" in another work of his, where it reads as fol-

[33] *Metaph.* X, 3, 1054a, 29–31; cf. Averroes, *Tafsīr*, X, Text. 10 (p. 1286, l. 2).

[34] *Top.* VII, 1, 152b, 30–32; cf. *Metaph.* X, 3, 1054a, 32–b, 3.

[35] *Defense*, p. 11, ll. 4–9. The bracketed additions are required by the context. In Périer's French translation of this treatise, the statement "as it is said in the Book *ṭaubīḳā*, which is the fifth" is left untranslated.

[36] *Defense*, p. 11, l. 15–p. 12, l. 3.

[37] *Ibid.*, p. 11, ll. 10–14.

lows: "One subject, according to their opinion, cannot be described by contradictory terms. But three, in its meaning, is contradictory to the meaning (*maʿnā*) of one, since three is many and one is not many; one is the principle of three and of every number, but three is not a principle of itself or of any other number; three is divisible, but one is not divisible . . . It has thus been demonstrated, they conclude, that these two predicates, namely, three and one, are contradictory, and, since the Christians apply both of them to the same subject at the same time, it must necessarily follow that their formula is contradictory and their doctrine is groundless." [38] In other words, they try to show that, by affirming of God both "three" and "one," the Christians at once both negate and affirm of God the same predicate; for by saying that He is three, they affirm that He is many and numerable and divisible, but by saying that He is one, they negate that He is many and numerable and divisible, and thus they violate the Law of Contradiction, which, as phrased by Aristotle, reads: "It is impossible for the same thing to belong and not belong at the same time to the same subject in the same respect." [39]

It is to be noted how in this passage the arguers, in order to show that the affirmation that God is both "three" and "one" is what Aristotle would describe as "contradictory," change the pair of terms "three" and "one" to the pairs of terms "many" and "not many," "principle of number" and "not principle of number," and "divisible and indivisible." This reflects Aristotle's statements to the effect that (1) "contradictory" is that which contains an "affirmation" and "negation" of the same subject [40] and that, (2) inasmuch as in any pair of contraries either one of them is the privation of the other and hence in a certain sense the negation of the other, the Law of contradiction applies also to contraries,[41] from which the ob-

[38] *Petits*, p. 46, l. 7–p. 47, l. 7; cf. p. 64, ll. 6–7.
[39] *Metaph.* IV, 3, 1005b, 19–20.
[40] *De Interpr.* 7, 17b, 16–18.
[41] *Metaph.* IV, 6, 1011b, 15–20.

jectors rightly infer that, inasmuch as in the affirmation that God is both "three" and "one," the term "three" means "many" and its contrary, the term "one," means "not many," the affirmation is contradictory.

In his refutation of this argument, Yaḥyā starts out by denying that the Christians use the term "one" in any of the three senses quoted above by Kindī from the *Topics*, adding that the classification of the meanings of the term "one" as reproduced by Kindī is incomplete.[42] He then proceeds to enumerate other meanings of the term "one" as well as of its opposite "many," out of which he selects two as suitable meanings of the term "one" used in the Trinitarian formula.[43] Finally, he tries to show that on the basis of his explanation of the use of the terms "one" and "three," the Trinitarian formula contains no contradiction, for God is said to be "one" from one point of view (*jihah*) or aspect (*wajh*), that is to say, with reference to "substance," and He is said to be "three" from another point of view or aspect, that is to say, with reference to "hypostases."[44] What Yaḥyā really does is to remind his opponent that, according to Aristotle's complete formulation of the Law of Contradiction, that Law holds only when the simultaneous affirmation and negation of the same thing of the same subject are "according to the same (κατὰ τὸ αὐτό),"[45] which in the Arabic translation of the *Metaphysics* is rendered by *bi-kull jihah*, "in every respect."[46]

The various meanings of the term "one" enumerated by Yaḥyā, on the basis of which he answers Kindī's objection, are six. They are as follows:

(1) One by relation or analogy (*bi'l-nisbah*),[47] of which he gives two examples: (a) "the relation of the source to the rivers which flow from it and the relation of the vital spirit in

[42] *Defense*, p. 12, ll. 4–6.

[43] Cf. below at nn. 47–69.

[44] *Petits*, p. 28, ll. 6–7; p. 42, ll. 4–8.

[45] *Metaph.* IV, 3, 1005b, 20.

[46] Averroes, *Tafsīr* IV, Text. 9 (p. 346, l. 3). Cf. above at n. 40.

[47] *Defense*, p. 12, l. 7. The Arabic term *nisbah* may stand here for either "relation" (πρός τι) or "analogy" (ἀναλογία). Cf. *Averroes: Tafsīr ma ba'd tabi'at*, Index D, a, s. v.

the heart to the vital spirit in the arteries are called one relation"; (b) "the relation of two to four and the relation of twenty to forty are one relation." [48] This interpretation is based upon two statements in Aristotle: first, his general definition of "one by analogy" (ἑν κατ᾽ ἀναλογίαν; Arabic: *wāḥid bi'l-musāwāh*) as "those which are related as a third thing to a fourth"; [49] second, his illustration of analogy by the comparison of the relation between the intellect and the soul to that between sight and the body.[50]

(2) One in the sense of the continuous (*al-muttaṣil*), as, for instance, body and surface and line, which are each said to be one, even though, insofar as they are each infinitely divisible, they are each many.[51]

(3) One in the sense of that which is indivisible (*mā lā yanḳasim*), such as the point, the unit, the instant, and the beginning of motion, which are each said to be one.[52]

These two meanings of "one" are based on Aristotle's statement that "the continuous (τὸ συνεχές) is one" and that "the indivisible (τὸ ἀδιαίρετον) is one," [53] supplemented by his statement that "line, surface, and body" are three of the five "continuous quantities" [54] and also his various statements with regard to the indivisibility of the point (στιγμή),[55] the unit (μονάς),[56] and the instant (νῦν).[57] As for Yaḥyā's mentioning of "the beginning (*mabda'*) of motion" as indivisible, it is probably a mistake for "the end (*tamām*) of motion," for, according to Aristotle, "there is an end (τέλος) of change," which is "indivisible," but "there is no beginning (ἀρχή) of change." [58] Or, perhaps, Yaḥyā has deliberately used the expression "the beginning of motion" in order to emphasize his own belief in the creation of the world against Aristotle's denial of it. If the world is assumed to have been created,

[48] *Defense*, p. 12, ll. 7–10.
[49] *Metaph.* V, 6, 1016b, 31–32, 34–35.
[50] *Eth. Nic.* I, 4, 1096b, 28–29.
[51] *Defense*, p. 12, ll. 11–13.
[52] *Ibid.*, ll. 13–14.
[53] *Phys.* I, 2, 185b, 7–8.
[54] *Categ.* 6, 4b, 23–25.
[55] *Phys.* VI, 1, 231a, 25–26.
[56] *Metaph.* V, 6, 1016b, 24–25.
[57] *Phys.* VI, 3, 233b, 33–34.
[58] *Ibid.*, 5, 236a, 10–15.

Aristotle himself would admit that it had a beginning and that the beginning was indivisible.

(4) One in the sense of that which "is said of things [which are called by many names, but] whose definitional formula (*al-ḳaul*), which signifies their quiddity or essence (*māhiy-yah*), is one," as, for instance, "wine," for which there are two Arabic names, *shamūl* and *ḫamr*; "ass," for which there are also two Arabic names, *ḥimār* and *ʿayr*; and "camel," for which again there are two Arabic names, *jamal* and *baʿīr*.[59] A similar example used by Yaḥyā in two of his other works is "man," for which in Arabic, as in some other languages, there are two names, *insān* and *bashar*, but whose quiddity or essence, as signified by the formula "rational mortal animal," is one.[60] In all these examples, the multiplicity is a multiplicity of names, and the unity is a unity of definitional formula or essence. In the corresponding passage in Aristotle, the examples used to illustrate that which is one in definitional formula (λόγος) or essence (τὸ τί ἦν εἶναι), but many in names, are "wine," for which he uses two Greek words, μέθυ and οἶνος,[61] and "garment," for which, again, he uses two Greek words, λώπιον and ἱμάτιον.[62] This meaning of one is approved of by Yaḥyā as an explanation of the Christian triunity.[63]

(5) One in the sense of "one in subject (*al-mauḍūʿ*) and many in the terms of its definition (*al-ḥudūd*), that is to say, one may affirm of the one subject many definitional terms, which in number correspond to the number of the *maʿāni* existing in that one subject and which are the definitional terms of those *maʿāni*. To illustrate: of Zayd, for instance, though he is one in subject, we may affirm the definitional term (*ḥadd*) animal and the definitional term rational and the definitional term mortal."[64] The basis of this meaning of one is a passage in which Aristotle tries to show that the parts of a definition (ὁρισμός), namely, the genus and differentia, are

[59] *Defense*, p. 12, ll. 14–16.
[60] *Trinity*, p. 132.
[61] *Phys.* I, 2, 185b, 9.
[62] *Ibid.*, 19–20.
[63] *Defense*, p. 12, l. 16 – p. 13, l. 3.
[64] *Ibid.*, p. 13, ll. 3–7.

many, and so he raises the question as to what constitutes the unity of a definition.[65] The answer given by him is that "the definition (ὁρισμός) is a single formula (λόγος)," and a formula "must be a formula of some one thing (ἑνός τινος)," which is a "this" (τόδε τι),[66] that is to say, it is one because it is a definition or definitional formula of one subject. This meaning of one is also approved of by Yaḥyā as an explanation of the Christian triunity.[67]

(6) One in the sense of "one in definition and many in subject, as, again, man, for instance, whose definition, so far as he is man, is one definition, but the subjects to which it may be applied are many, such as Zayd, ʿAbdallah, and Ḫālid, each of whom is a subject to be described as man." [68] The basis of this meaning of one is Aristotle's statement that "two things are called one, when the definitional formula (λόγος), which states the essence of one, is indivisible from another definitional formula, which shows the essence of the other, even though in itself every definitional formula is divisible [into genus and differentiae]." [69] This is later described by him as "one in species" (κατ' εἶδος; εἴδει) and is explained as referring to "those things whose definitional formula is one." [70] In one of his other works, Yaḥyā uses also the expression "one in species," [71] which he illustrates by the example of the application of the term "man" to "Zayd, ʿAmr, and Ḫālid," the same kind of example by which he also illustrates what he calls "one in definition and many in subject." This meaning of one is not considered by Yaḥyā as an answer to the question dealt with by him here, namely, why one god is described as three, for directly it is an answer to the question why three gods are described as one. Among the Church Fathers there was a difference of opinion with regard to this meaning of one as an explanation of triunity.[72]

[65] *Metaph.* VII, 12, 1037b, 8–23.
[66] *Ibid.*, 26–27.
[67] *Defense*, p. 13, ll. 7–8.
[68] *Ibid.*, p. 13, ll. 8–11.
[69] *Metaph.* V, 6; 1016a, 32–35.
[70] *Ibid.*, 1016b, 31–33.
[71] *Unity*, p. 131.
[72] Cf. *The Philosophy of the Church Fathers*, I, pp. 337, 348, 351.

This, then, is how Yaḥyā answers Kindī's two main objections. Against the objection that the hypostases could not be eternal because they are each composed of parts, he admits that they do each consist of parts but still they can be eternal because the parts of which they are each composed had never existed separately from each other, but have rather from eternity existed together in composition with each other. Against the objection that for a thing to be at once three and one is self-contradictory, he answers that this is possible if the thing is three and one from different points of view. He explains it by the following two meanings of the term one: (1) one in the sense of that which is one in definitional formula but many in names, as, for instance, the concept "man," of which the definitional formula is one in all languages, has in some languages, say, Arabic, two names, *insān* and *bashar*; (2) one in the sense of that which is one in subject but many in definitional terms, as, for instance, the term "Zayd" in the proposition "Zayd is a rational mortal animal."

But let us examine these two meanings and see what they imply.

According to the first meaning, the use of "one" in the Trinitarian formula is justified on the ground that the manyness of the hypostases is like the manyness of the two Arabic words for man or wine or ass or camel. This explanation quite evidently implies that the second and third hypostases are mere names and have no reality, which would thus make Yaḥyā a Sabellian. But Yaḥyā, as we have seen, is an outspoken believer in the reality of all the three hypostases.[73]

According to the second meaning, the use of "one" in the Trinitarian formula is justified by Yaḥyā on the ground that the manyness of the hypostases is likened by him to the manyness of the *maʿānī* by which he designates the mortality and rationality and animality which are predicated of one subject in the definitional proposition "Zayd is a mortal, ra-

[73] Cf. above at nn. 14 and 32.

tional animal." Now the term *maʿānī* may have been used by Yaḥyā here in either of two senses, either of which, however, would give rise to a difficulty. First, it may have been used by him in the sense of "things," for, in another work of his, he explains the "one" and the "three" in the Trinitarian formula by the analogy of the statement that "one thing (*shay'*)" may be described as being [in one respect] one thing and [in another respect] three things (*ashyā*), to which three things he subsequently refers as three *maʿānī* and as three *ṣifāt*.[74] But this would make this explanation the opposite of the explanation preceding it. Second, the term *maʿānī* may have been used by him here in the sense of an intellectual concept. But this would again make him a Sabellian.

Similar difficulties arise from his attempt in some of his other writings to explain the Trinity by other kinds of analogies.

One analogy used by him is the proposition "Zayd is a father, four cubits in height, and a physician." [75] A second analogy is the proposition "Zayd is a physician, geometrician, and scribe." [76] A third analogy is that of two mirrors which face each other. Any image in the first mirror will be reflected in the second mirror and thus produce in it image B. This image B will in turn be reflected in the first mirror and thus produce in it image C. These images, A, B, and C, are three insofar as each of them is distinguished from the one succeeding it by being related to it as cause to effect, but they are one insofar as images B and C are only reflections of image A.[77] This analogy, it may be noted, occurs in Abucara [78] and, before him, in Plotinus.[79] A fourth analogy is that of intellect (*ʿaḳl*, νοῦς), the act of intellection (*ʿāḳil*, νόησις), and the object of intellection (*maʿḳūl*, νοητόν, νοούμενον), which three are distinguishable from one another and yet all constitute one sub-

[74] *Petits*, p. 66, ll. 6–8, and p. 67, ll. 6–7.
[75] *Petits*, p. 49, ll. 1–9.
[76] *Trinity*, pp. 156, 167, 170.
[77] *Petits*, pp. 12–17; *Trinity*, pp. 157–160.
[78] Abucara, *Mimar* III, 21, p. 155.
[79] *Enn.* I, 1, 8.

stance.[80] A fifth analogy is that of packages on board a moving ship. In one respect, these packages may be described as being in motion, but in another respect they may be described as being at rest.[81] Now, of these five analogies, the first two correspond to what Aristotle calls "one according to accident," which he illustrates by the expression "the upright musician Corsicus." [82] But certainly Yaḥyā did not mean to imply by these analogies that the hypostases are accidents. As for the last three analogies, it is quite clear that, however the unity and the multiplicity in each of them may be described, the multiplicity in none of them has that kind of reality which, according to the orthodox Christian doctrine of the Trinity, is required by the multiplicity of the hypostases.

What, then, is the meaning of these analogies and what is Yaḥyā's own conception of the Trinity?

An answer to this question is furnished by Yaḥyā himself in one of his other treatises. In that treatise, Yaḥyā quotes first an anonymous opponent of Christianity as saying that all Christians, that is to say, all orthodox Christians, agree upon the formula "three hypostases (*aḳānīm*), one substance (*jauhar*)" [83] and then quotes him as arguing as follows: "If the Christians claim that the Father is like the sun which lightens with its light and warms with its heat, and the Son is like the rays of the sun, and the Spirit is like its heat, then they may be asked, Is this analogy based on the assumption that the rays and the heat are powers (*ḳuwā*) of the sun? If so, then, since the Son and the Spirit are, by the terms of this analogy, related to the Father in a similar way, they are excluded from the definition of hypostaticity and become two powers in God or two accidents in Him, and so, unlike Him, they are not hypostases." [84] In other words, while this Cappadocian formula, which is recited by all orthodox Christians, means that the hypostases are real beings, the analogy of the sun and its rays,

[80] *Petits*, pp. 18–20; *Trinity*, pp. 160–161.

[81] *Trinity*, p. 168.

[82] *Metaph.* V, 6, 1015b, 16–20.

[83] *Petits*, p. 36, l. 2. Cf. above n. 8.

[84] *Petits*, p. 38, l. 5–p. 39, l. 2.

which is equally used by orthodox Christians, implies that two of the three hypostases, namely, the Son and the Holy Spirit, are not real beings.

In refutation of this argument, Yaḥyā says: "The example of the sun and its rays is used by some Christian theologians only for the purpose of making their doctrine [of the Trinity] intelligible, by showing that among perceptible objects there is something which is one in one respect and more than one in another, and thereby thus refute the general opinion supposed and maintained by their opponents, namely, that nothing can be both one and many in any way or manner whatsoever. But it does not follow that when I apply a comparison to a thing with reference to a certain respect, the thing which is the object of comparison should resemble the thing to which it is compared with reference to all respects. Indeed, it is impossible to find two things between which there should be no difference at all, for multiplicity inevitably implies diversity, just as diversity implies multiplicity." [85] Again, "one must not assume that examples used by Christians are taken by them to resemble that to which they are likened in every respect." [86]

From the phrasing of the statement, it may be gathered that what Yaḥyā says here about the analogy of the sun and its rays is meant by him to be taken as a general principle which should be applied to all the other analogies used by him. In fact, his statement reflects the general attitude of the Church Fathers toward every analogy used by them in explaining the mystery of the Trinity.[87] Gregory of Nyssa has given expression to it in his statement: "Let one accept only what is fitting in the analogy but reject what is incongruous," [88] and Leontius of Byzantium has similarly given expression to it in his statement: "There is no exemplification but contains some unfitness." [89]

[85] *Ibid.*, p. 39, l. 3–p. 40, l. 4.
[86] *Ibid.*, p. 42, ll. 7–8.
[87] Cf. *The Philosophy of the Church Fathers*, I, pp. 428–429 and p. 304.
[88] *Oratio Catechetica* 10 (PG 45, 41 D).
[89] *Lib. Tres* I (PG 86^1, 1280 D).

But just as in the passage quoted about the sun and its rays Yaḥyā came out against the denial of the reality of the hypostases, so in another passage he comes out against a wrong interpretation of their reality. In that passage, he tries to answer an anonymous opponent of Christianity, whom he quotes as charging the Christians with the belief in three Gods on the ground of their assertion that God, who is one substance, is three hypostases and that each of the hypostases is God.[90] In answer to this charge, he says that it is only "the ignorant (*juhhāl*) among the Christians" against whom such a charge can be brought, for they erroneously and impiously suppose that "the three hypostases are essences (*dhawāt*) of three subjects (*mauḍūʿāt*) each of which differs from the other in itself," [91] and this, indeed, implies that "God is three substances (*jawāhir*) and three Gods." [92] By the expression "the ignorant among the Christians," I take it, he does not only mean the uneducated mass; he also means by it the followers of that doctrine known as Tritheism, for his description of these "ignorant among the Christians" reflects a passage in Photius, where the Tritheites are described as follows: "Some of the more shameless, having taken nature (*φύσιν*) and hypostasis (*ὑπόστασιν*) and essence (*οὐσίαν*) to mean the same, did not shrink from affirming also that in the Holy Trinity there are three essences (*οὐσίας*), whence they teach, if not in word, yet at least in thought, that there are three Gods and three Divinities." [93] The true Christian conception of the Trinity, Yaḥyā holds, is that of "the learned Imams" (*al-aʾimmah al-ʿulamāʾ*), that is to say, the Church Fathers, of whom he mentions "Dionysius [the Areopagite], Gregory [of Nazianzus or of Nyssa], Basil the Great, and John Chrysostom." [94] This

[90] *Petits*, p. 44, l. 8–p. 45, l. 2.
[91] *Ibid.*, p. 45, ll. 3–4.
[92] *Ibid.*, ll. 6–7.
[93] Photius, *Biblioth.* 230 (PG 103, 180 BC). The Greek *ὀυσία* means both "essence" and "substance" and, according to orthodox Christianity, in its sense of "essence," it is the same as "nature" but in its sense of "substance," it is the same as "hypostases."
[94] *Petits*, p. 53, ll. 4–6.

conception of the Trinity, he says, is acknowledged by "the three sects of the Christians,"[95] that is to say, the Malkites, the Nestorians, and the Jacobites. Elsewhere he makes it clear that the term "substance" in the expression "one substance" is to be taken to mean "essence" (*dhāt*)[96] or "quiddity" (*māhiyyah*)[97] and that the distinguishing properties of the three hypostases with reference to which the one God is three are paternity (*ubūwah*), filiation (*bunūwah*), and procession (*inbiʿāth*).[98]

From all this we gather that to the charge that the Christian affirmation that God is both one and three is an infringement on the Law of Contradiction Yaḥyā answers that there is no such infringement in that affirmation, inasmuch as the "oneness" is affirmed of God with respect to His essence and the "threeness" is affirmed of Him with respect to His hypostases. In justification of his answer Yaḥyā quotes certain propositions wherein one subject is in a similar way allowed to be described as being at once both one and many. None of these propositions, however, are taken by him to be completely analogous to the Trinitarian formula, that is to say, neither the oneness nor the manyness in these propositions is the same as the oneness and threeness in the Trinitarian formula. Underlying this is the common view of the Fathers of the Church that the Trinity is a mystery,[99] of which all the explanations attempted by them are not attempts to solve the mystery but only attempts to free the phrasing of its doctrinal formulation from the charge of being self-contradictory and meaningless, and they do this by showing how philosophers in a variety of ways justify the common practice of designating the many by the term "one."[100]

[95] *Ibid.*, p. 54, l. 8–p. 55, l. 1.
[96] *Petits*, p. 21, l. 7–p. 22, l. 3.
[97] *Defense*, p. 12, l. 15.
[98] *Petits*, p. 45, ll. 5–6.
[99] Cf. *The Philosophy of the Church Fathers*, I, pp. 287–288.
[100] *Ibid.*, pp. 309–310.

IV. An Unknown Splinter Group of Nestorians *

In Shahrastānī's account of the Christian sects that were known to the Muslim world, what is known as the orthodox Christian doctrine of the Trinity is to be found in his description of the doctrines of three main sects, the Malkites,[1] that is, the Byzantine Church, the Nestorians,[2] and the Jacobites,[3] that is, the Monophysites. Heretical conceptions of the Trinity are attributed by him to the Macedonians, Sabellians, and Arians.[4]

The conception of the Trinity held by all Christians who adhered to the orthodox doctrine, namely, the Malkites, the Nestorians, and the Jacobites, is described by Shahrastānī as follows: "They declare that God has three hypostases (*aḳā-nīm*). They say that the Creator is a single substance (*jauhar*) . . . one in substantiality and three in hypostaticality, and they mean by hypostases the attributes, such as existence, life, and knowledge, or the Father, the Son, and the Holy Spirit," knowledge being the Son or the Word, and of these three hypostases it is only the Son that is united with the body of Jesus by incarnation.[5] As against this common Trinitarian view of the three orthodox sects, Shahrastānī mentions the views on the Trinity of the three heretical sects. The common element in their heretical views is their refusal to believe in the eternity and reality of all the three hypostases, the Macedonians contending that the Holy Spirit was created, the Arians contending that both the Son and the Holy Spirit were created, and the Sabellians contending that God is "a single substance, a single hypostasis, having three properties, and united in its totality with the body of Jesus," the implication being that

* This section is based on my paper by the same title published in *Revue des Études Augustiniennes*, 6:249–253 (1960), supplemented by my paper "More about the Unknown Splinter Group of Nestorians," *ibid.*, 11:217–222 (1965).

[1] *Milal*, p. 173, ll. 4 ff.

[2] *Ibid.*, p. 175, ll. 9 ff.

[3] *Ibid.*, p. 176, ll. 19 ff.

[4] *Ibid.*, p. 178, l. 13–p. 179, l. 1.

[5] *Ibid.*, p. 172, ll. 8–11.

the three properties are not distinguished from each other nor from the single substance of hypostasis; they are thus mere names.[6]

Then under those who believed in the eternity and reality of all the three hypostases, Shahrastānī says of the Malkites that "they clearly state that the substance is other than the hypostases, the relation between them being like that between the bearer of an attribute and the attribute," [7] that is to say, the relation of the hypostases to the substance is like the relation of attributes to God as conceived by the Muslim Attributists. Of the Jacobite conception of the Trinity he says that "they believe in three hypostases, as we have mentioned," [8] that is to say, their view of the Trinity is like that of the Malkites, though, as he goes on, he tries to show that their view on Christology differed from that of either Malkites or the Nestorians. But in his description of the Trinitarian view of the Nestorians he starts out with the general statement that the founder of that sect, Nestorius, "said that God is one, possessing three hypostases: existence, knowledge, and life." This statement, so far, includes the Nestorians among the followers of the orthodox doctrine of the Trinity. Then, however, Shahrastānī goes on to report that, unlike the Malkites and the Jacobites who believe that "the substance [that is, the essence] is other than the hypostases," the Nestorians believe that "God is one possessing three hypostases (*aḳānīm*), existence and knowledge and life, but these hypostases are not superadded to the essence (*al-dhāt*) and they are not it (*huwa*),[9] that is to say, they are neither other than the essence nor the same as the essence, which means that they are neither existent nor

[6] *Ibid.*, p. 178, ll. 13–18.

[7] *Ibid.*, p. 173, ll. 18–19.

[8] *Ibid.*, p. 176, l. 19. Ibn Ḥazm (*Fiṣal* I, p. 49, ll. 9–10) describes the Jacobites as believing "that Christ was God and that God died, having been crucified." His description of the Jacobites is that of a special kind of Monophysite who approached Patripassianism.

[9] *Milal*, p. 175, ll. 11–12. The pronoun *huwa*, "he," has no antecedent here. It is probably a corruption of *hiya*, "she," of which the antecedent would be *al-dhāt*, "the essence." Hence, I translated it by "it." Cf. below at n. 31.

nonexistent. This conception of the hypostases in their relation to the essence is compared by him to the conception of "the modes (*aḥwāl*) of Abū Hāshim from among the Muʿtazilites," [10] referring thereby to the formulation of modes as being "neither God nor other than God" [11] and as being "neither existent nor nonexistent." [12]

According to Shahrastānī, then, the view of this group of Christians, described by him as Nestorians, stands midway between orthodox Trinitarianism and Sabellianism just as the Muslim Abū Hāshim's theory of modes stands midway between the realism of the Attributists and the nominalism of the Antiattributists. In Christianity, during the patristic period there was no distinction made between Modalism and Nominalism with regard to the problem of the Trinity.[13] There was no midway between the orthodox assertion of the reality of the second and third persons and the Sabellian denial of their reality. This group of Nestorians, however, has found an intermediate between these two extreme positions by attenuating the reality of the hypostases.

Then, having in mind the fact that the theory of modes originated primarily as a theory of universals and predication in general and that only afterwards was it applied to terms predicated of God,[14] he tries to compare the predication of God in the Nestorian Trinitarian formula to general logical predications. He starts his comparison by two preliminary explanations: (1) that the terms "knowledge" and "life" predicated of God in the Nestorian formula are predicated of Him in virtue of His being a knower, and a knower necessarily has life and knowledge; [15] (2) that the term "knowledge" predicated of God in the formula is what philosophers call "reason" (*nuṭḳ* = λόγος) and what in the New Testament is called "Word" (*kalimah* = λόγος).[16] He then goes on to say that

[10] *Ibid.*, ll. 15–16.
[11] *Farḳ*, p. 182, l. 14.
[12] *Ibid.*, l. 5; *Nihāyat*, p. 198, ll. 4–5.
[13] Cf. *The Philosophy of the Church Fathers*, I, p. 580.
[14] Cf. above, pp. 170–171.
[15] *Milal*, p. 175, ll. 17–18.
[16] *Ibid.*, l. 18.

"Nestorius' formula ultimately amounts to the assertion that God's being existent, living, and rational is as the philosophers say in the definition of man [that he is living and rational], except that in respect to man the things (*ma'ānī*) predicated of him differ, seeing that man is composite, whereas [in respect to God they do not differ], seeing that God is a simple substance, incomposite." [17] All this is in agreement with what we have seen is Abū Hāshim's theory of modes, according to which such terms as "living" and "rational," when predicated of man, are modes of the type he would call generic and specific attributes;[18] and, furthermore, such two or more terms, when predicated of man, would imply a multiplicity of modes in him, whereas all such terms, when predicated of God, would be reducible to the single mode of Godhood.[19] What this new conception of the Trinity means, according to Shahrastānī's interpretation, is that it gives modalistic interpretation to the Trinity, somewhat after the analogy of its modalistic interpretation of the meaning of the logical definition of man, thereby defending the Trinity against the Muslim charge that it was inconsistent with the unity of God.

But who were those Christians who held this new conception of the Trinity? Shahrastānī calls them "Nestorians." But he cannot mean by it the Nestorians as known to us from the history of Christianity and as also known to the Muslims. To begin with, we know that Nestorius was orthodox in his view on the Trinity. Then, we have the testimony of Mas'ūdī that the Nicene Creed constituted the creed of "the Malkites, the Jacobites, and the Ibādites or Nestorians, and it was recited by them daily in their liturgy." [20] Then, also, in Ibn Ḥazm's account of Christianity, the Nestorians are said to hold the same view as the orthodox Malkites on the doctrine of the Trinity.[21] Then, again, Yaḥyā Ibn 'Adī says that all the three Christian

[17] *Ibid.*, ll. 18–20.
[18] Cf. above, p. 187, at n. 16.
[19] Cf. above, pp. 172–174.
[20] Mas'ūdī, *Tanbīh*, p. 142, ll. 11–12 (196).
[21] *Fiṣal* I, p. 49, l. 5.

sects, that is, the Malkites, the Nestorians, and the Jacobites, are fully in agreement on the doctrine of the Trinity.[22] Finally, Shahrastānī describes the founder of these "Nestorians" of his as "*Nasṭūr al-ḥakīm*," that is, Nestorius the Wise or the Philosopher or the Physician, "who appeared in the time of Ma'mūn," [23] that is, during his reign (813–833). Ibn Athīr takes the Nestorius in this passage of Shahrastānī to refer to the historical founder of Nestorianism, who died in 451, and hence charges Shahrastānī with ignorance of the history of Nestorianism.[24] But such an ignorance on the part of Shahrastānī is unlikely. For one thing, a full account of the rise of Nestorianism is given in the works of such a well-known Arabic historian as Mas'ūdī (d. 912), where it is explicitly stated that Nestorius was Patriarch of Constantinople, that he flourished during the reign of Emperor Theodosius II, that he was a contemporary of Cyril of Alexandria, and that he was excommunicated at the Council of Ephesus.[25] It is inconceivable that Shahrastānī (d. 1153) should not have been acquainted with these facts. Then, also, Shahrastānī's detailed description of the founder of those whom he calls here Nestorians, such as the time in which he lived and his surname *al-ḥakim*, by which the historical Nestorius of Constantinople is not known to have been called, shows that he has reference here to a person who actually existed and was known as *Nasṭūr al-ḥakīm*, who flourished during the reign or the lifetime of Ma'mūn, who was himself a Nestorian, and whose followers continued to belong to the Nestorians, forming an indistinguishable group within the Nestorians. Now it happens that a Nestorian bishop, by the name of Nestorius, which in Arabic is Nastūr, flourished in Adiabene, on the Tigris, at about 800,[26] which corresponds exactly to Shahrastānī's "in

[22] Périer, *Petits*, p. 55, ll. 1 ff.

[23] *Milal*, p. 175, l. 9.

[24] Ibn al-Athīr, *Kitāb al-Kāmil fī al-Tārīḫ* (ed. C. J. Tornberg, I, p. 237, ll. 12–15. Cf. Sweetman, *Islam and Christianity*, II, 1, p. 28.

[25] *Murūj*, II, pp. 327, 328; *Tanbīh*, pp. 148–150 (204–207).

[26] Cf. *Dictionary of Christian Biography*, *s. v.* "*Nestorius* (6)"; *The*

the time of Ma'mūn." Nothing much is known about this Nestorian Bishop Nestorius, but he is as suitable a candidate as one could wish for that "Nestorius the Sage," who has given a new turn to the Christian doctrine of the Trinity, the followers of which are described by Shahrastānī as "Nestorians," and whose doctrine of Christology, as described by Shahrastānī, is Nestorian.

However, in Shahrastānī's account of the Nestorians' conception of the Trinity, one is to distinguish between his testimony as to their use of a new Trinitarian formula and his own view that this new formula for the Trinity is analogous with Abū Hāshim's formula for modes. With regard to his testimony, one may find confirmation for it in Juwaynī who says that, according to the Christians, "the hypostases are to the substance as the modes are to it, according to those Muslims who believe in modes." [27] Now there is no explanation for the ascription of such a modalistic conception of the Trinity to Christians in general except on the assumption that Juwaynī, who lived in Iran, had become acquainted with that new formulation of the Trinity through his contact with the Christians of Iran who were predominantly Nestorians. It is to be noted that even Shahrastānī, who in the passage quoted explicitly identifies only the Trinitarian formula of the Nestorians with the modalistic formula of Abū Hāshim, in two other passages [28] identifies the Trinitarian formula of Christians in general with Abū Hāshim's formula for modes, and this probably also because in Iran, where he lived, that was the prevailing formula used by Christians. Moreover, there is evidence, as I shall try to show later, which corroborates Shahrastānī's statement that this new Nestorian formula for the Trinity was introduced "in the time of Ma'mūn." With regard, however, to Shahrastānī's view, which, as we

---

Book of Governors: The Historia Monastica of Thomas Bishop of Marga, ed. and trans. F. A. W. Budge (1893), I, p. 279, l. 12; II, p. 506.

[27] *Irshād*, p. 28, ll. 14–15 (53).

[28] *Milal*, p. 34, ll. 19–20; *Nihāyat*, p. 198, ll. 2–6.

have seen above, is also the view of Juwaynī, that the new Nestorian formula for the Trinity is analogous to Abū Hāshim's formula for modes, I shall try to show that a formula analogous to the New Trinitarian formula had been used by orthodox Muslim Attributists as an expression of their belief in the reality of attributes. The same distinction is also to be made in Juwaynī's account of the general Christian doctrine of the Trinity.

Let us first examine Shahrastānī's statement that the new Nestorian formula for the Trinity is analogous to Abū Hāshim's formula for modes.

It happens that long before Abū Hāshim used the formula "not God and not other than God" for his unorthodox doctrine of modes, Sulaymān b. Jarīr used the same formula for the orthodox doctrine of attributes.[29] Since Sulaymān b. Jarīr died in 785, which is before the reign of Ma'mūn, during which reign the new Nestorian Trinitarian formula appeared, whereas Abū Hāshim died in 933, long after that reign, it is quite evident that it is in the light of the formula as used by Sulaymān b. Jarīr rather than in the light of the formula used by Abū Hāshim that the new Nestorian formula is to be studied.

Studied in the light of this orthodox Muslim formula, this new Nestorian formula, it can be shown, is no deviation from the orthodox Christian conception of the Trinity, though the change in its phrasing may be assumed to be an attempt at a verbal accommodation to the Muslim doctrine of attributes.

Let us now examine the two parts of this new formula.

As for the first part of the formula, namely, that the hypostases "are not superadded to the essence," if we assume that its phrasing was meant to correspond to that part of the orthodox Muslim formula which asserted that the attributes "are not other than God," we must also assume that it has the same meaning as its prototype in the Muslim doctrine. Now the expression "are not other than God" in the Muslim formula

[29] Cf. above, pp. 207 and 209.

means, as we have shown,[30] that the attributes are coeternal with God and that they are not separable from Him. Consequently, the expression "not superadded to the essence" must similarly mean that the hypostases are coeternal with the essence and that they are not separable from it. But this is good Christian doctrine; and thus the difference between the expression "not superadded to the essence" in the new Trinitarian formula and the expression "one essence" in the original Trinitarian formula is only verbal.

As for the second part of the new Nestorian formula, which we have taken to mean that the hypostases are "not the essence," even on the assumption that the phrasing was meant to correspond to that part of the Muslim formula which asserted that the attributes "are not God," we shall try to show that the framers of this new Nestorian formula did not deviate from the orthodox Christian conception of the Trinity, according to which each of the hypostases is God.

It will be noticed that the formula does not say that the hypostases are not God; it only says that the hypostases "are not it," that is, the *dhāt*, "the essence." [31] Now the Arabic term *dhāt*, "essence," stands here for the Greek *οὐσία* in the Cappadocian "one *ousia*, three hypostases." But according to the orthodox Christian conception of the Trinity, while the expression "one *ousia*" means not only that all three hypostases are coeternal and inseparable in *ousia* but also that they are one in Godhood, still the hypostases, by reason of their being really distinct from each other, are not assumed to be altogether the same as the essence; they are assumed to be in some respect distinct from the essence, as may be gathered from the analogies by which the Church Fathers tried to explain the relation between them and the essence. Thus, according to Basil and John of Damascus, both of whom identified the "essence" with the first hypostasis, the Father,[32] the relation between the essence and the hypostases is explained after the

[30] Cf. above, p. 210.

[31] Cf. above, p. 338, at n. 9.

[32] Cf. *The Philosophy of the Church Fathers*, I, pp. 352–353.

analogy of the relation between the species "man" and individual human beings, such as "Peter, Andrew, John, and James," mentioned by Basil,[33] or "Peter and Paul," mentioned by John of Damascus.[34] Similarly Augustine, to whom the "essence" is the common substratum of all the three hypostases and who rejects the analogy of the relation between species and individual, explains the relation between essence and hypostases and three statues made of gold.[35] Thus, according to either analogy, the hypostases in their relation to the essence are in some respect not altogether the same as the essence. Consequently, with regard to the statement in the second part of the new Nestorian formula, namely, that the hypostases "are not the essence," while to the Muslims it might have sounded like their own statement about the attributes — that they "are not God" — to the Nestorians themselves it meant that, while the hypostases are one in essence in the sense that they were one in Godhood, they "are not the essence" insofar as the essence is related to them either as a species to individuals or as gold to statues made of gold.

Corroborative evidence that the new Nestorian formula for the Trinity was modeled after the analogy of a Muslim formula as used by its orthodox Attributists and not as used by its unorthodox Modalists is to be found in a work by Joseph al-Baṣīr, who flourished either in Iraq or in Iran at the beginning of the eleventh century.

Two statements are quoted by al-Baṣīr in the name of "the Christians," which I shall reproduce here in reverse order. The second of these statements reads as follows: "In a similar way they say: Three hypostases, one substance (*jauhar*), one God." [36] This is an accurate restatement of the Cappadocian Trinitarian formula, in which the term *ousia* is translated, as it often is in Arabic versions of this formula, by "substance"

[33] *Epist.* 38, 2 (PG 32, 325 B); cf. 38, 3 (328 A).
[34] *De Fide Orthodoxa* III, 4 (PG 94, 997 A).
[35] Cf. *The Philosophy of the Church Fathers*, I, p. 351.
[36] *Ne'imot*, Arabic, p. 45a, ll. 2–3; Hebrew, p. 22b, l. 22.

rather than by "essence" (*dhāt*).[37] As for the phrase "one God," it is quite correctly added as an explanation of what is implied in "one substance." The first statement is embedded in the following passage: "The view of the Christians is analogous to the view of the Attributists. The Attributists assert that we do not describe the knowledge of God either as existent or as nonexistent, either as created or as eternal, either as the same as God or as other than God. The Christians likewise assert that, with regard to the hypostases, we do not say that they differ from each other and we do not say that they are each the same as the other, so that, with regard to the hypostasis of the Son, they do not say either that it is the same as the hypostasis of the Father or that it is other than it." [38]

In this latter quotation, the statement that "the hypostases are not different from each other and they are not each the same as the other," which al-Baṣīr quotes in the name of the Christians, reflects the formula quoted by Shahrastānī, and it points to the use of that formula by the Christians referred to by al-Baṣīr. But it will be noticed that the Muslim formula with which al-Baṣīr compares this statement of the Christians is ascribed by him not to Abū Hāshim but to "the Attributists," which Attributists he subsequently identifies with "Kullabites" (*kullābiyyah*),[39] that is, followers of Ibn Kullāb (d. 845), who was an orthodox believer in the reality of attributes [40] and, like his predecessor Sulaymān b. Jarīr, used a formula for the expression of his belief in real attributes, which was later adopted by Abū Hāshim as an expression for his belief in modes. Now, as far as I know, there is no reference anywhere to the use by Christians of the statement that "the hypostases are not different from each other and they are not each the same as the other," though it is not contrary to the Christian

[37] Cf. above, p. 128, n. 88.

[38] *Ne'imot*, Arabic, p. 44b, l. 14–p. 45a, l. 2; Hebrew, p. 22b, ll. 16–22.

[39] *Ne'imot*, Arabic, p. 45b, ll. 8 ff.; Hebrew, p. 23a, ll. 16 ff. (quoted in P. F. Frankl, *Ein Mu'tazilitischen Kalām aus dem 10. Jahrhundert* (1872), pp. 53–55.

[40] *Maḳālāt*, p. 169, ll. 10–13; p. 514, ll. 15–16; p. 546, ll. 9, 11; p. 548, ll. 1–2.

conception of the hypostases in their relation to each other. Undoubtedly, then, this statement was quoted by al-Baṣīr from Christians in his own locality, either Iraq or Iran, in either of which places the Christians were predominantly Nestorians. But the fact that he also quotes in their name the Cappadocian formula shows that they were orthodox in their conception of the Trinity. Furthermore, the fact that he compares this statement with a formula used by Muslims who believed in the reality of attributes shows that the Christians whose statement he quotes believed in the reality of the hypostases of the Trinity.

We thus have here corroborative evidence that among the Nestorians in Iraq and Iran there were those who, in an attempt to accommodate their doctrine of the Trinity to the Muslim doctrine of attributes, adopted a formula like that quoted by Shahrastānī, but that formula was used by them not in the sense in which it was used by Abū Hāshim — as an expression of a belief in modes — but rather in the sense in which it was used by some Attributists — as an expression of their belief in the reality of attributes. Those Nestorians, therefore, still continued to be orthodox in their Trinitarian belief: the accommodation was only verbal.

Now for the evidence which corroborates, as mentioned above, Shahrastānī's statement that the new Nestorian formula for the Trinity was introduced "in the time of Ma'mūn."

In a work written in Baghdad during the year 933, exactly a century after the death of Ma'mūn, in whose time, according to Shahrastānī, the new Nestorian formula for the Trinity made its appearance, Saadia discusses the Christology of four Christian sects.[41] The second of these sects can be identified as the historically known Nestorians. The fourth sect is described by him as that which "appeared only recently," and its Christology is reproduced as follows: "They assign to Jesus the position of a prophet only, and they

[41] Cf. my paper "Saadia on the Trinity and Incarnation." *Studies and Essays in Honor of Abraham A. Neuman* (1962), pp. 547–568.

interpret the sonship of which they make mention when they speak of him just as we interpret the Biblical expression 'Israel is My first-born son' (Exod. 4:22), which is merely an expression of esteem and high regard, or as others [= Muslims] interpret the description of Abraham as the 'friend' of God [Surah 4:124]." [42] Now by this fourth sect with its Ebionitic type of Christology, Saadia could not have meant the Samosatenians or the Arians or the Macedonians, all of whom held such a Christology, for all of them were known to Arabic-speaking peoples at the time of Saadia as old Christian sects, and Saadia could not have referred to any one of them as a sect which "appeared only recently." Quite evidently the reference is either to an old sect which had recently adopted this Christology or to an entirely new sect which had revived this Christology. Who, then, were the members of this sect?

An answer to this question may be found in that passage in Shahrastānī from which we have gathered our information about the splinter group of Nestorians who reframed their Trinitarian formula. In that passage, dealing with the Christology of the Nestorians, after reproducing the view that is traditionally ascribed to them, namely, that in the born Christ there are "two hypostases and two natures," [43] Shahrastānī discusses various Christological views held by various groups of Nestorians and in the course of his discussion he reproduces a view which he introduces by the words "And Photinus and Paul of Samosata say." [44] From the context, however, it is evident that these introductory words mean "And [some Nestorians, following] Photinus and Paul of Samosata, say." The view which ascribes to those Nestorians who followed Photinus and Paul of Samosata reads as follows: "The Messiah took his origin from Mary; he is a righteous servant and created, except that God has honored him and favored him because of his obedience and called him 'son' by adoption and not by begetting and union." [45] This is exactly like the Chris-

[42] *Emunot ve-De'ot* II, 7, p. 90, l. 21 – p. 91, l. 2.
[43] *Milal*, p. 176, l. 6.
[44] *Ibid.*, l. 11.
[45] *Ibid.*, ll. 11–13.

tological view ascribed by Saadia to the sect which "appeared only recently." What we have here then is, again, a report that a certain group of Nestorians — of whom Saadia knew that they "appeared only recently," that is, about seventy years before he was born (882), during the reign of Ma'mūn, and in the neighborhood of Baghdad, where Saadia wrote that statement — in an attempt to accommodate their belief about Jesus with that of the Muslims, according to whom Jesus was "only an apostle of God" (Surah 4:69), rephrased their common Nestorian Christology into an Ebionitic form of Christology. That they should have done so is not surprising. From its very beginning, Nestorianism was variously represented. Already during the lifetime of its founder, two Latin Church Fathers represented it as an Ebionitic Christology, like that we have quoted from Shahrastānī, even comparing it, like Shahrastānī, to the Christology of Photinus and Paul of Samosata. Thus Cassian compares the Nestorian heresy to the Ebionitic and Photinian heresies and describes it as believing that Christ is a mere man (*homo solitarius*),[46] and Marius Mercator finds that Nestorius, like Paul of Samosata, believed that Christ is the Son of God only as a reward of good actions and by adoption, not by nature (*pro meritis, et ex adoptione, non ex natura*).[47] Probably such a conception of Christology had already been vaguely floating about among the Nestorians in Iraq when it was crystallized by a splinter group among them during the reign of Caliph Ma'mūn.

V. Muslim Attributes in Medieval Christianity [1]

Though the doctrine of attributes in Islam originated under the influence of the Christian doctrine of the Trinity,[2] and

[46] *De Incarnatione Christi, Adversus Nestorium* I, 2 (PL 50, 18–19) and V, 2 (98 f.).

[47] *Epistola de Discrimine etc.* 2 (PL 48, 773 B).

[1] Based on pp. 49–64 of the chapter entitled "Extradeical and Intradeical Interpretations of Platonic Ideas" in my *Religious Philosophy*, pp. 27–68.

[2] Cf. above, pp. 112ff.

the controversy over attributes in Islam ran parallel to the controversy over the Trinity in Christianity,[3] there was no problem of attributes in Christianity, that is to say, there was no problem as to whether the various terms predicated of God in the two Scriptures implied the existence of any real things in God corresponding to those terms predicated of Him. Among the Fathers of the Church a distinction was drawn between the terms "Father," "Son," and "Holy Spirit," which were referred to as persons or hypostases, and all other terms predicated of God. As for the persons, they were regarded as real beings, which, though distinct from each other, were one in essence and thus constituted one triune God. As for all other terms, they were regarded as mere names descriptive of certain perfections of God, which were to be interpreted either as negations or as actions.

This was the situation in Christianity until about the middle of the ninth century. Then four events occurred which mark the history of the problem of attributes in Christianity.

The first event was a view with regard to Platonic ideas advanced by John Scotus Erigena (*c.* 800 – *c.* 877), which implied a theory of attributes like that held by the Attributists in Islam.[4] The second event was a view alleged to draw a distinction between the perfections predicated of God and the essence of God advanced by Gilbert de la Porrée (1076–1154), which again implied a theory of attributes like that held by the Attributists in Islam.[5] Both these views were condemned, the view of Gilbert by the Council of Rheims in 1148 and the view of Erigena by the Council of Paris in 1207.

Then something else happened. Early in the thirteenth century, certainly before 1235, there appeared a Latin translation of Maimonides' work *The Guide of the Perplexed*, which contained an account of the Muslim controversies over the problem of divine attributes and a presentation of his own

[3] Cf. above, pp. 133ff.

[4] Cf. *Religious Philosophy*, pp. 54–55.

[5] *Ibid.*, pp. 55–56.

elaborate theory in opposition to the reality of attributes. This Latin translation was made not from the original Arabic, in which the book was written, but from one of its two Hebrew versions. In that Hebrew version, the Arabic term *ṣifah*, which, as said above, reflects the Greek term τὸ χαρακτηριστικόν used in connection with the Trinity, was translated by two Hebrew terms, *middah* and *to'ar*. These two terms, in turn, are translated by three Latin terms: *dispositio*, *attributio*, and *nominatio*.[6] Of these three terms, each of which reflects one of the senses of the two Hebrew terms as well as of their underlying Arabic term, the term *attributio*, used in this translation in the sense of a divine predicate, is of special interest. By the time this translation was made, the Latin term *attributio* or *attributum* in the technical sense of "predicate" was not altogether unknown. According to the *Thesaurus Linguae Latinae* it was used in that technical sense by Cicero. But it was never used, as far as I know, as a designation of terms predicated of God, either in a work originally written in Latin or in a work translated from the Arabic into Latin. In the Latin translation of Ghazālī's *Maḳāṣid al-Falāsifah*, which was made in the twelfth century by John Hispalensis, the Arabic *ṣifah* is translated, not by *attributio* or *attributum*, but by *assignatio*.[7] The verb *attribuere*[8] and the noun *attributio*[9] do indeed occur in the Latin translation of Avicebrol's *Fons Vitae*, also made in the twelfth century by John Hispalensis, but from the context it may be gathered that in both its forms the term is used not in the sense of "predicate" and still less in the sense of "divine predicate" but rather in the sense of "gift," "addition," "cause."

This is event number three.

The fourth event is a double-header.

[6] Rabi Mossei Aegyptii, *Dux seu Director dubitantium aut perplexorum*, lib. I, cap. XLIX, fol. XVIIIa, l. 28; cap. LI, fol. XVIIIb, l. 41 (Paris, 1520).

[7] *Algazel's Metaphysics*, ed. J. T. Muckle (1933), p. 62, l. 2; cf. Arabic text: *Maqāṣid al-Falāsifah*, p. 149, l. 12.

[8] Avencebrolis (Ibn Gebirol), *Fons Vitae*, ed. Baeumker (1895), p. 92, l. 27.

[9] Albertus Magnus, *In I Sent.* III, 4.

Between the years 1245–1250 and between the years 1254–1256 Albertus Magnus and Thomas Aquinas respectively published their commentaries on the *Sentences* of Peter Lombard. In these commentaries, both of them for the first time used the term "attributes" instead of the traditional term "names" as a description of the various perfections predicated of God. Moreover, both of them, as soon as they introduced the term "attributes," raised the question, which, as phrased by Albert, reads: "Whether attributes in God are one or many?" [10] and, as phrased by Thomas, reads: "Whether in God are many attributes?" [11] The meaning of the question is whether or not the attributes are really distinct from God and from each other.

This is the succession of events in the history of post-Patristic Christian philosophy relating to the problem of attributes: (1) Erigena's theory of ideas; (2) the alleged Gilbert's view on the reality of the distinction between the perfections predicated of God and the essence of God; (3) the introduction into Christian Latin philosophy of the term "attributes" in the sense of divine predicates and withal a knowledge of the Muslim controversies about it; (4) the use of the term "attribute" and the raising of the problem of attributes by Albertus Magnus and Thomas Aquinas. The question naturally arises in our mind whether there is any causal connection between the first three events and the fourth event. In answer to this question, it may be said that with regard to the first two events there is an argument from silence showing that there is no connection between these two events and the fourth event. Neither Albert nor Thomas, throughout their discussions of the problem of attributes, makes any reference or allusion to Erigena or to Gilbert. Besides, while Gilbert was accused of believing in a real distinction between the perfection predicated of God and God, he was not accused of believing in a real distinction between the perfections them-

[10] *Ibid.*, p. 182, l. 9.
[11] Thomas Aquinas, *In I Sent.* II, 1, 2.

selves; quite the contrary, he is said to have believed that all the perfections predicated of God constitute one form in God.[12] There is, however, evidence of a connection between the new problem raised about attributes and the Latin translation of the work of Maimonides. First, there is St. Thomas himself, who in his commentary on the *Sentences*, after introducing the term attribute and raising the problem of attributes, quotes Maimonides and takes issue with him.[13] Second, there is Occam, who says: "The holy men of old did not use that word attributes (*attributa*) but in its stead they used the word names (*nomina*), whence, in contrast to certain moderns who say that divine attributes are distinct and diverse, the ancients and those who were at the time of the ancient masters said that divine names are distinct and diverse, wherefrom it follows that they laid down a distinction only with reference to names and a diversity only with reference to signs, but with reference to the things signified they assumed identity and unity"; [14] and in support of this Occam goes on to quote Augustine and Peter Lombard. The term "attributes" was thus regarded by Occam as a new-fangled term, of recent origin, which had come to replace the old traditional term "names," and he makes it unmistakably clear that there was no problem of the relation of attributes to God as long as "names" was used instead of "attributes," and that the problem arose only with the introduction of the term "attributes." Thus the use of the term attribute and the rise of the problem of attributes in medieval Christian philosophy had their origin in the Latin translation of Maimonides' *Guide of the Perplexed*.

[12] *Op. cit.* above, n. 94 (597 C–D).

[13] *In I Sent.* II, 1, 3c.

[14] *Quodlibet* III, 2 (Strasburg, 1491): "Sancti antiqui non utebantur isto vocabulo attributa, sed pro isto utebantur hoc vocabulo nomina. Unde sicut quidam moderni dicunt quod attributa divina sunt distincta et diversa, ita dicebant antiqui et qui erant tempore antiquorum doctorum quod nomina divina sunt distincta et diversa, ita quod non posuerunt distinctionem nisi in nominibus et unitatem in re significata et diversitatem in signis" (quoted with omissions by P. Vignaux in *Dictionnaire de Théologie Catholique*, vol. 11, col. 757).

This is how the Muslim problem of attributes was introduced into medieval Christian philosophy. From medieval Christian philosophy through Descartes [15] and from medieval Jewish philosophy through Spinoza [16] it was later introduced into modern philosophy.

[15] Cf. *Religious Philosophy*, pp. 65–66.
[16] *Ibid.*, pp. 66–67.

CHAPTER V

CREATION OF THE WORLD

I. Creation *Ex Nihilo*

1. HISTORICAL BACKGROUND

Through various sources, authentic and pseudepigraphic, the Mutakallimūn became acquainted with certain theories of the origin of the world of which they disapproved.[1] The theory which they approved of is that which is commonly known as creation *ex nihilo*, but which they describe as creation "not from something" (*lā min shay'*).[2] This theory is ascribed to "those who profess the unity of God" (*al-muwaḥḥidūn*),[3] by which is meant "the Muslims" (*al-muslimūn*).[4]

A conception of creation expressed explicitly in terms which mean creation *ex nihilo* is not to be found either in the Jewish or in the Christian or in the Muslim Scripture. The phrase *ex nihilo* is ultimately an interpretation of an expression which occurs in the Second Book of Maccabees 7:28, where God is said to have made heaven and earth and all that is therein οὐκ ἐξ ὄντων, "not from things existent," on the basis of which Church Fathers, to mention only the earliest one, the Pastor of Hermas, and the latest one, John of Damascus, in their formulation of the doctrine of creation, describe creation as being "from the nonexistent" (ἐκ τοῦ μὴ ὄντος).[5] From the context, however, it can be shown that by "nonexistent" they mean "nothing." It can be further shown that Philo[6] and some of the Church Fathers[7] who have adopted

[1] *Farḳ*, p. 346, ll. 8–17; *Uṣūl*, p. 59, l. 6 – p. 60, l. 11; *Fiṣal* I, p. 9, l. 17; p. 23, l. 16; p. 24, l. 21; p. 34, l. 13.

[2] Cf. below, p. 367. [3] *Uṣūl*, p. 70, l. 3. [4] *Ibid.*, p. 71, l. 10.

[5] *Hermae Pastor* II, Mand. I (PG 2, 913); *De Fide Orthod.* II, 5 (PG 94, 880 A).

[6] Cf. *Philo*, I, pp. 300–310.

[7] *Ibid.*, pp. 323–329, and my paper "Plato's Pre-existent Matter in Patristic Philosophy," *The Classical Tradition*, ed. Luitpold Wallach (1966), pp. 409–420.

the Platonic theory of creation out of a pre-existent matter made that matter to have been created out of nothing, thus indicating that the term "nonexistent" implied in Philo's description of creation as an act by which God brought into existence "things that were nonexistent" (τὰ μὴ ὄντα),[8] as well as the term "nonexistent" commonly used by the Church Fathers as a description of that out of which the world was created, were used by all of them in the sense of nothing. This use of the term "nonexistent" in the sense of nothing can be traced to two passages in Aristotle. In one passage, contrasting his own view with that of Platonists who have conceived of Plato's pre-existent matter as "the nonexistent" (τὸ μὴ ὄν),[9] he says that "matter" is nonexistent only "accidentally," whereas "privation" is nonexistent "essentially"[10] and, in another passage, having in mind that use of the term "nonexistent" described by him as being nonexistent essentially, he says that "the nonexistent" (τὸ μὴ ὄν) is "nothing" (μηδέν).[11] Explicitly, however, the first use of the phrase "out of nothing" as a description of creation occurs, in Latin, in Tertullian's *Adversus Marcionem*, composed at about 207, where creation is described by the phrase *de nihilo*,[12] and, in Greek, in Hippolytus' *Refutatio Omnium Haeresium*, composed not long after 222, where creation is described by the phrase ἐξ οὐδενός.[13]

Simultaneously with the formal speculation by the spokesmen of Christianity about the creation of the world and their explicit avowal of a belief in creation *ex nihilo*, there were informal discussions by the spokesmen of Judaism on the meaning of creation. In the Agadic literature of the time, there are references and allusions to attempts at interpreting

[8] *Opif.* 26, 81; *Mut.* 5, 46; *Mos.* II, 20, 100; cf. *Somn.* I, 13, 76.

[9] *Phys.* I, 9, 192a, 6–7.

[10] *Ibid.*, 4–5.

[11] *De Gen. et Corr.* I, 3, 318a, 15; cf. *Phys.* I, 19, 122a, 6.

[12] *Adv. Marcionem* II, 5. Later in the Latin translation of II Macc. 7:28 the phrase used reads *ex nihilo*.

[13] *Refut. Omn. Haeres.* X, 33, 8, p. 290, l. 8.

the story of creation in the Book of Genesis as meaning creation out of something, without making it clear whether that something was eternal or created or emanated from God.[14] The direct teachings of the rabbis, however, are always to the effect that the creation of the world was from nothing. One characteristic passage may be mentioned here. In answer to a challenge by one described as a "philosopher" who argued that certain terms in Genesis 1:2 refer to pre-existent eternal things out of which the world was created, the rabbi so challenged quoted scriptural verses to show that the things assumed by the "philosopher" to be pre-existent and eternal were really created.[15] Though it is not clear whether the rabbi admitted that they were pre-existent but only denied that they were eternal or whether he denied both that they were pre-existent and that they were eternal, it is quite clear that he was insistent upon what we call creation *ex nihilo*. However, no phrase literally corresponding to the Greek *ἐξ οὐδενός* or the Latin *de* or *ex nihilo* was coined by the rabbis to express their belief that creation was out of nothing.

Similarly the position of the Koran on the meaning of creation is vague. On the one hand, there is the verse, which would seem to imply creation out of something pre-existent. It is the verse which reads: "Then He applied himself to the [creation of] heaven, and it was smoke" (41:10). But this verse lent itself to two interpretations. According to Zamakhsharī, the pre-existent smoke itself was created, for, according to his interpretation of the verse, the smoke proceeded from the water under the throne of God, and the throne of God

[14] See Maimonides' speculation about one of these Agadot, that of R. Eliezer the Great in *Pirḳe de-Rabbi Eliezer* 3, as to whether the pre-existent light and snow were created or eternal. Modern scholars take these Agadot to imply creation out of something pre-existent which was emanated from God. See Neumark, *Geschichte*, I, i, pp. 52–53, 81–83, 87–93, 97–101; *Toledot*, I, pp. 51–52, 65–66, 71–75, 86–89; Altmann, "Note on the Rabbinic Doctrine of Creation," *The Journal of Jewish Studies*, 7:195–206 (1956).

[15] *Genesis Rabbah* 1, 5.

is one of the things created before the heavens and the earth,[16] thus suggesting a view like that held by Philo and some of the Church Fathers. According to Averroes,[17] however, the verse means that "the heaven was created from something," that is, from something eternal.[18] There is, indeed, in the Koran a statement which would seem to imply that creation was *ex nihilo*. It occurs in a Surah where Muhammad hurls a series of challenges at unbelievers who accused him of having forged the Koran himself (52:33). First, he says: "Let them then produce a discourse like it" (52:34). Then, he says: "Created they the heavens and earth?" (52:36). Between these two challenges, there is the following: "Were they created *min ghayri shay'in*?" (52:35). Now the phrase *min ghayri shay'in* could be taken to mean "from nothing" [19] and, if so taken, it would imply that the subsequent question, "Created they the heavens and earth?", means "Created they the heavens and earth from nothing?" However, the verse in question, with the phrase *min ghayri shay'in*, may be also taken to mean "Were they created by nothing?" [20] or "Were they created for no purpose?" [21] Similarly the tradition that prior to creation "God existed and there was nothing with Him" [22] does not by itself necessarily mean creation *ex nihilo*; it may only mean that God was the sole creator. Nor does the term *badī'u* which occurs in the twice-used expression "Creator (*badī'u*) of the heaven and the earth" (2:111; 6:101) necessarily mean creator *ex nihilo* on the mere ground, as explained by Jurjānī, that, in the case of God's creation of man, the term used is *ḫalaḳa*, "He created" (55:13).[23] Against this explanation one might argue that the fact that many more

[16] Quoted by Sale in a note on his translation of the Koran, on 41:10.
[17] *Faṣl al-Maḳāl*, p. 13, ll. 11–12.
[18] *Ibid*., ll. 6–7.
[19] So translated by Palmer and Ali.
[20] So translated by Sale and Rodwell.
[21] So translated by Bell.
[22] Buḫārī, *Saḥīḥ*, ed. Krehl, Vol. II, Bab I, p. 302, ll. 12–13.
[23] *Ta'rifāt*, p. 6, ll. 1–5.

times than twice is the term *ḫalaḳa* used in describing God as He "who created the heaven and the earth" (10:3, et al.) quite clearly indicates that, in those two verses in which the term *badīʿu* is used, the reason for its use there was not because the kind of creation meant to be conveyed by it differed from that which would have been conveyed by the term *ḫaliḳ*. On the whole, we may assume that, while early Muslims knew that creation meant opposition to eternity and while they may have thought of it as being out of nothing, they were not aware of the problem wheather creation was out of nothing or out of a pre-existent formless matter. An awareness of this problem, as we shall see, appeared later.

2. THE KALAM CONTROVERSY OVER THE NONEXISTENT (*al-maʿdūm*) AS A CONTROVERSY OVER *Ex Nihilo* *

The problem whether the world was created out of nothing or out of a pre-existent eternal matter appeared in the Kalam under the guise of the problem whether the nonexistent (*al-maʿdūm*) is nothing (*lā shay*) or something (*shay*). When and among whom this problem appeared and how far widespread it was may be gathered from the following three statements: (1) Baghdādī's statement that al-Ṣāliḥī (d. 890), though a Muʿtazilite, "agreed with the people of the Sunnah in their objection to calling the nonexistent something"; [1] (2) Ibn Ḥazm's statement that "all the Muʿtazilites, except Hishām b. ʿAmr al-Fuwatī [d. 840], believed that the nonexistents (*al-maʿdūmāt*) are somethings"; [2] (3) Shahrastānī's statement that "al-Shaḥḥām [d. 850] from among the Muʿtazilites originated the view that the nonexistent is something." [3] From all these statements we gather that the problem arose in the early

* Cf. my article "The Kalam Problem of Nonexistence and Saadia's Second Theory of Creation," *JQR*, n.s. 36:371–391 (1946).

[1] *Farḳ*, p. 164, ll. 1–2.

[2] *Fiṣal* IV, p. 202, ll. 2–3.

[3] *Nihāyat*, p. 151, ll. 2–3.

part of the ninth century, when the new view about "the nonexistent," introduced by one of the Muʿtazilites, was evidently contrary to an older view that had prevailed for some time among the orthodox. It is, however, to be noted that Ibn Hazm's statement that "all" the Muʿtazilites with the exception of only one dissenter followed the new view is to be taken to refer only to the immediate Muʿtazilite followers of the new view, seeing that Baghdādī, who preceded Ibn Ḥazm, mentions another later Muʿtazilite dissenter. From the scattered statements quoted in the names of various Mutakallimūn we get the impression that the problem of the nonexistent was dealt with in the form of a question whether in this world of ours the nonexistent, of which we ordinarily think as nothing, could really be something. But as to how the problem happened to arise no explanation is to be found in any of the sources. Five possible origins of the problem have been suggested by modern scholars.

First, the Vaiśeṣika philosophy. In this philosophy, it is said, just as among some of the masters of the Kalam, the nonexistent is regarded as something real.[4] Now, it happens that the discussion of the problem of the nonexistent in the Kalam is couched in terms borrowed directly from Greek philosophy and consequently, whatever influence the Vaiśeṣika philosophy may have had on the Mutakallimūn, the problem itself was consciously associated by them with certain problems in Greek philosophy, and it is this association with problems in Greek philosophy for which we are to look.

Second, Democritus and Leucippus.[5] Both of these philosophers, according to Aristotle, affirmed the existence of a void in addition to that of a plenum, calling the former nonexistent (τὸ μὴ ὄν) and the latter existent (τὸ ὄν); as a result they were led to say that "the existent is in no respect more existent than the nonexistent," [6] or, as it is reported directly in the name of Democritus, that "something (τὸ δέν) is in no

[4] Horten, *Systeme*, p. 4; cf. Pines, *Atomenlehre*, p. 116, n. 2.
[5] Schreiner, *Kalām*, n. 5 on pp. 8–9; cf. Horten, *Probleme*, p. 72, n. 1.
[6] *Metaph*. I, 4, 985b, 4–8.

respect more existent than nothing (τὸ μηδέν)."[7] Now, there can be no doubt that the Kalam in its discussion of the problem of the nonexistent has drawn upon the vocabulary used by Democritus and Leucippus, but the problem of the nonexistent discussed by the Kalam, as may be judged from the various contexts in which it occurs, has nothing to do with the question whether a vacuum does or does not exist.

Third, the Stoics.[8] In Stoicism, it is said, nonexistent things, such as centaurs and giants and other fictitious mythical beings, are described as an indefinite something (τί).[9] Here again, while the Stoic phraseology may have been used by those in the Kalam who discussed the problem of the nonexistent, this Kalam problem as to whether the nonexistent, prior to its coming into existence, is to be regarded as something is logically quite different from the Stoic view that fictitious concepts which never come into existence are to be regarded as something.

Fourth, Plato's theory of ideas. Plato, it is argued, believes that existence is only an accident supervenient to a thing, and consequently that things in their ideal existence, even before their acquisition of the accident of existence, are still things.[10] Now, to say that the "nonexistent" in the Kalam controversy refers to Platonic ideas, and that these ideas are called nonexistent because they have not yet acquired the accidental or temporal existence characteristic of sensible things, is an assumption which cannot be sustained. Plato himself never describes the ideas as nonexistent. On the contrary, the ideas in their totality are described by him as "true substance" (ἀληθινὴ οὐσία),[11] as "existing in reality" (ὄντως ὄν),[12] as "existing absolutely" (παντελῶς ὄν),[13] and as "existing eternally" (ἀεὶ ὄν).[14] How then could these Platonic ideas come to be described as "nonexistent"?

[7] Diels, *Die Fragment der Vorsokratiker*, 413, 11, quoting Plutarch, *Adv. Colot.* 4, p. 1108 F.

[8] Pines, *Atomenlehre*, p. 117.

[9] Seneca, *Epistola* LVIII.

[10] Horovitz, *Einfluss*, pp. 71–72.

[11] *Sophist* 246 B.

[12] *Phaedrus* 247 E.

[13] *Sophist* 248 E.

[14] *Timaeus* 27 D.

Fifth, Plotinus. Plotinus in the Arabic version of his work, it is said, compares the ideas to a seed which is described by him as first hidden (*ḫafiyyah*) in the earth and then appearing (*bān*) in the open and walking the road of existence (*kaun*) and actuality (*fiʿl*).[15] On the basis of this comparison it is argued that though, according to Plotinus, the ideas while "hidden" in the intelligible world are to be regarded as "nonexistent," still even in their nonexistence they are to be regarded as "something."[16] But here, again, as in the preceding interpretation, despite this comparison to a seed, Plotinus never describes the ideas as "nonexistent." On the contrary, like Plato, he describes them as "existent things" (ὄντα) and as "substances" (οὐσίαι).[17]

On the whole, the entire approach to the problem must be revised. We must not treat the Kalam discussion of whether the "nonexistent" is "something" or "nothing" as a mere collocation of terms, the origin of which is to be explained by some similar collocation of terms. We must assume that this discussion started with some real problem of vital importance to those who participated in it. In our study of this discussion, we must therefore first find the real and vital problem concealed behind it and then look for some reason why that problem was expressed in the form of a question as to whether the "nonexistent" is "something" or "nothing."

The real and vital problem, which to our mind is behind the discussion as to whether the "nonexistent" is "nothing" or "something," is the problem whether the world was created out of nothing or out of an antemundane matter. Islam, like Judaism and Christianity, started with a belief that this world of ours once had not existed and then came into existence. On this point the Koran is quite explicit. Restating the words of the Hebrew Scripture, it says: "We created the heavens and the earth and all that is between them in six days."[18] But

[15] *Uthūlūjiyya*, p. 78, ll. 6–12.
[16] H. S. Nyberg, *Kleinere Schriften des Ibn al-Arabi* (1919), pp. 51–52.
[17] *Enneads* V, 8, 5 (ll. 23–25).
[18] Surah 50:7; cf. also 11:9; 16:3.

as to the manner of creation, whether *ex nihilo* or from a pre-existent matter and, if the latter, whether that pre-existent matter was created or eternal, is, as we have seen, not clear.

Now we know that the earliest philosophical speculations about matters religious came to Islam through the Syrian Christians.[19] We may therefore assume that these Syrian Christians, on the basis of the Pastor of Hermas and John of Damascus,[19a] transmitted to the Muslims a creation formula, which in Arabic read that the world was created *min al-maʿdūm*, "from the nonexistent." This formula, we may assume, was accepted by the Muslims as an expression of their doctrine of creation.

We may also assume that the Syrian Christians, in transmitting that formulation of the doctrine of creation to the Muslims, transmitted to them also the traditional Christian interpretation of the term "nonexistent" as meaning "nothing," the Arabic for which was *lā shay*. This, too, we may assume, was accepted by the Muslims, not only because it agreed with their conception of God's absolute power but also because they may have found support for it in the tradition that "God existed and there was nothing with Him" quoted above.

The acceptance of this formulation of the doctrine of creation as being from *al-maʿdūm*, "the nonexistent," and the interpretation of "the nonexistent" as meaning "nothing" took place, we may further assume, before the appearance of Arabic translations of Greek philosophic works and even before the rise of Muʿtazilism.

Then with the translation of Plato's *Timaeus* before 808 and of Aristotle's *Physics* and *De Generatione et Corruptione* before the middle of the ninth century, the Muʿtazilites, who already existed by that time and who, according to Shahrastānī, "devoted themselves to the study of the works of the philosophers,"[20] became acquainted with Plato's theory of the creation of the world out of a pre-existent eternal matter

[19] Cf. above, pp. 51 f. [19a] Cf. above, p. 355. [20] *Milal*, p. 18, ll. 2–3.

and with Aristotle's theory of the eternity of the world. They learned also of Aristotle's view (1) that "nothing can come out of nonexistence (ἐκ μὴ ὄντος) in an absolute sense"; [21] (2) that matter is not nonexistent in an absolute sense, for, as Aristotle says, matter is only "accidentally" nonexistent; [22] it is "akin to substance in some sense," [23] and it is not "nothing" (μηδὲν) but "something" (τι); [24] (3) that matter is "the primary substratum of each thing, being that from which each thing comes into existence and which inheres in each thing." [25] We may, therefore, assume that, influenced by these philosophical views, the Muʿtazilites were reluctant to accept the already established belief that the world was created out of nothing. Still, as Muslims bound by the Koranic doctrine of the creation of the world, they could not accept the Aristotelian doctrine of the eternity of the world. They could, however, find nothing in the Koran, as we have seen,[26] directly opposed to the belief in a pre-existent eternal matter. So they accepted Plato's theory that the world was created out of a pre-existent eternal matter.

Now, according to Aristotle,[27] the Platonic pre-existent eternal matter out of which the world was created and which the Platonists call "the nonexistent" (τὸ μὴ ὄν) is not the same as his own eternal matter which is conceived by him as underlying the infinite succession of generated things in the eternal world and which, because it is conceived by him as being nonexistent only in an accidental sense, is called by him "something." The Muʿtazilites, however, we may assume, after the manner of the philosophic eclecticism which is characteristic of the Mutakallimūn in general, took Plato's pre-existent eternal matter to mean the same as Aristotle's substrative eternal matter, namely, as nonexistent only in an accidental sense and hence as something. In their conception of the Platonic pre-existent matter as being both "nonexistent"

[21] *Phys.* I, 8, 191b, 13–14.
[22] *Ibid.*, 9, 192a, 4–5.
[23] *Ibid.*, 5–6.
[24] *De Gen. et Corr.* I, 3, 318a, 15 ff.
[25] *Phys.* I, 9, 192a, 31–32.
[26] Cf. above, pp. 357 ff.
[27] *Phys.* I, 9, 192a, 6 ff.

and "something," they may perhaps have been influenced by Plotinus' description of his eternally emanated matter both as "nonexistent" (μὴ ὄν) and as "something" (τι).[28] As a result of this, while retaining the already established formula that the world was created *min al-maʿdūm*, that is, "from the nonexistent," the Muʿtazilites took "the nonexistent" (*al-maʿdum*) in the formula to refer to Plato's pre-existent matter, which, according to their interpretation, was, like Aristotle's substrative matter and perhaps also like Plotinus' emanated matter, something. Thus the controversy over the question whether the world was created out of nothing or out of a pre-existent matter took the form of a controversy over the question whether "the nonexistent" (*al-maʿdūm*) in the established creation formula was to be taken to mean "nothing" or "something." All the various other formulations of the problem of the nonexistent in the Kalam may be assumed to have grown out of the formulation of that original problem of the creation of the world, so that they always involve that problem, though it may be assumed that they have acquired also other meanings under the influence of other sources.

Evidence corroborating my attempt to show that the Kalam problem as to whether the "nonexistent" is "nothing" or "something" involves the problem as to whether the world was created from nothing or from a pre-existent eternal matter is to be found in three testimonies. First, there is the testimony of Baghdādī who in his *Farḳ*, after quoting a statement to the effect that the Muʿtazilites believed that God created the world from nothing,[29] argues that "the view that God creates a thing from nothing is true only according to the principle of the Ṣifātiyyah, our co-believers, who deny that the nonexistent is something."[30] Second, there is the testimony of Ibn Ḥazm who in his *Fiṣal*, after stating that "all the Muʿtazilites, except Hishām b. ʿAmr al-Fuwaṭī, believed

[28] *Enneads* II, 4, 16 (l. 3).
[29] *Farḳ*, p. 95, ll. 15–17.
[30] *Ibid.*, p. 96, ll. 3–5; cf. *Uṣūl*, p. 70, l. 15 – p. 71, l. 1, and p. 71, ll. 10–11.

that the nonexistents (*al-maʿdūmāt*) are things in the true sense of the term and are eternal and infinite," adds that "this marks it at once as a Dahrite view and as an affirmation of the existence of things which are infinite, eternal, and uncreated." [31] Third, there is the testimony of Shahrastānī who in his *Nihāyat*, after reproducing Avicenna's argument to the effect that if the world were created, then prior to its creation there would have had to be an eternal matter, adds: "This error is that which has plunged the Muʿtazilites into the belief that the nonexistent is something." [32]

Thus "all" the Muʿtazilites, who, with specified two exceptions,[33] believe that the "nonexistent" is "something," follow the Platonic belief in a pre-existent eternal matter. The question naturally arises in our mind whether, like Muḥammad b. Zakariyyā al-Rāzī,[34] these Muʿtazilites conceive of the pre-existent eternal matter as consisting of atoms. No direct answer to this question, as far as I know, is to be found. Indirectly, however, an answer to this question may be derived from the view expressed by, or ascribed to, certain Muʿtazilites in the following statements. Abū al-Hudhayl, referring to atoms as substances, speaks of substance and of accident as having been created by God.[35] Muʿammar, who denies that accidents are created by God, maintaining that only bodies are created by God,[36] says that, in contradistinction to accidents over which God has no power, God has power over substances,[37] that is, God creates substances. Abū Rashīd, in his discussion of the differences between the Muʿtazilites of Baṣra and the Muʿtazilites of Baghdad, ascribes to both these schools of Muʿtazilites the common belief that atoms are brought into existence by the Creator.[38] Finally,

[31] *Fiṣal* IV, p. 202, ll. 2–4.
[32] *Nihāyat*, p. 33, ll. 19–20.
[33] Cf. above, p. 359.
[34] Cf. Pines, *Atomenlehre*, pp. 34 ff.
[35] *Maḳālāt*, p. 363, ll. 10–13.
[36] *Farḳ*, p. 136, l. 18 – p. 137, l. 1, and p. 138, l. 12; *Milal*, p. 46, ll. 3–4.
[37] *Maḳālāt*, p. 548, ll. 9–10.
[38] *Masāʾil*, p. 23, l. 6 (German, p. 35 and p. 21, n. 1).

Maimonides represents the Kalam in general as believing that "God creates these substances constantly whenever He wishes." [39–46] Now the Mu'tazilites mentioned, or referred to, in these statements are certainly to be included among those almost "all" Mu'tazilites who follow the Platonic belief in a pre-existent eternal matter. Consequently, from the fact that atoms are held by them to be created it is to be inferred that the pre-existent eternal matter, according to them, does not consist of atoms.

With the appearance of this controversy over the meaning of the phrase *min al-ma'dūm* as a description of creation, the orthodox, as well as those who wished to refer to the orthodox belief in creation *ex nihilo*, could no longer use the vague and controversial phrase *min al-ma'dūm*. A new phrase had to be coined. Naturally we would expect that the new phrase would be *min lā shay'*, "from nothing," the phrase used many centuries later by Jurjānī.[47] To our surprise we find that the phrase which has come to be of general use reads *lā min shay'*, literally, "not from something." Thus one of the earliest creeds, the *Fiḳh Akbar* II, which, according to Wensinck, may have originated in the middle of the tenth century,[48] uses the formula: "God created things not from something (*lā min shay'*)," [49] and this phrase is also used by Alfarabi,[50] who died about 950, and by Mas'ūdī,[51] who died about 957. Whether there had been attempts at the use of some other expressions for the concept of *ex nihilo*, I do not know. Nor do I know of any explanations offered by Muslim writers for the use of this phrase rather than the phrase *min lā shay'*, "from nothing." One would be tempted to explain the placing of the negative particle *lā*, "not," before the preposition *min*, "from," in this Arabic formula *lā min shay'* as being due to the influence of

[39–46] *Moreh* I. 73, Prop. 1, p. 135, l. 29.
[47] *Ta'rīfāt*, p. 6, l. 1.
[48] Wensinck, *Muslim Creed*, p. 94.
[49] *Kitāb Sharḥ al-Fiḳh al-Akbar* II, p. 15, ll. 2–3.
[50] *Kitāb al-Jam'*, p. 23, ll. 15–16 (where *'an* is used for *min*.).
[51] *Murūj* IV, p. 110, ll. 3–4.

the formula οὐκ ἐξ ὄντων in Second Maccabees 7:28, where similarly the negative Greek particle for "not" is placed before the Greek preposition for "from"; and perhaps this is really the explanation. The use, however, of other Arabic expressions for *ex nihilo* and an explanation for the use of *lā min shay'* instead of *min lā shay'* are to be found in the Arabic works of two early Jewish philosophers.

Isaac Israeli, who flourished before the expression *lā min shay'* was used in the *Fiḳh Akbar* II and by Alfarabi, uses four Arabic phrases for *ex nihilo*.

In his *Book of Definitions*, of which we have the Arabic original, as well as a Latin and a Hebrew translation, he uses the following Arabic phrase:

1. *Min lays*,[52] of which the Latin translation is *ex non esse*,[53] "from nonexistence," and the Hebrew translation is *me-ayin*,[54] "from nothing." Both these translations are correct. In Arabic translations of Aristotle *lays* is used for the Greek μὴ εἶναι,[55] *non esse*, and in Saadia's Arabic translation of the Bible *lays* is used for the Hebrew *ayin* (Isa. 41:12). But in whichever of these two senses Israeli directly used this term, he used it in the sense of "nothing." This is made clear by him in the passage in which he contrasts the term *al-lays* with the term *al-ʿadam* (Latin: *privatio*; Hebrew: *ha-hefḳed*). The passage reads as follows: "*Al-ʿadam* (privation) takes place only after existence; thus, if a thing exists and then ceases to exist, it is said that such thing has been deprived (*ʿudim*, *privatum*, *nifkad*). . . . *Al-lays* (the nonexistent), however, cannot be described as being deprived, for the nonexistent has no form in thought (*fī al-wahm*, *in mente*, *ba-raʿyon*) so as to be described by existence or privation." [56]

In the back of the mind of Israeli as he was making these

[52] *Kitāb al-Ḥudūd*, p. 693, l. 5.
[53] *Liber Definitionum*, p. 4a, l. 68.
[54] *Sefer ha-Gebulim*, p. 140, ll. 29–30.
[55] Cf. Bouyges, *Averroès: Tafsir ma baʿd at-tabiʿat*, Index, D, *a*, *s.v.*
[56] *Ḥudūd*, p. 193, ll. 5–11; *Definitionum*, p. 4a, l. 68 – p. 4b, l. 6; *Gebulim*, p. 140, ll. 30–34.

statements about privation and the nonexistent were, I take it, two of the several meanings which Aristotle finds in the use of the term "privation" (στέρησις). In one of his works, privation is said by him to have as one of its meanings "the forcible removal of anything,"[57] that is to say, the act of depriving or the state of being deprived. In another work of his, dealing with "privation" as contrasted with "form" and "matter," that is, in the sense of the lack of form, he says that, in contradistinction to matter which is "nonexistent accidentally" and hence is existent in some sense, privation is "nonexistent essentially" and hence is in no sense existent[58] or, as he says of it in another work of his, it is "nothing" (μηδέν).[59] Accordingly, Israeli's statement that "the nonexistent has no form in thought so as to be described by existence or privation" is to be taken to mean that the term "nonexistent," as applied by Aristotle to the term "privation" as used by him in the sense of the lack of form, is, unlike matter, not to be described "by existence" in any sense whatsoever, nor does the term "nonexistent" of this use of the term "privation" mean simply "the forcible removal" of existence, which Aristotle finds to be the meaning of another use of the term "privation." The "nonexistent" (*al-lays*) of this use of the term "privation," Israeli wants us to conclude, means "nothing."

The other three phrases occur in his *Book of the Elements*, of which the Arabic original is not extant. I shall therefore quote the Latin and Hebrew phrases and try to identify their underlying Arabic phrases. In this work, Israeli starts with the general statement that the kind of "generation" which he describes as "creational" is the coming-to-be of a thing "from nothing" (*ex nihilo*, *me-ayin*).[60] Inasmuch as the phrase *lā min shay* commonly used at that time for *ex nihilo* is, as we shall see, used by him later in this work either in exactly that

[57] *Metaph.* V, 22, 1022b, 31–32.
[58] *Phys.* I, 9, 192a, 6–7.
[59] *De Gen. et Corr.* I, 3, 318a, 15; cf. above, p. 356.
[60] *Liber de Elementis*, p. 4d, ll. 5–7; *Sefer ha-Yesodot*, p. 8, ll. 1–3.

form or in the form *min la shay* and is translated respectively by *ex alio* and *mi-lo dabar*, the underlying Arabic phrase here for *ex nihilo* and *me-ayin* must have been *min lays*, the very same phrase which is used by him, as we have seen, in his *Book of Definitions* in the sense of *ex nihilo*. Then, in the course of his discussion, Israeli makes use of three other phrases as equivalents of the phrase for *ex nihilo* which he has just used. They are as follows:

2. *Non ex alio*,[61] Hebrew: *mi-lo dabar*.[62] On the basis of the Hebrew *dabar*, which is the Arabic *shay*, the Latin *alio* is undoubtedly a corruption of *aliquo*, which is also the Arabic *shay*. Accordingly, the original Arabic was either *lā min shay*, "not from something," according to the Latin, or *min lā shay'*, "from not something," according to the Hebrew.

3. *Ex privatione*;[63] Hebrew: *me-ha-he'der*;[64] of which the Arabic quite evidently was *min al-'adam*, "from privation." Israeli immediately goes on to explain that "privation is not something which exists in thought (*in mente*, *be-maḥashabah*) prior to the generation of things therefrom" — exactly the same explanation which in his *Book of Definitions* he gave of *al-lays* in contrast to *al-'adam*, "privation." This shows that "privation" is not used by him here in the sense of "the forcible removal of anything"; it is rather used by him here in the sense of the absence of form and hence in the sense of absolute nonexistence or nothing.

4. *Ex non existente*;[65] Hebrew: *mi-lo meṣi'ut*;[66] both of which are literal translations of the Arabic *min lā wujūd*, "from nonexistence." Since the term *wujūd* is used as a translation of the Greek τὸ εἶναι,[67] the phrase here would be in Greek ἐκ τοῦ μὴ εἶναι, which would be the equivalent of ἐκ τοῦ μὴ ὄντος, used in the sense of *ex nihilo*.

Thus Israeli uses for *ex nihilo* the following four phrases:

[61] *Elementis*, p. 9b, l. 14.
[62] *Yesodot*, p. 57, l. 5.
[63] *Elementis*, p. 10b, ll. 26–28.
[64] *Yesodot*, p. 69, ll. 22–23.
[65] *Elementis*, p. 10b, l. 27.
[66] *Yesodot*, p. 69, l. 22.
[67] Cf. Bouyges, *Averroès, Tafsir ma ba'd at-tabi'at*, Index D, a, *s.v.*

(1) *min lays*; (2) either (a) *lā min shay* or (b) *min lā shay*; (3) *min al-ʿadam*; (4) *min lā wujūd*. Of these, only 2a is the same as that used in the Muslim sources quoted above. Inasmuch as 1, 3, and 4 all ultimately reflect the Greek ἐκ τοῦ μὴ ὄντος, it shows that Israeli took the controversial term "nonexistent" to mean "nothing."

Saadia uses for *ex nihilo* the common Arabic expression *lā min shay* (*lo mi-dabar*).[68] But evidently because of knowing that the ordinary Arabic expression for "nothing" is *lā shay*, he raises in his mind the question why the technical phrase commonly used in Arabic for *ex nihilo* is *lā min shay* and not *min lā shay*. An answer to this question is given by him in his Commentary on *Sefer Yeṣirah* where, commenting upon a passage which in his Arabic translation from the Hebrew reads, "He created something not from something (*lā min shay*) and made that which was nonexistent (*lays*) into that which is existent (*ays*)," he says: "We say here 'He created something not from something (*lā min shay*)' and we do not say 'He created something from nothing (*min lā shay*)' for the same reason that we have translated the verse [in Job 26:7] to read 'He hangeth the earth not upon something (*lā ʿalā shay*)' and have not translated it to read 'He hangeth the earth upon nothing (*ʿalā lā shay*).' We thereby point to the fact that *lā shay* (nothing) is *shay* (something), whereas what is dealt with here [in *Sefer Yeṣirah*] is the belief that the Creator created the air *lā min shay* (not from something)." [69]

This passage would at first sight seem to be a mere quibble of words. But it really reflects a certain logical principle. According to Aristotle, whenever the negative particle "not" modifies a noun, such, for instance, as οὐκ ἄνθρωπος; Arabic: *lā insān*, "not-man," it is to be called an "indefinite noun" (ὄνομα ἀόριστον; Arabic: *ism ghayr muḥaṣṣal*).[70] Accordingly,

[68] *Emunot* I, 1, p. 32, l. 11.

[69] *Tafsīr Kitāb al-Mabādī*, p. 83, l. 16 – p. 84, l. 1. (106).

[70] *De Interpret.* 2, 16a, 30–32; Arabic translation by Isḥaḳ Ibn Ḥunayn in *Alfarabi's Commentary on Aristotle's De Interpretatione*, ed. Kutsch and Marrow, p. 22.

the ordinary Arabic for "nothing," which consists of two words, "not" and "something" (*lā shay*), may be taken logically as an "indefinite noun," to mean "not-something." Now, again, according to Aristotle, an "indefinite noun" applies "equally well to that which exists and to that which does not exist." [71] Accordingly, the phrase *min lā shay*, could, logically, be taken to mean "from not-something," in which case it would not mean "from nothing" but from an indefinite something which either exists or does not exist; or, rather, from an indefinite something, concerning which we do not know whether it exists or does not exist.[71a]

It is to be added that Maimonides' use of *baʿd al-ʿadam* (*aḥar ha-heʿder*), "after privation," as the equivalent of *lā min shay* (*mi-lo dabar*), "not from something," in the sense of *ex nihilo*,[72] reflects Aristotle's statement that "to come from (ἐκ) something" [73] may mean "to come after (μετά) something." [74] Reflecting both Maimonides and Aristotle, it can be shown, is St. Thomas' discussion of the meaning of *ex nihilo*, concerning which he says that it may mean (1) *post non esse*, "after nonexistence" or it may mean (2) *non fit ex aliquo*, "it is not made from something." [75] Similarly Crescas' explanation of *me-ayin*, "from nothing," as meaning *aḥar ha-heʿder*, "after privation," [76] reflects both Maimonides and Aristotle, and perhaps also St. Thomas, though, unlike both Maimonides and St. Thomas, Crescas uses the phrase "after privation" for the purpose of identifying *ex nihilo* with emanation." [77]

[71] *Ibid.*, pp. 22–23. This statement is omitted here in the Arabic translation as well as in two Greek manuscripts referred to by Bekker *ad loc.*, but it occurs later (3, 16b, 15) in connection with Aristotle's discussion of the "indefinite verb." Arabic students of this work, however, as may be gathered from Alfarabi's comment on 16b, 15–16 (p. 38), took this statement about the "indefinite verb" to apply also to the "indefinite noun." On the use of the indefinite predicate in Aristotle, see my paper, "Twice-Revealed Averroes," *Speculum*, 36:373–392 (1961).

[71a] Cf. pp. 387–389 of my article noted above, p. 359, starred note.

[72] *Moreh* II, 13 (1), p. 196, l. 6, and 13 (2), p. 198, l. 7.

[73] *Metaph.* V, 24, 1023a, 26.

[74] *Ibid.*, 1023b, 5–11.

[75] *Sum. Theol.* I, 45, 1, and ad 3.

[76] *Or Adonai* III, 1, 5, p. 69a, ll. 4–18 (ed. Vienna, 1859).

[77] Cf. my papers "The Meaning of *Ex Nihilo* in the Church Fathers,

II. Arguments for Creation *

Saadia, in a work written in Arabic and completed in the year 933 in Baghdad, lists four rational arguments for creation, of which he says that he has excerpted them out of many arguments by which he had found that the scriptural doctrine of creation could be supported.[1] More than two centuries later, during the second half of the twelfth century, Maimonides lists seven arguments for creation, which he describes as being those used by the Mutakallimūn.[2] Since of the four arguments used by Saadia — all of which, as we shall see, were known to the Arabs — only the first one is not used by Maimonides in his list of the Mutakallimūn's arguments, we have altogether eight arguments, of which seven are arguments used by the Mutakallimūn and one argument was not used by them.

In the interval between Saadia and Maimonides, some or all of the Mutakallimūn's seven arguments are reproduced also in the works of Ibn Suwār, Juwaynī, Ibn Ḥazm, Māwardī, Joseph al-Baṣīr, Jeshua ben Judah, Baḥya, Ibn Ṣaddiḳ, Halevi, Shahrastānī, and Averroes, and the one argument not used by the Mutakallimūn is reproduced also in the works of Ibn Suwār and Averroes. It is these eight arguments, of which some directly prove creation and others only refute eternity,[3] that are now the subject of our investigation. Starting with Saadia's first argument, which though not used by the Mutakallimūn was available to them, we shall arrange the seven arguments which were used by them in the order in

---

Arabic and Hebrew Philosophy, and St. Thomas," *Mediaeval Studies in Honor of Jeremiah Denis Matthias Ford* (1948), pp. 355–370; "Aṣilut ve-Yesh me-Ayin eṣel Crescas," *Sefer Asaph* (1953), pp. 230–236.

* This section is a completely revised and enlarged version of my paper "The Kalam Arguments for Creation in Saadia, Averroes, Maimonides, and St. Thomas," *Saadia's Anniversary Volume of the American Academy for Jewish Research* (1943), pp. 197–245.

[1] *Emunot* I, 1, p. 32, l. 16.

[2] *Moreh* I, 74, p. 150, l. 10.

[3] See below, Argument III, p. 386 at n. 1, and *Moreh* I, 71, p. 124, l. 11; I, 74, p. 150, ll. 12–13.

which they are listed by Maimonides, except for his second argument which we shall list with our fifth argument.

1. Argument from Finitudes and the Reconstruction of Its Original Form in John Philoponus.
2. Argument from the Analogy of Things in the World.
3. Argument from the Aggregation and Segregation of Atoms.
4. Argument from the Createdness of the Accidents of the Component Parts of the World.
5. Argument from the Impossibility of an Infinite by Succession.
6. Argument from Particularization.
7. Argument from Preponderation.
8. Argument from Immortal Souls.

I. ARGUMENT FROM FINITUDES AND THE RECONSTRUCTION OF ITS ORIGINAL FORM IN JOHN PHILOPONUS

The first argument listed by Saadia is described by him as the argument from "finitudes" (*al-nihāyāt*: *ha-takliyyot*).[1] This argument is later reproduced by Gersonides [2] from Averroes' Long Commentary on the *Metaphysics*,[3] where it is quoted in the name of John Philoponus. Prior to Averroes but after Saadia, the same argument is reproduced also in the name of John Philoponus by Ibn Suwār.[4] In Greek, the argument is reproduced in the name of John Philoponus by Simplicius in his Commentary on the *Physics*.[5]

[1] *Emunot* I, 1, 1st Theory (1), p. 32. l. 16 – p. 34, l. 7.

[2] *Milḥamot Adonai* VI, 1, 3, p. 296. Cf. Steinschneider, *Al-Farabi*, p. 162.

[3] Cf. below n. 15.

[4] French translation from an Arabic manuscript, with an Introduction by Bernhard Lewin, under the title of "La notion de *muhdat* dans le kalam et dans la philosophie," in *Donum Natalicum H. S. Nyberg Oblatum* (1954), p. 91 (8). Arabic original published a year later by A. Badawi entitled *Maḳālah l'Abī al-Ḫayir al-Ḥasan ibn Suwār al-Baghdādī* in *Neoplatonici apud Arabes* (1955), p. 246, l. 11. It is also referred to John Philoponus in a letter by Yaḥyā Ibn 'Adī (cf. S. Pines, "A Tenth Century Philosophical Correspondence," PAAJR, 115:24 (1955).

[5] Quoted by Bernard Lewin, *op. cit.*, p. 86 and n. 3. Cf. below n. 14.

The argument is based upon three propositions: first, the world is finite in magnitude; second, the force within the world, that "which preserves" (*al-ḥāfiẓah*: *ha-shomer*) the existence of the world, is finite; third, such a finite force cannot produce infinite existence. Out of these three propositions Saadia infers that the world must have "a beginning and end." In the course of his discussion, Saadia restates in his own way Aristotle's arguments in proof that the world is finite in magnitude [6] and that there is only one world.[7]

Now, it will have been noticed, the force within the body of the world which is said to be finite is described by Saadia as the force which causes the preservation of the world. In Aristotle, however, that finite force within the world is described as the force which causes the motion of the world.[8] The question may therefore be raised as to the reason for this change of terminology.

Then, also, the three propositions upon which Saadia's argument is based are all of Aristotelian origin. In the case of the first proposition, Saadia himself, as we have seen,[9] has reproduced Aristotle's arguments upon which it is based. Similarly his second proposition is based upon Aristotle's argument in proof that "an infinite force cannot reside in a finite magnitude," [10] and his third proposition is based upon Aristotle's argument in proof that "nothing finite can cause motion during an infinite time." [11] And yet the conclusions derived by them from these propositions differ. To Saadia these propositions lead to the conclusion that the world has "a beginning and end." To Aristotle these propositions only serve to prove that beyond the finite force within the body of the world there must be a force which is bodiless and infinite, and it is this bodiless and infinite force, called the immovable prime mover, that, according to him, causes the motion as well as the existence of the world to be infinite, that

[6] *Emunot* I, 1, 1st Theory (I), p. 32, ll. 17–21. Cf. *De Caelo* I, 5–7.
[7] *Ibid.*, l. 17 – p. 33, l. 10. Cf. *De Caelo* I, 8.
[8] *Phys.* VIII, 10, 266a, 13: κινεῖν; 266b, 4: κινήσει.
[9] Cf. above at n. 6. [10] *Phys.* VIII, 10, 266a, 24–25. [11] *Ibid.*, 12–13.

is, eternal.[12] The main issue, therefore, is not whether the finite force within the world produces infinite motion and existence, but rather whether there is a bodiless infinite force outside the world and whether that bodiless infinite force outside the world can produce the infinite motion and existence of the world. For Saadia, therefore, to argue against the eternity of the world from the mere fact that the force within the world must be finite would seem to fail to meet the real issue involved. Moreover, as can be shown,[13] Saadia had knowledge of Aristotle's theory of the immovable prime mover. Why then does he not make any reference to it here, even if only to refute it?

The answer to the first question is to be found in what may be inferred from Simplicius and Averroes as the original phrasing of the argument available to Saadia in the Arabic translation of John Philoponus' work.

Simplicius, after remarking that John Philoponus used Aristotle's demonstration that no finite body has an infinite force as the basis of an argument in support of his own view, restates that argument as follows: "For if the body of the heaven and of the world is finite, then it has a finite force, but that which has a finite force is immediately thought by him to be subject to corruption." [14]

In Averroes' Long Commentary on the *Metaphysics*, the argument reads as follows: "John the Grammarian has raised a grave and difficult doubt (*shakk*: *quaestio*) against the Peripatetics concerning this problem. He says: if every body has only a finite force and the heaven is a body, then the heaven has only a finite force. But anything finite is corruptible. Therefore, the heaven is corruptible." [15]

[12] *Ibid.*, VIII, 9, 266a, 6–9.

[13] *Emunot* I, 3, 7th Theory, p. 58, ll. 11–12.

[14] Simplicius in *Physica* VIII, 10, ed. Diels, p. 1327, ll. 14–16.

[15] In *Metaph.* XII, Comm. 41 (VIII, p. p. 324 B; Arabic, p. 1628, ll. 10–12): Joannes autem Grammaticus movit magnam quaestionem et difficilem Peripateticorum. Dixit nam si omne corpus habet potentiam finitam, et coelum est corpus: ergo habet finitam potentiam et omne finitum est corruptibile: ergo coelum est corruptibile.

This is the answer to the first question. For since on the basis of the finitude of the force within the world the argument in its original form as known to Saadia tried to prove not the createdness of the world but rather its corruptibility, it was quite natural for him to describe that force as one "which preserves" the world from being corrupted. Saadia's use of this argument for the corruptibility of the world as an argument for its createdness may be explained as being the result of a tacit inference by himself based upon Aristotle's statement that "whatever is corruptible is generated." [16] Thus also it is on the basis of this statement of Aristotle that from this argument for the corruptibiliy of the world Gersonides explicitly infers its createdness.[17]

In answer to the second question, I shall try to show that the reason why Saadia took no notice of Aristotle's explanation of the eternity of motion by his theory of the immovable prime mover is that John Philoponus' argument, which was known to Saadia in its original form, contained a refutation of that Aristotelian explanation. This I shall try to show by an attempt to reconstruct the original form of John Philoponus' argument on the basis of a comparison of Averroes' reproduction of it in his Long Commentary on the *Metaphysics* with parallel passages in three of his other commentaries on works of Aristotle.

The passage quoted above from Averroes' Long Commentary on the *Metaphysics*, in which John Philoponus is said to have raised a grave and difficult doubt against the Peripatetics concerning their belief in the eternity of the world, is followed by two other passages.

The first of these two passages consists of two parts, a tentative solution of the difficulty raised by John Philoponus and a refutation of that solution. It reads as follows: "If it is said that the absence of corruption in the heaven is acquired from the eternal incorporeal force [which is outside the heaven], then it will follow that something which has the possibility

[16] *De Caelo* I, 12, 28b, 2.

[17] *Milhamot Adonai* VI, 1, p. 296, ll. 1–2.

of corruption will be eternal, but that this is impossible has been shown by Aristotle at the end of the first book of *De Caelo*." [18] The tentative solution, it will be noticed, is exactly the solution that Aristotle would have offered for the difficulty, namely, attributing the incorrruptibility of the heaven to the prime mover. In the refutation of this tentative solution, the reference to "the first book of *De Caelo*" is to a passage in which Aristotle tries to show, on the basis of his own view that anything possible must become actual in infinite time,[18a] that a thing which has the possibility of corruption cannot be eternal, that is, it cannot exist for an infinite time, for, if a thing which is possible of corruption is assumed actually to exist for an infinite time, then such a thing will both exist for an infinite time and yet not exist, which is an impossible consequence.[19]

The second passage contains Averroes' own solution of the difficulty raised by John the Grammarian against the Peripatetics. The gist of his own solution is his adoption of the tentative solution of that difficulty and his rebuttal of the refutation of that tentative solution by his contention that, according to Aristotle one is to distinguish between the eternity of the motion of the celestial sphere, which is due to the Prime Mover, and the eternity of the existence of the celestial sphere, which is due to its own nature, for, according to Aristotle, he maintains, the celestial sphere, not being composed of matter and form, contains within it no possibility of corruption.[20]

Let us now compare these passages in the Long Commentary on the *Metaphysics* with their parallel passages in the Long Commentary on the *Physics*, the Long Commentary

[18] *In Metaph.* XII, Comm. 41 (VIII, p. 324 C; Arabic, p. 1628 ll. 13–15): Si igitur aliquis dixerit, quod privatio corruptionis est acquisita in coelo de potentia aeterna abstracta: continget ut aliquid possibilis corruptionis sit aeternum, quod autem est impossibile hoc, declaratum est in fine primi Coeli et Mundi.

[18a] Cf. my *Crescas' Critique of Aristotle*, p. 249 at n. 3, and p. 551, n. 3.

[19] *De Caelo* I, 12, 281b, 18–25; 282a, 21–25.

[20] *In Metaph.* XII, Comm. 41 (VIII, p. 324 CD; Arabic, p. 1629, ll. 1–15).

on the *De Caelo*, and the Middle Commentary on the *De Caelo*.

First, the very same difficulty which in the Long Commentary on the *Metaphysics* is quoted in the name of John Philoponus as having been raised by him against the Peripatetics [21] is in these three commentaries raised anonymously against Aristotle himself. Thus in the Long Commentary on the *Physics*, commenting directly on Aristotle's statement that "an infinite force cannot reside in a finite magnitude" and paraphrasing it to mean that "the force of every body is finite," Averroes says that "it is to be doubted whether this statement would include the celestial body or not, for, if it does include the celestial body, then the force of the celestial body will be finite, but whatever has a finite force is corruptible." [22]

The same question is also raised anonymously against Aristotle himself in the Long Commentary on the *De Caelo* [23] and in the Middle Commentary on the *De Caelo*.[24]

Second, the very same solution of this difficulty which in the Long Commentary on the *Metaphysics* is introduced tentatively with the word "if it is said" [25] is in these three commentaries quoted in the name of Alexander Aphrodisiensis. Thus in the Long Commentary on the *Physics*, it reads as follows: "In some of his treatises, Alexander, answering this objection, says that the celestial body has acquired eternity from its immaterial mover." [26]

The same solution is quoted in the name of Alexander also

[21] Cf. above at n. 15.

[22] *In Phys.* VIII, Comm. 79 (IV, p. 426 HI): "In propositine autem assumpta hic . . . dubitari potest, utrum contineat corpus celeste, aut non. Si enin continet corpus celeste, tunc corporis celestis erit potentia finita; cui autem est potentia finita, est corruptibile."

[23] *In de Caelo* II, Comm. 71 (V, p. 145 IK).

[24] *Paraphrasis in Primum de Caelo*, Summa X, Caput 2, Pars 8 (V, p. 293 G).

[25] Cf. above at n. 18.

[26] *In Phys.* VIII (p. 426 K); "Et Alexander in quibusdam suis tractatibus respondens dicit corpus celeste adeptum fuisse aeternitatem ab suo motore, qui non est in materia."

in the Long Commentary on the *De Caelo*[27] and in the Middle Commentary on the *De Caelo*.[28]

Third, the very same argument which in the Long Commentary on the *Metaphysics* is used as an anonymous refutation of the anonymous tentative solution of the original difficulty[29] is in these three commentaries presented as a refutation by John Philoponus of a solution by Alexander of the same original difficulty. Thus in the Long Commentary on *De Caelo*, after restating Alexander's solution of the original difficulty, Averroes says: "John has put this question to the Peripatetics in such a way that they cannot escape it, seeing that they admit that in the celestial body there is a finite force, for, if [as according to their assumption in their solution of the original difficulty], there would be two forces, namely, a finite force [within the celestial body] and an infinite force [outside the celestial body], it would follow that by the finite force the celestial body would be corruptible and by the infinite force it would be incorruptible [and thus it would be contrary to Aristotle's contention that that which has the possibility of corruption cannot be incorruptible]."[30]

So also in the Long Commentary on the *Physics*[31] and in the Middle Commentary on the *De Caelo*[32] is this argument described as a refutation by John Philoponus of a solution of the original difficulty, which is attributed to Alexander.

Fourth, as in the Long Commentary on the *Metaphysics*[33] so also in these three commentaries Averroes presents his own solution of the difficulties raised.[34]

[27] *In de Caelo* II (p. 145 K).

[28] *Paraphrasis in Primum de Caelo* (p. 293 GH).

[29] Cf. above at n. 18.

[30] *In de Caelo* II (p. 145 KL): "Ioannes autem dedit hanc quaestionem Peripatheticis tali modo, quod non possunt evadere ex ea, secundum quod concedunt quod in isto corpore celesti est potentia finita quoniam, si illic sint duae potentiae, finita scilicet, et infinita, continget ut secundum finitam sit corruptibile, et secundum infinitam incorruptibile."

[31] *In Phys.* VIII (p. 426 KL).

[32] *Paraphrasis in Primum de Caelo* (p. 293 I).

[33] Cf. above at n. 20.

[34] *In Phys.* VIII (p. 426 M f.); *In de Caelo* II (p. 145 L f.); *Paraphrasis in Primum de Caelo* (p. 293 I f.).

Thus in none of these three Commentaries is the name of John Philoponus mentioned in connection with the original difficulty raised against Aristotle. But in all of these three Commentaries, right after Alexander's solution of the difficulty raised against Aristotle, there follow passages which connect John Philoponus with the refutation of Alexander's solution.

On the basis of all these, we may now try to reconstruct the original form of John Philoponus' argument. It started, we may assume, with a restatement of an old difficulty afloat against Aristotle's theory of the incorruptibility of the world on the ground of the finitude of the force within it which preserves it from corruption. It then quoted in the name of Alexander and other Peripatetics a solution of that old difficulty based on the contention that the incorruptibility of the world was due to the prime mover. It finally concluded with John Philoponus' own refutation of Alexander's solution, in which he argued that, on the basis of a principle laid down by Aristotle himself, the world, which by its own nature is possible of corruption, could not be rendered incorruptible by the Prime Mover. Accordingly, in Averroes' Long Commentary on the *Metaphysics*, what follows after the words "He says" [35] is not Averroes' restatement of John Philoponus' own argument against "the Peripatetics" but rather a brief outline of the latter's entire discussion of the subjects, which falls into the following three topics: (1) Beginning with the words "if every body has only a finite force," [36] a restatement of an old difficulty raised against Aristotle himself; (2) beginning with the words "If it is said," [37] a restatement of Alexander's solution of the difficulty; (3) beginning with the words "than it will follow," [38] John Philoponus' refutation of Alexander's solution.[39]

[35] Cf. above at n. 15.

[36] *Ibid.*

[37] Cf. above at n. 18.

[38] *Ibid.*

[39] In the light of this reconstruction of the text in the lost work of John Philoponus the passage in Averroes' *De Substantia Orbis*, Caput 5 (IX, p. 11 A), which reads "Joannes autem dedit quaestionem, de qua plures consyderantes non potuerunt evadere. Dixit enim si mundus est finitus, debet

It is this argument of John Philoponus in its original form as it was found in his work against Aristotle's doctrine of the eternity of the world, which was available to Saadia in its Arabic version, that is the basis of his argument here. Thus relying upon John Philoponus' contention that the prime mover could not render the world incorruptible, he starts by arguing that the world must be corruptible. Then, drawing upon Aristotle's statement, quoted above, that "whatever is corruptible must be generated," he infers that the world must have been generated. The full force of the argument is thus to be restated by the use of two syllogisms, as follows:

A

Everything with a finite force in it is corruptible;
The world is with a finite force in it;
Therefore, the world is corruptible.

B

Everything corruptible is generated;
The world is corruptible;
Therefore, the world is generated.

2. ARGUMENT FROM THE ANALOGY [1] OF THINGS IN THE WORLD

Plato, who starts out with the unproved assumption that the world came into existence after it had not been in existence, tries to prove by the analogy of the things within the world, all of which always come into existence by some cause, that the world itself came into existence by a cause, surnamed creator.[2] The Mutakallimūn, pretending, unlike Plato, to try to prove by the analogy of the things within the

habere potentiam finitam, igitur est generabilis et corruptibilis" is to be taken as an abridged and incomplete restatement of the passage in his Long Commentary on the *Metaphysics* as well as of the passages in his other commentaries.

[1] Cf. below n. 7.

[2] *Tim.* 28 A.

world that the world itself is created, really try, like Plato, to prove by the analogy of the things within the world that the world itself has a creator, and it is only from this that they infer that the world was created. On the whole, as we shall see, some of the arguments — which are supposed to prove the creation of the world — directly prove the existence of a creator.

This type of argument is quoted by Shahrastānī in the name of "Abū al-Ḥasan," [3] who is quite evidently not the same as the one whom he calls "our master Abū al-Ḥasan al-Ash'arī" and to whom he ascribes the argument from the aggregation and segregation of atoms, to be quoted later. Schreiner suggests that the Abū al-Ḥasan is Abū al-Ḥasan al-Bāhilī.[4] In Shahrastānī's restatement of the argument, Abū al-Ḥasan starts out by showing how the birth and growth and development of man out of the seed could not be explained as being due to man himself or to his parents or to nature but rather to an eternal, powerful, and wise Creator, concluding that "whatever rules have been established with regard to any one individual or any one body holds true with regard to all, seeing that they all share in corporeality." [5] From this conclusion that there is a Creator he expects us to infer that the world is created.

Similarly Maimonides starts out to show how "one of the Mutakallimūn thought that from the case of one created thing one may infer that the world is created." [6] He then goes on to show, as does Abū al-Ḥasan, that no individual human being could have gone through all the stages of development from seed to manhood without some outside agent, adding that "the same syllogistic reasoning (*ḳiyās*: *heḳesh*) applies to a palm tree and to other things" and hence also "to the world as a whole," concluding, as in Shahrastānī's report of Abū al-Ḥasan, that "whatever rule may be found with regard

[3] *Nihāyat*, p. 12, ll. 1–2.
[4] Schreiner, *Kalām*, p. 51, n. 3.
[5] *Nihāyat*, p. 12, ll. 2–6.
[6] *Moreh* I, 74 (1), p. 150, l. 23.

to any one body must necessarily be applied to every body," [7] to which may be added, as in Shahrastānī, "seeing that they share in corporeality." The direct inference is, of course, that the world has a creator, which indirectly implies that the world is created. This argument, the commentator Efodi remarks, proves only that the world was created, but it does not prove that it was created *ex nihilo*.[8]

But there is another version of the argument from analogy which is reported by Averroes, similarly in the name of the masters of the Kalam, and in that version an attempt is made to prove not only creation but also creation from nothing. It reads as follows: "The Muslim Mutakallimūn, however, consider it as possible that something should be generated from nothing, and deny this principle [namely, that something must be generated from something].[9] The cause of their error is the fact of common observation that many things perceived by sight are generated from things not perceived by sight, as, e.g., fire from air, and so at first blush they came to imagine that something can be generated from nothing, for the common people understand by nonexistence only that which is not perceived by sight." [10]

Still another version of the argument from analogy, much

[7] *Ibid.*, ll. 23–29. This argument may be restated either as an argument by induction (*ḳiyās al-istiḳrā'*: *heḳesh ha-ḥippush*) or as an argument by analogy (*ḳiyās al-tamthīl*: *heḳesh ha-Hemshel*). Cf. *Millot ha-Higgayon*, Chap. 7. In the former case, it would be as follows: Inasmuch as most things corporeal are created, all things corporeal, including the world as a whole, must be created. In the latter case, it would be as follows: Inasmuch as the world as a whole and all individual things within the world are alike in their being corporeal, they must also be alike in their being created. From the phrasing of this argument here by Maimonides, it is evident that it is an argument by analogy. It is so taken by both Shem-ṭob and Efodi, who describe it as an argument by analogy.

[8] Cf. Efodi *ad loc.*

[9] Cf. *Phys.* I, 7, 190b, 9–10.

[10] *In Phys.* VIII, Comm. 4 (IV, p. 341 E): "Loquentes autem Saraceni habent pro possibili aliquid generari et nihilo, et negant hoc principium. Et causa erroris eorum fuit haec, quod sentitur quod multa comprehensibilia visu generantur ex rebus incomprehensibilibus visu. v. g. ignis ex aere: et sic imaginantur primo aspectu possibile esse aliquid generari ex nihilo. Vulgus nam non intelligit de non esse nisi illud, quod non comprehenditur visu."

like that given by Maimonides but with an attempt to prove that the creation is from nothing, may be discerned in Isaac Israeli's statement of his belief in the creation of the world. Starting with a restatement of a passage in Aristotle to the effect that "an element is a thing from which something is first generated," [11] he tries to show, from a study of the composition of the human body, how it is generated from sperm, blood, the two biles, and the phlegm, and how these in turn are generated from food, and how food is generated from the four elements, which are of the greatest simplicity, but how the four elements finally are generated from nothing except from the power of God.[12] He offers no proof for his conclusion that the four elements are created from nothing, though it is contrary to Aristotle, with whom he starts his discussion. But the proof which he had in mind, though not expressed, is implied in everything he says. It is an argument from analogy. All things in the world are created. Each thing is created from something simpler than itself. By analogy, the four elements must have been created from something simpler than the elements. Hence they must have been created from nothing.[13] Here then we have a proof for the creation of the world based upon the analogy of the creation of individual things — the same as in Maimonides' version of the Kalam proof from analogy. But, as we shall see later,[14] an argument of the same type, similarly proving creation from nothing, is ascribed by Maimonides to the Mutakallimūn and is based upon the impossibility of an infinite by succession.

[11] *Liber de Elementis*, p. 4a, ll. 10–12: "Philosophus . . . diffinivit elementum esse res ex qua generatione prima aliquid generatur." *Sefer ha-Yesodot*, p. 5, ll. 2–3. Cf. *Metaph*. I, 3, 983b, 8–9: ἐξ οὗ γίγνεται πρώτου.

[12] *Elements*, p. 4c, ll. 33–66; *Yesodot*, p. 6, l. 1 – p. 7, l. 8.

[13] With this interpretation of Isaac Israeli's argument, compare Neumark's interpretation in *Geschichte*, I, pp. 414–417; *Toledot*, II, pp. 88–91. Cf. my paper "The Meaning of Ex Nihilo in Isaac Israeli," *JQR*, n.s. 50:1–12 (1959).

[14] Cf. below, p. 426.

3. ARGUMENT FROM THE AGGREGATION AND SEGREGATION OF ATOMS

Shahrastānī, who divides the Mutakallimūn's arguments for the creation of the world into those which directly establish creation and those which only refute eternity,[1] reproduces an argument in refutation of eternity [2] based upon the common Mutakallimūn's view that the world is composed of atoms. He ascribes this argument to Ash'arī, to whom he refers as "our master Abū al-Ḥasan al-Ash'arī." [3] As phrased by Shahrastānī, it reads as follows: "If we assume the eternity of atoms, then one of these possibilities must also be assumed, namely, that the atoms are [eternally] either aggregated (*mujtami'ah*) or segregated (*muftariḳah*), or neither aggregated nor segregated, or both aggregated and segregated simultaneously, or some of them aggregated and some of them segregated. In general [however, in this world of ours] these atoms are not free from aggregation and segregation, or rather free from the possibility of the occurrence of aggregation [in some atoms] and segregation [in others], and from the possibility of the change of either one of them into the other. Now, by their own essence, the atoms can neither become aggregated nor segregated, for the essence, by the judgment of the intellect, does not undergo any change, whereas these atoms [by common observation] do undergo a change. Therefore, there must inevitably exist an aggregator and segregator [by whom the process of aggregation and segregation in this world of ours was created]. From the principles thus arrived at it follows that [the world, which is composed of atoms in the process of aggregation and segregation and which did not exist prior to the creation of that process, is created, for] whatever does not precede (*lā yasbiḳ*) that which is created is itself created." [4]

The gist of the argument is thus as follows: Given eternal

[1] *Nihāyat*, p. 11, ll. 5–6.
[2] *Ibid.*, ll. 12–13.
[3] *Ibid.*, l. 12.
[4] *Ibid.*, ll. 13–19.

atoms which from eternity could not by their own nature undergo the process of aggregation and segregation now observed in the world, it must necessarily follow that there is a creator who created this process, and hence the world, in which this process exists, is created. This argument thus proves only that this world of ours is created; it does not prove that the atoms out of which it is created are also created. In fact, Shahrastānī himself describes this argument as one aimed at "the refutation [of the eternity of the world]" [5] and not at the refutation of the eternity of atoms, which is the assumption with which, as we have seen, the argument begins. Similarly in his conclusion he says: "Therefore, there must inevitably exist an aggregator and segregator," which implies the existence of atoms that are to be aggregated and segregated.

The same argument as phrased by Maimonides reads as follows: "The atoms of the world [as it now exists] must inevitably be either aggregated or segregated and perhaps some atoms may be aggregated at one time and segregated at another. Now it is clear and manifest that in respect to their own essence . . . segregation is not more appropriate to them than aggregation, nor is aggregation more appropriate to them than segregation. The fact, therefore, that [in this world of ours] some atoms are aggregated, while others are segregated, and still others change from one of these states into the other, being aggregated at one time and segregated at another, is a proof that the atoms require someone that aggregates those that are aggregated and segregates those that are segregated [so that by his act of aggregation and segregation the world came into being after it had not been]. This, they say, is a proof that the world is created. It is thus clear to you that the author of this argument has used the first of the Mutakallimūn's propositions and all that necessarily follows from it." [6]

In this phrasing of the argument, too, the aggregation and

[5] *Ibid.*, l. 13.

[6] *Moreh* I, 74 (3), p. 151, ll. 17–27.

segregation by which the world came into existence could have taken place in atoms assumed to have been coeternal with God the Aggregator and Separator. The argument thus proves only creation, but not creation *ex nihilo*. It is evidently with reference to this limited scope of the argument that Maimonides has added the words "they say" in his restatement of the Mutakallimūn's conclusion that the world is created. It is evidently also because of this limited scope of the proof that Efodi, in his comment upon Maimonides' own comment at the conclusion of the argument, says: "Maimonides means thereby that this proof, even though based upon the Mutakallimūn's own propositions, may confirm the assumption of a pre-existent eternal matter." [7]

An argument like that ascribed to Ash'arī (d. 935) is used by his Jewish contemporary Saadia (d. 942), who describes it as being derived "from the aggregation (*jam'*: *ḳibbuṣ*) of parts (*al-ajzā'*: *ha-ḥalaḳim*) . . . I saw that bodies are combined parts (*ajzā' mu'allafah*: *ḥalaḳim meḥubarim*)." [8] Now the Arabic here for the expressions "aggregation of parts" and "combined parts" would seem to mean "aggregation" and "combination" of "atoms," [9] and thus the argument would seem to be based upon the conception of atoms like the argument quoted by Shahrastānī in the name of Ash'arī. However, Saadia's own illustration of the term "parts" by the example of the parts that make up the bodies of animals and plants and of the dust and stones and sand that make up the earth and of the successive layers of spheres, studded with stars, that make up the heaven [10] shows quite clearly that by the "parts" he does not mean "atoms." Besides, without himself believing in atoms,[11] he would not use an argument based on atoms in support of his own belief in creation. Then, also, it can be shown that the argument is nothing but a restatement in new

[7] Cf. Efodi *ad loc.*
[8] *Emunot* I, 1, 1st Theory, 2nd Proof, p. 34, ll. 8–9.
[9] Cf. *Moreh* I, 74, Prop. I, p. 135, ll. 19–22.
[10] *Emunot*, *loc. cit.*, p. 34, ll. 11–16.
[11] *Emunot* I, 3, 9th Theory, p. 62, ll. 9–20.

terms of the old argument of design, for, as he goes on, he says that in observing the aggregation of parts in the structure of the bodies of animals and plants, there were revealed to him in them "signs of the handiwork of the Maker, as well as of creation." [12] Similar evidence of design was found by him in the structure of the earth and still more in the structure of the heaven. In the corresponding argument in his Commentary on *Sefer Yeṣirah*, he similarly says: "As for the visible evidence of skillful work in the world, you only have to look at the stars and see how they are made each distinct from the other to arrive at the conclusion that there is a skillful worker who has purposely set about to cut them out according to a certain plan, making some of them great and others small and similarly causing some of them to be more luminous and others less luminous, some of them to be in a higher heaven and others in a lower heaven and some of them to have fast motion and others slow motion." [13]

Still this argument is like Ash'arī's argument both in the method of its reasoning and in the formulation of its conclusion. Both of them, though differing in what they mean by the parts of the world, argue from the aggregation of its parts to its creation. Again, both of them, though starting out to prove the creation of the world, end up by proving the existence of a Creator, which by implication is proved the creation of the world. Then, also, both of them, as is indicated by their respective authors, prove only that world was created, but not that it was created *ex nihilo*.

An argument for the creation of the world like this one by Saadia is contained in the third of the three propositions by which Baḥya proves the existence of God. As phrased by him, it reads as follows: "Everything combined (*mu'allaf*: *meḥubbar*) is indubitably composed (*murakkab*: *murkab*) of things more than one, and the things of which it is composed are prior to it in nature," [14] from which he infers the existence

[12] *Emunot, loc. cit.*, ll. 9–10.
[13] *Tafsīr Kitāb al-Mabādī*, p. 33, ll. 2–3 (pp. 53–54).
[14] *Ḥobot* I, 5, p. 45, ll. 8–9.

of God as the combiner of the composed things out of which the world was composed and hence created. Subsequently this proposition is expanded into an argument exactly like that used by Saadia. To begin with, the things out of which everything composed is made up (*murakkab*: *murkab*) are not atoms but rather "the four elements,"[15] each of which consists of "matter and form."[16] It is interesting to note that immediately after mentioning "matter and form" he adds "and they are the substance and the accident," as if he had meant to say that the ultimate composition of things are not that which the Kalam calls "substance and accident," namely, "atom and accident," but rather what the philosophers call "substance and accident," namely, "matter and form." Then, as he goes on, he makes it clear that the argument is an argument from design, for, beginning with the general statement that "we perceive with our senses and our reason that the world is like a house which has been built and fitted out with all its necessary equipment,"[17] he proceeds to describe in great detail the evidence of design and purpose in the various realms of nature.[18] Then also, being aware, like Saadia, that his argument proves only creation but not creation *ex nihilo*, he adds an extra proof that the creation was *ex nihilo*. But here, unlike Saadia, whose extra proof for *ex nihilo* is based on rational arguments, Baḥya's extra proof is based on two scriptural verses, Isaiah 44:24 and Job 26:7.[19] It is this scriptural proof for *ex nihilo* that Baḥya had in mind when, at the beginning of his discussion of the propositions by which he was to prove the existence of God, he referred to them as propositions by which he is to prove that "this world has a Creator who created it *ex nihilo*."[20]

Here then we have the same argument by two contemporaries, Ashʿarī and Saadia, each of them using it in accordance with his own view on the question of the existence of

[15] *Ibid.* I, 6, p. 47, l. 1.
[16] *Ibid.*, l. 14.
[17] *Ibid.*, p. 45, l. 19 – p. 46, l. 1.
[18] *Ibid.*, p. 46, l. 1 – p. 47, l. 5.
[19] *Ibid.*, p. 48, ll. 9–13.
[20] *Ibid.* I, 5, p. 43, l. 8.

atoms. One would naturally suspect that there must be some relationship between these two forms of the argument, but what is that relationship? That Ashʿarī's argument could not have been a modification of Saadia's is quite clear, for Saadia's Arabic work which contains that argument was written in Baghdad in 933, two years before Ashʿarī died in that city. As for Saadia's argument being a modification of Ashʿarī's, while that is not impossible, the question is whether we can find some kind of literary relationship between them. In answer to this question, it can be shown that the arguments used by Ashʿarī and Saadia to prove the existence of a Creator and hence also the creation of the world are based upon three arguments used by Abucara to prove the existence of a Creator.

In those arguments, starting by showing how the various things on earth and in the sea are all "aggregated (*jumiʿa*) and composed (*rukkiba*)" of the four elements,[21] Abucara says that "with regard to that which is composed, the parts thereof are prior (*asbaḳ*) to it in nature and often are in addition prior to it also in time." [22] He then goes on to show, by two arguments, how these four elements, prior to their having been composed into the various bodies in the world, were by their own nature moving in various opposite directions and possessing various opposite qualities, whereas in the bodies composed of them these opposite movements and opposite qualities are all neutralized. As this neutralization could not have been effected by their own nature, he concludes that it must have been effected by "the Powerful (*al-ḳawī*), whose power is indescribable," [23] and who is "the Almighty" (*al-ḍābiṭ al-kull*).[24] He then goes on to add a third argument, which reads as follows: "Moreover, from what we see of this Powerful One as to how out of these four parts (*ajzāʾ*) He has aggregated (*jamaʿa*) and composed (*rakkaba*) on the earth that which is incalculable and innumerable of the many kinds of trees and plants and mountains and metals and birds

[21] *Fī Wujūd al-Ḫāliḳ*, p. 762, ll. 13–16.
[22] *Ibid.*, p. 762, ll. 18–21; p. 763, ll. 4–6.
[23] *Ibid.*, p. 762, l. 23.
[24] *Ibid.*, p. 763, l. 14.

and creeping things that creep on the earth and in the seas, we know that He is wise and that His wisdom, like His power, is incalculable."[25] It is to be noted that these three arguments, like the arguments of Ashʿarī and Saadia, prove only the creation of the world out of something, in this case the something being the four elements, but do not prove that the elements themselves were created. That Abucara was aware of the limited scope of these three arguments is shown by the fact that subsequently he produced a new argument to show that the creation of the world was *ex nihilo*.[26]

Here then Abucara's three arguments make up one argument for the existence of God based upon the aggregation and composition of the four elements which are referred to as "parts"; and the God whose existence is proved by these arguments is described as He who "has aggregated and composed" these "parts" into various bodies in various parts of the world. This, as will be noticed, is the argument as used by Saadia, except for his additional conclusion that the proof of the existence of God as Aggregator proves the creation of the world. This argument of Abucara, again, as will be noticed, is the argument as ascribed to Ashʿarī, except for his taking the "parts" to mean "atoms" and except also for his additional conclusion that the proof of the existence of God as Aggregator and Segregator proves the creation of the world.

4. ARGUMENT FROM THE CREATEDNESS OF THE ACCIDENTS OF THE COMPONENT PARTS OF THE WORLD

An argument for the creation of the world based upon the accidents of its component parts described either as atoms or as bodies is ascribed by Averroes to the Ashʿarites,[1] by whom, as we shall see,[2] he means Juwaynī (d. 1065) and his associates. However, before Juwaynī this argument was used

[25] *Ibid.*, ll. 15–18.
[26] *Ibid.*, p. 264, ll. 9–24.

[1] Cf. below at n. 39.
[2] Cf. below, p. 396.

by the Ash'arite Bāḳillānī (d. 1013). As presented by him, the argument consists of a number of successive propositions, each of which is established by proof. Thus starting with the proposition that "the world, the upper and the lower, is inseparable (*lā yaḫruju*) from these two genera, namely, substances [that is, atoms] and accidents," [3] he proceeds to prove its creation by proving the following three propositions: (1) that accidents exist,[4] that is to say, they exist in both atoms and bodies; [5] (2) that "accidents are temporal events (*ḥawādith*)," [6] that is to say, they have a beginning and an end, whence they are created, which he proves by the observed fact that movement disappears at the arrival of rest; (3) that bodies are created, which he proves by the reasoning that "they do not precede (*lam tasbiḳ*) the temporal events (that is, the accidents in them) and do not exist before them, and whatever does not precede that which is created is created like it." [7] It is to be noted that, though from his first two propositions he could prove the createdness of atoms just as he does prove the createdness of bodies, still it is the proof of the createdness of bodies that he uses as the basis of his argument for the creation of the world.

This argument is next reproduced, together with a refutation, by a contemporary of Bāḳillānī, the Christian Ibn Suwār (b. 942), who ascribes it to the Mutakallimūn in general. As reproduced by him, it reads as follows: "A body is inseparable (*lā yanfakk*) from temporary events (*ḥawādith*) [later explained by him as meaning accidents] and does not precede (*lā yataḳaddam*) them. But whatever is inseparable from temporary events [that is, accidents] and does not precede them is created (*muḥdath*). Therefore, a body is created. This would be their syllogism if their reasoning were arranged according to the art [of logic]." [8] He then goes on to say that, in order to find out whether the premises are true, one must

[3] *Tamhīd*, p. 22, ll. 4–5.
[4] *Ibid.*, ll. 5–6.
[5] *Ibid.*, p. 17, l. 9; p. 18, ll. 4–5.
[6] *Ibid.*, p. 22, l. 6.
[7] *Ibid.*, p. 22, l. 10 – p. 23, l. 2.
[8] Ibn Suwār (cited above, p. 374, n. 4), p. 243, ll. 9–10 (1, p. 88).

first explain the exact meaning of each of the technical terms contained therein, and thereupon he explains the meaning of the Arabic terms for "body" and "temporal events" and "inseparable" and "does not precede" and "created." [9]

It is to be noted that the very fact that Ibn Suwār thought it necessary to explain the terms used by him in the argument shows that in his reproduction of the argument he has used the very same terms that were used by those Mutakallimūn to whom the argument is ascribed by him, and that the only change made by him in it was in reducing it to a syllogism. Now the terms used by him are not the same as those used by Bāḳillānī.[10] We may therefore infer that the Mutakallimūn to whom Ibn Suwār ascribes this argument are other than, and also prior to, his contemporary Bāḳillānī and his associates. Accordingly, on the assumption that Bāḳillānī, too, is reproducing an argument in the very same terms as used by others before him, we may further infer that the others whose argument he is reproducing are not the same as the Mutakallimūn to whom Ibn Suwār ascribes his argument. Then, also, since the terms used by Ibn Suwār in his argument are the same as those used by the Mutakallimūn to whom he ascribes the argument, it is quite evident that the term body used in it was meant by them to designate a body conceived of as being composed of atoms. Still no mention is made of atoms either in the syllogistic restatement of the argument or in Ibn Suwār's subsequent explanatory passage. Then, in that explanatory passage, there is to be noted the following peculiarity. While in the case of his explanation of the Arabic terms for "temporary events" and "inseparable" and "does not precede" and "created" he says that they are in accordance with what the Mutakallimūn mean by them, in the case of his explanation of the Arabic term for "body" he simply says:

[9] *Ibid.*, ll. 11–17 (2, p. 88).

[10] Ibn Suwār uses the terms (1) *lā yanfakk*; (2) *ḥawādith* (later explained by him as meaning *a'rāḍ*); (3) *yataḳaddam* (later explained by him as meaning *lā ḫālī* and *lā yasbuḳ*), whereas Bāḳillānī uses the terms (1) *lā yaḫruj*; (2) *al-a'rāḍ ḥawādith*; (3) *lā yasbuḳ*.

"body is length, breadth, depth." [11] Now the reason why he did not explain body in accordance with what the Mutakallimūn meant by it is quite clear. There was no explanation of body common to all the Mutakallimūn. In fact, Ashʿarī ascribes to them twelve explanations,[12] and the explanation given here by Ibn Suwār is one of them, that of Muʿammar.[13] Then, also, the reason why he selected this particular explanation is quite clear. It is an explanation which was also commonly used by philosophers who did not believe in atomism.[14] From all this it may be gathered that, while Ibn Suwār quoted this argument in the name of the Mutakallimūn and while he knew that they used the term body in it in the sense of its being composed of atoms, he also knew that the argument could be used, or that it was actually used, also by those who did not believe that a body was composed of atoms.

Ibn Suwār's refutation of the argument consists of three criticisms of which, as we shall see, the first and the third will prove to be of significance for the study of the historical background of this and the next argument respectively. In his first criticism, after explaining the Mutakallimūn's proposition that "a body is inseparable from accidents" to mean that in "every body" there is a "succession of movement and rest," he says "their opponents would not admit that movement and rest succeed each other in every body, for, according to their opinion, the heaven is [continuously] in motion, without being first without motion and then set in motion." [15] The third criticism reads as follows: "It is also necessary to remark that, even if it is admitted that a body is inseparable from accidents and that each of the accidents is created in time, it does not follow that the body is created in time, for it is possible that, despite the fact that each individual accident is created in time, the succession of these accidents would be

[11] Ibn Suwār, p. 243, l. 12 (2, p. 88).
[12] *Maḳālāt*, p. 301, ll. 2 f.
[13] *Ibid.*, p. 303, ll. 9–10.
[14] Aëtius, *De Placitis* I, 12, p. 310, ll. 9–10 (Arabic, p. 116, ll. 13–14).
[15] Ibn Suwār, p. 243, l. 18 – p. 244, l. 5 (3, pp. 88–89).

continued perpetually without an interval and without a temporal beginning." [16] It is to be remarked that of these two criticisms the first is based upon a refutation by Aristotle [17] of his own tentative objection to the eternity of the world [18] and the third is based upon an explanation by Aristotle of how an infinite by succession is possible.[19]

The next work in which this argument appears is the *Irshād* of Juwaynī. It is preceded there by the preliminary statement that, according to "those who believe in the unity of God" (*al-muwaḥḥidūn*),[20] . . . "the world consists of atoms and accidents" [21] and that, "when two atoms are combined, they form a body." [22] The argument then proceeds as follows: "The creation of atoms can be demonstrated by the establishment of certain principles: first, the establishment [of the existence] of accidents; second, the establishment of the creation of accidents; third, the establishment of the impossibility for atoms to be stripped (*taʿarrī*) of accidents; fourth, the establishment of the impossibility for created things to be without a first. When these principles have been established by proof, there follows therefrom that the atoms do not precede the created accidents, and that which does not precede that which is created is itself created." [23]

This is followed by a special demonstration for each of the four principles. From all this we are expected to draw the conclusion that, inasmuch as the constituent parts of the world, the atoms, are created, the world as a whole is created, on the self-evident ground that the whole does not precede the parts of which it consists.

[16] *Ibid.*, p. 244, l. 21 – p. 245, l. 3 (5, p. 90).

[17] *Phys.* VIII, 2, 252b, 28 – 253a, 2.

[18] *Ibid.*, 252b, 9–12.

[19] *Ibid.* III, 6.

[20] The term *al-muwaḥḥidūn* here refers to Muslims in general and not merely to the Muʿtazilites who are especially known as *aṣḥāb al-tauḥīd*, "the partisans of unity." So also is the Arabic term *al-muwaḥḥidūn* (Hebrew: *ha-meyaḥadim*) applied by Saadia (*Emunot* II, 3, p. 83, l. 21) and Maimonides (*Moreh* I, 75, 1st Argument, p. 157, l. 4) to Jews in general.

[21] *Irshād*, p. 10, l. 7 (28).

[22] *Ibid.*, ll. 11–12.

[23] *Ibid.*, ll. 12–16.

It will be noticed, however, that the direct proof for the creation of the world follows from the first three principles and that the fourth principle is not an integral part of it. Its purpose, as explicitly stated by Juwaynī himself in his demonstration, is only to refute a view opposite to that already established by the first three principles. He says: "It is a duty to attend to this [fourth] principle, for the establishment of what is aimed at by it shatters all the views of the unbelievers (*al-mulḥidah*). The fundamental view of most of them is that the world has always been as it is and that the revolution of the sphere has always been preceded by another revolution, without there having been a first. Then also there have always been events in the world of generation and corruption following one after the other in the same manner to infinity, so that every child is preceded by a parent, every grain is preceded by a seed, and every egg is preceded by a hen." [24] The reference here is quite clearly to Aristotle's view of the possibility of an infinite by succession which, as we have seen, is used by Ibn Suwār as a refutation of this argument for creation. And hereupon follows Juwaynī's refutation of this view of Aristotle.[25]

Another formulation of the argument is to be found in a work by a contemporary of Juwaynī (d. 1085) named Māwardī (d. 1085). It reads as follows: "The world consists of substances [that is, atoms] and bodies, which are inseparable (*lā tanfakk*) from created accidents such as aggregation (*ijtimā'*) and segregation (*iftirāḳ*) and motion and rest . . . and that which is inseparable from created accidents does not precede them." [26]

Evidently based upon a formulation of the argument like that used by Māwardī is the argument used by a contemporary of his, Joseph al-Baṣīr, who, as we have seen,[27] followed

[24] *Ibid.*, p. 14, l. 21 – p. 15, l. 4 (34). [25] *Ibid.*, p. 15, ll. 4 f.

[26] Quoted from a manuscript of Māwardī's *A'lam al-Nubuwwah* by Schreiner in his *Studien über Jeschua ben Jehuda*, p. 31, n. 2. Cf. printed edition (Cairo, 1330/1911), p. 6, l. 24 – p. 7, l. 3.

[27] Cf. above, p. 84.

the Mutakallimūn on the affirmation of the existence of atoms. The argument is presented by him in the form of proofs for the establishment of four propositions, the headings of which read as follows: "Proof of the first proposition, namely, the establishment of the existence [of accidents such as] aggregation and segregation [and motion and rest]." [28] "Proof of the second proposition, the creation of aggregation and segregation." [29] "Proof of the third proposition, namely, that a body is not devoid of aggregation and segregation." [30] "Proof of the fourth proposition, namely, that a body which is not devoid of that which is created is created like it." [31]

Joseph al-Baṣīr's pupil, Jeshua ben Judah, has five arguments for creation, of which the first one has the same logical structure as the argument of his teacher. It reads as follows: "We already know as a general rule that anything that cannot be released (*yigga'el*) from something created is created like that something. Therefore, if it proves true that a body is not devoid of something created, it necessarily follows that it is itself created." [32] And thereupon follow long proofs of the two premises contained in the argument.

Based on a version of this argument like that we have met with in Juwaynī, but quite evidently not based directly on Juwaynī in whose name he later quotes another argument, is the reproduction of this argument by Shahrastānī. He ascribes it simply to the Mutakallimūn and describes it as belonging to that type of the Mutakallimūn's arguments which directly establish creation, in contradistinction to the other type of their arguments which only refute eternity. As phrased by him, the argument reads as follows: "The generality of them (*'āmmatuhum*) followed the positive method of the establishment of creation (*ṭarīḳ al-ithbāt*) by the establishment of the existence of accidents in the first place, by the establishment of their creation in the second place, by the demonstra-

[28] *Ne'imot*, p. 4b; Arabic, p. 1a.
[29] *Ibid.*, p. 5b; Arabic, p. 3b.
[30] *Ibid.*, p. 6b; Arabic, p. 5a.
[31] *Ibid.*, p. 8a; Arabic, p. 8b.
[32] Hebrew text in Schreiner's *Studien über Jeschua ben Jehuda*, p. 29 f.; German translation, p. 31 f.

tion of the impossibility for atoms to be devoid (*ḫalā*) of accidents in the third place, and by the demonstration of the impossibility for created accidents to have a first in the fourth place. From these propositions it follows that whatever does not precede created things is itself created." [33]

It will be noticed, that, though he describes this argument as one used by the Mutakallimūn as a direct proof for creation, he reproduces Juwaynī's fourth proposition, which, according to Juwaynī himself, is only meant to refute eternity by refuting the possibility of an infinite by succession.[34]

In Judah Halevi, this argument is the second of two arguments described by him as being part of "concise restatements of the views which are considered as manifestly well-founded among those who are concerned with the principles of religion, whom the Karaites call: The Masters of the Kalam." [35] As phrased by him, the argument reads as follows: "The world is created, for the world is a body and a body is not devoid of motion and rest, both of which are accidents occurring to it successively one after the other, but that which occurs to the body of the world [in succession to something preceding it], by the very fact of its occurring [in succession of something preceding it] must inevitably be created and [so also] that which precedes it is created, for, if it were eternal, it [would have no beginning and hence] would not cease to exist [36] [and thus nothing would occur in succession to it, which is contrary to the facts of observation]. Therefore, both of them [namely, that which succeeds and that which precedes] are created. But that which is not devoid of successively occurring accidents is created, seeing that it does not precede its successive accidents and that these successive accidents are created. Therefore, the world [which does not

[33] *Nihāyat*, p. 11, ll. 7–10.
[34] Cf. above, p. 397.
[35] *Cuzari* V, 15.
[36] Reflects *De Caelo* I, 12, 282b, 31: "If ungenerated, it is by hypothesis indestructible."

precede the succession of accidents of which it is not devoid] is created." [37]

Two things are to be noted about this reproduction of the argument. First, the fact that it is ascribed to the "masters of the Kalam" indicates that the term body used in it is conceived of as being composed of atoms. Second, the fact that the accidents, upon the createdness of which the proof for the creation of the body of the world rests, are described as "occurring to it successively one after the other" indicates that, in phrasing this argument, its author was aware both of a refutation of it by Aristotle's view of the possibility of an infinite by succession and of a rebuttal of that refutation by an argument like that used by Juwaynī in refuting that view of Aristotle. Halevi himself, however, despite his belief in creation *ex nihilo*, declared that "the question of eternity and creation is baffling and the arguments on both sides are evenly balanced." [37a]

Averroes in his *Kashf* reproduces this argument twice, in two successive passages which are repetitious in their general content.[38] He ascribes it to the Ash'arites [39] and presents it as one of two arguments for the creation of the world used by the Mutakallimūn in order to prove thereby the existence of God, characterizing this argument as "that which is the better known and upon which the generality of them rely." [40] In the first passage, he says that "the creation of the world is according to them based upon the assertion [a] that bodies are composed of atoms and [b] that the atom is created and [c] that through its creation bodies are created." [41] In his long criticism of the use of this argument as proof for the existence of God he starts out by saying that "the method which they followed in proving the creation of the atom, called by them separate substance, is a method so difficult that it eludes many

[37] *Cuzari* V, 18, [2], p. 332, l. 28 – p. 334, l. 4; p. 333, ll. 19–24.
[37a] *Ibid.* I, 67, p. 28, ll. 22–23; p. 29, l. 22.
[38] *Kashf*, p. 29, l. 14 – p. 31, l. 17, and p. 31, l. 17 – p. 37, l. 15.
[39] *Ibid.*, p. 29, l. 17, and p. 32, l. 8.
[40] *Ibid.*, p. 31, ll. 18–19.
[41] *Ibid.*, p. 29, ll. 17–19.

people trained in the art of logical reasoning, not to speak of the common people." [42] In the second passage he says that the argument is based upon three propositions, as follows: "The first is that substances are inseparable from accidents, that is, they are not devoid of them; the second is that accidents are created; the third is that that which is inseparable from things created, that is, that which is not devoid of things created, is created." [43] Then, like Ibn Suwār, he refutes this argument by Aristotle's advocacy of the possibility of an infinite by succession. This refutation reads as follows: "It is possible to conceive of a single subject, namely, a body, upon which infinite accidents, as you were to say, infinite motions, whether opposed to one another or not opposed to one another, follow successively one after the other." [44] Then, having in mind the Stoic view of an infinite succession of temporarily limited worlds, he compares the view suggested by him to that "which many of the ancients held with regard to the world, namely, that it arose [after an infinite number of worlds had arisen] one after the other." [45]

This criticism is followed by a restatement of the Mutakallimūn's refutation of it by denying the possibility of any infinite by succession.[46]

In view of the fact that in his first passage Averroes criticizes the argument on the score of the unintelligibility of its proof of the createdness of the atom, and in view also of the facts that in his second passage the argument is based on the createdness of atoms and that he refers them both to the refutation of the argument by Aristotle's possibility of an infinite by succession and to the Mutakallimūn's rebuttal of this refutation, it is to be inferred that the "Ash'arites" to whom he ascribes the argument are Juwaynī and his associates rather than Bāḳillānī and his associates. So also it is Juwaynī who is explicitly said by Averroes to be the author of the second of the two arguments for creation mentioned by him

[42] *Ibid.*, ll. 19–21.
[43] *Ibid.*, p. 31, l. 18 – p. 32, l. 1.
[44] *Ibid.*, p. 35, ll. 19–21.
[45] *Ibid.*, p. 35, l. 21 – p. 36, l. 1.
[46] *Ibid.*, p. 36, ll. 1 f.

above as being used by the Mutakallimūn as proof for the existence of God.[47]

The same argument is reproduced by Maimonides as follows: "The world as a whole is composed of atom and accident and no atom is separated from one or several accidents. But all accidents are created in time, from which it must necessarily follow that the atom, which serves as their substratum, is likewise produced in time, for everything that is conjoined with things produced in time and is inseparable from them is produced in time. Therefore, the world in its entirety is produced in time." [48]

In his comments upon this argument, Maimonides discusses three refutations, of which two are as follows:

First, commenting upon the statement that "all accidents are produced in time," he says: "Now our opponent who maintains the eternity of the world contradicts us with regard to one accident, namely, circular movement, for Aristotle claims that circular movement is not subject to generation and corruption." [49] This refutation is based upon Aristotle's answer to his own tentative objection to the eternity of motion, which, as we have seen, is also drawn upon by Ibn Suwār as a refutation of this argument.

Second, commenting upon the statement that "everything that is conjoined with things produced in time and is inseparable from them is produced in time," from which it is inferred that the atom, which is inseparable from its temporally produced accidents, is produced in time, Maimonides says: "If someone argues, perhaps the atom itself is uncreated and only the accidents are produced in time, [but, though produced in time], these accidents are succeeding one another on the atom up to infinity, the Mutakallimūn reply that, in that case, there would be an infinite succession of temporarily produced things, but this they have already established to be impossible." [50] The refutation, based as it is upon Aristotle's

[47] Cf. above at n. 40 and below, pp. 436 f.

[48] *Moreh* I, 74 (4), p. 152, ll. 2–6.

[49] *Ibid.*, ll. 12–14.

[50] *Ibid.*, ll. 6–12.

view of the possibility of an infinite by succession, is used, as we have seen, without any rebuttal by Ibn Suwār and with a rebuttal by Juwaynī.

Stripped of its atomistic assumption as hitherto used by the Mutakallimūn, this argument is used by Ibn Ḥazm (d. 1064) and Joseph ibn Ṣaddiḳ (d. 1149), neither of whom believed in atomism,[51] as an argument for the creation of the world based upon the createdness of bodies not assumed to be composed of atoms. As phrased by Ibn Ḥazm, the argument reads as follows: "Every individual in the world and every accident in an individual and every [duration of] time is finite and has a beginning; [52] . . . and a whole composed of things which are finite and have a beginning is not something other than its parts, for the whole is not something other than the parts into which it can be resolved. . . .[53] Now the world as a whole, consisting as it does of its individuals and their places [text reads: its place] and their temporal durations (*azmānuhā*) and their [accidental] predicates (*maḥmūlātuhā*), is not something other than these things mentioned. But the individuals of the world and their places [text reads: its place] and their temporal durations and their [accidental] predicates have a beginning. Therefore, the world as a whole is finite and has a beginning." [54] As phrased by Ibn Ṣaddiḳ, the argument consists of the following four propositions: "[1] No things are separable (*yimmalṭu*) from substance and accident . . . and neither of these two is separable (*yimmaleṭ*) from the other. [2] Since the thing is so, either of these two alternatives is inevitable (*lo yimmaleṭ*), namely, either the accidents do not exist prior to the substance or the substance does not exist prior to the accidents, the result being that neither of them is prior to the other. [3] The accidents are created. [4] Whatever did not precede created things is created like them." [55] From all these he concludes that "the world as a whole is

[51] On Ibn Ḥazm, *Fiṣal*, V, p. 92, l. 17 ff.; on Ibn Ṣaddiḳ, cf. above, pp. 83–84.

[52] *Fiṣal*, I, p. 14, ll. 20–21.

[53] *Ibid.*, p. 15, ll. 4–6.

[54] *Ibid.*, ll. 7–9.

[55] *Olam Ḳaṭan* III, p. 48, l. 30 – p. 49, l. 6; cf. p. 49, ll. 15–18.

created." [56] Now the term "substance" here is not used by Ibn Ṣaddiḳ in the Kalam sense of atom but rather in the Aristotelian sense of body composed of matter and form, for he himself refers his readers here [57] to his own discussion of substance and accident in Part I of his work, and there his entire discussion is based upon Aristotle's views on matter and form and substance and accident.[58]

Two other forms of the same argument, both of them based upon the createdness of the accidents of bodies, are used by two contemporaries, Saadia (d. 942) and Alfarabi (d. 950), who flourished before Bāḳillānī and probably after the Mutakallimūn referred to by Ibn Suwār, and thus may have been acquainted with the Mutakallimūn's use of that argument.

In Saadia, the argument, which is described as being taken "from accidents," is used, like all his other arguments, to prove a conception of creation in which he himself believed. As phrased by him, it is based upon two pairs of propositions, one of these pairs dealing with accidents observed in celestial bodies. The first pair of propositions reads as follows: (1) "I found that no bodies are devoid (*taḫlū*) of accidents," [59] which accidents, he goes on to explain, appear and disappear, that is to say, they are created, but (2) "it is well known that whatever is not devoid (*yaḫlū*) of that which is created is [created] like it." [60] The second pair of propositions, dealing with celestial bodies, reads as follows: (1) "I observed them clearly, and beheld that they were inseparable (*lā tanfakk*) from created accidents," [61] and so, (2) "when I found . . . that they do not precede the created accidents (*lam tusabbiḳuha*), I was fully convinced that [they were created, for] whatever does not precede (*lam yusabbiḳ*) its created accident is [created] like it." [62]

In Alfarabi, the argument is presented only for the purpose

[56] *Ibid.*, p. 49, l. 18.
[57] *Ibid.*, p. 48, l. 31 – p. 49, l. 2; cf. p. 49, ll. 15–16.
[58] *Ibid.*, I, ii. p. 7, l. 1 – p. 9, l. 17.
[59] *Emunot* I, 1, 1st Theory, 3rd Argument, p. 35, ll. 4–5.
[60] *Ibid.*, ll. 9–10. [61] *Ibid.*, l. 11. [62] *Ibid.*, ll. 15–17.

of illustrating by a concrete example what is meant by a compound syllogism. Here is a simplified form of the seven syllogisms into which he has recast the argument: (1) "Every body is composite (*mu'allaf*) and anything composite is joined to an accident from which it is inseparable (*lā yanfakk*)," so that "every body is inseparably joined to an accident"; but "whatever is inseparably joined to an accident is inseparably joined to something created"; therefore, every body is inseparably joined to something created." (2) "Whatever is inseparably joined to something created is not preceding (*ghayr musābiḳ*) that something created," whence "no body is preceding something created"; but "whatever is not preceding something created comes into existence simultaneously with the coming into existence of that something created," whence "the coming into existence of every body takes place simultaneously with the coming into existence of something created." (3) But "the world is a body"; therefore, "the world is created." [63]

Neither Saadia nor Alfarabi indicates that the term "body" used by them refers to a body assumed to consist of atoms. In the case of Saadia, who uses this argument as proof for his own belief in creation, we may infer from his own disbelief in atoms that the term "body" in the argument is not used by him in the sense of a body consisting of atoms. In the case of Alfarabi, who uses this argument only for the purpose of illustration, we can only assume, on the ground of his not mentioning atoms, that the term "body" in the argument is used by him, as by his contemporary Saadia, not in the sense of a body consisting of atoms. Since both of them could have known of the use of this argument by the Mutakallimūn referred to by Ibn Suwār, and since also both of them use the reasoning based on the term *fakka* as used by Ibn Suwār and the reasoning based on the term *sabaḳa* as used by Bāḳillānī,[64]

[63] Alfarabi, *Al-Ḳiyās al-Ṣaghīr*, ed. Mubahat Türker, p. 262, l. 16 – p. 263, l. 7; Hebrew translation quoted by Ventura, *Saadia*, p. 104, n. 33.

[64] Saadia uses also the term *taḥlū* (p. 35, l. 4).

we may assume that both of them knew that the argument was used by the Mutakallimūn in the sense of a body consisting of atoms. In the case of Alfarabi, we may discern additional evidence of his knowledge of it in his use of the term *mu'allaf* in his opening statement "every body is composite (*mu'allaf*)," for the term *mu'allaf* rather than the term *murakkab* is mostly used in the Kalam in describing bodies as being composed of atoms.[65] In fact, Alfarabi himself, in one place, where he happens to refer to atomism, evidently the atomism of both the Greeks and the Mutakallimūn, began by using the term *murakkab* and then used the term *ta'līf*.[66] We may therefore assume that, though both Saadia and Alfarabi knew that the argument was used by the Mutakallimūn on the basis of the createdness of bodies assumed to be composed of atoms, they used it on the basis of bodies not assumed to be composed of atoms.

Surveying the various forms in which this argument is reproduced, we find that they fall into three types. The first type, the earliest one, which is used by Mutakallimūn, is that in which the argument is based upon the createdness of bodies assumed to be composed of atoms. The second type, which appeared later and is used by other Mutakallimūn, is that in which the argument is based upon the createdness of atoms. The third type, used by non-Mutakallimūn, is that in which the argument is based upon the createdness of bodies not assumed to be composed of atoms. Then we also find that the createdness of either the bodies or the atoms in all these three types of the argument is proved by the sensibly perceived creation of the accidents whether those of the bodies or those of the atoms. From these findings we may draw two conclusions with regard to the nature of this argument.

First, from the fact that of two groups of Mutakallimūn, both of them atomists, in trying to prove the createdness of

[65] *Maḳālāt*, pp. 302 f.; *Tamhīd*, p. 17, l. 8; cf. p. 12, l. 7; *Irshād*, p. 10, ll. 11–12; *Moreh* I, 73, Prop. I, p. 135, ll. 19–20.

[66] *'Uyūn al-Masā'il* 15, p. 61, ll. 13–15.

the component parts of the world by the sensibly perceived creation of their accidents, one of these two groups uses accidents of bodies and the other uses accidents of atoms, coupled with the fact that among the Mutakallimūn there was a difference of opinion as to whether atoms, in their isolation from bodies, could be perceived by the senses,[67–70] it is to be inferred that the difference between these two groups of Mutakallimūn in the use of the term accidents in their respective presentations of this argument is due to a difference of opinion between them as to the sensible perceptibility of atoms. Thus the Mutakallimūn who originally framed the argument as being based upon the createdness of bodies did so either because they themselves believed that the atoms of which bodies were composed could not directly be known by sense perception or because they wanted to frame the argument in such a way that it could be used even by those who believed that atoms could be directly known by sense perception, whereas those Mutakallimūn who later changed the argument to one based upon the createdness of atoms did so because they believed that atoms could be known directly by sense perception.

Second, from the fact that the component parts of the world — upon the createdness of which this argument for the creation of the world depends — are taken by those who use this argument to be either atoms or bodies assumed to be composed of atoms or bodies not assumed to be composed of atoms, it is to be inferred that what the component parts of the world happen to be assumed by one to be is not logically essential to the argument; what is logically essential to it is only the createdness of the component parts of the world.

So understood, the argument is analogous to an argument from the createdness of the component parts of the world used by three Greek Church Fathers, Basil (d. 379), Diodorus of Tarsus (d. c. 394), and John of Damascus (d. c. 754). As phrased by Basil, it reads: "Of what use are geometry . . .

[67–70] Cf. below, p. 491.

and far-famed astronomy . . . if those who pursue them cannot conceive that that of which the parts are subject to corruption and change must at some time by itself as a whole necessarily submit to the same incidents (παθήματα) that befall its parts." [71] Diodorus, as quoted by Photius, argues that "every change . . . spells corruption and a departure from the essence of that which is beginningless, and how then can things uncreated depend upon that which is created? . . . If one should say that change is uncreated, he utters something which is most impossible, for change is an incident (πάθος) which has a beginning, and so nobody can rightly speak of a beginningless change." [72] John of Damascus, starting with the general statement that "all things that exist are either created or uncreated," raises the rhetorical question: "Who, then, will refuse to grant that all existing things . . . are subject to change and alteration and movement of various kinds?" Expecting a negative answer, he concludes: "Things that are changeable are also wholly created." [73]

Now I have shown elsewhere that this Patristic argument is based upon Aristotle's tentative objection to the eternity of the world on the ground that "no change is eternal, for all change is from something to something" [74] and that one of the three Greek Fathers who used this argument, the earliest one, Basil, has taken note of Aristotle's refutation of it and rebutted it.[75] But, as we have seen above, both Ibn Suwār and Maimonides try to show how this argument of the Mutakallimūn for the creation of the world could be refuted by Aristotle's refutation of his own tentative objection to the eternity of the world.[76] The conclusion to be drawn therefrom is that, just as there is a relation between the Patristic argument and Aristotle's tentative objection, so there must

[71] *Hexaemeron* I, 3 (PG 29, 9 C–12 A).
[72] Photius, *Bibliotheca* 223 (PG 103, 833 BC).
[73] *De Fide Orthodoxa* I, 3 (PG 94, 796 A–C).
[74] *Phys.* VIII, 2, 252b, 9–10.
[75] Cf. pp. 352–354 of my article "Patristic Arguments against the Eternity of the World," *HTR*, 59:351–367 (1966).
[76] Cf. above, pp. 396; 402.

also be a relation between the Mutakallimūn's argument and Aristotle's tentative objection; and hence one is tempted to assume either that the Mutakallimūn's argument, like the Patristic argument, is based directly upon Aristotle's tentative objection or, what is more likely, that it is based upon the Patristic argument. Though there is no record of an Arabic translation of the work of Diodorus from which the argument is quoted by Photius and though also the *Hexaemeron* of Basil and the *De Fide Orthodoxa* of John of Damascus were translated into Arabic too late [77] to have been used by the Mutakallimūn referred to by Ibn Suwār, the Patristic argument may have become known to those Mutakallimūn, like some other Patristic teachings,[78] by oral transmission or it may have been reproduced in some Arabic work of that as yet unexplored vast Christian literature in Arabic. In our discussion of the preceding Kalam argument for the creation of the world we have seen how two versions of it have arisen out of an argument in an Arabic work by the Christian Abucara.[79] We have also seen how two of the Mutakallimūn's arguments for the unity of God, the argument from "mutual hindering" (*al-tamānu*ʿ) and the argument from "need" (*al-iftiḳār*), are traceable to John of Damascus,[80] though both arguments must have been known to the Mutakallimūn long before his *De Fide Orthodoxa* was translated into Arabic, for it can be shown that two arguments used by Saadia for the unity of God reflect these two arguments of the Mutakallimūn.[81] Similarly in our discussion later of the problem of free will and predestination we shall see how the conception in Islam of the non-causativity of God's foreknowledge is traceable to an Arabic work by the Christian Abucara, which is itself based upon John of Damascus.[82]

[77] On the dates of the translations of these works, see Graf, *Gesch. d. chridtl. arabisch. Litteratur*, II, pp. 56 and 52 for Basil and pp. 43 and 41 for John of Damascus.

[78] Cf. above, p. 129. [79] Cf. above, pp. 391–392. [80] Cf. above, pp. 49–50.

[81] *Emunot* II, 2, p. 82, (1) ll. 7–9, and (2) ll. 5–6.

[82] Cf. below, p. 663.

5. ARGUMENT FROM THE IMPOSSIBILITY OF AN INFINITE BY SUCCESSION

In our discussion of the preceding argument from the createdness of accidents, we have seen how Ibn Suwār raised a certain objection to it and how Juwaynī, Judah Halevi, Averroes, and Maimonides, after mentioning the same objection against that argument, refer to the Mutakallimūn's answer to that objection consisting in their denial of the possibility of an infinite by succession. Now it happens that the denial of the possibility of an infinite by succession which in Juwaynī and Judah Halevi and Averroes and Maimonides forms part of the argument from the creation of the accidents of atoms, where it is used as an answer to an objection raised against that argument, had been used before the time of Juwaynī by Naẓẓām and Saadia as an independent argument for the creation of the world, or rather as a refutation of its eternity, and that even after Juwaynī it is used as an independent argument by Ghazālī [1] and also by Maimonides,[2] in addition to his use of it as a reinforcing argument.[3] Averroes, in his Epitome of the *Physics*, indicates that the argument from the impossibility of an infinite by succession has its origin in John Philoponus' refutation of Aristotle's eternity of the world.[4] Still, despite his knowledge that the argument was originated by John Philoponus, he refers to it, both in his *Kashf* and in his *Tahāfut al-Tahāfut*,[5] as an argument of the Mutakallimūn. This, it would seem, is due to the fact that of John Philoponus' two arguments against eternity quoted or referred to by him, namely, (1) the argument from finitudes and (2) the argument from the impossibility of an infinite by succession, the latter — as may be gathered from the way it is introduced by those who happen to use it, such, for instance, as Halevi [6] and

[1] Cf. below, p. 422. [2] *Moreh* I, 74 (2) [3] *Ibid.* I, 74(4).

[4] Cf. Arabic text of the Epitome of the *Physics* (in *Rasā'il Ibn Rushd*, Hyderabad, A.H. 1366 [1947], p. 110, ll. 7–18; Hebrew translation, Riva di Trento, 1560, p. 40b, ll. 6–18.

[5] Cf. below, pp. 424; 425. [6] Cf. below, p. 423.

Shahrastānī [7] and Maimonides [8] — was of common use by the Mutakallimūn, whereas the former — as may be gathered from the way it is introduced by Ibn Suwār,[9] and from the fact that it is not included among the Mutakallimūn's arguments for creation listed by Halevi and Shahrastānī and Maimonides [10] and also from the fact that no mention of its use by the Mutakallimūn is made by Averroes in any of his references to it [10a] — was not used by the Mutakallimūn. An explanation of why no use was made by the Mutakallimūn of John Philoponus' argument from finitudes would seem to be found in the fact that this argument, as shown above, is directly not an argument for the createdness of the world but an argument for its corruptibility.[10b]

John Philoponus' arguments against Aristotle's view of the possibility of an infinite by succession occurred in two of his works, in his *Contra Aristotelem*, which is not extant in its original Greek, and in his *Contra Proclum*, which is extant in its original Greek. Both these works were translated into Arabic,[11] but the translations are not extant. However, one argument against this particular view of Aristotle is reproduced by Simplicius.[12]

As it is the Aristotelian conception of the possibility of an infinite by succession that the argument of John Philoponus is a refutation of, the target of that refutation may be restated as follows.

By a long argument Aristotle first arrives at the conclusion that "there is no body which is actually infinite." [13] He then raises a doubt: "Yet to suppose that the infinite does not exist in any way leads to many impossible consequences," and one

[7] Cf. below, p. 424. [8] Cf. below, pp. 425–426.
[9] See reference above, p. 374, n. 4.
[10] *Cuzari* V, 18; *Nihāyat*, p. 11, l. 5 ff.; *Moreh* I, 74.
[10a] See references above, pp. 378–379. [10b] Cf. above, pp. 376–377.
[11] Cf. Steinschneider, *Die arabischen Uebersetzungen aus dem Griechischen*, § 55 (79).
[12] *Simplicius in Physica*, VIII, 1, p. 1179, ll. 15–27. Cf. S. van den Bergh, *Averroes' Tahāfut al-Tahāfut*, II, p. 7, note to p. 9, 1.
[13] *Phys.* III, 5, 206a, 7–8.

of them is that "there will be a beginning and end of time." [14] In order to obviate that impossible consequence, he draws a distinction between an actual infinite and a potential infinite: an actual infinite, indeed, does not exist; a potential infinite does exist.[15] Of the potential infinite Aristotle mentions several kinds, but the one necessary for our purpose here is that which he describes as being infinite in the sense that the parts exist successively, in contrast to which the actual infinite is that whose parts exist simultaneously, and as an illustration of an infinite by succession he mentions the terms "day," "time," "men," and "movement." "Just as it is said that a day is . . . in the sense that one thing after another is always being generated, so also is the infinite." [16] Again: "The infinite exhibits itself differently in time, in men . . . For generally the infinite has this mode of existence: one thing is always being taken after another, and each thing that is taken is always finite, but always different." [17] Again: "Time indeed and movement are infinite . . . in the sense that each part that is taken does not remain." [18] In these passages, by the term "men," he means the generation of men from other men,[19] and by the terms "day," "time," and "movement," he means the revolutions of the celestial bodies.[20] Later in the same work Aristotle shows how all things that are moved are moved by something else,[21] and how the celestial bodies, because they are each moved by something else, are moved accidentally,[22] and how things in the world which are all moved by something else and in which sense they are moved accidentally

[14] *Ibid.*, 6, 206a, 9–11.

[15] *Ibid.*, 206a, 14 ff.

[16] *Ibid.*, 21–23.

[17] *Ibid.*, 25–29.

[18] *Ibid.*, 8, 208a, 20–21.

[19] Averroes, *In Phys.* III, Comm. 58 (IV, p. 112 F), has "in generatione" in place of "in hominibus" (IV, p. 111 I), the latter of which is a translation of Aristotle's *ἐπὶ τῶν ἀνθρώπων* (206a, 26).

[20] *Phys.* IV, 14, 223a, 33: "And it [that is, time] is simply the number of continuous motion," upon which Averroes remarks: "D. d. Est igitur propter hoc numerus motus, i. corporis coelestis" (*In Phys.* IV, Comm. 132 [IV, p. 203 F]).

[21] *Phys.* VIII, 4, 256a, 2–3.

[22] *Ibid.*, 6, 259b, 28–31.

terminate at the accidental circular motion of the celestial bodies which in turn are moved eternally by the eternal absolutely immovable first mover.[23]

John Philoponus' refutations, as may be gathered from his work against Proclus, fall into two parts.

In the first part, he begins by showing that "if the world is eternal, it will necessarily follow that, in this world, from the beginning to the present moment, the number of generated beings (*γενομένων*), of men or of plants or of other individuals (*ἀτόμων*) of every species, will be actually infinite. For if someone supposes a finite number of generated men or plants or any other individuals, then each one of them will have its existence in a finite [and hence generated] time, and the whole time will have to be finite [and hence generated], seeing that that which consists of finites is finite. If therefore the world is ungenerated and withal the generated [whole] time is actually infinite, it necessarily follows that the individuals generated in the infinite are actually infinite in number." [24]

Having thus established that if the world is eternal the succession of things within it would make an actual infinite, he goes on, in the second part, to summarize from his work against Aristotle two arguments to show that "in no manner whatsoever does an actual infinite exist — neither as existing all at once (*ἀθρόον*) nor as being generated bit by bit (*κατὰ μέρος*)," [25] for which two terms, *ἀθρόον* and *κατὰ μέρος*, he subsequently uses as their equivalents the terms *ἅμα*, "simultaneously," [26] and *διαδοχή*, "succession." [27]

In his first argument, inasmuch as he has already established that an infinite of which the parts are conceived to be generated in succession to each other is not a potential but an actual infinite, he tries to show that it is not to be distin-

[23] *Ibid.*, 7.
[24] *De Aeternitate Mundi contra Proclum*, p. 9, ll. 4–18.
[25] *Ibid.*, p. 9, ll. 20–22; p. 10, ll. 1–3.
[26] *Ibid.*, p. 10, l. 3.
[27] *Ibid.*, l. 23.

guished from an infinite of which the parts are conceived to exist simultaneously. There is a common reason, he says, for the impossibility of both these kinds of the infinite, the common reason being Aristotle's own principle that "it is impossible to traverse (διεξελθεῖν) an infinite." [28] And when he has explained how this principle of the intraversability of an infinite is to include the impossibility of the existence of an infinite number of things existing in succession of one after another, he uses this impossibility of an infinite by succession as an argument against the eternity of the world, as follows: "The infinite [by way of succession] thus being intraversable, if then the succession (διαδοχή) advancing from individual to individual of any given species arrives at things now existing through an infinite number of individuals, the infinite has been traversed, which is impossible." [29] The implication of this argument is that, on the basis of the principle that an infinite cannot be traversed, if we assume that there was in the past an infinite number of individuals of any species, no individual of that species could come into existence.

His second argument reads: "If the world is beginningless, then the generated number [of men] up to the time of Socrates, for instance, would be infinite; but if to that number were added the [men] generated from the time of Socrates to the present time, there would be something greater than the infinite, which is impossible." [30] And having in mind Aristotle's statement that "the same [infinite] thing cannot be many infinites," [31] with its implication that one infinite cannot be greater than another infinite,[31a] he similarly argues in his lost work against Aristotle, as quoted by Simplicius, that the assumption of eternity would lead to the absurdity that one infinite would be greater than another infinite. This form of

[28] *Ibid.*, ll. 3–5, based upon a combination of *Phys.* VIII, 8, 263a, 6, and VIII, 9, 265a, 19–20.
[29] *Ibid.*, p. 9, ll. 22–23.
[30] *Ibid.*, p. 11, ll. 2–6.
[31] *Phys.* III, 5, 204a, 25–26.
[31a] Cf. *Averroes in III Phys.*, Comm. 37, p. 102 C.

the argument is based upon the revolutions of the celestial spheres. Thus the sphere of Saturn completes its revolution in thirty years, the sphere of Jupiter in twelve years, the sphere of the Sun in one year, the sphere of the Moon in one month, and the sphere of the fixed stars in one day. Now, on the assumption of the eternity of the world, argues John Philoponus, each of these revolutions would be infinite, and yet, as compared with the revolutions of Saturn, those of Jupiter would be "almost three times as many" [that is, two and a half times as many], those of the Sun would be "thirty times as many," those of the Moon would be "three hundred and sixty times as many, and those of the sphere of the fixed stars would be "more than ten thousand times as many" [that is, 10,950].[32]

John Philoponus thus has two arguments in refutation of an infinite by succession, both of them based upon principles advanced by Aristotle himself, one based upon the principle that no infinite can be traversed and the other based on the principle that nothing can be greater than the infinite or that one infinite cannot be greater than another infinite, and in the unfolding of these arguments for the impossibility of an infinite by succession he uses the examples of the generation of men and the revolutions of the celestial spheres, the very same examples that are referred to by Aristotle by the terms "men"[33] and "movement,"[34] that is, the circular movement of the celestial spheres,[35] in the unfolding of his arguments for the possibility of an infinite by succession.

Let us now trace in chronological order the history of the various forms in which these two arguments for the impossibility of an infinite by succession were used, irrespective of whether both of them were used or only one of them was used, whether used directly as an argument for creation or whether used only as a reinforcement of the argument from the creation of the accident of atoms, and whether using for

[32] *Simplicius in Physica*, VIII, 1, p. 1179, ll. 18–22.
[33] *Phys.* III, 6, 206a, 26.
[34] *Ibid.*, 8, 208a, 20.
[35] *Ibid.*, VIII, 8.

the purpose of illustration the generation of men or the revolutions of the celestial spheres or of time or of movement in general.

Naẓẓām, as reported by Ḫayyāṭ on the basis of reports by Ibn al-Rāwandī, first refuted the Manichaean view of an infinite place, arguing that "the traversing (*ḳaṭ'*) of an infinite is impossible," [36] a statement which is based upon Aristotle's statement that "it is impossible to traverse (διελθεῖν) an infinite." [37] He then took up "the people who believed in the eternity of the world (*ahl al-dahr*)" [38] and tried to convince them that the successive movements of finite bodies must terminate at an act of creation.

He has two arguments.

His first argument reads as follows: "That which has passed of the traversing of bodies [that is, the past revolutions of the celestial bodies] must inevitably be either finite or infinite. If it is finite, it has a first, and this destroys your belief [in the eternity of the world]. And if it is infinite, it has no first, but that which has no first cannot arrive at any end [that is to say, it could have no succession of effects, or, more specifically, it could have no succession of revolutions up to some given day]. Therefore, the fact that that which has passed does arrive at some end is proof that it [has a first and] is finite." [39] From the context it is quite clear that Naẓẓām's argument here against the eternity of the world is an extension of his argument from the Aristotelian principle of the intraversability of an infinite previously used by him against the Manichaean infinite space. The two statements by which he tries to prove his contention against eternity, namely, that "if it is infinite, it has no first" and "that which has no first cannot arrive at some end," are explanations of how the Aristotelian statement about the intraversability of an infinite, in which the term "infinite" originally refers to infinite space, can be extended to include infinite motion. The two state-

[36] *Intiṣār* 19, p. 31, l. 21.

[37] *Phys.* VIII, 9, 265a, 20; cf. above n. 28.

[38] *Intiṣār* 20, p. 33, l. 2.

[39] *Ibid.*, ll. 3–6.

ments themselves are in fact based upon two statements in Aristotle, the former upon his statement that "in an infinite series there is no first," [40] and the latter upon his statement that "if there is no first there is no cause at all," [41] by which he means, as may be judged from the context, that without a first or cause, there can be no series of effects ending at any actual present time (νῦν).[42] It is quite possible that this additional explanation is taken from John Philoponus' lost work against Aristotle, for, as we have seen, there is a slight indication of it in the passage quoted above from his work against Proclus.[43]

The second argument is characterized by Ḥayyāṭ as "the best [argument] of the Kalam against those who believe in the eternity of the world." [44] It reads as follows: "Naẓẓām inquired of those who believed in the eternity of the world concerning the traversings of the stars [that is, concerning the infinite revolutions of the eternally revolving planets], saying: They must inevitably be either equal [in number] or unequal. If they are equal, then [inasmuch as] the number of one thing plus the number of another thing equal to it is greater than the number of the one thing separately, [the infinite revolutions of any two planets would be greater than the infinite revolutions of any one planet, and thus one infinite would be greater than another infinite, which is absurd]. And if they are unequal [one being more numerous than the other], then they are certainly finite with respect to revolutions, for the terms more and less are indications of finitude." [45]

In Saadia, the argument from the impossibility of an infinite succession is divided into two parts, one based on the premise that no infinite can be traversed and the other on the premise that no infinite can be greater than any other infinite.

[40] *Phys.* VIII, 5, 256a, 18–19. [41] *Metaph.* II, 2, 994a, 18–19.

[42] See Ross's Commentary on 994a, 18, and cf. *De Gen. at Corr.* II, 11, 337b, 28–29.

[43] Cf. above, pp. 413–414.

[44] *Intiṣār* 20, p. 33, ll. 18–19.

[45] *Ibid.*, ll. 13–16; cf. p. 33, l. 20 – p. 34, l. 1.

The first part constitutes the last of his four arguments for creation. It is presented by him in two forms, one of them playing upon the term "time" and the other upon the term "men," corresponding to the term "time" and "men" used by Aristotle in his discussion of the possibility of an infinite by succession.[46] Saadia, however, designates his entire fourth argument as an "argument from time."[47]

In the first form of the argument, conceiving of the flow of time from the past to the present as a sort of descent from the top of a place downward to the bottom and hence, conversely, conceiving of one's thinking backward to the past as a sort of ascent upward to the top, he says: "I know that time is threefold: past, present, and future. Although the present is smaller than any instant [that one can imagine], I take the instant [in time] as one takes a point [in space] and say: If a man should desire in his thought to ascend from that point upward (*ilā fauḳ*: *le-maʿalah*), it would be impossible for him to do so, inasmuch as time is now assumed to be infinite [in the past] and, with regard to that which is infinite [in this sense of having no beginning], thought (*al-fikr*: *ha-maḥashabah*) cannot proceed through it in that ascending manner and traverse it. The very same reason would make it impossible for the process of generation (*al-kaun*: *ha-havayah*=γένεσις) to course downward (*suflan*: *le-maṭṭah*) through the infinite and traverse it so as to reach us [and thus come to an end]."[48]

The general basis of this passage is the statement that "it is impossible to traverse the infinite," which occurs in several places in the works of Aristotle and to which reference has already been made above in connection with Naẓẓām.[49] But Saadia's use of the expression "thought cannot . . . traverse it," as well as his use of the adverbs "upward" and "downward," indicates that he had in mind here one particular statement of Aristotle, which reads that "it is impossible to traverse infinites in thought (νοοῦντα); consequently there are

[46] Cf. above, p. 412. [47] *Emunot* I, 1 (4), p. 36, l. 1. [48] *Ibid.*, ll. 1–7.
[49] Cf. above n. 28, and Bonitz, *Index Aristotelicus*, s. v. p. 74b, ll. 30–34.

no infinites either upward (ἐπὶ τὸ ἄνω) or downward (ἐπὶ τὸ κάτω)." [50]

In the second form of the argument, similarly conceiving of the process of "generation," that is, of the succession of causes and effects, as a descending process, he starts with the statement quoted above at the end of the first part of the argument that "it is impossible for the process of generation to course downward through the infinite and traverse it so as to reach us [and thus come to an end]," and then goes on to say: "But if the process of generation could not reach us, we could not come into existence. It would then necessarily follow that we and the multitude of all those who have come into existence would not have come into existence and existent things would not be existent. But since I find myself existent, I know that the process of generation has traversed the whole length of time until it reached me and that, if it were not for the fact that time is finite [in the past], the process of generation would not have traversed it. And unhesitatingly I affirm the same belief with regard to the future time as I did with regard to the past time." [51]

Later the same argument is restated by him more succinctly. If we assume, he says, that the existence of a thing were always conditioned upon its coming into being from another thing, then "the process would continue to infinity. But since the infinite required for our own coming into existence could not be completely traversed, the necessary conclusion would be that we do not exist. The fact is, however, that we do exist. Thus, if the things prior to our existence had not been finite, they could not have been completed so as to make possible our existence." [52] This argument reflects the Aristotelian statements already quoted above in connection with Naẓẓām.[53]

The second part of the argument, that based on the premise that no infinite can be greater than any other infinite, occurs as a refutation of the eighth of his thirteen theories of the

[50] *Anal. Post.* I, 22, 83b, 6–7.

[51] *Emunot* I, 1 (4), p. 36, ll. 6–7.

[52] *Ibid.*, 2, p. 40, ll. 18–20.

[53] Cf. above, p. 414.

origin of the world, which, as may be seen, is the Aristotelian theory of eternity. Starting with the self-evident premise that, on the assumption of the eternity of the world, the revolutions of each of the celestial spheres would be infinite, he presents the argument in two forms, corresponding to the two forms in which the argument is presented by John Philoponus. In its first form, it is described as an argument from "increase and diminution" and reads as follows: "Every day that elapses of the time of the revolution of the sphere constitutes an increase in past time and a diminution of the time to come. Now that which is susceptible of increase and diminution must be finite in power, and finitude necessarily implies creation." [54] In its second form, it is described as an argument from "the variation of the movements of the heavenly bodies," in which, having in mind the rotations of the uppermost sphere and the sphere of the Moon and the sphere of the Sun which are completed respectively in one day and in thirty days and in 365 days, he argues as follows: "When, therefore, we see that the movements of the heavenly bodies vary to such an extent that they are related to each other by the ratio of 1 to 30 or to 365 or more, we know that each of them is finite." He then also mentions the difference between the rotation of the uppermost sphere, which is completed in one day, and the rotation of the sphere of the fixed stars, which is completed once in 36,000 years, that is, in 13,140,000 days.[55]

In Juwaynī's *Irshād*, where the argument from the impossibility of an infinite by succession is used as a reinforcement of the argument from the creation of the accidents of atoms,[56] it is presented as only based on the principle that no infinite can be traversed as it was restated by Naẓẓām in the form of a demonstration showing that nothing can come into existence if its coming into existence had to be preceded by an infinite

[54] *Emunot* I, 3, 8th Theory, p. 60, ll. 11–14.

[55] *Ibid.*, p. 60, l. 16 – p. 61, l. 6. For the number 36,000 years, see *Rasa'il Iḫwān al-Ṣafa'*, 36, Vol. III, p. 251, ll. 1–2.

[56] Cf. above, pp. 396; 410.

number of causes. It reads as follows: "Let us take, for example, the revolution of the sphere witnessed by us now. According to the opinion of the unbelievers (*al-malāḥidah*), there have elapsed, before the revolution witnessed by us now, an infinite number of revolutions. But that which is infinite through the succession of one unit after another cannot be at an end. But the revolutions which preceded the revolution witnessed by us now are at an end. Therefore, the fact that they have elapsed and they have terminated proves that they are finite [and have a beginning]. This is sufficient for our purpose."[57] This, again, is based upon the Aristotelian statements quoted above in connection with Naẓẓām.

In corroboration of the conclusion to be drawn from this argument, namely, that nothing can take place if the taking place is conditioned upon a succession of infinite things preceding it, Juwaynī quotes certain keen reasoners (*muḥaṣṣilūn*) who argue that anyone who holds the opposite view is to be compared to one who says to another one: I will not give you a dirham unless I give you before it a dinar and I will not give you a dinar unless I give you before it a dirham."[58] By the terms of this condition, the argument concludes, neither a dinar nor a dirham will ever have to be given by the one who has made the offer.

Traces of the argument from the impossibility of an infinite by succession are to be found in Ibn Ḥazm. First, in the course of his fifth argument for creation, he makes the following statements: "There is no way for the second to exist except after the first and for the third except after the second, and so on forever;"[59] and so "if there were no first, there would be no last."[60] On the basis of these statements, he concluded that the world was created. Second, in the course of his third argument for creation, Ibn Ḥazm, having in mind the revolutions of the uppermost sphere and the sphere of

[57] *Irshād*, p. 15, ll. 6–10 (p. 34).
[58] *Ibid.*, p. 15, l. 17 – p. 16, l. 1 (p. 35).
[59] *Fiṣal* I, p. 18, ll. 20–22.
[60] *Ibid.*, p. 19, ll. 2–3.

Saturn, which are completed respectively in one day and in 10,950 days, argues that the assumption of the eternity of the world would lead to the conclusion that "one infinite is greater than another by well nigh 11,000 times, but that is absurd." [61]

In Ghazālī, the argument is presented in the form of a challenge to those who believe in eternity. It reads as follows: "By what reasoning will you refute your opponents in their argument that the eternity of the world is absurd on the ground that it will lead to the assumption that the revolutions of the spheres are infinite in number and that they cannot be numbered, despite the fact that the revolutions of the various spheres are related to each other as one sixth or one fourth or one half? For the sphere of Sun completes its revolution once in a year and the sphere of Saturn completes its revolution once in thirty years, whence the revolutions of Saturn are one thirtieth of the revolutions of Sun. Similarly the revolutions of Jupiter are one twelfth of the revolutions of Sun, for it completes its revolution in twelve years. But, according to you, just as the number of the revolutions of Saturn is infinite so also the number of the revolutions of Sun is infinite, despite the fact that the former is one thirtieth of the latter. Similarly the number of the revolutions of the sphere of the fixed stars, which completes its revolution once in 36,000 years, is infinite, just as is the number of the rising of Sun, which are each completed once during one day and night." [62]

In Baḥya, the argument is reflected in two statements which he makes in the course of his arguments for the creation of the world which he uses as a basis for his proofs for the existence of God. First, starting with the statement that "that which has no beginning has no end," [63] he proceeds to explain it on the ground that "it is impossible in that which has no beginning to reach an end at which one can stop." [64] Second, he adds: "If we conceive in our mind something that is ac-

[61] *Ibid.*, p. 16, l. 7 – p. 18, l. 10.
[62] *Tahāfut al-Falāsifah* I, 16, p. 31, l. 10 – p. 32, l. 6.
[63] *Ḥobot* I, 5, p. 44, l. 5.
[64] *Ibid.*, ll. 5–6.

tually infinite [as would be the case if we assume the world to be eternal] and we take off from it a certain part, then the remainder will undoubtedly be less than what it was before. Now if the remainder is infinite [as, again, would be the case if we assume the world to be eternal], then one infinite will be greater than another. But this is impossible." [65] Both these statements are quite evidently based on Saadia.

In Judah Halevi, as we have already seen, the argument from the impossibility of an infinite by succession is hinted at as a reinforcement of the argument from the creation of the accidents of atoms, which is the second of the arguments for creation which he quotes in the name of the Mutakallimūn.[66] As an independent argument, however, it is reproduced by him as the first of the Mutakallimūn's arguments for creation. It is presented in two forms.

First, on the basis of the principle that no infinite can be traversed, he argues: "If the past were infinite, then the individuals [that is, the individuals of any species] existing in the eternal past down to our own age would be infinite. But that which is infinite cannot pass into actuality; how, then, could those individuals have passed into actuality? . . . Inevitably, therefore, the past had a beginning and the existing individuals have a number which comes to an end . . . Hence the world had a beginning and the revolutions of the celestial sphere have a number which comes to an end." [67] Again, "if the creatures [that is, the individuals of the human species] were infinite in number, then how was that number brought to an end with us? For that which ends at something must inevitably have a beginning, seeing that otherwise each individual [human being] in order to come into existence would have to wait for the existence of an infinite number of individual [human beings] before him, with the result that no individual [human being] would ever come into existence." [68]

Second, on the basis of the principle that no infinite can

[65] *Ibid.*, ll. 13–15.

[66] *Cuzari* V, 15. Cf. above, pp. 399–400.

[67] *Ibid.*, 18 (1), p. 332, ll. 8–17; p. 331, l. 26 – p. 333, l. 7.

[68] *Ibid.*, p. 332, ll. 23–27; p. 333, ll. 14–18.

be greater than another, he argues: "For that which is infinite has no half nor double nor any numerical proportion. We know, however, that the revolutions of the sphere of the Sun are one twelfth of those of the Moon, and so do the other spheres stand in some numerical relation to one another, one being a part of the other. But of that which is infinite there is no part." [69]

In Shahrastānī, the argument is reproduced only as based on the principle that no infinite is greater than another,[70] and this is presented in its two forms.

In one of its forms, after quoting in the name of Avicenna the principle that one infinite cannot be greater than another, he argues that, on the assumption that the world is eternal, the past years before a certain given day and the future years after that day would be equal in infinity, but "if we took off a year from the past and added it to the future, then the past would be decreased and the future would be increased, even though they are both equal in infinity, whence it would result that the more would be equal to the less." [71]

In its other form, it reads as follows: "An argument raised against those who believe in the eternity of the world (*al-dahriyyah*) is that the movements of Saturn, which is in the seventh sphere, are equal to those of the Moon, which is in the first sphere, seeing that either one of them is infinite. But it is well known that [within the same given time] the movements of Saturn are less than the movements of the Moon. Thus the movements of the Moon are both equal to the movements of Saturn and greater than they. But this is utterly absurd and extremely self-contradictory." [72]

Averroes reproduces this argument in two of his works.

In his *Kashf*, it is reproduced in the name of "the later ones of the Mutakallimūn" as a reinforcement of the argument from the creation of the accidents of atoms. As reproduced there, it is based on the principle that no infinite can be

[69] *Ibid.*, p. 332, ll. 17–21; p. 333, ll. 7–11.
[70] Cf. above, p. 415. [71] *Nihāyat*, p. 26, ll. 11–16. [72] *Ibid.*, p. 29, ll. 11–15.

traversed, which he restates in the form in which it is to be found in Juwaynī, namely, as a demonstration showing that nothing can come into existence if its coming into existence has to be preceded by infinite causes. The argument then proceeds as follows: "An example illustrative of this principle is the motion of the celestial body which is taking place today. If there had to exist before it infinite motions, then of necessity this particular motion would not be in existence. They [the Mutakallimūn] compare it to the case of a man who said to another man: I will not give you this dinar until I have given you before it infinite dinars. In that case, it would be never possible for him to give to that other man the indicated dinar." [73] Averroes then proceeds to refute this argument.

In his *Tahāfut*, he refers to this argument as the greatest difficulty raised by the Mutakallimūn against an infinite by succession and quotes it as follows: "If the movements in the past are infinite, then no movement in the actual present can come into existence." [74]

In his *Tahāfut*, too, he quotes from Ghazālī's *Tahāfut* the argument based upon the principle that no infinite can be greater than any other infinite.[75]

In Maimonides the argument for creation from the impossibility of an infinite in succession is reproduced in two places.

First, in his argument from the creation of the accidents of atoms, he refers, as we have seen, to the Mutakallimūn's use of their denial of the possibility of an infinite by succession as a reinforcement of that argument and describes that argument together with its reinforcement as that which, "according to them, is the keenest and best of the arguments used for the purpose in question, so that it is regarded by many as a conclusive demonstration." [76]

Second, it is reproduced by him as an independent argument for creation, the second in his list of seven, where it is

[73] *Kashf*, p. 36, ll. 3–8.
[74] *Tahāfut al-Tahāfut* I, 29, p. 19, l. 15 – p. 20, l. 4.
[75] *Ibid.*, 26, p. 17, l. 12 – p. 18, l. 6; cf. above, p. 422.
[76] *Moreh* I, 74 (4), p. 152, ll. 9–10.

introduced as follows: "They say that by the fact one individual from among begotten individuals (*al-ashkhāṣ al-mutanāsilah*: *ha-ishim ha-noladim*) is created may be demonstrated that the world was created." [77] The expression "begotten individuals" used here seems to reflect the terms γενομένων and ἀτόμων used in the original of this argument by John Philoponus.[78] The argument which then follows may be summarized as follows: Suppose the world is eternal. It would then follow that in the case of men, for instance, the series of sons preceded by fathers would go on to infinity. "However, the Mutakallimūn have laid down as a principle that the existence of an infinity of this kind [that is, by succession] is impossible." [79] The conclusion we are expected to add in our mind is: Therefore, there was a first man and the world had beginning, both of them having come into existence by an act of creation.

Maimonides then supplements this argument by another argument, which may be summarized as follows: Suppose we ask ourselves, "from what was this first man created?" We would answer that he was created from dust and in answer to the question as to what that dust was created from, we would say that it was created from water, and so on. But this, as before, could not go on to infinity. The process must thus ultimately stop at something which came into existence after nonexistence. At the end, Maimonides remarks: "This, the Mutakallimūn say, constitutes a demonstration that the world came into existence after pure and absolute nonexistence." [80] What particular source Maimonides refers to here is unknown to me at the present writing.

An exposition of the Mutakallimūn's denial of the possibility of an infinite by succession, to which reference is made by Maimonides in both the preceding places, is to be found in his explanation of the eleventh of the twelve propositions in which he summarizes the physical theories of the Mutakal-

[77] *Moreh* I, 74 (2), p. 151, ll. 3–4.

[78] Cf. above, 413.

[79] *Moreh* I, 74 (2), p. 151, l. 7.

[80] *Ibid.*, ll. 8–14. Cf. above, p. 385.

limūn, namely, the proposition which reads that "the existence of that which is infinite in any manner whatsoever is impossible." [81] With regard to the impossibility of this kind of infinite, he adds: "Some of the Mutakallimūn seek to verify it, that is, to demonstrate its impossibility by an argument which I shall set forth for you later in this treatise, whereas others say that it is self-evident and immediately known and is in no need of any demonstration." [82] The promised argument which is set forth by him later is that based on the principle that no infinite can be greater than any other infinite. It is presented in two forms, corresponding to the two forms in which it is presented by John Philoponus, Saadia, and Shahrastānī.

The argument in its first form may be summarized as follows: Given an eternal world, it would follow that the number of the past successive individuals of any species up to a certain time would be greater than the number of the same past successive individuals of the same species up to some time before that, even though the number of the past successive individuals in each case is infinite. It would similarly follow that the number of the past revolutions of a certain celestial sphere up to a certain time would be greater than the number of the past revolutions of the same celestial sphere up to some time before that, even though the number of revolutions in each case is infinite.[83]

The gist of the argument in its second form is as follows: Given an eternal world, it would follow that the number of past revolutions of a certain fast-moving celestial sphere up to a certain date would be greater than the number of past revolutions of another slow-moving sphere up to the same date, even though the number of the past revolutions of each of these spheres up to that date was infinite.[84]

Both Averroes and Maimonides, independently of each

[81] *Ibid.*, 73, Prop. 11, p. 148, l. 19.
[82] *Ibid.*, p. 149, ll. 3–6.
[83] *Ibid.*, 74 (7), p. 155, ll. 17–25.
[84] *Ibid.*, ll. 25–30.

other,[85] refute the Mutakallimūn's denial of an infinite by succession.

In Averroes, the refutation of the argument from the intraversability of an infinite, with its implication that nothing can come into existence if its coming into existence is preceded by an infinite number of things on account of there being no first [86] occurs in his *Kashf*, in his *Tahāfut*, and in his commentaries on the *Physics*.

In his *Kashf*, the refutation starts with the statement that the Mutakallimūn's assertion, that "that which is to exist only after the existence of infinite things cannot come into existence, is not true in every respect" [87] and then goes on to mention two exceptions.

First, having in mind Aristotle's conception of the possibility of an infinite in the cyclical succession of things, which he illustrates by the cyclical succession of cloud and rain,[88] Averroes says that an infinite is possible in things which occur in a cyclical succession and he illustrates it by cyclical rising and setting of the sun and by the cyclical succession of cloud and rain.[89]

Second, having in mind Aristotle's conception of the possibility of an infinite also in the rectilinear succession of things, which he illustrates by the rectilinear succession of the generation of man,[90] and having also in mind Aristotle's statement that "man and the sun generates man," [91] as well as his description of the sun as "the generator," [92] he goes on to explain in what sense even a rectilineal succession can be infinite. It is true, he says, that an infinite rectilinear succession is impossible if the succession takes place essentially, as when in the case of men, for instance, it were assumed that each

[85] Cf. *Crescas' Critique of Aristotle*, p. 323.
[86] Cf. above, pp. 416–417.
[87] *Kashf*, p. 36, ll. 17–18.
[88] *De Gen. et Corr.* II, 11, 338b, 6–8.
[89] *Kashf*, p. 36, l. 20 – p. 37, l. 4.
[90] *Phys.* III, 6, 206a, 26; cf. above, p. 412.
[91] *Ibid.* II, 4, 194b, 13; cf. *Metaph.* XII, 5, 1071a, 13–16.
[92] *De Gen. et Corr.* II, 10, 336a, 18.

father is the sole and essential agent in generating the existence of his son, for then, indeed, the principle that "if there is no first cause, there is no last" holds true.[93] "But if it occurs by accident, as for instance, if man is really produced by some agent other than the man who is his father [namely, by the sun], so that the father is only in the position of an instrument in the hand of that agent [namely, the sun], then, if the agent continues an infinite action [as the sun in fact does], it is not impossible for it to produce [a succession of] infinite individuals by means of successively infinite instruments." [94]

In his *Tahāfut*, too, he refutes the argument by maintaining that "an accidental infinite, as distinguished from an essential infinite, is admitted by the philosophers; nay, this kind of infinite is in fact a necessary consequence of the existence of an eternal first principle," [95] and that "it is because the Mutakallimūn believed that that which is accidental is the same as that which is essential that they denied the existence of an accidental infinite and thus found the solution of their problem difficult and thought that their proof was logically cogent." [96]

In his Long Commentary on the *Physics*, after stating the view of "the Mutakallimūn of our religion" that nothing could come into existence if its coming into existence had to be preceded by infinite things, Averroes says: "We however say that this is impossible essentially, not accidentally, according to which, if there is a certain agent whose existence has no beginning [say the prime immovable mover], it will follow that his actions have no beginning, whence it will follow that prior to any action of his [that manifests itself in the world] there is an [other] action, so that prior to any action of his [in the world] there are infinite actions, but only by way of accident and not because some of them are essential to the existence of others. It is, therefore, only because the Mutakallimūn mistook that which is accidental for that which is essen-

[93] *Kashf*, p. 37, ll. 4–7.
[94] *Ibid.*, ll. 7–11.
[95] *Tahāfut al-Tahāfut* I, 30, p. 20, l. 16 – p. 21, l. 2.
[96] *Ibid.*, 32, p. 21, ll. 10–11.

tial that they said that events which have no first cannot take place." [97]

In his Epitome of the Physics, there is the following statement: "Plato and those who follow him from among the Mutakallimūn of our time and all those who believe in the creation of the world believed that that which is accidental is that which is essential and hence they denied the existence of an infinite regress of motion and affirmed their belief in a first motion coming into existence in time." [98] Then later there is a vague reference to "John the Grammarian" (that is, Philoponus) and his refutation of Aristotle "because he (that is, John Philoponus) has assumed that before any motion there is a motion essentially," and this is followed by the statement that "it is this which has forced Alfarabi to compose his treatise entitled "The Changeable Existing Things," for in that work he tried to inquire in what manner it is possible for one motion to precede another motion [to infinity]." [99]

In his refutation of the second argument, that based on the principle that no infinite is greater than any other infinite, which occurs in his *Tahāfut*, Averroes seems to have formulated Ghazālī's phrasing of the argument, which is the direct target of his assault, as follows: Given A, which completes one revolution in one month, and B, which completes 30 revolutions in one month, then the ratio of the whole of the revolutions of A in one year to the whole of the revolutions of B in one year would equal the ratio of 1 to 30. By this analogy Ghazālī argues that since Saturn completes one revolution in 30 years and Sun completes 30 revolutions in 30 years, the ratio of the whole of the revolutions of Saturn to the whole of the revolutions of Sun would be 1 to 30, but, since the whole of the eternal revolutions of Saturn is infinite and the whole of the eternal revolutions of Sun is also infinite, the ratio of the infinite revolutions of Saturn to the infinite

[97] *In Phys.* VIII, Comm. 15 (IV, p. 350 DE); cf. Comm. 47 (IV, p. 388 KL); V, Comm. 13 (IV, p. 218 I).

[98] Hebrew translation of the Epitome of the *Physics* VIII, p. 40b, ll. 6–9.

[99] *Ibid.*, ll. 16–22.

revolutions of Sun would equal the ratio of 1 to 30, thus leading to the absurdity that one infinite is greater than another infinite.

In his refutation of this argument, we may assume that Averroes had in the back of his mind passages in which Aristotle contends that the "infinite" is not the same as a "whole." Thus in one place Aristotle says "a whole (ὅλον: *al-kull*) is that which has beginning and middle and end,"[100] whereas an infinite, by the very meaning of the term, is that which has no beginning and no end; and in another place he says that "the infinite is that of which, however much one has taken, there is always more to take, whereas that of which there is nothing more to take is complete and whole (ὅλον)."[101] With this in the back of his mind, Averroes argues, in effect, that in such cases as the revolutions of Sun and Saturn, since their respective infinites are not wholes, there is no such ratio as that of the infinite revolutions of Sun to the infinite revolutions of Saturn and therefore one cannot speak of it as being equal to the ratio of 1 to 30. What one can only say is that the ratio of any finite number of revolutions completed by Sun in a given time to the finite number of revolutions completed by Saturn at the same time is equal to the ratio of 1 to 30.[102]

Maimonides does not reproduce the argument based on the principle of the intraversability of an infinite and hence does not directly refute it. But in his presentation of the difference between Aristotle and the Mutakallimūn on the question of an infinite by succession, he provides a refutation of that argument, which undoubtedly he had in mind.

In presenting the view of Aristotle, Maimonides starts out by saying that four kinds of *actually* and *simultaneously* existing infinites have been demonstrated by Aristotle to be impossible, namely, (1) a body infinite in magnitude; (2) an

[100] *Poetics*, 7, 1450b, 26–27.
[101] *Phys.* III, 6, 207a, 7–9.
[102] *Tahāfut al-Tahāfut* I, 27, p. 18, l. 7 – p. 19, l. 5.

infinite number of bodies each finite in magnitude; (3) an infinite number of bodies of which one is the cause of another; (4) an infinite number of unbodied beings of which one is the cause of another. These two kinds of *actually* and *simultaneously* existing series of causes and effects which Aristotle has demonstrated to be impossible are described by Maimonides as constituting "a natural and essential order." [103] Having in mind Aristotle's distinction between an actual infinite which is impossible and a potential infinite which is possible and having also in mind Aristotle's description of one kind of potential infinite as that in which one thing is taken after another [104] and that each part that is taken does not remain,[105] he refers to one kind of potential infinite [106] as "that which is infinite by succession (*bi'l-ta'āḳub*), and it is that which is called infinite by accident (*bi'l-'araḍ*), consisting in a thing coming to exist after the passing-away of another thing." [107] Finally, having in mind Aristotle's use of the examples of "time" and "movement" and "men" to illustrate this kind of potential infinite,[108] Maimonides mentions here as examples of this kind of potential infinite "time" [109] or "the succession of accidents in matter," [110] that is, movement, or "Zayd being the son of 'Umar, 'Umar the son of Ḫālid, Ḫālid the son of Bakr, and so on to infinity." [111] This kind of infinite, Maimonides says, is declared by Aristotle to be possible, for, "he who claims to have demonstrated the eternity of the world" also claims that the assumption of the existence of such an

[103] *Moreh* I, 73, Prop. 11, p. 148, l. 16.

[104] Cf. above n. 17.

[105] Cf. above n. 18.

[106] *Moreh* I, 74 (2), p. 148, l. 17.

[107] *Ibid.*, ll. 19–21. The two Hebrew versions translate both the Arabic term for "succession" and the Arabic term for "accident" by *miḳreh*, "accident." The term "succession" as a description of this kind of potential infinite does not occur in this chapter of Aristotle's *Physics* (III, 6), but, as we have seen, it is used by John Philoponus (cf. above at n. 29 and also at nn. 25 and 27). Nor is the description "by accident" used by Aristotle in this chapter, but it is implied in Aristotle's discussion analyzed above at nn. 21–23.

[108] Cf. above at nn. 37–41.

[109] *Moreh* I, 74 (2), p. 148, l. 24.

[110] *Ibid.*, ll. 24–25.

[111] *Ibid.*, p. 149, ll. 1–2.

infinite will lead to no "absurdity"[112] nor can any demonstration be advanced for its impossibility.[113] Disregarding the distinction made by Aristotle between the two kinds of infinite by succession, concludes Maimonides, the Mutakallimūn deny the possibility of any kind of infinite whatsoever.[114]

In this presentation of the contrast between Aristotle and the Mutakallimūn, it will be noticed how Maimonides emphasizes the distinction made by Aristotle between "actual" and "potential" and between "essential" and "accidental" and also Aristotle's declaration that no absurdity will follow his affirmation of the possibility of an infinite in succession and that no demonstration has been advanced against its possibility. All this provides a refutation of the first argument, parallel to the refutation so elaborately presented by Averroes.

Though Maimonides has reproduced the second argument, that based on the principle that no infinite can be greater than another infinite, he does not directly refute it. But he refers to the existence of a refutation of it, for right after his reproduction of that argument, as restated above,[115] he goes on to say as follows: "All these things are mere fictions and have no reality. Abū Naṣr al-Fārābī has demolished this proposition and has exposed the weak points in every one of its details, as you will clearly perceive when you earnestly and dispassionately study his well-known book *Al-Maujūdāt al-Mutaghayyirah*, 'The Changeable Beings.'"[116] What Alfarabi's refutation was we do not know, for the work mentioned by Maimonides is not extant.[117] But Narboni in his comment on this reference of Maimonides to Alfarabi's work, after stating that "this treatise has not reached us," suggests that Averroes' refutation of Ghazālī's use of this argument is based upon

[112] *Ibid.*, p. 148, l. 23. In this statement Maimonides evidently had in mind Aristotle's discussion in *Phys.* III, 6.

[113] *Ibid.*, l. 26. In this statement, Maimonides evidently had in mind Aristotle's discussion in *Phys.* VIII, 2–6.

[114] *Ibid.*, p. 148, l. 26 – p. 149, l. 3.

[115] Cf. above, p. 427.

[116] *Moreh* I, 74 (7), p. 155, l. 30 – p. 156, l. 3.

[117] Cf. Steinschneider, *Al-Farabi*, pp. 119–123.

Alfarabi's refutation of it in that treatise of his, for, he says, "undoubtedly Averroes saw that treatise of Alfarabi and summarized and organized its contentions in a manner most clear." [118]

Thus the argument which is only referred to by Maimonides, the systematizer, is parallel to that elaborately presented by Averroes, the commentator, both of them using the same source, in this case the work of Alfarabi.

6. ARGUMENT FROM PARTICULARIZATION

An argument which Maimonides describes as that of "particularization (*al-taḫṣīṣ*: *ha-hityaḥed*)" [1] occurs in Juwaynī in two forms.

First, in his *Irshād* it occurs not as an independent argument for the creation of the world but rather as supplementary to his combined argument from the createdness of the accidents of atoms and the impossibility of an infinite by succession [2] and as proving the creator of the world was a god endowed with an eternal free will. The argument reads as follows: "It has thus been established that the world was created and it has become clear that its existence had a beginning. But then, with regard to that which is created, [prior to its creation] its existence as well as its nonexistence was admissible (*jā'iz*) and [similarly, with regard to the time at which it was created, it is possible] that, at whatever time the creation of the world took place, its actual taking place could have been preceded by lengths of time and so it is also possible that it could have delayed by hours. When, however, the admissible existence rather than the admissible nonexistence has taken place [at a certain given time], reason immediately concludes that existence was in need of a particularizer (*muḫaṣṣiṣ*) to single it

[118] Narboni on *Moreh* I, 74 (7), p. 20a–b. For Averroes' refutation of their argument, see above at nn. 100–102.

[1] *Moreh* I, 74 (5), p. 152, l. 27.

[2] Cf. above, pp. 396–397; 410; 420.

out as the one which is to be realized [at a certain given time]." [3]

That particularizer, he goes on to say, must inevitably be one of the following three: (1) "something which necessitates the occurrence of the creation after the manner of a cause which necessitates its effect [that is, the view of the philosophers as represented by Avicenna]"; (2) "a natural power, which the Naturalists [that is, the Stoics] eventually wind up with"; (3) "an agent endowed with free choice." [4] He rejects the identification of the particularizer with either a necessary cause or a natural power on the ground that both these identifications would lead either to the absurdity of an infinite regress or to the eternity of the world, but, with regard to the latter, he says, "we have already furnished proof that the world is created." [5] The inevitable conclusion is, he maintains, that "the particularizer of created things is an agent who acts upon them by free choice, a particularizer who produced them with certain particular characteristics at certain moments." [6] Thus, in reverse of Avicenna who, having assumed that God acts by necessity, concluded that the world is eternal, and this because, on the assumption of creation, he could not explain why the world was created at a certain particular time and not at some other time, Juwaynī, who has already established that the world was created, that is, it was created at a certain particular time, concludes that God, the "particularizer," who created the world at a certain particular time in preference to some other possible time, does not act by necessity but rather by free choice.

His concluding statement that the particularizer, who is God, did by His free choice create the world at a certain time, taken by itself might mean that at a certain point in His infinite existence God by His free choice decided to create the world. This might imply that the choice, that is, the free

[3] *Irshād*, p. 16, ll. 10–14 (p. 36).
[4] *Ibid.*, ll. 16–18.
[5] *Ibid.*, p. 16, l. 18 – p. 17, l. 8 (pp. 36–37).
[6] *Ibid.*, p. 17, ll. 10–11.

will, by which He decided to create the world was itself something new which was created by God at the time the world was created. Such a view was current at the time of Juwaynī among the Muʿtazilite followers of Abū Hudhayl, who believed that the will to create the world was created by God outside Himself,[7] and among the Karrāmiyyah, who believed that that will was created by God in Himself.[8] In a later chapter, however, Juwaynī explicitly rejects the view of "some Muʿtazilites of Basra," that is, followers of Abū al-Hudhayl, that God wills to create things by a created incorporeal will,[9] and undoubtedly he would also reject the view of the Karrāmiyyah. His own conception of will is expressed by him in the statement that "God is willing in virtue of an eternal will," and this view he ascribes to "the Men of Truth," [10] that is, the Ashʿarites, to whom he belonged. Now what the Ashʿarites meant by attributing to God an "eternal will" may be gathered from a passage where their master Ashʿarī himself, after rejecting the view of "the Muʿtazilites" that "God is a willer by a created will," [11] maintains that "what God eternally knows will be at a given time, He eternally wills to be at that time, and what He eternally knows will not be, He eternally wills not to be." [12] In its application to the creation of the world it means that from eternity God had willed that the world should come into existence at a certain given time.

In another work of Juwaynī, referred to by Averroes briefly as *al-Niẓāmiyyah*,[13] the argument, which in the *Irshād* is based upon the contention that that which is admissible (*al-jā'iz*) requires a *muḫaṣṣiṣ* [14] and is used as a proof for the

[7] Cf. above, p. 141.

[8] Cf. above, pp. 145–146.

[9] *Irshād*, p. 37, ll. 17–19 (p. 67); p. 55, l. 12 – p. 56, l. 6 (pp. 93–96).

[10] *Ibid.*, p. 55, ll. 10–12.

[11] *Ibānah*, p. 60, l. 6; *Lumaʿ* 48.

[12] *Ibānah*, p. 60, ll. 3–5.

[13] *Kashf*, p. 37, ll. 15–16. The full title of Juwaynī's work is *Al-ʿAḳīdah al-Niẓāmiyyah fī'l-Arkān al-Islāmiyyah* (cf. Brockelmann, *Gesch. d. arab. Litt.*, *Supplementband*, I, p. 273 XIII. Cf. printed edition *Al-ʿAḳīdah al-Niẓāmiyyah*, p. 11, l. 1 – p. 13, l. 2.

[14] Cf. above at nn. 2–3.

existence of God dependent upon the proof for the creation of the world, is in this work given as an argument based upon the contention that admissibility (*al-jawāz*) [15] requires a *muḳtaḍin* [16] and is used as an independent argument in proof of the creation of the world. Now the term *muḳtaḍin* is quite evidently used by Juwaynī here in the sense of "necessitater" or "decider" and is thus used by him as the equivalent of the term *muḫaṣṣiṣ*, "particularizer" used by him in the *Irshād*. It was therefore quite natural for Averroes, in his restatement of this argument of the *Niẓāmiyyah*, to substitute the more precise term *muḫaṣṣiṣ* used in the *Irshād* for the less precise *muḳtaḍin* used in the *Niẓāmiyyah*.

We shall reproduce this argument of Juwaynī's for the creation of the world as it was recast by Averroes.[16a]

Averroes introduces his presentation of this argument by the statement that it is based upon two propositions.[17] The first proposition, as quoted by him, reads: "It is admissible (*jā'iz*) that the world with all that is in it should be the opposite of what it now is, so that it is admissible, for instance, that the world should be smaller than it is, or greater than it is, or of some other shape than that of which it is, or that the number of bodies in it should be different from that it now contains, or that the movement of any moving body in it should tend in a direction other than that in which it now tends, so that it would be possible for a stone to move upward and for fire downward and for an eastern movement to become a western and for a western to become an eastern." [18] The second proposition as quoted by him reads: "The admissible is created and it has a creator, namely, an agent, who out of two admissibilities turns it into one

[15] *Niẓāmiyyah*, p. 11, l. 5.

[16] *Ibid.*, l. 14 and *passim.* Later (l. 15 and p. 12, ll. 15 and 23) *mu'aththir* is used as the equivalent of *muḳtaḍin.* But the passive participle *muḫaṣṣaṣ* occurs on p. 12, l. 16, and there occur also *iḫtiṣāṣ* on p. 11, l. 18, and *yuḫaṣṣiṣu* on p. 12, ll. 12 and 13.

[16a] Cf. above, p. 400, at n. 40.

[17] *Kashf*, p. 37, l. 16.

[18] *Kashf*, p. 37, l. 16 – p. 38, l. 1. Cf. *Niẓāmiyyah*, p. 11, ll. 3–10.

rather than the other." [19] This second proposition is said by Averroes to have been explained by Juwaynī by means of three other propositions, which read as follows: "First, the admissible must needs have a particularizer (*muḫaṣṣiṣ*) who puts it into one of the admissible qualities rather than into the other; second, this particularizer cannot but be one who is endowed with will (*murīd*); third, that which exists [in one of two admissible qualities] because of a will is created in time." [20] Finally, referring again to Juwaynī, Averroes says: "From the fact that the world now existing in the place in the air (*al-jaww*) wherein it was created — meaning by the term air the void (*al-ḫalā'*) — could equally exist in another place in that void, he concluded that the world was created by a will." [21]

We thus have in Juwaynī two versions of the argument from particularization. (1) On the premise that the creation of the world has already been established by some other argument, the argument from the need of a particularizer is used in the *Irshād* to prove the existence of a Creator of the world who is endowed with eternal free will. (2) The same argument from the need of a particularizer (*muḫaṣṣiṣ*), or as

[19] *Kashf*, p. 38, ll. 1–2.

[20] *Ibid.*, p. 40, ll. 1–9. Cf. *Niẓāmiyyah*, p. 11, l. 10 – p. 12, l. 14.

[21] *Kashf*, p. 40, 9–11. It is to be noted that the use of the term "air" in the sense of "void" reflects Aristotle's references to the use of the term "air" in that sense (*Phys.* IV, 6, 213a, 30–31; *De Anima* II, 10, 419b, 34). Later on, in his criticism of this argument, Averroes makes it clear that he understood Juwaynī to mean that "the world is in a void by which it is surrounded" (*Kashf*, p. 40, l. 13), which, it may be noted, is in conformity with Juwaynī's known adherence to the Mutakallimūn's belief in atoms and a vacuum. The underlying passage in the *Niẓāmiyyah* (p. 12, ll. 9–14) reads: "The world in its totality abides in a given air (*jaww ma'lūm*), and the assumption that it is in this void (*dhalika al-ḫalā'*) implies an assumption that it could equally be in a void either rightwards or leftwards," from which Juwaynī goes on to prove that the world was created by "the will of an influencing factor (*mu'aththir*) endowed with choice" (*ibid.*, ll. 22–23). Had we not known that Juwaynī believed in atoms and a void, his statement that "the world in its totality abides . . . in this void" could be taken to mean, not that the world is surrounded by a void, but rather that the world occupies a void. On these two meanings of the term "void," see Avicenna's definition of *ḫalā'* in *Tis'u Rasā'il*, p. 94, ll. 10–11.

he calls it now a determiner or decider (*muḳtaḍin*), is used in the *Niẓāmiyyah* to prove that the world is created. This second version of the argument is based upon what is known as the Mutakallimūn's theory of "admissibility" (*al-jawāz*).[21a] Both these versions of Juwaynī's argument from particularization occur, as we shall see, in later works before the time of Averroes. But it is to be noted that whenever the second version occurs, the term *muḥaṣṣiṣ*, as in Averroes, is substituted for the term *muḳtaḍin*. Whether in all these cases, as in the case of Averroes, the writers' use of the second version is based exclusively on the *Niẓāmiyyah*, or whether they had for it some supplementary source, either some other work of Juwaynī or the work of some other author, I do not know at the present writing.

The first version is used by Judah Halevi in his *Cuzari*. It occurs, as in the *Irshād*, after the combined arguments for the creation of the world from the creation of the accidents of the atoms and the impossibility of an infinite by succession. It reads as follows: "That which is created must have a cause which created it, for that which is created must have been created at a particular time, which supposedly could have been either earlier or later. But the fact that it was created at that particular time to the exclusion of an earlier or later time necessarily implies the existence of a particularizer." [22] Subsequently he tries to show that the particularizer is endowed with will [23] and that the will is eternal.[24]

The second version is implied, though not directly restated, in Ghazālī's *Tahāfut*. Previously in that work, Ghazālī has stated his belief that the creation of the world as well as its creation at a certain time was determined by the eternal will of God.[25] He now takes up a possible objection that "the philosophers" who believe in eternity might raise against it.

[21a] Cf. below at nn. 43 and 44.

[22] *Cuzari* V, 18 [3], p. 334, ll. 5–7; p. 333, ll. 25–28.

[23] *Ibid.*, [9], p. 336, l. 1; p. 335, l. 25.

[24] *Ibid.*, [10], p. 336, l. 10; p. 337, l. 4.

[25] *Tahāfut al-Falāsifah* I, 8, p. 26, ll. 2–7.

In this objection, the philosophers are assumed to base themselves upon two premises: first, of two like things neither one of them can be given preference to the other except by a particularizer (*muḫaṣṣiṣ*), that is to say, by some agent who singles out one of the two like things and gives it preference over the other; [26] second, the eternal will of God cannot be such a particularizer.[27] On the basis of these two premises, the philosophers, says Ghazālī, could argue that if the world were created, then before its creation it was equally possible for it to be created at one time or at another time and to have one kind of shape or another; similarly it was equally possible for things in the world to be either white or black and in motion or at rest, but in none of these cases could the eternal will of God have been a "particularizer" to select one in preference to the other. Moreover, they could argue, if the world were created, then prior to its creation it was equally possible for it either to come into existence or not to come into existence, and the eternal will of God could not be the "particularizer" to select its coming into existence in preference to its not coming into existence.[28]

These two possible objections on the part of the philosophers Ghazālī answers with a denial of the premise that God's eternal will could not be the "particularizer" to choose between two like things. "The [eternal] will," he says, "is an attribute [of God] whose nature (*sha'n*) it is to distinguish something from its like," [29] so that it is this eternal will that is that "particularizer" (*muḫaṣṣiṣ*) which, according to the philosophers, "is needed to distinguish something from its like." [30] Consequently, he concludes, "it is by the [divine eternal] will that the world exists when (*ḥaythu*) it exists, according to the description in which it exists, and in the

[26] *Ibid.*, 28, p. 36, ll. 9–10.

[27] *Ibid.*, 29, p. 36, ll. 13–14.

[28] *Ibid.*, 28–29.

[29] *Ibid.*, 30, p. 37, ll. 10–11; cf. p. 38, ll. 1–2. For *sha'n* in the sense of "nature," see use of *min sha'n* for πέφυκε in the Arabic version of *Categ.* 10, 12a, 28.

[30] *Tahāfut al-Falāsifah* I, 30, p. 37, ll. 12–13.

place in which it exists." [31] Then, when the philosophers are represented by Ghazālī as finding fault with this conception of God's eternal will and as trying to show how they could explain the world as it is now constituted by their own belief in its eternity, he tries to find fault with the philosophers' explanation and to show the superiority of his own explanation.[32]

Here then we have an argument by Ghazālī for his belief in creation turning upon the term "particularizer."

The second version of the argument from particularization is used by Shahrastānī in his *Nihāyat*, where he ascribes it to "imām al-Ḥaramayn [al-Juwaynī]," without, however, mentioning the *Niẓāmiyyah*. It reads as follows: "The earth, according to our opponents, is surrounded by water and the water by air and the air by fire and the fire by the celestial sphere, and they are [all] localized bodies, occupying air (*jaww*) and space (*ḥayyiz*). But we of necessity know that it is not impossible to suppose that these bodies could each move to the right or to the left from what are now their respective places or that they could each become greater or smaller in figure and thickness. Now anything that is accorded one particular admissibility in preference to other alternative admissibilities, despite their all being equal admissibilities and similar possibilities, must by the necessity of reason be in need of a particularizer (*muḫaṣṣiṣ*)." [33] He then goes on to prove that the particularizer does not act by the necessity of nature but is endowed with power and choice, and he thus concludes by calling him maker of the world.[34]

This formulation of the argument differs from its formulation in the *Niẓāmiyyah*. In the *Niẓāmiyyah*, the conception of the structure of the world upon which Juwaynī's argument for its creation is based is that held by Juwaynī himself as a Mutakallim and believer in atoms and a vacuum. It is thus in accordance with this belief of his in the existence of a void

[31] *Ibid.*, ll. 9–10.
[32] *Ibid.*, 31–35, p. 38, l. 3 – p. 51, l. 3.
[33] *Nihāyat*, p. 12, ll. 8–13.
[34] *Ibid.*, p. 14, ll. 1–8.

that Juwaynī says that "the world in its totality abides in a given air (*jaww maʿlūm*)," immediately referred to by him as "this void" (*dhalika al-ḫalāʾ*), by which, as we have seen, he means, as rightly explained by Averroes, that "the world is in a void by which it is surrounded."[35] In the *Nihāyat*, however, the conception of the structure of the world upon which Juwaynī's own argument for its creation is based is said by Juwaynī himself to be "according to the opinion of our opponents," that is, the philosophers, by whom he means, as may be gathered from subsequent remarks of his, Avicenna and Aristotle,[36] who denied the existence of both atoms and a void. It is thus in accordance with their denial of the existence of a void that Juwaynī says of his "opponents" that they believed that the four elements and the celestial sphere which surround the earth are all "localized bodies, occupying air (*jaww*) and space (*ḥayyiz*)," without mentioning that they all in their totality abide in a void by which they are surrounded. Now, while it is possible that this new formulation of the argument is due to Shahrastānī's own revision of its formulation in the *Niẓāmiyyah*, it is more reasonable to assume that it has been drawn by him from some other work of Juwaynī.

A discussion of how the philosophers would refute this argument and how the philosophers' refutation could be rebutted occurs later in the *Nihāyat* where, referring to Avicenna's use of the term "providence" (*ʿināyah*) to mean God's knowledge of the order of existence which proceeds from Him by necessity,[37] Shahrastānī addresses the philosophers as follows: "Everything that you say concerning divine providence (*al-ʿināyah al-ilhāiyyah*) as bringing about by necessity that the order of existent things should be according to the most perfect arrangement, we predicate of the eternal will (*al-irādah al-azaliyyah*) which had decreed the particulariza-

[35] Cf. above n. 21.
[36] *Nihāyat*, p. 33, l. 1, and p. 35, l. 19.
[37] Cf. Goichon, *Lexique*, 468.

tion (*taḫṣiṣ*) of existent things according to the order known to it [from eternity]." [38] But then he goes on to refute the philosophic conception of necessary causality by showing that the conception of necessary causality could not explain the variety of shapes and species in the world.[39]

In Maimonides, the argument for the creation of the world from what he calls "particularization" is ascribed to the Mutakallimūn in general. But whatever sources he may have had for this argument, his presentation of it indicates that one of them was the *Niẓāmiyyah* of Juwaynī. Thus, like Juwaynī in the *Niẓāmiyyah*, who describes this argument as "the most useful and the choicest," [40] Maimonides describes it as one "to which they [the Mutakallimūn] accord very great preference" [41] and which "in my opinion is a most excellent argument." [42] Again, like Juwaynī in the *Niẓāmiyyah*, who begins this argument by indicating that it is based upon the theory that all things in the world "are alike in sharing the common description of admissibility (*al-jawāz*)," [43] Maimonides begins this argument by saying that it is based upon what earlier in his work he has described as the Mutakallimūn's theory of admissibility (*al-jawāz: ha-haʿabarah*).[44] Then, having noticed that the *Niẓāmiyyah* argument consists of a series of statements, each introduced by the term "the world," [45] in which, on the basis of the theory that it is admissible that the world could be different from what it is, Juwaynī arrives at the conclusion that "the world is an act which, without necessity, was brought into existence by the will of an influencing factor (*muʾaththir*) endowed with choice," [46] Maimonides says that "he [that is, Juwaynī] directs his thought

[38] *Nihāyat*, p. 43, ll. 6–9.
[39] *Ibid.*, p. 43, l. 17 – p. 44, l. 12; cf. above, pp. 440–441.
[40] *Niẓāmiyyah*, p. 13, l. 1.
[41] *Moreh* I, 74 (5), p. 152, l. 27.
[42] *Ibid.*, p. 153, l. 19.
[43] *Niẓāmiyyah*, p. 11, ll. 3–5.
[44] *Moreh* I, 74 (5), p. 152, ll. 27–28, and I, 73 (10), p. 144, l. 2.
[45] *Niẓāmiyyah*, p. 11, ll. 2 and 13; p. 12, ll. 2 and 15.
[46] *Ibid.*, p. 12, ll. 22–23; cf. l. 13.

to the world as a whole or to any part of it he likes" [47] and, believing as he does that it is admissible that the world could be different from what it is, he arrives at the conclusion that there exists "a particularizer endowed with choice" and hence that the world "is created." [48] Finally, having also noticed that in the sources used by him this argument is made to prove the existence of what they call "particularizer" (*muḫaṣṣiṣ*) or of what Juwaynī in the *Niẓāmiyyah* calls "determiner" (*muḳtaḍin*) and also "influencing factor" (*mu'aththir*) — entirely new terms used as a description of the conception of God as Creator — Maimonides adds: "For there is no difference between your saying particularizer (*muḫaṣṣiṣ*) and your saying agent (*fā'il*: *po'el*) or creator (*ḫāliḳ*: *bore'*) or bringer into existence (*mūjid*: *mamṣi'*) or innovator (*muḥdith*: *meḥaddesh*) or intender (*ḳāṣid*: *mekavven*). All these terms are meant to convey one and the same meaning." [49]

Though this argument is not directly refuted by Maimonides, a refutation of it is implied in his opening statement, quoted above, that this argument is based upon the theory of "admissibility" discussed by him in the Mutakallimūn's tenth proposition, as well as in his concluding statement that this argument "follows necessarily" from the tenth proposition,[50] for the theory of admissibility is refuted by him in his discussion of that tenth proposition.[51]

7. ARGUMENT FROM PREPONDERATION

Avicenna, who as a Neoplatonized Aristotelian believed that the world proceeded from God by a necessary causality, describes the world, by reason of its owing its existence to a cause, as being only possible of existence in virtue of its essence.[1] With this as a starting point, he tries to show that the procession of the world from God is beginningless, so

[47] *Moreh* I, 74 (5), p. 152, ll. 28–29.
[48] *Ibid.*, p. 153, ll. 4–6.
[49] *Ibid.*, ll. 6–8.
[50] *Ibid.*, l. 17.
[51] *Moreh* I, 73 (10).
[1] *Najāt*, p. 367, ll. 7–8.

that the world is coeternal with God. From his long zigzagging discussion,[2] we may carve out, insofar as it is necessary for our purpose, the following argument.

If we assume that the world proceeded into existence from God after it had not existed and that during its nonexistence it was possible for it either to continue in its nonexistence or to come into existence, then, "in order to make it necessary for existence to proceed from God or to give preponderance (*tarjīḥ*) to the procession of existence from Him [over its continuing in its nonexistence] there must inevitably appear a distinction occasioned by the occurrence in the meantime of something which did not exist when there was a preponderance of nonexistence [over the procession of existence from Him] and He was in a state of inactivity." [3] Avicenna then goes on to investigate what that something which occurred in the meantime might have been. He tentatively suggests that that something might have been a "will" as understood by those "who speak of a will and an object of will," [4] and as he goes on he says that he will forego the discussion "whether the will originates in God Himself or apart from Him," [5] the reference here being quite evidently to the Karrāmiyyah,[6] who believed in a created will created in the essence of God, and to Abū al-Hudhayl, who believed in a will created apart from God.[7] This suggestion is rejected by him on the ground that if the world was created in time by a created will, then the question arises why the will and hence the world were not created before [8] — a question which has been raised by philosophers ever since Parmenides whenever the belief of the temporal origin of the world came up for discussion.[9]

The crux of Avicenna's argument, then, is that on the assumption of the world's proceeding from God by necessity,

[2] *Ibid.*, p. 412, l. 5 – p. 418, l. 17.
[3] *Ibid.*, p. 416, ll. 7–8.
[4] *Ibid.*, ll. 9–10.
[5] *Ibid.*, p. 418, ll. 8–9.
[6] *Nihāyat*, p. 114, ll. 2–12.
[7] Cf. above, pp. 140–141 and 145–146.
[8] *Najāt*, p. 418, ll. 10–11.
[9] Cf. Diels, *Vorsokratiker*, under "Parmenides," Frag. 8, ll. 9–10.

it could not have proceeded from Him in time — and this on the ground that there is no adequate explanation why it proceeded at a certain given time and not sooner or later.

Avicenna's argument is freely reproduced by Ghazālī as the first of four arguments for the eternity of the world which he ascribes to "the philosophers," a term under which he is in the habit of restating the views of Avicenna. Briefly restated it runs as follows: If the world came into existence after it had not existed, then prior to its coming into existence it was possible for it either to continue in its nonexistence or to come into existence. Now, on the assumption of creation, the question why the world at first did not exist and then came into existence would have to be explained on the ground that at first there was no preponderator (*murajjiḥ*) to give preponderance to existence over nonexistence and then a preponderator emerged. But this explanation is open to the question: Why did the preponderator come into being at that particular time and not before? [10] If you say that the preponderator is the will of God and that that will of God to create the world did not at first exist in God and then it came into existence, then, besides the difficulty of assuming something new to come into existence in the Divine Being, there is, again, the question: "Why did that will come into being at that particular time and not before?" [11] In short, if the origin of the world is due to God's act of creation, then why was it created at that particular time and not sooner or later? [12] Having thus shown that the world could not have had a beginning, he concludes that the world must be eternal.[13]

To this question, Ghazālī answers with the following question: "How will you disprove him who says that the world was created by an eternal will which had decreed that its existence is to take place at the time at which it actually took place and that its nonexistence is to last until it actually lasted

[10] *Tahāfut al-Falāsifah* I, 3, p. 23, ll. 2–10.
[11] *Ibid.*, I, 3–4.
[12] *Ibid.*, 5, p. 24, ll. 9–10.
[13] *Ibid.*, 6, p. 25, ll. 5–6.

and that its existence is to begin when it actually began." [14] In other words, against Avicenna, who argues that the preponderator who determined the time of the creation cannot be the will of God, Ghazālī argues that the preponderator is the eternal will of God and that that eternal will, which is the preponderator, determined not only the *time when* the world should be created but also *the very fact that* the world should be created.

Here then, in his discussion of Avicenna's argument against creation, Ghazālī has introduced the term *murajjiḥ*, "preponderator," on the basis of Avicenna's use of the term *tarjīḥ*, "to give preponderance." In his refutation of Avicenna, then, Ghazālī has introduced a new argument for creation based upon the need of a preponderator to give preponderance to existence over nonexistence. But we have already shown above how Ghazālī has also made use of Juwaynī's argument for creation based upon the need of a particularizer.[15] Ghazālī thus has two arguments for the creation of the world, one based upon particularization, which he has borrowed from his teacher Juwaynī; the other based upon preponderation, which he himself has invented. The difference between the two arguments is that the former is based upon the Mutakallimūn's theory of "admissibility," whereas the latter is based upon Avicenna's theory of "possibility."

This new argument from preponderation, which was added by Ghazālī to Juwaynī's argument from particularization, is also used by Shahrastānī in addition to the argument from particularization, which has been reproduced by him previously in the name of Juwaynī.[16] As in Ghazālī, he presents this argument for creation as a revision of the same argument used by Avicenna against creation.

Starting with a restatement of Avicenna's argument and referring to Avicenna as "the opponent," he says: "The opponent admits that the world, which in virtue of its essence is only possible in respect of existence, is in need of a par-

[14] *Ibid.*, 8, p. 26, ll. 2–4. [15] Cf. above, p. 441. [16] *Ibid.*

ticularizer (*muḫaṣṣiṣ*) [or] a preponderator (*murajjiḥ*) to give preference to existence over nonexistence, but at the same time he says that the world existed from eternity alongside the particularizer or preponderator." [17] Now Avicenna himself, as we have seen, uses neither the term "particularizer" nor the term "preponderator"; Shahrastānī's ascription of the use of these terms to Avicenna is evidently based upon Ghazālī, who has put in the mouth of the philosophers the admission that "nothing can be distinguished from its like unless there is a particularizer (*muḫaṣṣiṣ*)," [18] and who himself, as we have seen, has introduced the term "preponderator" as the equivalent of the term "particularizer." Shahrastānī then gives his own version of the argument, starting with a proof that the world is only possible in respect of existence. His proof, in his own summary of it, reads as follows: "If a whole is composed of units, and if each of the units is only possible in respect of existence, then the whole must necessarily be only possible in respect of existence." [19] Since then the world as a whole is in virtue of its essence only possible in respect of existence, it follows, he goes on to say, that its existence is due to a preponderator (*murajjiḥ*) and that this preponderator must be necessary in respect of existence in virtue of its own essence. So far the conclusion of his argument agrees with that arrived at by Avicenna. But then he himself raises the question why he should not continue to agree with Avicenna in assuming that the world, dependent though it is upon the preponderator for its existence, should not coexist with that preponderator from eternity. In answer to this question he goes on to show by a number of arguments why he could not agree with Avicenna.[20]

In addition to his use of this argument from preponderation against those who believed in the eternity of the world, Shah-

[17] *Nihāyat*, p. 14, ll. 12–14.

[18] *Tahāfut al-Falāsifah* I, 28, p. 36, ll. 9–10.

[19] *Nihāyat*, p. 15, ll. 13–15; cf. p. 13, ll. 1–3. A similar kind of reasoning is used by Ibn Ḥazm (cf. above, p. 403). Cf. Diogenes, VII, 141.

[20] *Nihāyat*, p. 17, l. 14 – p. 23, l. 12.

rastānī uses it also against the Karramiyyah who believed that the will by which God created the world was itself created in the essence of God.[21] His argument reads as follows: "Anything created needs a creator, in view of the fact that by itself and with reference to its essence it is admissible of both existence and nonexistence. Consequently, when the side of existence has preponderated (*tarrajjaḥ*) over nonexistence, it necessarily needed a preponderator (*murajjiḥ*). Then, if this preponderator (*al-murajjiḥ*) were assumed to be created, it would need another preponderator, and so the matter would have to go to infinity." [22] And here we are expected to conclude that, since an infinite regress is impossible, the preponderator, that is, the will of God, must be eternal. Shahrastānī then goes on to say that the same argument also applies to those who say that the will is "created apart from God's essence," [23] by which he means Abū al-Hudhayl and his followers.[24] He finally remarks: "This is conclusive, for which there is no rebuttal." [25]

This is the historical background of the sixth argument in Maimonides' list of the seven Mutakallimūn's arguments for creation — the argument which he describes as being based upon "the preponderance (*tarjīh*: *hakra'at*) of existence over nonexistence" and which he ascribes to "one of the later ones (*ba'ḍ al-muta'aḥḥirin*: *eḥad min ha-aḥaronim*) who "thought that he had come upon an excellent method, superior to all the methods advanced before." [26]

Maimonides starts his restatement of the argument by quoting or summarizing its anonymous author as saying in effect that both those who believe in eternity and those who believe in creation believe that there is a God beyond the world and that the world differs from God in that it "is only possible in respect of existence, for, if its existence were necessary, it would be the God [that is to say, there would be no God

[21] *Ibid.*, p. 114, ll. 3–4.
[22] *Ibid.*, p. 116, ll. 8–12.
[23] *Ibid.*, ll. 12–5.
[24] Cf. above, pp. 140–141.
[25] *Nihāyat*, p. 116, l. 15.
[26] *Moreh* I, 74 (6), p. 153, ll. 22–23.

beyond the world], but we are discussing here only with those who affirm the existence of a God [beyond the world] and who at the same time maintain the eternity of the world." [27] He then goes on, again, to quote or to summarize his anonymous author on the meaning and implication of the concept of possibility, on the basis of which his argument for the creation of the world may be reduced to the following syllogism:

Everything that is only possible in respect of existence and that does exist must have been given preponderance of existence over nonexistence by a preponderator.

The world is only possible in respect of existence and it does exist;

Therefore, the world must have been given preponderance of existence over nonexistence by a preponderator.[28]

As to who is the "one of the later ones" of the Mutakallimūn to whom Maimonides ascribes this argument from preponderation, it is hard to tell. The expression "one of the later ones" used here by Maimonides may equally refer to either Ghazālī or Shahrastānī. Thus the expression "a skillful one from among the Mutakallimūn" [29] is used by him, as will be shown,[30] with reference to Ghazālī. But thus also the expression "one of the later ones" [31] is used by him, as has been shown,[32] with reference to Shahrastānī. From his statement, however, about what the "one of the later ones" here thought of this argument it would seem that the reference is to somebody other than either Ghazālī or Shahrastānī.

[27] *Ibid.*, ll. 24–25; cf. *Tahāfut al-Falāsifah* XVII, 5, p. 279, l. 12 – p. 280, l. 1.

[28] *Ibid.*, ll. 25–28. Schreiner (*Kalām*, p. 52, n. 6) identified this argument in Maimonides with Shahrastānī's argument on fol. 33b of the Leiden MS. of the *Nihāyat*, which corresponds to that on p. 116, ll. 8–15, in Guillaume's edition. This argument in Shahrastānī, as we have shown above (at nn. 21–25) is not an argument for the creation of the world but rather an argument against the Karramiyyah's view of the creation of the divine will in the divine essence.

[29] *Moreh* II, 14(4), p. 200, ll. 17–19.

[30] Cf. below, pp. 595–596.

[31] *Moreh* I, 75(5), p. 158, l. 16.

[32] Cf. above, p. 49, n. 41, quotations from Maimonides and Shahrastānī.

In his criticism of this argument, Maimonides starts out with two general observations. First, he characterizes the argument as being "very persuasive (*muḳni*ʿ: *maspiḳ*)," [33] by which he means, I take it, that it is only a "rhetorical" argument, for "rhetoric" is defined by Aristotle as the art of "persuasion." [34] Now, in Aristotle, arguments are said to be only rhetorical when they resemble "sophistical" [35] or "eristical" [36] discussions and thus lead to "false information" (συκοφαντία).[37] Therefore, by characterizing this argument here as "rhetorical," Maimonides means to say that he is going to show how the argument is sophistical and fallacious and leading to false information. Second, he shows that this argument has arisen from the argument based on particularization, the difference between them being that, whereas the argument from particularization tries to prove the need of a particularizer to give preference to one property over another in a thing already existing, this new argument from preponderation tries to prove the need of a preponderator to give preference to existence over nonexistence to something not yet in existence.[38] Therefore, by showing that the argument from preponderation has arisen from the argument from particularization, Maimonides means to say that he is going to show how this new argument shares in the fallaciousness of the argument from which it has risen.

To begin with, he says, taken with reference to its new formulation as an argument from preponderation, the argument is fallacious on two counts.

(1) It commits the fallacy of equivocation, for the minor premise in the syllogism to which this argument can be reduced, namely, the premise that the world is only possible in respect of existence and it does exist, means something dif-

[33] *Ibid* I, 74 (6), p. 153, l. 28.
[34] *Rhet.* I, 2, 1355b, 26–27.
[35] *Ibid.* I, 4, 1359b, 11–12.
[36] *Ibid.* II, 24, 1402a, 3.
[37] *Ibid.*, 15.
[38] *Moreh* I, 74 (6), p. 153, l. 28 – p. 154, l. 1.

ferent to different people. To those who believe in eternity it means that with reference to its own nature the world is only possible of existence, whereas to those who believe in creation it means that before it came into existence the world was only possible in respect of existence, and from each of these meanings of the premise a different conclusion is drawn. From its meaning as taken by those who believe in the eternity of the world, the conclusion drawn is that there must be a God who by His own essence is necessary in respect of existence and is the eternal cause of an eternal world. From its meaning as taken by those who believe in the creation of the world the conclusion drawn is that the world was created and that it was created by a God. Consequently the conclusion which the anonymous author of this argument meant to establish, namely, the creation of the world, could be established only if this premise were used in the sense in which it is understood by those who believe in creation.

(2) If the anonymous author of this argument meant to establish his conclusion from its premise as it is understood by those who believe in creation, then he commits the fallacy of begging the question (*petitio principii*), for the assumption in the premise that the world is created is the very thing which is to be demonstrated by the argument.[39]

Then, Maimonides goes on to say, taken with reference to its original formulation as an argument from particularization from which it has arisen, this argument from preponderation is fallacious on the ground that the theory of admissibility upon which the argument from particularization is based is itself based upon the Mutakallimūn's failure to distinguish between imagination and reason.[40]

8. ARGUMENT FROM IMMORTAL SOULS

In Maimonides, where the sixth argument, which is the argument from preponderance, is ascribed to "one of the

[39] *Ibid.*, p. 154, ll. 1–14.

[40] *Ibid.*, ll. 14–17.

later ones (*baʿḍ al-mutaʾakhkhirīn*: *eḥad min ha-aḥaronim*)," this argument, which is the seventh and last in his list of arguments, is introduced by the words "Said also one of the recent ones (*baʿḍ al-muḥdathīn*: *eḥad min ha-ḥadashim*)."[1] The identity of the author of this argument will be given later.

This recent Mutakallim is quoted by Maimonides first as claiming that "the creation of the world is established by what philosophers say regarding the survival of souls after death," and then as arguing as follows: "If the world were eternal, then the number of men who died in the infinite past time would be infinite and consequently there would be an infinite number of souls existing simultaneously. But this, that is to say, the simultaneous existence of an infinite number of numerable things, has been demonstrated beyond any doubt to be impossible."[2]

The history of this argument begins with a statement by Avicenna who, in the course of his discussion in his *Najāt* of the impossibility of things being infinite in number, says that an infinite number is possible in the case of things which, even though existing simultaneously, have no order either in position or by nature,[3] that is to say, which are neither corporeal nor interrelated as causes and effects. From this he concludes that "a certain species of angels and devils may be infinite in number."[4] It is evidently on the basis of this passage that Ghazālī in his *Maḳāṣid*, which is a sort of digest of the philosophy of Avicenna, says that "the human souls which are separated from the bodies by death may be infinite in number, even though they exist simultaneously, for . . . their simultaneous existence is without priority and posteriority either in position or by nature."[5] In his *Tahāfut*, Ghazālī argues against the eternity of the world on the ground that this would imply an infinite number of revolutions of the spheres, which he

[1] *Moreh* I, 74 (7), p. 154, l. 22.
[2] *Ibid.*, ll. 23–26.
[3] *Najāt* II, p. 203, ll. 6–7.
[4] *Ibid.*, ll. 9–10.
[5] *Maḳāṣid* II, p. 125, ll. 9–13.

contends to be impossible.[6] When the philosophers are quoted by him as retorting by saying that an infinite number of things is impossible only of things existing simultaneously but not of things existing successively,[7] he counters this by arguing that on the assumption of an eternal world there would be an infinite number of simultaneously existing surviving souls, concluding: "This opinion about [the possibility of an infinite number of surviving] souls is one adopted by Avicenna, and perhaps it is Aristotle's view, too." [8] His criticism of the infinity of surviving souls and hence also of the eternity of the world is twofold. First, referring to a statement made by him before in his argument from the revolution of the spheres that "number is bound to be either even or odd," [9] he argues that an infinite number of surviving souls could not be described as odd or even, and thus asks "how will you disprove a man who says that such a thing is a self-evident absurdity?" [10] Second, referring to the distinction made by Avicenna between things which have order either by nature or by position and things which have neither order by nature nor order by position, he asks: "Why did you declare one of these two cases of infinity as impossible and not the other? What proof is there for this distinction?" [11]

The next one to use this impossibility of an infinity of surviving souls as an argument against the eternity of the world and hence for its creation is Shahrastānī in his *Nihāyat.* He starts out by saying that "the easiest and best way of proving the creation of the world" is by first establishing that human souls are finite in number. From this, he argues, it would follow in succession that individual human beings are finite, that things composed of the mixture of the elements are created and finite, that the circular motion of the celestial spheres which brings about the composition of things out of the elements is finite, that the celestial movers of those circular mo-

[6] *Tahāfut al-Tahāfut* I, 16–19, p. 31, l. 10 – p. 33, l. 4.

[7] *Ibid.*, 20, p. 33, ll. 5–7.

[8] *Ibid.*, 22, p. 34, ll. 3–4.

[9] *Ibid.*, 21, p. 33, l. 8.

[10] *Ibid.*, 22, p. 34, l. 2.

[11] *Ibid.*, IV, 10, p. 137, ll. 9–10.

tions are finite, and hence that the world as a whole is created and has a beginning. "This," he concludes, "is the easiest and best method." [12] He then goes on to prove his original premise that souls must be finite in number on the ground that if they were infinite, it would follow that one infinite would be greater than another.[13]

This is the history of the argument against eternity from surviving souls. Here it would seem that "one of the recent ones" refers to Shahrastānī.

In his criticism of this argument,[14] Maimonides tries to show that among those who believe both in the eternity of the world and in the immortality of the soul there are (1) "some of the later philosophers," by whom he quite evidently means Avicenna and his followers,[15] who believe in the possibility of an infinite number of coexistent surviving incorporeal souls, and there are (2) Abū Bakr ibn al-Ṣā'igh (Avempace) and others who believe in the unity of the surviving souls.

III. The Kalam Arguments for Creation in Albertus Magnus, Thomas Aquinas, and Bonaventura *

Of all the works we have quoted as containing Kalam arguments for creation only Maimonides' *Moreh Nebukim* and Averroes' Long Commentaries on Aristotle were translated

[12] *Nihāyat*, p. 49, l. 18 – p. 50, l. 5.

[13] *Ibid.*, ll. 6–20.

[14] *Moreh* I, 74 (7), p. 155, ll. 1–11.

[15] Cf. above at nn. 7–8.

* In connection with what follows, cf. the following works: M. Joel, *Verhaltniss Albert des Grossen zu Moses Maimonides* (1863), pp. 35–38; Jacob Guttmann, *Das Verhaltniss des Thomas von Aquino zum Judenthum und zur judischen Litteratur* (1891), pp. 62–63; *Idem*, *Die Scholastik des dreizehnten Jahrhunderts in ihrem Beziehungen zum Judenthum und judischen Litteratur* (1902), pp. 98–100; Thomas Pegues, *Commentaire Français Litteral de la Somme Théologique* (1908), III, 87–97, on I, 46, 2; French translation of *Summa Theologica* I, 44–49, by A. D. Sertillanges (Appendice I, pp. 199–203; Appendice II, pp. 254–263), 2nd ed (1948); E. Gilson, *La Philosophie de Saint Bonaventure*, 2nd ed. (1943), pp. 155–157; *Idem*, *Le Thomisme*, 5th ed. (1947), pp. 211–213.

into Latin. When, therefore, we find that some of these arguments are included by Albertus Magnus, Thomas Aquinas, and Bonaventura [1] among the arguments quoted by them as having been advanced in proof of creation, we have to examine the relation of these arguments to the corresponding arguments quoted by Averroes and Maimonides. Both Averroes and Maimonides, as we have seen, refuted these arguments, the former because he did not believe in creation as traditionally interpreted by those whom he describes as "the *Loquentes* [that is, the Mutakallimūn] of the three religions existing nowadays"; [2] the latter simply because, as he says, these arguments "are subject to doubts and none of them constitutes a decisive demonstration except for those who do not know the difference between demonstration, dialectic [that is, probable reasoning], and sophism," [3] and are thus not valid enough to establish the belief in creation which is common, as he says, to "the three of us, namely, Jews, Christians, and Muslims," [4] Among these three Schoolmen, despite their belief in creation held by "these three religions," there was a difference of opinion as to the validity of these Kalam arguments, as well as of arguments advanced by others which they quote. Albertus Magnus and Thomas Aquinas reject them as invalid, the former describing them as "sophistical arguments," [5] and the latter as not being "of necessity conclusive, though not devoid of probability." [6] Bonaventura, however, accepts these arguments as valid, and, though he brings up objections against them, he answers those objections.

Of the eight arguments we have dealt with in the preceding section we shall deal here with three, two of which, (a) and (c), were actually used by the Mutakallimūn; the third, (b),

[1] Albertus Magnus, *In VIII Phys.*, Tract. I, Cap. XII; Thomas Aquinas, *Sum. Theol.* I, 46, 2; *Cont. Gent.* II, 38; *In II Sent.* Dist. I, Quaest. I, Art. V; *In VIII Phys.*, Lect. XXI; Bonaventura, *In II Sent.*, Dist. I, Pars I, Art. I, Quaest. II.

[2] Averroes, *In Metaph. XII*, Comm. 18 (VIII, p. 305 F).

[3] *Moreh* I, 71, p. 124, l. 5.

[4] *Ibid.*, p. 123, ll. 4–5.

[5] Albertus, *l.c.*, Heading of Cap. XII.

[6] *C.G.*, *l.c.*, Sed autem rationes.

though not actually used by them, was undoubtedly known to them.

(a) *Argument from Immortal Souls.*

One Kalam argument used by all these three Schoolmen can definitely be traced to Maimonides, and that is the argument from the surviving human souls.[7]

Each of them in his own way restates the contention of the argument that, on the assumption of an eternal world, there would be the simultaneous existence of an infinite number of surviving souls, which is contrary to the Aristotelian principle of the impossibility of the simultaneous existence of an infinite number of things." [8]

All of them, like Maimonides, try to show how those who believe in the eternity of the world would refute this argument. In their refutation they all reproduce Maimonides' refutation of it either as one single refutation or as two distinct refutations. Thus Albertus says that the argument fails to prove that those against whom it is directed believe that "souls survive after death and, if they survive, that they survive as numerically distinguished," for, he goes on to say, some philosophers, chief among them "a Moor by the name of Abouizer" (*Maurus nomine Abouizer*), while believing that souls survive, believes that only the intellectual parts of the soul survive and that all these survived intellectual parts are one.[9] The "Moor by the name Abouizer" is he whom Maimonides in his refutation of this argument refers to as "Abū Bakr ibn al-Ṣā'igh," [10] that is, Avempace. In the Latin translation of *The Guide of the Perplexed* used by Albertus, the same name is given as "Albumazer Maurus." [11] Similarly, Thomas Aquinas says that "those who hold the eternity of the world evade this argument in many ways," [12] and then

[7] Cf. above, pp. 452 ff.

[8] Albertus, *l.c.*, Alia est; Thomas, *S. Th.*, *l.c.*, Obj. 8; *C.G.*, *l.c.*, Rursus; *In II Sent.*, *l.c.*, Sed contra; Bonaventura, *l.c.*, Sed ad oppositum . . . Quinta.

[9] Albertus, *l.c.*, Quod autem.

[10] Cf. above, p. 455.

[11] *Dux seu Director dubitantium aut perplexorum* I, 73, fol. 73a, l. 34.

[12] *S. Th.*, *l.c.*, Ad octavum.

goes on to enumerate four views on immortality held by those who believed in the eternity of the world, each of which would invalidate the Kalam argument.[13] Among the four views enumerated by him, Aquinas reproduces the two mentioned by Maimonides. One of these is the view described by him as of those who "do not think it impossible that souls should be actually infinite in number," [14] seeing that they "have no order [either in space or position]." [15] Maimonides, as will be recalled, attributed this view to "some of the later philosophers"; [16] Aquinas refers it to "the *Metaphysics* of Algazel." [17] The other view is that of some "who say that of all souls only one will remain." [18] Maimonides, again, as will be recalled, attributes it to Avempace; Aquinas, in one place, attributes it to "the Commentator," [19] that is, Averroes.

Bonaventura, however, after reproducing the argument against eternity from surviving souls, raises tentatively an objection, in which he mentions two of the four views of immortality mentioned by Aquinas as being held by those who believe in eternity, one of which he phrases as the belief that "there is one soul for all men," but he characterizes it as being "much less acceptable" than the other view previously mentioned by him, namely, metempsychosis, which he has dismissed as being "an error philosophically." [20] Thus the twofold refutation of this argument is summarily dismissed by him.

(b) *Argument from Finitudes*

Thomas Aquinas, in his commentaries on the *Sentences* [21] and the *Physics*,[22] deals also with the argument from the finitude of things.[23] In his Commentary on the *Sentences*, he includes it among the arguments for creation which he con-

[13] *Ibid.*; *C.G.*, *l.c.*, Quod autem de animabus.

[14] *S. Th.*, *l.c.*

[15] *C.G.*, *l.c.*

[16] Cf. above, p. 455.

[17] *S. Th.*, *l.c.*; *Sent.*, *l.c.*, Solutio, Et quia ad rationes in contrarium, Ad Sextum. The reference is to the Latin translation of the *Makasid* (referred to above, p. 453, n. 5). Cf. *Algazel's Metaphysics*, ed. Muckle, p. 40, ll. 30 ff.

[18] *S. Th.*, *l.c.*; cf. *C.G.* and *Sent.*, *l.c.*

[19] Thomas, *In II Sent.*, *l.c.*

[20] Bonaventura, *l.c.*, Quinta.

[21] Thomas, *In II Sent.*, *l.c.*

[22] *Id.*, *In VIII Phys.*, *l.c.*

[23] Cf. above, pp. 374 ff.

siders as not being "of necessity conclusive, though not devoid of probability"; in his Commentary on the *Physics*, he deals with it purely as an objection to Aristotle's theory of the eternity of the world. The source from which he has derived that argument, as he himself indicates, is Averroes' Long Commentaries on the *Physics* (Book VIII, Comm. 79) and the *Metaphysics* (Book XII, Comm. 41).

In his commentaries on both the *Sentences* and the *Physics*, Thomas Aquinas starts by quoting the difficulty raised against the eternity of the world on the ground of the finitude of the force within it. In the Commentary on the *Sentences*, the argument is used to prove the impossibility both that "its motion should be for an infinite time" and that "its existence should endure for an infinite time." [24] In the Commentary on the *Physics*, it only tries to prove that "no body can endure infinitely." [25]

The subsequent treatments of this argument in his two commentaries differ.

In his Commentary on the *Sentences*, he quotes from Averroes' Long Commentary on the *Metaphysics*, Averroes' own solution of this difficulty by explaining that, according to Aristotle, the infinity of motion is due to the prime mover, and the infinity of existence is due to the incorruptibility of the celestial sphere by its own nature. Commenting on this distinction between the infinity of motion and the infinity of existence, which Averroes ascribes to Aristotle, St. Thomas maintains that, according to Aristotle, the infinity of existence is also due to the prime mover, and he supports himself by Averroes' own view in his *De Substantia Orbis*.[26] This, as will be recalled, is exactly the view of Alexander Aphrodisiensis, as quoted by Averroes in his Long Commentaries on the *Physics* and *De Caelo*.[27]

[24] Thomas, *In II Sent.*, *l.c.*, Sed contra 8.

[25] *Id.*, *In VIII Phys.*, *l.c.*, No. 6.

[26] *Id.*, *In II Sent.*, *l.c.*, Solutio, Et quia ad rationes in contrarium, Ad octavum.

[27] Cf. above, pp. 378–381.

In his Commentary on the *Physics*, however, he first quotes a solution of the difficulty as reported, he says, in the name of Alexander by Averroes in his [Long] Commentary [on the *Physics*]. As phrased by him, it reads as follows: "A celestial body receives its eternity [of existence] and its eternal motion from a separate mover of infinite power [that is, the prime mover]." [28] Then he goes on to show how Averroes in his [Long] Commentary on the *Physics* as well as on the *Metaphysics* refuted Alexander's solution of the difficulty. As phrased by him, it reads as follows: "It is impossible for a thing to receive eternity of being from another, for it would follow that what is corruptible in itself would become eternal." [29] It is to be noted that Averroes himself, as I have shown above,[30] admitted that the same refutation of Alexander's solution had been also advanced by John Philoponus. It is also to be noted that nowhere in his discussion of this problem does St. Thomas refer to John Philoponus, though his name is mentioned in Averroes' commentaries quoted by him. Finally, as in his Commentary on the *Sentences*, he quotes Averroes' own solution of the difficulty,[31] which he characterizes as being "contrary to the truth and to Aristotle's intention" and proceeds to prove it.[32]

(c) *Argument from an Infinite by Succession*

Then one argument, which is used by all three of these Schoolmen, and two arguments, which are used by only two of them, can be identified with some of the various forms in which the argument from the impossibility of an infinite by succession is presented in the Kalam.[33]

First, all of them use an argument which Thomas Aquinas and Bonaventura describe as being based on the Aristotelian principle that "it is impossible to traverse an infinite," [34] taking the term "infinite" in this principle to mean not only

[28] Thomas, *In VIII Phys.*, *l.c.*, No. 12.
[29] *Ibid.*
[30] Cf. above, pp. 378–381.
[31] Thomas, *In VIII Phys.*, *l.c.*
[32] *Ibid.*, Nos. 13–14.
[33] Cf. above, pp. 410 ff.
[34] *Phys.* VIII, 9, 265a, 19–20.

infinite space but also infinite motion.[35] In various ways, all of them argue that, on the assumption of the eternity of the world, the past revolutions of the celestial bodies would have to be infinite, with the result that the actual present revolution of the celestial bodies, and hence the actual present day, would not have arrived.[36] Both Albertus Magnus and Thomas Aquinas refute this argument, the former raising against it three objections; the latter only one objection.

Albertus, having in mind the distinction made by Averroes and Maimonides on behalf of Aristotle between an essential and an accidental infinite or between an actual and a potential infinite and their description of the accidental or potential infinite as an infinite by succession, argues in the first two of his three refutations that an infinite succession of celestial revolutions, which is an accidental or potential infinite, is not impossible.[37] His third refutation, I take it, is the same as the one refutation by Thomas.

Thomas' refutation of the argument, as phrased by him in his *Contra Gentiles*, reads as follows: "Though the infinite is not [traversed] when simultaneous and actual, it can be [traversed] when in succession [and in potentiality], since any part of such infinites (*infinitum*) taken is finite. Hence any part of the preceding revolutions taken could be traversed, since it is finite." [38] What he means to say is this. Aristotle's statement that an infinite cannot be traversed refers only to a continuous infinite extension which has neither beginning nor end, but in the case of an infinite by succession, such as infinite time or the infinite generation of man or the infinite division of magnitudes, which, according to Aristotle, means that "one thing is always taken after another, and each thing

[35] Cf. above, p. 416.

[36] Albertus, *l.c.*, Prima autem suarum demonstrationum est; Thomas, *S. Th.*, *l.c.*, Obj. 6; *C.G.*, *l.c.*, Adhuc, Quia; *In II Sent.*, *l.c.*, Sed contra 3; Bonaventura, *l.c.*, Tertia.

[37] Albertus, *l.c.*, Prima autem suarum demostrationum absque dubio nihil valet . . . Primum . . . Secundum . . .

[38] *C.G.*, *l.c.*

that is taken is always finite,"[39] there are parts which are traversed.

In his *Summa Theologica*, the same refutation is stated briefly as follows: "Passage is always understood as being from term to term. Whatever bygone day we choose, from it to the present day there is a finite number of days which can be traversed."[40]

In Bonaventura, a tentative refutation is raised only to be answered. This tentative refutation is not the same as the unanswered refutation in Albertus Magnus and Thomas Aquinas. It is something devised by Bonaventura himself. To make of it any sense we may assume that Bonaventura conceived of an opponent who had in his mind Aristotle's statement to the effect that time and movement are measured by each other, so that time units and movement units correspond to each other and that, if the movement units are infinite, the corresponding time units will also be infinite.[41] We may also assume that Bonaventura further conceived of his opponent as taking the Aristotelian statement that "it is impossible to traverse an infinite"[42] to mean that an infinite, whether an infinite space or an infinite succession of movements, cannot be traversed in finite time but that it can be traversed in infinite time. This, it will be recalled, resembles the reasoning in Aristotle's answer to Zeno's first argument against the infinite divisibility of space.[43] With all this in the back of his mind, Bonaventura hurls the following challenge: "If [in refutation of the argument] you should say that the infinite past revolutions of the spheres cannot indeed be traversed [in finite time] because they have no first but that they may still full well be traversed in infinite time [which similarly has no first], you will not get away with it."[44] Thereupon Bona-

[39] *Phys.* III, 6, 206a, 25–29.

[40] *S. Th.*, *l.c.*, Ad sextum.

[41] *Phys.* IV, 12, 220b, 14–32; VIII, 1, 251b, 10–28.

[42] *Phys.* VIII, 9, 265a, 10–20; cf. above n. 34.

[43] *Phys.* VI, 2, 233a, 24–31; cf. below, p. 516.

[44] Bonaventura, *l.c.*, Tertia. The text, slightly emended, reads as follows: "Si tu dicas quod non sunt pertransita, quia nulla fuit prima, sed (printed text: vel) quod etiam bene possunt pertransiri; per hoc non evades."

ventura goes on to rebut it. His rebuttal is based upon his attempt to disprove the view assumed in the refutation that infinite revolutions can be traversed in infinite time.[45] The chief points in his rebuttal are as follows. (1) Assuming that the world is eternal, Bonaventura raises the question whether we are able to fix a spherical revolution on some day which is infinitely prior to a given revolution on the present day or whether we are unable to fix any such revolution. (2) He shows the impossibility of either one of these alternatives. (3) Having thus shown that we are unable to fix a spherical revolution on some day which is infinitely prior to a given revolution on the present day, he expects us to conclude that the past infinite revolutions of the spheres in an assumed eternal world cannot be traversed in infinite time.[46]

Second, an argument used only by Thomas Aquinas[47] and Bonaventura[48] contends that, on the assumption of the eternity of the world, there would be an infinite number of efficient causes, but this, according to Aristotle himself in *Metaphysics* II. 2, is impossible. Aquinas illustrates it by the generation of one man from another man[49] as well as by the generation of one animal from another animal,[50] and Bonaventura illustrates it by the revolutions of the celestial bodies and by the generation of one animal from another animal.[51] Aquinas refutes this argument, and his refutation is based upon the distinction between an accidental and essential infinite,[52] which distinction in his Commentary on the *Sentences* is attributed by him to Averroes' Long Commentary on the *Physics*, Book VIII, Comm. 47. Bonaventura, referring to what has been hitherto referred to as "essential causes" in contrast to "accidental causes" as "things which are arranged

[45] Cf. Albertus, *In III Phys.*, Tract. II, Cap. V.
[46] Bonaventura, *l.c.*, Tertia.
[47] *S. Th.*, *l.c.*, Obj. 7; *C.G.*, *l.c.*, Amplius; *Sent.*, *l.c.*, Sed contra 5.
[48] Bonaventura, *l.c.*, Secunda.
[49] *S. Th.*, *l.c.*; *C.G.*, *l.c.*; *In II Sent.*, *l.c.*
[50] Thomas, *In II Sent.*, *l.c.*
[51] Bonaventura, *l.c.*, Secunda.
[52] *S. Th.*, *l.c.*, Ad Septimum; *C.G.*, *l.c.*, Quod etiam quinto; *In II Sent.*, *l.c.*, Solutio, Et quia . . . Ad quintum.

according to the order of causality," argues: "If you say that it is not necessary to assume a stop in the order [or succession] except in things which are arranged according to the order of causality, because in causes there must be a stop, then I ask: Why not in others?" [53] Thus, again, is the refutation of the argument summarily dismissed by him.

Third, an argument, again, used only by Thomas Aquinas and Bonaventura contends that, on the assumption of the eternity of the world, the past number of days or past number of revolutions to the present day would be infinite, with the result that with every additional day there would be additions to the infinite number of days and revolutions,[54] which would make something greater than the infinite. In his refutation, Thomas Aquinas, evidently drawing upon Aristotle's statement that "by addition, also, there is an infinite potentially, in the same way as an infinite by division, for it will always be possible to find something beyond the total for the time being," [55] says "that nothing hinders the infinite receiving an addition on the side on which it is finite." [56] This refutation of the argument is tentatively restated by Bonaventura in his own words only to be rebutted. His tentative restatement reads as follows: "If you say that the infinite is only in respect of the past, but in respect of the present, that is, the now, it is actually finite, and so on the side on which it is actually finite, may become greater, it does not invalidate the argument." He then goes on to show how, on the assumption of the eternity of the world, one infinite would be greater than another, even when the past infinite is finite in respect of any given present, for at any given present the infinite revolutions of the moon would always be twelve times as many as the infinite revolutions of the sun.[57]

[53] Bonaventura, *l.c.*

[54] *C.G.*, *l.c.*, Praeterea: *In II Sent.*, *l.c.*, Sed contra 4.

[55] *Phys.* III, 6, 206b, 16–18.

[56] *C.G.*, *l.c.*, Quod etiam quarto; *In II Sent.*, *l.c.*, Solutio, Et quia . . . Ad quartum.

[57] Bonaventura, *l.c.*, Prima.

Though none of these arguments which we have listed under "(c) *Argument from an Infinite by Succession*" are taken directly from the works of Averroes or from the work of Maimonides, still they show the unmistaken influence of the various presentations of the Kalam argument from the impossibility of an infinite by succession as these presentations could have come to be known to our three Schoolmen through Maimonides and Averroes.

CHAPTER VI

ATOMISM

I. Affirmation of Atomism

1. ORIGIN OF ATOMISM IN THE KALAM

In the early part of the ninth century there began to appear in the Kalam discussions of such philosophic concepts as body and substance and motion and accidents and the like.[1] Various meanings are given to these concepts, all of which can be traced to Greek sources — sources either genuine or spurious, of which some could have been known to the Mutakallimūn directly through translations and others only indirectly through hearsay.

It is from such Greek sources that the Mutakallimūn learned also about atoms. This is attested by the fact that the basic Arabic terms used by them in their first recorded discussions of atomism, during the early part of the ninth century, are all translations from the Greek. Thus the Arabic terms for atoms, *lā yatajazza'u* [2] and *lā yanḳasimu*,[3] are translations of the Greek terms ἄτομον [4] and ἀδιαίρετον.[5] So also the Arabic use of the term *al-jauhar*, "substance," by itself in the sense of "atom," [6] reflects Aristotle's statement that Democritus "makes magnitudes that are indivisible (ἄτομα) to be substances (οὐσίας)." [7] To this etymological evidence we may add the testimony of Ibn Ḥazm, who says that the atomism of the Kalam is to be traced to "some of the ancients (*al-*

[1] *Maḳālāt*, pp. 301 ff.

[2] *Ibid.* p. 59, l. 3.

[3] *Ibid.*, p. 307, l. 11.

[4] *Phys.* VIII, 9, 265b, 29.

[5] *De Gen. et Corr.* I, 1, 314a, 21; *Metaph.* V, 3, 1014b, 5. See "Glossarium" in Fobes' edition of the Latin version of Averroes' Middle Commentary on *De Gen. et Corr.* under the terms "indivisibilis" and "indivisibilia."

[6] *Maḳālāt*, p. 311, l. 15.

[7] *Metaph.* VII, 13, 1039a, 10–11. The Greek term οὐσία in the sense of atom occurs also in post-Aristotelian literature. Cf. Bailey, *The Greek Atomists and Epicurus*, p. 124, n. 6, and p. 345, n. 3.

awā'il)." [8] Similarly Maimonides ascribes the origin of Kalam atomism to "the ancient (*al-mutakaddimīn*: *ha-ri' shonim*; *ha-kadmonim*) philosophers." [9] By "some of the ancients" and "the ancient philosophers," they mean primarily the pre-Socratic Leucippus and Democritus, in which sense the term "ancients" (*al-kudamā'*) is used by Shahrastānī.[10] It is thus that Democritus is mentioned as the founder of atomism by Isaac Israeli,[11] Fahr al-Dīn Rāzī, Jurjānī, and Shīrāzī.[12] Epicurus is only referred to as the one who introduced into the atomic theory the view that the world came into being out of atoms by mere chance.[13] In Greek philosophy, Plutarch, after saying that Epicurus claims "to lay down the same principles [as Democritus]," ironically remarks that what Epicurus really did was "to steal from Democritus." [14]

It is strange, however, that atomism, which had been rejected by most of the Greek schools of philosophy, should have been accepted by all but a few of the early Mutakallimūn, the exceptions among them being the Mu'tazilite Naẓẓām, the Rafiḍite Hishām b. al-Ḥakam, and some other Rafiḍites, and, according to a late report, also the orthodox Ibn Kullāb.[15] In Greek philosophy, the earlier atomism of Leucippus and Democritus was rejected by both Plato and Aristotle, and the later atomism of Epicurus by all the schools of Greek philosophy which flourished in post-Aristotelian times. Nor was atomism favored by scriptural philosophers who preceded the Kalam. Both Philo [16] and the Church Fathers [17] align themselves with the dominant schools of Greek philosophy in rejecting atoms, evidently on purely

[8] *Fiṣal*, V, p. 69, l. 12.
[9] *Moreh* I, 71, p. 122, l. 26.
[10] *Milal*, p. 253, ll. 5–6; cf. p. 311, l. 8.
[11] Cf. *Yesodot*, p. 43, ll. 10–11; *De Elementis*, p. 8a, ll. 17–19.
[12] Cf. Pines, *Atomenlehre*, pp. 96–97.
[13] Cf., e.g., *Emunot* I, 3, 9th Theory; *Moreh* II, 13, p. 198, ll. 28–30.
[14] *Adversus Coloten* 8, 1111 B and C.
[15] Cf. below, p. 495, n. 1.
[16] Cf. *Philo*, I, pp. 166, 314–315.
[17] Cf. K. Lasswitz, *Geschichte der Atomistik*, I, pp. 11–30.

philosophic grounds, without making a religious issue out of it, even though occasionally they may find scriptural verses to support their rational choice.[18] The adoption of this generally discredited view by the Kalam and its being made by them into a religious doctrine requires an explanation.

An explanation may be found in the fact that in the ninth century, when the Muslims became acquainted with atomism, they also learned that those who believed in atoms denied causality, whereas those who believed in the infinite divisibility of matter affirmed causality. The denial of causality was thus in their mind associated historically with atomism. Whether that association meant to them also a logical association is doubtful, for, as we shall see, Muʿammar, who was an atomist, still believed in causality.[19] Now it happens that about a century earlier the Muslims had committed themselves to the view that the teachings of the Koran about the divine power do not allow the belief that God employs intermediate causes both in the actions of men and in the actions of all other things, and, while with regard to the actions of men there appeared in the Kalam the Muʿtazilite opposition to this view, with regard to the actions of all other things in the world there was no opposition to it in the Kalam except on the part of some individual Muʿtazilites.[20] Thus, barring the Muʿtazilite opposition with regard to human actions and the opposition on the part of individual Muʿtazilites with regard to actions in general, God was regarded by the Mutakallimūn as being the direct cause of everything that happens in the world, which meant a denial of causality. It is this denial of causality on purely religious grounds that made them predisposed to the acceptance of atomism, which in their minds was historically associated with the denial of causality,[21] even though at

[18] Cf. *Philo*, I, pp. 314–315.
[19] Cf. below, pp. 560; 566.
[20] Cf. below, p. 613.
[21] There seems to be a suggestion of this explanation by the Karaite

the same time, on similar purely religious grounds, as we shall see in the chapter on Causality, they rejected chance, despite its being historically associated with the atomism accepted by them. Evidently it was simpler for them to substitute their omnipotent God for chance than to harmonize Him with causality.

Once the theory of atoms was thus accepted by them on the ground of indirect religious considerations, they began to reinforce it by direct religious arguments.

The reinforcing religious arguments are based either upon a consideration of another aspect of God's power or upon a consideration of God's knowledge. The argument from power is reproduced by Ashʿarī in his account of the controversy over atoms among the Muʿtazilites. "They differed," he says, "as to whether the Creator is to be described as having the power to dissolve the whole aggregation of bodies so that they would be reduced to atoms. Al-Naẓẓām expressed himself in the negative, and so did also every one who denied the existence of atoms,"[22] whereas Abū al-Hudhayl, who believed in the existence of atoms, said that "it is possible for God to dissever a body and to annihilate whatever there is in it of aggregation, so that it becomes an atom."[23] The controversy over atoms is thus represented as a controversy over the question whether God could break up bodies into irreducible parts and also whether He could reduce them to one irreducible part. In Ibn Ḥazm the same argument from the power of God is stated as follows: "The proponents of atoms say: Is it not God who combines the parts of a body? Inevitably the

---

Aaron ben Elijah of Nicomedia in the following statement: "The sages of speculation [that is, the Mutakallimūn] do not agree with the aforementioned view, namely, that accidents have causes for their existence in bodies, maintaining that they come into being by the Prime Agent without the intermediacy of a cause, and therefore they admitted the existence of atoms of which bodies were supposed to be composed" (*ʿEṣ Ḥayyim* 4, p. 17, ll. 34–37).

[22] *Maḳālāt*, p. 586, ll. 1–3; cf. p. 59, ll. 4–7.

[23] *Ibid.*, p. 314, ll. 12–13; cf. p. 59, ll. 8–10.

answer is yes. They then say: Has God the power to divide these parts so that there would be nothing of a composition and nothing of parts in them, or has not God that power? If you say He has not the power, then your God is powerless. And if you say He has the power, then you have admitted the existence of an atom." [24] The argument from knowledge, in its simple form as restated by Baghdādī, tries to show that the infinite divisibility of a body, which is implied in the denial of atoms, "would force us to conclude that its parts are not limited in God's knowledge, but this involves a rejection of the Prophet's saying: 'And He counteth all things by number' (72:28)." [25] Reflecting all these religious arguments, Maimonides says that the theories of the atom and the void were accepted by the Mutakallimūn because they thought that these theories were "matters of common usefulness and premises which every follower of a revealed Law would be in need of." [26] There were also, of course, philosophic arguments in support of atomism,[27] but these appeared later and were used as auxiliary to the religious arguments. The original impetus for the adoption of atomism and the main support for it, as we have tried to show, are to be found in religious considerations.[28]

It must, however, be added that the argument from God's power is double-edged. For by the very same reasoning from God's power by which it is argued that God must have the power to break things up into parts no longer divisible, it

[24] *Fiṣal*, V, p. 94, ll. 14–16.

[25] *Fark*, p. 316, ll. 2–5; cf. p. 123, ll. 15–17. A parallel statement in the Wisdom of Solomon 11:20, which reads: "But in measure and number and weight Thou hast ordered all things" (cf. Isa. 40:12; Job 28:25), is used by St. Augustine to prove that, though material things are infinitely divisible, still they are all known to God (*De Civ. Dei* XII, 18). Cf. above, p. 169.

[26] *Moreh* I, 71, p. 122, ll. 28–29. Cf. Averroes, *In VIII Phys.*, Comm. 74, vol. IV, p. 418 IK, quoted below, p. 552 at n. 4.

[27] *Fiṣal* V, p. 93, ll. 2–3; p. 94, ll. 4–6; p. 96, ll. 3–12; *'Es Ḥayyim* 4, p. 14.

[28] Mabilleau, *Histoire de la Philosophie Atomistique*, p. 326, rejects Maimonides' explanation of a religious motive for Muslim atomism on the ground that he did not know what that religious motive was. Pines, *Atomenlehre*, p. 94, rejects a religious motive on the ground that it does not explain everything about the Muslim conception of atoms.

could also be argued that God should have the power to break things up into parts which are always divisible. In fact, Joseph al-Baṣīr, on becoming conscious of this argument, solved it by including the indivisibility of atoms among the impossibilities which do not come under God's power.[29] It may also be added that Ghazālī, who shared with the Kalam its denial of causality, rejected atomism.[30] To him, evidently, the historical association between the denial of causality and atomism did not mean a logical association. Nor was he daunted by either of the two religious arguments, just as Augustine was not daunted by one of these arguments,[31] and Joseph al-Baṣīr was not daunted by the other.[32]

But religious considerations which led the Kalam theologians to adopt atomism also made it impossible for them to adopt atomism in its original form as it was conceived in Greek philosophy.

First, with their belief in the creation of the world, the atoms, which to them were the component parts of the bodies of the world, had also to be created. This was not only the view of those who believed in creation *ex nihilo* but also the view of those who believed in creation out of a pre-existent eternal matter.[33]

Second, with their rejection of the infinite divisibility of matter on the ground that the infinite could not be known by God, they could not very well accept the view, held by all schools of Greek atomists, that the atoms were infinite in number. Thus of the exponents of the Kalam atomists in general it is said that one of their fundamental doctrines was that, in opposition to Aristotle, who believed in the infinite divisibility of matter and in some other kinds of infinity, they denied the existence of an infinite in any respect.[34]

[29] Cf. *Mahkimat* 1, p. 105b, ll. 4–5, and 21, p. 117b, ll. 11–21.
[30] Cf. above, p. 41. [31] Cf. above n. 25. [32] Cf. above n. 29.
[33] Cf. above, pp. 366–367. [34] *Moreh* I, 73, Prop. 11.

2. AN UNKNOWN PSEUDO-DEMOCRITEAN FRAGMENT AND THE UNEXTENDEDNESS OF ATOMS IN THE KALAM *

While religious considerations may account for the deviation of almost all Muslim atomists from Greek atomism on the problem of the eternity and the infinity of atoms, no religious consideration could account for the deviation of an entire school of Muslim atomists from Greek atomism on the problem of the magnitudinousness of atoms.

In Greek philosophy, the atoms, whether those of Leucippus and Democritus or those of Epicurus, are always presented as having magnitude. Of the atoms of Leucippus, Aristotle says that they have "bulk" (ὄγκος),[1] and of the atoms of Democritus, he says that they differ in "magnitude" (μέγεθος).[2] Of the Epicurean atoms, Epicurus himself says in his letter to Herodotus that "some variations of magnitude must be supposed," [3] and pseudo-Plutarch's *De Placitis Philosophorum*, which was translated into Arabic before the tenth century, says of the atoms of both Democritus and Epicurus that they are "bodies" and have "magnitude." [4] In the Kalam, however, there was a difference of opinion as to whether atoms are magnitudinous or not. The earliest Arabic doxography that we have, the *Maḳālāt* of Ashʿarī (d. 933), quotes the opinion of a number of Muslim theologians, all dating from the ninth century, on this question. With the exception of one, all of those quoted by him are for the unextendedness of atoms.[5] Somewhat later, in the early part of the tenth century, this was one of the topics upon which the schools of Baṣra and Baghdad held different views. The school of Baṣra, repre-

* Reprinted with some revisions from *Politische Ordnung und menschliche Existenz: Festgabe für Eric Voegelin* (1967), pp. 593–606.

[1] *De Gen. et Corr.* I, 8, 325a, 30.

[2] *Phys.* III, 4, 203b, 1.

[3] Apud Diogenes Laertius, X, 55.

[4] H. Diels, *Doxographi Graeci*², I, 3, 18, p. 285a, ll. 3 and 14.

[5] *Maḳālāt*, pp. 307–308. Cf. Otto Pretzl, "Die frühislamische Atomenlehre," *Der Islam*, 19:120 (1930).

sented by Abū Hāshim, maintained that the atom has measurement (*misāḥah*) [6] and occupancy of space (*mutaḥayyiz*),[7] whereas the school of Baghdad, represented by Kaʿbī, maintained that the atom was without measurement [8] and without occupancy of space.[9] By the time of Maimonides, in the latter part of the twelfth century, the denial of the extendedness of atoms seems to have become the prevailing view in the Kalam. He formulates it as follows: "The universe as a whole, that is, every one of the bodies that it contains, is composed of small particles which are indivisible on account of their smallness, and each of these particles is absolutely without quantity." [10]

The question is: Where did such a conception of unextended atoms come from? That it must have come from somewhere and could not have arisen spontaneously in Arabic philosophy is quite clear, for there is no conceivable reason, religious or rational, why Arabic philosophy should have departed on such a fundamental issue from its parent source.

The answer given by modern scholars is that it came from Indian philosophy. Mabilleau, who was the first to suggest this answer, goes still further by sweepingly asserting that the entire theory of atomism in Arabic philosophy had its origin in Indian atomism. In fact, he takes Indian atomism to be the source even of Greek atomism.[11] Pines, more judiciously, recognizes the Greek origin of Arabic atomism but finds that certain elements in it, among them the conception of non-extended atoms, owe their origin to Indian atomism.[12] But it seems to me that, while it is to be admitted that certain elements in Muslim atomism are of Indian origin, one may still question whether the concept of the unextendedness of atoms is among them. All the elements in Muslim atomism which have been shown to be of Indian origin are supplementary to elements derived from Greek philosophy, and not contradic-

[6] *Masāʾil*, p. 38, l. 15.
[7] *Ibid.*, p. 3, l. 21.
[8] *Ibid.*, p. 38, ll. 15–17.
[9] *Ibid.*, p. 41, l. 22 – p. 42, l. 2.
[10] *Moreh* I, 73, Prop. 1, p. 135, ll. 19–21.
[11] Mabilleau, *Histoire de la Philosophie Atomistique*, I, 51–60, 301–377.
[12] S. Pines, *Beiträge zur islamischen Atomenlehre* (1936), pp. 94–123.

tory to them. But the unextendedness of atoms is something contradictory to what is taught in Greek atomism. Consequently, if we admit, as we must, that the general theory of atomism in Islam is of Greek origin, there is no adequate reason, either philosophic or religious, by which we could explain why the Greek extended atoms were replaced by the Indian unextended atoms, especially since the latter view was subject to greater difficulty than the former. Inevitably, we must assume that unextended atoms somehow had a Greek origin. It is true, indeed, that nothing like it is to be found in Greek philosophy, but this is so only if by Greek philosophy is meant the teachings contained in the authentic writings of Greek philosophers. But these writings were not the primary source, and certainly not the only source, from which Muslims got their first knowledge of Greek philosophy. Prior to translation into Arabic of such authentic writings, Muslims picked up all sorts of fragmentary and often distorted information of Greek philosophy from spurious doxographies, either translated from the Greek or originally composed in Arabic. Oriental centers of Greek learning, such as Harran and Gondeshapur, were spawning grounds of various pseudepigraphs and forgeries. A specimen of this kind of spurious writing has been preserved in Shahrastānī's Doxography of Greek philosophers, which bears internal evidence of its being much older than the Arabic translations of the genuine works of Greek philosophers. This Doxography contains reports on the teachings of the two chief exponents of Greek atomism, two reports on Democritus and one on Epicurus. Let us study these reports and see what impression early Muslims could have gotten out of this Doxography about Greek atomism.

One of the reports on Democritus, which consists mainly of ethical maxims, contains also the following statement: "He has certain views on philosophy and characteristic views of his own on the principles of generation and corruption, and Aristotle gave preference to his opinion over the opinion of his teacher the divine Plato, in preferring which he did not act properly." [13] Here, then, one of the chief exponents of Greek atomism is represented as having characteristic views of his own on the principles of generation and corruption. We may reasonably assume that those of the early Muslims who could avail themselves of this Doxography already had some knowledge, derived from some other sources, about certain standard philosophic views, including a general and vague knowledge about Democritus' atoms and accidents. When, therefore, they read in this Doxography about characteristic views held by Democritus on the principles of generation and corruption they naturally identified them with his views on atomism. And when they further read in the same Doxography that the views held by Democritus with regard to atoms were favored by Aristotle in preference to the view of Plato they naturally got the impression that the atoms and accidents of Democritus are like the matter and form of Aristotle and not like the images and ideas of Plato. There is no use speculating as to what conception of atoms they could have gotten from this comparison between the atoms of Democritus and the matter of Aristotle. But knowing as we do that among Aristotelians there was a question whether the matter of Aristotle is extended or unextended, a question which had its repercussion in later Arabic philosophy,[14] we can readily see how from this Doxography it was possible for some of its readers to arrive at the conclusion that atoms were unextended.

The second report on Democritus is a medley of various views,[15] in which no trace is to be found of his theory of atoms.

The report on Epicurus in Shahrastānī's Doxography contains the following statement: "The principles are two, the vacuum and the forms (*al-ṣuwar*). As for the vacuum, it is empty space; but, as for the forms, they are over and above

[13] *Milal*, p. 305, ll. 3–5.

[14] Cf. my *Cresca's Critique of Aristotle* (1929), n. 18 on pp. 579–590, and summary on pp. 100–101.

[15] *Milal*, p. 294, ll. 12–20.

space and vacuum, and out of them arose all existent things and into them resolve all things that came into existence out of them, so that from them they had their beginning and unto them is their return."[16] The Arabic term *ṣūrah*, "form," is used as a translation of the Greek terms εἶδος and ἰδέα, and consequently the attribution here to Epicurus of a belief in a "vacuum" and "forms" reflects a Greek passage in which the atoms of Epicurus were referred to as ideas, for so, in fact, are the atoms of Democritus referred to in pseudo-Plutarch's *De Placitis Philosophorum*.[17] Here, too, there is no indication that the "atoms" called "forms" have magnitude. On the contrary, the term *ṣuwar*, to those who already had a smattering knowledge of philosophy, meant either Platonic "ideas" or Aristotelian "forms," neither of which had magnitude.

There is only one report in this Doxography in Shahrastānī, a combined report on Democritus and Epicurus, in which the atoms of both of them are explicitly said to have magnitude. But this report, as well as the report on Heraclitus and Hipassus immediately preceding it, can be shown, I believe, to be a later interpolation by some one who already had before him the Arabic translation of pseudo-Plutarch's *De Placitis Philosophorum*. These two reports are inserted in a section on Pythagoras, between a passage which contains a question addressed to Pythagoras and his answer[18] and a passage which begins with the statement: "Pythagoras had two well-guided (or wise) disciples."[19] The report on Heraclitus and Hipassus

[16] *Ibid.*, p. 297, ll. 10–12.

[17] Cf. Diels, *Doxographi Graeci*, IV, 5, 3, p. 388a, l. 4. The term ἰδέας in this passage of pseudo-Plutarch is undoubtedly used in the sense of σχήματα, "shapes," which is one of the characteristics of atoms (cf. below p. 487, n. 1). In the Arabic translation of pseudo-Plutarch, the term ἰδέας here is translated *shukūl*, "shapes" (singular *shakl* in the printed edition by Badawi, p. 158, l. 7). So also Nemesius in *De Natura Hominis* 2 (PG 40, 536 B; cf. Diels, *loc. cit.*), σχήματα as a description of atoms. In a passage quoted from Simplicius in Diels, *Die Fragmente der Vorsokratiker*, Demokritos B, 167, which was called to my attention by Professor Charles H. Kahn, the term εἶδος is used for atom. Here, too, εἶδος is undoubtedly used in the sense of σχῆμα.

[18] *Milal*, p. 277, ll. 1–4.

[19] *Ibid.*, l. 18.

and the combined report on Democritus and Epicurus which came between these two passages have nothing to do with Pythagoras. They are taken, as we shall see, from the Arabic translation of pseudo-Plutarch's *De Placitis Philosophorum*, where they chronologically follow a report on Pythagoras. But our interpolator, in order to explain why he inserted these reports into a report on Pythagoras, changed the opening words "Heraclitus and Hippasus of Metapontum," which occur both in the original Greek and the Arabic version of pseudo-Plutarch,[20] to read: "Heraclitus and Hippasus belonged to the Pythagoreans," [21] probably justifying himself for doing so on the ground of some rumors which he must have heard that both Heraclitus and Hipassus were of the school of Pythagoras.[22] But following faithfully the Arabic translation of pseudo-Plutarch's *De Placitis*,[23] our interpolator introduces his report on Democritus and Epicurus by the statement "Epicurus who philosophized in the days of Democritus," [24] for which the original Greek reads: "Epicurus, the son of Neoches, who philosophized in accordance with Democritus (κατὰ Δημόκριτον)." [25] Then, following again faithfully the partly inaccurate statement in both the original Greek and the Arabic translation of the pseudo-Plutarch's *De Placitis*, our interpolator says that, whereas Epicurus attributes to atoms "shape, magnitude, and weight," Democritus attributes to them only "magnitude and shape." [26]

Thus, barring the passage later interpolated from pseudo-Plutarch's *De Placitis*, there is nothing in this Doxography preserved by Shahrastānī, which is probably one of the earliest sources to have furnished the early Muslims some vague

[20] Diels, *Doxographi Graeci*, p. 283, ll. 17–18 (Arabic, p. 102, l. 4).

[21] *Milal*, p. 277, l. 4.

[22] Cf. Zeller, *Phil. d. Gr.* I⁴, n. 1 on pp. 568–569 and pp. 457–458; Diels, *op. cit.*, pp. 145, 152, 178.

[23] Arabic *De Placitis*, p. 102, l. 10.

[24] *Milal*, p. 277, l. 8.

[25] Diels, *op. cit.* n. 4, p. 285a, ll. 1–2.

[26] *Milal*, p. 277, ll. 10–11; cf. Diels, *op. cit.* n. 4, p. 285a, ll. 12–15 (Arabic, p. 102, ll. 14–16).

knowledge about Greek atomism, from which they could have learned that the atoms had magnitude. Quite the contrary, it could have suggested to them that the atoms had no magnitude.

But the Doxography preserved by Shahrastānī, we may assume, was not the only work of that type available to the early Muslims. There must have been many other doxographies, and among them there must have been those which contained distorted views about atomism, especially the atomism of Democritus. For Democritus is known to have been a favorite peg upon which to hang all kinds of views. Diels in his *Fragmente der Vorsokratiker* has more unauthentic fragments under Democritus than under all the others combined. Some of these fragments were brought to light only during the last century. To these numerous pseudo-Democritean fragments I am going to add one more — one which bears upon the question of a possible Greek source for unextended atoms.

The fragment is embedded in a passage in Isaac Israeli's work *De Elementis*, of which the original Arabic, written during the ninth or the tenth century, is lost, but of which there is a Latin translation, made in the twelfth century,[27] and a Hebrew translation, made in the thirteenth century.[28] The passage occurs in the course of Israeli's discussion of the meaning of Galen's definition of element, which Israeli quotes as reading that "the element is the minimum of the parts of a thing." [29] He discusses various possible meanings of the expression "the minimum of parts" used in Galen's definition.[30] He then makes a hypothetical interlocutor suggest that by "the minimum parts" in Galen's definition is meant those parts "into which a body is naturally divided and of which it is also

[27] *Liber de Elementis* in *Omnia Opera Isaac* (1515), fols. IIIIc-Xd.

[28] *Sefer ha-Yesodot*, ed. S. Fried (1900).

[29] *De Elementis*, fol. VIId, l. 13 (*Yesodot*, p. 40, l. 7); cf. Galen, *De Elementis ex Hippocrate* I, 1 (*Opera*, ed. Kühn, I, p. 413); *De Hippocratis et Platonis Placitis* VIII, 2 (V, p. 661).

[30] *De Elementis*, fol. VIId, l. 17 – fol. VIIIa, l. 5; *Yesodot*, p. 40, l. 9 – p. 43, l. 1.

composed, analogous to the division of a body into surfaces and of surfaces into lines and of lines into points." [31] In other words, the "minimum parts" are mathematical concepts like surfaces, lines, and points, of which Aristotle says that "all these are inherent in other things, and not one of them exists separately." [32] Israeli then makes his interlocutor say further that he can support such an interpretation of Galen's definition "by a statement of Democritus, for Democritus has said that body is composed of surfaces and surfaces are composed of lines and lines are composed of points." [33]

As no such statement is to be found in any of the extant fragments reporting the teachings of Democritus, Jacob Guttmann, in his monograph on Isaac Israeli, takes this statement as one composed by Israeli himself and declares it to be a misinterpretation on the part of Israeli of Democritus' theory of atoms.[34] This judgment, I believe, is inaccurate. Internal evidence shows that the statement is a quotation from some source.

The evidence is twofold.

First, there is the manner in which this statement of his hypothetical interlocutor is introduced by Israeli. According to the Latin translation, which seems to be a faithful literal reproduction of the original Arabic, it reads as follows: "And he corroborates it by a statement of Democritus, for Democritus has said." [35] In the olden time, before quotation marks were devised, such introductory words meant that what followed was a quotation.

Second, there is Israeli's own comment in refutation of his hypothetical interlocutor's suggestion. It reads as follows:

[31] *De Elementis*, p. 8a, ll. 5–11 (*Yesodot*, p. 43, ll. 1–5).

[32] *Metaph.* XI, 2, 1060b, 16–17.

[33] *De Elementis*, p. 8a, ll. 11–14 (*Yesodot*, p. 43, ll. 5–6): "et certificet super illud sermone Democriti, quoniam Democritus dixit quod corpus est compositum ex superficiebus et superficies compositae sunt ex lineis et lineae ex punctis."

[34] Cf. Jacob Guttmann, *Die philosophischen Lehren des Isaak ben Salomon Israeli* (1911), p. 13; p. 62, n. 1.

[35] Cf. above n. 33.

"We say to him: The statement of Democritus which you have quoted, namely, that, when points are put together, a line arises, is a statement which lends itself to two interpretations." [36] Israeli then goes on to explain what these two possible interpretations are. Now the very fact that Israeli suggests two possible interpretations of Democritus' statement, which he himself has put in the mouth of his hypothetical interlocutor, shows that the statement is not of Israeli's own composition, for certainly he would not suggest two possible interpretations of a statement which he himself has phrased. Undoubtedly, then, the statement is a quotation from a passage on Democritus in some doxography, which was either a translation from the Greek or originally composed in Arabic on the basis of Greek sources.

What the complete passage was from which the quotation in Israeli was taken may be reconstructed on the basis of two passages in Aristotle which, we shall try to show, are reflected in that quotation from Democritus.

The first of these passages occurs in the *Metaphysics*, where, speaking of the Platonists, Aristotle says that from one standpoint they treat unity, which is their first principle, as a mathematical "point," for "the unit is a point without position," and, when they do so, then "just like certain others," that is, the atomists Leucippus and Democritus, "they put things together out of that which is the smallest part." [37] Here, then, an analogy is drawn between the mathematical point and the atom of Democritus, though, when closely examined, the analogy is meant to be only with regard to indivisibility, namely, that both the mathematical point and the Democritean atom are indivisible; there is no indication in this analogy that the Democritean atom was to be, like the mathematical point, without any extension.[38]

[36] *De Elementis*, p. 8a, ll. 17–19 (*Yesodot*, p. 43, ll. 10–11): "Dicemus ei: Quod autem narrasti de sermone Democriti, quod cum puncta componuntur sit ex eis linea, est sermo habens duas intentiones."

[37] *Metaph.* XIII, 8, 1084b, 25–28.

[38] In *De Caelo* III, 4, 303a, 8–9, called to my attention by Professor Harold

The second passage occurs in the *De Anima*, in which Aristotle argues against a view, identified with that of Xenocrates, which maintains that the soul is a self-moving number, consisting of units. Aristotle's argument is divided into two parts. In the first part,[39] he assumes that the units, of which Xenocrates' soul-number consists, have no extension, but, in the course of his argument, from the fact that they are self-moving, he concludes that, even though they have no extension, they must have position, and hence are points, for, according to a statement of his elsewhere, a point is that which is indivisible, that is, unextended, but has position.[40] In the second part of his argument, Aristotle begins with a statement which, literally translated, reads: "Besides, it would seem to make no difference whether we say units or tiny corpuscles, for *if out of the little spheres of Democritus points be generated and quantity alone remain* (γὰρ ἐκ τῶν Δημοκρίτου σφαιρίων ἐὰν γένωνται στιγμαὶ, μόνον δὲ μένῃ τὸ ποσόν), there will still be in this, as in everything continuous, something which causes motion and something which is moved."[41] In this quotation from Aristotle, it is not quite clear what the statement, which we have italicized and of which we have reproduced the corresponding Greek, exactly means. But in Themistius' commentary on *De Anima*, which was translated into Arabic during the ninth century, this statement of Aristotle is paraphrased to read: "It will make no difference whether we say the soul consists of units or of tiny particles, which Democritus takes to be spherical, for *if any one assumes the spheres of Democritus to be no longer spheres but points which retained only their quantity*, nothing would prevent

---

F. Cherniss, Aristotle says that Leucippus and Democritus, by their theory of atoms, "in a way make things out to be numbers or composed of numbers." Here, too, the analogy of atoms to numbers only means that, like numbers, atoms are indivisible; it does not mean that, like numbers, they are also unextended.

[39] *De Anima* I, 4, 408b, 30 – 409a, 10.

[40] *Metaph.* V, 6, 1016b, 25–26, 30–31.

[41] *De Anima* I, 4, 409a, 10–13.

some of them from causing motion and others from being moved, as would be the case if they were small bodies." [42]

Perhaps the underscored paraphrase in Themistius of the underscored original statement in Aristotle is not as explicit as we would wish it to be, but the meaning is quite clear. It means to say: *If any one wishes to call the little spheres or atoms of Democritus points which possess magnitude*, he may do so. The interpretation of the passage in Aristotle is brought out more sharply by Averroes, who in his comment on the same passage in Aristotle, which is quite evidently based upon the comment of Themistius, says: "What Aristotle means thereby, as it seems to me, is this: And similarly he who assumes that it is possible for a point to be self-moving will admit that as a consequence of his assumption the point would be a body. Accordingly we may well say that the self-moving round atoms of Democritus are so very small that they are called points, for the point, according to its use in this assumption, is nothing but a body." [43] Undoubtedly this interpretation of the passage in Aristotle, as embodied in the commentaries of Themistius and Averroes, represents a traditional interpretation that was current in the various successive schools of philosophy, beginning with the schools of the Greek Peripatetics and continuing throughout the schools of their Arabic followers.

Let us then imagine a doxographer who wanted to transmit to his readers the view that Democritus, in contradistinction to the Aristotelian view of the infinite divisibility of matter,

[42] *Themistius in Libros de Anima Paraphrasis*, ed. R. Heinze (1899), p. 31, ll. 20–24: *οὐδὲν διοίσει μονάδας λέγειν ἢ σώματα σμικρὰ τὴν ψυχὴν, οἷα καὶ Δημόκριτος τὰ σφαιρικά· καὶ γὰρ εἴ τις ὑπόθοιτο τὰς Δημοκρίτου σφαίρας μηκέτι σφαίρας, ἀλλὰ στιγμάς, μόνον δὲ αὐτῶν τηροίη τὸ ποσόν, οὐδὲν κωλύει τὰς μὲν κινεῖν αὐτῶν, τὰς δὲ κινεῖσθαι, ὥσπερ εἰ μικρὰ σώματα ἦσαν.*

[43] *Averrois Cordubensis Commentarium Magnum in Aristotelis de Anima Libros I*, Comm. 69 (ed. Stuart Crawford [1953], p. 94, ll. 17–22): "Et intendit, ut mihi videtur: et similiter qui ponit quod possibile est ut punctus moveatur concedit ut contingat ei quod punctus sit corpus. Et ideo bene possumus dicere quod sphaerae Democriti, quae moventur ex se, adeo sunt parvae quod dicuntur puncta. Punctus enim secundum hanc positionem non est nisi corpus."

believed that things are ultimately composed of indivisibles called atoms. Let us further imagine that our doxographer, who undoubtedly knew that a mathematical point is indivisible, knew also of this statement of Aristotle that the atoms of Democritus could be loosely called points. Let us still further imagine that, knowing as he certainly did that besides points mathematicians also spoke of surfaces and bodies, he also knew of Aristotle's statement that surfaces are sections and divisions of bodies, and lines are sections and divisions of surfaces, and points are sections and divisions of lines.[44] Imagining that all this was in the back of our doxographer's mind, we can readily see how he could have drafted a statement on Democritus' view on atoms, which in its complete form, read as follows. "Democritus affirms that the principles of all things are little spheres which are indivisible like points, so that body is composed of surfaces and surfaces are composed of lines and lines are composed of points." It is the last part of this statement that is quoted by Israeli's hypothetical interlocutor.

Undoubtedly our doxographer had used the term "points" in that loose sense in which it is used in the two passages in Aristotle — in the sense of something which, while indivisible, is not unextended. But the early Muslim students of philosophy, who read his doxography, were more likely to have known the mathematical and philosophical commonplace that a point has position but no magnitude than the two above-quoted passages in Aristotle where the term "points" is loosely used in the sense of something which has magnitude. The impression they got from such a doxography was that Democritus' atoms were, like mathematical points, without extension.

Evidence that that doxographic statement could have led readers to assume that the atoms of Democritus were unextended is to be found in Israeli's own comment on it, to which we have referred above.

Israeli, who lived at a time when the physical writings of Aristotle and his *Metaphysics*, as well as pseudo-Plutarch's *De*

[44] *Metaph.* XI, 2, 1060b, 12–15.

Placitis Philosophorum, were already translated into Arabic, undoubtedly knew that the atoms of Democritus were extended and that Aristotle was opposed to atomism, and, as we shall see, he knew also why Aristotle was opposed to it. He certainly knew that in Islam, among those who believed in atoms, there were those who believed that the atoms were unextended and there were those who believed that they were extended, for, in his discussion of Muslim atomism, he mentions both these views and argues against both of them.[45] Presumably, however, he did not associate the term "points" in the statement of Democritus, which he puts in the speech of his hypothetical interlocutor, with the passages in Aristotle where the term "points" is used loosely in the sense of something indivisible but extended. And so, in his criticism of his interlocutor's explanation of the "minimum of parts" in Galen's definition of elements as meaning the same as the "points" or "atoms" in the statement quoted in the name of Democritus, he starts out by saying that "points" in Democritus' statements lends itself to two interpretations, neither of which is applicable as an explanation of Galen's "minimum of parts." The two explanations, as they emerge from his criticism of them, correspond to the two conceptions of atoms current in Islam, namely, that they are either (1) indivisible and also unextended or (2) indivisible but extended. His criticism of both the two Muslim conceptions of atoms and the two possible interpretations of the alleged statement of Democritus are based, as we shall see, upon two arguments used by Aristotle, one against the assumption that a body is composed of something that is both indivisible and unextended and the other against the assumption that something extended can be indivisible.

Aristotle's argument against the assumption that a body can be composed of something that is both indivisible and unextended occurs in several places. In one place, he argues that, since those things which are both indivisible and unextended

[45] Cf. *Yesodot*, p. 49, ll. 14 ff; *De Elementis*, p. 8c, ll. 53 ff.

have no parts, when they are in contact with one another, the contact will be "as whole with whole," but, if so, they cannot form a body, for a body, which is a continuous quantity, has distinct parts.[46] In another place, he argues that the constituent parts of a body cannot be points, for "when the points touch each other and exist together to form a single magnitude, they do not make the whole bigger . . . Hence, even if all the points were put together, they would not produce a magnitude." [47] In a third place, he simply queries: "And how can a magnitude be composed of indivisibles?" [48] So also Israeli argues that, on the assumption that the points in Democritus' statement are unextended, the conjunction between any such two points will be a conjunction of whole with whole, but "if . . . the conjunction of one point with another is a conjunction of whole with whole, then the two points will form one point and their place will be one place, for the whole of the one is the whole of the other, seeing that neither of them has extension nor is there between them any difference. And the same will hold true of the third point and the fourth and the others after it to infinity." [49] The conclusion of the reasoning which Israeli expects us to complete by ourselves is: Therefore no combination of such points could form a body.

And with regard to the assumption that the indivisibles out of which a body is composed have extension, Aristotle sums up his argument against it in his statement that "it is not true to speak of indivisible magnitudes." [50] So also Israeli, taking

[46] *Phys.* VI, 1, 231b, 2–5.

[47] *De Gen. et Corr.* I, 2, 316a, 30–34.

[48] *Metaph.* XIII, 8, 1083b, 15–16.

[49] *De Elementis*, p. 8a, ll. 21–27 (*Yesodot*, p. 43, ll. 11–17): "si . . . eius continuatio cum eo est continuatio cum toto, erunt duo puncta punctum unum, et erit ipsorum locus locus unus, quoniam totum cuiusque ipsorum erit totum alterius, cum nulli ipsorum sit divisio (Hebrew: *merḥaḳ* = Arabic *bu'd* = διάστασις, distance, exension dimension) neque differentia inter ea. Similiter secundum hanc similitudinem ratiotinatio etiam puncto tertio et quarto, et quae sunt post illud usquam ad infinitum." Cf. p. 8c, ll. 58–66 (*Yesodot*, p. 50, ll. 1–7) for the same argument against the Muslim unextended atoms.

[50] *Metaph.* XIII, 8, 1038b, 13–14.

up the assumption that the points in the Democritean fragment, though indivisible, are extended and have parts, so that when one point is conjoined with another, it is in conjunction with it as part with part, he argues as follows: "And, if the conjunction of one point with another is as part thereof with part of the other, then the division and dissection [of the point] would necessarily follow therefrom, but this would do away his claim [that a body is composed of points], for the point is indivisible." [51] Here, again Israeli expects us to supply the conclusion, as phrased by Aristotle, that "it is not true to speak of indivisible magnitudes."

And so, when we are told that the Kalam could not have gotten the conception of unextended atoms from Greek philosophy, we may say that it could have gotten it from that extant Doxography preserved by Shahrastānī in which the atoms of Democritus are allusively correlated with Aristotelian "matter" and covertly referred to as "simple spirits" and in which the atoms of Epicurus are more directly described as "forms" and as being "over and above space and vacuum," or it could have gotten it from that nonextant Doxography referred to by Israeli in which the atoms of Democritus are described as "points."

3. GREEK DESCRIPTIONS OF ATOMS AS REFLECTED IN THE ATOMISM OF THE KALAM

Having seen how Muslim atomists dealt with the Greek atomists' description of atoms as eternal and infinite and magnitudinous, let us now see how they dealt with some other characteristic descriptions of atoms used by Greek atomists,

[51] *De Elementis*, p. 8a, ll. 27–30 (*Yesodot*, p. 43, ll. 17–18): "Et si fuerit continuatio puncti cum puncto parte ipsius cum parte illius, sequitur ipsam divisio ac peremtio, et removebitur alteratio (evidently a misprint for *altercatio*, Hebrew: *ta'anah* = Arabic *da'wā*, assertion, claim, suit) ab eis, cum punctum sit cui pars non est." This last statement is a quotation from Euclid, *Elements* I, Def. 1. Cf. p. 8c, ll. 66–70 (*Yesodot*, p. 50, ll. 7–10) for the same argument against the Muslim extended atoms.

whether of the early Democritean type or of the later Epicurean type.

In the atomism of Democritus, as reported by Aristotle,[1] atoms are described as "existent" (ὄν), in contradistinction to the void, which is described as "nonexistent" (οὐκ ὄν), and they are also described as differing from each other in three ways: (a) they differ in position (θέσις) or "turning" (τροπή), as, for instance, "above and below, before and behind, [right and left]";[2] (b) they differ in shape (σχῆμα) or contour (ρυσμός), as, for instance, "angular, straight, and round"; (c) they differ in order (τάξις) or "inter-contact" (διαθιγή), as, for instance, any two atoms designated by the letters A and N may be arranged either in the order of AN or in the order of NA, so that the contact between them differs. All these descriptions, we shall try to show, are reflected in the Kalam discussions of atomism.

As for "existence," in the Kalam "existence" (*wujūd*) is taken by Abū Hāshim of the Baṣra school to be one of the essential attributes of the atom.[3]

As for "position" or "turning" (τροπή), by which is meant the contrasts of "above and below, before and behind, right and left," in the Kalam this topic is reflected in the discussion of *jihah*, "direction," in its relation to the atom,[4] the term "direction" being explained as meaning "right and left, above and below, before and behind."[5]

As for "shape," in the Kalam there is a discussion as to whether the atoms are each either like a square or round.[6]

As for "order" or "inter-contact," in the Kalam it is generally assumed that there is contact (*mass*) between atoms and hence presumably there is a difference of "order."[7]

[1] *Phys.* I, 5, 188a, 22–26; *Metaph.* I, 4, 985b, 4–19; VIII, 2, 1042b, 12–15.
[2] For the bracketed addition, see *Phys.* III, 5, 205b, 32–33.
[3] *Masā'il*, p. 3, 14 (20); p. 8, l. 8 (24).
[4] *Ibid.*, p. 40, l. 20; cf. *Maḳālāt*, p. 316, ll. 8–11.
[5] *Masā'il*, p. 41, ll. 5–6; cf. *Maḳālāt*, p. 316, l. 12.
[6] Cf. Horten, *Probleme*, p. 226.
[7] Cf. *Maḳālāt*, p. 302, l. 10 – p. 303, l. 3; Horten, *Probleme*, pp. 224–225; cf. Pines, pp. 8–9.

In Greek atomism, except for the properties of magnitude, shape, and weight, the eternal atoms before their collision are said to possess "none of the qualities belonging to things which come under our observation," [8] such as color and smell and taste and sound and cold and heat.[9] In the Kalam, there was a difference of opinion on this question. On the one hand, Abū al-Hudhayl,[10] Fuwaṭī,[11] and Abū Hāshim [12] maintained that it is possible for the created atom to be devoid of such accidents as color, taste, smell, and the like. On the other hand, Iskāfī [13] and Ka'bī [14] maintained, in the language of the latter, that "it is impossible for the atom to be devoid of color and taste and smell and warmth and cold and moisture and dryness." There seems to be no logical connection between the problem whether atoms have magnitudes and the problem whether they have accidents. Abū Hāshim, who says that atoms can be devoid of accidents, says that they have magnitudes; [15] Ka'bī, who says that they cannot be devoid of accidents, says that they have no magnitude; [16] and Abū al-Hudhayl, who says that they can be devoid of accidents, says that they have no magnitude.[17] Maimonides reproduces the prevailing view of the Kalam of his time as follows: "Each of the atoms created by God must inevitably have accidents, from which it is inseparable; such, for instance, as color, smell, and motion or rest; quantity, however, is an exception, for, according to their opinion, none of these substances has quantity; in fact, quantity is not designated by them as an accident and it is not conceived of by them in terms of accident." [18]

[8] Diogenes, X, 54.

[9] Lucretius, II, 730–859.

[10] *Maḳālāt*, p. 311, ll. 13–14; p. 312, l. 1.

[11] *Ibid.*, p. 304, ll. 6–7.

[12] *Masā'il*, p. 43, ll. 6–7.

[13] *Maḳālāt*, p. 302, ll. 8–9.

[14] *Masā'il*, p. 43, ll. 20–21. But in *Uṣūl*, p. 56, ll. 15–16, Ka'bī is said to hold that substance can be devoid of all accidents except color.

[15] *Masā'il*, p. 38, l. 15.

[16] *Ibid.*, ll. 16–17.

[17] *Maḳālāt*, p. 307, l. 10.

[18] *Moreh* I, 73, Prop. 5, p. 138, ll. 21–25. Cf. *Uṣūl*, p. 56, ll. 11 ff.; *Irshād*, p. 13, ll. 16 ff. (32).

In Greek atomism, again, the eternal atoms, while having no such qualities as color and smell and taste and sound and cold and heat, are still all in motion.[19] So also in Muslim atomism, even Abū al-Hudhayl, who believes that atoms may be devoid of such accidents as color, taste, smell, and the like, is reported to have said that they have motion and rest and what follows from them, such as aggregation and segregation.[20]

In Greek, or rather Epicurean, atomism, the eternal motion of the free atoms does not stop even when the atoms through their fortuitous collision are formed into compound bodies. Within compound bodies each of the constituent atoms is still in motion and, in fact, the motion of any compound body is the resultant of the total motions of its component atoms.[21] In his letter to Herodotus, Epicurus expresses himself on this point by saying that the atoms, when formed into compound bodies, "retain vibration (τὸν παλμὸν ἴσχυσιν)." [22] Though this letter was not translated into Arabic, this view was held by the Kalam atomists. Thus, those Kalam atomists who believed that atoms have not only motion but also all other kinds of accidents are reported by Maimonides to have held the following view: "With regard to accidents which exist in a body, none of them can be said to belong peculiarly to the body as a whole; rather does any of those accidents exist, according to their opinion, in each of the atoms of which the body is composed." As illustrations, Maimonides mentions such accidents as whiteness, motion, life, and sensation. In his use of motion as an illustration, he says: "Similarly they say with regard to a body in motion, that what is in motion is each of its component atoms and that only thereby is the body as a whole in motion." [23] The same view is also implied in the

[19] Aëtius, *De Placitis Philosophorum* I, 3, 18; I, 12, 5 (Arabic, p. 112, ll. 13–14; p. 117, l. 6); Diogenes, X, 43.

[20] *Makālāt*, p. 303, ll. 2–5; p. 311, ll. 11–15; p. 315, ll. 2–6. Cf. n. 50, below.

[21] See on this, Bailey, *Greek Atomists and Epicurus*, pp. 330 ff.

[22] Diogenes, X, 43.

[23] *Moreh Nebukim* I, 73, Prop. 5, p. 138, l. 26 – p. 139, l. 1.

following controversy reported by Baghdādī. Abū al-Hudhayl, he reports, maintained that "it is possible for a body consisting of many atoms to be moved by the motion which is inherent in some of the atoms . . . The rest of the Mutakallimūn say that only the atom in which the motion subsists is that which is moved by it, but not the whole body with all the other atoms . . . But, if the body as a whole is moved, then there was motion in each of its atoms." [24] The common assumption of both Abū al-Hudhayl and the other Mutakallimūn, despite the difference between them, is that the accident of motion exists in the atoms and not in the body.

Another point in Epicurean atomism, which may have been known to Arabic atomists, is the theory of the "swerve." This theory means that the atoms in their eternal motions downward were swerving somewhat aside from the perpendicular line of falling, for otherwise they could never form compound bodies and hence could not form the world. This Epicurean theory of the swerve is mentioned in two passages in pseudo-Plutarch's *De Placitis Philosophorum.* These passages, in their Arabic version, read as follows: (1) "As for Epicurus, he thinks that . . . atoms are moved, at one time perpendicularly (*ʿalā istiḳāmah wa-ḳiyām*, κατὰ στάθμην) and at another swervingly (*ʿalā mayl wa-inʿiṭāf*, κατὰ παρέγκλισιν)." [25] (2) "As for Epicurus, he believed in two species [of motion], one which is in parallel lines (*ʿalā al-istiwāʾ*, κατὰ στάθμην) and the other in swerving lines (*ʿalā al-mayl*, κατὰ παρέγκλισιν)." [26] In the exposition of their own theory of atoms, the Mutakallimūn do not mention the swerve, and this for the very good reason that in their own theory of atoms, wherein the atoms did not collide by mere chance but were combined by God, there was no need for a swerve to account for the combination. But in their exposition of the Epicurean theory of atoms, some of them, it would seem, did know of it. Thus both Saadia and

[24] *Farḳ*, p. 112, l. 7 – p. 113, l. 4.
[25] Aëtius, *De Placitis Philosophorum* I, 12, 5 (Arabic, p. 117, ll. 4–7).
[26] *Ibid.* I, 23, 4 (Arabic, p. 120, ll. 9–11).

Shahrastānī, in dealing with the atomism of Epicurus, seem to allude to his theory of the swerve, the former in his statement that the atoms "converged toward the space now occupied by the world and crowded and pressed together," [27] and the latter in his statement that the atoms "move according to every kind of direction of motion." [28]

In Greek atomism, the atoms are said to be apprehensible only by the "intellect" (*'aḳlan*, λόγῳ),[29] and it is maintained that "no atom has ever been seen by our sense." [30] Among the Mutakallimūn there was a difference of opinion about it, some of them maintaining that atoms can be seen and tasted or only seen, whereas others denied that atoms can be perceived by any of the senses.[31]

In Greek atomism, the atoms, though differing in shape or form, are said to be "of the same kind generically (τὸ γένος ἕν)." [32] So also in the Kalam, the school of Baṣra is reported as maintaining that "the atoms are all of the same kind generically." [33] Ka'bī, however, representing the school of Baghdad, maintains that they are both alike and different.[34] Similarly in Indian atomism, we are told, the atoms are not all ultimately homogeneous.[35] Maimonides represents the prevailing view of the Kalam of his time as maintaining that "all these atoms are similar, alike; there is no difference between them in any respect." [36]

As in Greek atomism, so also in the atomism of the Kalam,

[27] *Emunot* I, 3, 9th Theory, p. 61, ll. 15–16.

[28] *Milal*, p. 277, l. 14. See also his reference to the swerve in his *Nihāyat*, p. 123, ll. 8–11.

[29] Aëtius, *De Placitis Philosophorum* I, 3, 18, p. 285a, ll. 3 and 8 (Arabic, p. 102, ll. 11 and 13). Cf. Diogenes, X, 56; Lucretius, I, 268–270.

[30] Diogenes, X, 44.

[31] Horten, *Probleme*, p. 223.

[32] *Phys.* I, 2, 184b, 21.

[33] Masā'il, p. 2, l. 2 (German, pp. 17–18, and p. 18, n. 1). So also is the view of Jubbā'ī as reported in *Maḳālāt*, p. 308, ll. 9–11, where in l. 10, the word *bi-anfusiha*, which occurs twice, is evidently a corruption of *bi-a'arāḍiha*.

[34] *Ibid.*, ll. 2–4 (p. 18).

[35] Cf. Bailey, *The Greek Atomists and Epicurus*, p. 65.

[36] *Moreh* I, 73, Prop. 1; cf. Prop. 8.

bodies arise out of the combination of atoms, and this not only according to those of the Kalam who endow atoms with magnitudes but also according to those who make the atoms to be without magnitude. These latter fall into two groups. According to one group, the combination of nonmagnitudinous atoms form one magnitudinous body. According to another group, the nonmagnitudinous atoms through their combination with each other become magnitudinous bodies, with the result that the combination of atoms form not one body but rather many bodies, as many as the atoms that have entered into the combination.[37] How nonmagnitudinous atoms by mere combination can form a magnitudinous body, or can be transformed into magnitudinous bodies, is not explained, and Saadia has already criticized this view by arguing that it is utterly absurd to think that "what is neither long nor wide nor deep should be transformed into what has length and width and depth." [38] This argument, it may be remarked in passing, reflects Aristotle's argument that the constituent parts of a body cannot be points, on the ground that no body can be formed out of unextended points.[39] It is also like the argument in Greek philosophy against the assumption that atoms have no qualities, on the ground that, if atoms by themselves have no qualities, how could they acquire qualities by merely joining together? [40] These two views about what happens to the nonmagnitudinous atoms when they are combined into bodies, which are reported by Maimonides of the Kalam of his time, must have already existed during the ninth century, for some anonymous early atomists of the Kalam and also Iskāfī are reported by Ash'arī to have maintained, evidently in opposition to others, that "when atoms are combined, none of the individual atoms by itself becomes a body, for a body is formed out of two atoms united together." [41]

[37] *Ibid.*, Prop. 1.

[38] *Emunot* I, 3 (p. 43, ll. 2–3).

[39] *De Gen. et Corr.* I, 2, 316a, 30–34; cf. *Phys.* VI, 1, 231b, 2–5; *Metaph.* XIII, 8, 1083b, 13–14. Cf. above, p. 485.

[40] Plutarch, *Adversus Coloten* 8, 1111c.

[41] *Maḳālāt*, p. 302, ll. 6–7.

Greek atomism assumed the existence of a void in two senses: (1) in the sense of an infinite void,[42] within which an infinite number of finite worlds floated about,[43] so that outside each finite world there was a void; (2) in the sense of a void which was interspersed between the atoms of which the bodies within each finite world were composed.[44] In Arabic atomism, with regard to a void outside the one finite world which to the Mutakallimūn was created, there is an argument for creation by Juwaynī in which the *Jaww maʿlūm*, "given air," wherein the world is at first said by him to exist, is then immediately referred to by him as *dhalika al-ḫalāʾ*, "this void," on the basis of which Juwaynī is said by Averroes to believe that "the world is in a void by which it is surrounded." [45] With regard to a void within the world, there is a report by Abū Rashīd that Abū Hāshim of the school of Baṣra and the Ashʿarites accepted the existence of such a void, whereas Kaʿbī, representing the school of Baghdad, rejected it.[46] In Maimonides, the view prevailing among the Mutakallimūn of his time is presented as follows: "Those who are concerned with the fundamentals of religion [that is, the Mutakallimūn] also believe that there is a void, that is to say, one space or several spaces, in which there is nothing at all, being empty of all bodies and devoid of any substances [that is, atoms]." [47] By "one space," we may assume, Maimonides means a void outside the world, and by "many spaces" he means the many voids or interstices between the atoms within the world. Accordingly, when Ibn Ḫaldūn says that Bāḳillānī, who was an Ashʿarite, "affirmed the existence of the atom and of the void," [48] the term "void," we may assume, is used by him both in the sense of a void outside the world and in the sense of a void within the world.

[42] *De Caelo* III, 2, 300b, 8; Diogenes, X, 42.

[43] Diogenes, IX, 31 and 44.

[44] *De Caelo* I, 7, 275b, 29–30.

[45] *Nizāmiyyah*, p. 12, ll. 9–10, and *Kashf*, p. 40, l. 13; cf. above, p. 438 at n. 21.

[46] *Masāʾil*, p. 24, ll. 15–17 (36–37).

[47] *Moreh* I, 73, Prop. 2, 136, ll. 2–3.

[48] *Mukaddimah* III, p. 40, l. 9.

The atomism of Leucippus and Democritus, according to Aristotle, explained "generation (γένεσις) and corruption (φθορά)" by aggregation (σύνκρισις) and segregation (διάκρισις).[49] To the Kalam, too, according to Maimonides, "generation (*kaun*: *havayah*) is aggregation (*ijtimā'*: *ḳibbuṣ*) and corruption (*fasād*: *hefsed*) is segregation (*iftirāḳ*: *perud*)." [50]

In Greek philosophy, Aristotle has shown that spatial magnitude (μέγεθος), that is, distance (διάστημα),[51] and time (χρόνος), and motion (κίνησις) are either all infinitely divisible or are all composed of atoms.[52] The masters of the Kalam, generalizing as they did that everything in the world is composed of atoms, included under this generalization also distance, motion, and time. Thus Abū al-Hudhayl says that "the motion of a body is divided according to the number of its atoms . . . and the motion that befalls one atom is other than that which befalls another atom" and also that "motion is divided according to time, so that the motion which exists at one time is other than the motion which exists at another time." [53] Thus also Maimonides, restating the atomistic views prevailing in the Kalam of his time says that it maintained that "time is composed of nows (*ānāt*: *'atot* = τὰ νῦν) . . . distance (*al-masāfah*: *ha-derek*, *ha-merḥaḳ* = διάστασις) is not continuous but is composed of parts at which divisibility stops," [54] and "motion is the translation (*intiḳāl*: *he'teḳ* = φορά) of an atom, of those atoms [which constitute a body], from one atom [of the distance over which the body moves] to another atom next to it." [55]

[49] *De Gen. et Corr.* I, 2, 315b, 4–8.

[50] *Moreh* I, 73, Prop. 1, p. 135, ll. 25–26. These four are referred to in the Kalam by the term *al-akwān*, "the modes of being." Cf. *Irshād*, p. 10, ll. 9–10 (28).

[51] *Phys.* VI, 7, 237b, 35.

[52] *Ibid.*, 1, 231b, 18 ff.

[53] *Maḳālāt*, p. 319, ll. 10–13.

[54] *Moreh* I, 73, Prop. 3, p. 136, l. 12 and ll. 21–22. Cf. pseudo-Plutarch's *De Placitis Philosophorum* in Diels, *Doxographi Graeci*, I, 6, 4, p. 293a, l. 22, where ἀπόστασις (= διάστασις, διάστημα) is translated into Arabic (p. 107, l. 10) by *masāfah* (= *bu'd*).

[55] *Ibid.*, p. 137, ll. 1–2.

Such are some of the characteristics of Muslim atoms which can be traced to Greek philosophy. There are other characteristics by which atoms are described in Islam. Some of them have been traced to Indian influence;[56] but some, undoubtedly, have no other source than the playful fancy of their authors.

II. The Denial of Atomism and the Theories of Latency (*kumūn*) and the Leap (*al-ṭafrah*)

About the same time that atomism was introduced into the Kalam, there was introduced into it also the theory of the infinite divisibility of matter, which in Greek philosophy meant a theory in opposition to atomism. The exponents of this view in the Kalam were the Rafiḍite Hishām and the Muʿtazilite Naẓẓām,[1] both of them having flourished in the first half of the ninth century. Here are some of the earliest reports of their view.

As reported by Ḥayyāṭ, Naẓẓām admitted that "that which is infinite with respect to measurement and extension cannot be completely traversed,"[2] but still, while admitting that "a body is limited in the sense of having an end and limit with respect to measure and extension,"[3] he "denied that bodies are aggregates made up of indivisible parts, asserting that there is no part of a body which thought cannot divide into halves."[4] As reported by Ashʿarī, Hishām b. al-Ḥakam and some of the Rafiḍites assert that "a part is divisible for ever and that there is no part but that there is a part thereof, and to this there is no end except with respect to extension, for

[56] Cf. Pines, *Atomenlehre*, pp. 112 ff.

[1] Of the orthodox, Ibn Kullāb, according to a late report, was opposed to atomism (cf. Tritton, *Muslim Theology*, p. 108, based, as communicated to me by the author, on Ibn Taymiyyah, *Tafsīr Sūrat al-Iḫlāṣ*, p. 21). Orthodox thinkers who were disinclined to commit themselves to atomism are Ghazālī (see above, p. 41) and Fạhr al-Dīn Rāzī (cf. Taftāzānī, p. 47, l. 6).

[2] *Intiṣār* 19, p. 32, ll. 4–5 (p. 33, l. 1).

[3] *Ibid.*, 34, p. 47, ll. 4–5 (p. 55, ll. 17–18).

[4] *Ibid.*, 19, p. 32, ll. 7–9 (p. 33, ll. 5–7).

to the extension of a body there is an end but there is no end to its parts with reference to divisibility";[5] and similarly Naẓẓām is quoted by him as saying that "there is no part (*juz'*) but that there is a part thereof and there is no portion (*ba'ḍ*) but that there is a portion thereof and there is no half but that there is a half thereof, and a part may be divided by a divisor for ever, for it is infinite with respect to divisibility,"[6] the implication of the last remark being that with respect to extension a body is not infinite.

The distinction assumed in these passages between the impossibility of the infinite extension of a body and the possibility of its infinite division, and the explanation of the former on the ground that an infinite extension cannot be traversed, reflect statements in Aristotle's *Physics*[7] and *De Caelo*.[8] We may, therefore, assume that the infinite divisibility asserted by Naẓẓām and Hishām is, like the infinite divisibility asserted by Aristotle,[9] only potentially infinite but not actually so. That Aristotle's infinite divisibility was infinite only in a potential sense could have been known to both Naẓẓām and Hishām also from the Arabic translation of pseudo-Plutarch's *De Placitis Philosophorum*, where Aristotle's infinite divisibility is distinguished from that of the followers of Thales and Pythagoras by its being infinite only potentially and not actually.[10] It will have been noticed that in their respective reports on Naẓẓām's denial of atoms neither Ḫayyāṭ nor Ash'arī makes Naẓẓām dependent upon Hishām b. al-Ḥakam. Accordingly, when Baghdādī says of Naẓẓām that "from Hishām and from the heathen (*mulḥidah*) philosophers he took his view on the denial of atoms,"[11] his making Naẓẓām dependent upon Hishām is only a conjecture on his

[5] *Maḳālāt*, p. 59, ll. 4–7.
[6] *Ibid.*, p. 318, ll. 6–8; cf. p. 304, ll. 13–15.
[7] *Phys.* III, 6, 406a, 15–18; III, 4, 204a, 5; cf. *Metaph.* XI, 10, 1066a, 36–37.
[8] *De Caelo* I, 5, 271b, 2 ff.; III, 1, 299a, 17 ff.; III, 2, 300b, 4–5.
[9] *Phys.* III, 6, 206a, 14 ff.
[10] Diels, *Doxographi Graeci*, I, 16 (Arabic, p. 118, ll. 1–4).
[11] *Farḳ*, p. 113, ll. 16–17; cf. p. 50, ll. 15–16. On *mulḥidah* as referring to Aristotelians, see below, pp. 505–506.

part. Shahrastānī, in his report on Naẓẓām, merely says that "he agreed with the philosophers in the denial of atoms." [12] Ibn Ḥazm, who, in dealing with the Kalam theory of atoms, attributes it to "some of the ancients," [13] in dealing with those who denied atoms mentions "Naẓẓām and every one who is well versed in the teaching of the ancients." [14] By "the ancients" in both cases he means Greek philosophers in general, of whom in the former case the reference is especially to Democritus and Epicurus and in the latter case to Aristotle and all those who followed him in the denial of atoms.

With his rejection of atomism and his substitution for it of the Aristotelian theory of an infinitely divisible matter, Naẓẓām also rejected two theories which in his time were associated with atomism, namely, the atheistic Epicurean theory of chance and the orthodox Muslim extension of the Koranic teaching of creation into a theory of continuous creation.[14a] As a substitute for these two theories, and directly so against the theory of continuous creation, he adopted the Aristotelian theory of causality as expressed in Aristotle's statements that "all things that exist by nature have within themselves a principle of motion and rest," [15] that "nature is a principle and cause of motion and of rest in those things in which it inheres primarily," [16] that "motion is the actuality of that which is in potentiality in so far as it is in potentiality," [17] nature thus being inherent in things as the cause of transitions from potentiality to actuality, and that every motion of things in the world, which immediately is caused by that nature within the things themselves, is ultimately caused by a prime mover [18] who is God.[19] But, while Naẓẓām was willing to accept this Aristotelian view of a nature abiding in things of the world, he could not, as a Muslim who believed in the Koranic teach-

[12] *Milal*, p. 38, l. 19.
[13] *Fiṣal* V, p. 69, l. 12; cf. above, p. 467.
[14] *Ibid.*, p. 92, ll. 18–19.
[14a] Cf. below. pp. 561 ff.
[15] *Phys.* II, 1, 192b, 13–14.
[16] *Ibid.*, 21–22.
[17] *Phys.* III, 1, 201a, 10–11.
[18] *Ibid.*, VII, 10, 266a, 10 – 267b, 26.
[19] *Metaph.* XII, 7, 1072b, 26 – 1073a, 13.

ing of creation, accept the Aristotelian teaching that the world is coeternal with its prime mover, who is called by him God. And so he did with this Aristotelian theory of nature what other believers in creation before him, such as Philo, and following him the Church Fathers, had done with it: [20] he adjusted it to his own belief in a created world, and this he did by making nature something which God, the Creator of the world, implanted in the world at the time of its creation. This modified conception of the Aristotelian theory of nature is reflected in a statement, reported in the name of Naẓẓām, which reads as follows: "God stamped the stone with a nature and created it with an innate disposition, so that, when you throw it upwards, it flies upwards and, when the force of the throw is exhausted, the stone by nature returns to its place." [21] But Naẓẓām was not primarily interested in correcting an erroneous view of Aristotle. His primary interest was in ridding his coreligionists of what he considered their erroneous belief in continuous creation by explaining to them in nontechnical language how within the things created by God there is something, a nature, similarly created by God, which causes those things to be changed into other things or to give rise out of themselves to other things, thus creating in us the impression that in all things there is something hidden which nature causes to appear. In the reports of Naẓẓām's teachings, this view of his is represented as a theory of hiding (*kumūn*) and appearing (*ẓuhūr*),[21a] to which we shall refer as the theory of latency.

The earliest account of this theory of latency is to be found in the *Intiṣār* of Ḥayyāṭ (d. 902), who quotes it from a work by Ibn al-Rāwandī (d. 910), who in turn may have quoted it from a work by Jāḥiẓ (d. 869).

Ḥayyāṭ's account reads as follows: "Naẓẓām claimed that God created men and cattle and animals and minerals and plants all at one time and that the creation of Adam did not

[20] Cf. *Philo*, I, pp. 356–359.
[21] *Milal*, p. 38, ll. 16–17.
[21a] *Ibid.*, p. 39, ll. 13–14.

precede that of his children, nor did the creation of mothers precede that of their children. God, however, has hidden (*akman*) certain things in others, so that priority and posteriority have application only to the appearance (*ẓuhūr*) of those things from their places (*amākinhā*) and not to their creation and production." [22]

According to this account, Naẓẓām's theory of latency consists of three parts. First, it is an interpretation of the story of creation in the Koran, the main point in the interpretation being that the Koranic statement that God "created the heaven and the earth and all that is between them in six days" (50:37) should not be taken literally but should be interpreted to mean that all things were created simultaneously. And just as his theory of simultaneous creation is meant to be an interpretation of a verse in a Surah of the Koran, so also his enumeration of things thus created, namely, (1) "men," (2) "cattle," (3) "animals," (4) "minerals," and (5) "plants," reflects verses in a Surah of the Koran, in which God is said to have created the following things: (1) "man" (16:4), (2) "cattle" (16:5), (3) "horses and mules and asses" (16:8), (4) "whatever He has created in the earth of varied hues" (16:13), and (5) "trees . . . herbage and the olives and the palm-trees and the grapes . . . and all kinds of fruits" (16:10–11). Similarly, the statement that "the creation of Adam did not precede that of his children, nor did the creation of mothers precede that of their children" is meant to be an interpretation in terms of simultaneous creation of the verses: "He who created for you a single man, and from him brought forth his wife . . . He gave them a perfect [child]" (7:189–190). Second, not only were all things created simultaneously, but all the things that were so created contained in themselves all the variety of things that were ever to come into existence in the future. Third, since all things are "hidden" in the things created at the creation of the world, the emergence of any of these things from its hiding place is to be

[22] *Intiṣār* 31, p. 44, ll. 12–16.

regarded only as an "appearance" and not as something due to an act of "creation and production." Thus, while following the teaching of the Koran with regard to the creation of the world, he rejects the orthodox Muslim belief in continuous creation, according to which every change in a thing is a new act of creation by God. To him, everything has a nature, implanted in it by God, and it is this nature which causes every change in a thing, but, inasmuch as every change is a process of transition from potentiality to actuality, he describes all the changing phenomena in the world as a process of hiding and appearing.

An account of a different theory of latency is to be found in the *Maḳālāt* of Ashʿarī (d. 935). His account consists of four statements, of which the first and third are quoted from a report by Zurḳān (d. 910 or 891), but, as for the second and the fourth, it is not clear whether they are continuations of Zurḳān's report or whether they are taken from other sources.

Ashʿarī's account reads as follows: [23]

1. "Zurḳān reports that Ḍirār b. ʿAmr has said: Of things some are hidden (*kawāmin*) and some are not hidden. As for those which are hidden, they are oil in an olive and ointment in a sesame and juice in a grape, and all this is not according to the interpenetrability [of bodies] (*mudāḫalah*) maintained by Ibrahim [al-Naẓẓām].[24] As for those which are not hidden, they are fire in a stone and whatever is like this." [25]

2. "But many men of speculation said that that fire is hidden in a stone, so that al-Iskāfī and others claimed that it is hidden in firewood."

3. "And Zurḳān reports [further] that Abū Bakr al-Aṣamm said: Not a thing in the world of those mentioned by them is hidden in a thing."

[23] *Maḳālāt*, p. 328, l. 6 – p. 329, l. 3.

[24] Cf. below at nn. 33, 34, 37, 38.

[25] In *Fiṣal*, V, p. 61, ll. 23–24, Ibn Ḥazm says of Ḍirār, as does Ashʿarī here, that he denied latency only in the case of fire, but in *Fiṣal*, IV, p. 195, ll. 12–15, he says that Ḍirār denied latency altogether and that he ascribed every act to a direct creation of God.

4. "And Abū al-Hudhayl and Ibrāhīm [al-Naẓẓām] and Mu'ammar and Hishām b. al-Ḥakam and Bishr b. al-Mu'tamir said: Oil is hidden in an olive and ointment in a sesame and fire in a stone." The same, we may assume, would be true according to them also of "juice in a grape" and of "fire in wood."

Let us analyze this report of Ash'arī. To begin with, all the names mentioned in it are of contemporaries who flourished during the first half of the ninth century and, except for the Rafiḍite Hishām b. al-Ḥakam, they are all Mu'tazilites of both schools of Mu'tazilism; thus Ḍirār, Aṣamm, Abū al-Hudhayl, Naẓẓām, and Mu'ammar are Basraites, whereas Bishr b. al-Mu'tamir and Iskāfī are Baghdadians. Then, all those who are listed as affirming latency are described as affirming it only with regard to a limited number of things, which are marked by two outstanding characteristics. First, they are all things whose emergence from other things is brought about by some human act, such as squeezing in the case of juice out of a grape or of oil out of an olive or of ointment out of a sesame and such as striking with iron on a stone or rubbing one piece of wood with another in the case of fire out of a stone or out of a piece of wood. Second, they are all things whose presence in the things out of which they emerge is felt even before they are made to emerge by a human act. Thus the presence of the juice in the grape and of the oil in the olive and of the ointment in the sesame could be felt even before their emergence by the human act of squeezing, and similarly the presence of the fire in the stone and in the piece of wood could come to be felt by the gradual warming up of the stone and the piece of wood by the striking upon the former with iron and by the rubbing of the latter with another piece of wood.

We thus have reports of two theories of latency which appeared at about the same time, a comprehensive theory of latency, ascribed only to Naẓẓām, and a limited theory of latency, ascribed both to Naẓẓām and to six of his contemporaries. In the limited theory, the conception of latency is used only as an explanation of an observed fact that certain things were present in certain other things before their emergence from those other things by a certain human act. In the comprehensive theory, the conception of latency is used as an explanation in popular language of Aristotle's view that nature is inherent in things as the cause of their transition from potentiality to actuality; and the reason why Naẓẓām followed this Aristotelian explanation of all the changing events in the world is his rejection of the common orthodox Muslim explanation of it by the assertion of a belief in God's continuous creation.

Now it happens that Muʿammar, too, rejected the orthodox Muslim belief in God's continuous creation and, like Naẓẓām, adopted the Aristotelian term "nature," changed by him, as we have seen above, to the term *maʿnā*, as a designation of the inner cause of all the changing events in the world.[26] The question, therefore, arises why Muʿammar, who shares with Naẓẓām the limited theory of latency, does not share with him also the comprehensive theory. The answer to this question is to be found in the fact that, unlike Naẓẓām, Muʿammar did not follow Aristotle in rejecting atomism,[27] and consequently his conception of nature as the inner cause of all the changing events in the world differs from that of Aristotle as used by Naẓẓām. To Aristotle as well as to Naẓẓām, nature is the inner cause of all the changing events in the world in the sense that it is the inner cause of processes of transition from potentialities to actualities; to Muʿammar, nature, for which he also uses the term *maʿnā*, is the inner cause of all the changing events in the world, to which he usually refers as accidents, in the sense that it directly produces the accidents in bodies whenever they are formed by the aggregation of atoms.[28] Naẓẓām's rejection of the orthodox Muslim belief in God's continuous creation thus means two things: (1) changes are

[26] Cf. above, pp. 160–161, and below, p. 566.
[27] Cf. above, p. 158.
[28] Cf. above, pp. 158–161.

not new creations but only actualizations of potentialities; (2) these actualizations of potentialities are directly not caused by God but by nature. Muʿammar's rejection of the orthodox Muslim belief in God's continuous creation means only one thing, for, in agreement with the orthodox Muslims, he considers changes, or accidents, as new creations and not as mere actualizations of potentialities; he only maintains that they are caused not by God but by a nature, or a *maʿnā*, which is inherent in the atoms.[29] And so, corresponding to Naẓẓām's substitution of his comprehensive theory of latency for the rejected belief in God's continuous creation, Muʿammar substitutes his theory of *maʿnā* for that rejected belief in God's continuous creation.

These two theories of latency are thus not two contradictory versions of the same theory, with the inevitable consequence that one of them must be false; they are rather two different theories, arising from different considerations, so that it was possible for Naẓẓām to entertain both of them and for six of his contemporaries to entertain one of them without the other. And since these two theories existed side by side during the first half of the ninth century, it is to be assumed that neither Ḫayyāṭ nor Ashʿarī, each of whom reports only one of these theories, was ignorant of the theory which he does not happen to report. With regard to Ashʿarī, who survived Ḫayyāṭ by thirty-three years, it is inconceivable that he should have been ignorant of the comprehensive theory which is reported by Ḫayyāṭ. If Ḫayyāṭ does not happen to mention in his *Intiṣār* the limited theory of latency, it is presumably because it was not contained in Ibn al-Rāwandī's work, against which his *Intiṣār* was written; and if Ashʿarī does not happen to mention in his *Maḳālāt* Naẓẓām's comprehensive theory of latency,[29a] it is presumably because the *Maḳālāt* is not, and undoubtedly was not meant to be, a

[29] As we shall see later, to Naẓẓām, nature acts under divine supervision; to Muʿammar, nature, or rather *maʿnā*, acts without divine supervision. See below pp. 569 ff.

[29a] But see below at n. 46.

complete collection of all the views of every single one of the Mutakallimūn mentioned in it.

Naẓẓām's comprehensive theory of latency, as reported by Ḫayyāṭ, is reproduced by Baghdādī and Shahrastānī, and both of them suggest an Aristotelian origin for it, except, as we have seen, for the rejection of the Aristotelian view of eternity.

Baghdādī's suggestion may be gathered from a combination of two passages, one in his *Uṣūl* and the other in his *Farḳ*.

In the passage in the *Uṣūl*, he mentions two groups of people whom he describes as "the Eternalists of the Dahriyyah" (*azliyyah al-dahriyyah*) and, after reproducing the view of one of these groups, he says: "Others among them said that the accidents are eternal in bodies, except that they hide in bodies and appear, so that, when motion appears in a body, rest hides in it and, when rest appears, motion hides in it, and so every accident and its contrary appear and hide alternately in its substratum." [30] Now both these groups of Dahriyyah, described by Baghdādī as "Eternalists," are Aristotelians, for in another place in his *Uṣūl* he contrasts "the Dahriyyah known as Eternalists" with "the adherents of [eternal] matter," [31] where quite evidently the contrast is between Aristotelians and Platonists. Consequently, those among one of these two Aristotelian groups of Dahriyyah who are described by Baghdādī as believing that accidents "hide in bodies and appear" are Aristotelians.

In the passage in the *Farḳ*, he first reproduces Naẓẓām's comprehensive theory of latency almost verbatim from Ḫayyāṭ's *Intiṣār*.[32] Then, inasmuch as in Ḫayyāṭ's report as reproduced by himself latency is said by Naẓẓām to apply to "things" and "children" and also inasmuch as he himself has quoted Naẓẓām as holding that "color and taste and sound are bodies which penetrate each other in the same space," [33]

[30] *Uṣūl*, p. 55, ll. 11–15. [31] *Ibid*., p. 59, ll. 7–10.

[32] *Farḳ*, p. 127, ll. 1–7. In l. 5, *akthar*, "more numerous," is to be changed to *akman*, "has hidden," as in *Intiṣār* 31, p. 44, l. 14.

[33] *Ibid*., p. 122, ll. 14–15; cf. *Maḳālāt*, p. 327, ll. 10–11.

from which he infers that, according to Naẓẓām, "bodies are interpenetrable," [34] he argues as follows: "Al-Naẓẓām's view about appearing and hiding as applying to bodies, as well as his view about the interpenetration of bodies, is worse than the view of the Dahriyyah who claimed that all accidents are hidden in bodies," [35] that is to say, they claimed that only accidents, and not bodies, are hidden in bodies; for, according to them, as Aristotelians, accidents are not bodies.[36] There is here, then, an implied suggestion that, while Naẓẓām, following the Stoic view about accidents as bodies [37] and about the interpenetrability of bodies,[38] deviated from the views of the Aristotelian Dahriyyah on these two points, thereby making his own version of the theory of latency worse than their original version thereof, still it is the theory of latency of these Aristotelian Dahriyyah that is the source of Naẓẓām's theory of latency.

Now the Dahriyyah, whom Baghdādī himself includes among "the infidels before the days of Islam," [39] can be shown, I believe, to have consisted of an eclectic group of philosophers, among them Aristotelians, who flourished before the rise of Islam in the oriental centers of Greek philosophy, such as Harran and Gondeshapur.[40] It is they who used the terms hiding and appearing as a designation of the Aristotelian expression potentiality and actuality, and it is from them that it reached Naẓẓām.

It happens, however, that these Aristotelian Dahriyyah, that is, Eternalists, were known in Arabic also by the term Malāḥidah (or Mulḥidūn). Thus in Juwaynī's statement that "according to the theory of the Malāḥidah, the [celestial sphere], prior to its revolution we witness now, has already

[34] *Ibid.*, l. 16. Cf. also the same contrast on p. 55, l. 9 and l. 11.

[35] *Ibid.*, p. 127, ll. 15–16. In l. 16, *al-Zahriyyah* is to be changed to *al-Dahriyyah*.

[36] *Categ.* 8, 10a, 11; *Phys.* IV, 8, 216a, 27–33.

[37] Cf. Arnim, *Fragmenta*, II, 376 ff.

[38] *Ibid.*, II, 463 ff.

[39] *Farḳ*, p. 346, ll. 6–9.

[40] Cf. above, p. 474.

performed infinite revolutions,"[41] the Malāḥidah quite evidently are followers of Aristotle's theory of the eternity of the circular motions of the celestial spheres. Similarly in his statement that for the terms "substance" [that is, "atom"] and "accident" used in the Kalam the Mulḥidūn use the terms "matter" and "form,"[42] the Mulḥidūn are quite evidently Aristotelians.

It is no wonder, then, that one characterized as a Mulḥid should actually be found to have described the contrast between form and matter, that is, the contrast between potentiality and actuality, by the terms "hiding" and "appearing." Thus a contemporary of Naẓẓām, al-Ḳasim b. Ibrāhīm (d. 860), quotes in the name of a certain Mulḥid the following statements: (1) "You cannot deny that things continuously arise from other things nor can you deny that the thing which is their source is eternal." (2) "You cannot deny that the form of the date or of the [palm] tree is hidden (*kāmin*[*ah*]) in the seed and that, when it finds something that is similar to it, it makes its appearance (*zahara*.)" (3) "The seed is in material potentiality a date."[43] Of these three statements, the first statement quite evidently reflects Aristotle's theory of an eternal matter underlying the process of generation and destruction in our eternal world, and the second and third statements quite evidently reflect Aristotle's statement that "the seed . . contains the form potentially."[44] Thus also Ashʿarī reports as follows: "And many of the Mulḥidūn held that the colors and tastes and odors are hidden (*kāminah*) in earth and water and air; then they appear in unripe dates and other fruits by a translocation and by the conjunction of similarities (*al-ashkāl*) with one another. They compare it to a seed of saffron dropped into a jug of water, which, on being nourished by things similar to it (*bi-ashkāliha*), makes its appearance."[45]

[41] *Irshād*, p. 15, ll. 7–8 (34). [42] *Ibid.*, p. 13, ll. 20–21 (32).

[43] Cf. German translation from an Arabic manuscript by Pines in his *Atomenlehre*, n. 2 on pp. 99–100.

[44] *Metaph.* VII, 9, 1034a, l. 33 – 1034b, l. 1.

[45] *Maḳālat*, p. 329, ll. 4–7.

The theory of latency in this passage quite evidently belongs to what we have described as the comprehensive theory, even though it follows immediately after Ashʿarī's report on the limited theory of latency quoted above.[46]

More directly is the Aristotelian origin of Naẓẓām's theory of latency suggested by Shahrastānī. The subject is dealt with by him in two places in his *Milal*.

In one place, after reproducing Naẓẓām's theory of latency, like Baghdādī, from Ḫayyāṭ's *Intiṣār*,[47] where latency is applied to "bodies" rather than to "accidents," he says as follows: "This theory was taken by him from the exponents of hiding-and-appearing among the philosophers and always his inclination is more to adopt the view of the naturalists among them rather than that of the theists." [48] This last statement quite evidently means that, while in his theory of latency Naẓẓām follows the generality of philosophers, there is a difference between the "theists" and the "naturalists" with regard to some phase of this theory, and Naẓẓām follows the naturalists. Knowing as we do that in Shahrastānī, and in Arabic philosophy in general, "theists" refers to those who, like Plato and Aristotle, believe in the existence of incorporeal beings, and "naturalists" refers to those who, like the Stoics, deny the existence of incorporeal beings [49] and, knowing also that Naẓẓām's view that accidents are bodies and that bodies are interpenetrable has its origin in Stoicism,[50] we may take Shahrastānī's statement that Naẓẓām's view follows that of the "naturalists" rather than that of the "theists" to mean that Naẓẓām's theory of latency, insofar as it maintains that accidents exist in their subject potentially before they become

[46] Cf. above at note 23 and following.

[47] *Milal*, p. 39, ll. 9–13, where in l. 13 *makāminhā*, "their hiding place," is used instead of *amākinhā*, "their places," in the corresponding passage in the *Intiṣār* and the *Farḳ*.

[48] *Milal*, p. 39, ll. 13–15.

[49] See Ghazālī's characterization of "naturalists" and "theists" in his *Munḳidh*, pp. 19–20, and cf. Shahrastānī's characterization of "naturalists" (*Milal*, p. 202, ll. 13–14) and of Plato (*ibid.*, p. 283, l. 7).

[50] Cf. above at nn. 37, 38, and S. Horovitz, *Einfluss* (1899), pp. 10–11.

actual, is based upon Aristotle's theory of potentiality and actuality, but, insofar as it maintains that accidents are bodies and that bodies are interpenetrable, it is based upon the teachings of the Stoics. Elsewhere he similarly says of Naẓẓām that he "was inclined toward the naturalists among the philosophers in their teaching that the spirit is a body," [51] where, again, by the "naturalists" he means Stoics.[52] This is exactly like that which is implied in Baghdādī's comments on Naẓẓām's theory of latency.

In another place in the same work, after reproducing a report by Porphyry on the teaching of Anaxagoras, Shahrastānī says: "He is the first who advanced the theory of hiding-and-appearing insofar as he supposed that all things are hidden in the first body and their coming into existence is only their emergence into appearance out of that body as a species, a genus, a mass, a shape, and a denseness or a rareness, just as the ear of corn emerges into appearance out of a single grain, a stately palm out of small date-stone, a man, perfectly shaped, out of a paltry drop of sperm, and a bird out of an egg. All these are instances of the emergence of appearance out of hiding, of actuality out of potentiality, of form out of the disposition of matter. Creation (*al-ibdā'*), however, is only [of] one [thing], and it applies to no other thing except to that first body." [53]

Now, it will be noticed, in the passage quoted from Porphyry, upon which Shahrastānī makes his observation about Anaxagoras being the first who advanced the theory of "hiding-and-appearing," there is no mention of the terms "hiding" and "appearing." All that Porphyry is quoted as saying is that "the root of things is one single body" and that "from it proceed all bodies and bodily forces and species and genera." [54] The characterization of it as a theory of "hiding-and-appearing" was thus given to it by Shahrastānī himself because of its similarity to the theory of Naẓẓām, which was

[51] *Milal*, p. 38, ll. 11–12.
[52] Diogenes, VII, 156.
[53] *Milal*, p. 257, ll. 7–12.
[54] *Ibid.*, ll. 4–7.

widely known among Muslims. Moreover, even his statement that Anaxagoras was the "first" to advance a theory which was similar to Naẓẓām's theory of hiding-and-appearing should not be taken too literally, for shortly after his statement that Anaxagoras was "the first" to advocate a theory of latency, Shahrastānī himself says that Thales and Anaxagoras were at one "in the assumption of a prime matter and imaginable forms within it or of a primary body and existences hidden in it." [55] Furthermore, his use of the terms "prime matter" and "forms" as well as his description of Anaxagoras' theory of latency, in the passage quoted above, as that which teaches "the emergence . . . of actuality out of potentiality, or of form out of the disposition of matter" — terms characteristically Aristotelian — allusively suggests that, besides Thales and Anaxagoras, Aristotle also had a theory of latency.

What we really have in this passage is Shahrastānī's own opinion that the theory of latency, which in the passage he has quoted from Ḫayyāṭ's *Intiṣār* is ascribed to Naẓẓām, is in reality a theory which was held by certain Greek philosophers, such as Thales and Anaxagoras, who believed, as he says, in "a primary matter and in existences hidden in it," for all such philosophers believed in the "emergence of appearance out of hiding," which is only another way of restating Aristotle's belief in "a prime matter and in imaginable forms in it" or in the "emergence . . . of actuality out of potentiality."

The terms "hiding" and "appearing" are thus nontechnical equivalents of the Aristotelian technical term "potentiality" and "actuality" which were adopted by Naẓẓām from a certain group of eclectic non-Muslim philosophers who are usually referred to by Muslim writers as Dahriyyah, but in this particular case they also happen to be referred to as Malāḥidah or Mulḥidūn. That the use of the terms "hiding" and "appearing" as nontechnical equivalents of the Aristotelian technical terms "potentiality" and "actuality" was not

[55] *Ibid.*, p. 258, ll. 4–6.

uncommon may be evidenced by the following two examples.

First, there is the Arabic version of the *Enneads* of Plotinus, the so-called *Theology of Aristotle*. In that work, the author tries to show that nothing in nature stands still. He proves this by the analogy of the grain of seed (*badhr*) which, when planted in the ground, never ceases to grow, to change, and to become something else. For, he says, "in the seed lie high creative Logoi which are inseparably joined to it, but they are hidden (*ḫafiyyah*) and do not fall under our eyes. But when it performs its tasks and falls under our eyes its great and wonderful powers become apparent (*bānat*).[56] Here then we have the common philosophic conception that what seems to be a new creation is nothing but the unfolding of something which is already in existence described as the becoming "apparent" of that which was "hidden."

Second, there is the system of the Gnostic Simon as reproduced from his Great Announcement by Hippolytus. The system is represented by Hippolytus as a combination of Heraclitus, Plato, and Aristotle. Following Heraclitus, who was followed by the Stoics, Simon says that "fire is the principle of all things." [57] In this fire, there are, according to him, a double nature, "and of this double nature he calls one part hidden (κρυπτόν) and the other apparent (φανερόν)." [58] He then goes on to say that "the hidden parts have been in the apparent parts of the fire, and apparent parts of the fire have come into being from the hidden." [59] These hidden and apparent parts he identifies respectively with what Aristotle calls "potentiality" (δύναμις) and "actuality" (ἐνέργεια) and what Plato calls "intelligible" (νοητόν) and "sensible" (αἰσθητόν).[60] Here then the Aristotelian conception of potentiality and actuality is described as a transition from that which is "hidden" to that which is "apparent."

[56] *Uthūlūjiyya*, p. 78, ll. 6–8.
[57] Hippolytus, *Refutatio Omnium Haeresium* VI, 9, 3.
[58] *Ibid.*, 9, 5.
[59] *Ibid.*, 9, 6.
[60] *Ibid.*

In Ḥayyāṭ's account of Naẓẓām's theory of latency we have seen how Naẓẓām, in addition to his use of that theory as an interpretation of the Koranic version of the Biblical story of creation, has also interpreted the "six days" during which the creation took place as meaning that they were created "all at one time." Now this nonliteral interpretation of the expression "six days" was not in any way required by his desire to harmonize it with the Aristotelian theory of potentiality and actuality, for even by retaining the original meaning of this expression, he could say that in the things created during the six days there were hidden potentially all the things that were ever to appear in the future. The reason for this interpretation is to be found in external influence. It happens that by the time of Naẓẓām the interpretation of the scriptural story of the six days of creation as meaning simultaneous creation was current both in Judaism and in Christianity. In Judaism, there was Philo who said that the six days should not be taken as implying a sequence of time but rather as showing that the world was created according to a certain perfect order, and that it is to follow that perfect order, for in reality, he says, "all things took shape simultaneously (ἅμα)" or "at once (ὁμοῦ)."[61] There is something like it in a statement by the rabbis, according to which all the things that are said to have been created in six days were really created on the first day simultaneously with the creation of the heaven and earth but remained hidden until they each appeared on one of the six days.[62] In Christianity, beginning with Clement of Alexandria, the interpretation of the six days of creation as meaning simultaneous creation is discussed by various Church Fathers and there were among them those who accepted it.[63] It may have been from all these sources that the conception of simultaneous creation had reached Naẓẓām.

This is what seems to me to be the origin and history of Naẓẓām's theory of *kumūn*, "latency." It was first used by

[61] Philo, *Opif.*, 3, 13; 22, 67.

[62] *Genesis Rabbah* 12, 4.

[63] Cf. E. Mangenot, "Hexaméron," *DTC*, 6, cols. 2335–2338.

certain non-Muslim eclectic philosophers referred to as Mulḥidūn and Dahriyyah in an attempt to reproduce in nontechnical language Aristotle's conception of potentiality and actuality, which means his conception of causality. Naẓẓām took it up and used it as a substitute of the orthodox Muslim belief in continuous creation, just as Muʿammar used his theory of *maʿnā* as a substitute for it. But, in adopting this theory of latency, Naẓẓām introduced into it two changes. First, whereas originally it was applied to the Aristotelian doctrine of the eternity of the world, Naẓẓām applied it to the Koranic doctrine of the creation of the world. Second, whereas originally that which was hidden in bodies was described by the term "accident" or by terms which meant accidents, Naẓẓām, following the Stoic view that accidents were bodies and that bodies were interpenetrable, described that which was hidden in bodies by terms which meant bodies.

Let us now report on four other interpretations of Naẓẓām's theory of latency.

First, there is Steiner's interpretation. Without much ado, he states that Naẓẓām's theory of latency is based upon Aristotle's theory of potentiality and actuality.[64] This is exactly what I have been trying to prove.

Second, there is the interpretation of Horovitz.[65] This interpretation draws its support from the same texts that I have used in support of my interpretation. According to Horovitz, Naẓẓām's theory of simultaneous creation was taken from the rabbinic statement quoted above, and Naẓẓām's theory of latency is derived from the Stoic theory of the "seminal Logos," which is a sort of hidden generative power. In support of the Stoic origin of latency, he points to what he thought to be an analogy between Naẓẓām's statement that "the creation of Adam did not precede the creation of his children" and the Stoic doctrine that the primary fire is the seed of all the individual human beings, such as Socrates and

[64] H. Steiner, *Die Muʿtaziliten* (1865), pp. 66–68.
[65] S. Horovitz, *Einfluss*, pp. 21–24.

Xanthippe and Anytus and Meletes, who are to reappear in all the future cycles of the world.[66] In further support of the Stoic origin of the theory of latency, he refers to Shahrastānī's statement quoted above, where, in his critical comment on Naẓẓām's theory of latency, he says that Naẓẓām was more inclined to the view of the "naturalists" than to that of the "theologians," in which, taking the term "naturalists" to refer to the Stoics, he infers that, according to Shahrastānī, Naẓẓām's theory of latency was derived from the Stoics.[67] As for Shahrastānī's statement that Anaxagoras was the first to introduce the theory of latency, he thinks that this is an error on the part of Shahrastānī, due to his confusion of the term "seeds" (σπέρματα) of Anaxagoras and the term "seed" (σπέρμα) of the Stoics, even though the two have no connection with each other.[68]

Third, there is Horten's interpretation.[69] This interpretation, too, draws its support from the same texts that I have used in support of my interpretation. Horten makes Anaxagoras the direct source of Naẓẓām's theory of latency, admitting, however, that such a theory is to be found also in such pre-Socratic philosophers as Leucippus, Democritus, and Empedocles,[70] and that certain Stoic elements are also to be found in the reports of Naẓẓām's theory.[71] He is also aware of Shahrastānī's allusive application of the theory of latency to Aristotle's theory of potentiality and actuality and of matter and form, but, as for this, he thinks that this was Shahrastānī's own erroneous imposition upon Aristotle of a view foreign to him.[72] In support of his own explanation, Horten quotes the passage in which Shahrastānī himself characterizes Anaxagoras as the first who advanced the theory of latency [73]

[66] *Ibid.*, p. 24.
[67] *Ibid.*, p. 22.
[68] *Ibid.*, p. 23.
[69] M. Horten, "Die Lehre vom Kumūn bei Naẓẓām," *ZDMG*, 63 (1909), 774–792.
[70] *Ibid.*, p. 773.
[71] *Ibid.*, p. 776.
[72] *Ibid.*, p. 777, n. 1.
[73] *Ibid.*, p. 776.

and tries to show how the entire philosophy of Naẓẓām, which Horovitz has explained as Stoic, is based upon Anaxagoras.[74]

Fourth, there is the interpretation of Aptowitzer,[75] who dispenses with any philosophic origin, and for every statement in Naẓẓām's theory, as represented by Baghdādī and Shahrastānī, quotes some Jewish source. For simultaneous creation, he quotes rabbinic passages[76] and Philo,[77] but refers also to Christian parallels.[78] For the use of the term "hidden" or its equivalent, he quotes, again, rabbinic passages[79] and Philo.[80] For a phrase in Shahrastānī's restatement of Naẓẓām's theory of latency,[81] taken by him to mean that all things were created in their full-grown state, he quotes rabbinic passages,[82] the Fourth Book of Ezra,[83] and Philo.[84] For the statement that God "did not create Adam before creating his children," he quotes rabbinic passages where Adam is represented as including all the future generations of mankind.[85]

The theory of latency, as I have tried to show, was adopted by Naẓẓām as a substitute for the orthodox theory of continuous creation, which he had rejected together with his rejection of the orthodox theory of atoms. This means also that he rejected the atomic conception of space and time, for all of which he substituted the Aristotelian theory of the infinite divisibility of bodies as well as of space and time. Now the infinite divisibility of space was subjected by Zeno to a criticism consisting of four arguments, which are reproduced by Aristotle in his *Physics*. An answer, aimed, as we shall see, at Zeno's first argument and known as the theory of "the

[74] *Ibid.*, pp. 780 ff.

[75] V. Aptowitzer, "Arabisch-Jüdische Schöpfungstheorieen," *Hebrew Union College Annual*, 6 (1929), 205–217.

[76] *Ibid.*, n. 11.

[77] *Ibid.*, n. 12.

[78] *Ibid.*

[79] *Ibid.*, nn. 16 and 16a.

[80] *Ibid.*, n. 17.

[81] Cf. *Milal*, p. 39, l. 10.

[82] Aptowitzer, "Arabisch-Jüdische," n. 13.

[83] *Ibid.*, n. 14.

[84] *Ibid.*, n. 15.

[85] *Ibid.*, nn. 20 and 23.

leap" (*al-ṭafrah*), is ascribed to Naẓẓām. Though the same theory is ascribed also to Hishām b. al-Ḥakam in a report quoted by Ash'arī in the name of Zurḳān,[86] the theory is generally identified with the name of Naẓẓām. Thus Ibn Ḥazm introduces the theory of the leap as a theory which "some people from among the Mutakallimūn trace to Ibrāhīm b. al-Naẓẓām." [87] Baghdādī, after stating that "from Hishām and the heathen philosophers Naẓẓām took his view on the denial of atoms," adds: "Then upon this [that is, upon his denial of atoms] he built his theory of the leap, which no one before had thought of." [88] Similarly Shahrastānī, after stating that "Naẓẓām agreed with the philosophers in the denial of atoms," adds: "and he originated the theory of the leap." [89]

Zeno's first argument, as restated by Aristotle, reads as follows: "It is impossible for a thing to traverse infinite things or to touch (ἅφασθαι) infinite things one by one, in a finite time." [90] What he means to say is this: On the assumption of the infinite divisibility of distance, it would be impossible for an object to traverse any finite distance in finite time, for, since any finite distance is infinitely divisible, the object moving over it would have to traverse and touch an infinite number of parts of distance in a finite time, which Aristotle himself would have to admit to be impossible.

Naẓẓām's solution of this difficulty by his theory of the leap, as reported by Ash'arī in his *Maḳālāt*, reads as follows: "Al-Naẓẓām asserted that it is possible for a body to be in one place and then reach a third place without having passed through the second place, and this is done by means of a leap. He advanced for this several reasons. One of these is the case of spinning-tops, of which [the distances covered by] the motion of its upper part is more than [that covered by] the motion of its lower part and the former traverses a greater section than that traversed by their lower part or pivot, and

[86] *Maḳālāt*, p. 61, ll. 13–14.
[87] *Fiṣal* V, p. 64, l. 22.
[88] *Farḳ*, p. 113, ll. 17–18.
[89] *Milal*, p. 38, l. 19.
[90] *Phys.* VI, 2, 233a, 22–23; cf. VI, 9, 239b, 11–14; *Top.* VIII, 160b, 8–9.

this is due to the fact that their upper part touches (*yumāssu*) things which its opposite [the lower tip] cannot match." [91]

As reported by Shahrastānī in his *Milal*, Naẓẓām's solution of the difficulty reads: "He originated the theory of the leap, because his assumption of infinite divisibility would make it necessary that, if an ant walked over a rock from peak to peak, it would traverse an infinite [in finite time], but how can [one in] that which is finite [i.e., finite time] traverse that which is infinite? He explained it by saying that the ant traverses the distance partly by walking and partly by the leap." [92]

The term "touch" which occurs both in Aristotle's reproduction of Zeno's first argument and in Naẓẓām's theory of the leap as reproduced by Ash'arī shows quite clearly that it is as an answer to this argument of Zeno that Naẓẓām advanced his theory of the leap and also that it is from Aristotle's *Physics* that Naẓẓām learned of this argument from Zeno. Now it happens that Aristotle himself has answered this argument of Zeno,[93] and his answer is not the same as the theory of the leap by which Naẓẓām tried to answer it. Aristotle's answer is based on his view that alongside the infinite divisibility of space and magnitude is also the infinite divisibility of motion and time. Why Naẓẓām should have ignored Aristotle's answer and devised a new answer of his own cannot be explained. Certainly he could not have disagreed with Aristotle on the infinite divisibility of motion and time alongside the infinite divisibility of space and magnitude, and there is nowhere in the statements reported in his name evidence that he disagreed with Aristotle on this. The only plausible explanation is that, while he has learned by hearsay of Zeno's argument as restated by Aristotle in his *Physics*, he has not learned of Aristotle's answer to it. In fact, in none of the statements reported in the name of Naẓẓām with regard

[91] *Maḳālāt*, p. 321, ll. 6–10.
[92] *Milal*, p. 38, l. 19 – p. 39, l. 1.
[93] *Phys*. VI, 2, 233a, 24–31.

to his theory of the leap is there any indication that he had any knowledge of Aristotle's answer.

As for the soundness of Naẓẓām's theory of the leap, one would be tempted to discover in it some hidden physical or mathematical or metaphysical concept. But any such attempt would prove to be futile. The theory of the leap is nothing but a quibble of words. All there is to it is simply the statement that if the infinite parts into which a distance is divisible cannot be walked over, it can be jumped over. There are many things, Naẓẓām must have reasoned, which we cannot pass over by walking, but we can pass them over by jumping. Take a ditch, for instance, or a fence; we cannot walk through it, but we can jump over it. Why should we not say the same about the infinite parts into which a distance is divisible? indeed, we cannot walk through them, but why should we not be able to jump over them? The fallacy of this argument has been stated by Shahrastānī as follows: "He does not know that jumping is also the traversal of a distance which corresponds to another distance, so that the difficulty which follows from his view of the infinite divisibility of space is not removed by this theory. The difference between walking and jumping amounts only to a difference between the rapidity of time and its slowness." [94] And so even Ibn Ḥazm, who agreed with him on infinite divisibility,[95] refutes his theory of the leap.[96] "The theory of Naẓẓām," says Isfara'īnī, "has become a byword for every untrue, unacceptable theory." [97]

[94] *Milal*, p. 39, ll. 5–7.
[95] *Fiṣal* V, pp. 92, ll. 21 ff.
[96] *Ibid.*, p. 64, l. 21 – p. 65, l. 12.
[97] *Tabṣīr*, p. 68, ll. 7–8.

CHAPTER VII

CAUSALITY

I. Denial of Causality

1. THE DURATION AND DESTRUCTION OF THINGS

In the fictitious disputation between a Christian and a Muslim by John of Damascus, the Christian maintains that, after the six days of creation, all the normal processes of nature, such as the reproduction of men and plants and herbs, are the acts of God through intermediate causes, whereas the Muslim maintains that they are all the direct creations of God.[1] From this we gather that in the early part of the eighth century the Muslim already denied that God acts through intermediary causes.

How Muslims came to hold such a view can be explained on the ground of the belief held by the early Muslims that power is the primary and exclusive property of God. This belief they must have derived from the many verses in the Koran in which the true God of Islam is contrasted with the false pre-Islamic gods. The contrast is mainly between the true God who has power and the false gods who have no power. Here are a few representative verses. "What! Will they associate those with Him who cannot create anything, and are themselves created, and have no power to help them, or to help themselves" (7:191); "Say: Is there any of your associate-gods who produces a creature, then causes it to return to him? Say: God produces a creature, then causes it to return to Him" (10:35); "It is God who created you, then fed you, then will cause you to die, then will make you alive. Is there any of your associate-gods who can do aught of these things? (30:39); "Say: What think ye of your associate-gods whom you invoke beside God? Shew me what part of earth they have created, or have they any share in the heavens"

[1] *Disputatio Christiani et Saraceni* (PG 94, 1592 B – 1593 B).

(35:38). Power is thus the chief and exclusive characteristic of the true God.

This general conception of God as being the only one who has power to do things was still further enhanced by such verses as those in which God is spoken of specifically as being the cause of the various phenomena in the world. Here are a few representative verses. "It was We who rained down the copious rains, then cleft the earth with clefts, and made to grow therein the grain, and grapes and healing herbs, and the olive and the palm, and enclosed gardens thick with trees, and fruits and herbage, for the service of yourselves and your cattle" (80:25–32). "It is God who . . . sendeth down water from the heaven, and then bringeth forth therewith the fruits for your food; and He hath subjected to you the ships, so that by His command they pass through the sea" (14:37). "His command, when He willeth aught, is but to say to it, Be, and it is" (36:82).

The cumulative effect of these verses upon the mind of the early Muslims was that God, and God alone, by His own command and power, was the direct cause of all events in the world. Even verse 14:37, which, as quoted above, says that God, with the rain sent down by Him, bringeth forth fruits, must have been taken by them, from its context, to mean that God, by His command, directly makes the rain bring forth fruits. There is only one kind of created beings who are described in the Koran as being employed by God to perform certain acts, and that is angels; but angels are not what is usually meant by intermediate causes; they are only messengers of God who are especially commanded by Him to carry out His will on certain occasions,[2] though in one instance an angel is said to have disobeyed God's command (2:28–32; 38:71–74).

[2] On the conception of angels as being not causes but only deputies of God, see Ghazālī, *Tahāfut al-Falāsifah* XVII, 4–5, p. 279, ll. 1–2 and 10–11. On Ghazālī's view that not only angels but also human beings may act as deputies of God, see *Iḥyā'* XXXV, *Kitāb al-Tauḥīd w'al-Tawakkul*, Section *Bayān Ḥaḳīḳat al-Tauḥīd* (vol. IV, p. 250, ll. 31 ff).

This was the established Muslim belief during the early part of the eighth century, and to this there is no record of any opposition at that time.

About a century later, in the early part of the ninth century, Greek philosophic works were translated into Arabic. From these works Muslims became acquainted with two contrasting views among philosophers on the question of causality. On the one hand, there were those philosophers, and they were in the majority, who believed in the existence of a God conceived by them as a necessary remote cause of events in the world — a God who by the necessity of His own nature causes all events in the world to take place through the intermediacy of things which act as the immediate cause of those events. On the other hand, there were the Epicureans who denied the existence of any God at all and denied also that things are the immediate causes of events. To them all events in the world happen by mere chance. The Muslims could not approve of either of these two views completely, but they found something to approve of in each of these views. They approved of the belief in the existence of God affirmed in the first view, but they rejected its conception of God as a nonvolitional and remote cause and also its conception of things as having a causal power. As for the second view, that of the Epicureans, they approved of its denial of any causal power to things in the world, but they rejected its denial of the existence of God and also of its assertion that all events in the world happen by chance. To all of them, both orthodox and Muʿtazilites, with two outstanding exceptions among the latter,[2a] just as by His unrestricted power God created the world all by himself without any intermediary, so also by His unrestricted power does He govern the world all by himself without any intermediary causes. Everything in the world that comes into being comes into being directly by an act of creation by God.

[2a] Cf. below, pp. 560 ff.

But in the world as we know it things not only come into being but, after they come into being, they continue to be, and after they continue to be for some time, they cease to be. This gave rise in the Kalam to a problem designated by the terms "duration" (*baḳā'*) and "destruction" (*fanā'*), in the discussion of which both orthodox and Muʿtazilites participated. The discussion of this problem, in the passages to be examined, sometimes turns on the term "accidents" or "bodies"; but sometimes it turns on the term "things" or on the term "bodies" used interchangeably with the term "substances." Now to the Mutakallimūn the term "thing" (*shay'*) means anything created [3] and the term "substance," as we have seen above in the chapter on "Atomism," generally means to them "atom," and, with regard to atom, again as we have seen above in that chapter, they differ as to whether it is a body or not a body. When, therefore, the discussion about duration and destruction turns on the term "things," it has to be determined whether the term is used in the sense of "accidents" or in the sense of "bodies" or in the sense of "atoms." Similarly, when the discussion turns on the term "bodies" used interchangeably with the term "substances," it has to be determined whether the two terms so used, which are certainly meant to include "bodies" composed of atoms, are also meant to include "atoms" conceived of as bodies.[4]

The earliest listing of views with regard to continuance and cessation of existence occurs in Ashʿarī's *Maḳālāt* and Ḫayyāṭ's *Intiṣār*. In Ashʿarī, they are listed under the headings "People disagreed with regard to accidents whether they endure or not" [5] and "They differed as to whether accidents can be said to be destroyed or not." [6] In Ḫayyāṭ, the various views on both duration and destruction are introduced by the words "The discussion concerning the destruction of a

[3] Ashʿarī, *Maḳālāt*, p. 181, l. 3. Cf. the problem whether "the nonexistent" (that is, a thing prior to its creation) is a "thing," above, pp. 359 ff.

[4] Cf. below, nn. 19, 25, 32, 40, 57, 74, 87.

[5] *Maḳālāt*, p. 358, l. 1.

[6] *Ibid*., p. 360, l. 11.

thing." [7] Baghdādī in his *Uṣūl* deals with the problem under such headings as "Concerning the impossibility of the duration of accidents" [8] and "Concerning the manner of the destruction of that which is destroyed." [9] In Abū Rashīd, the problem is dealt with under the headings "An inquiry concerning the view that the duration of the substance cannot conceivably be due to a cause" [10] and "An inquiry concerning the view that the substance is destroyed by its opposite." [11] Ghazālī, in connection with his refutation of the view of the indestructibility of the world, quotes those whom he calls "the philosophers" as enumerating four views held by four groups of Mutakallimūn with regard to the belief of the destructibility of the world.[12] Brief accounts of various conceptions of duration and destruction occur also in other works.

Out of these sources I have selected a variety of statements which I have grouped together into eight main views. All these eight views, however they may differ on the particular problems of duration and destruction, start out with the common belief that, just as the world as a whole was created by God out of nothing by His utterance of the command "Be," so are all changing events in the world created by God out of nothing by His utterance of the command "Be," though in two of these views the command "Be" is given a special meaning.

Following are the eight main views.

I. A view in which a different explanation is given of the duration of accidents and of the duration of bodies.

With regard to the duration of accidents, Ashʿarī quotes some of his contemporary Muʿtazilites, among them Kaʿbī, as maintaining that "accidents, all of them, do not endure for two instants." [13] Later this view is ascribed by Baghdādī to

[7] *Intiṣār* 9, p. 22, l. 23 – p. 23, l. 1.

[8] *Uṣūl*, p. 50, l. 10.

[9] *Ibid.*, p. 230, l. 10.

[10] *Masāʾil*, p. 58, l. 18 (63).

[11] *Ibid.*, p. 69, l. 3 (70).

[12] *Tahāfut al-Falāsifah* II, 12, p. 86, ll. 5–6.

[13] *Maḳālāt*, p. 358, l. 1.

aṣḥābunā, "our fellow associates," that is, the Ash'arites, and to "al-Ka'bī," [14] and still later Rāzī ascribes it directly to the Ash'arites.[15] Commenting on this view as ascribed to the Ash'arites, Ṭūsī says: "As they saw with their own eyes that accidents which [according to their belief] do not continue in their existence [appear to continue to exist], they arrived at the conclusion that accidents are created anew at every instant." [16] Thus, according to this view, there is no real duration in accidents; their continuous creation, however, gives them the appearance of duration.

Since accidents have no real duration, they also have no real destruction. It is thus with reference to this view that Ash'arī reports: (1) "Some say, None of the accidents can be described as being destroyed, for that can be described as being destroyed which is capable of enduring": [17] (2) "Some say, [Accidents] are destroyed not by a destruction." [18] Here, again, later this view is ascribed by Baghdādī to *aṣḥābunā*, that is, the Ash'arites, restating it as a view which maintains that "every accident necessarily becomes nonexistent in the instant (*ḥāl*) following its creation." [19]

The same Ash'arites and Ka'bī who have been reported by Baghdādī on accidents are also reported by him on bodies. Thus referring directly to "Abū al-Ḥasan al-Ash'arī," he reports of him that with regard to "a body" his view is that

[14] *Uṣūl*, p. 50, l. 11. [15] *Muḥaṣṣal*, p. 75, l. 13.
[16] Ṭūsī on *Muḥaṣṣal*, p. 11, n. 2, ll. 6–7. [17] *Maḳālāt*, p. 360, ll. 12–13.
[18] *Ibid*., p. 361, ll. 6–7.
[19] *Uṣūl*, p. 230, ll. 11–12. It is probably with reference to this view that Ḥayyāṭ, using the term "thing" in the sense of "accident," reports the following: "Some people maintain that the destruction of a thing is not due to something other than the thing but rather to the fact that, if God wishes to destroy a thing, He brings about its destruction by not recreating the same thing" (*Intiṣār* 9, p. 23, ll. 2–3). This statement is evidently meant to be in direct opposition to the statement of Mu'ammar preceding it, which reads that "the destruction of a thing exists in something other than the thing" (*ibid*., p. 22, l. 19); but, inasmuch as the term "thing" in Mu'ammar's statement is used, as I shall show later (cf. below, p. 568), in the sense of "accident," we may assume that the term "thing" in this statement is similarly used in the sense of "accident."

"that which endures endures by a duration" [20] and that that duration is "a *maʿnā* added to the existence of the essence of that which endures" [21] or "a *maʿnā* which is something other than that which endures," [22] by which statements is meant that "duration" is a *maʿnā* in the sense that it is a "thing" which, like an "accident," exists in another thing, which other thing is its substratum.[23] Then, referring to Ashʿarī's view about the duration of a "body," Baghdādī goes on to say that "al-Kaʿbī from among the Muʿtazilites held a view similar to that of our master Abū al-Ḥasan, so that he affirmed that duration is a *maʿnā*," [24] by which is meant that in the case of a body duration is a *maʿnā* therein. Abū Rashīd, using the term "substance," that is "atom," instead of "body," says that, according to Kaʿbī, "a substance endures by a duration of which it is the substratum," [25] thus the view ascribed to Kaʿbī by Baghdādī with regard to body was held by him also with regard to substance. From a passage in Ghazālī, soon to be quoted, we shall similarly learn that the view ascribed to the Ashʿarites by Baghdādī was held by them also with regard to substance.

From the fact that the Ashʿarites and Kaʿbī — despite their belief that bodies and substances are not devoid of accidents [26] — explain the duration of bodies and substances by assuming that God creates in them a *maʿnā* of duration, it is

[20] *Uṣūl*, p. 230, ll. 13–15. [21] *Ibid*., p. 90, l. 5. [22] *Ibid*., p. 231, l. 3.

[23] On the use of the term *maʿnā* in the sense of a thing existing in another thing and hence called accident, see above, pp. 153 f. Throughout the passages quoted subsequently in this section, it will be noticed, both duration and destruction are invariably described as *maʿnā* (at nn. 38, 85, 87) and as "accident" (at nn. 39, 80, 81, 86) and as "existent thing" (at nn. 53, 68).

[24] *Uṣūl*, p. 231, ll. 9–10.

[25] *Masāʾil*, p. 59, l. 2 (63). It is probably this view about the duration of body and of substance that the following two anonymous statements quoted by Ashʿarī have reference to: (1) that accidents "endure by the duration of the body," which we assume means by the duration created in the body (*Maḳālāt*, p. 361, l. 2); (2) "that which endures endures by a duration" (*ibid*., p. 366, l. 14).

[26] For Ashʿarī, cf. *Uṣūl*, p. 56, ll. 11–14; for Kaʿbī, cf. above, p. 488.

to be inferred that, according to both the Ash'arites and Ka'bī, the continuous creation of accidents, by which they explain the apparent duration of accidents, would not be sufficient to explain the kind of duration which in their view is required in the case of bodies and substances. From the same fact it would at first sight also seem to be inferred that, according to the Ash'arites and Ka'bī, the *ma'nā* of duration imparts to bodies and substances a kind of duration which, unlike the apparent duration of accidents, is a real duration. This inference, however, is invalidated, as I shall try to show, by the statements of Ash'arī and Ka'bī with regard to the destruction of bodies, which, of course, express their view also with regard to substances.

As reported by Baghdādī, Ash'arī maintained that "God destroys a body by not creating in it a duration at the instant in which He wishes it to be destroyed." [27] Baghdādī then tries to show that Ka'bī's view on the destruction of a body is similar to that of Ash'arī by quoting Ka'bī as saying, almost in the words of the first part of Ash'arī's statement, that "a body is destroyed when God does not create in it a duration," [28] evidently expecting the reader to add the second part of Ash'arī's statement, namely, "at the instant in which He wishes it to be destroyed." Thus, according to both Ash'arī and Ka'bī, a body is destroyed by God not directly by an act of destruction but rather indirectly, as in the case of accidents, by God's "not creating in it a duration at the instant in which He wishes it to be destroyed." Now the expression "by not creating in it a duration at the instant in which He wishes it to be destroyed" means by ceasing to create in it a duration at the instant in which He wishes it to be destroyed and this explanation of the expression means by ceasing to create in the body that duration by the previous continuous creation of which the body has before that endured. This shows that the duration by which the body prior to its destruction has

[27] *Uṣūl*, p. 230, ll. 13–14.

[28] *Ibid.*, p. 231, ll. 11–12.

endured, being a *ma'nā*, that is, an accident, was itself, like all accidents, durationless and hence continuously created at every instant, so that the duration which it had imparted to the body was not a real duration but only an apparent duration, though its apparentness was not of the same kind as that of accidents. That such a view about the duration and destruction of bodies did actually exist at the time of Ash'arī and Ka'bī may be gathered from a report by their older contemporary Ḫayyāṭ, which reads as follows: "Some people maintain that at each instant (*waḳt*) God creates for the body a duration whereby the body endures. Then, when God desires to destroy that body, He does not create in it a duration, in consequence of which the body ceases to exist." [29]

In Ghazālī, this view, ascribed by him to the Ash'arites, reads as follows: "Accidents become nonexistent by themselves, and cannot be conceived as enduring. . . . As regards substances, they do not endure by themselves, but they endure by a duration added to their existence, so that, when God does not create a duration for them, they become nonexistent as a result of the nonexistence of the duration." [30]

According to this view, then, both accidents and bodies are continuously created without any interval of duration between any two of the creations. But whereas, in the case of accidents, the unintervaled continuous creations are creations only of durationless existences, in the case of bodies, the unintervaled continuous creations are creations of durationless existences and creations of nonenduring durations.

II. The view of Bāḳillānī. With regard to accidents, there is the following statement by himself. "Accidents are those of which the [affirmation of] duration is not proper. They are those which happen to come into existence in substances and bodies and cease to exist the instant after their coming into existence." [31] Thus, like the rest of his fellow Ash'arites,

[29] *Intiṣār* 9, p. 23, ll. 7–8.

[30] *Tahāfut al-Falāsifah* II, 15, p. 88, ll. 1–4.

[31] *Tamhīd*, p. 18, ll. 4–5.

Bāḳillānī believed that accidents have no duration and that they cease to exist when God ceases to create them again.

With regard to bodies and substances, there are in Baghdādī two reports in the name of Bāḳillānī. (1) "He declined to admit that duration is a *ma'nā* added to the existence of the essence of that which endures, whether visibly or invisibly, and he asserted that the destruction of a body is due not to the cutting off (*ḳaṭ'*) of the duration from it but rather to the cutting off of the modes of existence (*al-akwān*) from it." [32] (2) "The destruction of a substance is only by the cutting off of the modes of existence from it, for, when God does not create a mode of existence . . . in a substance, the substance ceases to exist; and Bāḳillānī does not posit duration as a *ma'nā* different from that which endures." [33] The term *akwān*, "modes of existence," it may be remarked, is used as a designation of "motion, rest, aggregation, and segregation," [34] which Bāḳillānī himself describes as belonging to the "genera of accidents," in connection with which he also mentions "colors." [35]

From these two passages we gather that Bāḳillānī substituted "the modes of existence" for his fellow Ash'arites' "*ma'nā* of duration" as an explanation of the duration of bodies and substances and that consequently he also substituted "the cutting off of the modes of existence" for his fellow Ash'arites' "cutting off of the *ma'nā* of duration" as an explanation of the destruction of bodies and substances. Now the expression "the cutting off of the modes of existence," taken by itself, might mean the destroying of the modes of the existence by a direct act of destruction, which in turn would imply that the modes of existence had themselves real duration and hence imparted to bodies and substances real

[32] *Uṣūl*, p. 90, ll. 5–7; cf. p. 45, ll. 16–17; p. 109, ll. 1–2; cf. also p. 67, ll. 4–7; p. 87, ll. 8–9, where the term "colors" is added to "the modes of existence" (cf. p. 231, l. 2, and below at n. 35).

[33] *Ibid.*, p. 231, ll. 1–3.

[34] *Irshād*, p. 10, ll. 9–10 (28).

[35] *Tamhīd*, p. 40, l. 18.

duration. But the explanatory statement "for, when God does not create a mode of existence . . . in a substance, the substance ceases to exist," which in the second passage immediately follows the expression "the cutting off of the modes of existence" shows quite clearly that by the expression "the cutting off of the modes of existence" is meant ceasing to create the modes of existence which up to that time have been continuously created. Thus the modes of existence, like the *ma'nā* of duration for which they are substituted are nonenduring, but continuously created, and hence, by their being continuously created, they impart to bodies and substances a duration which is not real but only apparent.

From all this we may gather that Bāḳillānī, while agreeing with his fellow Ash'arites on the durationlessness of accidents, differs from them on the explanation of the duration of bodies in that he substitutes an explanation by the use of the so-called "modes of existence" (*al-akwān*) for their explanation by the use of what they call a "*ma'nā* of duration." But once this substitution is made by him his explanation of the duration of bodies, and hence also of the destruction of bodies, is, *mutatis mutandis*, the same as that of his fellow Ash'arites.

In Ghazālī, this view, attributed to a "group of Ash'arites," is described as follows: "Accidents pass away by themselves, but substances pass away when God does not create in them motion and rest and aggregation and segregation, for it is impossible for a body to endure in its existence without being either in motion or at rest, and so it becomes nonexistent." [36]

According to this view, then, as according to the first view, both accidents and bodies are continuously created without any interval of duration between any two of the creations. But, whereas in the case of accidents the unintervaled continuous creations are creations only of durationless existences, in the case of bodies, the unintervaled continuous creations are creations of durationless existences and creations of nonenduring modes of existence.

[36] *Tahāfut al-Falāsifah* II, 16, p. 88, l. 19 – p. 89, l. 3.

III. The view of Ḳalānisī, whom, as we shall see, Baghdādī calls "our master," thus evidently regarding him as an Ashʿarite.[37] Here, again, from the fact that in Baghdādī only with regard to the destruction of bodies is he said to differ from the other Ashʿarites and no mention is made of a difference between them with regard to the durationlessness of accidents, it may be inferred that, with regard to accidents, he believed, as did the other Ashʿarites, that accidents are durationless, but continuously created, and hence they cease to exist when they cease to be created.[38] But what his view was with regard to bodies and substances calls for investigation.

As reported by Baghdādī, "Our master Abū al-ʿAbbas al-Ḳalānisī . . . affirmed the duration of a body to be a *maʿnā* other than the body." [39] This statement quite evidently means the same as the various similar statements of the Ashʿarites. On the face of it, therefore, it would seem to express a view which is the same as that of the Ashʿarites, namely, that the *maʿnā* of duration is itself nonenduring, but it is continuously created and hence the body in which it is created does not thereby become really durable; it becomes only apparently durable. His view, however, on the destruction of bodies and substances will show that he differs from the Ashʿarites also with regard to the durations of bodies and substances.

The view of Ḳalānisī on the destruction of bodies and substances is reported by Baghdādī as follows: (1) "Al-Ḳalānisī considers destruction as an accident subsisting in the body that is to be destroyed, so that the body is destroyed by it at the instant (*al-ḥālah*) following the instant (*ḥāl*) of the creation of the destruction in it." [40] (2) "Our master Abū al-ʿAbbas al-Ḳalānisī says that God destroys a substance

[37] See above, p. 34, n. 142, on the various dates of *Ḳalānisī*.

[38] For corroborative evidence, see next note.

[39] *Uṣūl*, p. 230, l. 16, and p. 231, ll. 8–9. Since, according to this statement, duration in bodies is due to a *maʿnā*, it corroborates the inference that, according to Ḳalānisī, accidents are durationless and hence continuously created, for, according to him, there can be no *maʿnā* in an accident (*Uṣūl*, p. 234, l. 3; cf. p. 45, ll. 7–8).

[40] *Ibid.*, p. 45, ll. 10–11.

only by a destruction which He creates in it, so that the substance is destroyed at the instant (*al-ḥāl*) following the instant (*ḥāl*) of the creation of the destruction in it."[41]

Now the fact that a body or a substance is said by Ḳalānisī to be destroyed only by the creation in it of a destruction, which means that it is not destroyed by the cessation of the creation in it of the *maʿnā* of duration, shows that, in his view, the body or the substance to be destroyed had real duration. But it could not have real duration unless the *maʿnā* of duration created in it, unlike the *maʿnā* of duration according to the view of the Ashʿarites, had continuance of existence. The duration created in bodies or in substances is thus itself durable and hence the bodies or the substances in which it is created do not cease to exist except by a direct act of destruction.

According to this view, then, accidents, as according to the first two views, are continuously created without any interval of duration between any two of their creations. But, in the case of bodies or substances, there is an interval of duration between any two of their creations.

IV. The view of the Muʿtazilite Abū al-Hudhayl. His is one of the two views referred to above in the introductory paragraph to this eightfold classification of views as giving the creative word "Be" a special meaning. The special meaning given to it by him is that the word "Be" itself is a created thing, created, as he says, "not in a substratum (*maḥall*),"[42] that is to say, it is a created incorporeal word outside the essence of God. Then, also, in contradistinction to the exponents of all the preceding views, Abū al-Hudhayl makes no distinction between accidents and bodies with regard to duration and destruction.

[41] *Ibid.*, p. 230, ll. 15–18. From these two reports by Baghdādī it is to be inferred that Ḳalānisī uses the term "substance" in the sense of "body." But whether the term substance in the sense of body is used by him also to include "atom" I am unable to tell, as I have been unable to find out what his view is on the problem of the extendedness of atoms.

[42] *Farḳ*, p. 108, ll. 6–7; *Milal*, p. 35, l. 2; cf. above, p. 141.

Abū al-Hudhayl's view on the duration of accidents and bodies, as reported by Ashʿarī, begins with the statement that "some accidents endure and some do not endure." [43] But, with regard to the duration of those accidents which endure, Ashʿarī reports Abū al-Hudhayl's explanation of it as follows: "He maintains that colors endure, and so do also tastes and smells and lives and power endure, all of them by a duration which does not exist in a spatial substratum (*makān*). And he explains that the [substratumless] duration is God's saying to a thing 'Endure.' The same holds true also of the duration of a body and of the duration of any of the durable accidents. And in the same way does he also maintain that pains and pleasures endure." [44] In another place, the same view, again quoted by Ashʿarī in the name of Abū al-Hudhayl, reads that "duration is something other than that which endures" and that "duration is God's saying to a thing 'Endure'." [45] Ashʿarī also quotes this view anonymously as maintaining that accidents, by which he quite evidently means accidents which endure, "endure by a duration which is not in a spatial substratum (*makān*)." [46] The report on this view by Baghdādī reads as follows: "Abū al-Hudhayl maintains that bodies and accidents which have duration endure only by reason of a duration not in a substratum (*maḥall*) and he explains that that [substratumless] duration is God's saying 'Endure'." [47] Here, too, as in the case of Ḳalānisī, it is not clear whether the created substratumless word "Endure" produces a durable duration or only a continuously created duration. But this vagueness is cleared up, again, as in the case of Ḳalānisī, by Abū al-Hudhayl's view on destruction.

Abū al-Hudhayl's view on destruction corresponds exactly to his view on duration. Thus Ashʿarī, coupling destruction with duration, in the latter of which, as we have seen, no distinction is made by Abū al-Hudhayl between accidents

[43] *Maḳālāt*, p. 358, l. 12.
[44] *Ibid.*, p. 359, ll. 1–4; cf. p. 366, l. 15; p. 367, l. 12.
[45] *Ibid.*, p. 366, ll. 14–15.
[46] *Ibid.*, p. 361, l. 3.
[47] *Uṣūl*, p. 51, ll. 3–5.

and bodies, describes Abū al-Hudhayl as maintaining that "duration and destruction have their existence not in a spatial substratum." [48] In another place, corresponding to his description of Abū al-Hudhayl as to what he maintained with regard to duration,[49] is his description of him as maintaining that "destruction is other than that which is destroyed . . . and that destruction is God's saying [to a thing] 'Perish'." [50] In still another place, corresponding to his quotation of the anonymous view reproduced above with regard to the duration of accidents by a substratumless duration,[51] which, as we have seen, is Abū al-Hudhayl's view with regard to durable accidents, is his quotation of an anonymous view with regard to "accidents" that "they are destroyed by a destruction which is not in a spatial substratum (*makān*)," [52] which, again, is Abū al-Hudhayl's view with regard to durable accidents. Now, the fact that, according to Abū al-Hudhayl, accidents and bodies are destroyed by the creation in them of the substratumless word "Perish," and not by the mere cessation of the creation in them of the substratumless word "Endure," shows that the duration produced in them by the creation in them of the substratumless word "Endure" is itself durable.

Nothing, as far as I know, is reported in the name of Abū al-Hudhayl about those accidents which, according to him, do not endure, such, for instance, as motion and desire.[53] Probably he would say that they are continuously created and that they are destroyed by the cessation of their being created.

According to this view, those accidents which have no duration are, as all accidents are according to the preceding

[48] *Maḳālāt*, p. 367, l. 12.
[49] Cf. above at n. 45.
[50] *Maḳālāt*, p. 366, ll. 14–15.
[51] *Ibid.*, p. 361, l. 3; cf. above at n. 46.
[52] *Ibid.*, l. 5.
[53] *Uṣūl*, p. 50, l. 18. With regard to "rest" he says that one kind does not endure and another kind does endure (*Uṣūl*, p. 51, ll. 1–2; *Maḳālāt*, p. 358, l. 13).

three views, continuously created without any interval of duration between any two of the creations. In the case of those accidents which have duration and also in the case of bodies, there is an interval of duration between any two of their creations.

The preceding four views, as will have been noticed, start out with the assumption that creation means only the bringing of something into existence but it does not involve the duration of that which is brought into existence. The next four views, we shall now see, start out with the assumption that the mere act of creation involves the duration of that which is brought into existence.

V. The view characterized by Abū Rashīd as that which maintains that "the duration of substances is not due to a cause." [54] By this is meant that the mere act of creation brings substances into an existence which is durable. Abū Rashīd presents this view as follows: "Among our masters [of the School of Baṣra] there is no difference of opinion on the view that the duration of bodies is not due to a duration [as its cause], adding that "our master al-Ḥusayn al-Ḫayyāṭ [of the School of Baghdad] supports this view." [55]

Corresponding to this view that God's creation involves duration is the view that destruction is the direct work of God. As reported by Abū Rashīd, it reads as follows: "Know that our master Abū al-Ḥusayn al-Ḫayyāṭ has said concerning substance that it passes out of existence by its being destroyed by God, thus allowing the power of God to extend to destruction." [56] So also Bāḳillānī, whose one view on destruction we

[54] *Masā'il*, p. 58, l. 18 (63).

[55] *Ibid.*, ll. 19–20. From Abū Rashīd's statement here and at n. 56 it is to be inferred that the term "substances" is used by him in the sense of "bodies." Whether the term is used by him here also to include "atoms" will depend upon the question whether all the Baṣraites were, according to him, in agreement with Abū Hāshim (cf. *Masā'il*, p. 38, l. 15) that atoms are extended and hence they are bodies.

[56] *Ibid.*, p. 69, ll. 4–5 (70); cf. p. 58, ll. 20–21 (63).

have reproduced above,[57] has at one time sponsored this view. As reported by Ṭūsī, it reads as follows: "As for the Ḳādī Abū Bakr [al-Bāḳillānī] . . . he says in one place of his writings that God as an agent who acts by free will destroys without any intermediary, and a similar view is also held by Maḥmūd al-Ḫayyāṭ." [58]

According to this view, then, in the case of bodies there is an interval of duration between their creations. Probably the same holds true also in the case of accidents.

VI. The view of the Karrāmiyyah. Their view on creation is somewhat like that of Abū al-Hudhayl in so far as they believe that creation is effected by God's created word "Be." But that word "Be" is created, or as they would say is occurring (*ḥādith*),[59] not as something substratumless outside of God but rather as something in God himself. Then, also, unlike Abū al-Hudhayl, they believe that creation involves duration, so that, according to them, there is no need for a created word "Endure." Corresponding to their conception of creation is their conception of destruction, which is effected, according to them, by the created word "Perish," which is occurring in God himself.

These conceptions of creation and destruction may be gathered from the following reports in Baghdādī: (1) "The Karrāmiyyah admit the possibility of the duration of all accidents," [60] maintaining that, "when God creates a body or an accident, its duration necessarily follows until He says to it 'Perish' and desires its annihilation." [61] (2) "They also held that no body or accident is created in the world without the occurrence (*ḥudūth*) of many accidents in the essence of God, such as the will that the event should take place and His saying to it 'Be'." [62] (3) "They likewise maintain that no accident perishes in the world without the occurrence of

[57] Cf. above, pp. 526 f.

[58] Ṭūsī on *Muḥaṣṣal*, p. 99, n. ll. 2–4.

[59] *Farḳ*, p. 204, ll. 16–17; cf. above, pp. 145–146.

[60] *Uṣūl*, p. 50, ll. 11–12.

[61] *Ibid.*, l. 14.

[62] *Farḳ*, p. 204, l. 17 – p. 205, l. 1.

many accidents in their God, of which one is His will that it perish and another is His command to that whose extinction He desires 'Become nonexistent' or the command 'Perish'." [63] The same view is reported by Ḫayyāṭ anonymously as follows: "Some maintain that, when God desires to destroy a thing, He creates for it a destruction and this destruction subsists in God." [64] As reported by Shahrastānī in the name of the Karramiyyah, it reads: "The nonexistent becomes nonexistent by an act of destruction which occurs (*al-wāḳiʿ*) in the essence of God by God's own power." [65]

In Ghazālī, this view reads as follows: "The Karrāmiyyah say that destruction is an act of God and that destruction means an existent thing which He brings about (*yuḥdithuhu*) in His essence, so that thereby the world becomes nonexistent." [66]

According to this view, then, in the case of both accidents and bodies there is an interval of duration between their creations.

VII. The view of Bishr b. al-Muʿtamir. As reported in his name by Ashʿarī, it reads: "Rest endures and it is not terminated except by the fact that that which is at rest goes over from rest to motion and so also blackness endures and it is not terminated except by the fact that that which is black goes over from blackness to its contrary, either whiteness or some other color; and the same holds true of the other accidents." [67] Elsewhere it is reported of him that, in contradistinction to Muʿammar's view that accidents are not created by God but are the acts of bodies either by choice, in the case of living beings, or by nature, in the case of non-living beings, Bishr b. al-Muʿtamir held that some accidents are the act of God and some the act of man.[68]

[63] *Ibid.*, p. 205, ll. 5–8.
[64] *Intiṣār* 9, p. 23, ll. 3–4.
[65] *Milal*, p. 81, l. 11.
[66] *Tahāfut al-Falāsifah* II, 14, p. 87, ll. 5–8.
[67] *Maḳālāt*, p. 360, ll. 7–8; cf. *Uṣūl*, p. 51, ll. 5–7.
[68] *Uṣūl*, p. 135, ll. 4–6 and 8–10; cf. below, p. 647.

Bishr's opening statement that "rest endures" and that "blackness endures," which he subsequently extends to include all other accidents, is to be taken to mean, I presume, that the very creation of accidents involves their duration. Such a view, as we shall see, was held by Jubbā'ī about both accidents and bodies and, as we shall also see, such a view is ascribed by Ash'arī not only to Jubbā'ī but also to some other people and is described by him as a view that "that which endures is enduring not by a duration." [69] So also, we may assume, does Bishr's view include bodies. Indirect evidence for this may be gathered from the following two reports by Ash'arī: (1) "Bishr b. al-Mu'tamir said: The creation of a thing is something other than the thing." [70] (2) "Those who believe that the creation of a thing is something other than the thing maintain that that which endures endures not by a duration." [71] From the combination of these two reports we thus gather that, with regard to a thing, by which in this context is meant a body together with its accidents, Bishr believed that creation involves duration.

With regard to Bishr's statement that rest or blackness or any other accident is not terminated, that is, destroyed, except by the fact that it goes over from what it happens to be to something which is its contrary, it is quite evident from the passage quoted above about his view regarding the creation of accidents that similarly here, of these contrary destructive accidents, some are the acts of God and some are the acts of man. Thus also, as we shall see later, a statement of his which reads that "movement may generate rest" [72] means that the agent of the rest which is generated by the movement may be either God or man, the former when the movement by which the rest is generated is an act of God and the latter

[69] Cf. below, p. 537.
[70] *Makālāt*, p. 364, l. 14.
[71] *Ibid.*, p. 366, l. 12. Here it would seem from the context that the term "thing" is used in the sense of anything "created" (cf. above at n. 3), thus including "atom" and "accident" and "body" composed of atoms.
[72] *Ibid.*, p. 413, l. 10; cf. below, p. 647.

when the movement by which the rest is generated is an act of man.

That there was among the Muʿtazilites a view like that of Bishr b. al-Muʿtamir with regard to both duration and destruction is corroborated by the testimony of the Karaite Aaron ben Elijah of Nicomedia, who says: "A group of Muʿtazilites maintain that, after the Creator brings an accident into existence, that accident endures in its existence by itself, without there being any need for the Creator to continue to bring it into existence. . . . And they maintain that for everything there is a contrary that reduces it to nothing, so that, when God wishes to destroy a thing, He brings that contrary into existence and thereby the thing is destroyed." [73]

Since, according to Bishr, it is God who destroys things after their duration, it is God who creates those things again after each of their destructions, and hence it is each of their creations that involves duration. According to this view, therefore, in the case of both accidents and bodies, there is an interval of duration between any two of their creations.

VIII. The view of Jubbāʾī. With regard to duration, Ashʿarī reports of him as follows: "He says that accidents which endure endure not by a duration and he thus also says concerning bodies that they endure not by a duration." [74] Similarly in another place, Ashʿarī reports as follows: "Some people, such as al-Jubbāʾī and others, say: "That which endures is enduring not by a duration." [75] Thus, according to Jubbāʾī, creation of existence involves duration.

[73] *ʿEṣ Ḥayyim* 4, p. 16, ll. 7–15. It is quite possible that it is to a view like this, namely, that a body is destroyed by its contrary, that Ḫayyāṭ has reference in his report that "some people maintain that the destruction of a thing exists in something other than the thing" (*Intiṣār* 9, p. 23, ll. 6–7), even though the same statement as quoted by him earlier in the name of Muʿammar (*ibid.*, p. 22, l. 19) has, according to my interpretation of it, another meaning (cf. above n. 19 and below, p. 541).

[74] *Maḳālāt*, p. 359, ll. 13–14. Jubbāʾī's list of the two types of accidents (*ibid.*, ll. 8–11) is about the same as that of Abū al-Hudhayl (*ibid.*, p. 358, l. 12 – p. 359, l. 349).

[75] *Ibid.*, p. 367, l. 3.

Distinguished from his view on duration and quite evidently also from his view on existence, in the creation of which duration, according to him, is involved, is Jubbā'ī's view on destruction. As reported by Ash'arī, it reads as follows: "Al-Jubbā'ī said, The destruction of a body exists [but] not in a spatial substratum [*makān*] and it is contrary to the body [which is to be destroyed] as well as to anything which is of the same kind as the body. He maintained that blackness which entered upon (*kāna fī*) the state of its existence after whiteness is the destruction of the whiteness, that in the same way anything which in its existence is the nonexistence [that is, the opposite] of something is the destruction of that something, and that the destruction of an accident takes up its abode (*yaḥullu*) in the body [in which the accident inheres]." [76] The reason for this last part of his statement, I take it, is the combination of Jubbā'ī's own view — as will appear in the next passage quoted — that the substratumless destruction is an "accident" with the Aristotelian view that "an accident cannot be an accident of an accident." [77] The same view, as reported by Baghdādī, reads in one place as follows: "Al-Jubbā'ī and his son maintained that God, when He desires the destruction of bodies, creates for them a destruction not in a substratum (*maḥall*) and this destruction is an accident contrary to all bodies, so that thereby all bodies are destroyed"; [78] and in another place, it reads as follows: "He and his son Abū Hāshim maintained that God, when He desires to destroy the world, creates an accident not in a substratum (*maḥall*), whereby He destroys all bodies and substances." [79]

Jubbā'ī's view on destruction, as thus reported by both Ash'arī and Baghdādī, is quite evidently nothing but a revision of Abū al-Hudhayl's view on destruction. Both of them start out with the assumption that destruction is something created by God outside the thing to be destroyed. Both of them assert

[76] *Ibid.*, p. 368, ll. 1–4.
[77] *Metaph.* IV, 4, 1007b, 2–3.
[78] *Uṣūl*, p. 231, ll. 12–14; cf. p. 45, ll. 11–13.
[79] *Farḳ*, p. 168, l. 17 – p. 169, l. 1; cf. p. 319, ll. 11–12.

that destruction is created "not in a substratum." But then they begin to differ. To Abū al-Hudhayl, the created substratumless destruction is God's created substratumless word "Perish"; to Jubbā'ī, it is a created substratumless accident. To Abū al-Hudhayl, God's created substratumless word "Perish" brings about destruction while retaining its status as a substratumless being; to Jubbā'ī, the created substratumless accident brings about destruction only on its becoming inherent in the body which is to be destroyed or the accidents of which are to be destroyed. Then there is also another difference between them, for Jubbā'ī explicitly says that "it is not within the power of God to destroy some of the [bodies and] substances, while letting all the others continue in their duration," [80] whereas Abū al-Hudhayl does not say that the power of destruction which he attributes to God is restricted to the destruction of the whole world only.[81] Thus, while they differ on the question whether it is "within the power of God," that is to say, whether God ever uses His power, to destroy only part of the world, they agree in a general way that it is within the power of God to destroy the whole world by a substratumless destruction created by Him for that purpose.

It is with reference to that upon which Jubbā'ī and Abū al-Hudhayl are agreed in a general way that Ghazālī says of the Mu'tazilites that they maintain that "the act proceeding from God is an existent thing, namely, a destruction, which He creates not in a substratum, so that thereby the whole world is destroyed all at once." [82]

[80] *Ibid.*, p. 179, ll. 1–2; cf. *ibid.*, p. 206, ll. 3–4; p. 319, ll. 10–11; *Uṣūl*, p. 45, ll. 13–14; p. 231, ll. 14–15.

[81] Cf. above, pp. 532–533.

[82] *Tahāfut al-Falāsifah* II, 13, p. 86, ll. 7–8. At the conclusion of his statement Ghazālī says that "the created destruction is destroyed by itself, so that it is in no need of another destruction and thus of an infinite regress" (ll. 8–9). Ash'arī's report on Jubbā'ī, however, concludes with the statement that "the destruction is not destroyed" (*Maḳālāt*, p. 368, l. 4). Evidently Ghazālī's text of the *Maḳālāt* had the reading that "the destruction is destroyed."

Another report by Ash'arī on Jubbā'ī's view on destruction reads as follows: "Some people, such as al-Jubbā'ī and others, said: . . . that which is destroyed is destroyed not by a destruction which is something other than that which is destroyed." [83] Now, taken as it stands, this statement would mean the destruction is created within that which is to be destroyed. But, if so taken, it would be contradictory to the statements of Jubbā'ī's view in the reports quoted from both Ash'arī and Baghdādī, according to which destruction is first created by God "not in a substratum," which means not in a body, including the body which is to be destroyed. I should, therefore, suggest that this statement contains only part of Jubbā'ī's view, that part in which he differs from Abū al-Hudhayl, and it is directly aimed at Abū al-Hudhayl. Thus aiming at Abū al-Hudhayl's view that his substratumless destruction brings about destruction in bodies and accidents while still in its state of substratumlessness and of its being outside any bodily object, Jubbā'ī contends that "that which is destroyed is destroyed not by a destruction which is [still substratumless and hence] something other than that which is destroyed." The conclusion which Jubbā'ī knew that those acquainted with the fullness of his view would draw from this fragmentary statement is that the destruction of a body, as well as the destruction of its accidents, is to be effected by that created substratumless destruction only after it has entered the body which is to be destroyed or of which the accidents are to be destroyed.

A view which is like that of Jubbā'ī's is the view of Ibn Shabīb.

With regard to duration, Baghdādī states in a context which deals with the duration of bodies that "Ibn Shabīb maintains that duration is not something other than that which endures," [84] which, like Jubbā'ī's statement that "that which

[83] *Maḳālāt*, p. 367, ll. 3–4.

[84] *Uṣūl*, p. 231, l. 9. With regard to accidents, Ash'arī reports in the name of Ibn Shabīb that both motion and rest are durationless (*Maḳālāt*, p. 359,

endures is enduring not by a duration," [85] means that creation involves duration.

With regard to destruction, his view, as reported by Ash'arī, reads as follows: "Muḥammad b. Shabīb said: The *ma'nā* which is a destruction and on account of which a body ceases to exist is not to be called the destruction of the body until the body has ceased to exist. The *ma'nā* takes up its abode in the body at the instant of its presence in the body, so that the body ceases to exist after the presence of that *ma'nā* [in it]." [86] In Baghdādī the same view is reported as follows: "Muḥammad b. Shabīb maintained that destruction is an accident other than that which is to be destroyed and that it takes up its abode in the body, so that the body is destroyed at the instant following the instant in which that accident of destruction takes up its abode in it." [87] A similar view, reported by Ḫayyāṭ anonymously, reads as follows: "Some people maintain that, when God desires to destroy a thing, He creates for it a *ma'nā* which takes up its abode in it, so that the thing is destroyed at the instant following the instant in which that *ma'nā* takes up its abode in it; and, when the thing is destroyed, that *ma'nā* is named destruction." [88]

From the combination of these three passages we gather that a *ma'nā* or an accident of destruction is created outside the body which is to be destroyed, and evidently also outside any other body; but that the destruction of the body does not actually take place until that *ma'nā* or accident takes up its abode in the body. This corresponds exactly to Jubbā'ī's view

---

ll. 6–7), which means, as may be judged from its context, that in the case of all other accidents, such as colors and tastes etc., he agrees with Abū al-Hudhayl (*ibid*., ll. 1–5) that they have duration, though quite evidently, unlike Abū al-Hudhayl, he believes that the duration of these accidents, like the duration of bodies, is involved in their creation.

[85] Cf. above at n. 77.

[86] *Maḳālāt*, p. 367, ll. 15–17.

[87] *Uṣūl*, p. 231, ll. 6–8.

[88] *Intiṣār* 9, p. 23, ll. 4–6. Here the term "thing," as may be judged from the corresponding statements by Ash'arī and Baghdādī quoted at nn. 85 and 86, is used in the sense of "body."

that an accident of destruction is created "not in a substratum," that is to say, outside any body, including the body of that which is to be destroyed; but that the destruction of the body does not actually take place until that substratumless accident of destruction becomes inherent in the body which is to be destroyed.

Since, according to both Jubbā'ī and Ibn Shabīb, it is God who destroys durational accidents and bodies after their duration, it is God who creates them again after each of their destructions, and hence it is that each of their creations involves duration. According to Jubbā'ī and Ibn Shabīb, therefore, in the case of both durational accidents and bodies, there is an interval of duration between any two of their creations.

There are thus three fundamental differences between the various exponents of these eight views. According to views I–II, there is no real duration and no real destruction. What appears to us as duration is merely the uninterrupted continuity of the durationless existence of things plus the creation of their nonenduring duration or plus the creation of their nonenduring modes of existence, and what appears to us as destruction is merely the cessation of the creation of the aforementioned durationless existence and durationless duration and durationless modes of existence. According to views III–IV, in addition to the creation of the durationless existence of things, there is the creation of a real duration of those things and the creation of a destruction of those durational things. According to views V–VIII, every creation of the existence of a thing involves its real duration, which real duration comes to an end by the creation of its destruction. Thus the expression "continuous creation," by which the Kalam conception of the origin of things and events in the world is commonly described, applies only to views I–II of these eight views. It is to be noted that, of these eight views, views I–II are attributed to Ashʿarites and a Muʿtazilite; [89] views III–IV are attributed

[89] Cf. above at nn. 13, 14, 25, 26, 30.

to an Ash'arite and a Mu'tazilite;[89a] views V–VIII are attributed to Mu'tazilites and the Karrāmiyyah.[90]

Then there is another difference between the various exponents of these eight views. To all the orthodox among them, just as the world was created by God out of nothing, so all things in the world continue to be created by Him out of nothing, and consequently the destruction of things in the world, however conceived of by them, means their being reduced to nothing, and it is out of that nothing that God creates them again. But among the Mu'tazilites there were many who contended that "the nonexistent is something" and by this, as I tried to show, they meant that the world was created out of a pre-existent matter.[91] We may, therefore, assume that to the Mu'tazilites among the exponents of these eight views, or at least to some of them, the creation of things in the world by God does not mean their being created out of nothing and similarly the destruction of things in the world, however conceived of by them, does not mean their being reduced to nothing; it rather means their being each changed into something else, and it is out of that something else that God creates each of them again.

Still, despite these differences, the exponents of all the eight views agree that, just as God created the world directly without any intermediaries, so does He continue to create every event in the world directly without any intermediaries, and it is in this general sense, with the reservation of the aforementioned differences in mind, that the expression "continuous creation" can be retained as a description of all these eight views. The common implication of these eight views is the denial of any causal nexus between successive events in the world.

This common implication of these various views is boldly affirmed by Ghazālī. Against those whom he calls "philos-

[89a] Cf. nn. 37 and 42.
[90] Cf. above, pp. 533–542.
[91] Cf. above, pp. 359 ff.

ophers" and who, he says, assert that "the connection observed between causes and effects is a necessary connection," [92] he declares that, "according to us, the connection between what is is usually believed to be a cause and what is usually believed to be an effect is not a necessary connection." [93] Taking up the case of "the burning of cotton on contact with fire," [94] which has already been used as an illustration by "Abū al-Hudhayl and Jubbā'ī and the majority of the people of the Kalām" in their denial of causality,[95] he argues that there is no proof that the fire is the cause of the burning, for "the only proof that the philosophers have is the observation of the occurrence of the burning when there is a contact with the fire, but observation proves only that the burning occurs when there is a contact with the fire; it does not prove that it occurs because of the contact with the fire." [96] He thus concludes that it is God who "by His will creates the burning of the cotton at the time of its contact with the fire," [97] and what is true of fire and its burning of cotton is true of any other succession of events.

2. THE THEORY OF CUSTOM (*'ādah*) AND ITS FORMULATION BY GHAZĀLĪ

Theoretically, the denial of causality and the reduction of every event in the world to something occasioned directly by the arbitrary will of God would have to lead to a denial of any justification on our part for anticipating any order and sequence in the happenings of the world. Still those in Islam who denied causality and explained every single act as a direct creation of God could not fail to observe that, practically, things in the world do happen according to a certain order

[92] *Tahāfut al-Falāsifah*, Phys., 5, p. 270, l. 13 – p. 271, l. 1.
[93] *Ibid.* XVII, 1, p. 277, ll. 2–3.
[94] *Ibid.* XVII, 2, p. 278, l. 6; 4, p. 278, l. 13 – 279, l. 1.
[95] Ash'arī, *Maḳālāt*, p. 312, ll. 11–13.
[96] *Tahāfut al-Falāsifah* XVII, 5, p. 279, ll. 3–5.
[97] *Ibid.* XVII, 10, p. 283, ll. 6–7.

of sequence and many of these things could be predicted in advance even by men who were not endowed by God with the gift of prophecy. What, then, is the explanation of this apparent order and sequence in the world.

Now a similar question must have been raised in the mind of the Epicureans who attributed everything to chance. They must have asked themselves, why is it that certain things, such, for instance, as the rising and the setting of the sun and the alteration of the seasons, happen according to a certain order? The answer given by them, as stated by Lucretius, is that it is due to a *foedus naturae certum*.[1] This expression, usually translated by "a fixed law of nature," should perhaps be translated by "a certain covenant of nature," that is to say, a fortuitous covenant or agreement of nature, for the expression means that the eternally swerving atoms in their fortuitous concourse, out of which the world arose, happened, as if by a covenant or agreement, to establish an equilibrium, the ἰσονομία attributed by Cicero to the Epicureans[2] — an equilibrium by which, as long as it lasts, events will follow in the same order of succession, even though, having been established by chance, it may by chance be upset at almost any moment.

Similar to the Epicurean explanation of the observable regularity in the sequence of certain events by the Greek term *isonomia* is the Kalam explanation of it by the Arabic term *'ādah*. This term often occurs as a translation of the Greek ἔθος and hence may be translated either "custom" or "habit," but I shall use for it the term "custom," reserving the term "habit" as a translation of *malakah* = ἕξις, which is used in a passage, to be quoted later, as something distinct from *'ādah*, thought related to it.[3] Now, in Aristotle, "custom" (ἔθος) is contrasted with "nature" (φύσις) in that "nature is conceived with that which is always (ἀεί); custom with that which is

[1] *De Rer. Nat.* V, 924.
[2] *De Nat. Deor.* I, 19, 50; I, 39, 109.
[3] Cf. below, p. 556, at n. 28.

often (πολλάκις)," [4] and hence it is also contrasted with "necessity" (ἀνάγκη), for "that which is necessity is at the same time always." [5] With this in the back of their minds, the masters of the Kalam, believing as they did that the regularity of the successive events in the world is subject to infringement by the miraculous working of God, found in the term custom, which refers to events occurring not always but only often, a suitable description of the regularity of the successive events which, according to them, may be infringed upon by miracles.

This conception of custom is ascribed by Ibn Ḥazm to the Ashʿarites, of whom he says that they used the term "custom" instead of "nature" as a designation of the normal course of events of which miracles are an infringement.[6] It is, therefore, this Ashʿarite conception of custom that Abū Rashīd, we may assume, has reference to in his tentative suggestion of the assumption of "an act of God by way of custom" [7] as a possible explanation of the phenomenon that fire is always produced by striking on a stone [8] and that air, under certain conditions, is always transformed into water.[9] Ṭūsī, much later, ascribes this conception of custom to Ashʿarī himself, whom he quotes as maintaining that "the repeated actions of God are performed by Him by causing the continuance of the custom (*bi-ijrāʾ al-ʿādah*)." [10]

There was thus a theory of custom among the Ashʿarites prior to the time of Ghazālī, for both Ibn Ḥazm (d. 1064) and Abū Rashīd (d. ca. 1068) died when Ghazālī (b. 1058)

[4] *Rhet.* I, 11, 1370a, 8–9.
[5] *De Gen. et Corr.* II, 11, 337b, 35.
[6] *Fiṣal,* V, p. 15, ll. 21–23; cf. p. 14, l. 23.
[7] *Masāʾil,* p. 36, l. 8.
[8] *Ibid.,* l. 7.
[9] *Ibid.,* p. 37, l. 17 – p. 38, l. 4.
[10] *Muḥaṣṣal,* p. 29, n. 1, l. 3. Literally, "by setting the custom *a-running,*" and so does Ḥarizi translate the expression *ajrā . . . al-ʿādah* (*Moreh* I, 73, Prop. 6, p. 140, l. 24) literally by "He set the custom a-running," whereas Ibn Tibbon translates it freely by "He instituted the custom?" The same Ibn Tibbon, however, translated the expression *jary ʿādah* (*Moreh* I, 73, Prop. 10, p. 144, l. 17) by *hemshek ʿādah,* "a continuance of custom."

was only a boy. This explains why the term custom is broached by Ghazālī allusively in such an offhand and casual manner and why, as will be noticed, it is treated by him as something already well known which he found to be useful in his attempt to solve a difficulty raised by himself tentatively against the denial of causality which he has just finished defending. The difficulty tentatively raised by him, it may be added, is to the effect that the denial of causality with its attribution of every event to the arbitrary will of God might lead to a denial of the reality of our sense perceptions. Thus — to quote but one of the several examples mentioned by him — a man might be led to believe that an object, which was a book when he left the house and which still appears to him to be a book on his return to the house, was really changed by God into a boy during his absence from the house and the reason that it still appears to him to be a book is that God did not create in him the faculty of seeing that which was once a book as it now really is.[11] It is in answer to this difficulty that Ghazālī makes use of the Ashʿarite theory of custom.

It happens, however, that this theory of custom in its original Ashʿarite formulation was criticized by both the non-Ashʿarite orthodox Ibn Ḥazm and by the Muʿtazilite Abū Rashīd. Their criticisms, though formally different, equally argue that the theory of custom, with its restrictive meaning of "often," does not fully explain the constancy observed in the regularity of the sequence of certain events which are not broken off by miracles. Thus Ibn Ḥazm argues that the term

[11] *Tahāfut al-Falāsifah* XVII, 11, p. 283, ll. 9 ff. It is interesting to note that the same argument that is used here by Ghazālī to prove the existence of custom was used before him by Saadia to prove, presumably against the Mutakallimūn, that God does not change the order of nature arbitrarily without some reason or purpose which He makes known to men beforehand. Cf. *Emunot* III, 4, p. 121, ll. 7–10: "For if we were to assume this [namely, that God changes things arbitrarily for no reason or purpose at all], then our confidence in the fixity of things would be shaken. None of us would then be sure, upon his returning to his dwelling and family, whether the All-Wise had not changed their essences and whether they were not different from the way in which he had left them." It would seem that Saadia and Ghazālī followed a common source.

"custom (*ʿādah*) in the Arabic language" is used with reference to something which may either be avoided or not be avoided, in contradistinction to the term "nature" which is used with reference to something the avoidance of which is impossible.[12] Abū Rashīd, evidently having in mind Aristotle's statement that "nature is concerned with that which is always; custom with that which is often," [13] argues that the theory of custom fails to explain why, for instance, in the production of fire by the act of striking on a stone, the effect "always occurs in the same way," [14] seeing that "if it were due to custom, it would not be impossible that there should be a stone from which no fire could at all be struck." [15] The argument behind the statements of both Ibn Ḥazm and Abū Rashīd is that, if one tries to explain the regularity in the sequence of events by an action on the part of God which, after the analogy of a certain type of regularity in human actions, is called custom, then the actions of God, like the actions of man, must be assumed to be subject to deviations — not deviations of the kind called miracles, but deviations which are not miraculous.

Ghazālī must have been aware of these criticisms of the Ashʿarite theory of custom, for the passage in which he introduces the theory of custom contains two statements which, as we shall see, try to show how the theory of custom can be made to explain the constancy of the real observable regularity in the order of the sequence of events. The two statements are as follows: (1) "God has created in us the knowledge that He will not do these things [that is, things like that of changing a book into a boy], although they are possible." [16] (2) "The continuous recurrence of the custom (*al-ʿādah*) in them again and again fixes in our mind the indelible impression that they will continue to follow a course of behavior in accordance with their past custom." [17]

That these two statements are attempts to explain both

[12] *Fiṣal*, V, p. 115, l. 24 – p. 116, l. 3.
[13] *Rhet.* I, 11, 1370a, 8–9.
[14] *Masāʾil*, p. 36, ll. 9–11.
[15] *Ibid.*, p. 36, ll. 11–12; cf. p. 38, ll. 5–7.
[16] *Tahāfut al-Falāsifah* XVII, 13, p. 285, ll. 9–10.
[17] *Ibid.*, ll. 11–12.

the reality and the constancy of the order observed in the sequence of events is clear. But what he means by "the knowledge" created in us and by "the impression" infixed in our mind calls for clarification. The first statement certainly cannot mean that God created in us some power by which we always know that the order of events observed by us in the past will not be changed in the future nor certainly can the second statement mean that it is the order of events observed by us in the past that creates in our mind the impression that it will continue in the future, for, if so taken, then these statements would be in opposition to Ghazālī's own view that the performances of the various faculties of the soul in furnishing us the various kinds of knowledge are "observable facts in which God has caused the continuance of the custom (*ajrā al-'ādah*)"[18] that is to say, they follow in each case a certain sequence of order by God's custom of creating them each directly in that order. These statements are, therefore, to be taken to mean that, ever since the creation of the world, whenever God creates certain events in succession to other events, He creates in men the knowledge or the impression that, barring miracles, the same events will continue to be created by Him in the future in the same order of succession.

It is thus not nature and causality — not even nature and causality implanted in things by God — but rather custom plus a repeatedly created knowledge that the custom will continue, that explains the regularity and the predictability of certain phenomena. When, therefore, Ghazālī in his Introduction to his *Tahāfut* argues in favor of the philosophers' explanation of the lunar eclipse as being caused by the interposition of the earth between the moon and the sun and of their explanation of the solar eclipse as being caused by the interposition of the moon between the observer and the sun, and when he also expresses his belief in the predictability of eclipses,[19] it does not mean that he agrees with the philos-

[18] *Ibid.* XVIII, 10, p. 303, l. 12.

[19] *Ibid.*, Intr., 13–16, p. 10, l. 14 – p. 13, l. 3.

ophers in the belief that there exists a causal nexus respectively between the lunar or the solar eclipse and the particular position of the earth or of the moon. What Ghazālī means to say is that it is the custom of God to create a lunar or a solar eclipse simultaneously with His creation of the particular position of the earth or of the moon, but it is also the custom of God, simultaneously with these two simultaneous creations, to create in our mind the knowledge or the impression that an eclipse either of the moon or of the sun will occur regularly at certain intervals under the same circumstances, unless He would will to change His custom.

It is to be noted, however, that in his *Iḥyā'* Ghazālī uses the term *sunnah* as the equivalent of *'ādah* with reference to the theory of custom and he uses the term "condition" (*sharṭ*) as a substitute for the rejected term "cause" (*sabab*, *'illah*). Thus, after stating that created things follow one another in a certain order of succession "in accordance with God's customary procedure (*sunnah*) with regard to His created things," [20] he goes on to explain that, in accordance with that customary procedure of God, "one created thing is a condition (*sharṭ*) for another," so that one is to say that "the creation of life is a condition for the creation of knowledge, not that knowledge is produced (*yatawallad*) by life." [21] It is to this passage in Ghazālī's *Iḥyā'* that Averroes quite evidently refers when in the course of his criticism of the denial of causality he says that "the Mutakallimūn acknowledge that there are conditions (*shurūṭ*) which are necessary to the conditioned, as when they say that life is a condition (*sharṭ*) of knowledge." [22]

It is also to be noted that in his *Iḥyā'* Ghazālī sometimes uses the term "cause" in the sense of what we have seen he uses the term "condition." Thus, after stating that "whatever the difference of the events may be, it points to a difference

[20] *Iḥyā'*, *Kitāb al-Taubah*, Section: *Bayān Wujūb al-Taubah* (IV, p. 6, ll. 9–10).

[21] *Ibid.* (ll. 15–18); cf. above at n. 18.

[22] *Tahāfut al-Falāsifah* XVII, 7, p. 521, l. 16 – p. 522, l. 1.

of the causes (*al-asbāb*), he goes on to say: "This is known from the customary procedure (*sunnah*) in making effects consequences of causes (*al-asbāb*)," [23] and thus also, when angel and Satan are each described by him as "cause," [24] the term is used by him loosely, for in reality neither of them is a cause; they are each only a messenger of God carrying out His bidding.[25] So also the Epicureans, as well as Hume, despite their denial of causality, do not hesitate to use the term cause in a loose sense.[25a]

It is similarly to be noted that, when in his *Iḥyā'* he describes the cleavage of water by a man's falling into it as a "natural act," [26] he uses the term "natural" in the sense of "customary."

3. AVERROES' CRITICISM OF THE DENIAL OF CAUSALITY AND OF THE THEORY OF CUSTOM

Criticisms of both the Mutakallimūn and Ghazālī for their denial of causality are to be found in several works of Averroes and in one of his works there is a criticism of the theory of custom aimed directly at Ghazālī's presentation of it. His criticisms of the denial of causality group themselves into five arguments; his criticism of the theory of custom makes up one of them. All these five arguments are used by Averroes to show that the views criticized by him are at variance with certain philosophic statements to which he alludes only slightly. In order, therefore, to bring out the full meaning of these arguments, I shall begin my exposition of each one of them with a reproduction of what I have reason to believe to be the philosophic statement alluded to in it and then I shall reproduce the argument itself either in full or in abridgment.

But before dealing with these five arguments individually,

[23] *Iḥyā', Kitāb Sharḥ Aja'ib al-Ḳalb*, Section: *Bayān Tasallūṭ al-Shayṭān* (III, p. 25, ll. 32–33).

[24] *Ibid.* (l. 35).

[25] Cf. above, p. 520.

[25a] Cf. *Religious Philosophy*, pp. 211–212, and above, p. 192.

[26] *Iḥyā', Kitāb al-Tauḥīd wa'l-Tawakkul*, Section: *Bayān Ḥaḳīḳah al-Tauḥīd* (IV, p. 248, l. 18).

I shall quote several passages, in one of which Averroes restates and criticizes one of those views of the Mutakallimūn on duration, of which, as we have seen, their view on the denial of causality is an indirect implication,[1] while in the others he restates directly that view of the Mutakallimūn on the denial of causality. All these passages are from his Commentaries on Aristotle.

In one passage, drawing upon Aristotle's statement that "the physicists" say that "things are always in flux and decay," [2] that is to say, things are constantly being destroyed, he comments that "the Mutakallimūn (*Loquentes*) of our religion are following the ancients therein and they thus say that accidents do not endure for two instants." [3] He then goes on to say: "But while the statement of the ancients is in accordance with the process of nature, the statement of the Mutakallimūn of our religion is groundless, for they have been driven to make this statement by no other reason except their desire to defend baseless principles, believing as they do that the revealed Law cannot be defended except by these principles." [4] In another passage, he reports of "the Mutakallimūn of the people of our religion" that "they say that there is one Agent for all existent things, one who attends to them personally without any intermediate.[5] . . . They thus deny that it is fire that burns and that it is water that moistens and that it is bread that satisfies hunger, maintaining that all these things require a Creator and Originator," [6] to which in a parallel passage he adds that the one Agent who acts without intermediation is "God" and that from this view of the Mutakallimūn it follows that "no existent thing has an action appropriate to it by nature." [7]

[1] Cf. above, p. 523.

[2] *Phys.* VIII, 8, 265a, 6.

[3] Averroes, *In VIII Phys.*, Comm. 74, p. 418 I K.

[4] *Ibid.*, K. Cf. Maimonides above, p. 55 at n. 65; p. 470, at n. 26.

[5] Averroes, *In XII Metaph.*, Comm. 18, Arabic: p. 1503, l. 16 – p. 1504, l. 1; Latin: VIII, p. 305 F.

[6] *Ibid.*, p. 1504, ll. 2–4; *ibid.*, p. 305 G.

[7] Averroes, *In IX Metaph.*, Comm. 7, Arabic: p. 1135, l. 15 – p. 1136, l. 1; Latin: VIII, p. 231 H.

Now for his five arguments against the Mutakallimūn's denial of a nature and causality.

First, in Aristotle there are the statements that "we suppose ourselves to possess unqualified scientific knowledge (ἐπίστασθαι) of a thing . . . when we think we know the cause (αἰτίαν) on which the fact depends" [8] and that "wisdom (σοφία) investigates into the cause of visible things." [9] With these statements in the back of his mind, Averroes says: "You should know that he who denies that causes, by the decree of God, influence things caused by them denies wisdom (*al-ḥikmah*) and scientific knowledge (*al-ʿilm*), for scientific knowledge is the knowledge of things by their causes and wisdom is the knowledge of invisible causes." [10]

Second, having in mind Aristotle's statement that "all men by nature desire knowledge (τοῦ εἰδέναι) [11] and that "knowledge" (τὸ εἰδέναι), that is, "scientific knowledge" (τὸ ἐπίστασθαι), is concerned with causes,[12] he says: "To deny causes altogether is to alienate from human nature that which properly belongs to it." [13]

Third, having in mind a certain statement by Ghazālī himself, he tries to show that by denying causality Ghazālī has invalidated his own statement. The statement of Ghazālī which Averroes had in mind here reads as follows: "Mankind is divided into two classes, one, the men of truth, who believe that the world came into being and know by logical necessity that that which comes into being does not come into being by itself but needs a Maker." [14] The reference here is to the Mutakallimūn, whose chief argument for the existence of God is based upon their belief in the creation of the world,

[8] *Anal. Post.* I, 2, 71b, 9–11; cf. *Phys.* I, 1, 184a, 10–14.

[9] *Metaph.* I, 9, 992a, 24–25; I, 1, 981b, 28.

[10] *Kashf*, p. 112, ll. 6–9; cf. *Faṣl*, p. 38, l. 17 – p. 39, l. 7; *Tahāfut al-Tahāfut* XVII, 6, p. 522, ll. 9–11.

[11] *Metaph.* I, 1, 980a, 21.

[12] *Phys.* I, 1, 184a, 10–11.

[13] *Kashf*, p. 112, ll. 9–10.

[14] *Tahāfut al-Falāsifah* IV, 1, p. 133, ll. 4–5; Averroes, *Tahāfut al-Tahāfut* IV, 1, p. 263, ll. 4–5.

which argument is reproduced by Averroes himself in one of his works,[15] where he characterizes it as the chief argument for the existence of God used by the Ash'arites. Now this argument for the existence of God from creation is exactly the argument used by Plato, and in Plato this argument is framed in terms of causality, reading: "All that comes to be must needs be brought into being by some cause."[16] With this in the back of his mind, Averroes says: "By denying causes in the visible world, one has no way of establishing the existence of an efficient cause in the invisible world, for judgment about the invisible in this matter is to be only in accordance with judgment about the visible, and consequently those who deny causality have no way of arriving at a knowledge of the existence of God, inasmuch as in consistency with their view they are bound not to admit the proposition which says that for every action there is an agent."[17]

Fourth, an argument consisting of three parts, each of them reflecting a statement in Aristotle.

Back of the first part of the argument is a statement by Aristotle to the effect that the "essence" (*τὸ τί ἦν εἶναι*) of a thing is the cause (*αἴτιον*) of why a certain one thing is a certain other thing or why a thing is subject to a certain action, as, for instance, in the inquiry as to "why man is an animal of such-and-such a kind" or in the question, "Why does it thunder?" or rather, "Why is sound produced in the clouds?"[18] Reflecting this statement, Averroes argues: "For it is self-evident that things have essences and attributes which determine the peculiar actions of each thing and through which the essences and names and definitions of things are differentiated, so that [conversely], if a thing had not its peculiar action, it would have no nature which is peculiar to

[15] *Kashf*, p. 29, l. 14 – p. 30, l. 2.

[16] *Tim.* 28 A.

[17] *Kashf*, p. 112, ll. 10–13; cf. *TaTahaf* XVII, 3, p. 519, ll. 12–15. See a similar argument by Baghdādī in *Uṣūl*, p. 138, l. 17 – p. 139, l. 1, quoted below, p. 652.

[18] *Metaph.* VII, 17, 1041a, 20–28.

it, and if it had not its peculiar nature, it would have no name and no definition peculiar to it, with the result that all things would be one."[19]

Back of the second part of the argument is Aristotle's statement that "the motion of a simple body is simple and a simple motion is of a simple body,"[20] upon which Averroes himself has commented that "inasmuch as the same [i.e., one] nature is the principle of one motion" . . . "bodies in which there are more than one nature ought to have more than one motion,"[21] from which he must have inferred that, conversely, if things have no motions they have no natures and hence if a thing [which is described as one] has no motion it has no nature and, having no nature, it is not one. Reflecting on these statements, Averroes continues to argue that, if particular things have no particular natures of their own, not only could they not be particular things, with names and definitions of their own, they could not even constitute one thing, "for it might be asked whether this one has one appropriate activity of its own or one appropriate passivity of its own, or whether it has not, and if it has an appropriate activity of its own, then there would indeed exist appropriate acts proceeding from appropriate natures, but if it had no single appropriate activity of its own, then the one would not be one."[22]

Back of the third part of the argument in Aristotle's statement that "being and unity are the same and are one nature in the sense that they are implied in one another as the terms principle and cause are."[23] Reflecting this statement Averroes concludes: "But if the nature of unity is denied, the nature of being is denied, and the consequence of the denial of being is non-being."[24]

[19] *TaTahaf*. XVII, 5, p. 520, ll. 10–15. The Arabic *li-mā* in l. 24 should be emended to read *lam*, corresponding to *lo* in the Hebrew version. Cf. the same argument in Averroes, *In IX Metaph*., Comm. 7, vol. VIII, p. 231 HI (Arabic, p. 1135, l. 15 – p. 1136, l. 15.

[20] *De Caelo* I, 2, 269a, 3–4.

[21] Averroes, *In De Caelo*, Comm. 8, p. 6 L.

[22] *TaTahaf* XVII, 5, p. 520, l. 15 – p. 521, l. 2.

[23] *Metaph*. IV, 2, 1003b, 22–24.

[24] *TaTahaf* XVII, 5, p. 521, ll. 2–3.

Fifth, the argument aimed at the theory of custom, in which Averroes tries to refute three possible meanings of the theory: (1) that it is the custom of God to act repeatedly in the same way; (2) that it is the custom of things to come into existence repeatedly in the same way; (3) that it is the custom of man to form a judgment that the coming of things into existence is repeatedly in the same way. His refutation of these three possible meanings is as follows:

(1) Having in mind Aristotle's statement that "things which are the result of custom are those which are done because they have been done often (πολλάκις)" [25] and using the Arabic phrase *'alā al-akthar*, which technically means "for the most part," [26] in the loose sense of "often," for which technically the Arabic is *kathīran*,[27] he argues that, if custom is used in the sense of its being the custom of God, it would follow that God had acquired the custom to act repeatedly in the same way by His having acted often in that same way, for "custom (*al-'ādah* = ἔθος) is a habit (*malakah* = ἕξις) which an agent acquires and from which a repetition of his act follows often (*'alā al-akthar*)." [28] But this, implying as it would a change in God, would be contrary to the Koranic teaching: "Thou shalt not find any change in the way of God; yea, thou shalt not find any variations in the way of God" (35:40, 41).[29]

(2) Having in mind Aristotle's statement that "inanimate objects perform each of their actions in virtue of a certain nature but artisans perform theirs through custom" [30] and remembering that occasionally in describing the actions of

[25] *Rhet.* I, 10, 1369b, 6–7.

[26] Thus the Greek ἐπὶ τὸ πολύ in *Anal. Pri.* II, 27, 70a, 2, where it is used as a description of probability, is translated by this Arabic phrase (see Arabic translation of the *Organon*, p. 301, l. 15). So also *aktharriyyah*: *me'odiyyim* in *Moreh Nebukim* II, 20, p. 217, l. 28, stands for the Greek ἐπὶ τὸ πολύ in *Phys.* II, 5, 196b, 11.

[27] So used as a translation of the Greek πολλάκις in *De Anima* III, 9, 417b, 30; see Arabic translation of *De Anima*, p. 81, l. 11.

[28] *TaTahaf.* XVII, 10, p. 523, ll. 5–6.

[29] *Ibid.*, ll. 6–7.

[30] *Metaph.* I, 1, 981b, 3–5.

inanimate objects Aristotle uses loosely the term custom in the sense of nature, as, for instance, in his statements that "it is the custom of moisture to combine with particles of water" [31] and remembering also that, according to Aristotle, "that which is the result of nature . . . takes place always or for the most part (ἐπὶ τὸ πολύ) in the same way," [32] he argues as follows: "If they mean that it is a custom in existent things, then [they are wrong, for] custom applies only to an animate being and, if it is used with reference to an inanimate object, it really means nature, but this is not being denied,[33] that is to say, [it is not at all denied by the philosophers] that existing things have a nature which determines the [action of each] thing either necessarily [that is, always] or for the most part (*aktharriy-yan*)." [34]

(3) The refutation of the third meaning of the theory of custom consists of two parts.

(a) Having in mind his own rephrasing of Aristotle's description of custom (*'ādah*=ἔθος) as "a habit (*malakah*=ἕξις) which an agent acquires" [35] and having in mind Aristotle's statement that the faculty by which the soul judges things is called "intellect" [36] and having also in mind that what the

[31] *De Plantis* II, 2, 823a, 33. [32] *Rhet.* I, 10, 1369a, 35 – 1369b, 2.

[33] On the basis of the Hebrew translation and the Latin translation from the Hebrew, which have here the reading *bilti mukḥash*, *non negamus* (p. 130 F), I take it that the Arabic here is to be *ghayr munkar*, "not being denied," instead of *ghayr mumkin*, "not possible," as it now stands in the Bouyges edition (p. 523, l. 9). Shem-ṭob Falaquera's paraphrase of this passage in his *Moreh ha-Moreh*, I, 73, Prop. 6, p. 57, has here *eno raḥok*, "it is not improbable," which similarly reflects the reading *ghayr munkar*. That this was the original reading of the text is supported by Averroes' own statement later that "custom . . . can be found . . . in existent things, and this, as we said, is what the philosophers designate by nature" (§ 24, p. 531, l. 16 – p. 532, l. 2). The reference in the last statement is to those passages in Aristotle alluded to by Averroes above, that what in animate beings is called custom is in inanimate beings called nature and that sometimes Aristotle describes that which is custom by the term nature (cf. at nn. 24–25 above). Van den Bergh, following the reading of the printed Arabic text, finds Averroes to be contradicting himself (see his note 6 to p. 325 of his translation).

[34] *TaTahaf* XVII, 10, p. 523, ll. 8–10.

[35] Cf. above at n. 21.

[36] *De Anima* III, 3, 428a, 3–5; 12, 434b, 3.

commentators of Aristotle call "the intellect in habit" (*al-'aḳl bi'l-malakah* = ὁ καθ' ἕξιν νοῦς) is defined by himself as "that which is the perfection of the material intellect" [37] or as that "in which the intelligible objects exist in actuality," [38] he argues as follows: "As for custom in the sense of our forming a judgment about existing things, custom used in this sense is nothing but an act of the intellect which is determined by its own nature and through which it becomes an intellect, but such a custom the philosophers do not deny," [39] that is to say, the philosophers have no objection to the description of man's judgment by the term custom.

(b) But, then, reasoning that, in view of the fact that custom is contrasted by Aristotle with necessity [40] and that hypothesis is similarly contrasted by him with necessity,[41] an act which is the result of custom is properly to be described as hypothetical, and, alluding to an earlier argument of his in which he tried to show that the Ash'arite denial of "necessity" in created things means a denial of "wisdom" both in created things and in the Creator,[42] Averroes goes on to argue against this third possible meaning of the theory of custom as follows: "The term custom is, as it were, a specious term. Underneath it, when closely examined, there is to be discerned no other meaning than that of its referring to a hypothetical act, such as when we say that it is the custom of so-and-so to act in such-and-such a way, by which is meant that he will act in that way for the most part (*fī al-akthar*). But if this were so, then all existing things would be hypothetical and there would not be [in them] any wisdom from which it might be inferred concerning the Creator that He is wise." [43]

[37] *Epitome of De Anima*, p. 83, ll. 6–7 (in *Rasā'il Ibn Rushd*, Hyderabad, 1366/1947); p. 85, ll. 17–18 (ed. Ahmed Fouad El Ahwani, Cairo, 1950).

[38] *Ibid*., p. 84, ll. 6–7; p. 87, l. 2.

[39] *TaTahaf* XVII, 10, p. 523, ll. 10–13.

[40] Cf. above, pp. 545–546.

[41] *Anal. Post.* I, 10, 76b, 23–24.

[42] *TaTahaf*. I, 169, p. 92, ll. 9–13. Cf. *Kashf*, p. 88, ll. 12–13: "He who maintains a denial of nature does away with a great part of things existing in the world which lead to the demonstration of the existence of the omniscient Agent."

[43] *TaTahaf*. XVII, 10, p. 523, l. 13 – p. 524, l. 1.

II. Affirmation of Causality *

In his exposition of the Mutakallimūn's views on duration and destruction and their denial of causality, Maimonides remarks: "Some of them asserted causality and were blamed for doing so." [1] As to who were those who asserted causality and were blamed for doing so, Maimonides does not say. Nor is there any record of an open controversy within the Kalam over the general problem of causality similar to the controversies over other problems, such, for instance, as the problems of attributes, the eternity of the Koran, and free will.[2] It happens, however, that the denial of causality is often expressed by certain circumlocutions or by certain terms used as the equivalent of causality. One of those terms is "nature." Thus Ghazālī, in his denial of causality against the philosophers who supported it, says that the philosophers believe that things affect each other by a nature which they possess,[3] and Averroes, in his refutation of Ghazālī, argues that the denial of causality is tantamount to a denial that things have a nature [4] and that the Mutakallimūn of the Ash'arites deny "the action of the natural powers which God has put in existent things." [5] Similarly Maimonides describes the denial of causality as a denial of the belief "that there exists a nature and that in any given body it is nature which determines that such and such an accident should accrue to it." [6] And so also Ibn Ḫaldūn, referring to the denial of causality by the Mutakallimūn, simply says: "They denied nature." [7] This use of

* Reprinted with many revisions and extended additions from *Mélanges Alexandre Koyré*, 1964, vol. II, pp. 602–618, where it appeared under the heading "The Controversy over Causality within the Kalam."

[1] *Moreh* I, 73, p. 141, l. 11.

[2] The section in Ash'arī's *Maḳālāt*, p. 389, l. 2 – p. 391, l. 7, under the heading "They Differ with Regard to Causes," does not deal with the problem of causality in general but with the problem of causality in human action, that is, with the problem of free will.

[3] *Tahāfut al-Falāsifah* XVII, 3, p. 278, ll. 10–13.

[4] *Tahāfut al-Tahāfut* XVII, 5, p. 520, ll. 12–13.

[5] *Kashf*, p. 88, ll. 4–5.

[6] *Moreh* I, 73, Prop. 6, p. 140, ll. 4–6.

[7] *Muḳaddimah*, III, p. 114, ll. 9–10.

the term nature in the sense of cause reflects, of course, Aristotle's definition of nature as "a certain principle and cause of motion and rest to that in which it is primarily inherent, essentially and not according to accident." [8]

And so, in order to find out who in the Kalam asserted causality and were blamed for doing so, let us look for those who asserted nature and were blamed for doing so.

Two candidates for the assertion of causality through their assertion of nature are to be found.

One of them is Muʿammar. Of him there are the following reports. First, "God created none of the accidents," [9] which brief statement is explained in a longer parallel statement as follows: "God created nothing but bodies. As for accidents, they are the products (*iḫtirāʿāt*) of the bodies themselves, either by nature, as burning is produced by fire, heat by the sun, and coloring by the moon, or by choice, as motion and rest and composition and separation are produced by living beings." [10] Second, "God is described as being powerful only with reference to substances, but, as for accidents, God cannot be described as powerful with reference to them; He did not create either life or death, either health or illness, either power or weakness, either color or taste or odor, all these being the act of substances by their nature." [11] Third, "every accident in a body results from the action of the body by its nature (*ṭabʿ*; *ṭibāʿ*)." [12] Fourth, "sounds, according to him, are the acts of bodies which are sonorous by their nature. The destruction of a body, according to him, is the act of the body by its own nature. The success of seed or its failure is an act of the seed itself, according to him. He also maintains that the destruction of any destructible thing occurs to it as an act by its own nature. He, furthermore, maintains that God exercises neither action nor power over accidents. And in

[8] *Phys.* II, 1, 192b, 20–23.
[9] Baghdādī, *Farḳ*, p. 137, ll. 4–5; *Maḳālāt*, p. 199, ll. 1–2.
[10] Shahrastānī, *Milal*, p. 46, ll. 3–6. Cf. Baghdādī, *Uṣūl*, p. 135, ll. 4–8.
[11] *Maḳālāt*, p. 548, ll. 9–12.
[12] *Farḳ*, p. 136, ll. 15, 16.

accordance with his view that God creates neither life nor death, he brands as false God's description of himself as one who gives life and causes death, for how can one who created neither life nor death give life or death?"[13] Fifth, "when atoms are aggregated, accidents necessarily result; the atoms produce them by the necessity of nature, each atom producing in itself whatever accident abides in it."[14] The cumulative effect of all these passages is that God, in the creation of the world, created only atoms and their aggregation into bodies; that in each atom there is a nature; that, when the aggregation of atoms formed a body, the totality of the natures of the atoms formed the nature of the body; so that, when each atom in that aggregation produces by its nature accidents in itself, also the body as a whole produces by its nature accidents in itself.

Another candidate for the affirmation of causality through an affirmation of nature is Naẓẓām. But concerning his view there are two contradictory statements in Ashʿarī, and so we shall first have to determine which of these two statements is to be followed.

One of these statements about Naẓẓām in Ashʿarī reads as follows: "He used to say, according to what is reported of him, that God created the bodies at one stroke[15] and that a body is created at every instant (*fī kulli waḳtin*)."[16] This quite evidently means a belief in continuous creation and hence a denial of causality. The other statement in Ashʿarī about Naẓẓām reads as follows: "He used to say that that which occurs outside the range of man is the work of God by the necessitation of a natural disposition[17] possessed by a thing, as, for instance, the moving forward of a stone when somebody throws it forward, or its moving downward

[13] *Ibid.*, l. 15 – p. 137, l. 3; *Maḳālāt*, p. 548, ll. 9–12.

[14] *Maḳālāt*, p. 303, ll. 10–11.

[15] Cf. above, p. 511.

[16] *Maḳālāt*, p. 404, ll. 10–11.

[17] On the basis of *Milal*, p. 38, l. 16, the term *ḫlkh* in *Maḳālāt*, p. 404, l. 5, is to have two dots on the final *h*, thus reading *ḫilḳah*, the same as the term which occurs later in l. 7.

when somebody throws it downward, or its moving upward when somebody throws it in an upward direction. . . . The meaning of this is that God has stamped the stone with a nature that, when somebody throws it forward, it moves forward, and so also with regard to the other consequences of things known as generated effects." [18] The same statement about Naẓẓām in Shahrastānī, quoted from a report by Ka'bī, who was a contemporary of Ash'arī, begins as follows: "Everything that goes beyond [the action of man who is] the subject of the power of the action is the work of God by the necessitation of a disposition (*al-ḫilḳah*);" [19] and here follows the same example of the throwing of a stone as in Ash'arī. This second statement in Ash'arī and the same statement quoted by Shahrastānī from a report by Ka'bī quite evidently mean that Naẓẓām rejected continuous creation and affirmed causality.

Here then we have two contradictory reports of Naẓẓām's view on causality. The question, therefore, is as to which of these statements represents his real view.

In answer to this question, I shall try to show (1) that Ash'arī's first statement, described by Ash'arī himself as being "according to what is reported of him," is only part of a longer statement quoted by Ash'arī's older contemporary, Ḫayyāṭ, from a statement about Naẓẓām by Ibn al-Rāwandī, who in turn quoted it from a report by Jāḥiẓ, who was a student of Naẓẓām; (2) that Ḫayyāṭ doubted the genuineness of this report by Jāḥiẓ; (3) that, whether genuine or not, this report by Jāḥiẓ, as fully quoted by Ḫayyāṭ, does not mean an expression of belief in continuous creation and hence Ash'arī's first statement based upon it does not mean continuous creation.

(1) The longer statement about Naẓẓām, as quoted by Ḫayyāṭ from Ibn al-Rāwandī, who quoted it from a report of Naẓẓām by Jāḥiẓ, reads as follows: "He [that is, Naẓẓām] used to assert that God creates the world and that which is in it at every instant (*ḥāl*) without destroying it and restoring

[18] *Maḳālāt*, p. 404, ll. 4–9.

[19] *Milal*, p. 38, ll. 15–16.

it." [20] Ash'arī's first statement, in which Naẓẓām, "according to what is reported of him," is quoted as having used to say that "a body is created at every instant," is quite evidently part of the longer statement quoted by Ḫayyāṭ.

(2) Ḫayyāṭ's doubting of the genuineness of this report is expressed as follows: "This view has been reported of Naẓẓām by none except by 'Amr b. Baḥr al-Jāḥiẓ; but his fellow students reproached him for it." [21] The fact that Ash'arī himself, in his statement quoted above, saw it necessary to add, parenthetically as it were, that this view of Naẓẓām is "according to what is reported of him" would seem to indicate that he was not quite certain about its genuineness.

(3) Now for the evidence that the statement reported by Jāḥiẓ of Naẓẓām, upon which Ash'arī's first statement is based, does not mean continuous creation and hence that also Ash'arī's first statement based upon it does not mean continuous creation. To begin with, the term "destruction" among those who believe that God directly creates every event in the world means, as we have seen, either that after the reduction of something to nothing God directly creates it again out of nothing or that after the transformation of something into something else God creates it again out of that

[20] *Intiṣār* 31, p. 44, ll. 19–20, quoted verbatim in *Farḳ*, p. 126, ll. 11–12. It is evidently this statement that is paraphrased by Ibn Ḥazm in his *Fiṣal* as follows: "It is reported of al-Naẓẓām that he has said that everything that God creates He creates at every instant (*fī kulli waḳtin*) without annihilating it" (quoted by Schreiner [*Kalam*, p. 48, n. 6] from the Leyden manuscript of the *Fiṣal* II, p. 195b). In the printed edition of the *Fiṣal* (V, p. 54, ll. 23–24) the reading is "at one instant" (*fī waḳtin wāḥidin*) instead of "at every instant," which is quite evidently a corruption. So also is the statement in Ṭūsī on *Muḥaṣṣal*, p. 20, l. 6 of n. 1, based either directly or indirectly upon the statement in the *Intiṣār*.

[21] *Intiṣār* 31, p. 44, l. 21; cf. *Farḳ*, p. 126, ll. 12–14. Similarly Ḫayyāṭ denies the authenticity of another report by Ibn al-Rāwandī, evidently also on the authority of Jāḥiẓ, that Naẓẓām maintained that "the fire in a wick does not stay in it the twinkle of an eye and that what one sees of it at one instant is different from what one has seen of it at a preceding instant" (*Intiṣār* 23, p. 36, ll. 3–5). The unreliability of Jāḥiẓ as a reporter of the view of others is attested by Ibn Ḥazm (*Fiṣal*, IV, p. 181, ll. 17–23). Cf. Israel Friedlaender, "The Heterodoxies of the Shiites in the Presentation of Ibn Ḥazm," *JAOS*, 28 (1907), pp. 50–51.

something else.[22] Consequently, when in his report Jāḥiẓ says that "God creates the world and that which is in it at every instant, without destroying it and restoring it," the phrase "without destroying it" quite evidently shows that the expression "God creates," supplemented by the phrase "at every instant," does not mean that continuously "God creates" things out of nothing; it rather means that continuously "God creates" something out of something, and hence but for the use of the term "creates" the statement would mean that God governs all the continuous changes in the world through intermediate causes. But, then, in Ash'arī's second statement, as well as in the statement quoted by Shahrastānī from Ka'bī's report, it will be noticed, the necessary causal process in the various movements of a stone is described by Naẓẓām as "the work of God," by which is quite evidently meant that the necessary causal process in the world is due to a nature which God implanted in the world at the time of its creation and over which He continues to exercise supervision. Consequently, again, if we assume that the expression "God creates" is used by Jāḥiẓ in the broad sense of the expression "the work of God" used by Shahrastānī, then it would not mean that God is the direct creator of all the changes in the world but rather that He is their ultimate creator, and this by reason of the fact that the cause of these changes is a nature which God created and implanted in the world at its creation and over which He continues to exercise supervision.

Corroboration of the foregoing suggestion that the expression "God creates" in Jāḥiẓ' report is not to be taken to mean that God directly creates is to be found in Baghdādī who, prior to his quoting that report of Jāḥiẓ, describes it as representing Naẓẓām's belief that "substances and bodies renew themselves (*tatajaddadu*) instant after instant." [23] His use of the expression "renew themselves" instead of "are created" or even "are renewed" seems to show that Baghdādī felt that the expression "God creates" used by Jāḥiẓ was not to be taken

[22] Cf. above, p. 543.

[23] *Farḳ*, p. 126, ll. 10–11.

as meaning that God is the direct creator of substances and bodies. In the light of this, it is quite possible that the reproach on the part of Jāḥiẓ's fellow students was only with regard to his use of the term "creates."

This, then, is the conception of causality common to both Naẓẓām and Muʿammar. According to both of them, there is a nature in every body, and this nature is the cause of all the changing events in it. As for the origin of that nature, it was, according to both of them, implanted by God in the bodies upon His creation of the world. In the case of Naẓẓām, this is explicitly stated by him in the passage quoted above, where he says that the nature or disposition of the stone to move downward was created by God and impressed upon the stone at the time of creation. In the case of Muʿammar, it is not so clear, for he does not explicitly say that the nature of bodies was created in them or bestowed upon them by God. But from the fact that bodies are said by him to have been created by God and that accidents are said by him not to have been created by God, it may be inferred that his conception of God is that of a Creator and that, when something was held by him not to have been created by God, he would explicitly say so. We may, therefore, reasonably assume that, since he did not explicitly say that the nature of bodies was not created by God, it is because he believed that it was created together with His creation of bodies. That this was the view of Muʿammar may be gathered from a statement by Ḫayyāṭ, who, in the course of his criticism of an interpretation by Ibn al-Rāwandī of a certain view of Muʿammar, says of Muʿammar that he believed that "God endowed bodies with a natural disposition whereby they produce their forms naturally." [24] From the manner in which he makes this statement it is clear that he assumes that Ibn al-Rāwandī is in agreement with this representation of the view of Muʿammar as to the origin of the nature possessed by bodies.

While both Muʿammar and Naẓẓām agree that bodies have

[24] *Intiṣār* 33, p. 45, ll. 22–24.

a nature and that their nature was created by God, they differ on two points in their otherwise common theory of nature.

First, they differ as to what that nature is.

To Muʿammar, believing as he does in atoms, that nature, which he calls *maʿnā*, is something which exists in the atoms and through the atoms in bodies, in the latter of which the totality of *maʿānī* of their constituent atoms form their *maʿnā* and nature. It is this *maʿnā* or nature that is the cause of all the changing events in bodies, as well as the cause of the regularity in the successive order of all these changing events in bodies. This successive order, however, is not conceived by Muʿammar as a process of transitions from potentiality to actuality. To him, each event in the order of succession is something actual. We have already discussed Muʿammar's *maʿnā* above.[25] To Naẓẓām, however, following as he does the Aristotelian conception of potentiality and actuality, that nature which he describes as being latent in bodies is, like the Aristotelian conception of nature, the cause of all the changing events in bodies, as well as the cause of the regularity in the successive order of all these changing events, in the sense of its being the cause of their transition from potentiality to actuality. All this is presented by him in his theory of latency (*kumūn*) which we have discussed above in connection with his denial of atomism.[26]

In the light of this difference in their conception of nature as a causal principle, we shall now try to interpret the statements about duration and destruction which are reported in their names.

Of Naẓẓām there is a direct report by Ashʿarī as to his view on both duration and destruction. It reads as follows: "Al-Naẓẓām said, That which endures endures not by a duration and that which is destroyed is destroyed not by a destruction." [27] Now, ordinarily, among those Mutakallimūn who deny nature as a causal principle, the use of the expression "not by a duration" as an explanation of how that which

[25] Cf. above, pp. 147 ff. [26] Cf. above, pp. 495 ff. [27] *Maḳālāt*, p. 367, l. 7.

endures is enduring means, as we have seen, that the very act of creation by which God directly creates every event in the world involves duration.[28] Similarly, among them, the use of the expression "not by a destruction" as an explanation of how that which is destroyed is being destroyed ordinarily means, as we have seen, that which is destroyed is destroyed by itself when God ceases to create it.[29] Knowing, however, as we do, that Naẓẓām is opposed to those who deny nature as a causal principle, we are to interpret these two statements of his in accordance with his own conception of nature as a causal principle. Consequently, his statement that "that which endures endures not by a duration" is to be taken to mean that it endures by that nature in it which causes in it that continuous process of change which Aristotle describes by the term "generation" (γένεσις, *kaun*). Similarly, Naẓẓām's statement that "that which is destroyed is destroyed not by a destruction" is to be taken to mean that it is destroyed by that nature in it which causes in it that continuous process of change which Aristotle describes by the term "corruption" (φθορά, *fasād*).

Of Muʿammar there are two statements in Baghdādī's *Farḳ*. (1) "Any accident of a body comes from the action of the body by its nature," [30] which, on the basis of a statement in both Ibn Ḥazm's *Fiṣal* [31] and Shahrastānī's *Milal*,[32] means that it is created by the action of the nature of the body. (2) "The destruction of a body, according to him, is the action of the body by its nature." [33] Now, knowing as we do that the term "nature" is used by Muʿammar in the sense of *maʿnā* and knowing also as we do that, according to him, bodies are created directly by God,[34] we are to take these two statements to mean that, while an "accident" is created by a *maʿnā* in the body in which the accident resides, a "body" is only destroyed by a *maʿnā* in it, for, as to its creation, it is created directly by

[28] Cf. above, p. 537.
[29] Cf. above, p, 523.
[30] *Farḳ*, p. 136, l. 15.
[31] *Fiṣal* IV, p. 194, ll. 12–13.
[32] *Milal*, p. 46, l. 4.
[33] *Farḳ*, p. 136, l. 16.
[34] Cf. above
[34] Cf. above, p. 158.

God. In the light of this, when in his *Uṣūl* Baghdādī reports Muʿammar as maintaining that "the creation of a thing is something other than the thing and so is also the duration and destruction of the thing something other than the thing,"[35] the term "thing" here means "accident" and thus the meaning of the statement is that the creation and duration and destruction of an accident are due to a *maʿnā* in the body in which the accident resides. So also in Ashʿarī's statement that "Zurḳān reports of Muʿammar that he maintained that the creation of a thing is something other than the thing,"[36] the terms "thing" and "something other" refer respectively to "accident" and *maʿnā*. When, however, Ḫayyāṭ reports that "as for Muʿammar, he maintains that the destruction of a thing consists in something other than the thing,"[37] the terms "thing" and "something other," as may be judged from the context, refer to "body" and *maʿnā*. Finally, when Ibn Ḥazm reports that "Muʿammar is of the opinion that destruction is an attribute consisting in something other than that which is to be destroyed,"[38] the terms "attribute" and "something other" refer to *maʿnā* and the expression "that which is to be destroyed" refers to both "body" and "accident."

Thus, according to Muʿammar, in this world of ours, of which only the bodies and the atoms constituting the bodies were originally created by God, all the accidents of bodies are created and are enduring and are destroyed by a nature or *maʿnā* inherent in those bodies. Bodies, however, are only destroyed by a *maʿnā*; their creation is directly by God; and, as for their duration, it is probably involved in their creation — a view dealt with above.[39]

So much for the first difference between Naẓẓām and Muʿammar in their otherwise common theory of nature, the difference as to what that nature is.

[35] *Uṣūl*, p. 231, l. 4.
[36] *Maḳālāt*, p. 364, l. 12.
[37] *Intiṣār* 9, p. 22, l. 19.
[38] *Fiṣal* V, p. 41, ll. 23–24.
[39] Cf. above, pp. 533 ff.

Second, they differ as to the manner in which nature operates in the world.

To Naẓẓām, nature in its operation in the world is dependent upon God and is subject to change by the miraculous power of God. His view is evident from the careful wording of his statement quoted above [40] that every act of the body is "the work of God in accordance with a natural disposition" in that body. Nature to him is thus only an instrument which acts at the bidding of God. This view is still more evident from his statements about miracles. For though he did not admit all the miracles vouched for by tradition, he did admit the possibility of miracles. Thus, when Baghdādī reports of him that he denied such traditional miracles as the splitting of the moon, the praising of God by stones in the hand of Muhammad, and the springing forth of water from between his fingers [41] or when Baghdādī also reports of Naẓẓām that he denied the inimitability of the excellence of the literary form of the Koran,[42] it does not really mean that he denied the possibility of those miracles or that he really denied the miraculous character of the Koran and the miraculous power of prophecy; it only means that, in the case of miracles which are reported only by tradition, he denied the authenticity of the tradition and, in the case of miracles which are mentioned in the Koran, he had a different interpretation of the passages in which the alleged miracle is mentioned.

In fact, of the miracle of the splitting of the moon there were two interpretations. According to one interpretation, based upon certain traditions, among them a tradition by Ibn Masʿūd, the splitting of the moon, which is mentioned in the Koran (Surah 54:1), refers to an event which had already taken place in the time of Muhammad. According to another interpretation, maintained by certain commentators of the Koran, it refers to an event which is yet to take place in the future,

[40] Cf. above, p. 561.
[41] *Fark*, p. 114, ll. 6–8.
[42] *Ibid.*, p. 128, ll. 5–14.

at the approach of the day of judgment.[43] Now, Baghdādī himself suggests,[44] and Shahrastānī expressly says,[45] that Naẓẓām's denial of the miracle of the splitting of the moon was due to his distrust of the tradition transmitted by Ibn Mas'ūd. Certainly, from this explanation of Naẓẓām's denial of the past miracle it cannot be inferred that he also denied that the miracle would occur in the future. Consequently, when Baghdādī accuses Naẓẓām of denying the veracity of Surah 54: 1,[46] he has overlooked its other interpretation. Such also may be the explanation of Naẓẓām's denial of the other two miracles mentioned by Baghdādī. Similarly, his denial of the inimitability of the excellence of the literary form of the Koran means only that he gave a different interpretation to the verses (2:21; 6:92; 11:16; 17:90) upon which the orthodox conception of the inimitability of the Koran was based. To him, the verses did not mean that men cannot actually imitate the style and eloquence of the Koran; they only meant that God deprived men of a desire to do so.[47] Naẓẓām's own belief in the miraculous power of prophecy as well as in the miraculous character of the Koran is explicitly affirmed by him in his acceptance as literally true the reports in the Koran of Muhammad's miraculous power to reveal things unknown, such as things past and future, things that are in the hearts of men, and things that men will say,[48] and also in his statement that the Koran, though not eternal, is "the work of God and His creation." [49]

On the whole, Naẓẓām's position on causality and miracles is analogous to that which Ghazālī ascribes to "the philosophers," by which in that particular context he means Alfarabi

[43] Cf. references to these two interpretations in the notes by Sale and Mulavi Muhammed Ali in their translations of the Koran *ad loc.*

[44] *Farḳ*, p. 135, l. 9.

[45] *Milal*, p. 40, ll. 16, 17.

[46] *Farḳ*, p. 135, ll. 8–11.

[47] *Maḳālāt*, p. 225, ll. 12–13; *Milal*, p. 39, ll. 15, 16–18.

[48] *Intiṣār* 15, p. 28, ll. 15–23; *Maḳālāt*, p. 225, ll. 11–12; *Farḳ*, p. 128, ll. 7–8; *Milal*, p. 39, ll. 15–16.

[49] *Maḳālāt*, p. 191, l. 12.

and Avicenna. These philosophers, according to Ghazālī, do not altogether deny the possibility of miracles; they only limit its scope, for, he says, they "affirm miracles that infringe upon the ordinary course of events only in three things" [50] and in the course of his discussion he mentions both those miracles which they deny and those which they affirm.

The miracles mentioned by Ghazālī as being denied by those philosophers are: first, the resurrection of the dead and the changing of the rod of Moses into a serpent, for, though both these miracles are recorded in the Koran, these philosophers, he says, interpret them figuratively; second, the splitting of the moon, which they denied, he says, because of their distrust of the tradition upon which it rested.[51] This is exactly, as we have seen, why Naẓẓām denied the miracle of the splitting of the moon. It is quite possible that under "the philosophers" Ghazālī meant to include Naẓẓām, for, though technically Naẓẓām is a Mutakallim and not a philosopher, he is described as one who "studied many philosophical works and mixed up their views with the views of the Muʿtazilites." [52]

The three miracles which Ghazālī says that the philosophers admit consist of what he describes as the extraordinary gifts of the prophets (1) to predict the future,[53] (2) to have a glimpse of the intelligibles,[54] and (3) to perform supernatural deeds in the outside world.[55] All these three gifts, according to Ghazālī, are admitted by the philosophers to be of a miraculous nature, even though they try to explain rationally how such miraculous powers of the prophets are not impossible. These miracles admitted by the philosophers are of the kind of miracles that, as we have seen, are ascribed by Naẓẓām to Muhammad. It is to be noted that Philo, who explicitly expresses his belief in miracles, does not accept all the extraor-

[50] *Tahāfut al-Falāsifah*, Phys., 7, p. 272, ll. 6–7.
[51] *Ibid.*, 6, p. 271, l. 10 – p. 272, l. 5.
[52] *Milal*, p. 37, ll. 5–6; cf. p. 38, l. 19; *Muḳaddimah*, III, p. 49, l. 5.
[53] *Tahāfut al-Falāsifah*, Phys., 7, p. 272, ll. 9–10.
[54] *Ibid.*, 9, p. 273, l. 12 – p. 274, l. 2.
[55] *Ibid.*, 11, p. 275, ll. 4–9.

dinary events recorded in the Hebrew Scripture as miracles; some of them are interpreted by him allegorically and some are explained by him rationally.[56]

Muʿammar, on the other hand, denies the possibility of miracles, for to him nature is independent of God and is not subject to any change by His will. This is evident from Muʿammar's own statements quoted above,[57] where, unlike Naẓẓām, he mentions only nature as that which produces accidents: no part in their production is assigned by him to God. It is still more evident from his statements, as quoted by Ibn al-Rāwandī, where he says that accidents, such as colors, tastes, odors, heat, and cold, and natural acts, such as motion, rest, aggregation, segregation, tangibility, separatedness, disease, illness, the blight of planets, life, and death, are all "the act of something other than God, and this act does not proceed from something living, powerful, and discerning, but rather from something inanimate, which is neither knowing nor powerful." [58] Even Ḫayyāṭ, who denies that Muʿammar attributed causality to nature alone, does not deny the authenticity of any of these statements attributed to Muʿammar. He only tries to vindicate Muʿammar from the charge of such extreme impiety by arguing that, inasmuch as God is admitted by Muʿammar to be the creator of nature, the God of Muʿammar may be regarded as a sort of remote cause of the accidents, a sort of an Aristotelian prime mover. Thus, in one place, after giving his aforementioned interpretation of Muʿammar, with which Ibn al-Rāwandī himself agrees, that "the forms of bodies are the natural acts of bodies in the sense that God endowed the bodies with a natural predisposition whereby they produce their forms naturally," he adds that "in spite of this," that is to say, in spite of Muʿammar's express statements that accidents, such, for instance, as the various colors of things, are produced by the nature of bodies, "he

[56] Cf. chapter on "The Immanent Logos, Laws of Nature, Miracles" in *Philo*, I, pp. 325–329.
[57] Cf. above at nn. 9–14.
[58] *Intiṣār* 33, p. 45, ll. 20–22; p. 46, ll. 1–4; 35, p. 47, ll. 7–8, 14.

believes that it is God who colors the heaven and the earth and everything else that is colored, in view of the fact that He created their natural disposition to produce color."[59] In another place, dealing with disease, illness, life, death, and the blight of plants, he does not deny the genuineness of the statement attributed to Muʿammar that they are the work of nature. He only argues that Muʿammar could not have meant that God had nothing to do with their production, and this because such a view would be against the Koranic verse that "He hath created death and life" (67:2).[60] Similarly, he does not deny the genuineness of the statement attributed to Muʿammar that "the Koran is not the work of God . . . but is the work of nature"; he only argues, evidently, again, on the ground of Muʿammar's belief that the nature of bodies was created by God, that, despite this express statement that the Koran is not the work of God but that of nature, "it is God who speaks through the Koran, the Koran is the word of God . . . and the Koran was created."[61] Finally, we have the testimony of Ibn Ḥazm, who, coupling Jāḥiẓ with Muʿammar, attributes to both of them the view that accidents are the work of nature, and from his discussion of that view it is quite evident that he took it to mean that it is the work of nature only, without any cooperation on the part of God.[62]

That a view like that we have found to be held by Muʿammar was current at his time may be gathered from the Karaite Abū (or Ibn) ʿAlī b. ʿAlī al-Baṣrī (Joseph ha-Levi). In an enumeration of various erroneous views current in the Arabic-speaking world, he mentions one which is exactly like that held by Muʿammar. He describes it as the view that "God, after creating the world, departed and left it to itself."[63] Though the author of this enumeration lived in the latter part

[59] *Ibid.* 33, p. 45, l. 24 – p. 46, l. 1.
[60] *Ibid.* 35, p. 47, ll. 7–8, 19–20.
[61] *Ibid.* 36, p. 48, ll. 2–5.
[62] *Fiṣal* III, p. 58, l. 21 – p. 59, l. 6; cf. below at nn. 57–61.
[63] Quoted from his commentary on the Minor Prophets; cf. S. Pinsker, *Likḳute Ḳadmoniyyot* [I], p. 26.

of the tenth century, the views enumerated by him date from an earlier period, for one of the views mentioned by him, namely, the denial of the resurrection of the body, is said by him to have been followed by the Karaite Mūsā al-Zaʿfrānī or al-Tiflisī (Moses ha-Parsi), who was a contemporary of Muʿammar.[64] The prototype of this view is to be discerned in the *Timaeus*. According to Plato in the *Timaeus*, the world was created, as he says, by the will of the Creator,[65] who upon its creation implanted in it a rational soul to govern it according to certain laws,[66] which may be called laws of nature, but these laws of nature were to be unchangeable, being described by their own Creator as "fated laws," [67] so that their Creator himself has no control over them.

According to Muʿammar, then, God who created the atoms and the bodies of the world and who created in them also a nature or *maʿnā* which is the principle of the laws of causality in the world, has abandoned these laws of causality, as it were, and allowed them to operate by themselves without any interference on His part. Muʿammar was aware, of course, of the Koranic teaching that God knows everything and is present everywhere (Surah 58:8), but this is taken by him to mean that God is present everywhere in the sense that it is He who has designed the laws of causality by which all things in the world take place and also in the sense that, despite the fact that He does not interfere in the operation of these laws, He knows all the things in the world that take place by their operation. This is what is to be taken to be the meaning of the statement which, as reported in the name of Muʿammar by Baghdādī reads that, "according to him, God is in every place in the sense of His being its designer (*mudabbir*) and of His knowing what is happening in it, but not in the sense of

[64] The statement that Mūsā al-Tiflisī himself believed that "God, after creating the world, departed, leaving it to be directed by itself" (*JE*, IX, 115, under "Musa of Tiflis") is based upon a misinterpretation of the text.

[65] *Timaeus* 29 E – 30 A.

[66] *Ibid.* 30 B, 48 A.

[67] *Ibid.* 41 E.

His settling down and taking up an abode in it." [68] Still, again, despite the fact that God knows all the things that transpire in the world, Muʿammar is reported to have refrained from saying "that God knows himself." [69] Accordingly, unlike the God of Aristotle who knows himself but does not know other things, [70] the God of Muʿammar knows other things but does not know himself.

There are thus in the Kalam three views with regard to causality. Briefly described, they are as follows:

First, the view implied in the eight views on duration and destruction held by most of the Mutakallimūn, both orthodox and Muʿtazilite, which, as formulated by Ghazālī, means, affirmatively, that God is the direct cause of every event in the world and, negatively, that there is no causal nexus between the events in the world. Historically, in so far as it affirms that God is the direct cause of every event in the world, it may be considered as a revision of the Philonic conception of causality in its relation to God by extending the creative power of God from its application to the origin of the world as a whole to the origin of all the individual events in the world; but, in so far as it denies any causal nexus between events in the world, it may be considered as a revision of the Epicurean theory of the denial of causality by ascribing the origin of the world as a whole, as well as of all the individual events within the world, not to chance but to the direct causation by God.

Second, the view of Naẓẓām, according to which the world is governed by laws of causality which, having been implanted in it by God at the time of its creation, operate under the supervision of God and are subject to His will. Historically, this represents the Philonic conception of causality in its relation to God.

Third, the view of Muʿammar, according to which the

[68] *Farḳ*, p. 140, ll. 14–16.
[69] *Ibid.*, p. 141, ll. 5–6.
[70] *Metaph.* XII, 9, 1074b, 15–35.

world is governed by laws of causality which, though implanted in it by God at the time of its creation, operate independently without any supervision by God and without their being subject to His will. Historically, this represents the Platonic conception of causality in its relation to God.

In the controversies over the problem of causality in the Kalam, as well as in Arabic philosophy in general, each of these views met with criticism. But, while the general denial of causality was criticized, as we have seen, by one who affirmed it [71] and, while the general affirmation of causality was criticized, again, as we have seen, by one who denied it,[72] the particular view of causality held by Muʿammar was criticized, as we shall see, both by one who denied causality and by one who, while affirming causality, held a conception of causality differing from that of Muʿammar.

The denier of causality who criticized Muʿammar is Shahrastānī. Referring to Muʿammar's statement that God created only bodies but that accidents are produced by the nature of bodies, he argues as follows: "If God does not create any accident, then He does not create . . . the body [bearing the accident], for creation is an accident; whence it would follow that no action at all should be ascribed to God." [73]

The affirmer of causality who criticized Muʿammar is Ibn Ḥazm. In one place in his work, he expresses his own belief in causality by rejecting the Ashʿarites, of whom he says: "They deny natural dispositions altogether. They say that in fire there is no heat, in snow no cold, and in the world as a whole no natural disposition whatsoever. They also say that in wine there is no nature which causes intoxication and in semen no power whereby one reproduces one's own kind. God, they say, can create out of semen whatever he pleases, so that it is possible for Him to create out of the semen of men a camel and out of the semen of a donkey a man and out of the seed of coriander a palm-tree." On this Ibn Ḥazm remarks: "We do not know of any argument by which they

[71] Cf. above, pp. 551 ff. [72] Cf. above, pp. 543–544. [73] *Milal*, p. 46, ll. 7–9.

strayed into this folly." [74] In another place, however, he opposes the particular conception of causality upheld by Muʿammar and also, according to him, by Jāḥiẓ. To quote: "As for the assertion of Muʿammar and al-Jāḥiẓ that all these [accidents mentioned in a preceding passage] result from the act of nature, it is a gross misunderstanding and an ignorance of the meaning of the term nature. The term nature only means the potency of a thing whereby the qualities therein, such as they are, come to pass, and of necessity we know that nature so defined has no intelligence. Accordingly, in the case of anything that has no deliberate choice, whether body or accident, such as stones and other inanimate things, if any one refers to the actions which appear from them as being their own, created by themselves, he is of the height of ignorance. Of necessity we know that, with regard to these actions, their creation is due to something outside those things from which they appear, and that is God, than whom there is no other." [75]

Back of this criticism by Ibn Ḥazm are certain statements of Aristotle about nature. To begin with, there are Aristotle's statements that "nature is in the same genus as potency (δύναμις, Arabic: *ḳuwwah*), because it is a principle of motion, not, however, in some other thing but in the thing itself, so far as it is itself" [76] and "that of things that come to be some come by nature." [77] It is this which is back of Ibn Ḥazm's statement here that "the term nature only means the potency (*ḳuwwah*) of a thing, whereby the qualities therein, such as they are, come to pass." Then, certain statements in Aristotle convey the view that nature, though working for an end, is something other than intelligence, such, for instance, as his statement that, at the sight of certain animals who seem to work for some end, people raise the question whether it is not "by intelligence (νῷ, *bi'l-ʿaḳl*)" that they so work,[78] or his statement that the cause of the existence or

[74] *Fiṣal* V, p. 14, l. 23 – p. 15, l. 4; cf. p. 62, ll. 20–23.
[75] *Ibid.* III, p. 58, l. 24 – p. 59, l. 6.
[76] *Metaph.* IX, 8, 1049b, 9–10.
[77] *Ibid.* VII, 7, 1032a, 12.
[78] *Phys.* II, 8, 199a, 20–23.

generation of animals and plants is "nature or intelligence (νοῦς) or something of the kind." [79] It is this, again, which is back of Ibn Ḥazm's statement here that "nature . . . has no intelligence (*lā yaʿḳul*)." But then, departing from Aristotle, he maintains, in still another place, that certain miraculous changes in the order of nature are possible [80] and that prophets have the power to perform miraculous acts which are contrary to the order of nature.[81]

III. Impossibilities

In the Hebrew Scripture, despite its teaching that all things are possible to God, which is so clearly expressed in Job's address to God, "I know that Thou canst do all things" (Job 42:2), there is also the teaching that certain things God will not do, which, again, is clearly expressed in such verses as that God "will not do unrighteousness" (Zeph. 3:5) and that "far be it from God, that He should do wickedness; and from the Almighty, that He should commit iniquity" (Job 34:10). This sentiment is re-echoed by Philo in a passage where his statement that "all things are possible to God" is preceded by the qualification that "God guides all things as He pleases in accordance with law and justice," [1] the implication thus being that, though all things are possible to God, He will do nothing that is contrary to what in His unfathomable wisdom is law and justice. Later in Christianity, Origen, referring to the New Testament statement that "with God all things are possible" (Matt. 19:26; Mark 10:27), says: "We maintain that God cannot do what is disgraceful (αἰσχρόν), since then He would be capable of ceasing to be God; for if He do anything that is disgraceful, He is not God." [2] In another place, commenting on the same New Testament verse, he says that "as far as His power is concerned, all things are possible; but as far as His justice is concerned, seeing that He

[79] *Ibid.* II, 4, 196a, 30.
[80] *Fiṣal* I, p. 60, ll. 3–5.
[81] *Ibid.* II, p. 181, ll. 16–17.

[1] *Opif.* 14, 46.
[2] *Contra Celsum* V, 23.

is not only powerful but also just, not all things are possible, but only those which are just." [3] In still another place, referring again to the same New Testament verse, he says that "in our judgment God can do everything which it is possible for Him to do without ceasing to be God and good and wise." [4] Pseudo-Dionysius, in answer to "Elymas the sorcerer" (cf. Acts 13:8), who found a contradiction between the Christian belief that "God is omniponent" and Paul's statement that "God cannot deny himself" (2 Tim. 2:13), says that a denial by God of himself would mean a denial that He is God, but God, though omnipotent, cannot do anything that would amount to a denial of His being God.[5]

In Islam, the question whether anything was impossible to God arose in the ninth century in the form of a debate among the Muʿtazilites on the question whether God had power over "injustice and lying." While it is generally admitted by the Muʿtazilites that God does not act unjustly and deceitfully, there is a difference of opinion among them as to why God does not act unjustly and deceitfully. According to Naẓẓām, who is described in one source as differing on this from his fellow Muʿtazilites,[6] but who is said in another source to have had some followers,[7] God does not act unjustly and deceitfully because He has no power over such acts.[8] According to Abū al-Hudhayl and to "most of the Muʿtazilites," God has the power to act unjustly and deceitfully [9] but He does not exercise that power, and this on account of "His wisdom and mercy" [10] or on account of its being disgraceful (*ḳabīḥah*) [11] or on account of its being a "diminution (*naḳṣ*) in

[3] *In Matthaeum Commentariorum Series* 95 (PG 13, 1746 C).

[4] *Contra Celsum* III, 70.

[5] *De Divinis Nominibus* VIII, 6 (PG 3, 904 C).

[6] *Milal*, p. 37, l. 8.

[7] *Maḳālāt*, p. 555, l. 1; cf. *Intiṣār* 28, p. 42, l. 23 – p. 43, l. 2.

[8] *Maḳālāt*, p. 555, l. 1–5; *Milal*, p. 37, ll. 7–9; *Farḳ*, p. 115, l. 18 – p. 116, l. 18; cf. *Intiṣār* 28, p. 42, ll. 21–23.

[9] *Maḳālāt*, p. 555, ll. 6–7, 9–10; cf. p. 200, ll. 7–8; p. 203, l. 14 – p. 204, l. 2; p. 560, ll. 4–8, and *Milal*, p. 37, ll. 8–9.

[10] *Maḳālāt*, p. 555, ll. 6–8.

[11] *Milal*, p. 37, l. 9; *Farḳ*, p. 188, ll. 13–14.

God."[12] In a debate which Naẓẓām is reported to have had with his fellow Muʿtazilites, he contended that there was no real difference between his own view that God has no power to act unjustly and deceitfully and their view that God has the power but does not exercise it.[13] According to Baghdādī, Naẓẓām's view that "the Author of justice has no power over injustice and lying" was taken from "the Dualists,"[14] that is, those who ascribe the good and the evil in the world to two distinct divine beings. Another kind of impossibility is attributed to both Naẓẓām and Abū al-Hudhayl as well as to all the other Muʿtazilites who believed that man was endowed by God with the power of free will. According to all of them, it is reported, "God cannot be described as having power over anything over which He has endowed man with power."[15] It is within this type of impossibilities that one is to include the view of those Muslim Libertarians who deny that God has foreknowledge of human actions.[16]

Besides these impossibilities which are due to the unwillingness of God to act contrary to what may be regarded as laws of ethical conduct, there are examples, reported in the name of Muʿtazilites, of impossibilities which are due to an unwillingness on the part of God to act contrary to certain laws of nature which He himself has established in the world. Thus Naẓẓām, to whom the observed order of nature is due to a principle of causality operating under the supervision of God,[17] is reported by Ibn al-Rāwandī to have said that it is impossible for God to create heat that would impart coldness and to create cold that would impart heat.[18] Abū al-Hudhayl, to whom the observed order of nature is directly created by God,[19] is reported by Ashʿarī to have said that "it is impossible

[12] *Maḳālāt*, p. 200, ll. 12–15.
[13] *Milal*, p. 37, ll. 17–20.
[14] *Farḳ*, p. 113, l. 18 – p. 114, l. 1.
[15] *Maḳālāt*, p. 549, ll. 7–8; p. 199, ll. 3–4; cf. above, p. 664.
[16] Cf. below, pp. 661–662.
[17] Cf. above, p. 569.
[18] *Intiṣār* 27, p. 41, ll. 13–14, 17–18.
[19] Cf. above, pp. 530–533.

for God to make the dead have knowledge or power or sight." [20] Mu'ammar, to whom the observed order of nature is due to a principle of causality operating without any supervision by God,[21] is reported by Ḫayyāṭ to have said that it is impossible that "God should destroy His creatures so that He should remain alone, just as He had been alone [before the creation of the world]." [22] It is within this type of impossibilities that one is to include the view of those Muslim Libertarians who deny that God has foreknowledge of any future events.[23]

Moreover, in the case of some impossibilities, the orthodox were in agreement with the Mu'tazilites. Thus Ḫayyāṭ reports that the orthodox were in agreement with Naẓẓām that it is impossible that God should create heat that would impart coldness and that He should create cold that would impart heat.[24] He similarly reports that many of the orthodox were in agreement with Mu'ammar that it is impossible that God should destroy all His creatures, basing their belief in such an impossibility on those Koranic verses wherein it is explicitly written that those who believe "will remain forever" in Paradise (43:69–73) and that those who are wicked "will remain forever" in the torment of Hell (43:74).[25]

The question whether it was really impossible for God to do certain things or whether God simply did not do certain things for some good reason, which, as we have seen, was debated by the Mu'tazilites in the ninth century, was revived a century later by the Iḫwān al-Ṣafā'. "Many learned persons," [26] they report, "maintain that God is powerless with

[20] *Maḳālāt*, p. 313, ll. 2–3.

[21] Cf. above, pp. 572–573.

[22] *Intiṣār* 9, p. 22, ll. 22–23. To this type of impossibilities belongs also Jubbā'ī's view that it is not within the power of God to destroy only some things in the world without destroying the whole world (cf. above, p. 539).

[23] Cf. below, pp. 661–662. Thus also Alexander Aphrodisiensis includes ignorance of future events among the things which are impossible for the gods (*De Fato* 30).

[24] *Intiṣār* 27, p. 41, ll. 17–19.

[25] *Ibid.* 9, p. 23, ll. 14–20.

[26] *Rasā'il Iḫwān al-Ṣafā'* 40, III, p. 357, l. 24.

regard to many things";[27] and if they are asked about the meaning of the Koranic verse that "God has power over everything" (2:19), they answer that this applies only to special things and it is not to be taken as laying down a universal principle.[28] Of the special things with regard to which those "many learned persons" maintained that God is powerless the Iḫwān al-Ṣafā' mention the following: "God is powerless to expel the devil from His kingdom; He is powerless to make a camel pass through (*yadḫulu*) the eye of a needle; He is powerless to make a man to be standing and sitting at one and the same time."[29] We are not told what their reasons were for these impossibilities, but we can guess what they were.

For the first impossibility the reason must have been based upon the Koranic statements that God has said to the devil "Get out of it [that is, of Paradise]" (15:34; 38:78; cf. 7:12), that Paradise is "as wide as the heavens and the earth" (3:127; 57:21), that "the kingdom of the heavens and the earth belongs to God" (2:101), and that "God is the one king of the kingdom" (3:25 and 3:1). Out of the combination of these statements, we imagine, those "many learned persons" inferred that, even though God expelled the devil from Paradise, He did not, and He could not, expel him from His kingdom, seeing that there is no place in the heavens above or on the earth below which was not included in His kingdom.

For the second impossibility the reason is quite evidently based upon the Koranic verse wherein, speaking of the doom of those who reject the apostles of God, it says that "heaven's gates shall not be opened to them, nor shall they enter Paradise, until the camel passes through (*yalija*) the eye of the needle" (7:38; cf. Matt. 19:24).

Of the third impossibility the reason is quite evidently based upon pseudo-Plutarch's statement that God could not make "him who is sitting to be [at the same time] upright."[30]

[27] *Ibid.*, p. 358, l. 2. [28] *Ibid.*, ll. 9–10. [29] *Ibid.*, ll. 3, 5, 6.

[30] *De Placitis Philosophorum* I, 7, 3, p. 299, ll. 9–10 (Arabic, p. 112, ll. 1–3).

This reflects a rule which, as phrased by Aristotle, reads: "To say that at the same time one is both standing and sitting . . . is to say not only what is false but also what is impossible," [31] that is to say, it is in violation of the Law of Contradiction, for, according to Aristotle,[32] the Law of Contradiction applies not only to "contradictories" (ἀντιφάσεις, *naḳā'iḍ*), such as the proposition "A is standing and not standing at the same time," but also to "contraries" (ἐναντία, *ḍiddani*), such as the proposition "A is standing and sitting at the same time."

In opposition to these "many learned persons," the Iḫwān al-Ṣafā' maintain that each of these impossibilities is due to its matter: the matter, in the case of the expulsion of the devil, is the "Kingdom"; in the case of the camel, it is the "eye of the needle"; and in the case of standing up and sitting down it is the "man." [33] With God, they insist, all these things are possible. They admit only one impossibility, namely, for God to create His equal. But this does not imply any lack of power on the part of God, for being equal with God, they argue in effect, spells nonexistence (*'adam*), whence for God not to be able to create His equal means not to be able to create nonexistence, but such an inability does not mean a shortcoming in God's power to act, for nonexistence is not one of the objects included in the universe of discourse of an agent's power to act and to produce [34] — in arguing which, it may be remarked, the Iḫwān al-Ṣafā' quite evidently allude to what was known to them as a generally accepted principle, namely, that "an agent does not act to produce nonexistence, for nonexistence does not require an agent." [35]

Thus, according to the Iḫwān al-Ṣafā', except for the creation of another God equal with himself, nothing is impossible for God, though, of course, working through matter, God

[31] *De Caelo* I, 12, 281b, 12–14.

[32] *Metaph.* IV, 6, 1011b, 15–22.

[33] *Rasā'il* 40, III, p. 357, ll. 22–23; p. 358, ll. 3–4, 5, 6–8.

[34] *Ibid.*, p. 358, ll. 11–14.

[35] *Moreh* I, 73, Prop. 6, p. 140, l. 11; cf. *Tahāfut al-Falāsifah* II, 12, p. 85, l. 7 – p. 86, l. 4; *Tahāfut al-Tahāfut* II, 24, p. 131, ll. 5–8; *'Eṣ Ḥayyim* 4, p. 16, ll. 1–2.

does not do certain things in this material world, and this, they would probably say with Origen and Abū al-Hudhayl, is on account of "His wisdom."

A systematic presentation of impossibilities, partly under the influence of the Iẖwān al-Ṣafā', is to be found in Ibn Ḥazm, who opens his discussion with the statement that "the impossible (*al-muḥāl*) falls into four parts, and there is no fifth part." [36]

The first part is described by him as "impossible in a relative sense," such as a beard grown on a boy of three or a logically ordered discourse delivered, and a metrically perfect poem composed by an unlettered person.[37] The second part is described by him as "impossible with reference to existence," such as something inanimate changed into an animate being or an animate being changed into something inanimate or one kind of animate being changed into another kind or a stone endowed with the power of speech and bodies endowed with the power of creating other bodies.[38] These two types of the impossible, however, are declared by him to be only impossible for us; they are not impossible for God; they are therefore subject to the miraculous working of God.

Historically the first two kinds of impossibilities, which to Ibn Ḥazm are possible for God and are subject to His miraculous working in this world, correspond to the common traditional conception of miracles, such as the making of things happen in a way in which they do not ordinarily happen or the changing of things into things into which they are not ordinarily changed or endowing things with powers which they do not ordinarily possess. Some of the concrete examples used by Ibn Ḥazm here are those which pagan philosophers, who did not believe in miracles, described as being unqualifiedly impossible. Thus, according to Ibn Ḥazm, by a miracle something inanimate can be changed into an animate being, whereas, according to Galen, God could not make a man out

[36] *Fiṣal* II, p. 181, l. 8.

[37] *Ibid.*, ll. 10–12.

[38] *Ibid.*, ll. 12–17.

of a stone; [39] again, according to Ibn Ḥazm, by a miracle one kind of animate being can be changed into another kind, whereas, according to Palaephatus, it was impossible for the goddess Artemis to change Actaeon into a deer — the story was an invention of the poets in order to inspire veneration for the gods; [40] and also, according to Ibn Ḥazm, by a miracle bodies may create other bodies, whereas according to Aristotle, "man is born from man, but not bed from bed." [41]

The third part of the impossible [42] is described by Ibn Ḥazm as "impossible with reference to that which we clearly and distinctly understand by the constitution of our intellect," that is to say, that which is contrary to what is rationally or logically self-evident, as, for instance, that a man should be sitting and standing at the same time or that God should make a man to be sitting and not sitting at the same time. By his use of these two examples of impossibilities of the same kind, he thus, like the Iḫwān al-Ṣafā', follows Aristotle in making the Law of Contradiction to apply both to "contradictories" and to "contraries." [43] Then, like the first two types of the impossible, this third type, too, is said by Ibn Ḥazm to be impossible only for us, but possible for God. Unlike the first two types, however, this type is not subject to the miraculous working of God in this world; only in another world will God exercise His power over it. In other words, like Origen and Abū al-Hudhayl, Ibn Ḥazm would say that while God has the power to do these things, He does not do them, at least in this world of ours, on account of His unfathomable wisdom.[44]

The fourth part of the impossible [45] is described by Ibn Ḥazm as "absolutely impossible," such as anything that would require that "the essence of God should undergo a change,"

[39] *De Usu Partium Corporis Humani* XI, 14 (ed. Kühn, vol. III, p. 905).

[40] *De Incredilibus* 3. Cf. R. M. Grant, *Miracles and Natural Law in Graeco-Roman and Early Christian Thought*, pp. 128 f.

[41] *Phys.* II, 1, 193b, 8–9.

[42] *Fiṣal* II, p. 181, ll. 17–24.

[43] Cf. above at nn. 28–30.

[44] Cf. above, pp. 578; 579.

[45] *Fiṣal* II, p. 181, l. 24 – p. 182, l. 1.

and this is impossible even for God himself, for it is "impossible by its own essence" and, should it be conceived as possible, "one part of it would contradict another," that is to say, it would be contrary to the unity of God. This quite obviously reflects what we have quoted above from the Church Fathers with regard to ascribing to God any action that would cause Him to cease to be what He is.[46]

According to this view, then, there are only two kinds of impossibilities which are not subject to miraculous work on the part of God, namely, those which are contrary to the Law of Contradiction and those which would imply a change in the essence of God. Of these only the second one is an absolute impossibility; the first one is to be considered as within God's power and it is called impossible only in the sense that God would not perform such things in this world of ours — and this quite evidently, as Origen and Abū al-Hudhayl say, because of the wisdom of God.

The next discussion of impossibilities is to be found in Ghazālī. After ascribing to philosophers the belief that among those things which they describe as possible there is room for miracles, which are explained by them rationally, and after also admitting his own belief in impossibilities, he says that the philosophers may raise the following question: "We agree with you that everything possible is in the power of God, and you agree with us that anything impossible does not fall under the category of power. Now of things, there are some whose impossibility is known, there are others whose possibility is known, and there are still others about which reason hesitates and does not decide whether they are impossible or possible. What, then according to you, is the limit of the impossible?"[47] In other words, what do all those who believe in God's power to work miracles consider as impossibilities and as not subject to miraculous action on the part of God?

In his answer, Ghazālī says that impossibilities are things

[46] Cf. above, pp. 578; 579.

[47] *Tahāfut al-Falāsifah* XVII, 24, p. 292, ll. 2–5.

which infringe upon the Law of Contradiction, of which Law he gives three formulations: "[1] the simultaneous affirmation and negation of a thing, or [2] the simultaneous affirmation of the particular [of a certain general] and the negation of the general, or [3] the simultaneous affirmation of two things and the negation of one of them." [48] This is followed by descriptions of four concrete cases of impossibilities, which were presumably meant by Ghazālī to be used as illustrations of his three formulations of the Law of Contradiction. In presenting these four concrete cases, I shall reduce each of them to a proposition.

The first two cases, which were meant to illustrate the first formulation, may be reduced to the following propositions:

(1) A is simultaneously black and white; [49]

(2) A is simultaneously in the house and in another place.[50]

Evidently knowing that these propositions are contraries and not contradictories, but knowing also Aristotle's explanation why the Law of Contradiction applies also to contraries, an explanation according to which "in each pair of contraries one is a privation," that is, a "negation," [51] Ghazālī tries to show how these two contrary propositions are really contradictory. He thus argues in effect that in the first part of the first proposition, namely, "A is black," the affirmation of blackness implies the negation of whiteness, and similarly in the first part of the second proposition, namely, "A is in the house," the affirmation of A's being in the house implies the negation of his being in another place. Thus, the two propositions, though contrary in form, are really contradictory in meaning.

The third case, which was meant to illustrate the second formulation, may be reduced to the proposition: A is simultaneously seeking (or pursuing) and is not knowing what

[48] *Ibid.* XVII, 27, p. 293, ll. 5–7.
[49] *Ibid.*, 28, p. 293, ll. 8–11.
[50] *Ibid.*, ll. 11–13.
[51] *Metaph.* IV, 6, 1011b, 18–19.

he is seeking (or pursuing).[52] Now, according to Aristotle, "will" originates in "knowledge"[53] and "pursuit" originates in "will,"[54] which means that "pursuit" is a particular of "knowledge" the general. Reflecting such a view, Ghazālī argues that this proposition consists of the simultaneous affirmation of the particular of knowledge, namely "seeking (or pursuing)," and the negation of the general knowledge, namely, "not knowing," and thus it is the simultaneous affirmation and negation of knowing.

The fourth case, which was meant to illustrate the third formulation, may be reduced to the proposition: A is simultaneously an inanimate object and is knowing.[55] Starting out with the general premise that to be inanimate implies to have no knowledge,[56] Ghazālī argues that while the proposition in question affirms of A two things, namely, "inanimate" and "knowing," it negates of it one of these things, namely "knowing," seeing that its negation is implied in the term "inanimate," and thus it is the simultaneous negation and affirmation of knowing.

Another kind of impossibility mentioned by Ghazālī is that of "the transformation (*ḳalb*) of genera [into one another]."[57] As an example of this kind of impossibility he mentions the transformation of "blackness" into "power."[58] Then, with regard to this kind of impossibility, Ghazālī remarks that "some Mutakallimūn say that it is in the power of God."[59] The reference is to the following passage in Ash'arī's *Maḳālāt*: "Some say, . . . God has power to trans-

[52] *Tahāfut al-Falāsifah* XVII, 28, p. 293, l. 13 – p. 294, l. 1. The active participle and imperfect of the Arabic *ṭalaba*, "seeks," are used in the Arabic version of *De Anima* III, 7, 431a, 9–10 and 16, as translations of the Greek διώκει, "pursues."

[53] *Eth. Nic.* III, 3, 1111a, 23–24.

[54] *Ibid.* VI, 2, 1139a, 25–26.

[55] *Tahāfut al-Falāsifah* XVII, 28, p. 294, ll. 1–4.

[56] Cf. Aristotle's statement that "it is sensation primarily which constitutes the animal" (*De Anima* II, 2, 413b, 2). Cf. also *De Gen. Anim.* II, 2, 436a, 30–31.

[57] *Tahāfut al-Falāsifah* XVII, 29, p. 294, l. 4.

[58] *Ibid.*, l. 6.

[59] *Ibid.*, ll. 4–5.

form bodies into accidents and accidents into bodies. . . . And some say, The description of God as having power over this is impossible, for the transformation [over which God has power] is only that which is the destruction in a thing of one set of accidents and the creation in it of another set of accidents." [60] The names of two Mutakallimūn who believed in the possibility of such a transformation may be gathered from Shahrastānī, who reports that Ḍirār and Ḥafṣ al-Fard said that "it is possible for God to transform accidents into substances." [61]

And so the only impossibilities admitted by Ghazālī are those which involve a violation of the Law of Contradiction. Otherwise, all things are possible with God and are subject to the miraculous workings of God.

Taking Ibn Ḥazm and Ghazālī as reproducing the common view of the Kalam on impossibility, we may arrive at the conclusion that three types of impossibilities were admitted by the Kalam: (1) things in violation of the Law of Contradiction; (2) things contrary to what is considered as the nature of God; (3) by some also the transformation of genera into one another.

IV. Repercussions in Christianity

1. St. Thomas on the Kalam Denial of Causality

The Kalam denial of causality became known to St. Thomas Aquinas through two sources: (1) the Latin translation of Maimonides' *Guide to the Perplexed*, which was made from Ḥarizi's Hebrew translation; (2) the Latin translations of Averroes' Long Commentaries on several works of Aristotle, made directly from the Arabic. How this view is presented by Averroes we have shown above.[1]

In his reproduction of this view of the Kalam, St. Thomas,

[60] *Maḳālāt*, p. 567, ll. 7–9 and 11–12.
[61] *Milal*, p. 63, ll. 12–13.
[1] Cf. above, pp. 551 ff.

as we shall see, draws mainly on Maimonides, but occasionally also on Averroes.

The earliest reference in St. Thomas' writings to the Mutakallimūn's denial of causality occurs in his Commentary on the *Sentences*, where, in his discussion of the question "whether anything other than God produces anything," he enumerates what he calls three "positions" (*positiones*). Of these, the first position is that "God operates all things immediately (*immediate*), so that nothing else is the cause of anything, and this to such an extent that its exponents say that fire does not make hot (*calefaciat*), but it is God who does it, and that the hand does not move itself, but it is God who causes its motion, and so they say also about other actions." [2] This certainly represents the view of the Mutakallimūn. Which of his two available sources was drawn upon here by St. Thomas, may be determined by the following considerations. The expression "God operates all things immediately (*immediate*)" suggest Averroes' statement that "the One produces all things without intermediation (*sine medio*)." [3] The statement that the Loquentes say that "fire does not make hot (*calefaciat*)" reflects a combination of Averroes' statement that the Mutakallimūn "denied that fire burns (*comburere*)" [4] and Maimonides' statement that the Mutakallimūn say that "the fact that fire burns (*comburentem*)" is only "a custom" [5] and not a law of nature. His statement that the Loquentes say that "the hand does not move itself, but God causes its motion" (*nec manus movetur, sed Deus causat eius motum*) reflects Maimonides' statement that, according to the Mutakallimūn, "the motion of the hand which [in our opinion] moves a pen is an accident created in the hand" (*motus manus moventis pennam est accidens creatum in manu*).[6] Finally, his description of the view of the Loquentes, as well

[2] *In II Sent.*, d. 1, q. 1, a. 4, *Solutio quarum una est.*
[3] *In XII Metaph.*, Comm. 18, p. 305 F.
[4] *Ibid.*, p. 305 G.
[5] *Moreh* I, 73 (72), Prop. 10, p. 144, ll. 21–22; Latin, fol. 34v, ll. 36–37.
[6] *Ibid.*, Prop. 6, p. 141, ll. 2–3; Latin, fol. 34r, l. 6.

as of each of the other two views, by the term *positio* would seem to reflect the term *positio* in the Latin translation of the *Guide of the Perplexed*, where it is used as the equivalent of *anticedens* (= Hebrew *hakdamah*; Arabic: *mukaddimah*) in the sense of "proposition" and where every one of the twelve "propositions" into which Maimonides divides the teachings of the Mutakallimūn is described as a *positio* or an *antecedens*.[7] But in connection with this, too, it happens that Averroes uses the term *positio* as a description of a certain view of the Loquentes.[8]

Then in his *Summa contra Gentiles*, toward the end of his arguments in support of his view "that God preserves things in existence," St. Thomas concludes: "Hereby is excluded the position of certain Mutakallimūn in the Law of the Moors (*quorumdam loquentium in lege maurorum positio*)." [9] This manner of referring to the Mutakallimūn is evidently based upon a combination of the Latin of Maimonides' *a loquentibus Maurorum* [10] and the Latin of Averroes' *loquentibus nostrae legis*.[11] After this introduction of the Loquentes, St. Thomas attributes to them the following views or positions:

1. "All forms are accidents." This reflects the *octava positio* in Maimonides, according to which the Loquentes maintain "that there exists nothing but substance and accident, since (*quoniam*; Hebrew and Arabic: "and that") the natural forms are accidents." [12]

2. "No accident lasts (*durat*) for two instants (*per duo instantia*)." This reflects the *sexta positio* in Maimonides,

[7] Thus in the Latin of *Moreh Nebukim* I, 73 (72), the twelve propositions are at the beginning of the chapter described as *antecedentia . . . duodecim*, but then, in Propositions 4, 5, 6, 8, 10, and 12, the term used is *positio*, whereas in all the other Propositions the term used is *antecedens*. It is to be noted in Propositions 6 and 10, wherein the denial of causality is dealt with, the term used is *positio*.

[8] *In VIII Phys.*, Comm. 15, p. 349 I.

[9] *Cont. Gent.* III, 65, ad *Per hoc autem*; cf. III, 69, ad *Ex praemissis autem quidam*, and *quidam etiam*.

[10] *Moreh* I, 71 (70); Latin, fol. 29r, l. 31.

[11] *In XII Met.*, Comm. 18, p. 305 F.

[12] *Moreh* I, 73 (72), Prop. 8, p. 143, l. 9; Latin, fol. 34v, l. 5.

according to which "an accident does not last (*durat*) for two instants (*per duo instantia*)." [13] In Averroes the *Loquentes nostrae legis* are reported as saying that "accidents do not remain (*remanent*) for two times (*per duo tempora*)." [14–15]

3. "In order to be able to maintain that the world needs to be preserved by God," that is to say, that the continuance of the world's existence depends upon God, the Loquentes had to resort to the view that "the formation of things" (*rerum formatio*), that is, the successive change of forms or accidents observed in things, is "always in a process of being made" (*semper . . . in fieri*), that is, it is always a succession of new creations.[16] This reflects the statement in Maimonides that, according to the Loquentes, after the perishing of a certain accident, "God creates another accident of the same kind, which also perishes, and after that He creates again, and so it goes on always, so long as God wills that that kind of accident be preserved." [17]

After thus reproducing the view of those whom Maimonides describes as the view "of the most" of the Mutakallimūn with regard to the continuance of accidents and hence of things in the world, St. Thomas reproduces the views of two other classes of Loquentes.

First, "some of them are said to have maintained" that the atoms, which together with accidents make up bodies, "would be able for a time to remain in existence, if God were to withdraw His government from things." [18] This refers to the view which Maimonides attributes to "some of the masters of speculation from among those Loquentes," which is to be identified as the view of Muʿammar and his followers, according to which "if we could conceive of the passing-away of the Creator, it would not necessarily follow the passing-away of the things created by Him, namely, the world." [19]

[13] *Ibid.* I, 73 (72), Prop. 6, p. 139, l. 33; Latin, fol. 33v, l. 27.

[14–15] *In VIII Phys.*, Comm. 74, p. 418 K.

[16] *Cont. Gent.* III, 65, ad *Per hoc autem.* Cf. *De Verit.* 5, 2, ad 6.

[17] *Moreh* I, 73 (72), Prop. 6, p. 138, ll. 27–29; Latin, fol. 33v, ll. 31–32.

[18] *Contra Gentiles* III, 65, ad *Per hoc autem.*

[19] *Moreh* I, 69 (68), p. 117, ll. 23–24; Latin, fol. 28r, ll. 29–30. Cf. above, pp. 572 ff.

Second, "some of these say indeed that things would not cease to exist unless God caused in them the accident of termination (*accidens decisionis*)." [20] This reflects the statement in Maimonides that "there are others who say that if He wished to destroy the world, He would create an accident of termination (*accidens finis*) and the world would be destroyed." [21] This, as we have seen, represents the view of Jubba'ī and his son.[22]

In his *De Potentia*, the next work in which St. Thomas mentions the Mutakallimūn's denial of causality, he introduces it by the expression "some Loquentes in the Law of the Moors, as Rabbi Moses (Maimonides) reports." [23] Finally, in his *Summa Theologiae* he ascribes it simply to "some" (*aliqui*).[24] In both these places the illustration used is that of their assertion that it is not fire that gives heat (*ignis non calefacit* or *calefaceret*).

2. NICOLAUS OF AUTRECOURT AND GHAZĀLĪ'S ARGUMENT AGAINST CAUSALITY *

At about the time St. Thomas came out against the Loquentes and reasserted the established Christian belief that God acts both naturally through secondary causes and miraculously without secondary causes, there appeared in Christianity those known as Averroists who were accused of having said that "God cannot produce the effect of a secondary cause without that secondary cause." [1] As such a belief would lead to the denial of miracles, it was quite natural for Schoolmen, in their attempt to defend the possibility of miracles, to try to show how it was possible for God to produce things without the intermediacy of secondary causes. One of them, Nicolaus of Autrecourt, went so far as to deny that God ever acts by

[20] *Cont. Gent.* III, 65, ad *Per hoc autem.*

[21] *Moreh* I, 73 (72), Prop. 6, p. 140, ll. 16–17; Latin, fol. 33v, ll. 46–48.

[22] Cf. above, p. 538.

[23] *De Potentia*, q. 3, a. 7c.

[24] *Sum. Theol.* I, 105, 5c.

* Reprinted from *Speculum*, 44:234–238 (1969).

[1] Cf. J. R. Weinberg, *Nicolaus of Autrecourt* (1948), p. 87, quoting Chart. Univ. Paris, Tome I: Condemnations 1270.

means of secondary causes, thus arriving at a view like that of the Muslim Loquentes criticized by St. Thomas. This view of Nicolaus as to the denial of causality is expressed by him in a variety of statements. One of them, refuting an argument for causality based upon the observation of the burning of flax (*stuppa*) on its contact with fire, advanced by Bernard of Arezzo,[2] reads as follows: "This consequence, namely, 'fire is next to flax and there is no impediment, hence the flax will be consumed,' is not evident by an evidence deduced from the first principle." [3] This refutation of the argument, it has been rightly suggested, is similar to Ghazālī's refutation of those whom he calls philosophers and to whom he ascribes the view that fire is the real cause of combustion.[4] The question, however, is rightly raised as to whether Ghazālī's refutation could have been known to Nicolaus, for the only known source from which he could have learned of that refutation is the 1328 Latin translation of Averroes' *Tahāfut al-Tahāfut* (*Destructio Destructionis*), which embodies Ghazālī's *Tahāfut al-Falāsifah* (*Destructio Philosophorum*), but the date of that translation is too close to 1327, the year in which Nicolaus began to lecture at the University of Paris, though it is admitted that he could have subsequently obtained knowledge of Ghazālī's refutation "from this source had he read it." [5]

Addressing myself solely to the question whether Ghazālī's refutation was known to Nicolaus, I shall try to show two things: (1) that a knowledge of Ghazālī's *Tahāfut al-Falāsifah* was somehow available to Latin Schoolmen long before the Latin translation of Averroes' *Tahāfut al-Tahāfut* in 1328; (2) that the example of the burning of flax mentioned by Bernard in his argument for causality and by Nicolaus in

[2] Cf. *ibid.*, p. 34, n. 6, quoting J. Lappe, *Nicolaus von Autrecourt* (1908), p. 11*, ll. 29–30.

[3] Cf. *ibid.*, p. 65, n. 18, quoting Lappe, p. 32*, ll. 16–19.

[4] *Tahāfut al-Tahāfut* XVII, 5, p. 279, ll. 3–5; cf. Weinberg, *op. cit.*, p. 85, n. 4.

[5] Cf. Weinberg, *op. cit.*, p. 86.

his refutation of the argument is based upon passages in Ghazālī's *Tahāfut al-Falāsifah* where it is quoted in the name of the philosophers.

(1) That a knowledge of Ghazālī's *Tahāfut al-Falāsifah* had been available to the Schoolmen long before the 1328 Latin translation of Averroes' *Tahāfut al-Tahāfut* can be shown by a passage in Albertus Magnus' Commentary on Aristotle's *Physics*. In that Commentary, Albertus reproduces seven arguments used by those who believe in the eternity of the world, of which arguments he says that they have been collected by Maimonides (*a Moyse Egyptio Judaeorum Philosopho*) from various places in the works of Aristotle [6] and from other works.[7] Against one of these arguments, the fourth, which involves the concept of impossibility, Maimonides quotes tentatively a refutation, of which the Latin translation as known to Albertus would read in English as follows: "However, a skillful one from among the later Mutakallimūn said that he had solved this problem, maintaining that the possibility under consideration was in the agent, but not in that which is acted upon." [8] Both the argument and the refutation, it can be shown, are based upon Ghazālī's *Tahāfut al-Falāsifah*, in which the passage underlying the refutation reads as follows: "The meaning of possibility with reference to something created is that its creation is possible for an agent who has the power to create it, so that possibility is an attribution to the agent." [9] Albertus, in restating this refutation, also only tentatively, introduces it as follows: "There was, however, a certain person among those who defended the belief that the world had a beginning, one by the name

[6] Albertus Magnus, *Liber VIII Physicorum*, Tract. I, Cap. 11, Opinio Aristotelis et ejus rationes, end.

[7] *Ibid*., Secunda ratio, end.

[8] *Rabi Mossei Aegyptii Dux seu Director dubitantium aut perplexorum* II, 15, Quarta via: "Unus autem de intelligentibus postremis loquentibus dixit quod ipse solverat hanc quaestionem, dicens quod ista possibilitas erat in agente, sed non in operato." Cf. *Moreh Nebukim* II, 14, p. 200, ll. 17–19.

[9] *Tahāfut al-Falāsifah* I, 99, p. 77, ll. 3–4.

of Algazelus, who said that he had solved this argument." [10] Now Albertus could not have known that the anonymous Mutakallim referred to by Maimonides was Ghazālī unless he had a knowledge of the *Tahāfut al-Falāsifah*. So also, we may assume, both Bernard and Nicolaus could have had a knowledge of the *Tahāfut al-Falāsifah*, even if the 1328 Latin translation of Averroes' work had not yet reached them.

(2) That the example of the burning of flax by fire used by Bernard in his argument for causality and by Nicolaus in his refutation of that argument is based upon passages in Ghazālī can be shown by the following considerations: First, in none of the works known to have been available to Bernard and Nicolaus, works in which the example of burning by contact with fire is used in connection with the problem of causality, is there any mention of any particular object as that which is burned on its contact with fire. Thus Averroes and Maimonides and St. Thomas, in reproducing the Mutakallimūn's view on causality, quote them as denying that "fire burns" [11] or that "fire makes hot," [12] without mentioning anything as that which the fire burns or makes hot. But Bernard, in his argument that fire is the cause of burning, and Nicolaus, in his refutation of that argument, do mention something as that which fire burns. Now the only one, possibly known to them, who mentions that which fire burns in his discussion of causality is Ghazālī, for he uses the example of the burning of "cotton" (*al-ḳuṭun*) by fire both in his restatement of the philosophers' belief in causality [13] and in his refutation of that belief.[14] Though Bernard and Nicolaus

[10] Albertus Magnus, *op. et loc. cit.*, Quarta ratio: "Fuit autem quidam ex defendentibus quod mundus incepit, nomine Algazelus, qui dixit se solvisse hanc rationem per hoc quod dixit . . ."

[11] Averroes, *In XII Metaph.*, Comm. 18, VIII, p. 305 G: "ita quod negant ignem comburere" (cf. above, p. 590, n. 4). Maimonides, *Moreh Nebukim*, Latin: 1, 72, Decima positio, fol. 34v, ll. 36–37: "vel esse ignem comburentem" (cf. above, p. 590, n. 5).

[12] St. Thomas, *Sum. Theol.* I, 105, 5c: "puto quod ignis non calefaceret." Cf. *In II Sent.*, d. I, q. I, a. 4c; *De Potentia* III, 7c.

[13] Ghazālī, *Tahāfut al-Falāsifah* XVII, 2, p. 278, l. 6.

[14] *Ibid.* XVII, 4, p. 278, l. 13 – p. 279, l. 5; 10, p. 283, ll. 6–7.

mention not "cotton" but rather "flax" as that which fire burns, a study of the Latin translations of the Arabic term *al-ḳuṭun* will show, I believe, that the term *stuppa*, "flax," used by Bernard and Nicolaus goes back to the term *al-ḳuṭun* used by Ghazālī.

In the 1328 Latin translation of Averroes' *Tahāfut al-Tahāfut*, made directly from the Arabic, the term *al-ḳuṭun* used by Ghazālī is translated by the term *bombax*[15] (= *bombyx*, *βόμβυξ*) — a term of which the original meaning is "silkworm" and hence "silk." How that Arabic term came to be translated by *bombax* can be explained by a passage in Pliny's *Naturalis Historia* and a comment on it by the French Jesuit Jean Hardouin in his edition of the *Naturalis Historia* (Paris, 1658). In that passage in his *Naturalis Historia* dealing with "Egyptian flax (*linum*)," Pliny refers to that which we nowadays call cotton as that which some people call *gossypion* and describes it as a "silky substance" (*bombyx*) inside a fruit grown on a shrub, "the down of which is spun into threads."[16] Jean Hardouin, in his comment on this passage, says that the Italians call it *bombace*, but "we," that is, the French, call it *coton*, and then he quotes Iacobus de Vitriaco (d. 1240) as reporting in one of his books that the *bombax* produced in the East is called by the French *coton* both in Latin and in their own language.[17] It is, therefore, quite understandable how the French Jew, Kalonymus ben Kalonymus, who was the 1328 Latin translator of Averroes' *Tahāfut al-Tahāfut*,[18] knowing that the term *coton* was only a transliterated form of the Arabic *ḳuṭun*, preferred to translate that Arabic term by the Latinized Greek term *bombax*.

[15] MS. Vat. Lat. 2434, fol. 53r, Col. 1, l. 9.

[16] *Naturalis Historia* XIX, 2, 14.

[17] Commenting on the text *ex interiore bombyce*, Jean Hardouin says: "Hoc est, lanugine, quam Itali *Bombace* appellant, nos *Coton* dicimus . . . Jacobus de Vitriaco, lib. I, cap. 85. *Sunt ibi* in oriente *praeterea arbusta quaedam quae seminantur, ex quibus colligunt bombacem, quae Francigenae Cotonem seu Coton appellant*" (quoted from the second edition, 1723, vol. II, p. 156, n. 30).

[18] Steinschneider, *Hebr. Uebers.*, p. 330.

Two centuries later, however, in 1527, when an Italian Jew by the name of Kalonymus ben David,[19] published in Venice a new translation of Averroes' *Tahāfut al-Tahāfut*, this time made from its Hebrew translation, he translated the Arabic term *al-ḳuṭun* through the Hebrew *ha-ṣemer gefen*,[20] by *stuppa* (= στύππη).[21] Since *stuppa* means "flax," or rather flax of an inferior quality,[22] it would at first sight seem that the use of this term by the translator for *ṣemer gefen* was either (1) because he did not know that there was a Latin word for "cotton" or (2) because he thought the Hebrew *ṣemer gefen* meant flax. But neither of these reasons would explain why he used a word which means flax. As for the first reason, he certainly knew of the use of the term *bombax* for cotton in the 1328 Latin translation, for he alludes to that translation, though rather uncomplimentarily, in his dedicatory letter to Cardinal Hercules Gonzaga; [23] and undoubtedly also he must have known of the Italian use of *bombace* in the sense of cotton, for the Italian use of *bombace* in that sense a century and a half later, as testified by Jean Hardouin in 1685, must have gone back at least to the time of this translator. As for the second reason, the Hebrew *ṣemer gefen*, literally, "wool of a vine tree," [24] is an old and widely used Hebrew expression for cotton.[25] In fact, a countryman of that translator, Rabbi Obadiah Bertinoro (d. 1500), the author of a well-known commentary on the Mishnah, in his comment on the expression *ṣemer gefen* in *Kil'ayim* VII, 2, explains its meaning by the use of the Arabic *ḳuṭun*, quite evidently taken from the Hebrew translation of Maimonides'

[19] *Ibid*., p. 333.

[20] The definite article *ha* is so adjoined to the construct *ṣemer* in the MS. of the Bibliothèque Nationale, Heb. 910[3], fol. 162r, Col. 1, l. 3.

[21] *Destructio Destructionum*: In Physicis, Disputatio Prima, in Junta's ed. of *Aristotelis . . . opera*, Vol. IX (1573), p. 129 B.

[22] Pliny, *Natur. Hist.* XIX, 3, 17.

[23] Quoted by Steinschneider in *Hebr. Uebers*., p. 333.

[24] Cf. Pliny's description of cotton-trees as "woolbearing trees" (*lanigerae arbores*) whose leaves, but for their smallness, might be taken for those of the "vine" (*Nat. Hist.* XII, 21, 38).

[25] Cf. Immanuel Löw, *Die Flora der Juden*, II, pp. 238 ff.

Arabic commentary on the Mishnah, thus assuming that the Italian Jewish reader of his commentary would know enough to associate the Arabic *ḳuṭun* as an explanation of *ṣemer gefen* with the Italian *cotone.*

It would thus seem that, despite his knowledge that *ṣemer gefen* could be translated by *coton* or by *bombax*, the 1527 Latin translator was disinclined to use either one of these terms — the term *coton* probably for the same reason that, as I have suggested above, it was not used by the 1328 Latin translator and the term *bombax* probably because of its double meaning, for the same term, thus spelled, was used in Latin also as an exclamation of ironical astonishment. The term *stuppa* seemed to him to be a most fitting substitute for either of these two terms as that which is to be used as an example of something which is sure to be burned at its contact with fire, for he certainly could have known that in Lucretius the term *stuppa* is used as an example of that which easily catches fire [26] and that in Pliny it is described as that which is used for "wicks of lamps"; [27] and perhaps he was also influenced by the use of the Italian *stoppa* as an example of something which is easily inflammable, as, for instance, its use in the popular saying *spegnere il fuoco colla stoppa*, "to extinguish the fire with hards of flax," by which is meant to make of a small evil a greater one. And perhaps also he did not want to use any term meaning cotton as an example of that which people use for burning purposes because cotton did not grow in Italy and as something imported it was too expensive to be used for burning purposes. It is to be noted that Judah Halevi, who flourished in Spain during the early part of the twelfth century, in a passage in his *Cuzari*, which I have shown to be aimed at Ghazālī's denial of causality, substituted "a piece of wood" for Ghazālī's "cotton" as an example of that which is burned at its contact with fire.[28] The reason for

[26] *De Rerum Natura* VI, 880. Cf. also the use of *stupa* in the Vulgate of Isaiah 1:31 (suggested by Professor Morton Smith).

[27] *Natur. Hist.* XIX, 3, 17.

[28] Cf. above, *Cuzari V*, 20, p. 338, l. 6; p. 339, l. 3.

the substitution in the case of Halevi is presumably the same as the last reason that I have suggested in the case of the use of "flax" as a substitute for "cotton" in the case of the 1527 Latin translator.

In the light of all this, we have reason to assume that the term *stuppa* in Bernard and Nicolaus had its origin similarly in its use as a substitute for a term meaning "cotton" used by Ghazālī in his discussion of the problem of causality. This may have happened in either of two ways. The term *stuppa* may have been substituted for the Arabic *al-ḳuṭun* in that earlier Latin source of information of Ghazālī's *Tahāfut al-Falāsifah* referred to by Albertus Magnus — if we assume that that was the source of Bernard's and Nicolaus' knowledge of Ghazālī's use of it as an example of causality. Or the term *stuppa* may have been substituted by Bernard and Nicolaus themselves for the term *bombax* in the 1328 Latin translation of Averroes' *Tahāfut al-Tahāfut* — if we assume that that translation was the source of their knowledge of Ghazālī's use of it as an example of causality.

CHAPTER VIII

PREDESTINATION AND FREE WILL

INTRODUCTION

In the Koran there is a marked distinction between its statements about the power of God over what happens in the world, including what happens to human beings, and its statements about God's power over the actions of human beings. With regard to the former, there are such general statements as the following: "His is the kingdom of the heavens and the earth; He maketh alive and killeth; and He hath power over all things; . . . and He knoweth all things" (57: 2–3); "He it is who created you of clay, and then decreed the term of your life" (6: 2); "There is no moving thing on earth but on God is its sustenance" (11: 8). But with regard to God's power over human actions, there are contradictory statements. To begin with, there are statements which affirm absolute predestination, as, for instance, the following: "No soul can believe but by the permission of God" (10: 100); "This truly is a warning: And whoso willeth, taketh the way to his lord. But will it ye shall not, unless God will it" (7: 29–30). Predestination is also implied in such verses as the following: "And whom God shall please to guide, that man's breast will He open to Islam; but whom He shall please to make go astray, strait and narrow will He make his breast" (6: 125); "Their hearts and their ears hath God sealed up" (2: 6). An implication of predestination may also be discerned in the statement: "God is fully cognizant of what ye do" (63: 11). But complete freedom is affirmed in such verses as the following: "The truth is from your Lord: let him then who will, believe; and let him who will, disbelieve" (18: 28); "But truly I am forgiving to whomsoever repents and believes and acts uprightly, and lets himself be guided" (20:84). Free will is also implied in verses in which guidance and making to go astray and sealing up are represented as following upon one's free-will actions. Thus: "As for those who believe not in the signs of God, God will not guide them" (16: 106); "None will He make go astray thereby except the wicked" (2: 24); "Thus God sealeth up every heart which is arrogant and haughty" (40: 37).

I. The Predestinarians

The first attempt at the formulation of a doctrine of human action was based upon those verses which emphasize predestination. What form that doctrine took may be gathered from three sources, all coming from a period before the middle of the eighth century: first, a group of traditions transmitted by a succession of individuals in the name of Muhammad; second, a statement of the doctrine of predestination by Jahm b. Ṣafwān; third, a fictitious disputation between a Christian and a Muslim by John of Damascus.[1]

In the traditions, stress is laid upon the equality, with respect to predestination, of the actions of human beings and the things that happen to human beings. One of the traditions, which occurs in several versions, begins, in one of the versions, with the following statement: "As for any one of you, his generation in the womb of his mother is affected in the course of forty days . . . afterwards an angel is commissioned to breathe the living spirit into him."[2] Then the angel is said to ask a question of God concerning the destiny of "the seed" which, in one of the versions, reads as follows: "O my Lord, miserable or blessed? Whereupon one or the other is written down. O my Lord, male or female, when one or the other

[1] Cf. Edward E. Salisbury, "Materials for the History of the Muhammadan Doctrine of Predestination and Free Will," *AJOS*, 8(1866), 103–182. The passages referred to in nn. 2, 3, 4 below are quoted on pp. 123–124 and those in n. 9 below on p. 139. Cf. also Wensinck, *Muslim Creed*, pp. 54–56; Watt, *Free Will*, pp. 17–19.

[2] Muslim, *Ṣaḥīḥ* IV, *Ḳadar*, 1, p. 2036, ll. 6–8.

is written down. He also writes down his manner of conduct, his deeds, his term of life, his sustenance. Then [it is said to the angel]: Roll up the leaves, for no addition shall be made thereto, nor anything taken therefrom."[3] Finally there comes the conclusion, which, to quote again the version cited, reads as follows: "Therefore, by Him beside whom there is no God, any one of you may even conduct himself as those destined for Paradise, until there is only a cubit between him and it, and yet the registered decree shall prevent him, so that he shall conduct himself as do those destined for Hell, and accordingly enter therein; and any one of you may even conduct himself as do those destined for Hell, until the distance between him and it is only a cubit, and yet the registered decree shall prevent him, so that he shall conduct himself as those destined for Paradise, and accordingly enter therein."[4]

The significance of these Muslim traditions comes out when compared with the following rabbinic traditions: "R. Johanan said . . . The Holy One, blessed be He, beckons to the angel in charge of conception, whose name is Laylah, saying unto him: know that on this night a man is formed out of the seed of so and so. Know thou it for thy good and take care of this drop. . . . Thereupon the angel takes up the drop and brings it before Him by whose word the world came into being, and says unto Him: I have done according to all that Thou hast commanded me; but now what shall be decreed concerning this drop? Thereupon the Holy One blessed be He decrees concerning it what it is to be in the end, whether male or female, whether weak or strong, whether poor or rich, whether short or long, whether ugly or handsome, whether thick or thin, whether insignificant looking or of imposing bulk, and in a similar way God decrees concerning all things that will happen to him. But He does not decree whether the man is to be righteous or wicked, for this choice He leaves into the power of man himself, as it is written. See,

[3] *Ibid.*, 2, p. 2037, ll. 7–8.

[4] *Ibid.*, 1, p. 2036, ll. 9–12.

I have set before thee this day long life and good, and death and evil (Deut. 30:15). Thereupon the Holy One blessed be He beckons to the angel in charge of [living] spirits, saying unto him: Bring me the spirit of so and so, which is now in Paradise. . . . Thereupon the angel goes and brings the spirit in the presence of the Holy One blessed be He. . . . At once the Holy One blessed be He says unto the spirit: Enter into the drop held by angel so and so." [5]

A parallel statement by Ḥanina b. Papa, probably based upon the preceding statement, reads as follows: "The name of the angel who is in charge of conception is Laylah. He takes up a drop and places it in the presence of the Holy One, blessed be He, saying: O Lord of the universe, what is in store for this drop? Is it destined to produce a strong man or a weak man, a wise man or a foolish man, a rich man or a poor man? He does not, however, inquire whether it is to produce a wicked man or righteous man. It thus bears out the view of R. Ḥanina [b. Ḥama], for R. Ḥanina [b. Ḥama] said: "Everything is in the power of Heaven except the fear of Heaven." [6]

Then there are also the following two pertinent rabbinic statements:

"Forty days before the embryo is formed, a heavenly voice goes forth and says: The daughter of so and so for so and so." [7]

" 'God also has set the one over against the other' (Eccl. 7:14). This refers to Hell and Paradise. What is the distance between them? A handbreadth." [8]

[5] *Tanḥuma*: *Peḳude* 3.

[6] *Niddah* 16b. It is not clear whether the last two sentences are part of the original statement by R. Ḥanina b. Papa or whether they are an editorial comment upon that statement. I have translated them as if they were part of the original statement.

[7] *Soṭah* 9a; *Sanhedrin* 27a.

[8] *Ecclesiastes Rabbah* on Ecc. 7:14. Cf. *Pesiḳta Rabbati* (ed. F. Friedmann), p. 201 a.

The similarities between the Muslim traditions and the rabbinic passages in motif as well as in literary form are quite striking. There is the angel inquiring of God as to the future destiny of the seed. There is also the angel in charge of spirits which are breathed into the seeds either by the angel himself, in the Muslim tradition, or by God himself, in the rabbinic lore. There is the forty days either before the conception, in the Muslim tradition, or before the formation of the embryo in the rabbinic lore. Then there is the distance of a cubit between the sinner and Hell or between the righteous and Paradise, in the Muslim tradition, and the distance of a handbreadth between Hell and Paradise, in the rabbinic lore. But there is an outstanding difference, theologically, between the Muslim tradition and the rabbinic lore. In the rabbinic lore, a distinction is made between what happens to man and what man does, and while the former is predestined, the latter is left to man's free choice. In the Muslim tradition, no such distinction is made. Human action is as predestined as the events of human life. On the basis of all this one would be tempted to suggest that the Muslim traditions were formulated with a knowledge of the rabbinic sources and in opposition to them.

The same choice on the part of the early Muslims of the predestinarian passages in the Koran in preference to the libertarian ones is also clearly indicated in many other traditions. Here is a most striking one, which again occurs in several versions. One of these versions reads as follows: "The Apostle of God . . . said: Adam and Moses disputed with each other. Said Moses: O Adam, it is thou, our father, who didst frustrate our destiny and eject us from Paradise; to whom Adam replied: It is thou, O Moses, whom God did especially favor with converse with Himself and for whom He traced lines of writing with His own hand — dost thou blame me for doing that which God predestined for me forty years before He created me? Therefore Adam got the better of Moses in the dispute." [9] Ash'arī, after reproducing this and other traditions, concludes: "These traditions prove that what God knows will be, will be, and He writes it down; and that He writes down the people of the Paradise and the people of Hell, and creates them as two groups: a group for Paradise, and a group for flame." [10]

Just as the traditions try to show that there is no difference between things that happen to human beings and the actions of human beings, so does Jahm b. Ṣafwān try to show that there is no difference between things that happen in the world in general and the actions of human beings. All of them, he maintains, are continuously and directly created by God. If man is spoken of as acting, it is only by way of metaphor, just as we say that the stone moves, the spheres revolve, the sun rises and sets, the tree bears fruit, the water runs, the heaven is cloudy and rains, the earth stirs and produces plants, and the like.[11] Indeed man is said to differ from inanimate beings in that he possesses power and will and choice, but here, again, it is God who creates in man the power (*ḳuwwah*) and the will (*irādah*) and the choice (*iḫtiyār*) by which he acts, just as "He creates for man the height by which he is tall and the coloring-matter by which he is colored." [12] In short, "man is compelled (*majbūr*) in his actions, having no power (*ḳudrah*) and no will and no choice." [13] Then also, according to Jahm, "reward and punishment, like human actions, are subject to compulsion (*jabr*)," and furthermore, "if compulsion is to be maintained, religious obligation must also be subject to compulsion." [14]

The same emphasis on the denial of any difference between the actions of human beings and the things that happen in the world as being the chief characteristic of the Muslim

[9] Muslim, *Ḳadar*, 13, p. 2042, l. 17 – p. 2043, l. 2.
[10] *Ibānah*, p. 87, ll. 8–10.
[11] *Maḳālāt*, p. 279, ll. 3–6; *Milal*, p. 60, l. 20 – p. 61, l. 4.
[12] *Maḳālāt*, p. 279, ll. 7–9.
[13] *Milal*, p. 60, ll. 19–20.
[14] *Ibid.*, p. 61, ll. 4–5.

doctrine of predestination is to be found in the fictitious disputation of John of Damascus. In that fictitious disputation the problem, as formulated by the question put by the Saracen to the Christian, is as follows: "Are you endowed with free will, and are you able to do whatever you wish?" [15] The Christian maintains that he has been formed by God with free will, and that the free will with which he was formed enables him to do either good or evil, and that because of his freedom of the will he is deserving reward for doing good and evil for doing evil. In the course of his discussion, he also mentions the fact that man in his doing of evil is instigated by the devil. He does not, however, mention that in his doing of good man is sometimes helped by God. The Muslim, in contradistinction to this, maintains, as his view is formulated for him by the Christian, that "[the doing of] good and evil" comes at the command of God,[16] that is to say, they are decreed by God beforehand.

From the same Disputation it may be gathered that the problem of freedom in man was part of the general problem whether God acts in the world through intermediate causes. The Christian, in that Disputation, maintains that after the six days of creation all the normal processes of nature are performed by God through intermediate causes, and man, as one of the intermediate causes, acts by free will. The Muslim, in contradistinction to this, maintains that even after the six days of creation God directly creates every normal process of nature, so that every act of man, which the Christian attributes to man himself as a free agent, is attributed by the Muslim to God.[17]

In the course of the Disputation, the Christian raises what, as we shall see, is the stock argument against the denial of free will. If man is not free, he argues in effect, then "God will be found unjust" in punishing, or in ordering to punish, those

[15] John of Damascus, *Disputatio Christiani et Saraceni* (PG 94, 1589 C).
[16] *Ibid.* (1592 A). [17] *Ibid.* (1592 B–1593 B).

who do evil.[18] Another argument hinted at by the Christian is the inconsistency between the assumption that God had willed beforehand for the sinner to commit certain sins and the fact that God does not will the sinner to commit those sins, which is implied in the revealed prohibitions of those sins.[19]

This in broad outline is what we may gather from John of Damascus as to the prevailing earliest Muslim view on predestination and free will. There is no difference between human action and any of the acts of nature: human action, like any other act of nature, both good and evil, was predetermined by God and is directly created by God.

From these accounts, internal as well as external, we gather that the original form of predestinarianism was that which Jahm himself emphatically describes by the term compulsion. But here quite naturally the following question comes up. In the Koran, as we have seen, there are libertarian passages as well as predestinarian ones. How did it happen that the early Muslims chose to follow the predestinarian rather than the libertarian passages? An answer to this question was suggested by Schreiner in 1900. On the basis of evidence adduced by several scholars, among them Goldziher, as to the existence of a belief in fatalism among pre-Islamic Arabs, he says: "With reference to the teaching of free will, there is no doubt that among the heathen Arabs the conception of fate was widespread, and the statements of the Koran [to the contrary] were not capable to do away with them." He then goes on to say that later, in the case of the predestinarian views of Ashʿarī, there was the additional influence of the Persian fatalism.[20] Evidently having in mind the same fatalistic belief of the pre-Islamic Arabs, to which he refers as a "mythological tradition," Goldziher in 1910, speaking of the controversy over the problem of free will in Islam, says: "Although the Koran could supply both parties with argu-

[18] *Ibid.* (1592 AB). [19] *Ibid.* (1593 C).

[20] Schreiner, *Studien über Jeschʿa ben Jehuda*, p. 11.

ments, still a mythological tradition, which either developed very early as a kind of hagadah in Islam, or perhaps first appeared in the course of these debates — exact dates cannot be furnished — favored the determinists."[21] Watt goes further.[22] He finds in Muslim tradition not a choice in preference of the predestinarian to the libertarian passage in the Koran but a departure even from the predestinarian passages of the Koran itself. "The Qur'ān," he says, "is through and through theistic," whereas "the Traditions, though they mention God, at times tend to be atheistic." "These impersonal and rather atheistic conceptions," he goes on to say in effect, are a survival of the pre-Islamic belief in an impersonal Fate, and to prove that pre-Islamic Arabs believed in an impersonal Fate he draws upon some modern students of Islam who tried to show that the personification of time in pre-Islamic poetry really involves a conception of fate like that found in Greek mythology.

There is no doubt, I suppose, that if one started out to prove that the predestinarian view of Muslim tradition is a survival of a pre-Islamic atheistic fatalism, he could easily train his senses to discern an atheistic trend in Muslim tradition despite its mentioning God. But I do not believe that any one who, without such a preconceived purpose, reads the pious utterances of the traditions could find in them any deviation from the theism of the Koran. Quite the contrary, to the ordinary reader they all seem to be attempts to aggrandize and to exemplify the power of God spoken of in the Koran. Nor do I believe that any one not acquainted with later orthodox Muslim predestinarianism and with the earlier Greek belief in the mythological three Fates would see in the pre-Islamic poetic personification of time a fatalistic belief of sufficient strength to survive in the new religious setting inaugurated by the rise of Islam. Besides, one should like to know why there was no similar survival of fatalism among

[21] Goldziher, *Vorlesungen*, III, 4, pp. 95–96 (English, p. 101).
[22] Watt, *Free Will*, pp. 19ff.

the early Greek converts to Christianity, who before their conversion believed either in the fate of the popular religious kind or in the fate of the rationalized philosophic kind expressed in terms of a belief in inexorable laws of nature. If fatalistic pagan Greeks, on their coming in contact with the Philonic conception of freedom, could without any qualms of conscience adopt that view, why could not the so-called fatalistic pagan Arabs do the same on their coming in contact with a similar Christian conception of freedom?

A more likely explanation for the preference given by the early Muslims to the predestinarian verses is to be found in those verses in the Koran in which the true God of Islam is contrasted with the false pre-Islamic gods as a God who has power with gods who are powerless,[23] as, for instance, in such verses as the following: "Thy Lord is powerful. Yet beside God they worship what can neither help nor hurt them" (25:56–57). "It is God who created you, then fed you, then will cause you to die, then will make you alive. Is there any of your companion-gods who can do aught of these things?" (30:39). "Say: Is there any of the gods whom ye add to God who produceth a creature, then causeth it to return to him? Say: God produceth a creature, then causeth it to return to Him" (10:35). Power is thus the chief characteristic of the true God, and so all the passages which speak of God's power, including the passages which speak of His power over the actions of man, were to be taken as establishing the standard of true belief. Even in Judaism, with all the emphasis by rabbis on the belief in the freedom of the will, there is still the testimony of Maimonides that, despite the fact that there was no open opposition to this belief among the Jews, "most of the uninformed (*golemim*) among the Jews say that God decrees concerning man at the beginning of his formation [in his mother's womb] whether he should be righteous or wicked."[24] Simple-mindedness and excessive zeal for the power of God

[23] Cf. above, pp. 518 ff.
[24] *Mishneh Torah, Teshubah* V, 2.

has thus led these Jews to a belief in predestination which was contrary to the teaching of their religion. It is simple-mindedness and excessive zeal for the power of God, it would seem, that is taken by Maimonides to be also the reason for Muslim predestinarianism, for in the same passage, quite evidently referring to the Predestinarians in Islam, he couples them with those "most of the uninformed among the Jews" and describes them as "the uninformed (*tippeshim*) among the gentiles." The Hebrew term *tippeshim* here, as I have explained above,[25] is used by Maimonides as the equivalent of the Arabic term *bulh* and *jāhilūn* or *juhhāl* which are used by himself as a description of ignorant persons who do not apply reason to the teaching of tradition and perhaps also as the equivalent of the Arabic *ḥumuḳ* which was used in a similar sense by the Muʿtazilites as a description of their opponents who refused to apply reason to tradition.

It is thus the contrast between the powerfulness of the true God of Islam and the powerlessness of the false pre-Islamic gods so often dwelt upon in the Koran that has led to the preference given to the predestinarian verses in the Koran over the libertarian verses. We have similarly suggested how the contrast between the true God of Islam and the pre-Islamic idols dwelt upon in the Koran has contributed to the preference given by the early Muslims to the anti-anthropomorphic verses in the Koran over the anthropomorphic verses.[26] And as in the case of the preference for the anti-anthropomorphic verses,[27] so also in the case of the preference for the predestinarian verses, all the verses contrary to those given preference to, we may assume, were at first declared to be inexplicable and any discussion of them was branded as heresy but later some method of interpretation made its appearance. Such a method of interpretation was, as we shall see, the theory of acquisition which was adopted by them and used in various ways.[28]

[25] Cf. above, pp. 95 f.
[26] Cf. above, pp. 8 f.
[27] Cf. above, pp. 206 ff.
[28] Cf. below, pp. 684 ff.

This is how the predestinarian verses in the Koran were given preference over the libertarian verses and the Koranine predestinarianism was described by Jahm as compulsionism. In the course of time, as we shall see,[28a] spokesmen of predestinarianism rejected the term compulsionism, referring to it disdainfully as the obsolete view of the Jahmiyyah. Still the predestinarians continued to believe that man's acts were created by God, and so they were constantly reminded of the two arguments against predestination already raised by John of Damascus, namely, the argument that it would be an injustice on the part of God to punish men for deeds which He himself compelled them to do and the argument that it would be an inconsistency on the part of God to command men to do certain things which He likes and not to do certain other things which He does not like and at the same time to compel them to disobey those commands. But in the course of time these arguments were answered. As quoted by Averroes in the name of the Ashʿarites, the answers with regard to the two arguments run as follows.

With regard to the argument from injustice, the Ashʿarites, according to Averroes, say in effect that no act is either just or unjust in itself. An act is just or unjust only with reference to its being in obedience to the will of God or in disobedience to it. One cannot, therefore, say that God acts unjustly when by the decision of His will He punishes man for doing something which He himself willed that he should do.[29] In other words, God has a conception of justice which is unknowable to us.

With regard to the argument that Predestination implies that God compels man to do what God himself does not like, the Ashʿarites, again, according to Averroes, boldly assert that "it is conceivable that God should do that which He does not like and that He should decree that which He does not wish." [30]

[28a] Cf. below, pp. 690 ff.

[29] *Kashf*, p. 113, ll. 9–15.

[30] *Ibid.*, p. 114, ll. 8–10.

II. The Libertarians

While in the fictitious debate between a Christian and a Muslim composed by John of Damascus during the early part of the eighth century the Muslims are represented only by a Compulsionist,[1] there is evidence that by that time there had already existed among Muslims those who maintained man's free will or, as the expression goes, man's power to act. The first to start the discussion about the power of man is said to be Maʿbad al-Juhanī, who died in 699. What his view on the subject was is not known.[2] Nor is much known about the view of his disciple al-Ḥasan al-Baṣrī.[3] But beginning with Ghaylān al-Dimashḳī (d. 730) reports on the views of those who believed in free will are extant.[4]

Before we proceed to discuss the Libertarians' view on man's power, let us try to state their position on God's power. As a rule, the Libertarians accepted all the Koranic teaching with regard to God's absolute power over the order of nature. With the exception of Naẓẓām and Muʿammar, who believed in laws of nature and secondary causes,[5] they believed with the rest of the Mutakallimūn in the principle of continuous creation.[6] They also accepted the Koranic teaching on the preordination of man's term of life. This we have on the authority of Ashʿarī, who says that if the Libertarians were asked whether they would accept the Koranic teaching on this point they "would necessarily answer yes." [7] Similarly

[1] Cf. above, pp. 606 ff.

[2] A. J. Wensinck, *The Muslim Creed*, p. 53; Watt, *Free Will*, pp. 48, 53–54.

[3] Ritter, "Geschichte der Islamischen Froemmigkeit," *Der Islam*, 21 (1933), 1–83; Tritton, *Muslim Theology*, p. 58; Watt, *Free Will*, p. 54–55.

[4] Cf. Watt, pp. 40–41, 54–55.

[5] Cf. above, pp. 559 ff.

[6] This may be gathered from the statement that it is possible for a stone in the air to remain at rest and for cotton on its contact with fire not to burn which is attributed to "Abū al-Hudhayl and Jubbāʾī and the majority of the followers of the Kalām," by which is meant, as may be judged from the context, the majority of the Muʿtazilites (*Maḳālāt*, p. 312, ll. 10–13). Cf. above, p. 544.

[7] *Ibānah*, p. 76, l. 5.

they, or at least some of them, accepted the Koranic teaching of the preordination of man's sustenance. This, too, we have on the authority of Ashʿarī who says of the Muʿtazilites in general that they believed that "God created bodies and likewise the means of their sustenance,"[8] though, according to another authority, only "a group" of the Libertarians admitted the preordination of the term of life and of sustenance.[9] They parted from the established orthodoxy of their time only on the question of the preordination of human action. Human action is taken by them to differ from any other action in the world. And just as all those Muʿtazilites who denied causality and believed that every action in the world is directly created by God made an exception of human action, so also Naẓẓām and Muʿammar, the two Muʿtazilites who affirmed causality and believed that every action in the world is determined by an antecedent cause, made an exception of human action and both of them, each in his own way, affirmed free will.[10]

The fact that all the Libertarians with the exception of Naẓẓām and Muʿammar agreed with the generality of Muslims in denying intermediate causes in all the so-called natural actions, and in maintaining that those actions are all directly created by God, raises the question why they should have made an exception of human actions and why in opposition to the generality of Muslims they should have preferred the libertarian verses in the Koran to its predestinarian verses. The explanation that suggests itself is that it must have been due to some external influence and that the external influence must most probably have been Christianity, for from the fictitious debate between a Christian and a Muslim by John of Damascus it may be gathered that Christians urged upon Muslims their own belief in the freedom of the will. Indeed in that fictitious debate the Christian urges not only the belief

[8] *Maḳālāt*, p. 257, l. 9.

[9] Cf. Malaṭī, *Tanbīh*, p. 134, ll. 14–15.

[10] For Naẓẓām, see below, pp. 628 ff. For Muʿammar, see *Maḳālāt*, p. 331, l. 13 – p. 332, l. 3; *Fiṣal* IV, p. 199, ll. 18–19; V, p. 74, ll. 9–11; *Milal*, p. 47, ll. 1–9.

of free will in man but also the belief of intermediate causes in nature, and one may wonder why those Muslims who yielded to Christians in the matter of free will did not also yield in the matter of intermediate causes. The answer is to be found in the difference between these two beliefs. The belief in intermediate causes, which means a belief in the existence of laws of nature, is primarily a philosophic principle which was adopted by scriptural philosophers, the Church Fathers, and before them Philo, as a concession to philosophy, even though they sought and found support for it in Scripture.[11] The belief in absolute free will, however, is primarily a scriptural belief, which scriptural philosophers, the Church Fathers, and before them Philo, defended by scriptural teachings, occasionally with the help of philosophic reasoning.[12] This difference between the two beliefs must have become known to the Muslim Libertarians from their discussions with Christians, and so, while they were willing to follow the Christians in the belief of free will, for which they could find explicit support in the Koran, they saw no need of following them in the belief of intermediate causes, for which they could find no explicit support in the Koran.[13] The only possible support in the Koran for what may be taken to mean intermediate causes is its ascription to angels the function of carrying out the will of God; but angels, we imagine, as their name implies, were considered by them as being only messengers of God, appointed by Him each time to perform a certain given mission, and were not to be regarded as what is generally understood by intermediate natural causes.[14]

[11] Cf. *Philo*, I, chapter on "The Immanent Logos, Laws of Nature, and Miracles" and the corresponding chapter in *The Philosophy of the Church Fathers*, II.

[12] Cf. *Philo*, I, chapter on "Free Will" and corresponding chapter in *The Philosophy of the Church Fathers*, II.

[13] Cf. above, p. 601.

[14] On the conception of angels as not being causes but only deputies of God, see Ghazālī, *Tahāfut al-Falāsifah* XVII, 4–5, p. 279, ll. 1–2, and ll. 10–11. On the view that not only angels but also men may act as deputies of God, see Ghazālī, see *Iḥyā'* XXXV, *Kitāb al-Tauḥid wa'l-Tawakkul*, Section: *Bayān Ḥaḳīkat al-Tauḥīd* (Vol. IV, p. 250, ll. 31 ff.).

The chief argument used by Muslim Libertarians in support of free will was that it was required by divine justice. Already one of the earliest of Muslim Libertarians, the Ḳadarite Ghaylān al-Dimashḳī, advances this argument in the form of a series of questions addressed by him to Caliph ʿUmar b. ʿAbd al-ʿAzīs. They read as follows: "Hast thou ever found, O ʿUmar, anyone wise who blames (*yaʿīb*) that which he does, or does that which he blames, or who punishes for that which he has prescribed or prescribes that for which he will punish? Or have you found anyone of discernment who summons men to true religion and then leads them astray from it? Have you found anyone merciful who imposes upon his servants difficult tasks beyond their capacity or who punishes them for obedience? Or have you found anyone just who incites men to injustice and wrongdoing? Or have you found anyone truthful who incites men to falsehood and deceitfulness?" [15] It is later repeatedly used by the Muʿtazilites. Thus Wāṣil, the founder of Muʿtazilism, maintains that "God is wise and just and it is impossible that evil and injustice should be referred to Him and hence it is impossible that He would make men do the opposite of what He had commanded and that He should ordain something for them and then recompense them for it; it thus follows that that man is the doer of good and evil, belief and unbelief, obedience and disobedience . . . God has endowed him with power over all this." [16] Similarly Thumāma argues that, if man's action is determined by God, then man deserves "neither reward nor punishment and neither praise (*madḥ*) nor blame (*dhamm*)." [17] It is because of this rejection of preordination in the actions of men that the Muʿtazilites, of whom Wāṣil was the founder, are known as "the partisans of justice," just as, on account of their rejection of attributes they are known as the "partisans of unity."

This argument, that, if man was not free, divine justice

[15] *Al Muʿtazilah*, p. 16, ll. 8–13 (p. 26, ll. 3–7).
[16] *Milal*, p. 32, ll. 7–10.
[17] *Al Muʿtazilah*, p. 35, ll. 15–16 (p. 63, ll. 8–9).

could not "blame" and "punish" man for his wrong deeds nor could man be "praised" for his good deeds, has its historical origin in the discussion of the problem of freedom from its earliest appearance in literature. Aristotle, whose conception of free will is only relative, says that for feelings which are without choice we are neither praised (ἐπαινούμεθα) nor blamed (ψεγόμεθα).[18] The "praise" and "blame" used here by Aristotle are human praise and blame. Philo, in support of his conception of absolute free will, argues that it is only because of the absolute human freedom of the will that "man very properly receives blame (ψόγον) for offenses which he designedly commits and praise (ἔπαινον) for the good actions which he intentionally performs" [19] and also that it is because the human soul is endowed with freedom that "it will deservedly suffer the inevitable punishment dealt out to ungrateful freedmen." [20] The "blame" and "praise" and "punishment" used here by Philo are, as evident from the context, divine blame and praise and punishment. Similarly John of Damascus says that "voluntariness, then, is assuredly followed by praise (ἔπαινος) and blame (ψόγος)" [21] and that, if man is not free, "God will be found unjust" in punishing, or in ordering to punish, those who do evil.[22] And so also Abucara, in his Arabic work, argues in effect that, if man "is compelled to do what he does . . . then how can God in His justice . . . hold out to man the expectation of reward for his obedience and punishment for his disobedience." [23] The Muslim version of the argument, we may reasonably assume, came directly from Christians, with whom Muslims are known to have debated the problem.

Another argument in support of freedom, the like of which occurs in ancient philosophy, is used by Wāṣil b. ʿAṭāʾ in his statement that "man knows within himself that capacity

[18] *Eth. Nic.* II, 4, 1105b, 32; 1106a, 2–3.
[19] *Immut.* 10, 47. [20] *Ibid.* 10, 48.
[21] *De Fid. Orth.* II, 24 (PG 94, 953 A).
[22] *Disputatio Christiani et Saraceni* (PG 94, 1592 AB).
[23] Abucara, Mimar IX, 3.

(*iḳtidār*) and action exist and that whoever denies this denies [that which is known by] necessity."[24] This argument, ascribed to the Muʿtazilites, is characterized by Juwaynī as an argument based on "the perception of the intelligent." The opening statement of the argument reads as follows: "One with native intelligence distinguishes between that which is within his own power and that which is not within his own power and perceives a difference between his movements which are voluntary and his colors over which he has no power."[25] The same argument, similarly ascribed to the Muʿtazilites, is phrased by Shahrastānī as follows: "Man knows within himself that the occurrence of an act is in accordance with intentions that it is to occur and intentions that it is not to occur, so that, if he wants movement, movement will take place and, if he wants rest, rest will take place."[26] As phrased by Alexander Aphrodisiensis, the argument reads as follows: "It is rather absurd and against all evidence to say that necessity extends even to" movements performed by human beings, for "all the time we see . . . that not all things are bound to such causes as these [that is, as those to which necessity is bound]." He then goes on to argue that, while "fire, for example, is incapable of receiving cold, . . . it is possible for the man who is seated, to stand up, for the man in motion to come to rest, and for the man who is speaking, to remain silent."[27] Strikingly similar to this argument as thus phrased by Alexander is the phrasing of the same argument by two Jewish philosophers writing in Arabic. In Saadia it reads: "As for the argument from sense perception, I find that a human being feels conscious of his own power either to speak or to remain silent."[28] In Judah Halevi it reads: "For thou perceivest that thou hast power over either speaking or remaining silent."[29]

[24] *Milal*, p. 32, ll. 12–14.
[25] *Irshād*, p. 113, ll. 19–21 (183–184).
[26] *Nihāyat*, p. 79, ll. 10–12.
[27] Alexander, *De Fato* IX. Cf. Cicero, De Fato V.
[28] *Emunot* IV, 4, p. 152, ll. 10–11.
[29] *Cuzari* V, 20, p. 340, ll. 10–11; p. 341, ll. 5–7.

The influence of Greek terminology through the Church Fathers may be discerned in the use of the Arabic term *ḳadariyyah* as a designation of those who believed in free will. Originally in the Koran God is described by various forms of the verb *ḳadar*, "to possess power," "to determine," "to decree." Thus God is described as "powerful (*ḳadīr*) over all" (2:19), as "the powerful" — *al-ḳadīr* (30:53), as "having the power (*ḳādir*) to send down a sign" (6:37), and Moses is said to have come to Midian by God's *ḳadar*, "decree" (20:42). But, when the question of free will was raised, the term *ḳadariyyah* was applied not to the Predestinarians, who believed that power belongs only to God, but rather to the Libertarians, who believed that "God is not to be described as having power (*ḳudrah*) over a thing over which men have power (*yaḳdur*)." [30] Why that name was given to those who assigned power to man has been variously explained. A collection of these various explanations was made by Nallino,[31] in which is included Goldziher's explanation that the deniers of God's *ḳadar* are called *ḳadariyyah* in the sense of *lucus a non lucendo*.[32] Nallino himself accepts Haarbrücker's explanation [33] that they were called *ḳadariyyah* because they were the first to discuss the meaning of the term *ḳadar* which was used in the Koran. A new explanation offered by Watt is that the term *ḳadariyyah* started as a nickname by which the Predestinarians and Libertarians called each other, but which ultimately stuck only to the Libertarians.[34] I should like to suggest that the use of the term *ḳadariyyah* as a description of the Libertarians, with the implied new use of the term *ḳadar* as meaning the power of man to determine his own actions, was due to the influence of Greek philosophic vocabulary. It happens that in the report by John of Damascus of

[30] *Maḳālāt*, p. 549, ll. 9–10.

[31] C. A. Nallino, "Sul nome di 'qadariti'," *Rivista degli Studi Orientali*, 7 (1916–18), 461–466.

[32] Goldziher, *Vorlesungen über den Islam*, 4, p. 95 (English, p. 101).

[33] Haarbrücker's translation of Shahrastānī's *Milal*, vol. II, p. 387.

[34] Watt, *Free Will*, pp. 48–49.

the disputation between the Christian and the Muslim the term used for one being endowed with free will is *αὐτεξούσιος*,[35] which literally means "in one's own power," and hence "one's own master," "free agent." We may assume that in the debates between Muslims and Christians on the problem of freedom of the will the term *αὐτεξούσιος* was translated into Arabic by *ḳādir bi-nafsihi*, "powerful by his own self." Once the term *ḳādir*, "powerful," was thus used in a phrase describing man's own power, it was quite natural to use the term *ḳadariyyah* as a description of those who believed in man's own power to determine his actions.

Thus the very name Ḳadarites by which the early Libertarians came to be called is owed to the influence of Greek philosophic terminology through Christian sources.

As to whether there was also a Jewish influence upon Muslim Libertarianism, Isfarā'inī states explicitly that Muslim Libertarians have acquired their belief in free will from Jewish Libertarians.[36] Two modern Jewish scholars, Schreiner and Neumark, think that Wāṣil's statement to the effect that everything is predestined "except goodness and wickedness, nobleness and baseness, which belong to men's acquisitions (*aksāb*)"[37] reflects the influence of the rabbinic statement that "everything is in the power of Heaven except the fear of Heaven."[38] It is, however, to be noted that, even if we assume that Wāṣil's statement has been influenced by the rabbinic statement, there is still the following difference between them. According to Wāṣil, to be predestined means to be created by God directly;[39] according to the rabbis, to be "in the power of Heaven" means to be created by God indirectly through intermediate causes.

Though the Mu'tazilites from their very beginning fol-

[35] John of Damascus, *op. cit.* (PG 94, 1589 BC).

[36] *Tabṣīr*, p. 133, ll. 7–10; cf. above, p. 70. Cf. also above, p. 605.

[37] *Milal*, p. 32, l. 19 – p. 33, l. 1. On the use of the term "acquisitions" here, see below, p. 666.

[38] *Berakot* 33b.

[39] Cf. above at n. 6.

lowed the Ḳadarites in affirming that man has power over his action, they were not certain as to whether that power entitles him to be described as the creator of his action. Thus Ash'arī, in an early part of his *Maḳālāt*, reports that there was a difference of opinion among the Mu'tazilites as to whether man creates (*yaḫluḳu*) his actions or not.[40] Later in the same work he reports that all the Mu'tazilites, except one, affirmed that man is in the real sense of the terms a *fa'il*, "agent," and a *muḥdith*, "innovator," and a *muḫtari'*, "inventor," and a *munshi'*, "causer of rising." [41] The term *ḫāliḳ*, "creator," is significantly omitted from the list of terms upon which all the Mu'tazilites, except one, agreed that they may be applied to man in their real, and not merely in their metaphorical, sense. An explanation of this difference of opinion among the Mu'tazilites with regard to the term "creator" is to be found in the following statement of Juwaynī: "The early Mu'tazilites refrained from calling man creator (*ḫāliḳ*) because of the closeness of their contact with the early Muslims who unanimously declared that there is no creator but God. The later Mu'tazilites, however, became bold and called man creator in [what they considered to be] the real sense of the term." [42] As to who these later Mu'tazilites were and why they had no scruples in applying to man the term creator, we are informed by Taftāzānī in the following statement: "The early Mu'tazilites refrained from using the term *ḫāliḳ*, creator, with reference to man, and only used the terms *mujid*, bringer into existence, *muḫtari'*, inventor, and the like. But when al-Jubbā'ī and his followers saw that the terms all meant the same, namely, the one who causes a transition from nonexistence into existence (*al-muḫrij min al-'adam ilā al-wujūd*), they became bold and used term *ḫāliḳ*, creator." [43] What this last part of the statement means is that Jubbā'ī and his followers

[40] *Maḳālāt*, p. 228, ll. 5–11.
[41] *Ibid.*, p. 539, ll. 12–13.
[42] *Irshād*, p. 106, ll. 11–13 (173–4).
[43] Taftāzānī, p. 96, ll. 3–6. For Jubbā'ī's own statement as to why he applied to man the term "creator," see below, pp. 680–681.

came to consider the difference between the term "creator" and the other terms as being only verbal. This view of Jubbā'ī would seem to have become prevalent among the Muʿtazilites, for Shahrastānī, in his exposition of the views of the Muʿtazilites in general, says that "they are in agreement that man is a possessor of power (*ḳādir*) and creator (*ḫāliḳ*) of his actions, the good and the bad." [44]

The description of man as having power over his action, commonly used by the Muʿtazilites in expressing their belief in free will, even when added by the description of man as being a creator, does not mean that man's action is entirely independent of God, for, while indeed man has the power to act, that power comes to him from God. As to how that power (*ḳudrah*) or, as it is also called, capacity (*istiṭāʿah*), comes to man from God, there were two views.

According to one view, man *qua* man is from birth endowed by God with the power to act. It is this view which is reported by Ashʿarī in the name of the Maymūniyyah, of which he says that it is in accordance with the view of the Muʿtazilites. It reads as follows: "God has entrusted (*fawwaḍa*) men with acts and has conceded to them (*jaʿala lahum*) the capacity to perform all the duties imposed upon them, so that both unbelievers and believers are in a position to carry them out, and God has no will in men's actions and men's actions are not created by God." [45] Historically, this conception of free will was first formulated by Philo [46] and was followed by all the early Church Fathers.[47]

According to another view, man *qua* man is not endowed from birth with the power to act, but with each act God creates in man a power which enables him to act freely of

[44] *Milal*, p. 30, ll. 16–17.

[45] *Maḳālāt*, p. 93, ll. 7–10. Cf. definition of *tafwīḍ*, "entrustment," "delegation," quoted by Franz Rosenthal, in his *Muslim Conception of Freedom*, p. 21, n. 50, from As-Sarakhsī's *Uṣūl* (Cairo, 1372), I, 122: "Delegation (*tafwīḍ*) means delegation of the divine will to a person, giving him the right to choose and thus making him responsible for his actions."

[46] Cf. *Philo*, I, pp. 424–428.

[47] Cf. *ibid.*, I, pp. 458–459, and my *Religious Philosophy*, pp. 158–161.

his own accord. That there was such a view among Libertarians as distinct from the preceding view is explicitly stated by Maimonides who — in contrast to "those" of whom he simply says that they assert that "man has capacity (*istiṭāʿah*)," [48] by which he undoubtedly means the view ascribed by Ashʿarī to the Maymūniyyah — mentions "the Muʿtazilites," of whom he says that they assert that "man acts in virtue of a power (*ḳudrah*) created in him." [49] Undoubtedly this direct statement of Maimonides is based upon some source which is unknown to me at the present writing. An implication of a difference of opinion among the Muʿtazilites on this question is to be discerned, I believe, in Ashʿarī's discussion of the difference of opinion among the Muʿtazilites on the question whether capacity (*istiṭāʿah*) has duration or not. Most of the Muʿtazilites, he reports, say it has, but some say it has not.[50] Underlying this difference of opinion, I take it, is the question whether capacity is an inborn endowment in man, so that it precedes every act of man and hence has duration, or whether it is created simultaneously with each act and, inasmuch as acts are continuously created, the capacity for an act has no duration.[51] Consequently, whenever Muʿtazilites happen vaguely to speak of man as having power to act, they may mean thereby either a power with which man *qua* man is endowed from birth or a power which God creates in man with each act.

Then there was another difference among the Libertarians in their conception of freedom. According to most of them, the power to act which man derives from God in either of the two ways mentioned is a power to perform either noble acts and goodness or base acts and wickedness. According to one group of Libertarians, however, only "wickedness and base acts are from men themselves," whereas "noble acts and goodness are from God." [52] What this view means, we may assume,

[48] *Moreh* III, 17 (4), p. 337, l. 24.
[49] *Ibid.* I, 73 (6), p. 141, l. 20.
[50] *Maḳālāt*, p. 230, ll. 1–8.
[51] Cf. below, p. 670.
[52] Malaṭī, *Tanbīh*, p. 126, l. 15.

is that one is free either to follow or to resist the inducements of Satan, which are the source of man's base and wicked actions, but one is not free to resist the grace of God, which is the source of man's noble and good actions. It is not clear, however, whether the divine grace by which, according to this group of Libertarians, man is enabled to do good is a power with which man *qua* man is endowed by God at his birth or whether it is a power which God creates in man with each act he is about to perform. A similar vagueness with regard to the use of divine grace occurs later in the discussion of Ḫāṭirāni.[53]

III. The *Ḫāṭirāni* in the Kalam and Ghazālī as Inner Motive Powers of Human Actions *

The controversy in Islam between the Predestinarians and the Libertarians as to whether man in his doing of evil is a free agent or not means whether man is free to resist some power that prompts him to do evil. In the Koran, that power is called Satan, who, though created by God (7:11), has set himself up, evidently with the permission of God, as the beguiler of man (7:15–17) and is described as "an enemy, openly leading astray" (28:14) and as one whose "incitement" incites man (41:36). This incitement of Satan is, according to the Predestinarians, irresistible, whereas, according to the Libertarians, it is resistible, so that when man, without resisting it, does the evil which he is incited to do, he does it of his own free will.

This description of Satan as enemy and evil inciter of man reflects both the Biblical and the Rabbinic conception of Satan. In the Bible, though mostly Satan is represented as the adversary, that is, the enemy, of man, he is also described as

[53] Cf. below, p. 636.

*Reprinted from *Studies in Mysticism and Religion*, presented to Gershom G. Scholem, 1967, pp. 363–379.

the inciter of man to do something wrong.[1] In Rabbinic literature, Satan continues to be the adversary or enemy of man, but his role as the evil inciter of man is much greater, and he is specifically described as one who "goes down [from heaven] and leads [man] astray."[2] But in this role of his as inciter of evil he is identified with the evil *yeṣer*[3] who, like Satan, is called "enemy"[4] and is described as "inciting" man to evil,[5] but, unlike Satan, is said to exist within man himself, in his heart.[6] In the Koran, however, there is no explicit mention of an evil motive power within man himself corresponding to the Rabbinic evil *yeṣer*, though there may be an allusion to some such motive power in the statements that "his soul permitted (*ṭawwaʿaṭ*) him to slay his brother" (5:33) and "the soul is wont to command evil" (12:53).

Nor is there in the Koran any explicit mention of a good motive power within man himself corresponding to the Rabbinic good *yeṣer*. The only good motive power explicitly mentioned in the Koran as the opponent of Satan is God himself. Thus: "But for the goodness and mercy of God towards you, you would have followed Satan, except a few" (4:85); "But for the goodness and mercy of God, not one of you would be ever pure, but God purifies whom He will" (24:21); "And if an incitement from Satan incites thee, then take refuge in God" (41:36); "I take refuge in the Lord of men . . . from the evil of the Whisperer" (114:1, 4); "Verily no power has he over those who believe" (16:101). Here, again, the Koranic conception of God as the cause of man's doing of good is taken by the Predestinarians to mean that God compels man to do good, whereas by the Libertarians it is taken to mean that the power of freedom of choice possessed by man is ultimately traceable to God who has created it within him.

Gradually, however, new conceptions of powers that move

[1] I Chron. 21:1; cf. II Sam. 24:1.
[2] *Baba Batra* 16a.
[3] *Ibid.*
[4] *Sukkah* 52a.
[5] *Ibid.* 52b.
[6] *Ibid.* 52a.

man to good or to evil action appeared in Islam. First, there appeared, as a counterpart of Satan, a new good motive power, who, like Satan, was a creation of God external to man. Second, both for the doing of good and the doing of evil there appeared two new motive powers, both creations of God within man himself.

The reference to a created good motive power external to man occurs in a tradition which reads as follows:

> Man has two visitations (*lammatāni*), a visitation (*lammah*) from the angel and a visitation from Satan. As for the visitation of the angel, it portends good and a belief in the Truth and a benignancy of the soul; as for the visitation of Satan, it portends evil and a denial of the Truth and a malignancy of the soul.[7]

Thus from among the angels who in the Koran are said to act as God's messengers one angel has been selected to act for God as the opponent of Satan.

Two motive powers for the action of man, vaguely described by terms which lend themselves to different interpretations, appear in another tradition.[8] The difference of interpretation of those terms is brought out in four translations of this tradition, two in English and two in French. I shall quote these translations in chronological order and in the first of these translations I shall insert within parentheses the vague Arabic terms which lend themselves to those different interpretations.

> 1. E. E. Salisbury, 1866: "There is made to succeed no successor (*mā istuḫlīfa ḫalīfah*) [in human descent] who has not two inclinations (*biṭānatāni*), one prompting him to good, and impelling him thereto, and the other

[7] Quoted in *Lisān al-'Arab*, Vol. 16, p. 26, ll. 12–13; cf. Fritz Meier, *Die Fawā'iḥ al-Ǧamāl wa-Fawātiḥ al-Ǧamāl des Naǧm ad-Dīn al-Kubrā* (1957), p. 127, n. 3.

[8] *Ḳadar* VIII, p. 255, ll. 2–4, in Buḫārī, *al-Ṣaḥīḥ* (ed. Krehl and Juynboll).

prompting him to evil, and thereto impelling him; and he is secured whom God secures." [9]

2. A. de Vlieger, 1903: "Chaque prince s'entoure de deux espèces de confidents. Il y a des confidents qui lui conseillent le bien et qui l'y incitent; il y en a d'autres qui lui conseillent le mal et qui l'y incitent. Et celui-là est bien protégé que Dieu protège." [10]

3. O. Houdas, 1914: "Tout vicaire institué par Dieu possède deux sentiments innés: l'un qui lui ordonne le bien et l'excite à le faire; l'autre qui lui ordonne le mal et l'excite à le faire. Celui-là seul est préservé que Dieu préserve." [11]

4. W. M. Watt, 1948: "There is no 'calif' who does not have two courtiers, one ordering and inciting him to good, and one to bad; and the protected is he whom God protects." [12]

Of these four translations, the second and the fourth take the good and the evil inciter to exist outside of man, thus identifying them probably with the angel and Satan of the other tradition. The first and the third translations take them to exist within man himself, and the first translation, that of Salisbury, I shall try to show, is based upon an identification of these two inner motives for human action with the Jewish traditional two *yeṣarim*, the good *yeṣer* and the evil *yeṣer*. Let me write a sort of commentary on Salisbury's translation.

First, Salisbury's translation of the expression *mā istuḫlīfa ḫalīfah* by "there is made to succeed no successor [in human descent]," which means "there is no human being," is evidently based upon the Koranic verses "I am making a successor (*ḫalīfatan*) on earth" (2:28) and "It is He who made you successors (*ḫalā'ifa*) on earth" (6:165; 35:37), in the former

[9] "Muhammadan Doctrine of Predestination and Free Will," *Journal of the American Oriental Society*, 8 (1866), p. 137.

[10] *Kitāb al Qadr*, p. 64.

[11] *El-Bokhari: Les Traditions Islamiques*, IV, 324.

[12] *Free Will and Predestination in Early Islam*, p. 27.

of which Adam is called "successor" and in the latter men in general are called "successors."

Second, his translation of the term *biṭānatāni*, which literally means "inner sides," by the term "inclinations" is probably based on the assumption that the passage reflects the Rabbinic view that in every man there is a "good *yeṣer*" and an "evil *yeṣer*," that is, a good inclination and an evil inclination.

A view explicitly affirming the existence of two motive forces within man himself, referred to by the term *ḫāṭirāni*, which is the dual form of the singular *ḫāṭir*, was, according to reports in Ashʿarī's *Maḳālāt*, introduced by Naẓẓām (d. 845). The reports read as follows:

> 1. Ibrāhīm al-Naẓẓām said: There must needs be *ḫāṭirāni*, of which one bids advancing (*al-iḳdām*) and the other bids desisting (*al-kaff*), so that one's choice between them may be a genuine choice. Ibn al-Rāwandī reported of him that he had said the *ḫāṭir* of disobedience (*al-maʿṣiyah*) is from God, except that God produced it for the sake of causing just action and not in order to stir up disobedience.[13]

> 2. Ibrāhīm al-Naẓẓām maintained that man has no power [of free choice] over that for which he has no *ḫāṭirāni* (*lā yuḫtar*) in his heart.[14]

Ashʿarī's first report quite evidently implies that the original statement of Naẓẓām consisted of two parts, the first part dealing with the need of *ḫāṭirāni* for the proper exercise of free choice between advancing and desisting and the second part dealing with the need of *ḫāṭirāni* for the proper exercise of free choice between obedience and disobedience. But it is

[13] *Maḳālāt*, p. 427, l. 16 – p. 428, l. 1; The first part of the report is reproduced by Shahrastānī, *Milal*, p. 41, ll. 2–3, on which see the comment by S. Horovitz in *Ueber den Einfluss der griechischen Philosophie auf die Entwicklung des Kalam* (Breslau, 1909), p. 26.

[14] *Maḳālāt*, p. 239, l. 5.

not clear what the relation between these two parts was. On the one hand, the two parts may have referred to two different kinds of acts, the first part referring to what may be called secular acts, described by the terms advancing and desisting, by which was simply meant doing and not doing, and the second part referring to what may be called religious acts, described by the terms obedience and disobedience, by which was quite evidently meant obedience and disobedience to divine commands. On the other hand, the second part may have been only an extension of the first part, explaining that by advancing and desisting was meant obedience and disobedience to divine commands. However, from a report by Baghdādī on Naẓẓām's theory of *ḫāṭirāni* soon to be quoted,[14a] a report evidently based either on Ashʿarī's first report or on the same source that was used by Ashʿarī in that first report, it may be inferred that the first report of Ashʿarī dealt only with acts of obedience and disobedience to divine commands and that hence *ḫāṭirāni* were required by Naẓẓām only in connection with religious acts. Accordingly, in his brief second report on Naẓẓām's theory of *ḫāṭirāni*, which is evidently based on his longer first report and is couched in his own language, Ashʿarī did not feel the need of specifying that the acts for which Naẓẓām required *ḫāṭirāni* were only religious acts. From still another report by Ashʿarī on Naẓẓām we gather that, in contradistinction to the *ḫāṭir* of disobedience, who is described here by Naẓẓām as one who was created in the heart of man and who only "bids" (*ya'mur*) man to desist from obedience to divine commands, Satan is described by him as one for whom it is impossible to enter into the heart of man and who "restrains" (*nahā*) [15] man from performing acts of piety and charity.

Thus in connection with religious acts there are within man two opposite motive powers called *ḫāṭirāni*. What according to Naẓẓām were the two opposite motive powers within man in connection with secular acts may be gathered

[14a] Cf. below, p. 631.
[15] *Ibid.*, p. 436, ll. 12–15.

from two other reports on him by Ashʿarī. The reports read as follows:

1. Al-Naẓẓām said: All bodies are in motion and motion is twofold, motion in the sense of an inclination to motion (*iʿtimād*) and motion in the sense of locomotion (*nuḳlah*), and both of them are motion in reality, whereas rest exists only in speech.[16]

2. Ibrāhīm al-Naẓẓām said: (a) There is no action of man but motion [and similarly desistance from action, which is rest, is motion]; (b) man does not produce an act of motion [in his body unless there is a corresponding motion] in the soul; (c) prayer and fasting [which are religious acts of the body], desires and aversions and knowledge and ignorance [which are acts of the soul], truthfulness (*al-ṣidḳ*) and falsehood (*al-kadhib*) [spoken about matters of belief, which are religious acts of the body], a man's speech and his silence [which are secular acts of the body], and the rest of the acts of man are motions.[17]

Combining these two reports with reports quoted above, we gather that, in the case of all opposite acts of the body, whether secular or religious, there must be corresponding opposite acts of the soul, but, whereas in the case of secular opposite acts of the body, the corresponding opposite acts of the soul may be such opposites as desires and aversions or knowledge and ignorance, in the case of religious opposite acts of the body, the corresponding opposite acts of the soul are the *ḫāṭir* of obedience and the *ḫāṭir* of disobedience.

[16] *Ibid.*, p. 324, ll. 12–13. On the term *iʿtimād*, see S. Pines, "Études sur Awḥad al-Zamān Abu'l Barakāt al-Baghdādī," *Revue des Études Juives*, 103 (1938), pp. 45 ff. and Goichon, *Ibn Sīnā: Livre des Directives et Remarques*, pp. 284–285, n. 2.

[17] *Ibid.*, p. 403, ll. 14–16. Cf. *Milal*, p. 38, l. 7: "Knowledge in its various forms and desires are motions of the soul." Cf. also the terms *kadhib* and *ṣidḳ* in such verses of the Koran, for instance, as (3:69) "They speak falsehood (*al-kadhiba*) about God" and (33:8) "He might ask the speakers of the truth as to their truthfulness (*ṣidḳihim*)."

Baghdādī in his report referred to above assigns to Naẓẓām's theory of *ḫāṭirāni* a foreign origin. According to him, it was borrowed by Naẓẓām from the Brahmans, whose view is described by him as follows:

> As for the Brahmans, they acknowledge the unity of the Creator but deny the Messengers [sent by Him] and they maintain . . . that the heart of no human being is devoid of *ḫāṭirāni*. One of the *ḫāṭirāni* is from God, and this one calls man's attention to that which makes it necessary for him to know concerning the knowledge of God and concerning the duty of his giving thanks to God, and it prompts him to speculation and to the seeking of information concerning God from His signs (*āyāt*) and demonstrations (*dalā'il*).[18] The second *ḫāṭir* is from Satan, and this turns man away from obedience to the *ḫāṭir* which is from God.[19]

Baghdādī then goes on to show how Naẓẓām has introduced certain changes in this theory of *ḫāṭirāni*, among them the view that both the *ḫāṭir* of obedience (*al-ṭā'ah*) and the *ḫāṭir* of disobedience (*al-ma'ṣiyah*) were created by God in the heart of man.[20]

Now Baghdādī's brief account here of Brahmanism is on the whole similar to the longer accounts of it in Ibn Ḥazm[21] and Shahrastānī.[22] But neither in Ibn Ḥazm nor in Shahrastānī is there any mention of *ḫāṭirāni*, nor is there in them any mention of a being corresponding to the Satan here in Baghdādī. In fact, Brahmanism, I am told by Professor Daniel H. H. Ingalls, has no conception of two opposite motive powers in

[18] Cf. Saadia's translation of the Hebrew *otot u-mofetim* (signs and wonders [τέρατα]) by *āyāt u-barāhīn*, signs and demonstrations (Deut. 6:22 *et passim*) and Koran (2:86): "Moses came to you with demonstrations (*bi'l bayyinati*)." Cf. Kaufmann, *Attributenlehre*, p. 15, n. 28.

[19] *Uṣūl*, p. 26, ll. 6–12; p. 154, l. 16 – p. 155, l. 3.

[20] *Ibid.*, p. 27, ll. 2–3; p. 155, ll. 10–11. In *Farḳ*, p. 338, ll. 6–7, Baghdādī attributes the theory of *ḫāṭirānī* to the "Brahmans and Ḳadariyyah."

[21] *Fiṣal*, I, p. 69, l. 4 ff.

[22] *Milal*, p. 444, l. 10 ff.

man. Accordingly, while we may assume that Baghdādī had some source — some spurious oral or written account of Brahmanism — from which he derived his information about the Brahman's *ḫāṭirāni*, the fact that no mention is made of these *ḫāṭirāni* by Ibn Ḥazm and Shahrastānī shows quite clearly that Baghdādī's source of information was not generally known and, if known at all, was not widely used, and hence one may doubt whether it could have been the source of Naẓẓām's theory of *ḫāṭirāni*. From Baghdādī's report, however, it may be inferred that Naẓẓām's theory of *ḫāṭirāni* was considered by Baghdādī, and undoubtedly also by others, as being of foreign origin. Let us then try to find out what that foreign origin may have been. Three possibilities suggest themselves.

First, there is the Zoroastrian doctrine of the "Twin Spirits" which lead man to choose good or evil. The text, quoted from a literal translation, reads as follows: "Now, in the beginning were these two Spirits (*tā mainyū*), who had revealed themselves as Twin, well-working; in thoughts, and in words also, and in deeds, these two show themselves as good and bad; and of these two the wise rightly do choose, but not so the unwise" (Yasna XXX, 3).[23] The similarity between the Zoroastrian *tā mainyū* and Naẓẓām's *ḫāṭirāni* is striking. The fact that Naẓẓām is said to have associated himself in his youth with "the sect of Dualists" [24] would seem to corroborate the assumption of a Zoroastrian influence upon him. Moreover, the term *ḫāṭir* has among its several meanings also the meaning of "thought," "mind"; and so does also the term *mainyū*.

Second, there is the Jewish doctrine of the two *yeṣarim* mentioned before. Not only is there a general similarity between the Jewish doctrine and Naẓẓām's doctrine, but there is also a connection between the Arabic *ḫāṭir* and the Hebrew

[23] *The Divine Songs of Zarathushtra* translated by Irach J. S. Taraporewala (Bombay, 1951), p. 136.

[24] Baghdādī, *Farḳ*, p. 113, ll. 13–14.

yeṣer, for, though the roots of these two terms have different meanings, both of these terms have acquired the same derivative meanings of "thought," "desire," and "inclination." In fact, Saadia, in his Arabic translation of the Pentateuch, renders the Hebrew *yeṣer* (Gen. 6: 5; 8:21; Deut. 31: 21) by the Arabic *ḫāṭir*. Then there are especially striking similarities between the *ḫāṭir* of disobedience in Naẓẓām and the evil *yeṣer* in Judaism. Just as the *ḫāṭir* of disobedience is said by Naẓẓām to have been created by God, so is the evil *yeṣer* said by the rabbis to have been created by God himself,[25] and just as the *ḫāṭir* of disobedience is said by Naẓẓām to have been created for a good purpose, so is the evil *yeṣer* said by the rabbis to have been created for a good purpose and to have been included among the things created by God which are described as "very good" (Gen. 1: 31).[26]

Third, as the term *ḫāṭir* has also the meaning of "soul," the distinction between the *ḫāṭir* of obedience and the *ḫāṭir* of disobedience may reflect Plato's distinction in the human soul between two parts, the rational (λογιστικόν) and the irrational (ἀλόγιστικον) or concupiscent (ἐπιθυμητικόν), of which the former is that which restrains (τὸ κωλῦον) man from something noxious and the latter is that which prompts (τὸ κελεῦον) him to it.[27] Or, in its meaning of "desire," the term *ḫāṭir* may reflect Aristotle's use of the term ὄρεξιζ, "appetency," which, when combined with intellect (νοῦς), is used "in accordance with reason" and yields "rational wish" (βούλησις), but, when combined with imagination and used contrary to reason, yields concupiscence (ἐπιθυμία),[28] thus corresponding to Naẓẓām's *ḫāṭir* of obedience and *ḫāṭir* of disobedience.

It would be futile to speculate as to which of these sources was that from which Naẓẓām derived his theory of *ḫāṭirāni*. Ecclecticism is characteristic of Naẓẓām as of all the other Mutakallimūn, and we may therefore assume that his theory of *ḫāṭirāni* had its origin in a combination of all these sources.

[25] *Berakot* 61a.
[26] *Genesis Rabbah* 9, 7.
[27] *Republic* IV.439 CD.
[28] *De Anima* III, 10, 433a, 9–30.

A combination of the Jewish *yeṣarim* with the philosophic rational and irrational desires, or rational and irrational souls, is already to be found in Philo [29] and, it can be shown, also in Christianity. Accordingly, in whatever sense the term *ḫāṭir* is used by Naẓẓām, whether in its sense of desire or inclination or intellect or soul, the *ḫāṭirāni* are conceived by him as two special inner motive powers which prompt man to opposite religious acts, as distinguished from some general inner motive powers which prompt man to opposite secular acts. In both these kinds of acts, Naẓẓām, as a Muʿtazilite, believed that man is free to make his own choice between the two opposite promptings.

The theory of *ḫāṭirāni* introduced by the Muʿtazilite Naẓẓām met with various reactions among his fellow Muʿtazilites. As reported by Ashʿarī "Abū al-Hudhayl and [some of] the rest of the Muʿtazilites" adopted it but they made the *ḫāṭir* of disobedience to come from Satan.[30] Others, however, rejected them altogether. The reports on the latter read as follows:

> (1) Bishr b. al-Muʿtamir said: He who is free to choose his action, and as he chooses it, is in no need of the *ḫāṭirāni*, and as proof of this he proffered the first Satan, for there is no tradition that Satan had a *ḫāṭir* (*yuḫṭar*).[31]

The reference is to the verses in the Koran where Satan, or rather Iblis, is said to have been created by God and to have disobeyed Him (7: 10–11; 38: 77) but where no mention is made of a *ḫāṭir* by which he was led to disobey God.

> (2) Some people said that, in the case of action which man by his own nature is apt to perform and which he has a mind to perform, towards which he has an inclination and for which he has a liking, there is no need for a

[29] Cf. my *Philo*, II, 288–290.

[30] *Maḳālāt*, p. 429, ll. 1–2. For the reason of my adding within brackets the qualifying "some of," see below, n. 33.

[31] *Ibid.*, p. 428, ll. 5–6; cf. *Milal*, p. 45, ll. 16–18.

ḫāṭir to urge him to perform them. As for actions, however, which man dislikes and for which he has an aversion, when those actions are divine commands, God creates in man such a number of motive powers as will counterbalance his dislike for those actions and his aversion to them. And if the actions toward which man has an inclination and for which he has a liking were instigated by Satan, then God equips man with certain motive powers and an incitement which counterbalance the instigation of Satan and bar his way to victory. And if God wishes that an action which man dislikes and to which by his nature he has an aversion should be liked and desired by him, He creates motive powers and an incitement and an intimidation and an augmentation (*taufīr*) [32] which surpass that which there is in him of a dislike for that action, with the result that he is inclined to that to which he is [now] urged and which by nature he is [now] made to desire. Ibn al-Rāwandī states that this view is the same as his own view.[33]

The difference between these anonymous "people," with whom Ibn al-Rāwandī agrees, and Naẓẓām may be restated as follows: As Mu'tazilites, who believe in free will, they admit with Naẓẓām that, in the case of secular acts, free will means man's power to choose between the opposite promptings of a natural inclination and a natural aversion; but, in disagreement with Naẓẓām who, in the case of religious acts, takes free will to mean man's power to choose between the opposite promptings of a *ḫāṭir* of obedience and a *ḫāṭir* of

[32] The reading *taufīr* here, as may be seen from its variants, is doubtful. It is probably a corruption of *taufīḳ* which is used elsewhere in the *Maḳālāt* (p. 263, l. 1; p. 283, l. 10) in the sense of divine help or favor or grace.

[33] *Maḳālāt*, p. 428, ll. 7–15. It is undoubtedly these two types of opponents of Naẓẓām, who specifically opposed his requirement of *ḫāṭirāni* for religious acts, that Ash'arī had in mind when immediately after his second report on Naẓẓām (p. 239, l. 5; cf. above at n. 14) he says that "[some of] the rest of the Mu'tazilites" disagreed with him (p. 239, ll. 6–7). For the reason of my adding within brackets the qualifying "some of," see above at n. 30.

disobedience, they believe that, even in religious acts, free will means man's power to choose between the opposite promptings of a natural inclination and a natural aversion. Like Naẓẓām, however, they believe that, in religious acts, there is for disobedience also an external instigator, and that is the Koranic Satan. Again, as Muʿtazilites, they admit with Naẓẓām that God who has endowed man with the power of free will does not interfere in human actions,[34] but they add that under certain circumstances God may help man toward the exercise of his power of free will. This auxiliary divine grace, they say, manifests itself in three ways. In the case of the instigation of Satan to disobedience, (1) God may create in man new motive powers which would counterbalance the Satanic instigation, so that man would be enabled to exercise his power of free will and make his own choice. In the case of the prompting to disobedience by a natural aversion, either (2) God may, again, create in man new motive powers which would counterbalance that prompting of the natural aversion, so that man would be enabled to exercise his power of free will and make his own choice, or (3) God may transform that prompting to disobedience into a prompting to obedience. It is not clear, however, whether this auxiliary divine grace is conceived of by these anonymous "people" and Ibn al-Rāwandī as a free grace or as a merited grace.

Among the orthodox Mutakallimūn, Naẓẓām's theory of *ḫāṭirāni*, used in the sense of two inner motive powers one inciting to good actions and the other inciting to evil actions, was adopted by Muḥāsibī, who, though regarded by the Ṣūfī as one of them, is included by Baghdādī and Shahrastānī and others among the orthodox Mutakallimūn.[35] But, while accepting Naẓẓām's theory of *ḫāṭirāni*, as a Predestinarian, Muḥāsibī did not believe that man was free to follow the prompting of either of the one or the other of the *ḫāṭirāni*, and so,

[34] *Ibid.*, p. 549, ll. 9–11.

[35] *Kitāb al-Riʿāya Liḥuqūq Allāh* by . . . al-Muḥāsibī, edited by Margaret Smith, Introduction, p. [xv]. Cf. paragraph on Muḥāsibī by Fritz Meier (cited above, n. 7), pp. 127–128.

as if for the purpose of changing the original unorthodox meaning of the theory, he does not use the term *ḫāṭirāni*, which is the dual of *ḫāṭir*, nor does he speak of a contrast between one kind of *ḫāṭir* and another kind of *ḫāṭir*; instead he uses the term *ḫaṭarāt*, which is the plural of *ḫaṭrah*, and he speaks of a contrast between one kind of *ḫaṭarāt* and another kind of *ḫaṭarāt*, the singular *ḫāṭir* being used by him only in the sense of one of the sources of one of those two kinds of *ḫaṭarāt*.[36] Thus, reflecting Naẓẓām's statement that "there must needs be *ḫāṭirāni*, of which one bids advancing [that is, obedience] and the other bids desisting [that is, disobedience]," he says that "the keeping of the laws of God is in accordance with the *ḫaṭarāt* of the heart, which incite to every good and evil." [37] But, whereas according to Naẓẓām both *ḫāṭirāni* come from God and according to Abū al-Hudhayl and others the *ḫāṭir* of disobedience comes from Satan, Muḥāsibī gives a different explanation of the origin of his good and evil *ḫaṭarāt*.

His explanation of the origin of the good *ḫaṭarāt* is twofold. First, they come "from the intellect (*al-ʿaḳl*) after God has aroused it." [38] The first part of the statement quite evidently reflects Aristotle's statement that rational wish arises from appetency plus the intellect.[39] The second part is an attempt to harmonize the Aristotelian and the Koranic teaching by making the intellect only that which carries out the bidding of God.

Second, explains Muḥāsibī, this rousing of the intellect consists partly in that "God recalls to the mind of man [a remembrance of God] by the creation of a *ḫāṭir* which He installs in the man's heart" and partly in that "He commands the angel to recall to the mind of man [that remembrance of God]." [40] In connection with the angel, Muḥāsibī quotes in the name of ʿAbdallah b. Masʿūd the tradition quoted above

[36] Cf. below at n. 40.
[37] *Op. cit.* n. 35, p. 44, ll. 3–4.
[38] *Ibid.*, l. 9.
[39] Cf. above at n. 27.
[40] *Op. cit.*, p. 44, ll. 15–16.

about the visitation (*lammah*) from the angel,[41] upon which he remarks that in one tradition ascribed to ʿAbdallah b. Masʿūd it is said that the visitation from the angel means God.[42] All this would seem to be an attempt to harmonize Naẓẓām's *ḫāṭir* of obedience with the angel of tradition and God of the Koran.

His explanation of the origin of the evil *ḫaṭarāt* is also twofold.

First, they come "from the passionate desire (*hawan*) of the soul." [43] This, we may assume, means that the evil *ḫaṭarāt* come from what Aristotle calls "concupiscence," that is, passionate desire, which, according to him, arises from appetency plus imagination by which man is apt to be moved contrary to reason; [44] or it means that they come from what Plato calls "the irrational or concupiscent" part of the soul.[45] That this has a reference to a philosophic view is evident from Muḥāsibī's subsequent statement that "one of the philosophers (*al-ḥukamāʾ*) said: If you want the intellect to rule over passionate desire (*hawan*) do not undertake an act of pleasure until you consider the end." [46] Whatever the immediate source of this quotation, ultimately it rests on Plato's advice that "all passionate desires" (ἐπιθυμίαι) should be controlled by "knowledge and reason" (ἐπιστήμῃ καὶ λόγῳ) [47] plus Aristotle's statement that rational wish is that which is guided by the practical intellect which is always directed to some end.[48] As proof-text of this philosophic explanation of the origin of evil deeds he quotes two Koranic verses, which literally read that "his soul (*nafsuhu*) permitted him to slay his brother" (5:33) and that "the soul (*al-nafsa*) is wont to command evil" (12:53) but in which the term "soul" is taken by him to mean the irrational or concupiscent soul.[49]

Second, they come "from the enemy," [50] that is, from

[41] Cf. above at n. 7.
[42] *Op. cit.*, p. 44, ll. 16–18.
[43] *Ibid.*, ll. 8–9.
[44] Cf. above at n. 28.
[45] Cf. above at n. 27.
[46] Muḥāsibī, p. 45, ll. 7–9.
[47] *Republic* IX, 586 D.
[48] *De Anima* III, 10, 433a, 13–14 and 22–25.
[49] *Op. cit.*, p. 44, ll. 20–21.
[50] *Ibid.*, l. 9.

"Satan," [51] for which he quotes as proof-texts several Koranic verses.

Here then we have an attempt to combine a somewhat modified form of Naẓẓām's *ḥāṭirāni* not only with God and Satan of the Koran and with the angel and Satan of tradition but also with the intellect and the irrational soul or desire of philosophy.

The identification of Naẓẓām's *ḥāṭirāni* with some philosophic concepts followed by their combination with the angel and Satan of tradition and with the intellect and the irrational soul or desire of philosophy is to be found in Ghazālī's *Iḥyā'*, Book XXI, entitled "Exposition of the Wonders of the Heart." [52] Using, at least once, Naẓẓām's term *ḥāṭirāni*,[53] the dual of *ḥāṭir*, and speaking, like Naẓẓām, of a contrast between one kind of *ḥāṭir* and another kind of *ḥāṭir*, he also uses the term *ḥawāṭir*, the plural of *ḥāṭir*, and speaks also of a contrast between one kind of *ḥawāṭir* and another kind of *ḥawāṭir*.

Ghazālī starts his discussion of *ḥāṭir* by trying to explain its meaning in terms of what in his *Maḳāṣid al-Falāsifah* he described as "the faculties of the animal soul" [54] and previously in this Book XXI of the *Iḥyā'* he described as "the armies of the heart." [55] Now the faculties of the soul are divided by him after Aristotle [56] and Avicenna [57] into "perceptive faculties" and "motive faculties," [58] concerning which

[51] *Ibid.*, p. 44, l. 21 – p. 45, l. 1.

[52] *Kitāb Sharḥ 'Aja'ib al-Ḳalb* in *Iḥyā'*, ed. Cairo 1358/1939, vol. III, pp. 2–47. German: *Die Wunder des Herzens* by Karl Friedrich Eckmann, Mainz 1960, where n. 2 on p. 54 contains the following references to those who have dealt with the term *ḥāṭir*: R. Hartmann, *Al-Ḳuschairīs Darstellung des Ṣūfītums*, pp. 80–81; R. A. Nicholson, *Kashf al-Maḥjūb*, p. 387, Section: Technical Terms of the Ṣūfīs; J. Obermann, *Der philosophische und religiöse Subjektivismus Ghazālīs*, p. 158.

[53] *Ibid.*, Section: *Bayān Tasallūṭ al-Shayṭān 'ala'l-Ḳalb bi'l-Waswās*; III, p. 25, l. 30; cf. below at n. 76.

[54] *Maḳāṣid al-Falāsifah*, Cairo, n. d., p. 276, l. 5.

[55] *Bayān Junūd al-Ḳalb*, III, p. 5, l. 4.

[56] *De Anima* III, 9, 432a, 15–17.

[57] *Najāt*, p. 259, l. 2; *Shifā'*: (1) ed. J. Bakoš, *Psychologie d'Ibn Sīnā*, 1956, p. 41, ll. 7–8; (2) ed. F. Rahman, *Avicenna's De Anima*, 1959, p. 41, l. 4.

[58] *Maḳāṣid*, p. 276, ll. 7–8.

he says in his *Maḳāṣid* that, coming as these faculties do from one source, the soul, their functions are connected with each other.[59] And so here he is trying to show how *ḫāṭir* is a motive faculty of the soul, but one which has its origin in the perspective faculty of the soul.

As for its having its origin in the perceptive faculty of the soul, he says that the *ḫawāṭir* are the impressions left upon the soul by two vanished internal senses, namely, memory and cogitation. "Cogitation," it may be remarked, is an internal sense the function of which is to construct out of images of real things new fictitious images.[60] To quote Ghazālī's own words: "The particular impressions which arise in the heart are the *ḫawāṭir*. I mean by *ḫawāṭir* that which arises in the heart from cogitations (*al-afkār*) and memories (*al-adhkār*), and by this I mean that the heart's perception of knowledge is either by way of producing something new or by way of recollection. They are called *ḫawāṭir* because they occur (*taḫṭur*) after the heart has paid no attention to them." [61]

As for its becoming a motive faculty of the soul, his discussion here reflects his previous discussion of the motive faculty under the heading "The Armies of the Heart," where, following Avicenna,[62] he subdivides the motive faculty into two other faculties: (a) that which incites (*baʿath*) in the heart the emotions of desire and irascibility or of pursuit and avoidance; (b) that which actually produces physical movements in the limbs and muscles and nerves.[63] These two sub-faculties of the motive faculty are described by him respectively by the terms "will" [64] (*irādah*) and "power"

[59] *Ibid.*, ll. 9–10.

[60] Cf. pp. 91–92 of my paper "The Internal Senses in Latin, Arabic, and Hebrew Philosophic Texts," *Harvard Theological Review*, 28 (1935), 69–133.

[61] *Iḥyā'* (ed. Cairo, 1358/1939), Section: *Bayān Tasallūṭ al-Shayṭān*, in *Iḥyā'*, ed. cit., III, 25, ll. 24–26.

[62] *Najāt*, p. 259, ll. 3–13; *Shifā'*: (1) p. 41, l. 8 – p. 42, l. 4; (2) p. 41, ll. 5–16.

[63] *Iḥyā'*, Section: *Bayān Junūd al-Ḳalb*; III, p. 6, ll. 30–33.

[64] *Ibid.*, l. 31.

(*ḳudrah*)[65] — terms used by him elsewhere in the *Iḥyā'* as a description of similar two-motive sub-faculties in connection with human action.[66] In the *Maḳāṣid*, however, there is no special term for the second sub-faculty of the motive faculty corresponding to *ḳudrah*; and, with regard to the first sub-faculty, Ghazālī uses for it there a term other than *irādah*. Prefatory, however, to his naming that other term for the first-sub-faculty, he starts out by saying that "*irādah*, will, cannot come into being except from *shahwah*, desire, and *nuzū'*, impulse."[67] He then goes on to say that *nuzū'*, impulse, may be either a desiderative faculty (*ḳuwwah shahwāniyyah*) bent on pursuit or an "irascible faculty" (*ḳuwwah ghaḍabiyyah*) bent on avoidance.[68] He finally concludes that "the impulsive faculty (*al-ḳuwwah al-nuzū'iyyah*) is that which incites (*bā'ithah*) and orders."[69] The term *nuzū'* or *ḳuwwah nuzū'iyyah* is thus used by him in the *Maḳāṣid* as a description of the first sub-faculty of the motive faculty. Incidentally it can be shown that the term *nuzū'* reflects the Greek term ὁρμή as used by Aristotle in his statements that the principle of motion is in animals impulse (ὁρμή) accompanied by appetency and in man impulse accompanied by appetency and reason.[70] Thus also is the term *ishtiyāḳ* used in that sense of that Greek term in the Arabic translation of a lost Greek work by Alexander Aphrodisiensis.[71]

It is this term *nuzū'*, impulse, for which previously in the *Iḥyā'*, under the heading of "The Armies of the Heart," he

[65] *Ibid.*, l. 32.

[66] *Iḥyā'*: *Kitāb al-Taubah*, Section: *Bayān Wujūb al-Taubah*; IV, p. 6, l. 19 and l. 27.

[67] *Maḳāṣid*, p. 276, l. 12. On the basis of the Hebrew and Latin translations of the *Maḳāṣid*, the printed Arabic text is to be emended by the insertion between *al-shahwah*, at the end of l. 12 on p. 276, and *wa'l-nuzū'*, at the beginning of l. 13, another *wa'l-nuzū'*. My quotation is translated from the reading as emended.

[68] *Ibid.*, ll. 13–16.

[69] *Ibid.*, p. 277, l. 3.

[70] *Ethica Eudemia* II, 8, 1224a, 16–30.

[71] Cf. pp. 73–74 of my paper "The Problem of the Souls of the Spheres from the Byzantine Commentaries on Aristotle through the Arabs and St. Thomas to Kepler," *Dumbarton Oaks Papers*, No. 16 (1962), 65–93.

substituted the term *irādah*, that now, under the heading "Satan's Domination of the Heart by Means of Temptation," he substitutes for it the term *ḫāṭir* in its capacity as that which incites certain movements in the soul, which subsequently lead to movements in the body, with the general statement that "the *ḫawāṭir* are the movers of the wills (*al-irādāt*)" and that "the *ḫawāṭir* are the starting point of actions." [72] Then, having in mind his own use elsewhere in the *Iḥyā'* of the expression "the decision (*jazm*) of the will" for the term "will," [73] and his own statement there that movements of the body, of which he mentions the movement of the hand, must be preceded by "a strong decisive (*jāzim*) inclination (*mayl*) in one's soul called intention (*ḳaṣd*)" [74] and using terms which, though not the same, mean the same things, he says: "Then the *ḫāṭir* moves the craving (*al-raghbah*), the craving moves the decision (*al-'azm*), the decision moves the intention (*al-niyyah*), and the intention moves the limbs." [75]

Thus far Ghazālī has dealt with the *ḫāṭir* as a motive faculty which incites man to various kinds of secular actions. Now he is to take up the discussion of the *ḫāṭir* as a motive faculty which incites man to various kinds of religious actions. Of the *ḫawāṭir*, he says, some lead to actions which from a religious viewpoint are good and others lead to actions which from a religious viewpoint are evil. Accordingly these *ḫawāṭir* fall into two contrasting groups, each of them constituting collectively a single *ḫāṭir* and the two of them forming a dualism, a *ḫāṭirāni*, of which one *ḫāṭir* is "a praiseworthy *ḫāṭir* named divine inspiration" and the other *ḫāṭir* is "a blameworthy *ḫāṭir* named Satanic whispering"; and both the praiseworthy *ḫāṭir* and the blameworthy *ḫāṭir*, he goes on to say, are created by God in the hearts of men, but they are created there by means of two different causes, the cause of "the *ḫāṭir*

[72] *Iḥyā'*, *op. cit.*, Section: *Bayān Tasallūṭ al-Shayṭān;* III, p. 25, ll. 26–28.
[73] *Ibid.*, *Kitāb al-Taubah*, Section: *Bayān Wujūb al-Taubah*; IV, p. 6, l. 16 and l. 19.
[74] *Ibid.*, l. 27.
[75] *Ibid.*, Section: *Bayān Tasallūṭ al-Shayṭān*; III, p. 25, ll. 26–28.

which gives rise to good" being an angel and the cause of "the *ḫāṭir* which gives rise to evil" being Satan.[76] Later, in the course of this discussion, he adds to the good *ḫāṭir* and the evil *ḫāṭir* two other inner motive powers, namely, intellect and irrational soul or desire.[77]

And so the praiseworthy *ḫāṭir* and the blameworthy *ḫāṭir* of Ghazālī are like the *ḫāṭir* of obedience and the *ḫāṭir* of disobedience of Naẓẓām and like the good *yeṣer* and the evil *yeṣer* of the rabbis. Still there is a difference between them. To Naẓẓām and the rabbis man by his own power is free to allow the prompting of either the one or the other of the two opposite motive powers within him. Not so to Ghazālī. According to him, all "acts of obedience and disobedience" [78] take place "by the decree of foreordainment of God." [79] In a passage which reminds one of Augustine's statement that there are those "whom God has predestined to eternal life" and there are those "whom He has predestined to eternal death," [80] he says that "God created the paradise and He created people for it and He keeps the people preoccupied with the performance of good deeds; He created hellfire and He created people for it and He keeps the people preoccupied with the commitment of sins." [81]

But here Ghazālī seems to become conscious of a difficulty. If all human actions are predestined, what need is there for all these so-called armies of the heart, the praiseworthy and the blameworthy *ḫāṭir*, the angel and Satan, the intellect and the irrational soul? And as if he were trying to provide an answer in anticipation of such a question, he goes on to present what would seem to be an exposition of what he considered to be the purpose of these armies of the heart. Their purpose,

[76] *Ibid.*, ll. 31–35.

[77] *Ibid.*, Section: *Bayān Sur'at Taḳallub al-Ḳalb*; III, p. 45, ll. 5–7, 21–22; p. 46, ll. 6–7.

[78] *Ibid.*, p. 46, l. 27.

[79] *Ibid.*, ll. 33–34.

[80] *De Anima et Ejus Origine* IV, xi, 16; cf. *De Civitate Dei* XV, i, 1; *Enchiridion* 100. Cf. my *Religious Philosophy*, pp. 175–176.

[81] *Iḥyā'*: *op. cit.*, Section: *Bayān Sur'at Taḳallub al-Ḳalb*; III, p. 47, ll. 1–2. Cf. quotation from Muslim's *Ṣaḥīḥ*, above, p. 603, at n. 4.

he seems to say, is to serve as means by which God moves in His various mysterious ways His foreordained wonders to perform, for, though from eternity it has been decreed by Him what the actions of every human being are to be, it is not His will that the life of the predestined saint should be one monotonous stretch of dull saintliness and the life of the predestined sinner should be one continuous riot of exciting sinfulness. By His unfathomable wisdom, the road to the predestined end of both saint and sinner is to be paved with good and bad intentions and with conflicting desires and wills and actions. In illustration thereof, Ghazālī depicts the hearts of men as stages upon which dramatic plays are enacted by a resident company of noble and villainous *ḫawāṭir* and intellects and irrational souls and by two guest stars, an angel and Satan. There are plots and counterplots, culminating sometimes in happy endings and sometimes in unhappy endings.[82] And when the curtain falls, Ghazālī seems to address the audience: Think not that the actors you have watched are free agents moving by their own power toward endings of their own choosing; no, they are only toy figures moved by an unseen hand in the performance of prescribed parts calculated to lead to predetermined endings devised by God the great playwright.

IV. Generated Effects (*al-mutawalladāt*)

In their teaching that human actions are free, the Muʿtazilites were faced with the problem as to what constitutes human actions. A classification of such actions is vaguely suggested by the founder of Muʿtazilism, Wāṣil b. ʿAṭāʾ, in his statement that "the actions of man are ranged under movements, rests, inclinations (*iʿtimādāt*), speculation, and knowledge."[1] A formal classification is made by Abū al-Hudhayl in his distinction between "the acts of the heart

[82] *Iḥyāʾ*, *ibid.*, p. 45, l. 3 – p. 46, l. 28.
[1] *Milal*, p. 32, ll. 10–11.

(*afʿāl al-ḳulūb*) and the acts of the bodily organs (*afʿāl al-jāwariḥ*)," [2] both of which are included by him in what he describes as "acts within man himself." [3] A third kind of human acts is described by him as "that which is generated from a man's act," [4] briefly referred to by the term *al-tawallud* [5] or by the term *al-mutawalladāt*,[6] that is to say, the theory of "generated effects." Though the distinction between acts of the heart and acts of the bodily organs would not seem to have been generally accepted, the distinction between a man's acts in his own body, that is, in himself, and his acts in another body, that is, generated effects, was, as we shall see, generally assumed. Such a distinction, it may be noted, is implied in the combination of several statements of Aristotle. Thus, in one place, Aristotle says in effect that appetency combined with intellect or imagination produces movement in the body in which the soul resides by means of something "corporeal" (*σωματικόν*),[7] which something "corporeal" is explained by him elsewhere as meaning "a certain power (*δύναμιν*) and force (*ἰσχύν*)." [8] In another place, he says that "power (*δύναμις*, *ḳuwwah*) means a source of movement or change which is in another thing [than the thing moved or changed] . . . as, for instance, the art of building is a power which is not in the thing built," [9] according to which, the "power" (*δύναμις*) or "force," whereby appetency combined with intellect or imagination is said by Aristotle to move the body in which the soul resides,[10] does, according to him, also move another thing than the body moved.

Now, with regard to acts produced by man within himself,

[2] *Ibid.*, p. 35, l. 15.

[3] *Maḳālāt*, p. 402, l. 12.

[4] *Ibid.*, l. 8; *Milal*, p. 35, ll. 18–19.

[5] *Maḳālāt*, p. 400, l. 15.

[6] *Ibid.*, p. 405, l. 6.

[7] *De Anima* III, 10, 433b, 13–19; cf. Hicks, *ad loc.*

[8] *De Motu Animalium*, 10, 703a, 9.

[9] *Metaph.* V, 12, 1019a, 15–17. Though the Arabic translation of the *Metaphysics* seems to have had here a different, or rather defective, reading, the meaning is the same. Cf. text in *Averroes*: *Tafsir ma baʿd at-tabiʿat*, ed. Bouyges, Dal, Text. 17, p. 577, l. 15 – p. 578, l. 1; cf. also Avicenna, *Najāt*, p. 348, ll. 14–16.

[10] Cf. above at n. 7.

it is generally assumed by the Muʿtazilites that man is their agent.[11] But with regard to generated effects, the question arose among them as to whether they should be considered as being the same or as not being the same as man's acts within himself. Ashʿarī enumerates eight Muʿtazilite views on this question with regard to generated effects. Following his order of presentation, I shall first describe these views, either singly or in pairs, by a brief quotation from Ashʿarī's own descriptions of them and then, whenever necessary, add some comment.

The first view is that of Bishr b. al-Muʿtamir. It is described by Ashʿarī as follows: "That which is generated from our act . . . is our act, originating from causes which proceed from us [as their conscious agents]." [12] He illustrates it by the examples of "the flight of a stone when thrown and the flight of an arrow when shot and the perception which originates when we open our eyes," [13] to which he later adds: "color . . . and sweetness . . . and smell and pain and pleasure and health and illness and desire." [14] Baghdādī introduces his report on him as follows: "He carried to the furthest extreme his view about generated effects, so that he claimed it possible for a man to create, by way of generation, color and taste and smell and sight and hearing and the rest of the sensations, provided he is the [conscious] agent of that which causes them, and the same is true of his view of heat and cold and wetness and dryness." [15] Shahrastānī introduces his report on him as follows: "He was the originator of the theory of generated effects, which he carried to the furthest extreme." [16] Thus, according to Bishr, the effects in generated effects apply not only to movements and changes but also to accidental qualities and sensations and emotions.

In my translation of the quotation from Ashʿarī, it will have been noticed, I added the bracketed expression "as their

[11] Cf. above, pp. 614 ff.

[12] *Maḳālāt*, p. 401, l. 5.

[13] *Ibid.*, ll. 9–10.

[14] *Ibid.*, p. 402, ll. 5–6.

[15] *Farḳ*, p. 143, ll. 5–8.

[16] *Milal*, p. 44, ll. 14–15.

conscious agent" after the expression "originating from causes which proceed from us" and similarly in my translation of the quotation from Baghdādī I added the bracketed word "conscious" before the expression "agent of that which causes them." [16a] I did so purposely in order to show that a generated effect is, according to Bishr, man's own act only when it was consciously intended by the man to proceed from his act within himself, but that, without such a conscious intention, the generated effect is to be regarded as any act in the world which, according to Bishr as according to most of the Muʿtazilites, is the direct creation of God. It was necessary to bring out this distinction in Bishr's view of generated effects because by means of it we are able to explain certain other statements quoted in his name. Thus when Baghdādī in his *Uṣūl* quotes Bishr as saying with regard to accidents, of which he mentions colors and tastes and smells and sights and hearings, the very same accidents which are described by him here as generated effects, that "some of them are the action of God and some of them the action of man," [17] it is to be assumed that the latter are those of them which proceed from causes of which man is a conscious agent, whereas the former are those of them which proceed from causes of which man is not the conscious agent. Similarly, when Ibn Ḥazm quotes Bishr as saying that "God never created color and taste and smell and touch . . . but men created all these," [18] again, the very same accidents which are described by Bishr here as generated effects, it is to be assumed that they are said to be created by men only when they proceed from causes of which men are conscious agents. So also when Ashʿarī quotes Bishr as saying that "movement may generate rest," [19] it is to be assumed that the author of the rest which proceeds from the movement as its cause may be either man or God, depending upon whether man was the conscious agent of that movement or not its conscious agent.

[16a] Cf. below at n. 20.

[17] *Uṣūl*, p. 135, ll. 8–10.

[18] *Fiṣal*, IV, p. 197, ll. 6–8.

[19] *Maḳālāt*, p. 413, l. 10.

The second view is that of Abū al-Hudhayl and those who follow him. It is described by Ashʿarī as follows: "Everything that is generated from a man's act, when he is aware of what is to follow from his act, is his own act."[20] In Baghdādī this is said to be the view of "the majority of the Libertarians."[21] So far this is the same as the view of Bishr b. al-Muʿtamir. However, again according to Ashʿarī, Abū al-Hudhayl, in contradistinction to Bishr, makes an exception of "pleasure and colors and tastes and smells, heat and cold, wetness and dryness, cowardice and courage, hunger and satiety, and comprehension and knowledge occurring in another by his act, for all this is, according to him, the act of God."[22] Thus according to Abū al-Hudhayl, the effects in generated effects apply only to movements and changes; they do not apply to accidental qualities nor to sensations and emotions and cognitions.

The third and fourth views are those of Naẓẓām and Muʿammar respectively. Naẓẓām's view is described by Ashʿarī as follows: "That which occurs outside the range of man is the act of God by the necessitation of a natural disposition [here *ḫlḳh* is to be read *ḫilḳah*] possessed by a thing, as, for instance, the flight of a stone [forward], when somebody throws it forward, or its flight downward, when somebody throws it downward, or its flight upward, when somebody throws it in an upward direction, and in the same way perception is the act of God by the necessitation of a natural disposition (*al-ḫilḳah*). The meaning of this is that God has stamped the stone with such a nature that, when somebody throws it forward, it flies forward, and so also with regard to the other instances of generated effects."[23] Muʿammar's view is described by Ashʿarī as follows: "Generated effects and whatever abides in bodies, such as movement and rest, color and taste and smell, heat and cold, dryness and wetness, are

[20] *Ibid.*, 402, ll. 8–9.
[21] *Uṣūl*, p. 137, ll. 11–12; *Farḳ*, p. 328, ll. 12–13.
[22] *Maḳālāt*, p. 402, ll. 14–16.
[23] *Ibid.*, p. 404, ll. 4–9.

each the act of the body in which it abides by the nature of that body." [24]

In these two views, as will be noticed, there is a common element as well as a difference. The common element in them is their assertion that generated effects are due to a nature within the body of that in which the effect is generated. The difference, on the mere face of their statements just quoted, would seem to be twofold. First, in Naẓẓām, a stone, and for that matter any other body, is clearly said to owe its nature to God; in Muʿammar, a body is simply said to have a nature, without any indication how it got that nature. Second, in Naẓẓām, an effect that is generated in a body is said to be the act of God by means of the nature which the body owes to Him; in Muʿammar, an effect that is generated in a body is said to be the act of the body by means of the nature which it has. But, as I have shown above, Muʿammar, just like Naẓẓām, believed that the nature in bodies was created by God; [25] the only difference between them is that, according to Naẓẓām, the nature in bodies acts under the supervision of God, whence its act is described here as that of God, whereas, according to Muʿammar, the nature in bodies, though created by God, acts independently of God and without any supervision by Him.[26]

The fifth view is that of Ṣāliḥ Ḳubbah. It is described by Ashʿarī as follows: "Man acts only within himself, and whatever occurs at the time of his act, as the flight of a stone when thrown and the burning of wood upon contact with fire and the feeling of pain at a blow, is created by God." [27]

The sixth and seventh views are those of Thumāmah and Jāḥiẓ respectively. Thumāmah's view is reported by Ashʿarī as follows: "Man has no action except the act of willing (*al-irādah*); whatever is other than it takes place without an originator (*muḥdith*), such as the flight of a stone when thrown, an act which, Thumāmah maintains, is brought in

[24] *Ibid.*, p. 405, ll. 6–5.
[25] Cf. above, p. 565.
[26] Cf. above, pp. 569; 572.
[27] *Maḳālāt*, p. 406, ll. 6–8.

relation with men metaphorically." [28] Ashʿarī's report of Jāḥiẓ' view reads as follows: "Whatever is after the act of willing is [the act] of man by his nature and is not by choice, and no action proceeds from man by choice except the act of willing." [29]

In Ashʿarī's reports of these two views four things are to be observed. (1) While Thumāmah simply says that "man has no action except the act of willing," Jāḥiẓ says that "no action proceeds from man by choice except the act of willing." (2) While Thumāmah illustrates his expression "whatever is other than will" by the example of "the flight of a stone when thrown," thus indicating that he means by it that which is commonly called "generated effect," Jāḥiẓ simply uses the unexplained expression "that which is after the will," which by itself may mean the act within one's own body, which comes after the act within one's heart or within one's soul. (3) While Thumāmah says that "whatever is other than will originates without an originator" and "is brought in relation with man metaphorically," Jāḥiẓ says that "that which is after will is [the act] of man by his nature." (4) When Jāḥiẓ says that "no action proceeds from man by choice except will," it is not clear whether (a) it refers to his previous statement that "that which is after the will is [the act] of man by his nature and not by choice," the omission of the phrase "by his nature" being only accidental, or whether (b) it refers to some other kind of act, one which, while not being "by choice," is also not "by his nature."

The question which naturally arises in our mind as to whether these differences in phrasing imply a difference of view is solved negatively by a statement which, as reported by Baghdādī in the name of followers of Jāḥiẓ, reads as follows: "They say that al-Jāḥiẓ agreed with Thumāmah that men have no action except the act of willing and that the rest of their acts are ascribed to men only in the sense that

[28] *Maḳālāt*, p. 407, ll. 9–11; *Farḳ*, p. 157, ll. 13–14; *Milal*, p. 50, ll. 5–6.
[29] *Maḳālāt*, p. 407, ll. 12–13; *Farḳ*, p. 160, ll. 8–10; *Milal*, p. 52, ll. 6–7.

they proceed from them by nature and are necessitated by their will."[30] Similarly Shahrastānī, after rephrasing Jāḥiẓ' view by saying that "men have no acquisition (*kasb*) except the act of willing, their actions taking place by nature," adds the words "as Thumāmah said."[31] The expression "proceed from them by nature and are necessitated by their will" used here by Baghdādī is quite evidently another way of phrasing Jāḥiẓ's original statement, "is [the act] of man by nature and is not by choice," as given by Ashʿarī.

On the basis of this testimony of the followers of Jāḥiẓ as to his agreement with Thumāmah, one is justified, I believe, in trying to explain certain unclear statements of one of them by corresponding clear statements of the other, as follows. (1) Thumāmah's statement that "man has no action except the act of willing" is to be taken to mean the same as Jāḥiẓ' statement that "no action proceeds from man by choice except the act of willing." (2) Jāḥiẓ' expression "whatever is after the act of willing" is to be taken to refer to generated effects as does Thumāmah's expression "whatever is other than it [that is, the act of willing]," which is explicitly explained by the example of such a generated effect as "the flight of a stone when thrown." Hence, from the fact that both of them speak only of the act of willing and generated effects and make no mention of man's action within himself, which comes after the act of willing and before generated effects, and also from the fact that both of them as Muʿtazilites are to be assumed to believe in the freedom of any human act unless explicitly disapproved, it is to be inferred that man's action within himself is included by them in the act of willing. Thus, according to both of them, man's action within himself, like the act of willing and unlike generated effects, proceeds from man by choice. (3) Thumāmah's statement that "whatever is other than it [that is, the act of willing] takes place without

[30] *Fark*, p. 160, ll. 8–10.

[31] *Milal*, p. 52, l. 7. On the use of *kasb* here in the sense of free act, see above, p. 620, and below, p. 666.

an originator" is to be taken to mean the same as Jāḥiẓ' statement that "whatever is after the act of willing is [the act] of man by his nature and is not by choice"; that is to say, the expression "without an originator" is not to be taken literally; it is to be taken to mean that generated effects are without an originator like the originator of the act of willing, who acts by choice. (4) Jāḥiẓ' statement that "no action proceeds from man by choice except the act of willing" is to be taken to mean that no generated effects but only the act of willing and man's action within himself proceed from man by choice. There thus results a complete agreement between the two views. It is to be noted, however, that, despite the fact that both Baghdādī and Shahrastānī state, each of them in his own way, that Jāḥiẓ agreed with Thumāmah, neither of them assumes so complete an agreement between them as that which I have tried to establish. Thus Baghdādī takes Thumāmah's statement that "whatever is other than it [that is, the act of willing] takes place without an originator" to mean literally that it takes place "without an agent (*fāʿil*)" and hence he argues that such a view would invalidate the proof for the existence of a "creator" (*ṣāniʿ*) from the premise that the world is created.[32] Similarly Shahrastānī takes that statement of Thumāmah literally.[33] Thus, again, Baghdādī takes the term "no action" in Jāḥiẓ' statement that "no action proceeds from man by choice except the act of willing" to include both man's acts within himself, such as praying and fasting, and generated effects, such as stealing and killing, and hence argues that such a view would lead to the conclusion that man should not be held responsible for his actions.[34] According to my interpretation, both Thumāmah and Jāḥiẓ are immune from Baghdādī's criticisms.[35]

The eighth view is that of Ḍirār, who is quoted by Ashʿarī as maintaining "that man may act outside the range of his own

[32] *Uṣūl*, p. 138, l. 17 – p. 139, l. 1.
[33] *Milal*, p. 49, ll. 14–17.
[34] *Farḳ*, p. 160, l. 13 – p. 161, l. 3.
[35] For their immunity from Baghdādī's second criticism, see below, p. 655.

self and whatever is generated from that act of his, such as motion or rest [in another body], is an acquisition (*kasb*) with respect to man and a creation with respect to God." [36] What Ḍirār does here is to apply to generated effects his theory of acquisition, which, as we shall see later,[37] is his own modification of the Muʿtazilite belief in the freedom of human action; whence, just as man's action within his own body has two agents, man and God, so also an effect in another body generated from a man's act within his own body has two agents, man and God. A variation of Ḍirār's view is the view of Murdār who, unlike Ḍirār to whom both man's acts in himself and generated effects have two agents, maintains that only generated effects have two agents, whereas a man's acts in himself are the man's own acts. This may be gathered from the following sources: (1) A report reproduced by Ḫayyāṭ from Ibn al-Rāwandī who reports it in the name of Abū Zufar who quotes Abū Mūsā [al-Murdār] as saying that "it is possible for an act to proceed from two agents by way of generation (*tawallud*)," [38] that is to say, as a generated effect; (2) Baghdādī's comment on this report saying that Murdār "held this view in spite of the fact that he rejected the view of the Sunnites that an act could proceed from two agents one of them being creator and the other acquirer," [39] that is to say, in spite of his not using the same theory of acquisition as an explanation of man's acts in himself, which, according to Baghdādī, was the theory so used not only by Ashʿarī but also originally by all the Sunnites; [40] (3) Shahrastānī who, after stating that Murdār was a pupil of Bishr b. al-Muʿtamir, says that "his view on generated effects was like that of his master [that is to say, they are the acts of man], adding thereto that one act may proceed from two agents by way of generation (*tawallud*)." [41]

And so the question which the Muʿtazilite exponents of the

[36] *Maḳālāt*, p. 408, ll. 4–6.
[37] Cf. below, pp. 667 f.
[38] *Intiṣār* 43, p. 54, ll. 1–2.
[39] *Farḳ*, p. 152, ll. 5–6.
[40] Cf.
[41] *Milal*, p. 48, ll. 14–15.

eight views enumerated by Ash'arī have set out to answer, namely, the question whether generated effects are to be considered, with respect to their agentship, as being the same or as not being the same as man's acts within himself, is answered by them in two ways. According to the exponents of three of those eight views, generated effects are the same as man's acts within himself, with respect to their agentship,[42] whereas, according to the exponents of five of those eight views, generated effects are not the same as man's acts within himself, with respect to their agentship. Of the exponents of those five views, one considers generated effects as being the acts "of God by the necessitation of a natural disposition [in things]"; [43] one considers them as being the acts "of the body . . . by the nature of that body"; [44] one considers them as being "created by God"; [45] two consider them as being the acts "of man by his nature and are not by choice." [46]

Now, with regard to the acts of man within himself, the exponents of all the eight views, including Ḍirār with some qualification,[47] consider them as free acts of man, for which man is to be held responsible and hence, in accordance with divine justice, is to be punished. Consequently, those three of the eight exponents who consider generated effects as being the same with respect to their agentship as man's acts within himself are to be assumed to consider them also as free acts of man for which man is to be held responsible, whereas those five of the eight exponents who do not consider generated effects, with respect to their agentship as being the same as man's acts within himself are to be assumed not to consider them as free acts of man for which man is to be held responsible. But to assume that generated effects, which constitute such a great part of human action and include such acts as stealing and killing, were held by any group of Mu'tazilites as not being free acts of man and as not being acts for which

[42] Bishr b. al-Mu'tamir (first), Abū al-Hudhayl (second), Ḍirār (eighth).
[43] Naẓẓām (third). [44] Mu'ammar (fourth).
[45] Ṣāliḥ Ḳubbah (fifth).
[46] Thumāmah (sixth) and Jāḥiẓ (seventh). [47] Cf. above at n. 37.

man was to be held responsible is something unthinkable, knowing as we do the Muʿtazilite insistence upon divine justice and hence upon man's freedom to act and his responsibility for all his actions. I shall, therefore, try to show how even those who do not consider generated effects as being the same as man's acts within himself with respect to their agentship may still consider them as being the same as man's acts within himself with respect to man's responsibility for them. A generated effect, it will be recalled, is described as "that which is generated from a man's act." [48] This means, of course, that a generated effect is dependent upon man's free act within himself to such an extent that, without such a free act by man, no generated effect would take place by any of those means by which they are said to take place. Therefore, inasmuch as without man's own free act within himself no generated effect could take place, man is to be held responsible for any of his generated effects just as he is for any of his own acts within himself — and this irrespective of how the generated effect in itself is being produced.

V. Antinomies of Free Will

With their assertion of free will, whether in the choice of both good and evil or only in the choice of evil, the Libertarians were confronted with two difficulties. First, how would they explain those verses in the Koran which either directly or indirectly ascribe to God control over human action? Second, how would they reconcile the description of God in the Koran as all-knowing and all-powerful with their conception of man's free will? Their attempt to solve these difficulties or antinomies will be presented under five headings.

1. FREE WILL AND PREDESTINARIAN VERSES IN THE KORAN

The Koran contains condemnations of two sinners, one, Abū Lahab, explicitly mentioned by name (111: 1–5), and

[48] Cf. above at n. 4.

the other, Walīd b. Mughīra, only alluded to (74: 11–26). With the belief in a preëxistent Koran, even in a preëxistent created Koran,[1] it means that these sinners were condemned long before they were born, with the inevitable implication that they were predestined to be sinners. Moreover, at the conclusion of the predestined condemnation of Walīd for his predestined sin there is the verse, "Thus God leads astray whom He pleases and guides whom He pleases" (74: 34), which is a direct denial of man's freedom in both his doing of evil and his doing of good. These verses troubled the mind of the Libertarians. Of one of the early Libertarians, ʿAmr b. ʿUbayd, it is told that he denied the genuineness of the verses concerning Abū Lahab and Walīd b. Mughīra.[2] Of another Libertarian, Hishām b. ʿAmr al-Fuwaṭī, it is reported that he prohibited the description of God by those Koranic terms which imply a denial of free will.[3]

Most of the Libertarians, however, instead of prohibiting the use of predestinarian terms as descriptions of God, only rejected their literal meaning and tried to interpret them in accordance with their own belief in freedom. An account of such interpretations is given by Ashʿarī.[4] Here are two examples of their interpretations of terms describing God as making people go astray. According to one interpretation, such terms should be taken to mean that God "is naming them and judging them goers astray," [5] that is to say, "since God finds them going astray, He tells us that He makes them go astray, just as it is said, 'So-and-so made so-and-so a coward,' when he found him to be a coward." [6] According to another interpretation, such terms should be taken to mean "that God ceases to produce the kindness and the guidance and the lastingness that He gives to the faithful, and it is the cessation of these things that is called making to go astray." [7]

[1] Cf. above, pp. 236 ff. and pp. 264 ff.

[2] Cf. Schreiner, *Aš'aritenthum*, pp. 92–93.

[3] *Fark*, p. 146, ll. 13 ff.; *Milal*, p. 50, ll. 15 ff.

[4] *Maḳālāt*, p. 256, l. 4 ff.

[5] *Ibid.*, p. 261, ll. 10–11.

[6] *Ibid.*, ll. 15–16.

[7] *Ibid.*, ll. 12–14.

2. FREE WILL AND THE APPOINTED TERM (*ajal*)

Ash'arī in his *Ibānah*, taking it for granted that the Mu'tazilites accepted the Koranic teaching of an appointed term of life, that is, of the *ajal* (6:2), surmises that they would also accept the Koranic teaching that the *ajal* is inexorable (7:32; 63:11).[1] Then, having in mind the Mu'tazilite belief in the freedom of the will, including the freedom of the will to kill, he says that the Mu'tazilites may be asked: "Tell us then about him whom someone kills violently — do you think he is killed in his appointed term, or rather at his appointed term?" [2] He thus confronts the Mu'tazilites with a dilemma,[3] which may be restated as follows: If one believes in an inexorable appointed term, then the act of killing had to take place at the appointed term, whence it is not a free act; and, if one believes in free will, then the act of killing could take place at any time it pleased the killer, whence the appointed term is not inexorable.

The Mu'tazilites' solution of this dilemma is reported by Ash'arī in his *Maḳālāt* in the form of what amounts to four views on the question of what would happen to the killed person if the killer, by the exercise of his free will, does not kill him at what is supposed to be his appointed term. Presenting these four views in a slightly different order, I shall quote in each case Ash'arī's description of it and then try to determine what particular conception of the *ajal* it implies.

One of these four views is described by Ash'arī as that "of certain ignorant members of the sect," who maintain that "a man's *ajal* is the time until which God knows that he will last, if he is not killed, and not the time at which he is killed." [4] What this view means is that there is an *ajal* as taught in the Koran, but a killer, by his free act of killing, can undo that divinely decreed *ajal*. In his *Ibānah*, where this view is suggested by Ash'arī only hypothetically as one which might be

[1] *Ibānah*, p. 76, ll. 4–5.
[2] *Ibid.*, l. 6.
[3] *Ibid.*, ll. 7–8.
[4] *Maḳālāt*, p. 256, ll. 8–9.

tried by the Muʿtazilites in solving the dilemma, it is dismissed by him as "impossible" on the ground that it is contrary to the Koranic teaching of the inexorability of the *ajal*.[5] Such a view, it is to be noted, is ascribed by Ḥillī to "some of the Baghdadians" [6] and by Ījī to the generality of the Muʿtazilites.[7] It is this view also that Taftāzānī means by his reference to "some of the Muʿtazilites, who say that the killer cut short his [that is, the killed person's] appointed term." [8]

Another view is ascribed by Ashʿarī to Abū al-Hudhayl, which is described as follows: "The man would die at this time, even if he were not killed." [9] What this view would seem to mean is (1) that the *ajal* is inexorable; (2) that God has a foreknowledge of the act as well as of the time of the killing, but that that foreknowledge is not the cause of either the act or the time of the killing,[10] so that the killing at that particular time is the free choice of the killer; (3) that God synchronizes the *ajal* with the freely chosen time of the killing foreknown to him.

This view is presented by Nasafī in his Creed as that of orthodox Islam; [11] Ḥillī ascribes it to the "Compulsionists" (*al-mujbirah*); [12] and Ījī ascribes it to "the People of Truth" (*ahl al-ḥaḳḳ*).[13] Inasmuch as none of these share with the Muʿtazilite Abū al-Hudhayl in his belief in free will, what this view, as professed by them, would seem to mean is (1) that the *ajal* is inexorable; (2) that God has a foreknowledge of the act as well as of the time of the killing, and that that foreknowledge is the cause of both the act and the time of the

[5] *Ibānah*, p. 76, ll. 8–16.

[6] Ḥillī, *Kashf al-Murād*, quoted by Weil in *Sefer Asaf*, p. 274, n.

[7] Jurjānī, *Sharḥ al-Mawāḳik*, VIII, p. 170, ll. 13–15 (ed. Th. Sorensen, p. 127, ll. 10–12).

[8] Taftāzānī, p. 108, l. 10. See Elder's n. 8, on p. 94 of his translation for the change of "Allah" of the printed Arabic text to "the killer."

[9] *Maḳālāt*, p. 257, ll. 1–2.

[10] Cf. below, pp. 662 f.

[11] Taftāzānī, p. 108, l. 6.

[12] *Op. cit.* (above, n. 6).

[13] *Op. cit.* (above, n. 7), p. 170, ll. 10–11 (p. 127, l. 7).

killing; (3) that God synchronizes the *ajal* with the killing caused by His foreknowledge.

A third view is described by Ashʿarī simply by saying that "others believe that, if the murderer did not kill him, he might either die or live." [14] This view, as phrased, could be interpreted either as implying a denial of the *ajal* or as a denial of God's foreknowledge of the murderer's free act of killing. According to the first-mentioned interpretation, without there being any *ajal*, the unkilled man's natural death might take place either at the time he would have been killed or at some subsequent time, whence the statement that, "if the murderer did not kill him, he might either die or live." According to the second-mentioned interpretation, without there being a foreknowledge on the part of God of the free act of killing, His decreed *ajal* might have happened either to coincide with the time the man would have been killed or to come into effect at some time after that, whence, again, the statement that, "if the murderer did not kill him, he might either die or live." Inasmuch, however, as the *ajal* is explicitly taught in the Koran, whereas God's foreknowledge of all future events is, as we shall see, not explicitly taught in the Koran,[15] we may conclude that the second-mentioned interpretation is more likely to be the right one.

The same view is ascribed by Hillī to "the Verifiers" (*al-muḥaḳiḳḳūn*).[16] Inasmuch as the term "the Verifiers" refers to orthodox Mutakallimūn,[17] — who do not share with the Muʿtazilites their belief in free will — the view ascribed to them by Ḥillī, though the same in expression with the view ascribed by Ashʿarī to a group of Muʿtazilites, could not be the same in meaning. We may therefore assume that this view, as professed by "the Verifiers," has reference to the tradition which, according to Taftāzānī, "mentions the fact

[14] *Maḳālāt*, p. 257, l. 3.
[15] Cf. below, pp. 660–661.
[16] *Op. cit.* (above, n. 6).
[17] Cf. Elder, p. 65, n. 17, of his translation of Taftāzānī, referring to *Dict. of Tech. Terms*, p. 327.

that some acts of obedience prolong one's span of life." [18] Accordingly, if the unkilled man deserves a prolongation of his span of life by reason of "some acts of obedience," he will live; if not, he will die at the time at which he would have been killed, which to "the Verilers" is also the time of his *ajal*.

The fourth view is described by Ash'arī as follows: "Still others consider the preceding view as impossible." [19] Their objection to the third view, we may assume, is on the ground of its denial, as we have seen, of God's foreknowledge of the time of the murderer's free act of killing. We may therefore further assume that these still others who reject the third view agree with the second view, the view of Abu al-Hudhayl.

So much for the antinomy of man's free will and the appointed term (*ajal*).

3. FREE WILL AND PREORDAINED SUSTENANCE

Preordained sustenance (*rizḳ*), is another principle taught in the Koran.[1] Its antinomy with free will may be stated as follows: Given free will, a thief who steals for a living acts of his own free will and his sustenance therefore is not preordained by God. But given preordained sustenance, the sustenance which comes from stealing must be preordained by God. The answer given by the Libertarians is summed up in their saying that "God does not provide the forbidden," [2] that is to say, only legitimate earnings are preordained by God; illegitimate earnings are not preordained by God.

4. FREE WILL AND GOD'S FOREKNOWLEDGE

In the Koran, while omniscience is ascribed to God explicitly in such statements as "He knows all things" (57:3) and "He is fully cognizant of what ye do" (63:11), God's

[18] Taftāzānī, p. 108, ll. 12–13, for which Elder (p. 94, n. 9) gives reference to Ibn Ḥanbal's *Musnad*, III, 229 (ed. Cairo, A.H. 1313).

[19] *Maḳālāt*, p. 257, l. 4.

[1] Surah 2:208; 24:38; 42:18.

[2] *Maḳālāt*, p. 257, ll. 8–9; *Ibānah*, p. 77, ll. 4–5; *Taftāzānī*, p. 109, l. 14.

prescience is mentioned only with reference to five things (31:34), which are spoken of in tradition as "the five keys of secret knowledge," [1] and of these five things none is a human action. When, therefore, the Libertarians began to speculate on the bearing that God's foreknowledge may possibly have upon man's free action, they came up with two views.

One view, as was to be expected, restricted God's foreknowledge to the five things, or to the five kinds of things, with reference to which it is mentioned in the Koran, thus denying it of all other things or, at least, of human actions. We thus find that to the Libertarians (*al-ḳadariyyah*) is ascribed the general view that "God does not know a thing until it is" [2] and of a particular group of Libertarians, the Shabībiyyah, it is reported that they "deny that [God's] knowledge exists antecedently to what men are doing and what they are becoming." [3] A similar denial of God's foreknowledge either of all future things or only of future human actions was maintained by others who may be assumed to have been Libertarians. Thus one group of Rafiḍites, evidently those Rafiḍites who were Libertarians,[4] said that "God knows what will be before it is, except the acts of men, for He knows them only in the state of their existence." [5] Hishām b. al-Ḥakam, a Rafiḍite whose particular conception of free will will be discussed later,[6] quite evidently denies God's foreknowledge of any future events, for he explicitly says that "one cannot properly be a knower, unless an object of knowledge is already existent"; [7] and, with regard to God's not having a foreknowledge of the acts of men, he has the following additional argument: "If God had foreknowledge of what men would do, there would be no test (*al-miḥnah*) and no free choice (*al-iḫtiyār*)." [8] Presumably, the exponents of these

[1] Cf. Sale's note in his translation of the Koran *ad loc.*

[2] *Ibānah*, p. 85, ll. 10–11.

[3] Malaṭi, *Tanbīh*, p. 133, ll. 32–33, quoted by Watt, *Free Will and Predestination*, p. 52.

[4] *Maḳālāt*, p. 41, l. 7.

[5] *Ibid.*, p. 38, ll. 15–16.

[6] Cf. below, pp. 672–673.

[7] *Maḳālāt*, p. 494, l. 4; *Farḳ*, p. 49, l. 18.

[8] *Maḳālāt*, ll. 4–5; *Farḳ*, p. 50, ll. 1–2.

views would include the lack of foreknowledge on the part of God either of all future events or of only human actions among those impossibilities which are due to the unfathomable wisdom of God.[9]

But it would seem that some Muʿtazilites, instead of denying God's foreknowledge of human action, denied only its causative function. We have for this the testimony of Judah Halevi who, in dealing with the antinomy of God's foreknowledge and free will, wherein he refers to an act of free will as that which is possible, says as follows: "The Mutakallimūn have dealt with this matter in detail and have arrived at the conclusion that the knowledge of that which is possible is accidental, so that the knowledge of such a thing is not the cause of the generation of that thing. Accordingly, God's knowledge does not compel things yet to be generated — despite His knowledge of them, it is possible for them either to be generated or not to be generated, for the knowledge of what may be generated is not the cause of its being generated, just as the knowledge of what has been generated is not the cause of its having been generated."[10] Undoubtedly Judah Halevi's statement is based upon some sources which at the present writing are unknown to me. Indirectly such a view is implied in the statement attributed to the Muʿtazilites that a man of whom it is foreknown by God that he would not believe has the power to become a believer.[11] A direct ascription to the Muʿtazilites of a view like that quoted in their name by Judah Halevi is to be found in Tahānawī (1745) who, in his *Kashf Iṣṭilāḥāt al-Funūn* quotes the Muʿtazilites as maintaining that "the fact that God knows beforehand that one's span of life (*ajal*) will be terminated by some cause does not necessitate that that span of life should be terminated in

[9] Cf. above, pp. 578 ff.

[10] *Cuzari* V, 20, p. 240, ll. 20–26; p. 241, ll. 17–23. Prior to Halevi, the uncausativeness of God's foreknowledge was discussed by Saadia (*Emunot* VI, 4, p. 154, ll. 11–20), without reference to the Kalam.

[11] *Maḳālāt*, p. 243, l. 15.

that way, for knowledge is consequent on that which is known but does not effect it or direct it." [12]

But, though the principle that God's foreknowledge does not compel was quite certainly used by the Muʿtazilites as a solution of the antinomy of God's foreknowledge and man's free will, it was not new with them. It has an old history. At about the time of the rise of Muʿtazilism, it was used by the Christian Abucara who, in an Arabic work of his, after showing that God has foreknowledge of His own actions and that it is impossible for that foreknowledge to make it necessary for God to do that which is foreknown to Him, he goes on to say: "So also is it impossible that God's foreknowledge should transform into necessity that free will with which He had equipped man and which at the creation of man He had ordered it for man's good." [13] Shortly before Abucara, it was briefly expressed by John of Damascus as follows: "God foreknows all things but does not predetermine them." [14] Much earlier it was expressed by Rabbi Akiba in the apothegm: "Everything is foreseen, yet freedom of choice is given." [15]

5. FREE WILL AND GOD'S POWER: THE THEORY OF ACQUISITION (*kasb*; *iktisāb*)

a. Pre-Ashʿarite Acquisition

(1) Three theories of acquisition

Divine power is still another principle taught in the Koran.[1] Its antinomy with free will may be stated as follows. Given divine power, it must mean infinite power, and so everything

[12] Cf. *Dictionary of Technical Terms in the Sciences of the Mussalmans*, ed. A. Sprenger and W. Nassau Lees, II, p. 1317, ll. 8–10 (quoted by G. Weil in his "Teshubato shel Rab Hai Gaon ʿal ha-Ḳeṣ ha-Ḳaṣub la-Ḥayyim," *Sefer Asaf* [1955], p. 272, n. 49).

[13] Graf, *Die arabischen Schriften des Theodor Abu Qurra*, Mimar IX, pp. 234–235.

[14] *De Fide Orth.* II, 30 (PG 94, 969 B).

[15] *M. Abot* III, 15.

[1] Cf. above, pp. 518–519; 601–602.

must be within the power of God. But given man's free will, it means that man's power to choose between two kinds of action is not within the power of God. This antinomy is phrased by Ash'arī in the form of a question raised by the Mu'tazilites as to "whether God has power over that over which He has endowed men with power." [2] Two views are reported by him in two places in his *Maḳālāt*.

One view is attributed by him in one of these places to "most of the Mu'tazilites" [3] and in the other place it is attributed by him to "Ibrāhīm [al-Naẓẓām], Abu al-Hudhayl, and all the Mu'tazilites and Ḳadarites except al-Shaḥḥām." [4] As reproduced by him in the latter place, the statement of this view consists of two parts, which read as follows: "God is not to be described as having power over a thing over which He has endowed [5] men with power, and it is impossible that one thing should be the object of power of two possessors of power." [6] In the other place, the statement of the view consists of only one part, which reads: "God is not to be described as having power in any respect whatsoever over that over which He has endowed (*aḳdar*) men with power." [7]

The first part of the first statement quite evidently means that man is endowed by God with the power to act freely and of that power he cannot be deprived even by God himself, the implication being that for God to deprive man of the power to act with which He himself has endowed him is one of the impossibilities which, as we have seen above,[8] it was believed that God in His wisdom would never render possible. The second part of the statement would seem to be

[2] *Maḳālāt*, p. 199, ll. 3–4; cf. p. 594, ll. 7–8.

[3] *Ibid.*, p. 199, l. 5.

[4] *Ibid.*, p. 549, ll. 9–10. Isfarā'inī, however, includes Abū al-Hudhayl among those who believed in acquisition (cf. Horten, *Systeme*, p. 339, n. 2).

[5] The text reads *yuḳdir*, "endows with power," but this seems to be a corruption of *akdar*, "has endowed with power"; cf. p. 549, l. 12, and p. 199, l. 5.

[6] *Maḳālāt*, p. 549, ll. 10–11.

[7] *Ibid.*, p. 199, ll. 5–6.

[8] Cf. above, pp. 578 ff.

an addition by Ash'arī himself, pointing out in advance the contrast between the view he had just quoted and the view of Shaḥḥam he was about to quote.

The second view, that of Shaḥḥām, is reproduced in its main part, with a few slight verbal changes, in both places in the *Maḳālāt*. That main part reads in one of the places as follows: "God has power over that over which He has endowed (*aḳdar*) men with power and that one movement, as an object of power, is the object of power of two possessors of power, namely, God and man, so that, if [God] the eternal does it (*fa'alahā*), it is by necessity (*iḍṭirāran*) and if [man] the created does it (*fa'alahā*), it is by acquisition (*iktisāban*)." [9] Note the terms "one movement" and "does it," which quite clearly indicate that the term "power" dealt with in these passages refers only to the "power to act" and does not include the "power to will to act," so that whatever Shaḥḥām says about the power with which God has endowed man refers only to the power to act and does not refer to the power to will to act.

This statement quite evidently means that, in opposition to his teacher Abū al-Hudhayl and all the other Mu'tazilites of his time, Shaḥḥam maintained that, even though man has been endowed by God both with the power to will to act and with the power to act, God either may deprive him of the power to act, without necessarily depriving him also of the power to will to act, or may allow him to retain both these powers. Consequently, if God has deprived man of the power to act, then every act performed by man thereafter is not a free act of his own; it is created for him by God; so that, as Shaḥḥām puts it, "if [God] the eternal does it, it is by necessity." But, if God has not deprived man of the power to act, then every act is performed by man in virtue of that power to act which he has acquired by his having been endowed with it by God and of which God has not deprived him, so that, again, as Shaḥḥām puts it, "if [man] the created does it, it is by acquisi-

[9] *Maḳālāt*, p. 549, ll. 12–14; cf. p. 199, ll. 7–9.

tion." The term "acquisition" is thus used by him in the sense of man's free action. Hence Baghdādī, after stating that "Shaḥḥām allowed the possibility for one thing to be the object of power of two possessors of power," explains it to mean that "either one of them, instead of the other, could produce that object." [10]

The term acquisition had a twofold history before Shaḥḥām.

First, by the early Libertarians the term acquisition in the plural was used as a description of man's actions, all of which they regarded as free because of the power to act freely with which man was endowed by God, that is to say, acquired from God. Thus, in a passage dealing both with the pre-Muʿtazilite Ḳadariyyah and their Muʿtazilite followers, Baghdādī ascribes to them the view that "God is not the creator of the acquisitions (*aksāb*) of men" [11] and that "it is men who determine their acquisitions (*aksāb*)." [12] There is no reason to doubt that Baghdādī is quoting the original terminology of the Ḳadariyyah described by him. Similarly there is no reason to doubt that Shahrastānī also is quoting the original terminology of Wāṣil when he says of him that he described "goodness and wickedness, nobleness and baseness" as belonging to men's acquisitions (*aksāb*)." [13] This use of the term acquisitions as a description of the free actions of men is quite evidently based upon those Koranic verses which begin by saying (4:110) "whosoever does (*yaʿmal*) evil" and then go on to say (4:111) "whosoever acquires (*yaksib*) a sin" (4:112) "whosoever acquires (*yaksib*) a fault or sin," or of which one (52:16) reads: "Ye shall be recompensed only for what ye have been doing (*kuntum taʿmalūna*)" and the other (52:21) reads: "Every man is held pledge [that is, responsible] for what he has acquired (*kasaba*)." To those who believed that man was endowed by God with the power of free will, these verses meant that man's free actions are his acquisitions.

Second, from other passages in Ashʿarī's *Maḳālāt* we gather

[10] *Farḳ*, p. 163, ll. 8–9.

[11] *Ibid*., p. 94, l. 7.

[12] *Ibid*., l. 8.

[13] *Milal*, p. 32, l. 20 – p. 33, l. 1.

that, prior to Shaḥḥām, Ḍirār was excluded from the Mu'tazilite sect on account of his belief in a theory of acquisition,[14] and also that a theory of acquisition was held by Najjār.[15] Similarly, when Ash'arī's contemporary Ḫayyāṭ ascribes to "Ḍirār and Ḥafṣ al-Fard" a view with regard to "that which is created,"[16] the reference, as we shall see, is to the theory of acquisition. Finally, when all these three, Ḍirār and Ḥafṣ and Najjār, are described by Shahrastānī in his *Milal* as belonging to those Mu'tazilites whom he calls "middlings" (*mutawassiṭūn*) and as differing from most of the Mu'tazilites on certain problems,[17] one of these problems is quite evidently that of acquisition.

Let us now unfold the full views of Ḍirār and Najjār on acquisition as may be gathered from Ash'arī and others.

With regard to Ḍirār, Ash'arī reports as follows: "The reason for which Ḍirār b. 'Amr separated himself from the Mu'tazilites was his assertion that the acts of man are created and that one act comes from two agents (*fā'ilūn*), one of whom creates it, namely, God, while the other acquires (*iktasaba*) it, namely, man, and that God is the agent (*fā'il*) of the acts of men in reality and men are also the agents of them in reality."[18] In Shahrastānī the same view is ascribed to both Ḍirār and Ḥafṣ b. al-Fard and is restated as follows: "They both say that the acts of men are created by God in reality and man acquires them in reality and they both consider it as possible that the taking place of an act should be the joint product of two agents."[19]

Ash'arī then goes on to quote Ḍirār as follows: "And he asserts that capacity (*istiṭā'ah*) is before the act and together with the act and it is a part of the possessor of the capacity,"[20] which last statement, according to another report by Ash'arī on Ḍirār, means that "capacity" is part of the "body" of the possessor of the capacity.[21] In Shahrastānī, the same view, as

[14] *Maḳālāt*, p. 281, ll. 2–3.
[15] *Ibid.*, p. 566, ll. 14–15.
[16] *Intiṣār* 91, p. 98, ll. 4–5.
[17] *Milal*, p. 19, ll. 14–15.
[18] *Maḳālāt*, p. 281, ll. 2–5.
[19] *Milal*, p. 63, ll. 11–12.
[20] *Maḳālāt*, p. 281, ll. 5–6.
[21] *Ibid.*, p. 345, ll. 12–14.

ascribed to both Ḍirār and Ḥafṣ, reads: "Capacity and incapacity are part of the body . . . and that part undoubtedly lasts [at least] two units of time [that is, instants]." [22] Baghdādī's restatement reads that Ḍirār "agreed with the Muʿtazilites that capacity exists before the act and he even went further by maintaining that it exists before the act and together with the act and after the act and that it is part of the possessor of the capacity." [23]

In another place, Ashʿarī quotes Ḍirār as asserting "that a man may produce an action in something outside his reach and that that which is generated from his act in himself in something other than himself, whether motion or rest, is an acquisition of his and a creation of God." [24]

It is this conception of acquisition, on account of which Ashʿarī says that Ḍirār separated himself from the Muʿtazilites, that Ḫayyāṭ means by his statement that one of the views held by Ḍirār and Ḥafṣ, on account of which "they are not Muʿtazilites," that is to say, they are no longer Muʿtazilites, is "their view with regard to that which is created," that is to say, their view that men's acts are created by God but only acquired by men. Consequently when Ḫayyāṭ goes on to quote Bishr b. Muʿtamir's tirade against these two renegade Muʿtazilites, starting with the statement "we disown them" and concluding with the statement "their master is al-Jahm," [25] by this concluding statement he does not mean literally that Ḍirār and Ḥafṣ are Jahmite Compulsionists; he only means that their assertion that man's acts are created by God, even though qualified by the statement that they are acquired by man, is to his own way of thinking in no wise different from the outright Compulsionism of Jahm.[26] So also does Shahrastānī place them together with the Jahmiyyah under the Jabariyyah, that is, the Compulsionists,[27] even though he explicitly ascribes to them the theory of acquisition.[28]

[22] *Milal*, p. 63, ll. 13–14. [23] *Farḳ*, p. 201, ll. 13–15.

[24] *Maḳālāt*, p. 408, ll. 4–6; cf. p. 407, l. 15 – p. 408, l. 3.

[25] *Intiṣār* 91, p. 98, ll. 5–8.

[26] Cf. above, pp. 606; 608. [27] *Milal*, p. 63, l. 6. [28] *Ibid.*, ll. 11–12.

So much for Ḍirār's conception of acquisition. Now for Najjār's conception of it.

Of Najjār, Ashʿarī reports that he maintained "that the deeds of men are created by God, whereas men are the agents (*fāʿilūn*) thereof" [29] and that "man has power over acquisition (*al-kasb*), but is powerless with regard to creation." [30]

In Baghdādī, this view of Najjār is restated in two passages as follows: (1) "God is the creator of the acquired acts of man"; [31] (2) "with regard to terming the acquirer an agent . . . al-Najjār applied that term [to him] in a general way (*aṭlaḳahu*)," [32] that is to say, without the additional phrase "in reality" which is used by Ḍirār.

Ashʿarī then continues to report Najjār as maintaining "that capacity cannot precede the act, that the help of God is created at the instant of the act, simultaneously with (*maʿa*) the act, and that this is capacity; that no two acts are produced from one capacity and that for every act a capacity is created simultaneously with (*maʿa*) the creation of the act; that a capacity does not endure; that with its coming into existence, the act comes into existence, but that during its nonexistence the act does not exist." [33] The simultaneity of the capacity with the act is also mentioned by both Baghdādī [34] and Shahrastānī [35] as characteristic of the view of Najjār.

Continuing, Ashʿarī also reports Najjār as maintaining that "man does not act in another but produces actions only in himself; . . . he does not effect any action in a thing by way of generation." [36] Baghdādī similarly reports that "al-Najjār held a view with regard to generated effects like that held by our fellow-associates [that is, the Ashʿarites], namely, that they are God's acts by choice." [37]

From all this it is clear that though Ḍirār and Najjār agree

[29] *Maḳālāt*, p. 283, l. 3.
[30] *Ibid.*, p. 566, l. 14.
[31] *Farḳ*, p. 195, l. 14.
[32] *Ibid.*, p. 197, ll. 5–6.
[33] *Maḳālāt*, p. 283, ll. 6–10.
[34] *Farḳ*, p. 195, l. 15.
[35] *Milal*, p. 62, ll. 6–7.
[36] *Maḳālāt*, p. 284, ll. 9–12.
[37] *Farḳ*, p. 197, ll. 9–10.

that man's acts are created by God and man is only their acquirer, their conception of acquisition is not the same. The differences between their views, as we have seen, are three: (1) with regard to the use of the expression "in reality" as a description of the term "agent"; (2) with regard to the description of "capacity" in its relation to the "act"; (3) with regard to the authorship of "generated effects."

Of these three differences the most fundamental one is that with regard to the description of "capacity" in its relation to the "act." To Ḍirār, man's capacity or power to acquire any act created for him by God exists before the act and is part of his own body. By this is meant that from birth man is endowed by God with a capacity or power to acquire by himself any act which is to be created for him by God, so that his act of acquiring is a free act of his own. To Najjār, however, that capacity or power to acquire the act is created in him by God simultaneously with His creation of the act, so that not only man's power of acquiring but his very act of acquiring is created by God.

This difference between them with regard to capacity leads to the two other differences between them. Since according to Ḍirār man by his own power or capacity acquires the act created for him by God, by that same power he can also acquire generated effects. To Najjār, to whom man's act of acquiring is created by God, that created act of acquiring is limited to acts in man's own body and does not extend to generated effects. Then the difference in regard to capacity also leads to the difference with regard to the use of the phrase "in reality." To Ḍirār, to whom man's act of acquiring is created by man himself, man may be called both an acquirer and an agent in reality. To Najjār, however, to whom man's act of acquiring is created by God, man may be called acquirer and agent but not acquirer and agent in reality.

The term "acquisition," as used by those who, like Ḍirār and Najjār, believed that God is the creator and man is only an acquirer, is explained by Ghazālī as having its origin in the

Koran,[38] by which he quite evidently means those verses which we have quoted above. By this, I take it, Ghazālī does not mean that those referred to by him were the first to use the term acquisition; he only means that they were the first to use the term acquisition in the sense that that which is acquired by man is created for him by God. In view of the fact that the term *kasab*, "to acquire," has been shown to be one of the commercial terms in the Koran,[39] we may assume that this theory of acquisition was conceived by those referred to by Ghazālī after the manner of a commercial transaction, such as this. A man enters a workshop, say a pottery. He sees the potter working on his wheel and molding clay into pots of various shapes and sizes. He orders a pot of a certain shape and size, and, when the potter has made it for him in accordance with his specification, he pays for it and takes it home. The pot is thus his acquisition and legally his property, but it is the potter's creation.[40]

From all this we gather that, in opposition to the use of acquisition among the Muʿtazilites in the sense of irrevocable free human action, there appeared among the Muʿtazilites three distinct theories of acquisition, that of Ḍirār, that of Najjār, and that of Shaḥḥām. Both Ḍirār and Najjār rejected the Muʿtazilite view that man is the creator of his own acts, maintaining that their creator is God, man being only their acquirer. They differ, however, as to the creatorship of the acquisition by which man acquires the acts created for him by God. To Ḍirār, the creator of the acquisition is man himself; to Najjār its creator is God. In opposition to both of them,

[38] Quoted by A. v. Kremer in *Geschichte der herschenden Ideen des Islam's*, II, p. 306, n. 26, from Ghazālī's *Iḥyāʾ*, IV, 312, ed. Cairo, 1279 (cf. ed. Cairo, 1358, IV, p. 249, ll. 19–20).

[39] Cf. Torrey, *The Commercial-Theological Terms in the Koran*, pp. 27–29.

[40] It is to be noted that Joseph Schacht quotes a passage dating from about 150/725 in which the term *iktisāb* is taken by him to mean "responsibility" (cf. pp. 31–32 of his "New Sources for the History of Muhammadan Theology" in *Studia Islamica*, 1:23–42 (1953). As for the meaning of the expression *fāʿil kāsib* used by Māturīdī, as quoted by Schacht (*ibid.*, p. 32), it will be discussed later (see below, pp. 711 f).

Shaḥḥām retained the Muʿtazilite view that man is endowed by God to create freely his own acts and hence these acts are described by him as acquisitions. He differs, however, from the Muʿtazilites by maintaining that God may deprive man of that endowed power, so that, when this happens, it is God who creates man's acts for him. Thus, while, according to Ḍirār and Najjār, every act of man is always at once both a creation of God and an acquisition of man, according to Shaḥḥām, every human act may be either wholly a creation of God or wholly an acquisition of man.

Theories of acquisition like those of Ḍirār and Najjār can be shown to have been reported respectively in the names of the Rāfiḍite Hishām b. al-Ḥakam and the Sunnite Ibn Kullāb, the former probably a contemporary of Ḍirār and the latter a contemporary of Najjār.

With regard to the Rāfiḍah, Ashʿarī, after stating that "Hishām b. al-Ḥakam" belonged to a group of Rāfidah who held that "the acts of men are created by God," [41] goes on as follows: "Jaʿfar b. Ḥarb reports of Hishām b. al-Ḥakam that he has said that the acts of a man are his choice (*iḫtiyār lahu*) in one respect and necessity (*iḍṭirār*) in another; they are his choice in that he wills (*arāda*) them and acquires (*iktasaba*) them and they are necessity in that they do not proceed from him except at the origination of the inciting cause (*al-sabab al-muhayyij*) for those acts." [42] What is meant by "the inciting cause" is explained in a subsequent passage in which Ashʿarī reports in the name of "the associates of Hishām b. al-Ḥakam" [43] that "the arriving inciting cause" is that "by reason of which the act takes place" [44] and that "when that cause exists and God has created it, the act takes place inevitably." [45] Thus the report quoted by Jaʿfar b. Ḥarb in the name of Hishām b. al-Ḥakam means that the acts of man are an acquisition on the part of man in the sense that they

[41] *Maḳālāt*, p. 40, ll. 12–13.

[42] *Ibid.*, p. 40, l. 13 – p. 41, l. 3.

[43] *Ibid.*, p. 42, l. 12.

[44] *Ibid.*, l. 16.

[45] *Ibid.*, p. 43, ll. 2–3.

are "his choice" and that "he wills them" by a power with which he has been endowed by God, but that they are a creation on the part of God in the sense that they do not proceed from man unless God creates the "inciting cause" by reason of which the acts take place inevitably and by necessity. According to this report, then, the theory of acquisition held by the Rāfiḍite Hishām b. al-Ḥakam was exactly like that held by the Muʿtazilite Ḍirār and perhaps there was some connection between them. It is in the light of this conception of free will that one is to understand Hishām b. al-Ḥakam's use of the expression "free choice" in his statement, as quoted elsewhere by Ashʿarī, that, "if God had foreknowledge of what men would do, there would be no test (*al-miḥnah*) and no free choice (*al-iḫtiyār*)." [46]

With regard to the Predestinarians among the Sunnites, there are two passages quoted by Ashʿarī in the name of Ibn Kullāb. In one of these passages, after stating that what is recited of the Koran subsists in God from eternity, he says that "the recital of it is originated and created [by God], and it is an acquisition (*kasb*) on the part of man." [47] In the other passage, he says "that speech may be by necessity and it may be by acquisition (*iktisāban*)." [48] The wording of the first of these two passages suggests a conception of acquisition like either that of Ḍirār or that of Najjār and the wording of the second passage would seem to suggest a conception of acquisition like that of Shaḥḥām. Inasmuch, however, as Ibn Kullāb belonged to the orthodox who were Predestinarians, we may assume that his conception of acquisition was like that of Najjār's and consequently it is in that sense that the first passage is to be taken. As for the second passage, it happens to follow immediately after a passage in which Abū al-Hudhayl is reported as saying that "speech" may occur either "by necessity" or "by choice." [49] Consequently what this

[46] *Ibid.*, p. 494, ll. 4–5; cf. *Farḳ*, p. 49, l. 18, and above, p. 661.
[47] *Ibid.*, p. 602, ll. 1–2; cf. above, p. 249.
[48] *Ibid.*, p. 605, ll. 5–6. [49] *Ibid.*, ll. 2–3.

second passage of Ibn Kullāb means is that, in contrast to Abū al-Hudhayl, who as a Libertarian believed that there was a kind of speech that was "by choice," Ibn Kullāb, as a Predestinarian who adopted Najjār's theory of a created acquisition, declared that that kind of speech which Abū al-Hudhayl described as being "by choice" should be described as being "by acquisition."

Thus at about the middle of the ninth century, apart from the earlier use of acquisition as a description of free human action, there were three theories of acquisition, that of Ḍirār, that of Najjār, and that of Shaḥḥām. All these three theories of acquisition were rejected by the Muʿtazilites. Outside the Muʿtazilites, a theory of acquisition like that of Ḍirār is reported in the name of the Rāfiḍite Hishām b. al-Ḥakam and a theory of acquisition like that of Najjār is reported in the name of the Sunnite Ibn Kullāb. What happened to this earlier use of acquisition and to these three theories of acquisition subsequently may be gathered from two sets of passages in Ashʿarī's *Maḳālāt*, which was composed in the early part of the tenth century.

(2) Spread of acquisition among Libertarian groups and individuals

In one set of passages, Ashʿarī deals with the theory of acquisition among the Libertarians. This set of passages falls into four parts.

The first part consists of a passage, which reads as follows: "The Baghdadians among the Muʿtazilites said: God is not to be described as having power over the action of men or over anything in a class [of actions] over which He has empowered men, and He is not to be described as having power to create for men belief by which they shall be believers, nor unbelief by which they shall be unbelievers, nor disobedience by which they shall be disobedient, nor acquisition (*kasb*) by which they shall be acquirers." [1]

[1] *Maḳālāt*, p. 550, ll. 9–12.

From this passage we gather that, while these Baghdadians (1) used the term "acquisition," they believed (2) that God has empowered man with the power to act; (3) that God does not deprive man of that power; (4) that God does not create the actions of man, exemplified by such actions as belief and unbelief and disobedience; (5) that God does not create the acquisition of man. All this shows that, though these Baghdadian Muʿtazilites use the term "acquisition," they do not follow the theory of acquisition as it was held by Ḍirār, to whom man is only the acquirer of his action but God is its creator,[2] nor do they follow the theory of acquisition as it was held by Shaḥḥām, to whom God may deprive man of his endowed power to act and create for him his action.[3] Like Naẓẓām and Abū al-Hudhayl, they believed that all human actions are at all times freely performed by man in virtue of that power with which God has empowered him,[4] but they preferred to describe those freely performed actions as being by acquisition in order to indicate that the freedom with which man performs them is ultimately acquired by him from God. The Ḳadariyyah [5] and Wāṣil,[6] as we have seen, have used the term acquisition in this sense.

The second part consists of a passage in which Ashʿarī reports that a certain Shīʿite sect, known as the Zaydiyyah, was divided into two groups on the question of predestination and free will, one of them believing that men's actions are created by God and another one of them believing that "men's actions are not created by God nor originated by Him as new things; rather are they an acquisition (*kasb*) of men, who originate them, produce them as new things, give them a beginning, and make them." [7] From the wording of their statement it is clear that they believed that men's actions are free, but, like the preceding Baghdadians among the Muʿtazilites, they described the free actions of men by the term acquisition. Inas-

[2] Cf. above, p. 667.
[3] Cf. above, p. 665.
[4] Cf. above, p. 664.
[5] Cf. above, p. 666.
[6] *Ibid.*
[7] *Maḳālāt*, p. 72, ll. 11–12.

much as the founder of this sect, Zayd b. ʿAlī b. al-Ḥusayn, is said to have been a pupil of Wāṣil b. ʿAṭāʾ,[8] we may assume that Zayd himself, followed by some of his adherents, adopted Wāṣil's theory of free will and, like Wāṣil, described the free actions of man by the term acquisition, which term they continued to use in that old general sense, even when later, with the rise of the theory of acquisition in its technical sense, the term assumed a new specific meaning. It will, however, be noticed that in the passage quoted above, while the Zaydiyyah explicitly deny that men's actions are "created (*maḫlūḳah*)" by God, they do not say that they are "created (*maḫlūḳah*) by men; instead they merely say that men "originate them (*aḥdathūhā*), produce them as new things (*iḫtarʿaūhā*), give them a beginning (*ābdaʿūhā*), and make them (*faʿalūhā*)." The reason for this is that, as we have seen above, the early Muʿtazilites refrained from describing man as the creator of his actions, even though they denied that God was their creator.[9]

The third part consists of four passages, which read as follows:

1. "Al-Nāshī said: God is . . . an agent (*fāʿil*) in reality and man is . . . an agent in a metaphorical sense." [10]

2. "And he used to say that man is not an agent in reality nor an originator (*muḥdith*) in reality." [11]

3. "And he used to say that God does not originate (*aḥdath*) man's acquisition and man's action." [12]

4. "And he used to say that God does not originate man's acquisition." [13]

From a comparison and combination of these four passages, and leaving out for the time being the question as to whether the term "action" should be omitted in passage 3 or added in passage 4, we may reduce the four statements con-

[8] Cf. I. Friedlaender, "The Heterodoxies of the Shiites in the Presentation of Ibn Ḥazm," *JAOS*, 29 (1908), 11.

[9] Cf. above, pp. 620–622.

[10] *Maḳālāt*, p. 184, ll. 6–8.

[11] *Ibid.*, p. 501, ll. 6–7.

[12] *Ibid.*, l. 7.

[13] *Ibid.*, p. 539, l. 15.

tained in these four passages to the following two statements: 1. God is an agent and originator in reality, so that He does not originate in a mere metaphorical sense. 2. Man is an agent and originator only in a metaphorical sense, so that he originates only in a metaphorical sense.

What Nashī means by the contrast between "in reality" and "in a metaphorical sense" may be gathered from a passage where he explains as follows the difference between the application of such terms as knowing and powerful and the like to God "in reality" and their application to man "in a metaphorical sense": "When *ṣandal* which is imported from its place of origin is called by us *ṣandal* [sandalwood, imported from India], that term applies to it in reality, but when we call man *ṣandal* [robust], that term is applied to him in a metaphorical sense."[14] Evidently the Arabic term *ṣandal* in the sense of the adjective "robust" is taken by Nashī to have been derived from the use of the same term in the sense of "sandalwood," and so *ṣandal* in its original sense is called by him *ṣandal* "in reality," whereas *ṣandal* in its derivative sense is called by him *ṣandal* "in a metaphorical sense." Accordingly, when he says that God is both an agent and originator in reality, whereas man is both an agent and originator metaphorically, he means that God is the ultimate origin and source of every action that is performed in the world directly by some agent, whereas man, though he performs every action of his directly, derives his power to act from God and therefore is an agent and originator only in a metaphorical sense. By the same token, when in passages 3 and 4 Nashī says that "God does not originate," which, as we have seen, amounts to his saying that God does not originate in a mere metaphorical sense, he means thereby that God is not the direct cause of origination but rather its ultimate cause, which to him means its cause in reality.

In passages 1 and 2, where God in contrast to man is said by Nashī to be an agent and originator in reality, that is to

[14] *Ibid.*, p. 500, l. 14 – p. 501, l. 1; cf. p. 184, l. 16 – p. 185, l. 1.

say, an ultimate agent and originator, which by implication means that God is not a direct agent and originator, it is not clear whether this denial of God's being a direct agent and originator means that He is not the direct agent and originator only of man's actions or whether it means that He is not the direct agent and originator also of any other kind of action that occurs in the world. Should this denial mean the latter, then Nashī would have aligned himself with Naẓẓām and Muʿammar in their affirmation of a belief in causality, that is, a belief in intermediate causes,[15] contrary to the belief of almost all the other Muʿtazilites, who, in the case of all actions other than human actions, agreed with the orthodox Mutakallimūn that God is their direct originator.[16] This vagueness, however, is cleared up in passages 3 and 4. In these passages, stating negatively that "God does not originate," by which is meant, as we have seen, that God does not originate directly, Nashī says explicitly that what God does not originate directly is "man's acquisition and man's action" (passage 3) or "man's acquisition" (passage 4), from which we have reason to infer that, in the case of all other actions in the world, he believed that they are originated by God directly, thus aligning himself with most of the Muʿtazilites in denying causality.

But it will have been noticed that, while in passage 3 Nashī says that God does not directly originate both "man's acquisition and man's action," in passage 4 he says that God does not originate directly "man's acquisition," without mentioning "action," which might be taken to imply that, while God does not create man's acquisition, He creates man's action. Now of these two statements, that of passage 3 is, as we have seen, a denial of acquisition in any of its conceptions,[17] whereas that of passage 4, with its possible implication, is an affirmation of acquisition as conceived of by Ḍirār.[18] Consequently, of passages 3 and 4, only one can be taken to represent the genuine view of Nashī. But which one is it? Fortunately an

[15] Cf. above, p. 613.
[16] *Ibid.*
[17] Cf. above at nn. 1–6.
[18] Cf. above, pp. 667 f.

answer to this question is to be found in a statement by Ibn Ḥazm, according to which, Nashī "agreed with the Muʿtazilites on the question of free will (*ḳadar*)," [19] which means that Nashī held that God does not create or originate man's action. The omission of "and man's action" in passage 4 is, therefore, a scribal error.

From all this we gather that, while Nashī (1) used the term "acquisition," he believed (2) that God has empowered man with the power to act; (3) that God does not deprive man of that power; (4) that God does not create the acquisition of man; (5) that God does not create the action of man. His view is thus exactly like that of the Baghdadian Muʿtazilites and others discussed above [20] who use the term acquisition only as descriptive of the freely performed human actions in order to indicate that the freedom with which man performs them is ultimately acquired by him from God.[21]

The fourth part consists of three passages, which read as follows.

1. "When God has empowered men with power over motion or rest or some other action, He has power over that which is of the kind of that over which He has empowered men with power, and this is the view of al-Jubbāʾī and groups of the Muʿtazilites." [22] In this passage Jubbāʾī, as reported by Ashʿarī, repeats almost verbatim the words of his teacher Shaḥḥām and thus joins him in coming out against Naẓẓām and Abū al-Hudhayl and all the other Muʿtazilites who, as we have seen above, are reported as saying that "God is not to be described as having power over a thing over which He has endowed a man with power." [23] We may thus infer that, like Shaḥḥām, Jubbāʾī believed that God may deprive man of the power to act with which He has empowered him,

[19] Quoted from a manuscript copy of Ibn Ḥazm's *Fiṣal* (II, 141r) by Schreiner in his *Zur Geschichte des Aš'aritenthums*, p. 89, n. 4. This statement is omitted in the printed editions of the *Fiṣal* (Cairo, 1317–27, IV, 194, l. 23; and Cairo, 1347–48, IV, p. 148, l. 12).

[20] Cf. above, pp. 674 f.

[21] Cf. above, p. 666.

[22] *Maḳālāt*, p. 199, l. 16 – p. 200, l. 2.

[23] Cf. above, p. 664.

without necessarily depriving him also of his equally empowered power to will to act,[24] in which case thus the act willed by man is created for him by God. Nothing, however, is said here by Jubbā'ī to indicate whether also, like Shaḥḥām, he would describe man as acquirer of his actions in the case he had not been deprived by God of his empowered power to act.

2. "Al-Jubbā'ī said: The meaning of acquirer is one who acquires something beneficial or something harmful, something good or something bad, or, in other words, his acquisition is of an object which is outside himself, as his acquisition of wealth and the like, for the wealth which he acquires is outside himself, so that the wealth is an acquisition of his in the real sense of the term, even though it is not an action of his." [25] In this passage, Jubbā'ī's insistence that the term "acquisition" is to be used only in the sense of getting or having possession of an object which is "outside" the acquirer and is not an "action" of his quite evidently is meant to be in opposition to Shaḥḥām's use of the term "acquisition" as a description of the "action" performed by man in virtue of a power to act with which he has been empowered by God. But still nothing is said by Jubbā'ī here to indicate how man is to be described in relation to such an action.

3. "Al-Jubbā'ī said: The meaning of saying that God is a creator is that He does things in a predetermined manner and [similarly], with regard to man, when he performs deeds in a predetermined manner, he is a creator." [26] No reason is given by Jubbā'ī for his new explanation of the meaning of the term "creator." But I believe he had a reason for that. He must have inferred it from three verses in the Koran, which in his mind were arranged in the form of an argument as follows: Though the Koran says (12:3) that "God begets not (*lā yālid*)," still it describes God as saying to men (49:13): "O men! verily, we have created you (*ḫalaḳnāhum*) a male and

[24] Cf. above, p. 665.

[25] *Maḳālāt*, p. 542, ll. 4–7.

[26] *Ibid*., p. 195, ll. 4–6; p. 539, ll. 6–9.

a female," and this quite evidently on the ground of its saying elsewhere (35:12; 41:47) that "no female conceives (*taḥmilu*) or is delivered without His knowledge." Thus, according to the Koran, he must have reasoned, God, who does not directly beget human beings, is called the creator of human beings only because no human being is born without His knowledge, which means that all human beings are born according to His foreknowledge, and will, and predetermination. And so, he must have argued, inasmuch as God has endowed man with the power to act with foreknowledge and will and predetermination, man may be called the creator of his acts.

(3) *Acquisition among the* Ahl al-Ithbāt

In another set of passages in the *Maḳālāt*, Ashʿarī deals with a group of people whom he describes as *Ahl al-Ithbāt*, "The People of Affirmation," and as followers of the theory of acquisition.

This set of passages falls into three parts.

The *first part* consists of two passages, as follows:

1. "Many of the People of Affirmation said that man is an agent (*fāʿil*) in reality in the sense of his being an acquirer, but they do not admit that man is an originator (*muḥdith*)." [1]

In their describing man as being "an agent in reality" these "many People of Affirmation" follow Ḍirār.[2] In not describing man as an "originator" they show that they share in the view said to be held by "the People of Affirmation" that the term *muḥdath*, "originated," means the same as the term *maḫlūḳ*, "created," [3] whence, inasmuch as man is not the creator of his actions, he is also not their "originator."

2. "It has come to my ears that some of them said that he is an originator (*muḥdith*) in reality in the sense of his being an acquirer (*muktasib*)." [4]

Quite evidently these "some" People of Affirmation did

[1] *Maḳālāt*, p. 540, ll. 1–2.
[2] Cf. above, p. 667.
[3] *Maḳālāt*, p. 541, ll. 11–12.
[4] *Ibid.*, p. 540, ll. 2–3.

not share in the view said to be held by the People of Affirmation that the term "originated" means the same as the term "created," whence they argued that, just as man is an agent in reality, he is also an originator in reality.

The *second part* consists of three passages, as follows:

1. A passage in which Kūshānī, who is at first introduced as one of "the many People of Affirmation"[5] and then is said to be a follower of Najjār,[6] is presented as one who, in contrast to those who described man as "an agent in reality," declined to say that man is an agent in the sense of an acquirer.[7] Inasmuch as Najjār is known to have denied only that man is "an agent in reality" but did not deny that man is "an agent,"[8] we may assume that what Kūshānī declined to say is only that man is an agent in reality.

2. "Among the People of Affirmation there were some who said that God really does (*yafʿal*) in the sense of His being one who creates (*yaḫluḳ*) and that man does not really do but only really acquires, for one does not do unless he creates, seeing that the meaning of the term doer or agent (*fāʿil*) in the [Arabic] language is the same as that of creator (*ḫāliḳ*), and if man could create some one acquisition of his, he could create every acquisition of his."[9]

The implication of the statement of these some People of Affirmation that "man does not really do" is that, like Najjār, they would describe man simply as "an agent" but not as "an agent in reality."

3. "All the People of Affirmation, except Ḍirār, say that man has no action in that which is other than himself and they declare this as impossible."[10]

Since one of the three differences between Ḍirār and Najjār in their conception of acquisition is, as we have seen, that Ḍirār extended man's acquisition of his act to generated effects, whereas Najjār denied it,[11] this report shows that all

[5] *Ibid.*, ll. 4 and 9.
[6] *Ibid.*, p. 541, ll. 3–4.
[7] *Ibid.*, p. 540, ll. 4–9.
[8] Cf. above, p. 669.
[9] *Maḳālāt*, p. 541, ll. 6–10.
[10] *Ibid.*, p. 408, ll. 6–7.
[11] Cf. above, pp. 668; 669; 670.

the People of Affirmation agreed with Najjār on this aspect of the theory of acquisition.

The *third part* consists of two passages, as follows:

1. The People of Truth (*Ahl al-Ḥaḳḳ*) and Affirmation (*wa'l-Ithbāt*) said that God has the power to create belief by which men shall be believers and disbelief by which they shall be disbelievers and acquisition by which they shall be acquirers and obedience by which they shall be obeyers and disobedience by which they shall be disobeyers." [12]

2. "Most of the People of Affirmation denied that God is to be described as having power to force men to belief by which they shall be believers and to disbelief by which they shall be disbelievers and to justice by which they shall be just and to injustice by which they shall be unjust." [13]

It is to be noted that the contrast between "the People of Truth and Affirmation" and "Most of the People of Affirmation" is only with reference to the question whether God has the power to force men in matters of belief and disbelief and of justice and injustice, the implication thus being that, with reference to any human action which is not a matter of religion or morality, all the People of Affirmation are in agreement with the People of Truth and Affirmation that "God has the power to create . . . acquisition by which men shall be acquirers," that is to say, they follow Najjār in believing that man's act of acquiring is created by God.

From all this we may gather that the People of Affirmation, who on the whole are to be included among the Predestinarians,[14] adopted the theory of acquisition as formulated by Ḍirār and Najjār, many of them following Ḍirār and some of them following Najjār, though with regard to generated effects all of them followed Najjār.

This, then, is the story of acquisition prior to the time of

[12] *Maḳālāt*, p. 551, ll. 15–17.

[13] *Ibid.*, p. 552, ll. 1–3. The qualifying term "most" is explainable by the fact that there were "People of Affirmation" who held other opinions on God's power over unbelief and injustice (cf. *Maḳālāt*, p. 554, ll. 12–16).

[14] Watt, *Free Will*, p. 112.

Ashʿarī. The original use of acquisition as a description of free human action was continued by the Baghdadian Muʿtazilites, by a group of Zaydiyyah, and by Nashī. Shaḥḥām's theory of acquisition was followed by his pupil Jubbāʾī, who, however, did not use the term acquisition. Ḍirār's and Najjār's respective theories of acquisition found followers among those Predestinarians known as the People of Affirmation.

b. Acquisition in Ashʿarī, Bāḳillānī, and Juwaynī

We have thus described the status of the theory of acquisition both among the Libertarians and among the Predestinarians in the early part of the tenth century, when Ashʿarī was still a Muʿtazilite and pupil of Jubbāʾī. Then in 912, when Ashʿarī broke away from the Muʿtazilites and joined the ranks of the orthodox, he accepted their belief in Predestination and, like some of them, he also adopted the theory of acquisition. What his conception of the theory of acquisition was may be gathered from his own works.

In his *Lumaʿ*, Ashʿarī starts his discussion of the problem of *ḳadar*, "predestination," with the question, "Why do you claim that the acquisitions of men are created by God?," [1] thus introducing the term "acquisition," used by him here in the sense of human "action," as a term already of common knowledge which needed no explanation.[2] So also in his *Ibānah*, introducing the term acquisition as something already well known, he says that "there cannot be, under the authority of God, any acquisition on the part of men that God does not will," [3] by which he means that every acquisition of men is created by God, for, according to Ashʿarī himself, the Koranic verse, "Doer of what He wills" (11:109, 85:16) means that God is the creator of what He wills.[4]

[1] *Lumaʿ* 82, p. 37, l. 3.

[2] Once before in the *Lumaʿ* (47) he introduces the term "acquisition" without any explanation.

[3] *Ibānah*, p. 63, ll. 17–18.

[4] *Ibid.*, p. 2, ll. 4–5; *Lumaʿ* 49, p. 24, ll. 7–8.

Later in answer to a challenge, he explains that by acquisitions he means acquired acts or movements as distinguished from necessary movements, illustrating the former by such movements as "going and coming and approaching and receding" and the latter by such movements as "the trembling from palsy and the shivering from fever." [5] That there is a distinction between these two kinds of movement, he says, "a man knows . . . by a necessary knowledge which leaves no room for doubt" [6] — a statement which is analogous to the statement of the Libertarians with regard to their own belief in the absolute freedom of human action that "man knows within himself" that the voluntary actions of his are within his own power.[7]

How man acquires the acts which are created for him by God is described by Ashʿarī in two sets of passages.

In the first set, using the term "power" (*ḳudrah*, *ḳuwwah*), he makes the following statements.

First: "The acquirer acquires a thing because the acquiring takes place in virtue of his created power (*ḳudrah*) over it." [8]

Second: "The true meaning of acquisition is that the thing proceeds from the acquirer in virtue of a certain power (*ḳuwwah*)." [9]

Third: "The occurrence of an act which is an acquisition has no agent in reality save God and no one is with power over it so that it will be with power over it in its reality, in the sense that he creates it, save God." [10] The first part of this statement is quite evidently in opposition to Ḍirār, who held that man is an agent in reality.[11]

Fourth: "Does a man, then, acquire a thing as it really is? . . . This is an error. He acquires . . . only in virtue of a created power." [12]

Fifth: "When God empowers us over acquired motion it must be He who creates it in us as an acquisition." [13]

[5] *Lumaʿ* 92, p. 41, ll. 15–16.
[6] *Ibid.*, ll. 10–16.
[7] Cf. above, p. 618.
[8] *Lumaʿ* 89, p. 40, ll. 7–8.
[9] *Ibid.* 92, p. 42, ll. 1–3.
[10] *Ibid.* 87, p. 39, ll. 10 and 13–14.
[11] Cf. above, p. 667.
[12] *Lumaʿ* 90, p. 40, ll. 11 and 12.
[13] *Ibid.* 95, p. 43, ll. 12–13.

In the second set of passages, using the terms "power" and "capacity" (*istiṭā'ah*) interchangeably, he makes the following statements:

First: "Man is capable in virtue of a capacity which is distinct from him." [14] This is in direct opposition to Ḍirār's view that capacity is part of the body of the man who is capable.[15]

Second: "The capacity cannot precede the act" [16] but "is simultaneous with the act." [17] This is in opposition to the view of Ḍirār [18] and in agreement with the view of Najjār.[19]

Third: "The power does not endure." [20] This, again, is in opposition to Ḍirār [21] and in agreement with Najjār.[22]

Fourth, his denial of the view that "the power over a thing is a power over both it and its contrary," [23] the reason for this being that, in accordance with his denial of free will, the expression "the power over a thing" means with him the power by which man must necessarily produce the thing for which that power was created in him by God and cannot produce any other thing, whence his denial of the view that "the power over a thing" is also the power over "its contrary." This denial is in opposition to the Mu'tazilites who, in accordance with their belief in free will, maintain, as quoted by Ash'arī in his *Maḳālāt*, that "capacity is a power over the act and its contrary, and it does not necessitate the act," [24] that is to say, man by his capacity or power may freely choose to produce either one of the two contrary acts.

Fifth: His denial of the view that "there may be one power over two volitions, or over two motions, or over any similar pairs of things." [25] The reason given by him is that "a power is power only over that which exists with the power in the

[14] *Ibid.* 122, p. 54, l. 3.
[15] Cf. above, p. 667.
[16] *Luma'* 123, p. 54, ll. 10–11.
[17] *Ibid.* 128, p. 56, l. 17.
[18] Cf. above, p. 667.
[19] Cf. above, p. 669.
[20] *Luma'* 125, p. 55, l. 4.
[21] Cf. above, p. 667.
[22] Cf. above, p. 669.
[23] *Luma'* 126, p. 55, ll. 10–11.
[24] *Maḳālāt*, p. 230, ll. 12–13; cf. *Metaph.* IX, 5, 1048a, 7–15.
[25] *Luma'* 127, p. 56, ll. 6–7.

abode (*maḥall*) of the power."[26] What the statement here means is that the created power in man can acquire only a movement which is created by God in the man's own body, when the same body is the abode of both the power which acquires and the movement which is acquired, but that that created power in man cannot acquire a movement which is technically called a "generated effect," that is to say, a movement generated by man in something outside his body. That this is meant to be a denial of the application of the theory of acquisition to generated effects can be shown by the following statement in Baghdādī's *Uṣūl*: "Our fellow associates (*asḥābunā*) [that is, the Ash'arites] say that that which the Libertarians call generated effects is the act of God. Man cannot be properly said to be an agent of that which is not in the abode (*maḥall*) of his power, for it is possible that a man would stretch the string of a bow and the arrow would be sent forth by his hand and still God would not create departure in the arrow. Man is not an acquirer. It is only action which is within the abode of his own power that can be predicated of man as an acquisition."[27] This statement is thus, again, in agreement with Najjār[28] and in opposition to Ḍirār.[29]

From all this we gather that Ash'arī's conception of acquisition is fully in agreement with that of Najjār, so that, according to him, despite his use of such language as "the acquirer acquires a thing because it takes place in virtue of his created power over it,"[30] it is God who simultaneously with the creation of the thing creates in man the power to acquire as well as the act of acquiring. And so in his *Maḳālāt*, speaking for himself, Ash'arī says that, "in the case of everything concerning which God is described as having power to create it as an acquisition for men, God has the power to force men to it,"[31] by which is meant that the "acquisition,"

[26] *Ibid.*, ll. 7–8.

[27] *Uṣūl*, p. 138, ll. 6–11; cf. his *Farḳ*, p. 328, ll. 10–13.

[28] Cf. above, pp. 669 f.

[29] Cf. above, pp. 667 f.

[30] *Luma'* 89, p. 40, ll. 7–8.

[31] *Maḳālāt*, p. 552, ll. 8–9.

namely, the object acquired, is forced upon men by God, whence it follows that the act of acquiring has no influence upon the object acquired, whence it further follows that the very act of acquiring is created by God. Thus Averroes, referring to the Ash'arite conception of acquisition, describes it as follows: (1) "Man has acquisition (*kasb*), but that which is acquired (*al-muktasab*) and that which brings about the acquisition (*al-muksib*) are created by God." [32] (2) "Man has no acquisition (*iktisāb*) and no action (*fi'l*) that has an influence upon existent things," [33] by which he means that both the act of acquiring and the object acquired are created by God.[34]

It is this view of Ash'arī on acquisition as expressed by himself in his *Luma'* that is reproduced by Juwaynī in his *Irshād* as the view of "the People of Truth" (*ahl al-ḥaḳḳ*).[35]

Juwaynī opens his discussion with the statement that "all created things are created by the power (*ḳudrah*) of God, without any distinction between those with which human power is connected and those over which the Lord is alone in His power." [36] Subsequently "created things . . . over which the Lord is alone in his power" is referred to by him as "necessary movement," [37] illustrated by the trembling of the hand,[38] and "created things . . . with which human power is connected" is referred to by him as the movement which "man has chosen and acquired," [39] illustrated by man's intentional movement of his hand.[40] In the course of his discussion he makes the statement that "man has power over his acquisition" [41] and that man's knowledge of the distinction between the trembling of the hand and the intentional movement of the hand is a "necessary known thing," [42] that is to say, man knows it intuitively.[43]

[32] *Kashf*, p. 105, ll. 19–20.
[33] *Tahāfut al-Tahāfut* III, 24, p. 156, ll. 9–10.
[34] Cf. quotation from Averroes below at n. 65.
[35] *Irshād*, p. 106, l. 4 (173).
[36] *Ibid.*, ll. 4–5.
[37] *Ibid.*, p. 122, l. 15 (197).
[38] *Ibid.*, l. 14.
[39] *Ibid.*, l. 15.
[40] *Ibid.*, l. 14.
[41] *Ibid.*, l. 10 (196).
[42] *Ibid.*, ll. 13–16 (197).
[43] *Ibid.*, ll. 8–9 (198).

All these quite evidently reflect Ashʿarī's *Lumaʿ*.

Then, as Ashʿarī does in the *Lumaʿ*, he makes the following statements about the power of acquiring.

First: "It is impossible to attribute the difference between human necessary motion and human motion of choice simply to the one who apparently performs the motion, without the addition of some other thing," [44] which other thing, he goes on to explain, is a "power" created within the apparent performer of the motion as something distinct from him.[45]

Second: "The created power . . . does not endure." [46]

Third: "The created power is simultaneous with the creation of its object and does not precede it"; [47] again: "Capacity is simultaneous with the act." [48]

Fourth: "The created power is attached to only one object," [49] by which is meant that it is not attached to "two contraries." [50]

Fifth: "The created power applies only to that which exists in the abode (*maḥall*) of the created power; that which takes place outside the abode of the [created] power is not an object of that power but takes place by an act of God." [51] This statement is the same as that we have quoted above from Ashʿarī's *Lumaʿ*,[52] which I have explained to mean a denial of the application of the theory of acquisition to generated effects.[53]

From all this it is clear that, while Ḍirār and Najjār and Ashʿarī all use the same formula, namely, that the acts of men are created by God and acquired by men, there are differences between its use by Ḍirār and its use by Najjār, and Ashʿarī follows Najjār's use of it. In the light of this, when Baghdādī says of Ḍirār that "he agrees with our fellow associates [that

[44] *Ibid.*, p. 122, l. 23 (197).
[45] *Ibid.*, p. 123, ll. 3–4 (198); cf. *Lumaʿ* 122.
[46] *Irshād*, p. 123, l. 16 (198); cf. *Lumaʿ* 125.
[47] *Irshād*, p. 124, ll. 13–14 (200).
[48] *Ibid.*, p. 125, l. 5 (201); cf. *Lumaʿ* 123–124 and 128.
[49] *Irshād*, p. 127, l. 5 (204).
[50] *Ibid.*, ll. 5–6; cf. *Lumaʿ* 126.
[51] *Irshād*, p. 131, ll. 5–7 (210).
[52] *Lumaʿ* 127, p. 56, ll. 7–8.
[53] Cf. above, pp. 686–687.

is, the Ash'arites] in [their view] that the acts of men are created by God and acquired by men," [54] his statement is to be taken to mean that, even though they differ in their conceptions of acquisition, they agree in the use of this formula in so far as it expresses their common opposition to the Mu'tazilite denial that the acts of men are created by God. So also, and more evidently so, in the sequel to his statement, in which Baghdādī says that Ḍirār also agrees with the Ash'arites "in repudiating the view [of Burghūth cited by him before] concerning generated effects," [55] he quite evidently means that, even though Ḍirār and the Ash'arites differ with regard to the authorship of generated effects,[56] they agree in their opposition to the view of Burghūth, according to whom generated effects are "God's acts by necessity." In the case of Najjār, however, it will be noted, Baghdādī does not merely quote the common formula for acquisition; he rather says specifically that his followers agreed "with our fellow associates" in the view that "God is the creator of the acquisitions of men," [57] that is to say, He is the creator of both "the acts of acquiring" and "the acts acquired."

In adopting the theory of acquisition, Ash'arī, a former Mu'tazilite, like Ḍirār and Najjār, who were also former Mu'tazilites, aimed it directly at the Mu'tazilite denial that the acts of men were created by God. Thus in his *Luma'* it is the Mu'tazilites who are behind the question, "Why do you claim that the acquisitions of men are created by God?" [58] with which he opens up his discussion of Ḳadar. But also, having in mind the Compulsionists,[59] he throughout the *Luma'* emphasizes in a variety of ways his view that acquisition is due to a power in man, as, for instance, in the following

[54] *Farḳ*, p. 201, ll. 11–12.

[55] *Ibid.*, ll. 12–13. Burghuth's view is cited before on p. 197, ll. 6–8.

[56] Cf. above on Ḍirār, p. 668; on Ash'arī, p. 687.

[57] *Farḳ*, p. 195, l. 14.

[58] *Luma'* 82.

[59] That Ash'arī was conscious of the existence of Compulsionists is evidenced by his reference to the *jabr* of the Jahmī (*Maḳālāt*, p. 41, l. 4) and to the *Mujbirah* (*Maḳālāt*, p. 430, l. 2), and cf. above, p. 612.

passages quoted above:[60] "The acquirer acquires a thing because the acquiring takes place in virtue of his created power over it" and "the true meaning of acquisition is that the thing proceeds from the acquirer in virtue of a created power." So also Juwaynī, in his reproduction of Ashʿarī's theory of acquisition, while constantly contrasting it with the view of the Muʿtazilites, points out that Ashʿarī's theory is to be contrasted with the view of "the Compulsionists" (*al-jabariy-yah*),[61] that is to say, those who deny that man has any power. Nowhere, however, does Ashʿarī explain what exactly he means by that "power" possessed by man over his acquisition when he himself explicitly says that "God has the power to force man to it."[62]

As was to be expected, this last statement quoted gave rise to the objection that a power to acquire an act created by God which enables man neither to acquire that act nor to create it cannot in any sense whatsoever be described as a power possessed by man.

This objection is quoted by Juwaynī in the form of a question addressed anonymously to the Acquisitionists. It reads as follows: "Your belief that man is an acquirer is unintelligible (*ghayr maʿḳūl*), for if a power has no influence over its object (*fi maḳdūrihā*) and if that object is not brought into existence by it, then the assumption that the power bears any kind of relationship to its object is meaningless."[63] Baghdādī similarly reports that the Libertarians grumbled that the theory of acquisition was "unintelligible to them."[64] So also Averroes argues against the Ashʿarite conception of acquisition as follows: "This view is meaningless, for, if both the acquisition (*al-iktisāb*) [that is, the act of acquiring] and that which is acquired (*al-muktasab*) are created by God, then man is compelled in that acquisition of his."[65]

[60] Cf. above, p. 685.
[61] *Irshād*, p. 122, ll. 10–13 (196–197).
[62] Cf. above, p. 687 at n. 31.
[63] *Irshād*, p. 118, ll. 20–21 (F p. 190).
[64] *Uṣūl*, p. 133, ll. 8–9.
[65] *Kashf*, p. 105, ll. 20–21.

It must have been this kind of objection to the theory of acquisition as conceived by Ashʿarī that induced Bāḳillānī, a follower of Ashʿarī, to revise the theory of acquisition. While admitting with the acquisitionists that man's actions are created by God, he tries to show how acquisition is a power in man and is not without influence upon the actions of man. In every human act, he says in effect, one is to distinguish between the generic subject of the act and the specific forms it may assume in any of its operations, to which he refers as the "mode" (*ḥāl*) of the act. Thus, for instance, the act of movement may assume in its actual operation the mode of sitting down or of standing up or of walking or of prostrating oneself in prayer. Now, maintains Bāḳillānī, while the generic subject of the act, such as the movement itself, is indeed directly created by God, the mode of the operation of that movement, such as sitting down or standing up or walking or prostrating oneself, is not created by God; it is acquired by the power of man.[66] In the *Muḥaṣṣal*, this view of Bāḳillānī is briefly restated by Rāzī as follows: "The Ḳāḍī [Bāḳillānī] asserts that the essence of the act occurs by the power of God but its becoming obedience or disobedience is by the power of man." [67] Thus, while man's power does not influence the existence of the act, it does influence its mode of existence. Bāḳillānī has thus introduced into human action an element of freedom.

This explanation of how man's free will may be harmonized with God's power reminds one of Chrysippus' attempt by using the illustration of the motion of a wheel or a top or a cylinder caused by its being initially propelled by man to explain how *adsensio*, "assent," which is the Greek συγκατάθεσις,[68] is the free action of man, even though it is produced by an anterior cause. The motion of the wheel or the top or the cylinder, he says, is undoubtedly caused by the

[66] *Milal*, p. 69, l. 9 – p. 70, l. 12; *Nihāyat*, p. 73, l. 1 – p. 75, l. 15.

[67] *Muḥaṣṣal*, p. 140, l. 23.

[68] Cf. A. Yon's Introduction to his edition of Cicero's *De Fato* (1933), p. XXVIII, n. 3.

man who propelled it, but the particular form of rotation assumed by the motion is not caused by the man who propelled it but rather by the particular force (*vi*) and nature (*natura*) of the object moved. So also, he argues, "the object which strikes our sense-perception imprints and engraves, as it were, its image in our soul, but our assent is in our own power." [69] This is exactly the explanation offered here by Bāḳillānī. God directly creates in man the motion, but man by his own power determines what form the motion should assume.[69a]

Bāḳillānī's revision of Ash'arī's conception of acquisition must have had followers among certain Ash'arites, for Juwaynī reproduces it, without mentioning the name of Bāḳillānī, as a view held by some of the orthodox teachers.[70] Juwaynī, however, refutes this revised conception of acquisition, concluding his refutation with the statement that the acceptance of this conception "is a turning away from the path of truth and salvation and an opening of the way to things causing corruption in matters of fundamental religious beliefs." [71]

With his rejection of Bāḳillānī's revision of Ash'arī's conception of acquisition, Juwaynī tries his hand at solving the difficulty that has led Bāḳillānī to his revision. Reasserting Ash'arī's view that "the created power has no influence at all on the object of power," Juwaynī justifies the use of the term "power" by arguing as follows: "It is not a necessary condition for the connection which an attribute has with an object that the attribute should influence the object connected with it, for, in the case of knowledge, its connection with an object of knowledge is indisputable, even though it has no influence upon the object of knowledge. By the same token, the human will, though connected with the act of man, has

[69] Cicero, *De Fato*, 17, 39 – 19, 43.

[69a] But see Ludwig Stein, who in his "Antike und mittelalterliche Vorläufer des Occasionalismus," *Arch. f. Gesch. d. Philos.*, n.s. 2:205–221 (1889), relates Chrysippus' view with the theory of *kasb* as conceived of by Ash'arī.

[70] *Irshād*, p. 118, ll. 22 ff (F pp. 190–191).

[71] *Ibid.*, p. 119, l. 13 (p. 191).

no influence upon the act." [72] What Juwaynī means may be restated as follows. The term "power" is used here by Ash'arī not in the sense of a power to acquire but in the sense of a power to will to acquire, and to will in relation to its object is analogous to knowledge in relation to its object. Now, when God creates in man a knowledge of some existent thing, it means that the very creation of the knowledge implies its having that existent thing as its object, so that the knowledge itself has no influence either on the existence of the thing or on its having it as its object. So also, when God creates in man a power to will to acquire something created by Him, it means that the very creation of the power to will to acquire implies its having that created something as its object, so that the power to will itself has no influence, though it is called power.

While, in his *Irshād*, Juwaynī endorses and justifies Ash'arī's use of acquisition as a moderate kind of interpretation of the traditional belief in predestination, in another work, quoted but unnamed by Shahrastānī,[73] he offers another interpretation, similarly moderate, of the same traditional belief in predestination.

As reported by Shahrastānī, Juwaynī opens up his discussion by disposing of three views. First, as in the *Irshād*, he rejects "the denial of power and capacity," that is, compulsionism, on the ground that "both reason and sense-perception reject it." [74] Second, contrary to his view in the *Irshād*, he rejects "the affirmation of a power which has no influence whatsoever," that is, Ash'arī's conception of acquisition, on the ground that, "it is like the denial of power altogether." [75] Third, again, as in his *Irshād*, he rejects "the affirmation of an unintelligible influence upon a mode," that is, Bāḳillānī's version of acquisition, on the ground that "it is like the denial of an influence in a special sense," [76] by which is meant that,

[72] *Ibid.*, ll. 14–16.
[73] *Milal*, p. 70, ll. 12–13.
[74] *Ibid.*, ll. 13–14.
[75] *Ibid.*, ll. 14–15.
[76] *Ibid.*, ll. 15–16.

inasmuch as a mode is defined as that which is neither existent nor nonexistent,[77] Bāḳillānī's version means neither the denial nor the non-denial of influence. But, it will be noticed, no mention is made here of an objection to Bāḳillānī's view on religious grounds like that raised against it in the *Irshād*.[78]

Juwaynī's own view, as presented by Shahrastānī, is based upon the following propositions: (1) man knows within himself that he has power but that that power does not enable him to create independently, all by himself, the existence of something; (2) man's action depends for its existence upon his power, which acts as its immediate cause; (3) this power of man depends for its existence upon another cause, which one in a series of causes; (4) this series of causes culminates in God, the Uncaused Cause; (5) God, the Uncaused Cause, is "the Creator of the causes and the caused ones," by which is meant that God is the remote cause or creator of each caused cause in the series of which the immediate cause is its immediately preceding caused cause in the series; (6) every caused cause in the series is to be considered as independent (*mustaghnin*) with respect to its being the cause of that which follows it, but it is to be considered as dependent (*muḥtāj*) with respect to its being caused by that which precedes it, whereas the Creator is the Absolute Independent One (*al-ghanī al-mutlaḳ*).[79] In the *Muḥaṣṣal*, this view of Juwaynī is briefly restated by Rāzī as follows: "The Imām al-Ḥaramayn [al-Juwaynī] maintains that God [as a remote cause or creator] produces for man the power and will and these two then bring about by necessity the existence of the object of the power. This is also the view of the philosophers and among the Muʿtazilites the view of Abū al-Ḥusayn al-Baṣrī. The majority of the Muʿtazilites, however, are of the opinion that man produces his actions not by way of necessitation but rather by way of choice." [80]

[77] Cf. above, p. 171 at n. 21.
[78] Cf. above at n. 71.
[79] *Milal*, p. 70, l. 16 – p. 71, l. 4; *Nihāyat*, p. 78, l. 11 – p. 79, l. 7.
[80] *Muḥaṣṣal*, p. 141, ll. 1–4.

What we have here is a new view of the orthodox Muslim doctrine of predestination. All actions of man are indeed, as according to the common orthodox view, predetermined by God from eternity, but whereas, according to the common orthodox view followed by Juwaynī himself in his *Irshād*, these eternally predetermined actions are brought into existence by their being directly created by God, according to this new view of his they are produced by the necessary causality of a power in man which is the last in a series of causes of which God is the ultimate cause conceived of as Creator. Inasmuch as according to this new view the "power" in man is considered as "independent" with respect to its being the cause of the human actions which follow it, thus implying that it has an influence upon human actions, this view is advanced by Juwaynī in opposition to all the three orthodox views criticized by him, namely, the view of the Compulsionists which was criticized by him for denying power and capacity altogether, the view of Ashʿarī which was criticized by him for affirming a power which has no influence whatever, and the view of Bāḳillānī which was criticized by him for affirming an unintelligible influence upon a mode which has neither existence nor nonexistence.

Underlying this new interpretation of the orthodox Muslim doctrine of predestination is, I believe, a new turn given to a view expressed by Alfarabi in a passage dealing with the problem of free will. In that passage, quite evidently having in mind the Muʿtazilite belief in free will, Alfarabi comes out in opposition to it by asserting that in human action there is no "choice" (*iḫtiyār*) without a "cause" that ascends to the "cause of causes," [81] and then goes on to show how God is the ultimate cause of all human actions by the intermediacy of a series of interconcatenated causes, of which man's choice is the last cause in that intermediate series of causes.[82] Now, according to Avicenna, in every cause in a series of inter-

[81] *Fuṣūṣ al-Ḥikam* 48, p. 78, ll. 6–8.
[82] *Ibid.* 49, p. 78, l. 12 – p. 79, l. 1.

mediate causes there is the distinction of its being possible with respect to its own self and its being necessary with respect to its cause,[83] so that in man's choice, of which Alfarabi says that it is not without a cause, there is a distinction between a possible aspect and a necessary aspect. What Juwaynī, therefore, has done here is to rename the Avicennian distinction between an aspect of necessity and an aspect of possibility as a distinction between an aspect of dependence and an aspect of independence and to advance this conception of man's power to choose, which originally was advanced by Alfarabi in opposition to the Mu'tazilite belief in free will, as a new interpretation of the orthodox Muslim doctrine of predestination.

Most interesting are Shahrastānī's three comments on this view of Juwaynī.

First, he explains, what Juwaynī did was to take a principle from "the metaphysical philosophers" and dress it up "in the garb of the Kalam" [84] in order to avoid "the utter folly of compulsion." [85]

Second, Shahrastānī argues, the philosophic principle of causality drawn upon by Juwaynī as an explanation of human action is not restricted by its original exponents to human action. It is applied by them to every process of coming-into-being. The underlying meaning of this principle, he says, is the conception of an order of nature throughout which there is a concatenation of cause and effect. But such a conception of causality, he concludes, "is not what is believed by Muslims of whatever sect they may be." [86] In other words, the philosophic conception of God as acting indirectly through intermediary causes, even though God, "the Uncaused Cause," is by some sleight of language called "the Creator of the causes and of the caused ones" in the series of causes and effects, is contrary to the common Muslim belief that God is the direct

[83] *Najāt* III, p. 368, ll. 8–9.
[84] *Milal*, p. 71, ll. 4–5; cf. *Nihāyat*, p. 78, ll. 16–18.
[85] *Nihāyat*, p. 78, ll. 16–17.
[86] *Milal*, p. 71, ll. 5–8.

creator of everything that happens. As will be recalled, even the Muʿtazilites, with the exception of Naẓẓām and Muʿammar, denied causality.[87]

Third, Shahrastānī tries to show that the philosophic principle of causality which Juwaynī has drawn upon to establish a view, in opposition not only to the views of Ashʿarī and Bāḳillānī but also to the view of the Compulsionists, really implies compulsion. To quote: "Compulsion must most necessarily follow as a corollary from the conception of the concatenation of causes, for the following reason. Every kind of matter, according to this conception, is predisposed to a special kind of form, and all forms flow from the Giver of Forms upon successive kinds of matter by way of compulsion. This process goes on continuously, so as to result that the choice between two alternatives is compulsion, that the power over two possibilities is compulsion, that the realization of man's actions by means of causes is compulsion, and that the sequence of actions and reward is compulsion. All this is like sickness resulting from an uneven temper, like well-being resulting from an even temper, like knowledge resulting from the mind's freeing itself of sluggishness, and like an image appearing in a mirror on its being polished. In fine, intermediate causes only predispose [something to existence], but are not the authors of existence, for that which in virtue of its own essence has only the nature of possibility cannot be the author of existence in the true sense of the term."[88] In other words, the possible aspect which Juwaynī finds in Alfarabi's causally determined man's "choice" is not sufficient to account for the kind of "power" which Juwaynī wants to attribute to man against the Compulsionists who deny it of man.

c. Acquisitionism in Ghazālī

Ghazālī discourses on the problem of free will and acquisition in three places in his *Iḥyāʾ*, in Book II, entitled "Founda-

[87] Cf. above, p. 613.

[88] *Nihāyat*, p. 78, ll. 17 – p. 79, l. 7.

tions of the Articles of Creed" (*Kitāb Ḳawā'id al-'Aḳā'id*), in Book XXXI, entitled "Repentance" (*Kitāb al-Taubah*), and in Book XXXV, entitled "The Unity of God and the Trust in God" (*Kitāb al-Tauḥīd wal-Tawakkul*).

In his first discourse, Ghazālī starts with a statement of the view commonly agreed upon by all Predestinarians, namely, that God, who created man and his powers and his movements, created also all his actions and that all his actions remain dependent upon God's power.[1] In support of this common belief of the Predestinarians, he advances two arguments: First, since the power of God is perfect and unrestricted, it cannot but be that the actions of man are created by God. Second, since man's actions are dependent upon the movements of his body and all the movements of man's body are by their essence equally dependent upon the power of God, there is no reason for differentiating in this respect some movements, called actions, from other movements.[2] This second argument is evidently aimed at those Libertarians who would distinguish between certain actions over which God has power and certain actions over which God has no power; such, for instance, as the distinction made by some of them between God having power over the movements and rests of men but not over their belief and unbelief [3] or the distinction between noble acts as created by God and base acts as created by man.[4]

He then goes on to say that "the fact that God is alone in the creation of the movements of man does exclude them from being objects of man's power by way of acquisition (*iktisāb*)." [5] What he means by acquisition emerges from his following discussion.

To begin with, "God created at once the power (*al-ḳudrah*) and the object of power (*al-maḳdūr*) and He created at once

[1] *Iḥyā'* II: *Kitāb Ḳawā'id al-'Aḳā'id*, Section III, Principle 3, vol. I, p. 116, ll. 1–3.

[2] *Ibid.*, ll. 7–9.

[3] Ash'arī, *Maḳālāt*, p. 551, ll. 3–12. Cf. above, p. 683.

[4] Cf. above, p. 623.

[5] *Iḥyā'*, *loc. cit.*, ll. 13–14.

the choice (*al-iḫtiyār*) and the object of choice (*al-muḫtār*)." [6] From Ghazālī's subsequent statements it becomes clear that by "power" he means the power to move, used in the general sense of the power to act, that by "choice" he means the choice between moving and not moving, and that by "object of power" and "object of choice" he means a movement performed by the power to move as a result of a choice to move rather than not to move; in other words, a voluntary movement, in the general sense of a voluntary action. Thus in every voluntary movement of man, such, for instance, as the raising of his hand, three things are involved: (1) the power to move; (2) the choice between moving and not moving; (3) the movement performed by the power as a result of the choice. Each of these three things is, according to him, created in man by God. Referring to the created power to move as well as to the created movement as an attribute (*ṣifah*) created in man by God, Ghazālī distinguishes between the power and the movement as follows: "The power is an attribute (*waṣf*) of man and a creation of God but is not an acquisition (*kasb*) of man, whereas the movement is a creation of God and an attribute (*waṣf*) of man but is also an acquisition of man, for it is created as an object of power by [another] power [namely, the power to choose]; which is to him [also] an attribute. The movement thus has a relationship to another attribute which is to be called power, and it is with reference to this relationship that movement is called acquisition." [7] In short, acquisition is any movement of man preceded regressively by a power to move and by a power to choose, that is, to will, to use that power to move, plus the assumption that the movement itself and the power to move and the will to use that power to move are all created by God.

Ghazālī then goes on to show how acquisition conceived as such a movement, regardless of the assumption that it is created by God, cannot be exclusively a compelled act nor

[6] *Ibid.*, ll. 14–15.

[7] *Ibid.*, ll. 15–17.

can it be exclusively a free act. It cannot be exclusively a compelled act, for "how could a movement [which is preceded by a power to will to use a power to move] be pure compulsion when man is necessarily conscious of a distinction between a movement which is the object of a power [such as the raising of the hand] and the movement of the uncontrollable trembling [of the hand]?" [8] The conclusion we are expected here to draw is that, since the latter kind of movement is quite obviously one of pure compulsion, the former kind of movement cannot be of pure compulsion. It may be noted that the same argument had been used by Ghazālī's teacher, Juwaynī, in refutation of compulsionism [9] and, as we have seen above, it had also been used by Ashʿarī.[10] Nor, Ghazālī goes on to say, can it be exclusively a free act of man, for "how could that movement be the creation of man, when man does not encompass the knowledge of the different constituent parts of the acquired movements and their numbers," [11] that is to say, in order for a man to be the exclusive author of his movement, he would have to have foreknowledge and control of every conceivable circumstance that makes it possible for that movement to come about, but no man has such knowledge and control. Ghazālī, therefore, concludes: "Since both these extremes are untenable, there remains only to adopt a middle course with regard to the belief under consideration, namely, that the movement is determined by the power of God by way of creation and by the power of man by way of another kind of relationship, that which is designated by the term acquisition (*iktisāb*)." [12] In short, acquisition is a description of any act resulting from man's choice under the assumption that man's power to choose to act and man's power to act and the act resulting from man's exercise of these two powers are all created by God. Thus acquisition, by way of which man's acts are said to be objects

[8] *Ibid.*, ll. 17–18.
[9] *Irshād*, p. 123, ll. 8–9 (F p. 198); cf. above, p. 688.
[10] Cf. above, p. 685 at n. 5.
[11] *Iḥyā'*, *loc. cit.*, ll. 18–19.
[12] *Ibid.*, ll. 19–20.

of his power,[13] is created in man by God. This is in agreement with the conception of acquisition as held by Najjār and Ash'arī.

Finally, Ghazālī adds the following statement: "It is not necessary that the relation of the power to the object of power should be that of creation only, seeing that the power of God was related to the world from eternity, although the actual creation of the world by that power did not as yet take place and, when its creation did actually take place, the power became related to it by another kind of relationship. It is thus clear that the assertion of a relationship between a power [and an object of power] does not apply exclusively to cases where the object of power has been actually brought into existence by the power." [14]

In this passage, I take it, Ghazālī anticipates the following objection: How could acquisition justify the description of man's act as an object of man's power, when acquisition itself is said to be created in man by God and as such quite evidently has no influence upon man's actions? It will be recalled that the same objection to the theory of acquisition is mentioned by his teacher Juwaynī.[15] His answer to this objection is like that given by Juwaynī, except for the change of Juwaynī's analogy of man's knowledge for the analogy of God's eternal power. Juwaynī, as we have seen, tried to show that just as man's knowledge of something existent does not influence that existent something so also man's power to will to acquire something does not have to influence that something acquired.[16] Ghazālī similarly tries to show that just as God had from eternity the power to create the world, without the world having been created from eternity, that is to say, without there having been from eternity an object influenced by that power, so also man's power to will to acquire something does not have to influence that something acquired.

So much for Ghazālī's treatment of the problem of free will

[13] Cf. above at n. 5.

[14] *Iḥyā', loc. cit.*, ll. 20–23.

[15] Cf. above, p. 691.

[16] Cf. above, pp. 693–694.

and acquisition in his first discourse on the subject. What Ghazālī has done here is to explain Ash'arī's description of man as having power to acquire the acts created for him by God, even though that power has no influence on man's acquiring those acts.

In his second discourse, Ghazālī begins by laying down his own conception of free will in the form of an answer to a question. "If you ask: Hasn't man choice (*iḫtiyār*) in action and in abstention from action? I answer yes, but this does not contradict our assertion that everything is due to the creation of God, for the choice itself is also due to the creation of God and man is forced into the choice which he makes." [17]

He then goes on to explain this statement by a detailed analysis of the process of eating. This process is shown by him to involve a number of things created by God, of which he mentions the following: hands by which man can handle food; the food; a feeling of hunger; a knowledge that food will appease the hunger; a sense of precautionary inquiry as to whether the food is fit for eating; a knowledge that the food in question is fit for eating; the decision (*injizām*) of the will (*irādah*) to take the food; the movement of the hand in the direction of the food. It is the "decision of the will," he says, that is called "choice" (*iḫtiyār*) and this like all the other steps in the process of eating is created by God.[18] Then, following his own view, already discussed above, that the ordinary succession of events observed in the world is not due to causal relationship between them but rather to a custom (*'ādah*) on the part of God to create things continuously in the same order of succession [19] and, by only changing the term *'ādah* for the term *sunnah*, he says here: "These created things, however, follow one another in an order of sequence in accordance with which God's custom (*sunnah*) proceeds

[17] *Iḥyā'* XXXI: *Kitāb al-Taubah*, Section: *Bayān Wujūb al-Taubah wa-Faḍluhā*, vol. IV, p. 5, l. 26 – p. 6, l. 1.

[18] *Ibid.*, p. 6, ll. 1–9.

[19] Cf. above, pp. 548–549.

in His creation, and in this procedure of God's custom there is no change." [20]

Bringing this to bear upon the problem of free will, he tries to show that this conception of continuous creation as a divine custom means the following: "One of the created things is the condition (*sharṭ*) for another, so that one must precede and the other must follow, as, for instance, will is created only after knowledge, knowledge is created only after life, and life is created only after body. Accordingly, the creation of body is a condition to the origination of life, not that life is produced (*tatawallad*) by body; the creation of life is a condition for the creation of knowledge, not that knowledge is produced (*yatawallad*) by life, but rather that the abode or substratum (*maḥall*) is not predisposed to the reception of knowledge except when it has life; and the creation of knowledge is a condition for the decision (*jazm*) of the will, not that knowledge produces (*yūlid*) will, but rather that only a living and knowing body can be the recipient of will." [21] Then, after stating that this manner of succession of continuously created things is according to a fixed and immutable order predetermined by God's generosity and His eternal power, he goes on to show that human actions are subject to the same "procedure of divine foreordainment and divine decree" that govern all the so-called natural events in the world. He illustrates this by showing how a man's act of writing is created by God by His creating in the man who has a desire to write "four things," namely, (1) by His creating in the soul of the man a knowledge (*ʿilm*) of that toward which he has a desire, a knowledge called comprehension (*idrāk*) and cognition (*maʿrifah*)"; (2) by His creating, again, in the soul of the man "a [will (*irādah*), that is, a] strong and decisive inclination (*mayl ḳawīy jāzim*) called intention (*ḳaṣd*)"; (3) by His creating in the hand of the man "an appropriate attribute called power (*ḳudrah*)," that is to say, a power to write; (4) by His creating, again, in the

[20] *Iḥyāʾ*, *loc. cit.*, ll. 9–10.

[21] *Ibid.*, ll. 15–20.

hand of the man "a movement (*ḥarakah*)," that is to say, the act of writing,[22] with the implication that, as he has said before, these "four things" are not each successively produced as an effect by that which precedes it as its cause but rather that, in man as the "abode," each of these "four things" follows the one preceding it as something conditioned follows that which precedes it as a condition.

Finally, after stating that "these four things" appear in the body of man, that is, in their "abode," as from "the interior of the invisible world," [23] he goes on to say: "And therein are perplexed the minds of those who idle away in the easy life of the visible world. Some say that man's action is sheer compulsion (*jabr*); some say it is [man's own] creation (*iḫtirā'*); and some who steer a middle course favor the view that it is acquisition (*kasb*). But if there were opened to them the gates of heaven and they looked at the invisible world above, it would become clear to them that each of their views is true only from a certain aspect." [24]

Thus the theory of acquisition, which in the first discourse is definitely adopted by him as a solution of the conflict between absolute compulsion and absolute freedom, is now in this second discourse included by him among those theories which he describes as held by "those who idle away in the easy life of the visible world" and as one of those theories which one could find to be "true only from one aspect." Somehow one gets the impression that in this discourse it is not the term "acquisition," and what it stands for, that is offered by him as a resolution of the conflict mentioned by him but rather the term "abode," which is used by him as a description of the relation of man to the successive conditions preceding the act created in him by God. But how the use of this term would explain the difficulty raised by him is not made clear here. This, I shall now try to show, is made clear by him in his third discourse.

In that discourse, Ghazālī again poses the question of how

[22] *Ibid.*, ll. 26–28. [23] *Ibid.*, ll. 28–29. [24] *Ibid.*, ll. 32–35.

man could be described as simultaneously acting both under compulsion and with choice.[25] In answer to this question, he divides human action into three types: (1) action of choice (*fiʿl iḫtiyārī*), illustrated by the act of writing; (2) volitional action (*fiʿl irādī*), illustrated by the act of breathing and also by the act of closing one's eyelids when a needle is aimed at the eyes; (3) natural action (*fiʿl ṭabīʿī*), illustrated by cleaving the water when one plunges himself into it.[26]

This threefold division of human action, despite the difference of terminology in the description of the second and third types, is the same as the threefold division used by Ashʿarī and by Ghazālī's own teacher Juwaynī. The first type, which Ghazālī describes as "action of choice" and illustrates by the act of writing, is exactly like the first type in Ashʿarī and Juwaynī, who illustrate it by the act of going and coming [27] and by that of intentional movement.[28] The second type, which he describes as "volitional" — a term which, as will appear subsequently, he uses in the sense of "instinctive" — corresponds to that which is described by Ashʿarī and Juwaynī as "necessary" and is illustrated by the movements of trembling and shivering.[29] The third type, which he describes as "natural" — a term which quite evidently he uses here loosely in the sense of "customary" [30] corresponds to what Ashʿarī and Juwaynī refer to as generated effects, that is, an action produced by man in something outside his own body.[31] Then, just as Ashʿarī and Juwaynī maintain that, though God is the creator of all these three types of action enumerated by them, man has a part in the first type by being an acquirer, so also Ghazālī tries to show that, though all the three types of human action enumerated by him are, as he says, "in reality the same with respect to necessity (*al-iḍṭirār*) and compulsion (*al-jabr*)," [32] by which he means that they are all created by God,

[25] *Ibid.* XXXV: *Kitāb al-Tauḥid wa'l-Tawakkul*, Section: *Bayān Ḥaḳiḳat al-Tauḥīd*, vol. IV, p. 248, ll. 11–12.

[26] *Ibid.*, ll. 15–16 and 22–23.

[27] Cf. above, p. 685.

[28] Cf. above, p. 688.

[29] Cf. above, pp. 685; 688.

[30] Cf. above, p. 551.

[31] Cf. above, pp. 686–687.

[32] *Iḥyā'*, *loc. cit.*, ll. 16–17.

still the first of these three types of action is due both to compulsion and to choice, that is to say, man has a part in it.

In his attempt to show how man's part in action of "choice" differs from his role in "volitional" action, Ghazālī goes on to analyze and compare these two types of action. Now in his second discourse, as will be recalled, he has shown how such an action of choice as man's writing is created by God by His creating in man "four things," namely, knowledge (*'ilm*), will (*irādah*), power, and movement.[33] With these "four things" in the back of his mind, he opens his discussion here by saying in effect that both action of choice and volitional action start out with a knowledge (*'ilm*) which, on the basis of its judgment that the action will be beneficial, is followed by a will (*irādah*) which leads to that action.[34] He then goes on to show how the "knowledge" as well as the "will" which follows it differs in these two types of action. In the case of volitional action, such as the closing of the eyelids when the needle is aimed at the eyes, the knowledge that the closing of the eyelids will be a beneficial act is instantaneous, "without perplexity and hesitation"[35] and "without deliberation and cogitation,"[36] so that this kind of action, he says, "takes place by the will,"[37] that is to say, simply by the will, for the will acts simultaneously with the instantaneous knowledge. In other words, the term "will" (*irādah*) is used here by Ghazālī in the sense of an instinctive action like that which he elsewhere describes by the term "estimation" (*wahm*) and which he illustrates by the example of the lamb's instinctive fear of the wolf and its instinctive running away from him.[38] In the case of action of choice, such as the act of writing, say the writing of a letter to somebody, man does not know instan-

[33] Cf. above, p. 704.
[34] *Iḥyā'*, *loc. cit.* n. 25, p. 248, l. 28.
[35] *Ibid.*, l. 29. [36] *Ibid.*, l. 32. [37] *Ibid.*
[38] *Maḳāṣid al-Falāsifah*, III, p. 285, ll. 10–11; *Tahāfut al-Falāsifah* XVIII, 3, p. 299, ll. 1–11; *Mīzān al-'Amal*, p. 19, l. 19 – p. 20, l. 2; cf. pp. 86–104 in my paper "The Internal Senses in Latin, Arabic, and Hebrew Philosophic Texts," *Harvard Theological Review*, 28 (1935), 69–133.

taneously whether it will do good or harm and the will to write or not to write will not follow instantaneously. The action of the will in such a case takes place slowly and hesitatingly and only when, after "deliberation and cogitation" [39] with the aid of the "discerning faculty and the intellect," [40] man has come to know whether the action will be beneficial or harmful. "And so," etymologizes Ghazālī, "inasmuch as the will [in this case] is roused to do [only] that which becomes evident to the intellect as good, this will is called in Arabic *iḫtiyār*, choice, a term derived from the term *ḫayr*, good, that is to say, the will is roused to do [only] that which has become evident to the intellect as good." [41] He thus concludes that it is "the same will" that becomes choice [42] or rather that "choice is a mode of expression for a special kind of will." [43] In his second discourse, it will be recalled, "knowledge" (*ʿilm*) in the case of the act of writing is said by him to mean "comprehension" (*idrāk*) and "cognition" (*maʿrifah*) and similarly "will" (*irādah*) in that type of action is said by him to mean "a strong and decisive inclination (*mayl ḳawīy jāzim*) called intention (*ḳaṣd*)." [44] He finally concludes his analysis of man's action of choice in a passage where, using the term "subservient" in the sense in which a thing conditioned may be described as being subservient to the condition preceding it, he says: "The incitement of the will is made subservient by the judgment of the intellect and sense perception, the power is subservient to the incitement of the will, and the movement is subservient to the power. All this is determined in man by necessity, without his being aware of it, so that he is only an abode (*maḥall*) and a channel of these things; but, as for their proceeding from him, that is by all means to be denied." [45]

[39] *Iḥyāʾ*, *loc. cit.* n. 25, p. 248, l. 33.
[40] *Ibid.*
[41] *Ibid.*, p. 248, l. 35 – 249, l. 1. The same etymological explanation of *iḫtiyār* is quoted from an earlier source by Franz Rosenthal in *The Muslim Concept of Freedom*, p. 19.
[42] *Iḥyāʾ*, *loc. cit.* n. 25, p. 249, ll. 1–2.
[43] *Ibid.*, ll. 3–4.
[44] Cf. above at n. 22.
[45] *Iḥyāʾ*, *loc. cit.*, p. 249, ll. 14–16.

With this analysis of man's action of choice and his statement that man is an abode of the conditions that lead up to the act created in him by God, Ghazālī goes on to show how the concept of "abode" is used by him as a substitute for the concept of "acquisition" as an answer to the question posed by him, namely, the question of how man could be described as simultaneously acting both by compulsion and with choice. He says: "The sense in which man is compelled is that all this is indeed produced within him but produced by something other than himself and not by himself, and the sense in which he is the possessor of choice is that he is the abode (*maḥall*) of a will which takes place in him by compulsion after the judgment of the intellect that the action which is to follow is good, pure, and beneficial, the judgment of which, too, having taken place by compulsion. Man is thus under compulsion alongside the choice by which he is acting, so that, while the action of fire in burning, for instance, is pure compulsion and the action of God is pure choice, the action of man is in an intermediate position between these two positions, for it is compulsion alongside choice. Accordingly, the People of Truth tried to find a fitting third designation for man's action, inasmuch as it is a third kind of action. Following the example of the Book of God, they called it acquisition (*kasb*), which, to him who understands it aright, is not contradictory to either compulsion or choice but it combines the two of them."[46] This conception of man as the abode of the conditions that lead up to the act of which God is the agent, Ghazālī adds subsequently, makes man also an agent of the act, though not in the same sense in which God is its agent. "The sense in which God is an agent (*fāʿil*) is that He is the Creator (*al-muḫtariʿ*) of that which exists, but the sense in which man is an agent is that he is the abode in which God has created the power after He had created in it the will [and has created in it the will] after He had created in it the knowledge. The power is connected with the will and the will is

[46] *Ibid.*, ll. 16–21.

connected with the knowledge as the conditioned is connected with the condition. And it is the power of God with which the connection of [any so-called] effect with [any so-called] cause or the connection of [any so-called] created thing with [any so-called] creator is connected. In the case of anything [say, any act] connected with power, whatever that connection may be, the abode of that power is to be called its agent." [47] In support of this last statement, he quotes Koranic verses, in which certain acts of which God is the real agent are sometimes treated as if angels or men are their agents, the reason for this being, Ghazālī wishes us to understand, that angels and men are treated in those verses as agents only because they are abodes of powers created in them by God.[48]

What Ghazālī has really done in his third discourse is to revise Juwaynī's new explanation of the element of choice in human action [49] by eliminating from it the objectionable theory of causality. Thus, whereas to Juwaynī man's act is preceded by a series of causes and effects of which man's power is the immediate cause of his act, to Ghazālī man's act is preceded by a series of conditions of which man's power is the immediate condition of his act. Again, whereas to Juwaynī God is the ultimate cause conceived of as the indirect creator of every cause in the series as well as of man's act, to Ghazālī God is the direct creator of every condition in the series as well as of man's act. Finally, whereas to Juwaynī man's act, despite its being brought into existence by the necessary causality of his power, contains an element of choice because of his view that man's power, which is the immediate cause of his act, is "independent" with respect to its being the cause of that act, to Ghazālī man's act, despite its being directly created by God, contains an element of choice because of his view that man's power, though created by God in man as the immediate condition of his act, has man as its "abode." So also Augustine, despite his belief that man

[47] *Ibid.*, p. 250, ll. 26–29. [48] *Ibid.*, ll. 31 ff. [49] Cf. above, pp. 694 ff.

acts by necessity, still maintains, reflecting a view of Aristotle, that man has free will, and this because the necessity does not come from outside man but from within man, which means that man is the "abode" thereof.[50]

d. Acquisition in Māturīdī

When late in the preparation of the manuscript of this work I decided to deal with Māturīdī's view on acquisition, I had of his own writings one English translation by Schacht of a single sentence from one of his works and two German paraphrases by Götz of passages from two of his works.

Schacht's English translation was of a sentence in Māturīdī's *Al-Tauḥīd* which reads that "each person knows by a sort of intimate persuasion that he chooses to do what he does and that he is a responsible agent (*fāʿil kāsib*)." [1]

This statement, taken by itself, lends itself to two interpretations. (1) Its first part may be taken to reflect the statement quoted above in the name of the Muʿtazilites to the effect that man knows by an "intellectual perception" or that he "perceives within himself" that he is free to perform certain acts all by himself.[2] Taken in this sense, then the term "agent" in the second part would have to be taken to mean that man is the creator of his acts and hence the term *kāsib* would presumably have been used by Māturīdī in the same sense as the terms *aksāb* and *kasb* have been used respectively by Wāṣil [3] and Shaḥḥām,[4] namely, in the sense that man *qua* man has acquired from God the power to create his own acts. Such an interpretation would make Māturīdī a Libertarian. (2) But the first part of the statement may also be taken to mean the same as Ashʿarī's statement that man "knows by a necessary knowledge which leaves no doubt" that over certain movements of his he has power and that of such

[50] Cf. *Religious Philosophy*, pp. 170–176.

[1] J. Schacht, "New Sources for the History of Muhammadan Theology," *Studia Islamica*, 1: 32 (1953).

[2] Cf. above, pp. 617–618.

[3] Cf. above, p. 666.

[4] Cf. above, pp. 665 f.; 672.

movements he is an acquirer.[5] Taking it in this sense, we may further take it that Māturīdī, like Ashʻarī, followed Najjār's conception of acquisition and hence, like Najjār, he describes man the acquirer by the term "agent," meaning thereby simply "agent" but not "agent in reality."

Of Götz's two German paraphrases one is of a passage, again, in Māturīdī's *Al-Tauḥīd*, which reads as follows:

> Seinen Darlegungen zufolge besitzt Gott die Macht (qudra)[7]) über alles Geschaffene, mithin auch über das Tun der Menschen (ḫalq al-ʻibād). Der Mensch kann also nicht von sich aus etwas erschaffen, wenn Gott nicht zuvor in ihm die Kraft und die Fähigkeit (istiṭāʻa)[8]), eine bestimmte Handlung auszuführen, geschaffen hat. Mit anderen Worten, der Mensch wird erst von Gott dazu in den Stand gesetzt, das von ihm frei gewählte Tun (fiʻl muḫtār) sich aneignen (kasb — iktisāb) und ausführen zu können.[6]

This passage, too, lends itself to two interpretations. (1) If we take the Arabic expression *ḫalq al-ʻibād* literally to mean "the creation by men" and if we also assume that the German terms "auszuführen" and "ausführen," of which the English is "to carry into effect," "to realize," "to bring about," stands here for some such Arabic term as *taḥṣīl*, used in the sense of "to cause something to happen," or as *takmīl*, used in the sense of "to carry out," then the meaning of this passage would be the same as the first interpretation of the preceding statement. It would mean that God prior to any human act creates in man the power to create that act by himself and that man acquires that power and causes the act to happen, that is, he himself creates that act. Māturīdī would thus appear to follow those Muʻtazilites who believed that the power with which God endows man to create his acts is implanted in him

[5] Cf. above, p. 685 at n. 6.

[6] M. Götz, "Māturīdī und sein Kitāb Ta'wīlāt al-Qur'ān," *Der Islam*, 41: 54–55 (1965).

by God prior to each act.[7] (2) But if we take the Arabic expression *ḫalq al-ʿibād* to mean, as translated into German by Götz, "das Tun der Menschen," "the action of men," and if we also assume that the Arabic term underlying Götz's German terms "auszuführen" and "ausführen" is *taḥṣīl*, but to be taken not in the sense of "auszuführen," "to carry into effect," but in the sense of "erwerben," sich aneignen," "to acquire," "to appropriate to oneself," then the meaning of this passage would be the same as the second interpretation of the preceding statement. It would mean that the acts of man are created by God but man acquires them and appropriates them to himself. It would, however, leave it unexplained as to whether the acquisition is to be taken in the Ḍirārite sense or in the Najjārite sense.

The second of Götz's two German paraphrases is of the *Kitāb Taʾwīlāt al-Qurʾān*, which Abū al-Maʿīn Maimūn al-Nasafī (d. 1114) ascribes to Māturīdī [8] and which, according to ʿAlāʾ al-Dīn Abū Bakr al-Samarḳandī (d. 1145), was composed by students of Māturīdī on the basis of his oral teachings.[9] The paraphrase reads as follows:

> Seiner Ansicht nach ist Gott der Schöpfer alles Seins, also auch des menschlichen Tuns, aber Gott erschafft in dem Menschen den freien Willen (iḫtijār), der ihn befähigt, zwischen dem von Gott Befohlenen und Verbotenen frei zu wählen und das zu erwerben, was er will, m.a.W. Gott hat dem Menschen die Fähigkeit gegeben, die Erwerbung (kasb, iktisāb) der ihm von Gott geschaffenen Handlung zu wählen und sie zu wollen.[10]

This passage, taken by itself, makes it quite clear that Māturīdī is an acquisitionist and is opposed to the Muʿtazilite view that man is the creator of his own acts. Man to him is only the acquirer of his acts. But whether he is an acquisitionist of the Najjārite type or of the Ḍirārite type is not

[7] Cf. above, pp. 622–623.

[8] Götz, *op. cit.*, p. 29.

[9] *Ibid.*, pp. 30–31.

[10] *Ibid.*, p. 52.

clear, for the passage lends itself to two interpretations. First, it may mean that simultaneously with His creation of man's act God creates in man the power and the act of choosing between two alternative acts as well as the act of acquiring that which he has chosen and willed. This would make him an acquisitionist of the Najjārite type. Second, it may mean that before each human act God first creates in man the power of choosing all by himself between two alternative acts and thereby to acquire again all by himself the act chosen by him, and it is then that God creates the act that has been chosen and acquired by man himself. This would make Māturīdī an acquisitionist of the Ḍirārite type.

A work entitled *al-ʿAḳāʾid*, "Articles of Belief," was written by a contemporary of ʿAlāʾ al-Dīn Abū Bakr al-Samarḳandī, named Najm al-Dīn al-Nasafī (d. 1142), from the theological standpoint of the Maturidites.[11] Strangely enough the term "acquisition" is not used by him in connection with human actions; instead he uses the term "choice." His conception of the respective parts of God and man is thus expressed by him in the following two statements: "God is the creator of the actions of human beings whether of belief or of unbelief, of obedience or of disobedience";[12] (2) "human beings have actions of choice (*afʿāl iḫtiyāriyyah*) for which they are rewarded or punished."[13] Taken by themselves, these two statements mean that in actions of belief and unbelief or of obedience and disobedience, in which there is a choice between two alternative acts, man has the power to choose which alternative act to follow and God creates that act for him.

About two centuries later, Taftāzānī (1322–1389/95), in his commentary on Nasafī's work, tries to point out tentatively a contradiction between Nasafī's statement just quoted that "human beings have actions of choice," of which he says

[11] Cf. Elder's Introduction to his English translation of Taftāzānī, pp. XIX and XXII.

[12] Taftāzānī, p. 96, l. 2.

[13] *Ibid.*, p. 100, ll. 1–2.

that it would have no meaning "unless man be one who brings his action into existence," [14] and a statement of Nasafī earlier in his work that God, "the originator of the world," [15] that is, of "the world in the totality of its parts," [16] is "one," [17] which means, "as it has already been shown,[18] that God is alone (*mustakill*) in creating actions and bringing them into existence." [19] Taftāzānī seems to resolve this seeming contradiction by taking the term "choice" in Nasafī's statement to mean to choose to acquire, for he explains Nasafī's statement with regard to the respective parts of God and man in human action to mean that "God is the creator (*al-ḫāliḳ*) of everything and man is an acquirer (*kāsib*)." [20]

Now it happens that Taftāzānī counted himself as an Ash'arite but had been in close contact with Maturidites.[21] We may therefore assume that he certainly knew of Ash'arī's theory of acquisition and that he also knew that the theory of acquisition was used by Māturīdī. The question therefore arises whether his interpretation of Nasafī in terms of acquisition was meant by him to be an interpretation of Nasafī in terms of what he knew what Ash'arī's conception of acquisition was [22] or whether it was meant by him to be an interpretation in terms of what he may have understood to be Māturīdī's conception of acquisition.

An answer to this question is to be found in one of the several explanations of acquisition which are advanced by Taftāzānī. One of these explanations reads as follows: "Man's directing (*ṣarf*) his power and will to the act is acquisition; God's bringing the act into existence following upon (*'akīb*) that [acquisition] is creation." [23] Now this explanation of acquisition bears a striking resemblance to an explanation of acquisition ascribed to the Maturidites in the work of a certain other al-Nasafī quoted by Abū 'Udhbah (d. 1713) in

[14] *Ibid.*, p. 101, ll. 6–7.
[15] *Ibid.*, p. 52, ll. 2–3.
[16] *Ibid.*, p. 42, ll. 3 and 5–6.
[17] *Ibid.*, p. 55, l. 4.
[18] *Ibid.*, p. 55, l. 4 – p. 58, l. 6.
[19] *Ibid.*, p. 101, l. 7 – p. 102, l. 2.
[20] *Ibid.*, p. 102, l. 4.
[21] Cf. Elder's Introduction, p. XXIII.
[22] Cf. Elder's translation, p. 85, n. 12.
[23] Taftāzānī, p. 102, l. 5.

the following passage: "Acquisition, according to the opinion of the Maturidites, as al-Nasafī has stated (in *al-Iʿtimād* and in *al-Iʿtiḳād*), is [man's] directing (*ṣarf*) his power to one of two possible acts, and it is not created [by God]." [24] In this passage, the printed parenthetically enclosed reference to what seems to be titles of two books attributed vaguely to one of the several authors known as al-Nasafī is quite evidently a corruption of the title of one book, *al-Iʿtimād fī al-Iʿtiḳād*, the author of which is Ḥāfiẓ al-Dīn al-Nasafī,[25] who died in 1310, thus about eighty years before Taftāzānī and about two hundred years after Najm al-Dīn al-Nasafī, upon whose work Taftāzānī wrote his Commentary. Thus what Taftāzānī has done in his Commentary is to show that under the guise of the statement that "human beings have actions of choice," al-Nasafī has really given expression to the Maturidite theory of acquisition. Moreover, the latter part of Taftāzānī's comment, which says in effect that God's creation of the act "is following upon (*ʿaḳīb*)" man's acquisition, shows that the Maturidite theory of acquisition attributed by Taftāzānī to Nasafī is of the Ḍirārite type, according to which the power of acquiring, which is created in man by God, and the act of acquiring, of which man is an agent in reality, are both prior to the creation of the act.[26] When, therefore, shortly afterwards Taftāzānī says that "man's action is by God's creating and bringing it into existence [simultaneously or in conjunction] with (*maʿa*) what man has of power and action," [27] the Arabic preposition *maʿa*, "with," is not to be taken here in the sense of "simultaneously with" [28] but rather in the sense of "in conjunction with," that is to say, "man's action" is due both to "God's creating and bringing it into existence" and to "what man has of power and action," namely, to man's act of acquiring.

[24] *Rauḍah Bahiyyah*, p. 26, ll. 13–14.

[25] Cf. Brockelmann, *Geschichte der arabischen Litteratur*, II, p. 107.

[26] Cf. above, pp. 667–668.

[27] Taftāzānī, p. 102, ll. 8–9.

[28] For the use of *maʿa* in the sense of "simultaneous with" in the case of Najjār's view, see above, p. 669.

Though the theory of acquisition which Taftāzānī attributes to Nasafī is quite evidently derived from a Maturidite source, he does not hesitate to supplement his Maturidite explanation of acquisition by explanations drawn from other sources. Here are two of such explanations. First, "acquisition is that which occurs by the use of some instrument; creation is without an instrument." [29] This reflects certain contrasting descriptions of acquisition and creation found in Ashʿarī's *Maḳālāt*.[30] Second, "acquisition is an object of power which occurs in the abode (*maḥall*) of its power; creation is an object of power not in the abode of the power." [31] This reflects Ashʿarī's and Juwaynī's statements, quoted above, that acquisition applies only to an act which is attached to the "abode of the power," that is to say, an act in man's own body, such as the movement of one's own hand, but an act which occurs outside "the abode of the power," that is, a movement produced by man in some other body, technically known as a generated effect, is created by God.[32]

In that work of Abū ʿUdhbah, right after the brief statement that "acquisition, according to the opinion of the Maturidites," as stated in a work by Ḥāfiẓ al-Dīn al-Nasafī, "is [man's] directing (*ṣarf*) his power to one of two possible acts, and it is not created [by God]," there comes a passage about which it is not clear whether, as a whole or in part, it is a continuation of the preceding quotation or a comment by Abū ʿUdhbah based on some other places in the same work of Ḥāfiẓ al-Dīn al-Nasafī. The passage reads as follows: "For all that which constitutes the action of the bodily organs, namely, movements; and similarly abstention from bodily action (*al-turūk*), which constitutes the action of the soul, namely, inclination (*al-mayl*) and incitement (*al-dāʿiyyah*) and choice (*al-iḫtiyār*), is by the creation of God, on which the power of man has no influence. Man is the abode (*maḥall*) of

[29] Taftāzānī, p. 102, ll. 9–10.
[30] *Maḳālāt*, p. 539, ll. 4–5; p. 542, ll. 2–3.
[31] Taftāzānī, p. 102, l. 10.
[32] Cf. above, pp. 686–687; 689.

his power only with reference to his decision (*'azmihi*) following upon (*'akīb*) God's creation of these things within him — a resolute decision without hesitation and a sure turning toward the action looked for by him. When man experiences (*wajada*) that decision, God creates for him the act, so that the act is related to God in so far as it is motion and it is related to man in so far as it is he who commits adultery and similar other kinds of acts of disobedience. And in the same way acts of obedience, such as prayer, for instance, are also acts which in their true sense are related to God in so far as they are movements and to man in so far as they are prayer, for man's turning the movement created by God into prayer is an attribute [of man], being the upshot of the resolute decision. This is in conformity with the view of Ḳādī Bāḳillānī, which maintains that the power of God pertains to the root of the action and the power of man pertains to the characterization thereof as being either obedience or disobedience." [33]

On the basis of this passage, the theory of acquisition held by these Maturidites may be restated as follows. God creates in man such faculties of the soul as "inclination," "incitement," and "choice," by which is meant faculties which lead man to the choice between two possible alternative actions. As a result of God's creation in man of these faculties, man becomes the "abode" of the "power" of a "resolute decision" to obtain that one of the two possible alternative actions which he has chosen. As soon as man experiences within himself that "resolute decision," God creates in him a general movement toward those two possible alternatives of the action, and man, in virtue of his being the abode of that power of resolute decision, turns that general movement created in him by God toward either one or the other of the two possible alternatives of the action. It is this power of resolute decision in man to turn the general movement created in him by God into either one of its two possible directions that these Maturidites call

[33] *Rauḍah Bahiyyah*, p. 26, l. 14 – p. 27, l. 6.

"acquisition," which, as quoted above, they say "is [man's] directing his power to one of two possible acts, and it is not created [by God]."

This report of Abū ʿUdhbah calls for two comments. First, the manner in which he introduces the use of the description of man as an "abode" as an explanation of the Maturidites' theory of acquisition shows the influence of, as well as a deviation from, Ghazālī's use of the same description for the same purpose.[34] Thus, whereas according to Ghazālī every one of the powers of which man is the abode is created in him directly by God,[35] according to these Maturidites the "power" of the "resolute decision" of which man is the abode arises in man following upon God's creating in him certain faculties of the soul. Second, in a report by Ḳāḍī Zādeh (d. 1582) of the Maturidites' theory of acquisition, evidently based upon the same work of Najm al-Din al-Nasafī as that used by Abū ʿUdhbah, the "resolute decision" is described as being created in man by God.[36]

[34] Cf. above, pp. 609–610.
[35] Cf. above, p. 708 at n. 45.
[36] Cf. A. de Vlieger, *Kitāb al Qadr*, p. 178.

CHAPTER IX

WHAT IS NEW IN THE KALAM?

The story of the Kalam is the third version of a thrice-told tale based on the same plot. The plot is "Scripture meets philosophy." The two first met at the dawn of the Christian era in Alexandria under the aegis of Philo, and as a result of that meeting there emerged a new type of philosophy, a scriptural philosophy, of which the first version was that of Philo, the second version that of the Church Fathers, and the third version that of the Kalam.

In the following pages, we shall try to show briefly how the six Kalam problems dealt with in this work are related, both in their resemblances and in their differences, to the problems dealt with by Philo and the Church Fathers in their attempts to interpret Scripture in terms of philosophy and to revise philosophy in conformity with Scripture.

I. ATTRIBUTES

At the first meeting, the unity of God, which in the Hebrew scripture means only a denial of the plurality of gods, under the influence of Greek philosophic discussion of the various meanings of the term "one," came to mean with Philo what may be called absolute unity or simplicity, that is to say, the denial of any kind of distinction of parts in God. Similarly under the influence of Greek philosophy, the description of God in the Hebrew scripture as being unlike anything in the world came to mean with Philo the denial with regard to God of what the philosophers call corporeality.

At the second meeting, the Fathers of the Church, like Philo, started with the belief in the unity and unlikeness of God as taught in the Hebrew scripture. But on the basis of the teachings of their Greek scripture, the New Testament, they started also with the belief in a pre-existent Christ, called the Son of God or the Word of God, and the belief in a pre-existent Holy Spirit.

In the course of time there arose among the Church Fathers two main views with regard to the pre-existent Christ and the pre-existent Holy Spirit and their relation to God called the Father.

First, there was the view of the generality of the Church Fathers, who believed that the Pre-existent Christ and Holy Spirit are real beings, coeternal with God the Father, having from eternity originated from Him, and that each of them is to be called God like God the Father. Their view is expressed by the formula that God is one essence and three Persons. In justification of their view they argued that the unity of God, in which they confessed to believe, is not to be taken in the sense of absolute unity but only in the sense of relative unity.

Second, there were their opponents, whom we shall call the Sabellians. Insisting that the unity of God is to be taken in the sense of absolute unity, they denied that the pre-existent Christ and the pre-existent Holy Spirit are real beings, maintaining that they are mere names of God.

There was no sectarian controversy among the Church Fathers with regard to the problem of the incorporeality of God, but among the orthodox Fathers there was one, Tertullian, who, evidently following the Stoic denial of incorporeality, interpreted the Scriptural unlikeness of God to mean that God is a body unlike other bodies.

At the third meeting, Islam, like Philo and the Church Fathers, started with the belief in the unity and the unlikeness of God as taught in their Arabic scripture, the Koran. But on the basis of the Koran, Islam started also with a denial of the Christian Trinity. This denial of the Trinity led to debates between Christians and Muslims soon after the Muslim conquest of Syria in 635. In such debates, we have reason to assume, the Christians tried to explain that by the second and third Persons of the Trinity they merely meant that such terms as "life" and "knowledge," or "life" and "power," or "knowledge" and "power," which even in the Koran are attributed to God, are real things in God, distinct from the essence of God, though coeternal with it and inseparable from it, and, being coeternal with the essence of God, they are each to be called God. In the course of such debates, the spokesmen of Islam were somehow led to express their willingness to admit that "life," "knowledge," and "power," attributed in the Koran to God, are real eternal things in God distinct from the essence of God, but insisted upon denying that they are each to be called God. Soon the admission of the reality of the terms "life," "knowledge," and "power" attributed in the Koran to God led to the extension of the same reality to other terms attributed to God in the Koran or in both the Koran and the Sunnah. This is the origin of that which ever since the Latin translation of Maimonides' *Guide of the Perplexed* in the thirteenth century has been known as the orthodox Muslim doctrine of divine attributes, which doctrine became a problem and a subject of discussion in medieval Latin philosophy and hence in the philosophy of Descartes and Spinoza.

With the rise of the Kalam, this belief in real attributes was adopted by the generality of its followers, but the Muʿtazilites among them, insisting as they did upon the absolute unity and indivisibility of God, denied the reality of attributes, declaring all the terms predicated of God to be mere names of God.

A view intermediating between the views of the Attributists and the Antiattributists was introduced among the Muʿtazilites and is known as the theory of Modes. Denying the view of the Attributists that attributes are real things—that is, they are existent—and denying also the view of the Antiattributists that attributes are mere names—that is, they are nonexistent—this new theory maintains that attributes are neither existent nor nonexistent. When it was objected that this formulation of modes is an infringement on the Law of Excluded Middle, the answer was given that the existence which is negated in the first part of the proposition means extramental existence and that the existence which is negated in the second part of the proposition means verbal existence; and, since between extramental existence and verbal existence there is an intermediate kind of existence, namely mental existence, there is no infringement of the Law of Excluded Middle by the formulation of modes, for it is this mental existence that is indirectly affirmed by the formulation. It is to be noted that this conception of mental existence as distinguished from extramental existence and verbal existence is analogous to a view which appeared later with Abelard in the medieval problem of universals of which he made a theory of conceptualism as distinguished from realism and nominalism.

As in Christianity, there was no sectarian difference in Islam on the incorporeality of God, but some individual Mutikallimūn arrived at a view which, like Tertullian's, maintained that God is a body unlike other bodies.

2. THE KORAN

Related to the controversy in the Kalam over attributes is the controversy in it over the Koran.

In the Koran, the Koran presents itself as having existed prior to its revelation and even prior to the creation of the world. By this pre-existence of the Koran, it can be shown, was meant in the Koran itself and by the earliest followers of the Koran, a pre-existent created Koran. Then also in the Koran, the Koran describes itself not only by the term "Koran" but also by such terms as "word," "wisdom," and "knowledge"—that is to say, the word of God, the wisdom of God, and the knowledge of God. It was, therefore, quite natural that, with the rise of the belief that terms predicated of God are real eternal attributes, the Koran, described as it is as the Word of God and the Wisdom of God and the Knowledge of God, should come to be considered as an eternal attribute in God prior to its revelation to man. This, it may be assumed, is how the belief in the eternity or uncreatedness of the Koran arose. But evidently the original belief in a pre-existent created Koran continued to be held by certain individuals in Islam. When, therefore, the Muʿtazilites formally declared their opposition to the reality of eternal attributes, they also denied that the pre-existent Koran was an eternal, real attribute in God, declaring themselves in favor of the surviving original conception of a pre-existent created Koran. Thus, when early in the eighth century John of Damascus in his prescriptive model for debates between Muslims and Christians assumes that the Muslim spokesman would affirm that the Word of God in the sense of a pre-existent Koran is uncreated and refers to Muslim heretics who believe that it is created, the Muslim spokesman is to be taken to be an orthodox Mutakallim, whereas the Muslim heretics are to be taken to refer to the Muʿtazilites.

Now, from John of Damascus' prescriptive model for debates between Muslims and Christians we may gather that from actual debates on the Trinity Muslims learned from Christians two things. First, they learned that Christians compared their own belief in "the Word of God" used in the sense of the pre-existent Christ with the Muslim belief in "the Word of God" used in the sense of the pre-existent Koran. Second, they learned that among the Christians there existed a problem as to the relation of the pre-existent Christ to the born Christ, and that, while the generality of Christians solved that problem by the belief that the pre-existent Christ was incarnate in the born Christ with the result that in the born Christ there were two natures, a divine and a human, there were those who denied such an incarnation, so that in the born Christ there was only one nature, a human nature. Under the influence of this new knowledge, some Muslims, we imagine, must have raised to themselves the question as to the relation of the pre-existent Koran to the revealed Koran. While indeed there is no evidence that such a question was actually raised, there are many Kalam passages which seem to contain opposite answers in anticipation of such a question. According to one kind of answer, analogous to the Christian incarnation, that is, enfleshment of the pre-existent Christ in the born Christ, there came to be in Islam an inlibration, that is, embookment of the pre-existent Koran in the revealed Koran; so that in every Koran made by man's reciting it, or hearing it, or memorizing it, or writing it down, there are two natures, that of the pre-existent Word of God and that of man's impression or expression or imitation of it. According to another kind of answer, there is no inlibration, so that every man-made Koran is only an impression or expression or imitation of the pre-existent Koran.

3. CREATION

At the first meeting between Scripture and philosophy, Philo started with the belief in the creation of the world as taught in the Hebrew scripture. In his attempt to explain the meaning of this scriptural belief philosophically, he expresses himself in two ways. In one place, he says that God has created all things out of matter (ὕλη), which would ordinarily be taken to reflect what is generally known as the Platonic pre-existent eternal matter. In another place, evidently following an expression used in II Maccabees 7:28, he says that God has brought into being "things that were non-existent (τὰ μὴ ὄντα)," in which the term "non-existent," according to Aristotle's use of it, may be taken to mean either "matter" or "nothing." In his interpretation, however, of the story of creation in the opening of the Book of Genesis, Philo makes it quite clear that, while indeed he follows Plato's conception of creation as being out of a pre-existent matter, he takes that pre-existent matter itself to have been created out of nothing.

At the second meeting, the Fathers of the Church, like Philo, started with the belief in the creation of the world as taught in the Hebrew scripture. Then, while in their attempt to explain the meaning of the scriptural creation, they—again like Philo in that aforementioned one place—express themselves by saying that the world was created "from the non-existent (ἐη τοῦ μὴ ὄντος)," they make it quite clear that they use that expression in the sense of creation from nothing. Later, in the third century, a phrase literally meaning "from nothing" as a description of creation was coined almost simultaneously by two Church Fathers, one in Latin (*de nihilo*) and one in Greek (ἐξ οὐδενός). In the writings of the Church Fathers, moreover, we find both an explicit rejection of creation out of a pre-existent eternal matter and explicit affirmations of creation out of a pre-existent created matter.

At the third meeting, the Muslims started with the belief in the creation of the world as taught in their Arabic scripture, the Koran, which in its main outline is the same as that taught in the Hebrew scripture. Whatever the early Muslim conception of creation may have been, it is reasonable to assume that the technical phrase "from nothing" used later by the Mutakallimūn as a description of creation came to them from their contact with Christians, whose aforementioned ἐη τοῦ μὴ ὄντος was translated to them by the Arabic *min al-maʿdūm*. This is reflected in reports to the effect that the orthodox Mutakallimūn who affirmed that the non-existent (*al-maʿdūm*) is nothing were those who believed that creation was out of nothing. Then, with the translation of Greek philosophic works into Arabic, the Muʿtazilites, on becoming acquainted with what was known as the Platonic theory of creation out of a pre-existent eternal matter, began to explain the phrase *min al-maʿdūm* in the above-mentioned Arabic translation of the Patristic Greek formula for creation to mean from a matter which is eternal. This is reflected in reports to the effect that almost all the Muʿtazilites affirmed that the non-existent (*al-maʿdūm*) is something and that on account of this they were accused of believing in an eternal matter.

Thus, while among the Church Fathers the belief in creation out of a pre-existent eternal matter was rejected, in Islam there were those who accepted it. This acceptance quite evidently points to a belief that it could be reconciled with the Koranic doctrine of creation. It is to be noted that among contemporary Arabic-speaking Jews there were those flourishing long after the rise of the Muʿtazilites who explicitly declared that creation out of a pre-existent eternal matter was reconcilable with the scriptural teaching of creation.

In the reports on the Kalam special mention is made of the various Mutakallimūn's attempts to frame arguments for creation. Seven such arguments are enumerated. Of these seven arguments, one is used as proof either for creation not necessarily out of nothing or for creation out of nothing;[1] another one is used as proof for creation out of nothing;[2] still another one implies its use as proof of creation not necessarily out of nothing;[3] all the others can be taken to imply their use as proofs for creation out of nothing. Two of the last type of arguments became subjects of discussion among the Schoolmen.

4. ATOMISM

At the first meeting of Scripture with philosophy, Philo learned that among the philosophers there were two views with regard to the constitution of bodies. According to the prevailing view among them, bodies were constituted of an eternal infinitely divisible matter and this view implied a belief in a theory of causality and a belief in the existence of God as the prime cause. According to the other view held by some among the philosophers, bodies were constituted of atoms, which atoms, in infinite number, had existed from eternity prior to their formation into bodies, which formation into bodies happened by mere chance. Finding in Scripture no objection to the prevailing view of the philosophers either on the score of the infinite divisibility of matter or on the

[1] Cf. above, pp. 384–385.
[2] Cf. above, p. 426.
[3] Cf. above, pp. 387ff.

score of its causality but only on the score of its eternity, he adopted that prevailing view of the philosophers, modifying it only to affirm that the infinitely divisible matter was created by God.

At the second meeting, for reasons quite evidently like those of Philo, the prevailing view among the philosophers was adopted by the Church Fathers.

At the third meeting, the Mutakallimūn, it may be reasonably assumed, became acquainted with the two contrasting philosophic views on the constitution of bodies, not from authentic works of Greek philosophers but from spurious doxographies of Greek philosophy. Since, unlike Philo and the Church Fathers, these Mutakallimūn were opposed, on religious grounds, to infinity and causality, both these philosophic views on the constitution of bodies were objectionable to them—the theory of an infinitely divisible matter on the score of its eternity, infinity, and causality; the theory of atoms on the score of its eternity, infinity, and chance. Still they felt that they could not altogether ignore the philosophic speculations about the constitution of bodies and that they had somehow to make a choice between the two views.

Finding that in the case of atomism it was possible to eliminate from it all its three objectionable features, whereas in the case of the infinitely divisible matter it was impossible to eliminate two of its three objectionable features—namely, those which were on the score of infinity and causality—they quite naturally adopted atomism with certain modifications. Thus the atoms, according to them, were created by God as the constituent parts of bodies at the time of His creation of the world, and they were finite in number.

Now it happens that the description of atoms in those spurious doxographies, unlike their description in the authentic works of the Greek philosophers, makes no mention of the extendedness of the atoms. Quite the contrary; from certain terms used in those doxographies as descriptions of atoms, readers could have gotten the impression that they were unextended. Moreover, it can be shown that one of those doxographies conveyed to its readers the definite impression that the atoms of Democritus were, like mathematical points, unextended. Because of all this, the first Mutakallimūn, in their adoption of atomism, conceived of the atoms as being unextended. Later, however, with the spread of translations of the authentic works of Greek philosophers, there arose in the Kalam two schools with regard to the problem of the unextendedness of atoms. One school, that of Baghdad, retained the original view that atoms were unextended; another school, that of Basra, maintained that atoms were extended.

Atomism, once adopted by the Kalam, continued to be one of the beliefs that characterized its followers as a class. Individual dissenters, however, did exist. One of the best known is Naẓẓām. Rejecting atomism, he adopted Aristotle's view that bodies are infinitely divisible, with its implication that all change in bodies is a transition from potentiality to actuality. This Aristotelian conception of change as a transition from potentiality to actuality is described by Naẓẓām as a conception that all change is a process of hiding (*kumūn*) and appearing (*zuhūr*), a description evidently borrowed from the spurious doxographies where it was used as a substitute in popular language for Aristotle's technical description in terms of potentiality and actuality. Naẓẓām's view, generally referred to as Naẓẓām's theory of *kumūn*, may be referred to in English as his theory of latency.

5. CAUSALITY

At the first meeting, Philo, in his attempt to scripturalize philosophy, modified the philosophic conception of causality so that, according to him, God at the creation of the world implanted in it certain laws of causality whereby the world was governed under His supervision, but these laws could be suspended by God by His creation of what came to be called miracles.

At the second meeting, a scripturalized conception of causality like Philo's was adopted also by the Church Fathers.

At the third meeting, Muslims started with Koranic verses on the basis of which they formed the belief that every event in the world is directly created by the arbitrary will of God—a belief which came to be referred to as continuous creation. This belief was opposed by them not only to the philosophic conception of causality but also to the scripturalized conception of causality which they had learned from Christians. Thus when in the early part of the eighth century John of Damascus in his prescriptive model for debates between Muslims and Christians instructs the Christian to argue that after the six days of creation all normal processes of nature are the acts of God through intermediate causes, the Muslim is expected by him to maintain that all the so-called normal processes of nature are directly created by the arbitrary will of God. This original Muslim belief was retained by all the followers of the Kalam, including the Muʿtazilites, except that among the Muʿtazilites there were two dissenters.

Against the aforementioned belief of continuous creation there arose in the Kalam the following question: How on the basis of this belief can one explain the commonly observed fact that, barring unpredictable miracles, events in the world follow a certain regular order of sequence? The explanation given was that the regularly sequential events between unexpectedly occurring miracles is due to the fact that in the case of those events God acts in a manner like that which in the case of human action is called "custom." The term custom here is quite evidently borrowed from Aristotle, who uses it as a description of events which occur not "by nature" nor "by necessity" nor "always" but only "often," and thus the term custom seemed to certain masters of the Kalam to be an appropriate description of the regularly sequential events which, according to them, were not "by nature" nor "by necessity" and were subject to interruption by miracles. When the objection was raised that the term custom applies to regularly sequential events which are described not only as occurring "not always" but also as occurring "only often," whereas regularly sequential events between any two occasionally occurring miracles are said to occur "always," the answer given was that, simultaneously with His direct creation of any sequence of events, God creates in the mind of man the knowledge that, barring miracles, the same sequence of events will continue to be created by Him in the future.

It is, however, to be noted that, though the Mutakallimūn believed that every event in the world is directly created by God, they still believed that certain events God will never create. In other words, like the Church Fathers and Philo before them, they believed in impossibilities—that is to say, acts which for some good reason God would not perform.[4] Among the various attempts made to enumerate such impossibilities, two are especially mentioned, those which would imply a change in the nature of God and those which are contrary to the law of contradiction.

The two Muʿtazilite dissenters referred to above with regard to the denial of causality are Naẓẓām and Muʿammar. Both of them, like Aristotle, believe that things have a "nature" which is the cause of the successive changes in them; and, like the Church Fathers and before them Philo, they believe that that nature was implanted by God in things at the time of the creation of the world. They differ, however, in two things with regard to that nature.

First, they differ as to what that nature is. Naẓẓām, by his rejection of the Kalam atomism, adopted Aristotle's distinction of matter and form and hence the distinction of potentiality and actuality. The nature of a thing, as in Aristotle, applies to the form of the thing, and when nature is said to be the cause of motion in the thing the meaning is that nature is the cause of a transition from potentiality to actuality. Muʿammar, by his retention of the Kalam atomism, rejected

[4] Cf. above, p. 580 at n. 13. I take Naẓẓām's statement to mean that his differences from his opponents is only verbal.

Aristotle's distinction of matter and form and hence also the distinction of potentiality and actuality. The Aristotelian term nature is used by him in the sense of what he calls *maʿnā*, which *maʿnā* exists in atoms and through the atoms in bodies and, when nature in the sense of *maʿnā* is said by him to be the cause of motion in things, it means that it is the cause of a transition from one state of actuality to another state of actuality.

Second, these two dissenters differ as to how nature operates in the world. To Naẓẓām, nature, which was implanted by God in things at the creation of the world, continues to operate in the world under the supervision of God and hence the orderly succession of changes of which it is the cause may be suspended by God on His creation of miracles. To Muʿammar, nature, or its substitute *maʿnā*, though implanted in things by God at His creation of the world, operates in the world without any supervision of God and hence there is no suspension of its operation in the form of miracles. Such a view, it can be shown, has its origin in Plato's *Timaeus;* it had been known in Islam as a heretical view prior to Muʿammar and it is analogous to what is known in the later history of philosophy as Deism.

The Kalam denial of causality was not without its impact upon the history of philosophy. St. Thomas Aquinas discusses it in several of his works and repudiates it. Nicolaus of Autrecourt's argument that there is no causal nexus between the burning of "flax" and its contact with fire can be shown to be based upon Ghazālī's argument that there is no causal nexus between the burning of "cotton" and its contact with fire. Thus also Hume's contention that the mind is "determined by custom" to infer that there is some causal nexus between two successive events is based upon Averroes' contention that the "custom" which the Kalam attribute to God as an explanation of the sequential order of things created by Him is only "an act of the mind." [5]

[5] See my *Religious Philosophy*, pp. 209–210.

Some historians assume that the occasionalism of the seventeenth century is somehow connected with the orthodox Kalam view on causality,[6] but whether there is any literary connection between them is yet to be shown.

6. PREDESTINATION AND FREE WILL

At the first meeting, Philo became acquainted with three Greek philosophic views on man's action. First, the view of the generality of the philosophers, according to which man's action, like all the actions in the world, is determined by the eternal necessary internexus of causes; man's action is called free only when it is performed without external compulsion and without ignorance. Second, the view of the Epicureans, according to which, with their denial of causality, human action, like all the actions in the world, is free. Third, the view of the Stoic Chrysippus, according to which the eternal necessary internexus of causes, in which he believed, does by the necessity of its nature, cease to function at certain acts in the world, and similarly also at the will of man, so that man's action, by the cessation of causality, is free. Philo in his effort to philosophize Scripture as well as to scripturalize philosophy arrived at a view according to which, while man's action, even when free from external physical compulsion, is still determined by an internexus of divinely created internal psychical causes, man from birth is endowed by God with miraculous power to break that nexus of psychical causes and to act freely contrary to their determination.

At the second meeting, the same view, in its main contention, was adopted by the Greek Church Fathers. But among the Latin Fathers, Augustine arrived at the view that the original freedom with which Adam had been endowed by God at his creation was lost with his fall, so that his descendants thereafter act by necessity—the necessity of concupiscence when they act sinfully and the necessity of divine grace when they

[6] See my reference above, p. 693, n. 69a.

act righteously. But still, following Aristotle, who describes a necessary act as voluntary if the necessity flows only from psychical causes within man himself, he describes man, though acting by necessity, as being free, inasmuch as his necessity flows from within himself.

At the third meeting, the Muslims started with two sets of Koranic verses, one of a predestinarian nature and the other of a libertarian nature. Their first attempt to formulate a doctrine of human action was based upon the predestinarian verses. Then toward the end of the seventh century, probably under the influence of Christianity, libertarian views began to penetrate into Islam which gradually caused a division within it between those who retained the original predestinarian views and those who, under the name of Ḳadariyyah, adopted the newly arisen libertarian views. This division continued within the Kalam, wherein the generality of its followers retained the original predestinarian views of Islam whereas the Muʿtazilites adopted the libertarian views of the Ḳadariyyah.

The difference between these Predestinarians and Libertarians may be stated as follows:

According to the Predestinarians, there is no distinction between the actions that occur in the world, including the actions which occur to man, and the actions which are performed by man. All of them are directly created by God. This conception of predestinationism in its early stages was described by one of its exponents as compulsionism—a description which was rejected by later exponents of predestinationism.

According to the Libertarians, there is a distinction between actions that occur in the world—including actions which occur to man—and actions performed by man. The former actions are admitted by all but two of the Libertarians to be directly created by God; the latter actions are taken by them to be performed by man's free will. With regard to their common belief in free will, there were the following differences among them. Some of the Libertarians believed that man from birth was endowed by God with the gift of free will. Others believed that before each act God endowed man with such a power. Inasmuch as, according to all these Libertarians, the free will which man enjoyed was acquired by him as a gift from God, they referred to human action as "acquisition" (*aksāb*), evidently having in mind the fact that sometimes in the Koran the term *kasaba*, "to acquire," is used synonymously with the term *ʿamila*, "to do."

Their assertion of free will confronted the Libertarians with five antinomies, of which two are the antinomy of free will and God's foreknowledge and the antinomy of free will and God's power.

As for the antinomy on the score of God's foreknowledge, it happens that in the Koran there is no direct reference to God's foreknowledge except with reference to five things, and so some Libertarians allowed themselves to assert that God has no knowledge of future events. Evidently to them this was one of the impossibilities which God in His wisdom established in the world.

As for the antinomy on the score of God's power, there were three solutions, of which the second solution consisted of two versions, and this second solution in its two versions and the third solution are referred to as theories of acquisition.

One solution is attributed to most of the Muʿtazilites. As expressed by them it reads that "God is not to be described as having power over a thing over which He has endowed man with power"; that is to say, for God to exercise His power in cases involving man's free will is one of the impossibilities which God in His wisdom established in the world.

A second solution of the antinomy was introduced by two Muʿtazilites, Ḍirār and Najjār. Drawing upon the distinction commonly made in ordinary speech between the artisan who makes a thing and the purchaser who acquires the thing and thus becomes its owner, they applied that distinction to human actions. Every human action is created by God but is acquired by man, and it is in the sense that man is the acquirer of the act that he may be called its agent. Accordingly, every human act comes from two agents, namely God the creator and man the acquirer.

But, while Ḍirār and Najjār are in agreement as to the description of the human act as an acquisition in this new sense of the term, they differ as to the origin and meaning of this acquisition. According to Ḍirār, man from birth is endowed by God with the power to acquire the act which is to be created for him by God, so that the power to acquire and the act of acquiring are to be ascribed to man's own free will; man, therefore, is to be called an agent in reality and the description of man as acquirer is to apply also to generated effects. According to Najjār, the power to acquire as well as the act of acquiring is created in man by God simultaneously with His creation of the act for man, so that both man's power to acquire and his act of acquiring are created for him by God; man, therefore, is to be called simply an agent but not an agent in reality and the term acquirer is not to be applied to man in the case of generated effects.

A third solution of the antinomy is that of Shaḥḥām. Unlike "most of the Muʿtazilites," he believes that God may deprive men of the free will with which He has endowed them, and, unlike Ḍirār and Najjār, he retains the original Libertarian use of the term acquisition as meaning the act of man's free will with which he has been endowed by God. Thus in contradistinction to the view common to both Ḍirār and Najjār as described above, his view may be described as meaning that every act of man may come from either one of two agents, namely, God, in the case He has deprived man of his freedom, in which case man's act is "by necessity," or man, in the case God has not deprived man of his freedom, in which case man's act is "by acquisition," that is to say, it is a free act of man's will.

The Ḍirār-Najjār solution was rejected by their fellow Muʿtazilites. The Shaḥḥām solution was followed by his pupil "al-Jubbāʾi and groups of the Muʿtazilites," but he, and probably also his followers, have rejected the term "acquisition" as a description of man's free action, substituting for it the term "creation." The Ḍirār–Najjār solution, however, found followers among the Predestinarians; evidently they saw in it an explanation of the libertarian verses in the Koran. Thus of Ibn Kullāb, a Predestinarian, it is reported that he applied to certain human actions the term "acquisition," which presumably he used in the Najjārite sense; of a group of Predestinarians named "The People of Affirmation" it is reported that many of them followed Ḍirār's version of acquisition and some of them followed Najjār's version of it, though with regard to generated effects all of them followed Najjār; finally, Ashʿarī, speaking for himself, makes it quite clear that he follows the Najjārite version of acquisition.

It happens, however, that Ashʿarī, in his attempt to show that acquisitionism is against both compulsionism and libertarianism, emphasizes on the one hand that acquisition is a "power" and on the other hand that it is "created" in man by God and that "God has the power to force man to it." As was to be expected, the question arose how acquisition could be called a "power" when it has no influence upon the object of the power.

Attempts to answer this question were made by Bāḳillānī, Juwaynī, and Ghazālī.

Bāḳillānī's answer is a revision of the theory of acquisition by distinguishing in every human action between the act itself and its mode of operation. The former is created by God and the latter is within the power of man, and it is the latter to which the term acquisition is to be applied. Bāḳillānī's cessation of God's direct creativity of human action at the mode of the operation of that action may be compared to Chrysippus' cessation of the necessary process of causation at human action, except for the following difference: To Bāḳillānī the cessation is by the will of God; to Chrysippus it is by the necessity of nature.

Juwaynī, using the term power in the sense of will, tries to show that power in the sense of will does not have to influence its object. He tries to show this by comparing will to knowledge and by arguing that, just as one may be said to be knowing something without his influencing the existence of that something, so one may also be said to be willing something without influencing the existence of that something.

Ghazālī does not discuss this question directly, but provides answers for it in two of his three discourses in which he deals with acquisition.

The answer provided by him in the first of his three discourses on acquisition is one in which, like Juwaynī, he tries to show how power need not have an influence upon its object. But whereas Juwaynī tries to show it by the analogy of man's power, in the sense of man's will to acquire, to man's knowledge of something, Ghazālī tries to show it by the analogy of man's power to acquire to God's eternal power to create, for prior to the creation of the world God's eternal power to create was a power without an object influenced by it.

The answer provided by Ghazālī in the third of his three discourses on acquisition is contained in his explanation of how what "the People of Truth" call acquisition is a combination of "compulsion" and "choice." The explanation given by Ghazālī is that acquisition is a "choice" despite its being also a "compulsion," because man is the "abode" of the compulsion as he is of the choice, that is to say, because the compulsion in the case of acquisition comes from within man himself and not from something external to man. Though no allusion whatsoever is made here by Ghazālī to philosophy, his explanation may be taken to reflect Aristotle's contention that an act performed by "necessity" may be described as being "voluntary" if the necessity comes from within man himself and not from something external. So also Augustine, who insists that man is free despite his contention that man sins by the necessity of concupiscence and does good by the necessity of divine grace, reflects that view of Aristotle.

CONCLUSION

We have thus seen that out of the six problems dealt with in this book, four are exactly the same as those encountered in the first two meetings between Scripture and philosophy and the other two have grown out of problems discussed in the second meeting; we have seen also that each of these six problems, whatever its origin, has an independent development in the Kalam, and finally that in the independent development of the problems in the Kalam the treatment of each problem is an attempt to explain Scripture in the terms of philosophy. And so the Kalam belongs to that new type of philosophy, the scriptural philosophy, which, having been built up by Philo, continued to flourish in various versions until the seventeenth century when it was pulled down by Spinoza.

BIBLIOGRAPHICAL NOTE

The Bibliography is in five sections: I. Muslim Works and Writers; II. Jewish Works and Writers; III. Greek and Latin Works and Writers; IV. Christian Works and Writers; V. Periodicals, Series, and Reference Works.

These lists by no means constitute a full bibliography: they are designed primarily to supplement the footnote citations in identifying editions that Professor Wolfson used and wanted mentioned.

The following abbreviations refer to works of Aristotle and are expanded in the Index of References, part III.

Anal. Post.	*De Gen. Anim.*	[*De*] *Soph. Elench.*	*Poet.*
Anal. Pri.	*De Gen. et Corr.*	*Eth. Nic.*	*Rhet.*
Categ.	*De Interpr.*	*Metaph.*	*Top.*
De Anima	*De Long. et Brev. Vitae*	*Phys.*	
De Caelo			

Abbreviations for periodicals, series, and certain standard reference works are expanded in section V of the Bibliography.

Short titles frequently cited are listed with their authors below. Further information will be found under the author's name in the section of the Bibliography designated: I (Muslim), II (Jewish), III (Greek and Latin), or IV (Christian).

Al-Ḳiyās al-Ṣaghīr: Alfarabi I
Al-Muʿtazilah: Ibn al-Murtaḍa I
Anwār: Ḳirḳisānī II

Buḫārī, *Ṣaḥīḥ*: Buḫārī I

C.G., *Cont. Gent.*: Thomas Aquinas IV
Cuzari: Judah Halevi II

De Elementis: see *Liber de Elementis*
De Placitis: Aëtius III
De Substantia Orbis: Averroes I
Definitionum: see *Liber Definitionum*
Dux seu Director . . . : see *Rabi Mossei Aegyptii . . .*

Elementis: see *Liber de Elementis*
Emunah Ramah: Abraham Ibn Daud II
Emunot: Saadia II

Eshkol ha-Kofer: Judah Hadassi II
ʿEṣ Ḥayyim: Aaron ben Elijah II

Farḳ: Baghdādī I
Faṣl al-Maḳāl: Averroes I
Fiḳh Akbar: Abū Ḥanīfah I
Fiṣal: Ibn Ḥazm I
Fī Wujūd al-Ḫāliḳ: Abucara IV
Fuṣūṣ al-Ḥikam: Alfarabi I

Gebulim: see *Sefer ha-Gebulim*

Ḥobot: Baḥya II
Ḥudūd: see *Kitāb al-Ḥudūd*

Ibānah: Ashʿarī I
Iḥyāʾ: Ghazālī I
Iḳtiṣād: Ghazālī I
Intiṣār: Ḫayyāṭ I
Irshād: Juwaynī I
Ishārāt: Avicenna I

Ḳadar: Muslim I
Kashf: Averroes I
Kifāyat: Faḍālī I
Kitāb al-Ḥudūd: Isaac Israeli II
Kitāb al-Jam': Alfarabi I
Ḳobeṣ: Maimonides II

Liber Definitionum: Isaac Israeli II
Liber de Elementis: Isaac Israeli II
Luma': Ash'arī I

Maḥkimat Peti: Joseph al-Baṣīr II
Maḳālāt: Ash'arī I
Maḳāṣid al-Falāsifah: Ghazālī I
Masā'il: Abū Rashīd I
Milal: Shahrastānī I
Millot ha-Higgayon: Maimonides II
Mi'yār al-'Ilm: Ghazālī I
Mīzān al-'Amal: Ghazālī I
Moreh: see *Moreh Nebukim*
Moreh Nebukim: Maimonides II
Mughnī: 'Abd al-Jabbār I
Muḥaṣṣal: Rāzī I
Muḳaddimah: Ibn Ḥaldūn I
Munḳidh: Ghazālī I
Murūj: Mas'ūdī I

Najāt: Avicenna I
Ne'imot: Joseph al-Baṣīr II
Nihāyat: Shahrastānī I
Niẓāmiyyah: Juwaynī I

'Olam Ḳaṭan: Joseph Ibn Ṣaddiḳ II
Opif.: Philo II

Placita: Aëtius III

Rabi Mossei Aegyptii . . . : Maimonides II
Rasā'il Iḫwān al-Ṣafā': Iḫwān al-Ṣafā' I
Rauḍah Bahiyyah: Abū 'Udhbah I

Ṣaḥīḥ: Buḫārī I
Ṣaḥīḥ: Muslim I
Sefer ha-Gebulim: Isaac Israeli II
Sefer ha-Yesodot: Isaac Israeli II
Shemonah Peraḳim: Maimonides II
Siyāsāt: Alfarabi I
S. Th., *Sum. Theol.*: Thomas Aquinas IV

Tabsīr: Isfarā'inī I
Tabyīn: Ibn 'Asākir I
Taftāzānī: Taftāzānī I
Tahāfut al-Falāsifah: Ghazālī I
Tahāfut al-Tahāfut: Averroes I
Taḥrīm: Ibn Ḳudāmah I
Tamhīd: Bāḳillānī I
Tanbīh: Malaṭī I
Tanbīh: Mas'ūdī I
Ta'rīfāt: Jurjānī I
Tatahaf: see *Tahāfut al-Tahāfut*
Teshubot ha-Rambam: Maimonides II
Tis'u Rasā'il: Avicenna I

Uṣūl: Baghdādī I
'Uyūn al-Masā'il: Alfarabi I
Uthūlūjiyya: Pseudo-Aristotle I

Waṣiyyah: Abū Ḥanīfah I

Yesodot: see *Sefer ha-Yesodot*

BIBLIOGRAPHY

I. MUSLIM WORKS AND WRITERS

For translations of the Koran into English by Bell, Muhammed Ali, Palmer, Rodwell, Sale, and Wherry, see the List of Editors, Translators, and Authors of Secondary Works.

'Abd al-Jabbār, *Al-Mughnī fī Abwāb al-Tauḥīd wa'l-'Adl*, VII, Cairo, 1381 A.H. [1963].

Abū Ḥanīfah, *Fiḳh Akbar* II (spurious), in *Kitāb Sharḥ al-Fiḳh al-Akbar*, Hyderabad, 1321 A.H.

English trans. by A. J. Wensinck in his *The Muslim Creed*, Cambridge, England, 1932.

——*Kitāb al-Waṣiyyah* (spurious), Hyderabad, 1321 A.H.

English trans. by Wensinck in *The Muslim Creed.*

'Abū Rashīd [of Nīshāpūr], *Kitāb al-Masā'il fī al-Ḥilāf bain al-Baṣriyyīn wa'l-Baghdādiyyīn*, ed. and trans. into German by Arthur Biram (German title: *Die atomistische Substansenlehre aus dem Buch der Streitfragen . . .*), Leiden, 1902.

Abū 'Udhbah, *Al-Rauḍah al-Bahiyyah*, Hyderabad, 1322 A.H. [1904].

Alfarabi, *Fuṣūṣ al-Ḥikam*, ed. Friedrich Dieterici in his *Alfārābī's philosophische Abhandlungen*, Leiden, 1890.

——*Kitāb al-Jam' bain Ra'yay al-Ḥakīmayn*, ed. Dieterici in *Alfārābī's philosophische Abhandlungen.*

——*Kitāb al-Ḳiyās al-Ṣaghīr*, ed. Mubahat Türker, "Fārābī'nin bazi mantik eserleri," *Revue de la Faculté de Langues, d'Histoire et de Géographie de l'Université d'Ankara*, 16: 165–286 (1958).

English trans. by N. Rescher, *Al-Fārābī's Short Commentary on Aristotle's Prior Analytics*, Pittsburgh, 1963.

——*Kitāb al-Siyāsāt al-Madaniyyah*, Hyderabad, 1346 A.H.

——*Sharḥ Kitāb al-'Ibārah*, ed. W. Kutsch and S. Marrow (English title: *Alfarabi's Commentary on Aristotle's De Interpretatione*), Beirut, 1960.

——*'Uyūn al-Masā'il*, ed. Dieterici in *Alfārābī's philosophische Abhandlungen.*

Ash'arī, *Kitāb al-Ibānah 'an Uṣūl al-Diyānah*, Hyderabad, 1321 A.H. [1903].

English trans. by W. C. Klein, *The Elucidation of Islām's Foundation*, New Haven, Conn., 1940.

——*Kitāb al-Luma'*, ed. and trans. into English by R. J. McCarthy in his *The Theology of al-Ash'arī*, Beirut, 1953.

——*Kitāb Maḳālāt al-Islāmiyīn wa-Iḫtilāf al-Muṣallīn*, ed. Hellmut Ritter, Constantinople, 1929–1930.

Averroes, Epitomes of Aristotle's works:

Of the *Physics*. In *Rasā'il Ibn Rushd*, Hyderabad, 1366 A.H. [1947]. Hebrew, *Kiẓẓure Ibn Roshd 'al Shema' Tibe'i le-Aristoteles*, Riva di Trento, 1560.

Of *De Anima*. In *Rasā'il Ibn Rushd*; ed. by El Ahwani in his *Talḫīs Kitāb al-Nafs*, Cairo, 1950.

—— *Kitāb Faṣl al-Maḳāl*, ed. M. J. Müller in his *Philosophie und Theologie von Averroes*, Munich, 1859.

—— *Kitāb al-Kashf 'an Manāhij al-Adillah*, ed. Müller in the same.

—— Long Commentaries on Aristotle's works:

On the *Physics*. Latin in *Aristotelis omnia quae extant opera . . .*, Venetiis, apud Iuntas, 1562–1574, vol. IV.

On *De Caelo*. Latin in same, vol. V.

On *Metaphysics*. Arabic: *Tafsīr ma ba'd al-Ṭabī'ah*, ed. M. Bouyges, Beirut, 1938–1952. Latin in *Aristotelis omnia quae extant opera*, vol. VIII.

On *De Anima*. Latin, ed. S. Crawford: *Averrois Cordubensis Commentarium Magnum in Aristotelis de Anima*, Cambridge, Mass., 1953.

—— Middle Commentaries on Aristotle's works:

On *De Caelo*. Latin in *Aristotelis omnia quae extant opera*, vol. V (Latin title: *Paraphrasis in Primum de Caelo*).

On *De Generatione et Corruptione*. Latin, ed. F. H. Fobes, Cambridge, Mass., 1956.

—— *Sermo de Substantia Orbis*, in *Aristotelis omnia quae extant opera*, vol. IX.

—— *Tahāfut al-Tahāfut*, ed. M. Bouyges, Beirut, 1930.

Latin: trans. (A.D. 1328) by Kalonymus b. Kalonymus, MS. Vat. Lat. 2434; trans. (1527) by Kalonymus b. David: *Destructio Destructionum* in *Aristotelis omnia quae extant opera*, vol. IX.

Eng. trans. by S. van den Bergh, *The Incoherence of the Incoherence*, London, 1954.

Avicenna, *Al-Ishārāt wa'l-Tanbīhāt*, ed. J. Forget, Leiden, 1892.

French trans. by A.-M. Goichon, *Ibn Sīnā: Livre des directives et remarques*, Beirut and Paris, 1951.

—— *Al-Najāt*, Cairo, 1331 A.H. [1913].

—— *Al-Shifā': Psychology*, ed. F. Rahman, *Avicenna's De Anima*, London, 1959.

Ed. and trans. into French by J. Bakoš, *Psychologie d'Ibn Sīnā*, Prague, 1956.

—— *Tis'u Rasā'il fī al-Ḥikmah wa'l-Tabī'iyyāt*, Cairo, 1326 A.H. [1908].

Baghdādī, 'Abd al-Ḳāhir Ibn Ṭāhir, *Al-Farḳ bain al-Firaḳ*, ed. M. Badr, Cairo, 1328 A.H. [1910].

English trans. by Kate C. Seelye, *Moslem Schisms and Sects*, Part I, New York, 1920; Abraham S. Halkin, *Moslem Schisms and Sects*, Part II, Tel-Aviv, 1935.

—— *Kitāb Uṣūl al-Dīn*, Istanbul, 1346 A.H. [1928].

Bāḳillānī, *Al-Tamhīd*, ed. R. J. McCarthy, Beirut, 1957.

Buḫārī, *Al-Jāmi' al-Ṣaḥīḥ*, ed. M. Ludolph Krehl and Th. W. Juynboll (French title: *Le Recueil des traditions mahométanes*), Leiden, 1862–1908.

French trans. by O. Houdas and W. Marçais, *El-Bokhari: Les Traditions islamiques*, Paris, 1903–1914.

Faḍālī, *Kifāyat al-'Awāmm min 'Ilm al-Kalām*, Cairo, 1315 A.H.

English trans. by D. B. MacDonald in his *Development of Muslim Theology, Jurisprudence and Constitutional Theory*, New York, 1903.

Ghazālī, *Iḥyā' 'Ulūm al-Dīn*, Cairo, 1358 A.H. [1939].

——— *Kitāb al-Iḳtiṣād fī al-I'tiḳād*, Cairo, n.d.

——— *Maḳāṣid al-Falāsifah*, Cairo, n.d.

Latin trans. by John Hispalensis, ed. J. T. Muckle: *Algazel's Metaphysics*, Toronto, 1933.

——— *Mi'yār al-'Ilm*, Cairo, 1329 A.H.

——— *Mīzān al-'Amal*, Cairo, 1342 A.H.

——— *Kitāb al-Munḳidh min al-Ḍalāl*, Beirut, 1959.

——— *Tahāfut al-Falāsifah*, ed. M. Bouyges, Beirut, 1927.

Ḫayyāṭ, *Kitāb al-Intiṣār*, ed. and trans. into French by A. N. Nader (French title: *Le Livre du triomphe et de la réfutation d'Ibn al-Rawandi l'hérétique*), Beirut, 1957.

Ibn 'Asākir, *Tabyīn Kadhib al-Muftarī*, Damascus, 1347 A.H. [1928–1929].

Summary English translation by R. J. McCarthy in his *The Theology of al-Ash'arī*, Beirut, 1953.

Ibn al-Athīr, *Al-Kāmil fī al-Ta'rīḥ*, ed. C. J. Tornberg, Leiden, 1851–1874.

Ibn Ḫaldūn, *Al-Muḳaddimah*, ed. É. M. Quatremère (French title: *Prolégomènes d'Ebn-Khaldoun*), Paris, 1858.

English trans. by F. Rosenthal, *The Muqaddimah: An Introduction to History*, New York, 1958.

Ibn Ḥazm, *Kitāb al-Fiṣal fī al-Milal wa'l-Aḥwā' wa'l-Niḥal*, Cairo, 1317–1327 A.H.

Ibn Ḳudāmah, *Taḥrīm al-Naẓar fī Kutub Ahl al-Kalām*, ed. and trans. into English by G. Makdisi (English title: *Censure of Speculative Theology*), London, 1962.

Ibn al-Murtaḍā, *Kitāb al-Milal wa'l-nihal*, ed. T. W. Arnold (English title: *Al-Mu'tazilah: being an extract from the Kitābu-l milal wa-n nihal*), Leipzig, 1902.

Ed. by S. Diwald-Wilzer (German title: *Die Klassen der Mutaziliten*), Beirut, 1961.

Iḫwān al-Ṣafā', *Rasā'il Iḫwān al-Ṣafā'*, Beirut, 1377 A.H. [1957].

Isfarā'inī, *Al-Tabṣīr fī al-Dīn wa-Tamyīz al-Firḳah al-Nājiyah 'an al-Firaḳ al-Hālikīn*, Cairo, 1374 A.H. [1955].

Jurjānī, *Sharḥ al-Mawāḳif*, ed. Th. Sörensen (Latin title: *Statio quinta et sexta et appendix libri Mevakif. Auctore el-Īgī cum commentario Gorgānii*), Leipzig, 1848.

——— *Kitāb al-Ta'rīfāt*, ed. G. Flügel, Leipzig, 1845.

Juwaynī, *Al-Irshād fī Uṣūl al-I'tiḳād*, ed. and trans. into French by J. D. Luciani, Paris, 1938.

——— *Al-'Aḳīdah al-Niẓāmiyyah fī al-Arkān al-Islāmiyyah*, Cairo, 1367 A.H. [1948].

Malaṭī, *Kitāb al-Tanbīh wa'l-Radd 'alā Ahl al-Ahwā' wa'l-Bida'*, ed. S. Dedering, Leipzig, 1936.

Mas'ūdī, *Murūj al-Dhahab wa-Ma'ādin al-Jauhar*, ed. and trans. into French by C. Barbier de Meynard and Pavet de Courteille (French title: *Les Prairies d'or*), Paris, 1861–1877.

——— *Al-Tanbīh wa'l-Ishrāf*, ed. M. de Goeje, Leiden, 1894.

Māwardī, *A'lām al-Nubuwwah*, Cairo, 1330 A.H. [1911].

Muḥāsibī, *Kitāb al-Ri'āya Liḥuqūq Allāh*, ed. Margaret Smith, London, 1940.

Muslim Ibn al-Ḥajjāj, *Ṣaḥīḥ Muslim*, Cairo, 1374 A.H. [1955]. *Ḳadar* in vol. IV.

Pseudo-Aristotle, *Kitāb Uthūlūjiyya Arisṭūṭālīs*, ed. Fr. Dieterici (German title: *Die sogenannte Theologie des Aristoteles*), Leipzig, 1882.

See also Plotinus.

Pseudo-Plutarch, *De Placitis Philosophorum* (*Al-Ārā' al-Ṭabī'iyyah*), Arabic trans. by Ḳustā Ibn Lūḳā, ed. 'Abd al-Raḥmān Badawī in his *Aristotelis De Anima et Plutarchi De Placitis Philosophorum*, Cairo, 1954.

See also Aëtius.

Rāzī, *Muḥaṣṣal Afkār al-Mutaḳaddimīn wa'l-Muta'aḫḫirīn*, Cairo, 1323 A.H. [1905].

Shahrastānī, *Kitāb al-Milal wa al-Niḥal*, ed. W. Cureton (English title: *Book of Religious and Philosophical Sects*), London, 1846.

German trans. by Th. Haarbrücker, *Scharastani's Religionspartheien*, Halle, 1850–1851.

——— *Nihāyat al-Iḳdām fī 'Ilm al-Kalām*, ed. and trans. into English by A. Guillaume (English title: *The Summa Philosophiae of al-Shahrastānī*), London, 1934.

Ṭabarī, *Annales quos scripsit . . . at-Tabari*, ed. M. J. de Goege, Lugd. Bat., 1879–1901.

Taftāzānī, *Sharḥ al-'Aḳā'id al-Nasafiyyah*, Cairo, 1335 A.H.

English trans. by E. E. Elder, *Sa'd al-Dīn al-Taftāzānī on the Creed of Najd al-Dīn al-Nasafī*, New York, 1950.

Ṭūsī, *Commentary on Faḫr al-Dīn al-Rāzī's Muḥaṣṣal*, in 1905 edition of *Muḥaṣṣal*.

II. JEWISH WORKS AND WRITERS

References to the Mishnah, Talmud, and Midrash are to the standard editions unless otherwise noted. Certain texts written in Arabic by Jewish authors have been cited throughout the book by their Hebrew titles. In such instances, the Arabic title is given below, followed by the familiar Hebrew title in brackets.

Aaron ben Elijah of Nicomedia, *'Eṣ Ḥayyim*, ed. F. Delitzsch and M. Steinschneider, Leipzig, 1841.

Abraham Ibn Daud, *Emunah Ramah*, ed. and trans. into German by S. Weil, Frankfurt a. M., 1852.

Avicebrol (Ibn Gabirol), *Fons Vitae* (Latin trans. by John Hispalensis), ed. C. Baeumker, Monasterii Aschendorff, 1895.

Baḥya Ibn Paḳuda, *Al-Hidāyāh 'ilā Farā'iḍ al-Ḳulūb* [Hebrew: *Ḥobot ha-Lebabot*], ed. A. S. Yahuda, Leiden, 1912.

Hebrew trans. by Judah Ibn Tibbon, Wilna, n.d.

English trans. by M. Hyamson, *Duties of the Heart*, New York, 1925–1945.

Crescas, Hasdai, *Or Adonai*, Vienna, 1859.

Efodi, Commentary on Maimonides' *Moreh Nebukim*, in the Wilna, 1914, edition of that work.

Falaquera, Shem-ṭob ben Joseph, *Moreh ha-Moreh*, Pressburg, 1837.

—— *Reshit Ḥokmah*, ed. M. David, Berlin, 1902.

Gersonides, *Milḥamot Adonai*, Leipzig, 1866.

Ibn Janaḥ, *Kitāb al-Luma'* [Hebrew: *Sefer ha-Riḳmah*], ed. J. Derenbourg, Paris, 1886.

Hebrew translation by Judah Ibn Tibbon, ed. M. Wilensky, Berlin, 1929.

Isaac Israeli, *Kitāb al-Ḥudūd wa'l-Rusūm*, ed. Hartwig Hirschfeld, *JQR* 15 (1902–1903), 689–693.

Hebrew: *Sefer ha-Gebulim*, ed. Hirschfeld in *Festschrift zum 80. Geburtstag Moritz Steinschneiders*, Leipzig, 1896.

Latin: *Liber Definitionum*, in *Omnia Opera Ysaac*, Lyon, 1515.

—— *Sefer ha-Yesodot*, ed. S. Fried (German title: *Das Buch über die Elemente*), Drohobycz, 1900.

Latin: *Liber de Elementis*, in *Omnia opera Ysaac*, Lyon, 1515.

Joseph al-Baṣīr, *Kitāb al-Muḥtawī*, MS., Budapest.

Hebrew: *Sefer ha-Ne'imot*, MS. Leiden.

Kitāb al-Muḥtawī, ed. M. Klein and E. Morgenstern, Budapest, 1913.

—— *Tamyīz*, MS. British Museum.

Hebrew: *Maḥkimat Peti*, MS. Leiden.

Joseph Ibn Ṣaddiḳ, *'Olam Ḳaṭan*, ed. S. Horowitz (German title: *Der Mikrokosmos des Josef Ibn Ṣaddiḳ*), Breslau, 1903.

Judah b. Barzillai, *Perush Sefer Yeṣirah*, ed. S. J. Halberstam, Berlin, 1885.

Judah Hadassi, *Eshkol ha-Kofer*, Eupatoria, 1836.

Judah Halevi, *Cuzari*, Arabic with Hebrew translation by Judah Ibn Tibbon, ed. by Hartwig Hirschfeld (German title: *Das Buch al-Chazari*), Leipzig, 1887.

English: *Judah Hallevi's Kitāb al-Khazari*, by H. Hirschfeld, revised edition, London, 1931.

Ḳirḳisānī, *Kitāb al-Anwār wa'l Marāḳib*, ed. Leon Nemoy, New York, 1939–1943.

Maimonides, Abraham, *Milḥamot ha-Shem*, in *Ḳobes Teshubot ha-Rambam*, ed. A. L. Lichtenberg, Leipzig, 1859, vol. III, pp. 15a–21b.

Maimonides, Moses, *Ḍalālat al-Ḥa'irīn* [Hebrew: *Moreh Nebukim*], ed. I. Joël, Jerusalem, 1930–1931.

Hebrew translation by Samuel Ibn Tibbon, Wilna, 1914.
Hebrew translation by Judah al-Harizi, ed L. Schlossberg, 3 vols., London, 1851, 1876, 1879.
Latin translation [from Harizi's Hebrew]: *Rabi Mossei Aegyptii Dux seu Director dubitantium aut perplexorum*, Paris: A. Justinianus, 1520.
French: *Le Guide des Égarés*, Arabic text, ed. and tr. into French by Salomon Munk, Paris, 3 v., 1856–1866.
English: *The Guide of the Perplexed*, tr. and ed. by Michael Friedlaender, London, 3 vols., 1881–1885.
English: *The Guide of the Perplexed*, tr. S. Pines, Chicago, 1963.
German: *Führer der Unschlüssingen*, tr. and ed. by Adolf Weiss, Leipzig, 1923.
——— *Maḳālah fī Ṣinā'at al-Manṭiḳ* [Hebrew: *Millot ha-Higgayon*], Arabic and Hebrew ed. and trans. into English by I. Efros (English title: *Maimonides' Treatise on Logic*), New York, 1938.
——— *Maḳālah fī Teḥiyyat ha-Metim* [Hebrew: *Ma'amar Teḥiyyat ha-Metim*], Arabic with Hebrew translation by Samuel Ibn Tibbon, ed. by Joshua Finkel (English title: *Maimonides' Treatise on Resurrection*), *PAAJR*, 9:57 ff., 1939.
——— *Teshubot.*
Ḳobeṣ Teshubot ha-Rambam we-Iggerotaw, ed. A. L. Lichtenberg, Leipzig, 1859.
Teshubot ha-Rambam, ed. A. H. Freimann, Jerusalem, 1934.
——— *Thamāniyah Fuṣūl* [Hebrew: *Shemonah Peraḳim*], ed. and trans. into German by M. Wolff (German title: *Mūsā Maimūnī's Acht Capitel*), 2nd. ed., Leiden, 1903.
Hebrew trans. by Samuel Ibn Tibbon, ed. and trans. into English by J. Gorfinkle (English title: *The Eight Chapters of Maimonides on Ethics*), New York, 1912.
Naḥmanides, *Iggeret ha-Ramban*, in *Ḳobeṣ Teshubot ha-Rambam*, ed. A. L. Lichtenberg, Leipzig, 1859, vol. III, pp. 8a–10b.
Narboni, *Beur le-Sefer Moreh Nebukim* (Commentary on Moreh Nebukim), ed. J. Goldenthal, Vienna, 1852.
Philo. *Philo* [complete works], with an English translation, ed. F. H. Colson and G. H. Whitaker (Loeb Classical Library), 12 vols., 1955–1963.
Saadia, *Kitāb al-Amānāt wa'l-I'tiḳādāt* [Hebrew: *Emunot we-De'ot*], ed. S. Landauer, Leiden, 1880.
Hebrew trans. by Judah Ibn Tibbon, Yosefov, 1885.
English: *The Book of Beliefs and Opinions*, tr. Samuel Rosenblatt, New Haven, 1948.
——— *Tafsīr Kitāb al-Mabādī* (*Commentary on Sefer Yeṣirah*), ed. and trans. into French by M. Lambert (French title: *Commentaire sur la Séfer Yesira*), Paris, 1891.
Taḳu, Moses, *Ketab Tamim*, in *Ozar Nechmad* III, Vienna, 1860, pp. 58–99.

III. GREEK AND LATIN WORKS AND WRITERS

Citations of Aristotle follow the numbering of Immanuel Bekker's edition, *Aristotelis Opera*, Berlin, 1831–1871. Greek texts of Aristotle cited are available with English translation on facing pages in the Loeb Classical Library, as are the texts cited of Cicero, Diogenes Laertius, Lucretius, Plato, Pliny, Plutarch, and Seneca. Works of which other editions have been used or specifically mentioned are listed here.

Aëtius (pseudo-Plutarch), *De Placitis Philosophorum*, in H. Diels, *Doxographi Graeci*, 3rd ed., 1929.

Arabic translation by Ḳusṭā Ibn Lūḳā, *Al-Ārā' al-Tabī'iyyah*, ed. 'Abd al-Raḥmān Badawī in his *Aristotelis De Anima et Plutarchi De Placitis Philosophorum*, Cairo, 1954.

Alexander Aphrodisiensis, *De Fato*, in *Alexandri Aphrodisiensis praetor commentaria scripta minora*, ed. Ivo Bruns, part II, Berlin, 1892.

Aristotle, *De Anima* [*LCL*].

Aristotle: De Anima, ed. R. D. Hicks, Cambridge, England, 1907.

Arabic translation by Isḥāḳ Ibn Hunain, *Fī al-Nafs*, ed. 'Abd al-Raḥmān Badawī in his *Aristotelis De Anima et Plutarchi De Placitis Philosophorum*, Cairo, 1954.

——— *De Interpretatione* [*LCL*].

Arabic translation by Iṣhāk Ibn Hunain: *Fī al 'Ibārah*, ed. I. Pollak in *Abhandlungen für die Kunde des Morgenlandes*, Bd. 13, no. 1, Leipzig, 1913; and in *Alfarabi's Commentary on Aristotle's De Interpretatione*, ed. W. Kutsch and S. Marrow, Beirut, 1960.

——— *Aristotle's Metaphysics*. A revised text with introduction and commentary by W. D. Ross, Oxford, 1924.

——— *Organon Aristotelis in versione Arabica antiqua* [Arabic title: *Manṭiḳ Arisṭū*], ed. 'Abd al-Raḥmān Badawī, Cairo, 1948–1952.

Damascius. *Damasci philosophi Platonici Quaestiones de primis principiis*, ed. Joseph Kopp, Frankfurt am Main, 1826.

Diogenes Laertius, *Lives of Eminent Philosophers with an English translation*, by R. D. Hicks. 2 vols. 1925 [*LCL*].

Euclid. *Euclidis Opera Omnia*, ed. I. L. Herberg and H. Menge [Greek and Latin], 8 vols. Leipzig, 1883–1916.

Galen. *Claudii Galeni opera omnia*, vols. I, III, V, in the series *Medicorum Graecorum Opera quae exstant*, ed. C. G. Kühn, 26 vols., Leipzig, 1821–1830.

Palaephatus. *Palaephati Peri Apiston* [*De Incredilibus*], ed. Nicolaus Festa, in *Mythographi Graeci*, vol. III, fasc. II (Leipzig, 1902).

Pliny, *Naturalis Historia* [*LCL*].

Caii Plinii Secundi Naturalis historiae libri xxxvii. interpretatione et notis illustravit Joannes Hardainus . . . in usum Serenissimi Delphini, Paris, 1685.

Plotinus, *Enneads* I–III, ed. and tr. into English by Arthur H. Armstrong (*LCL*).

Enneades I–V, in *Plotini opera*, ed. Paul Henry and H. R. Schwyzer, vols. I and II, Brussels, 1951, 1959.

English: *Plotinus: The Enneads*, trans. by Stephen McKenna; 4th ed., rev. by B. S. Page, London, 1969.

——— *Uthūlūjiyya* ("the Arabic version of his work"), see pseudo-Aristotle, List I above.

Plutarch, *Adversus Coloten*, in *Plutarch's Moralia*, vol. XIV, ed. and tr. B. Einarson and P. H. DeLacey (*LCL*, 1967).

Porphyry. *Porphyrii Isagoge et in Aristotelis Categorias commentarium*, ed. Adolphus Busse [Commentaria in Aristotelem Graeca, vol. IV, part I], Berlin, 1887.

Proclus, *Institutio Theologica . . . The Elements of Theology. A revised text, with translation, introduction, and commentary* by E. R. Dodds. Oxford, 1933.

——— *Procli Diadochi in Platonis Timaeum Commentaria* [Greek and Latin], ed. Ernest Diehl. Leipzig, 1903.

——— *Procli successoris Platonici in Platonis Theologiam*, Hamburg, 1618. Greek text, ed., with Latin translation, by Aemilius Portus.

——— *The Six Books of Proclus . . . on the Theology of Plato* translated from the Greek . . . by Thomas Taylor, 2 vols. London, 1816.

Simplicius. *Simplicii in Aristotelis Physicorum libros quattuor priores commentaria*, ed. H. Diels, Berlin, 1882, and . . . *libros quattuor posteriores* . . . , ed. Diels, Berlin, 1895 (vols. IX and X, respectively, in Commentaria Aristotelem Graeca).

Themistius. *Themistii in Libros Aristotelis De Anima Paraphrasis*, ed. R. Heinze [Commentaria in Aristotelem Graeca, vol. V, part III], Berlin, 1899.

IV. CHRISTIAN WORKS AND WRITERS

Texts of many of the Church Fathers are cited from J. P. Migne's *Patrologia Latina* (*PL*) or his *Patrologia Graeca* (*PG*); English translations of a number of these are included in *The Ante-Nicene Fathers* (*AN*), ed. A. C. Coxe, or in the two series of *A Select Library of Nicene and Post-Nicene Fathers of the Christian Church* (*NPN*), ed. Philip Schaff and Henry Wace. Other editions used or specifically mentioned are described in this list.

Abucara (Abū Qurra, Theodore, Bishop of Harran), *Fī Wujūd al-Ḫāliḳ wa'l-Dīn al-Ḳawīm*, ed. Louis Cheikho in *Al-Mashrik* 15:758–774 (1912).

German translation by Georg Graf, *Des Theodor Abū Kurra Traktat über den Schöpfer und die wahre religion* (Beiträge zur Geschichte der Philosophie des Mittelalters, Bd. 14, Heft 1), Münster, 1913.

——— *Mimar*. In *Les Oeuvres arabes de Théodore Aboucara*, ed. C. Bacha, Beyrouth, 1904, supplemented by Opuscula XXV and G. Graf's German translations in "Die arabischen Schriften des Abū Qurra," in *Forschungen zur christliche Literatur- und Dogmengeschichte* 10:67–78 and 188–191 (Paderborn, 1910).

——— *Opuscula ascetica* in Migne, *PG* 97.

Albertus Magnus, *Opera omnia*, Paris, 1890–1899 (vol. III, *Physicorum*; vols. XXV–XXX, *Commentarii in libros quatuor Sententiarum Petri Lombardi*).

Athanasius, *Epistola de synodis Arimini in Italia, et Seleuciae in Isauria, celebratis*, *PG* 26.

"On the Councils of Ariminum and Seleucia," J. H. Newman's translation, revised, *NPN* 2 ser. V.

——— *Orationes contra Arianos*, *PG* 26.

"Four Discourses against the Arians," *NPN* 2 ser. V.

Athenagoras, *Supplicatio pro Christianis* . . . ed. Ludwig Paul. Halis, 1856.

Legatio pro Christianis, *PG* 6.

"A Plea for the Christians," *AN* II.

Augustine, *De Civitate Dei*, *PL* 41; *LCL*; *NPN* II.

——— *De Trinitate*, *PL* 42; *NPN* III.

——— *De Anima*, *PL* 44; *NPN* V.

——— *Enchiridion*, *PL* 40.

"On Faith, Hope, and Love," *NPN* III.

Basil, *Epistolae*, *PG* 32; *LCL*.

English: *Letters*, tr. by Sister Agnes Clare Way, with notes by Roy J. Deferrari, 2 vols., New York, 1951, 1955 (The Fathers of the Church, a new translation, vols. 13, 28).

——— *Hexaemeron*, in *PG* 29; *NPN* 2 ser. VIII.

——— *Homilia*, in *PG* 31.

Bonaventura, *Opera Theologica Selecta*, ed. L. M. Bello, Tom. II: *Liber II Sententiarum*, Firenze, 1938.

Elias of Nisibis (Eliā Bar Sināyā), *Kitāb al-Burhān 'ala Ṣaḥīḥ al-Imān*, trans. into German by L. Horst, *Des Metropoliten Elias von Nisibis Buch vom Beweis der Wahrheit des Glaubens*, Colmar, 1886.

Epiphanius, *Adversus Octoginta Haereses, opus quod inscribitur Panarium sive Arcula*, in Migne, *PG* 41.

——— *Panarion*, ed. Karl Holl, Leipzig, 1933. (Die griechischen christlichen Schrifsteller der ersten drei Jahrhunderte).

Gregory of Nyssa, *Oratio Catechitica Magna*, *PG* 45.

"The Great Catechism," *NPN* 2 ser. V.

Hermas, *Pastor*, *PG* 2.

"The Pastor of Hermas," *AN* II.

Hippolytus, *Contra Haeresin Noëti*, *PG* 10.

——— *Refutatio omnium haeresium* (*Philosophumena*), ed. Paul Wendland, Leipzig, 1916, in *Hippolytus Werke*, vol. III (Die griechischen christlichen Schriftsteller der ersten drei Jahrhunderte).

("Philosophumena" in *PG* 16 was still ascribed to Origen.)

"The Refutation of All Heresies," *AN* V.

Ibn Suwār, *Maḳālah l'Abī al-Ḫayir al-Ḥasan Ibn Suwār al-Baghdādī*, ed. 'Abd al-Raḥmān Badawī in his *Neoplatonici apud Arabes*, Cairo, 1955.

French translation by B. Lewin, in *Donum Natalicium H. S. Nyberg Oblatum*, Uppsala, 1954.

Irenaeus, *Adversus Haereses*, *PG* 7.

English: *Five Books of S. Irenaeus, Bishop of Lyons, against Heresies*, translated by the Rev. John Keble, Oxford, 1872.

John Philoponus, *Ioannes Philoponus De aeternitate mundi contra Proclum* editit Hugo Rabe, Lipsius, 1899 (Bibliotheca scriptorum graecorum et romanorum Teubneriana).

——*Joannis Philoponi De opificio mundi libri VII*, recensuit Gualterus Reichardt, Lipsiae, 1897 (Bibliotheca . . . Teubneriana).

Justin Martyr, *Dialogus cum Tryphone Judaeo*, *PG* 6.

Nicolaus of Autrecourt.

Nicolaus von Autrecourt: Sein Leben, seine Philosophie, seine Schriften, ed. Joseph Lappe (Beiträge zur Geschichte der Philosophie des Mittelalters, Bd. VI, Heft 2), Münster, 1908.

Occam. *Quod libeta septum una cum tractatu de sacramento Altaris Venerabilis inceptaris fratris Guilhelme de Ockham*, Argētine [Strasbourg], 1491.

Origen, *Contra Celsum*, *PG* 11.

Gegen Celsus, ed. Paul Koetschau, in *Origenes Werke*, vols. I, II, Leipzig, 1899 (Die griechischen christlichen Schriftsteller der ersten drei Jahrhunderte).

English: *Origen: Contra Celsum*, tr. with intro. and notes by Henry Chadwick, Cambridge, 1953; Origen against Celsus, *AN* IV.

——*In Joannem Commentarii*, *PG* 14.

Der Johanneskommentar, ed. Erwin Preuschen, in *Origines Werke*, vol. IV, Leipzig, 1903 (Die griechischen christlichen Schriftsteller der ersten drei Jahrhunderte).

Origenes. Commentary on St. John's Gospel; the text revised with a critical introduction and indices, by A. E. Brooke; 2 vols., Cambridge, 1896.

English translation: *AN* X.

——*In Matthaeum Commentariorum Series*, *PG* 13.

Paul Rahib [the Monk] of Antioch, Bishop of Sidon. Letter to a Muslim Friend [Arabic text], in *Vingt Traités*, ed. L. Cheikho, pp. 15–26; ed. and tr. into French by Louis Buffat, *Revue de l'Orient Chrétien* 8:388–425 (1903).

——*Maḳālah fī al-Firaḳ al-Muta'ārafah baina al-Naṣārā*, in *Vingt Traités*, pp. 27–34.

German translation by G. Graf in *Jahrbuch für Philosophie und Spekulativ Theologie* 20:172–179 (1905).

Tertullian, *Liber adversus Hermogenem*, *PL* 2:220–263.

——*Libri quinque adversus Marcionem*, *PL* 2:263 ff.; *Liber secundus*, 307–347.

——— *Liber adversus Praxeam*, *PL* 2:175–220.

English translations, *AN* III.

Theodore of Mopsuestia. *Theodori Episcopi Mopsuesteni in Epistolis B. Pauli Commentarii*, the Latin version with the Greek fragments, ed. H. B. Swete, vol. I, Cambridge, 1880.

Thomas Aquinas. *Doctoris Angelici ordinis Praedicatorum Opera Omnia*, Parmae, 1852–1873. (Photographic reprint with intro. by V. J. Bourke, 25 vols., New York, 1948–1949).

——— [*Summa*] *de veritate catholicae fidei contra gentiles*, vol. V in Parma edition.

——— *De Potentia Dei*, vol. VIII, *ibid.*

——— *De Veritate*, vol. IX, *ibid.*

——— *In octos libros physicorum expositio*, vol. XVIII, *ibid.*

——— *Scriptum in quatuor libros Sententiarum Magistri Petri Lombardi* [I and II], vol. VI, *ibid.*

——— *Summa Theologica* I, vol. I.

English: *Summa Theologica* . . . Literally translated by Fathers of the English Dominican Province, London, 1911–1922.

Timothy, Nestorian patriarch of Antioch. "The Apology of Timothy the Patriarch before the Caliph Mahdi," Syriac text, ed. and tr. into English by Alphonse Mingana, in *Bulletin of the John Rylands Library*, Manchester, England, January 1928, pp. 137–298. Reprinted in *Woodbrooke Studies*, vol. 2 (1928).

Yaḥyā Ibn ʿAdī, see note on p. 351, above.

V. PERIODICALS, SERIES, AND REFERENCE WORKS

[*AN*]. *The Ante-Nicene Fathers*, 10 v., New York, 1885–1896; American reprint, revised by Arthur Cleveland Coxe from *The Ante-Nicene Christian Library*, Edinburgh, 1867–1872, ed. Alexander Roberts and James Donaldson.

Archiv für Geschichte der Philosophie, Berlin, 1888+.

[*DCB*]. *Dictionary of Christian Biography, Literature, Sects and Doctrines during the first eight centuries*, 4 v., London, 1877–1887; ed. William Smith and Henry Wace.

[*DTC*]. *Dictionnaire de Theologie Catholique*, 15 v. in 23, Paris, 1903–1950; ed. A. Vacant and E. Mangenot; continued under E. Amann.

[*EI*]. *Encyclopaedia of Islam*, 4 v., Leiden and London, 1913–1934; Supplement, 1938.

New edition, Leiden, 1954——.

[*ERE*]. *Encyclopaedia of Religion and Ethics*, 13 v., Edinborough and New York, 1908–1927; ed. James Hastings.

[*HTR*]. *Harvard Theological Review*, Cambridge, Massachusetts, 1908+.

Islam, Der, Berlin, 1910+; text in English, French, and German.

[*JE*]. *Jewish Encyclopedia, The*, 12 vols., New York and London, 1901–1906 (new edition, copyright 1925).

[*JQR*]. *Jewish Quarterly Review*, v. 1–20, London, 1888–1908; new series, Philadelphia, 1910+.

Journal Asiatique, Paris, 1822+.

[*JAOS*]. *Journal of the American Oriental Society*, New Haven, Connecticut, 1843+.

[*JRAS*]. *Journal of the Royal Asiatic Society*, London, 1834–1863; n.s., 1864–1889; 3 ser., 1889+.

Lisān al-'Arab, by Ibn Manẓūr, 20 v., Bulaq, Egypt, 1300–1308 A.H. [1882–1889].

[*LCL*]. Loeb Classical Library, Cambridge, Massachusetts, and London, 1912+.

Mashrik [*Al-Machriq*], Beirut, 1898+; issued under the direction "des Pères de l'Université St Joseph." French title page, Arabic text.

[*MGWJ*]. *Monatsschrift für Geschichte und Wissenschaft des Judentums*, Breslau, 1851+.

Muslim World, The (Hartford Seminary Foundation), New York and London, 1911+; (1911–October 1947 as *Moslem World*).

Ozar Nechmad, 4 numbers, Vienna, 1856–1863.

[*PG*]. *Patrologia Graeca*, ed. J. P. Migne, Paris, 1845–1866.

[*PL*]. *Patrologia Latina*, ed. J. P. Migne, Paris, 1844–1865.

[*PAAJR*]. *Proceedings of the American Academy for Jewish Research*, Philadelphia, 1928+.

Revue de l'Orient Chrétien, v. 1–30, Paris, 1896–1946.

Revue des Études Augustiniennes, Paris, 1955+.

[*REJ*]. *Revue des Études Juives*, Paris, 1880+.

[*NPN*]. *A Select Library of Nicene and Post-Nicene Fathers of the Christian Church*, [two series] New York, 1886–1890 and 1890–1900, ed. by Philip Schaff and Henry Wace.

Studia Islamica, Paris, 1953+.

[*ZDMG*]. *Zeitschrift der Deutschen Morgenländischen Gesellschaft*, Leipzig, 1863+.

Zeitschrift für Assyriologie und vorder-asiatische Archäologie, Leipzig, 1886+.

INDEX OF REFERENCES

I. MUSLIM WORKS AND WRITERS

The Koran

Ṭabarī

Taftāzānī

Ṭūsī

II. JEWISH WORKS AND WRITERS

Scripture

III. GREEK AND LATIN WORKS AND WRITERS

XII, 4..22 | 5..428 | 6..1 | 7..226, 232, 499 | 9..232, 575 | 10, ..1 | Comm. 41..376
XIII, 8..480, 485, 492

Ethica Nicomachea I, 4..22, 291, 328 || II, 4..617 || III, 3..588 || V, 6..22 || VI, 2..588

Ethica Eudemia II, 6..641

Rhetorica I, 2..33, 451 | 4..451 | 10..556, 557 | 11..546, 548 | 15..33 || II, 24..451 || III, 10..24, 291

Poetica 7..431 || 21..24, 291

De Motu Animalium 10..645

De Generatione Animalium II, 2..588

De Plantis II..557

CICERO

De Natura Deorum..12, 545

De Fato..618, 693

DAMASCIUS

Philosophi Platonici 54..123

DIOGENES LAËRTIUS

De Vita et Moribus Philosophorum VII, 141..448 | 156..508 || IX, 22..159 | 31 and 44..493 || X, 42..493 | 43..489 | 44..491 | 54..488 | 55..472 | 56..491

EUCLID

Elements I..486

GALEN

De Usu partium corporis humani IX, 14..585

De Elementis ex Hippocrate I, 1..478

De Hippocratis et Platonis Placitis VIII, 2..478

LUCRETIUS

De Rerum Natura I, 268–270..491 || II, 730–859..488 || III, 348, 502..192 || V, 924..545 || VI, 880..599

PALAEPHATUS

De Incredilibus 3..585

PLATO

Phaedrus 247 E..361

Republic IV, 439 CD..633 | IX, 586 D..638

Sophist 246 B..361 | 248 E..361 | 254 E..151

Timaeus 27 D..361 | 28 A..382, 554 | 29 E–30 A..574 | 30 B, 48 A..574 | 41 E..574

PLINY

Naturalis Historia XII, 21, 38..598 || XIX, 2, 14..597 | 3, 17..598, 599

PLOTINUS

Enneads I, 1, 8..332 || II, 4, 16..365 || V, 8, 5..362 || *Uthūlūjiyya* ..362, 510

PLUTARCH

Adversus Coloten 4, p. 1108F..361 || 8, 1111B, C..467 | 1111C..492

PORPHYRY

Isagoge..154, 187, 196, 197

PROCLUS

Institutio Theologica..124, 142

In Timaeum..124, 142

In Platonis Theologiam..124, 142

SENECA

Epistola I, 8..361

SIMPLICIUS

In Physica VIII, 1..411, 415 | 10..374, 376

THEMISTIUS

In De Anima..481, 482

FRAGMENTS

Ammonius (Arnim)..202

Democritus..361, 477, 478

Galen? (Arnim)..286, 505

Parmenides..445

IV. CHRISTIAN WORKS AND WRITERS

EDITORS, TRANSLATORS, AND AUTHORS OF SECONDARY WORKS

This is not in any sense a complete list of materials used; it is intended primarily to complement information given in the footnotes. An asterisk (*) by a page number indicates that further information is to be found on that page; a dagger (†) by a name means that information will be found in the Bibliography under the name designated. Entries with neither symbol nor page reference record works Professor Wolfson used but did not have occasion to cite specifically in the book as it now stands.

Carra de Vaux, C. M. B., *Gazali*, Paris, 1902 . . 41
Chadwick, Henry, tr. Origen.†
Cheikho, Louis, ed. *Vingt Traités théologiques d'auteurs arabes Chrétiens, ixe–xiiie siècles*, 2nd ed., Beyrouth, 1920 . . 121, 122, 128–129
Corbin, Henry, *Histoire de la Philosophie Islamique*, Paris, 1964.
Crawford, Stuart, ed. Averroes † . . 482
Cureton, William, ed. Shahrastānī.†
Cherniss, Harold . . 480–481

Davidson, Herbert A., "John Philoponus as a Source of Medieval Islamic and Jewish Proofs of Creation," *JAOS* 89:357–391 (1969).
Dedering, Sven, ed. Malatī.†
Deferri, Roy J., ed. Basil.†
Delitzsch, F. and Steinschneider, M., ed. Aaron b. Elijah.†
Derenbourg, J., ed. Ibn Janāh † . . 93
Diels, Hermann, ed. Aëtius † and Simplicius.†
——— *Doxographi Graeci*, Berlin, 1879; 3rd ed., 1929; see Aëtius.
——— *Die Fragmente der Vorsokratiker*, Berlin, 1912 . . 361, 476
Dieterici, Friedrich, ed. Alfarabi † and pseudo-Aristotle.†
Diwald-Wilzer, Susanna, ed. *Ibn al-Murtaḍā*.†

Eckmann, Karl Friedrich, tr. Ghazālī . . 639 *
Efros, Israel, ed. and tr. Maimonides.†
Elder, Earl Edgar, tr. *A Commentary on the Creed of Islam; Sa'd al-Din al-Taftāzānī on the Creed of Najm al-Dīn al-Nasafī*, New York, 1950 . . 94, 215, 282, 659, 714, 715

Fakhry, Majid, *A History of Islamic Philosophy*, New York, 1970.
Finkel, Joshua, ed. Maimonides † . . 107
Flügel, G., ed. Jurjānī.†
Fobes, Francis Howard, ed. Averroes † . . 466
Forget, J., ed. Avicenna.†
Frank, Richard M., "Al-Ma'anā, some Reflections on the Technical Meaning of the Term and its use in the Physics of Mu'ammar," *JAOS* 87:248 (1967).
Frankl, P. F., quotes Joseph al-Baṣīr † . . 113,* 346 *
Freimann, A. H., ed. Maimonides † . . 95, 107
Fried, S., ed. Isaac Israeli . . 478 *
Friedlaender, Israel . . 91, n. 35 [*for* 1:602, n. 5 *read* 1:187, n. 6], 209,* 315,* 563,* 676 *
Friedländer, Michael, tr. Maimonides † . . 55

Gardet, Louis and M. M. Anawati, *Introduction à la Théologie Musulmane*, Paris, 1948 . . 19, 40, 41, 61, 63, 64, 119
Geiger, Abraham, *Was hat Mohammed aus dem Judenthume aufgenommen?* Bonn, 1833; 2 rev. aufl. Leipzig, 1902 . . 305

——— [*Kalam*] *Ueber den Einfluss der griechischen Philosophie auf die Entwicklung des Kalam*, Breslau, 1909 . . 65, 164, 167, 182, 628 *
——— *Die Psychologie bei den jüdischen Religions-Philosophen des Mittelalters von Saadia bis Maimuni*, 4 v., Breslau, 1898, 1900, 1906, 1912.
Horst, L., ed. Elias of Nisibis † . . 304,* 315
Horten, Max, *Die Philosophie des Islam*, Munich, 1924 . . 182
——— [*Probleme*]. *Die philosophischen Probleme der spekulativen Theologie im Islam*, Bonn, 1910 . . 141, 360, 487, 491
——— *Die philosophischen Systeme des spekulativen Theologen im Islam*, Bonn, 1912 . . 34, 35, 66, 67, 112, 115, 164,* 182, 258, 360, 664
——— articles in periodicals . . 67,* 115,* 164,* 167,* 182,* 513 *
Houdas, O. and W. Marçais, tr. Buḥārī †: *El Bokhari: Les Traditions islamiques*, Paris, 1903–1914, . . 627

Ibn Ḥunayn, Isḥaḳ, tr. Aristotle . . 371
Ibn Tibbon, Judah, tr. Baḥya Ibn Pakuda † and Saadia † . . 96
Ibn Tibbon, Samuel, tr. Maimonides † . . 56, 96

Joël, I., ed. Maimonides.†
Joel, M., *Albert*, Breslau, 1863 . . 455 *
Justinianus, A., ed. Maimonides.†

Kahn, Charles H. . . 476
Kalonymus b. David, tr. Averroes . . 598
Kalonymus b. Kalonymus, tr. Averroes . . 597
Kaufmann, David, *Geschichte der Attributenlehre in der jüdischen Religionsphilosophie des Mittelalters von Saadja bis Maimûni*, Gotha, 1877 . . 98, 122, 631
Keble, John, tr. Irenaeus.†
Klein, W. C., tr. Ash'arī.†
Kopp, Joseph, ed. Damascius . . 123 *
Krehl, M. Ludolf, and Th. W. Juynboll, ed. Buhārī † . . 626
Kremer, Alfred von, *Culturgeschichtliche Streifzüge auf dem Gebiete des Islams* [Arab. & Pers.], Leipzig, 1873 . . 61 *
——— *Geschichte der herrschenden Ideen des Islam*, Leipzig, 1868 . . 671
Kuhn, C. G., ed. Galen.†
Kutsch, W., and S. Marrow, ed. Alfarabi † . . 371

Lambert, M., ed. and tr. Saadia.†
Landauer, Samuel, ed. Saadia.†
Lappe, Joseph, ed. Nicolaus † . . 594
Lasswitz, Kurd, *Geschichte der Atomistik vom Mittelalter bis Newton*, Hamburg and Leipzig, 1890 . . 467
Lewin, Bernhard, tr. Ibn Suwār . . 80,* 374 *
Lichtenberg, A. L., ed. Maimonides.†

Löw, Immanuel, *Die Flora der Juden*, Vienna and Leipzig, 1928 . . 598
Luciani, J. D., ed. and tr. Juwaynī.†

Mabilleau, Léopold, *Histoire de la philosophie atomistique*, Paris, 1895, . . 59, 67, 470, 473
McCarthy, R. J., ed. and tr. Ash'arī †; ed. Bakillānī †; tr. Ibn 'Asākir.†
Macdonald, Duncan Black, *Development of Muslim Theology, Jurisprudence, and Constitutional Theory*, New York, 1903, 26, 62, 63, 167, 283, 289
——— tr. Faḍālī's *Kifāyat*.†

Madkour (Madkūr), Ibrahim, *L'Organon d'Aristote dans le monde Arabe*, Paris, 1934 . . 21
Makdisi, George, ed. Ibn Ḳudāmah † . . 96
Malter, Henry, *Saadia Gaon: His Life and Works*, Philadelphia, 1921 . . 89, 98
Mangenot, E. . . 511
Margoliouth, David Samuel . . 7 *
——— *The Early Development of Mohammedanism*, London, 1914 . . 13
Meier, Fritz [Friedrich Max] . . . (Wiesbaden, 1957) . . 626
Mingana, Alphonse, ed. and tr. Timothy † . . 311–313
Muckle, J. T., ed. Ghazālī † . . 351,* 458
Müller, M. J., ed. Averroes.†
Muhammed Ali, Maulvi, tr. *The Holy Qur-án, containing the Arabic text with English translation and commentary*, Woking, England, 1917 . . 305, 311, 358, 570
Munk, Salomon, ed. and tr. Maimonides: *Le Guide des égarés* publié pour la première fois dans l'original Arabe et accompagné d'une traduction française et de notes critiques, littéraires, et explicatives par S. Munk, 3 tom. Paris, 1856–66 . . 55, 85, 89, 90, 91, 113, 167
——— *Mélanges de philosophie juive et arabe*, Paris, 1859 . . 167
——— "Notice sur Abou'l-Walid Merwan Ibn-Djana'h" . . 93 *

Nader, Albert N., ed. and tr. Ḫayyāṭ.†
——— *Le Systeme Philosophique des Mu'tazila*, 1956 . . 167,* 182
Nallino, C. A. . . 19,* 619 *
Nemoy, Leon, ed. Ḳirḳisānī.†
Neumark, David, *Geschichte der jüdischen Philosophie des Mittelalters nach Problemen dargestellt*, Berlin, 1907–1928; Hebrew translation: *Toledot ha-Filosofiah be-Yesra'el*, 2 v., New York, 1921, 1929 . . 69, 70, 357, 385
Nöldeke, Theodor, *Sketches from Eastern History* translated by J. S. Black and revised by the author (London 1892) . . 307
Nyberg, H. S. . . 362 *

Palmer, E. H., tr., *The Qur'ān*, Oxford, 1880 . . 358
Patton, Walter M., *Aḥmad Ibn Ḥanbal and the Miḥnah*, Leiden, 1897 . . 31, 240, 241, 252, 253, 264, 294, 297

Pegues, Thomas, *Commentaire*, 10 v., Toulouse, 1907–1915 .. 455 *
Périer, Augustin, ed. Yaḥyā Ibn 'Adī .. 1, 55, 80, 81, 321 *
——— *Petits Traités apologétiques de Yahyâ ben 'Adî*; Texte arabe édité pour la première fois d'après les manuscrits de Paris, de Rome et de Munich et traduit en Français .. Paris, 1920 (Arabic and French)
——— *Yahyâ ben 'Adî, un philosophe arabe chrétien du Xe siècle*, Paris, 1920.
——— "Un Traité de Yahyâ ben 'Adī, Défense du Dogme de la Trinité contre les objections d'al-Kindi," *Revue de l'Orient Chrétien* 22:3–21 (1920–21).
Pines, Shlomo (Salomon), *Beiträge zur islamischen Atomenlehre*, Berlin, 1936 .. 67, 220, 221, 360, 361, 366, 467, 470, 473,* 487, 495, 506
——— "A Tenth Century Philosophical Correspondence," 90,* 374
——— article in *Revue des Études Juives*, 1938 .. 630 *
——— tr. Maimonides' *Guide* † .. 55
Pinsker, S., *Likkute Kadmoniyyot* [i], Vienna, 1860 .. 573, 574
Pocock, E. .. 113 *
Pollak, Isidor, ed. Arabic tr. of Aristotle's *De Interpretatione* † .. 115
Poznanski, S. .. 306 *
Pretzl, Otto .. 472 *
Preuschen, Erwin, ed. Origen, *In Joan.*† .. 304

Quatremère, E. M., ed. Ibn Ḫaldūn.†

Rabe, Hugo, ed. John Philoponus.†
Rahman, F., ed. Avicenna † .. 639, 640
Reichart, G., ed. John Philoponus.†
Rescher, Nicholas, tr. Alfarabi.†
Ritter, Hellmut .. 613 *
——— ed. Ash'arī.†
Rodwell, J. M., tr. *The Koran; translated from the Arabic, the Surahs arranged in chronological order, with notes and index*, London, 1861 .. 358
Rosenthal, Franz, tr. Ibn Ḫaldūn † .. 13, 254
——— *The Muslim Concept of Freedom Prior to the Nineteenth Century*, Leiden, 1960 .. 13, 254, 622, 708
Ross, Sir William David, *Aristotle's Metaphysics*, a revised text with introduction and commentary, 1924 .. 417

Sale, George, tr. *The Koran* (London, 1734) .. 304, 305, 358
Salisbury, Edward E., in *Journal of the American Oriental Society* .. 602, 627
Schacht, Joseph, *The Origins of Muhammadan Jurisprudence*, Oxford, 1950; corrected ed., 1953 .. 7, 13, 29
——— "New Sources for the History of Muhammadan Theology," 1953 .. 671,* 711
Schmölders, Augustus, *Essai sur les Écoles philosophiques chez les Arabes*,

et notamment sur la doctrine d'Algazzali [with a polemical treatise of his in Arabic and French], Paris, 1842 . . 59, 66–67, 167, 182
Schreiner, Martin, *Zur Geschichte des Aš'aritenthums*, Leiden, 1890 . . 40, 656, 679
——— *Der Kalam in der jüdischen Literatur*, Berlin, 1895 . . 59, 69, 70, 89, 159, 263, 265, 360, 383, 450
——— "Studien über Jeschu'a ben Jehuda," *Bericht über die Lehrenstalt für die Wissenschaft des Judenthums in Berlin*, 18 (1900) . . 61, 397, 398, 608
——— [*Polemik*]: "Zur Geschichte der Polemik zwischen Juden und Muhammedanern," *ZDMG* 42:591–675 (1888) . . 75, 91
Seelye, Kate C., tr. Baghdādī.†
Sell, Charles Edward, *The Faith of Islam*, 3rd ed., London, 1907 . . 283
Sertillanges, A. D., tr. Thomas Aquinas' *Summa Theologica* . . 455
Smith, Margaret, ed. Muḥāsibī,† London, 1940 . . 636
Sörensen, Th., ed. Jurjānī † . . 658
Spitta, Wilhelm, *Zur Geschichte Abu'l-Hasan al-As'arī's*, Leipzig, 1876 . . 23
Stein, Ludwig . . 693
Steiner, Heinrich, *Die Mu'tazaliten oder die Freidenker in Islâm*, Leipzig, 1865 . . 512
Steinschneider, Moritz, *Al-Farabi*, in *Mémoires de l'Académie Impériale des Sciences de Saint-Petersbourg*, VII, 13, 4 (1869) . . 374, 433
——— *Die arabische Literatur der Juden*, Frankfurt, 1902 . . 82, 89, 90
——— *Die arabischen Übersetzungen aus dem Griechischen*, Leipzig, 1897 . . 22, 54, 148, 224, 411
——— *Die hebraeischen Uebersetzungen des Mittelalters und die Juden als Dolmetscher* (Berlin, 1893) . . 79, 597, 598
——— *Polemische und apologetische Literatur in arabische Sprache zwischen Muslimen, Christen und Juden* (Leipzig, 1877) . . 75, 305
——— with F. Delitzsch, ed. Aaron b. Elijah of Nicomedia,† *'Es Ḥayyim.*
Sweetman, J. W., *Islam and Christian Theology*, 2 v., 1945–1955 . . 61, 62, 115, 121, 341
Swete, H. B., ed. Theodore of Mopsuestia † . . 318

Taraporewala, Irach J. S. . . 632 *
Tornberg, C. J., ed. Ibn al-Athīr † . . 265, 266, 341
Torrey, Charles C., *The Commercial-Theological Terms in the Koran*, Leiden, 1892 . . 671
Tritton, Arthur Stanley, *Muslim Theology*, London, 1947 . . 34, 63, 167, 258, 495, 613
Türker, Mubahat, ed. Alfarabi † . . 405
Twersky, Isadore, *Rabad of Posquières*, Cambridge, Mass., 1962 . . 110

Ventura, Moïse, *La Philosophie de Saadia Gaon*, Paris, 1934 . . 405
Vignaux, P., article on Nominalism, *DTC* . . 353
Vlieger, A. de, ed. and tr. *Kitāb al Qadr* [Buḫārī, *al-Ṣaḥīḥ*], 1903 . . 627, 719

Watt, W. Montgomery, "Early Discussions" . . 264, 302 *
——— *Free Will and Predestination in Early Islam* (London, 1948) . . 61,* 602, 609, 613, 619, 627, 661, 683
Weil, G., in *Sefer Assaf*, ed. V. Cassuto, J. Klausner, and J. Gutmann, Jerusalem, 1952–53 . . 663 *
Weil, Salomon, ed. and tr. Abraham Ibn Daud.†
Weinberg, Julius Rudolph, *Nicolaus of Autrecourt, a Study in 14th Century Thought*, Princeton, 1948 . . 593, 594
Weiss, Adolf, tr. Maimonides † . . 55
Wendland, Paul, ed. Hippolytus.†
Wensinck, Arent Jan, *The Muslim Creed; Its Genesis and Historical Development*, Cambridge, England, 1932 . . 61, 62, 63, 94, 214, 245, 280, 367, 602, 613
——— "Lawh" in *Encyclopedia of Islam* . . 245
Wherry, E. M., *A Comprehensive Commentary on the Qurán, comprising Sale's translation and preliminary discourse with additional notes and emendations*, 1882 . . 304, 305
Wilensky, M., ed. Ibn Janaḥ † . . 93
Wolff, M., ed. and tr. Maimonides.†
Wolfson, Harry Austryn, *Crescas' Critique of Aristotle: Problems of Aristotle's Physics in Jewish and Arabic Philosophy*, Cambridge, Mass., 1929 . . 378, 428, 475
——— *Philo: Foundations of Religious Philosophy in Judaism, Christianity, and Islam*, 2 v., Cambridge, Mass., 1947 . . 11, 74, 76, 133, 134, 174, 219, 222, 224, 276, 355, 467, 468, 498, 512, 615, 622, 634
——— *The Philosophy of the Church Fathers: Volume I, Faith, Trinity, Incarnation*, Cambridge, Mass., 1956 . . 74, 129, 134, 138, 147, 217, 236, 246, 247, 276, 287, 295, 299, 304, 306, 311, 317, 320, 324, 330, 334, 336, 339, 344, 345, 615
Volume II (unpublished) . . 49
——— *Religious Philosophy: A Group of Essays*, Cambridge, Mass., 1961 . . 11, 19, 26, 118, 147, 217, 349, 350, 354, 551, 643, 711
——— Papers, 21, 22, 23, 49, 109, 140, 147, 160, 199, 205, 206, 219, 224, 232, 291, 337, 347, 355, 359, 372, 373, 385, 408, 472, 559, 593, 640, 641, 707

Yahuda, A. S., ed. Baḥya.†
Yon, Albert, ed. and tr. Cicero: *Traité du destin* (Latin and French, Paris, 1933) . . 692

Zeller, Eduard, *Die Philosophie der Griechen* (Tübingen, 1844–1852); many editions . . 123, 477